D1532279

Praise for *The Optimism Advantage*

"In life we have controllables and uncontrollables. Dr. Terry Paulson does a masterful job in *The Optimism Advantage* of supporting the thesis that we control our attitude and our actions. Read and study every chapter of this book and you will increase the probability of having a great life of happiness and achievement!"

—Don Hutson, coauthor of the #1 *New York Times* Best-Seller,
The One Minute Entrepreneur; and CEO of U.S. Learning,
Memphis, TN

"Terry Paulson is refreshing in that he teaches what he practices. His panoramic view of the research on optimism coupled with his thoughtful insight and experiences as a psychologist make this a book we can all benefit from reading. He goes beyond hyperbole and hype to address the principles and practices of optimism."

—Mark Sanborn, Leadership Expert and Author of *The Fred Factor*,
You Don't Need a Title to be a Leader, and *The Encore Effect*

"I am optimistic that this book will be a best seller. Henry Ford once said, '*Whether you think you can or whether you think you can't, you're right.*' Terry Paulson's newest book, *The Optimism Advantage*, will show you how you *can* see the opportunity in every encounter!"

—Dr. Tony Alessandra, Author of *Charisma*,
and Hall-of-Fame Keynote Speaker

"Terry Paulson's book *The Optimism Advantage* reminds us that optimism is a learned skill. This book is not the traditional self-help hype but a book that provides tried-and-true principles that inspire personal responsibility for living the life you have always dreamed about, as only an optimist can do. I thoroughly enjoyed this book and plan on having my 13-year-old daughter read it as well."

—Jodi Walker, CSP, Professional Speaker and
Author of *Share A Kind Word: How to Use the Infinite
Power of Words to Enhance Your Life
at Home and at Work*

"Shifting one's perspective in life requires more than a positive attitude. Rather, it's an approach to living with optimism and ambition. Dr. Terry Paulson lays out a clear and attainable vision for purposeful and joyous living. His tremendous expertise and meaningful insights contribute measurably to this insightful book."

—Dr. Nido Qubein, President, High Point University, and Chairman, Great Harvest Bread Company

"No psycho-babble here. Paulson puts it plainly and pleasantly: Life as a leader, boss, parent, partner, or spouse can drive you crazy unless you master your attitudes and actions. His book provides the perfect prescription."

—Dianna Booher, Author of *The Voice of Authority: 10 Communication Strategies Every Leader Needs to Know* and *Booher's Rules of Business Grammar: 101 Fast and Easy Ways to Correct the Most Common Errors*

"This book is about creating personal hope, filled with lessons and truths that will inspire you to not just believe, but confirm that the glass is more than half full."

—Shep Hyken, Best-Selling Author of *The Cult of the Customer*

"What an important book for such a time as this! This is not just a simple self help book that says to think differently—Terry tells us how to actually take the steps to change your attitude and your life. To live and to succeed, this is a must read."

—Bert Decker, CEO, Decker Communications, Inc.

"This is the best time for you to take advantage of what Terry has to say about optimism. He is the master, and this book is a must! Don't let setbacks keep you from the progress you deserve."

—Thomas J. Winninger, Founder of Winninger Institute for Market Resilience, Author of six books, including *Get Out of the Boat: Discover the Purpose of Your Life*

"Results! That's the key that Terry Paulson shares in *The Optimism Advantage*. This book is filled with more than *Truths*. It actually shows you how to turn those *Truths* into *Results*. If you're stuck, this book is the starter's pistol. Pull the trigger—buy it—read it—get results."

—W Mitchell, CPAE, '08–'09 President of the Global Speakers Federation

"*The Optimism Advantage* will motivate and inspire you to do your best and be your best, no matter what's happening around you, no matter your current circumstances. I highly recommend it."

—Robert B. Tucker,
Author of *Innovation Is Everybody's Business*

"Optimism can be a chosen habit and a learned skill. Take Dr. Paulson's message to heart and learn to cultivate a healthier, more productive mindset. In all challenges we can learn to see opportunities. We can learn to overcome the emotions of gloom and guide others to a better path. Make this *your* advantage; read this book often!"

—Jim Cathcart, Author of *Relationship Intelligence*®

"*The Optimism Advantage* is clear, succinct, and has great transferable concepts that the reader can implement immediately. This is a valuable resource for professionals and leaders alike."

—H. James Zinger, CSP, President, Hypmovation, Inc.

"*The Optimism Advantage* is a must read! This landmark book may be the most important book you read this year. Each chapter is a road map to navigate current circumstances and take dominion of both attitude and actions. Important truths spring alive with profound stories and are then made actionable. Read this book and discover a more deeply fulfilling life."

—Eli Davidson, M.A., Reinvention Expert,
International Best-Selling Author of *Funky to Fabulous*

"A leader's job is to keep hope alive. Before executives can ever expect to inspire others, they have to manage their own attitudes and actions. *The Optimism Advantage* gives leaders all the practical insights and ammunition they need to maintain a positive attitude and energize every communication."

—Patricia Fripp, Keynote Speaker and Executive Speech Coach

"In order to turn your setbacks into comebacks, it will take faith, focus, and follow through . . . and all these require the power of optimism! Terry Paulson has written a book that will change your inlook, uplook, and outlook! Read *The Optimism Advantage* and tell all your friends to read it! You will change your life and the lives of those you love! I highly recommend this book!"

—Willie Jolley, author of *Turn Setbacks into Greenbacks:*
7 Secrets for Going Up in Down Times

THE OPTIMISM ADVANTAGE

You make A Difference!

Terry Paulson

THE OPTIMISM ADVANTAGE

50 Simple Truths to

Transform Your Attitudes

and

Actions into Results

TERRY L. PAULSON, PhD

WILEY

John Wiley & Sons, Inc.

Published by John Wiley & Sons, Inc., Hoboken, New Jersey.
Published simultaneously in Canada.

For general information on our other products and services or for technical support, please contact our Customer Care Department within the United States at (800) 762-2974, outside the United States at (317) 572-3993, or fax (317) 572-4002.

Wiley also publishes its books in a variety of electronic formats. Some content that appears in print may not be available in electronic books. For more information about Wiley products, visit our web site at www.wiley.com.

Library of Congress Cataloging-in-Publication Data:

Paulson, Terry L., 1945–
The optimism advantage: 50 simple truths to transform your attitudes and actions into results/by Terry L. Paulson.
  p. cm.
Includes bibliographical references and index.
  ISBN 978-0-470-55475-3 (cloth)
1. Optimism. 2. Attitude (Psychology) I. Title.
BF698.35.O57P38 2010
153.1—dc22

                                        2009038778

Printed in the United States of America

10 9 8 7 6 5 4 3 2 1

CONTENTS

ACKNOWLEDGMENTS

This book is a culmination of personal and professional experiences, and study over the years. As such, there are many to acknowledge for their contribution.

For my parents, Ann and Homer, who challenged me with loving encouragement, modeled optimism every day, and made laughter and faith welcome companions on our family's joy ride through life, thank you for shaping and encouraging my optimistic attitude.

For my wife, Lorie, son, Sean, grandchildren, Micah, Jeremiah, Naomi and Chloe, and other members of my whacky and wonderful family, thank you for teaching me that the relationships you have in life make the ride worthwhile. Thanks for the love, memories, and the experiences yet to come.

For the thousands of audiences who have graced me with their presence, attention, laughter, applause, insights, and stories, thank you for helping me fill this book with tested insights that make a difference. You have taught me much of the wisdom I value and share.

For my speaking colleagues from Speakers Roundtable, Gold Coast Speakers, and the National Speakers Association, thank you for your years of inspiration, collaborative support, engaging quotes, and encouragement. You are the hope merchants who provide the motivation and messages that help others live their dreams and invent a better future.

For Nancy Lefkowitz, who has provided the steady office grounding, needed editing, and business support that made this work possible, thank you for your years of friendship and service.

For the team at John Wiley & Sons, Inc., my editor, Lauren Lynch, and production editor, Lauren Freestone, thank you for optimistically nurturing this title from conception to publishing birth. I knew that your compliments, criticisms, and deadlines were evidence of caring enough to produce a product we can all be proud of.

For Dr. Martin Seligman for the pioneering and continuing work he has inspired and completed in the study of positive psychology. More than merely understanding pathology, his work and leadership have challenged us to understand and promote constructive mental health habits.

Finally, I thank God for his sustaining grace and empowering presence in my life. You fuel my purpose, affirm my value, and give me an enduring hope. Thank you for providing faith in a community that's always there for us. To God be the glory in all that I do.

CHAPTER 1

Trade Being Your Own Worst Enemy to Become Your Own Best Supporter

"Get busy living, or get busy dying!"
—Morgan Freeman as "Red" in *The Shawshank Redemption*

Every book has a beginning, so let's start where every book ought to begin—what's in it for you?

I'm assuming that you picked up this book because you want practical insights you can use right away to better your life on and off the job. You want to be affirmed for what you do well, and you want to be better for having invested the time in reading this book.

You also read self-help books to know that you're not alone. You want to know that you're not the only one who struggles with making life work, and you want a few new, tried-and-true insights that you can use to make your life's journey just a little more satisfying and successful.

> "I prepare for the tough times by reading biographies. It reminds me that famous people never had it easy. Their lives are all stories of people who had to overcome obstacles over and over again. In his first court experience, the judge told Richard Nixon that he was the worst prepared lawyer he'd ever seen. George Patton was dyslexic and graduated last in his class at West Point. They persevered; I have to persevere!"
> —Randy Voeltz

We're facing some challenging circumstances, and people are looking for positive answers. Every age has its share of struggles, but when the tough times hit, they have a way of getting everyone's attention.

Facing continued downsizing and more layoffs, a manager at one of my leadership training events added a sharper edge to an enduring cliché: "When they hired me, I *was* promised a rose garden. But they forgot to tell me that these rosebushes have some pretty nasty thorns. I hope you're going to provide some pruning shears to help me find a way out of this mess!" When you're encountering difficult situations, you want answers. When life gives you a headache, you want something to take away the pain, and you want to avoid getting another one!

Although you'll find plenty of useful answers and practical advice in this book, getting advice is probably not your primary problem. You've received more than your share of good advice from other authors, friends, teachers, and passing gurus. The challenge lies in *making* that good advice work for your life and your career. That's why this book won't coddle you; it'll challenge you with some unsettling truth telling that's designed to help you transform your attitudes, relationships, habits, and choices. Those changes will help you experience the optimism advantage. But for optimism to work, you have to do the work to think and act differently!

Truth #1: Life Is Difficult

The first truth in the great game of life is worth memorizing—life is difficult! So get over it. No sweet-talking politician, fairy godmother, or genie is coming to sprinkle stardust or grant three wishes. Embracing optimism is about embracing self-reliance, personal responsibility, and the work of changing your thought patterns and your actions. It doesn't mean that you're denying reality; it's simply about positively coping with that reality to succeed in the face of life's challenges.

If you're lucky, you had parents, teachers, and bosses who cared enough to let you experience the natural consequences of your choices. They expected a lot from you. They also encouraged you, but they didn't give you grades you didn't deserve. They let you win and lose on your own. They made you cope with your own falls and failures and earn the rewards you received.

Protective cocoons may work for caterpillars, but they don't work for people. Shielding children from all of life's natural pains and setbacks doesn't allow them to gain the confidence that they need to cope with the even bigger challenges they will face later in life. In the great game of business, there is no eighth-place trophy for a salesperson who loses a critical account to a competitor. If the quality of your product or service is substandard, you don't get a passing grade. You lose the business.

So if you think optimism means adopting a Pollyanna mind-set where everything turns out right, then you've got the wrong idea. That's simply self-help hype! *True* optimists have earned their positive attitude from a proven track record of overcoming real obstacles. They did it the old-fashioned way; they earned confidence one obstacle, one challenge, and one victory at a time!

> "What lies behind us and what lies before us are tiny matters compared with what lies within us."
> —Oliver Wendell Holmes

If you are to become a true optimist, start by being a realist. Accept that life is difficult, and then get busy learning as much as you can about the challenges you face. Why? Because you've overcome problems in the past, you have every reason to believe that you've got what it takes to overcome whatever problems life deals you.

Life Is a Self-Help Project, but You're Not Working on It Alone

Developing maturity at any age is all about realizing that life is essentially a self-help project. Now, that's a good thing, because it's *your* life. How you define success, nurture your own education and career, respond to your problems, and make your choices allows you to shape your life the way you want it lived. That's both a life-affirming opportunity and a personal responsibility, but, as you realize, it also comes with your share of frustrating challenges. As an optimist, you'd want it no other way.

But optimists are not alone, and neither are you. Contacts in your local community, family, professional network, and fellow members of your faith community can help you make your way on life's journey. Although all of these people can support you, it's up to you to develop and tap those resources. Optimists don't merely settle for the relationships that find them. To claim your own optimism advantage, you need to realize who matters, who never did, who shouldn't anymore, who still does, and who you want to add to your team. The bottom line is simple: Seek out relationships that encourage and support the person you want to be.

Self-reliance doesn't require you to discount or dismiss the importance of others. It's simply about building healthy relationships that work for both parties. If you give value, you usually get value. Good relationships are like deposit systems in many ways; you tend to get back what you put in. Perhaps it doesn't always happen immediately, or in exactly the way you expected, but when you find a way to do your part to serve others, people have a tendency to serve you back. When you help a small, struggling customer when they are growing, they may just remember you when they're big and profitable. In short, take time to cultivate the right relationships, and you'll soon become more optimistic and accomplish more on and off the job.

Optimists Everywhere Claim Their Version of the American Dream

For people of every age and in every country, the optimistic belief that they can have a dream and make it happen has become a powerful source of hope and motivation. As the United States has become the influential nation that it is today, the importance of self-reliance in achieving personal dreams has been reinforced over and over again. The history of our country is ripe with stories of individual Americans who took risks, overcame challenges, bounced back from setbacks, and earned their own version of the American Dream.

This in no way limits the dreams of other world citizens. After I mentioned the American Dream at a leadership presentation in Singapore, an apology seemed appropriate for what some might label a clear *diversity disaster!* But a manager from

> "Children everywhere need the encouragement to dream big dreams. I'd like to think we could help them do just that. I love hearing the excitement in their voices when they realize they can do something new."
> —Tiger Woods

Hong Kong addressed my concern when he announced to all in attendance: "Please remember that the American Dream is not just your dream; it's the world's dream. The world looks to America and hopes that they, too, can have the freedoms and the opportunities you can easily take for granted. You have no need to apologize for referring to the American Dream. Please protect it for all of us."

Throughout the world today, free, optimistic people everywhere share a version of that dream. Many do everything within their power to come to America to achieve it. Some wait years for a visa; others cross treacherous borders. In America, the gate swings in, because opportunities still remain. You certainly don't meet a lot of people trying to get out!

Rest assured that no matter what the country, *hope* is a sweet-sounding word in any language. Even in the toughest economic times, some world citizens find ways to do quite well. Instead of watching the negative drone of bad news, people with an optimistic attitude and a compelling dream get busy taking advantage of available opportunities. Instead of worrying about the global economy, they get busy making an impact on their own personal economy one day at a time.

This book is full of hope, optimism, and suggestions on what you can do to live your dreams—dreams that don't always involve big paychecks or newspaper headlines. Many millionaires who were B and C students were the ones who had the guts to start a small business, live in a nice little house, and save more than they spend. They live frugally and are very self-confident and self-sufficient.

Challenge yourself to become one of these dreamers. To deliver on that dream, you're going to have to get down to work! Success *does* come, but often, it doesn't come easy!

Choose Learned Optimism over Learned Helplessness

If this is getting a bit too optimistic for you to believe, then maybe you've already fallen victim to what has been called the depression of our age, *learned helplessness*. This depression comes from the belief that nothing you can do will better your situation. Modern-day living has a way of reinforcing how little you control and making it far too easy to become a victim.

Victims feel that they can't do anything to make a difference in what happens to them. Since they have no confidence in their own ability to cope with adversity and earn their own success, they avoid seemingly useless constructive actions, preferring instead to wait for fate to deal its hand. Both their headaches and their happiness come from what happens to them, instead of as a result of their own actions. Victims look for ways to blame those who contribute to their pain.

> "Everything can be taken from a man but one thing . . . to choose one's attitude in any given set of circumstances."
> —Viktor Frankl

Optimists are the opposite of victims. With positive attitudes built on a personal track record of overcoming adversity, they believe in their own ability to achieve their goals and overcome whatever obstacles hinder them. When dealt a poor hand, they look for ways to play it well. They take pride in their achievements and look forward to life's challenges.

The choice is yours. You can trade your victim thinking and learned helplessness for the optimistic attitudes and actions that will help you develop your own resilience, persistence, resourcefulness, and results. Every page you read and every step you take to alter your thinking will make you more optimistic.

The Study of Optimism and a New Emphasis on Positive Psychology

Some refer to him as the father of positive psychology, but whatever you call him, you can't talk about *learned optimism* without giving credit to the pioneer who provided the vision, the early research, and the road map on how to apply the truths discovered. Martin E. P. Seligman, PhD, is a psychologist, a University of Pennsylvania professor, the author of *Learned Optimism* and *Authentic Happiness*, and a past president of the American Psychological Association. His earlier works are well worth reading, and his insights will be evident throughout this book.

Before Seligman became president of the American Psychological Association in 1997, an analysis of negative versus positive topics in psychology journals from 1967 to 1997 found 41,416 references on anxiety, 54,040 on depression, 1,710 on happiness, and 415 on joy. It was time to balance the books by studying and learning more from the resilient souls who seem to cope with stress— and effectively and consistently handle the demands placed on them both on and off the job.

When he became APA president, Seligman challenged

> "Psychology has, since World War II, focused on the question of how can we cure mental illness? It's done very well. There are by my count at least 14 mental illnesses which we can now treat or relieve, either with psychotherapy or with drugs. But that's half the battle. We've ignored the other side, which is to ask: How can we take what we are strongest at and build them up in such a way that they become great buffers against our troubles?"
>
> —Martin E. P. Seligman

psychologists to increase their study of positive psychology. Historically, psychologists had learned a lot about mental illness and how people break down in the face of life's challenges. But why do some in the same situations remain resilient, resourceful, and optimistic? Seligman wanted researchers to find out.

So *can* you change your attitude and your actions to become more optimistic? You bet you can! Researchers have shown that you can significantly alter the way you think and act and become more like the optimist you want to be.

At one of my presentations on the optimism advantage, a woman approached me after the program and confessed, "I wish I had your attitude." My reply was immediate: "Take it. Your taking my attitude certainly won't stop me from keeping mine!"

Star in Your Own Positive Soap Opera

Unfortunately, claiming your own optimism advantage takes more than the mere decision to do so. It requires a long history of changing how you think and act. This isn't a movie that's all wrapped up in a fancy bow in two hours. This is a soap opera, and you're the only star who counts. Your challenge as you read this book and apply the insights learned is to make your life's soap opera as positive as possible. As already discussed, you'll want to fill your cast with people who will encourage and support you, and steer clear of those who belittle and doubt you.

> "Make a point that you will not sign up, line up, or whine up about the recession. Instead, stand up and fight for your dreams and goals, and never, ever give up on you and the incredible possibilities that are within you!"
>
> —Willie Jolley

Like any soap opera, there'll be challenges, setbacks, victories, defeats, laughter, tears, joy, grief, record profits, and sizable losses. Your job is to keep making progress in claiming the life you want to live, one day at a time, one choice at a time. This book will help you write your positive script and find your supportive cast of characters.

Why is this book a must-read at this point in your life? Some clichés are so wise that they're worth repeating: "Today is the first day of the rest of your life!" Life is way too precious to waste boring yourself in an existence that isn't satisfying, and there's no time like the present to take responsibility for changing your situation. Waiting won't make it any easier, and it won't make success any more likely.

Stop being your own worst enemy and start becoming your own best advocate. Take the time to learn how to trade your negative thoughts and unproductive worries for the positive attitudes and constructive actions that will help you produce winning results.

Truth #2: Control What You Can, and Accept and *Use* What You Can't

Cultivating optimistic attitudes and actions is this book's focus, but one of its guiding truths comes from what has been affectionately called the Serenity Prayer, a simple but powerful statement that was written by theologian Reinhold Niebuhr. Taken aback by the impact of his words, he confessed in *The Essential Reinhold Niebuhr: Selected Essays and Addresses*: "The embarrassment, particularly, was occasioned by the incessant correspondence about a prayer I had composed years before, which the old Federal Council of Churches had used and which later was printed on small cards to give to soldiers. Subsequently Alcoholics Anonymous adopted it as its official prayer. The prayer reads: 'God, give us grace to accept with serenity the things that cannot be changed, courage to change the things that should be changed, and the wisdom to distinguish the one from the other.'"

The Serenity Prayer has been shortened, memorized, and repeated privately and publicly—because it captures important truths that *work*. Treasured statements like these that stand the test of time deliver wisdom with a simplicity that makes every word count. Whether you believe in God or not, this book will help you appreciate the value and depth of this statement and the sentiments it promotes.

As an optimist in training, you must learn how to accept and maximize your reaction to the both the blessings and the adversity that come your way and take responsibility for managing your own motivation, attitudes, and actions in a way that makes a difference in the quality of your life.

Optimism Is Important on and off the Job

Optimism can have a profound impact on both your personal life and your professional life. Graduating with a doctorate in clinical psychology prepares men and women to provide therapy, but it seldom teaches therapists to appreciate the importance of one's work life to one's mental health. Therapists are ready to deal with abusive parents and struggling marriages, but what about bosses and dysfunctional teams who can drive someone crazy? Both worlds are important to you and to this book because optimism can make a difference to you in both situations.

> "Perpetual optimism is a force multiplier."
> —Colin Powell

A leader without influence and an ability to drive strategic change really isn't a leader. A professional who can't translate her gifts and skills into results that serve won't last in this competitive global economy. To be effective in either role requires you to have the right skills, the right attitudes, and the right motivation. And while advancing in your career and making a difference for those you serve is important, there is more to life than work. Few people would want on their tombstone: "I finished everything on my to-do-list!" Life is about cultivating good relationships, being a good parent or partner, making a difference to your community—and, most important, enjoying the journey.

Everyone complains about the difficulty of finding the right work-life balance. Maintaining such a stable balance will always require a healthy tension that appreciates the importance of both areas of your life. Honor the importance of achievement and business results, and honor the importance of lasting and satisfying relationships with those you love. This book is committed to helping you do both.

Faith and Faith Communities Can Impact Your Optimism

The month before making a presentation to an executive forum at a major national newspaper, *One Minute Manager* author Ken Blanchard had presented to the same group. Executives were still talking about one of his comments.

"Ken's program was exceptional," the meeting planner confessed. "But it was his response to a question that had people talking. During the Q&A, one of the executives asked, 'You spend your life motivating audiences. How do you motivate yourself?'"

"I'm so glad you asked," Ken replied with a smile. "Every morning I rise early for time to study the Word of God and for prayer. I know faith is important to many. For me, faith centers and motivates me in a way that nothing else can."

That simple, authentic disclosure about how faith affected Blanchard's life and attitude surprised and challenged many of the executives present. It gave them permission to discuss more openly the role spiritual faith played in their own lives.

Although not a primary focus of this book, research and surveys have found that religious faith has consistently been a reliable source of hope and optimism for many people. For centuries, believers have written and witnessed to its impact in their lives. To leave out references to the difference faith and faith communities can have on your attitudes and actions would not do justice to the breadth of insights available to you. Explore this area of life for yourself, and never discount its importance to many very optimistic believers.

> "In our study, we looked at 11 major religions in America and how hopeful and optimistic the adherents were. We looked at the level of optimism in stories the children were told, as well as in the liturgy and sermons. We found strict Calvinists, Roman Catholics and Orthodox Jews were the most hopeful and optimistic, while Unitarians and Reformed Jews tended to be more pessimistic. The fundamentalist religions simply seem to offer more hope for a brighter future than do the more liberal, humanistic ones."
>
> —Martin E. P. Seligman

Don't Just Read This Book—Devour It

Remember: The books you buy and put on the shelf won't affect your thinking or your life. This book is full of proven strategies that work,

> "All truly wise thoughts have been thought already thousands of times; but to make them truly ours, we must think them over again honestly, until they take root in our personal experience."
>
> —Goethe

but strategies don't work unless you use them. Start by promising to devour this book. Write in the margins. Test and use the strategies that make sense to you, consistently, over time—until they become habits.

Don't just read this book once; that is a lesson my grandmother imparted to me when I was very young. With sparkling eyes and an inquisitive mind, she nurtured her children's offspring with stories and quotes that left a lasting legacy. She often gave us her version of a Swedish massage, and while working my back, she would share quotes and Scripture from memory. I once asked her, "How do you remember so many quotes?"

Grandma Vera said something I've treasured since: "If you read something often enough, no one can take it away from you."

How many great books have you underlined and treasured but never read again? If you were to bet on this book or on years of negative thinking habits, which would you bet on? The good money in Vegas is on your past habits. The only way you change that is to diligently nurture and review content that will provide you the ammunition and encouragement for the changes you want to make.

Don't just read this book; reread the chapters that speak to what you need to change. Summarize what you've learned for your friends and family. Share your favorite short quotes and key statements on your social networking websites. By doing so, you can become a force for positive change for all your friends. When you risk being contagious for what's working for you, you'll soon find you're practicing and remembering what you're sharing!

One final note: I promise not to bore you with lengthy references or scientific jargon. I'll even add some timely humor, relevant stories you can relate to, and inspiring quotes to keep you turning the pages.

I've written this book to provide you with examples and tools you can use now to make a difference in your at-

> "The future belongs to those who show up for it."
> —Mark Steyn

titude and your life. It's self-help-lite, and it's word-reduced to make it a quick and worthwhile read. With that in mind, let's get on to the next chapter.

CHAPTER 2

Deal with the Hand You're Dealt

"If you're too consumed with the one door in your life that closes, you'll never reach the open door."

—Tommy Lasorda

Life deals you both bad and good hands. You—and countless others—struggle with the tough times and can easily take for granted life's many blessings. As an optimist, you'll learn to play both well.

You don't need this book to tell you that life is difficult; that truth is impossible to avoid. After all, the bad hands are the ones that that tend to get your attention. Even when the worst happens to others, we often say, "But by the grace of God go I!" In short, that could have just as easily been you or me!

The late M. Scott Peck's transforming work, *The Road Less Traveled*, continues to sell thousands of books every year. It starts with an affirmation of the same assertion: "Life is difficult. This is a great truth, one of the greatest truths. It is a great truth because once we truly see this truth, we transcend it. Once we truly know that life is difficult—once we truly understand and accept it—then life is no longer difficult. Because once it is accepted, the fact that life is difficult no longer matters."

Everybody has and will continue to experience bad days—an unwelcome diagnosis, a stock market fall, a terminated job, a lost loved one, a game you should have won, personal rejections, customers who go to a competitor, and natural disasters you

> "The business world's most revered figures, from Bill Gates on down, almost invariably overcame overwhelming odds. They didn't surf easily to the top on a big societal wave of applause. In fact, they spent most of their pre-success years being shouted down by naysayers. Yet they persisted. It was incredibly hard, and that's the whole point: I'm not saying that it's not as easy to succeed as it used to be. I'm saying it never was."
> —Rob Walker

couldn't have planned for. You hope for more, but you aren't thrown by less because we are all in this together.

Why Do Bad Things Happen to Good People?

For centuries, people have struggled with a vexing question: "If there is a just and all-powerful God, why do bad things happen to good people?" Books have been written to explore this difficult question. Some reject faith, because no answer seems adequate. Others choose to trust that God has a plan they will someday understand. Still others look for the good that may emerge through facing the adversity with optimism, courage, and faith. But through all the mental and emotional gymnastics that facing reality requires, the fact remains that bad things do happen to good people!

Years ago, a cancer survivor shared with a friend his struggle with the question

> "The God I believe in does not send us the problem; he gives us the strength to cope with it."
> —Rabbi Harold S. Kushner

"Why me?" After a moment's silence, his friend asked, "Did you ever think to ask yourself 'Why not me?'" It had never occurred to him to even ask that question.

That question unleashed a liberating insight. He realized that life is neither fair nor unfair; it's simply life. Bad things can happen to anyone. "Why me?" assumes I should be exempt from the pain everyone else feels. "Why not me?" is humbling and appropriate. It introduces us to the reality that life's challenges happen to everyone. Difficult days are facts of life, but learning to deal well with those difficult times can help you become stronger.

Find Perspective and Get on with Life

> "In the middle of difficulty lies opportunity."
> —Albert Einstein

Faced with a diagnosis of Parkinson's Disease, award-winning actor and author of *Always Looking Up* Michael J. Fox had to find a way to accept this painful reality and continue to make the best of his life. When commenting on his optimistic attitude in an ABC special, Michael said, "The answer had very little to do with protection and everything to do with perspective. The only unavailable choice was whether or not to have Parkinson's. Everything else was up to me. I could concentrate on the loss or just get on with life and maybe see if the holes started filling in for themselves."

Michael's optimistic journey from adversity to a renewed appreciation for life can be applied to your life as well. As bad as his disease can be, Fox found a way to make it a gift. Taken with the right perspective, even adversity can be a blessing that opens unseen doors and a new appreciation for life. When we are confronted by death, disease, or an accident, the value of a day takes on an entirely new meaning.

Disappointment Can Launch New Dreams

You don't have to face a terminal diagnosis to appreciate the perspective gained by failure and setbacks. Experienced sales professionals have

learned the hard way the importance of staying in the game to
earn the sale. To the best sales
professionals, "NO" is just "ON"
spelled backwards!

> "Experience is not what
> happens to you. It is what you
> do with what happens to you."
> —Aldous Huxley

When my teenage son, Sean, asked if I'd give him a car, I quickly replied, "No." He immediately protested, "Everyone gets a car!" And I replied, "That will be everyone minus one!" His face said it all. I'm sure he was wondering how unfortunate he was to be born to this father!

But Sean persisted. With his birthday coming up, he decided to settle for even a partial payment. He asked how much I would give him toward his car for a birthday present. I responded with a borrowed line from Bill Cosby: "I'll match what your friends will give you!"

Though my son left that conversation disappointed, he found that disappointment can be a tough but valuable teacher. Out of Sean's frustration came the motivation to find a way to earn the money he needed for his car—no matter what.

When he announced his decision to write a book about favorite family lectures, we initially laughed. He was sixteen, and we were sure that writing a term paper and charging readers a quarter might be a more realistic goal. But after explaining his plan and making a good case for my joining him on the project, a dream was launched.

Sean took surveys from hundreds of teens. He became the co-author of his first self-published book, *Secrets of Life Every Teenager Needs to Know*. He helped earn his new car the old-fashioned way—by working for it. Disappointments can launch dreams. For optimists, good things can come out of even the toughest parents.

Truth #3: Face the Brutal Reality but Never Lose Faith

Leaders must be able to authentically drive a rock-solid optimistic vision while being willing to face the brutal facts—the un-comfortable truths of the obstacles they face in today's competitive

> "You must maintain unwavering faith that you can and will prevail in the end, regardless of the difficulties—and at the same time, have the discipline to confront the most brutal facts of your current reality, whatever they might be."
>
> —Jim Collins

and treacherous global economy. Such free markets ensure both success and failure—winners and losers. Companies that were once successful can lose out to competitors in developing countries who are able to produce similar products at half or even a quarter the price.

Those who are successful in adapting, survive; those who don't fall by the wayside. In challenging times, companies go under and people lose jobs, but out of that crisis, the seeds of new opportunities emerge. Resources are reinvested. Companies are refocused and people are retooled. Small businesses get launched because people have mortgages and no way to pay them off. We want painless progress, but pain and change often make economies stronger. Someone is always making tough economies work; it might as well be you and your company!

We like to think that we are the only age that has had to deal with constant change. We are not. Spectacular booms have always been accompanied by brutal competition, followed by glaring busts every time something truly new has come on the scene.

> "Creative destruction is not just an unfortunate side effect of free-market capitalism; it is the very engine of capitalistic prosperity. Unprofitable methods, firms and industries must be liquidated to release resources for new enterprises. Investment is not enough. There has to be disinvestment as well."
>
> —Edward Luttwak
> Author of *Turbo Capitalism*

From the canal mania in the 1830s to the dot.com craze of the 1990s, investors invariably got burned for letting their exuberance get ahead of reality. But when the smoke cleared, new innovations were left for new booms to ride! Railroad tracks helped create a national mass market. Telegraph lines facilitated the rise of modern big business. Electricity grids revolutionized manufacturing and extended the working day. The dot.com busts unleashed the Internet and new digital platforms that serve us today. Destruction is part of the foundation for economic and societal growth.

The struggle to survive produces stress, but stress is the spice of life. It's overcoming those storms and the stress they create that makes the ride worthwhile. After all, stress is created by the demands placed on us—the challenges to make a difference with our time and our skills. The absence of stress is death! Wouldn't you rather have a demanding day? Good leaders and professionals love days with a lot of important things to accomplish. Time flies when you're making meaningful things happen.

> "The world is too big for us. Too much is going on. Too many crimes, too much violence and excitement. Try as you will, you get behind in the race in spite of yourself. It is an incessant strain to keep pace, and still you lose ground. Science empties its discoveries on you so fast you stagger beneath them in hopeless bewilderness. . . . Everything is high-pressure. Human nature can't endure much more."
>
> —*Atlantic Journal* Editorial, June 16, 1833

Beware of the Status Quo

So don't dread the difficult days; expect them. In fact, learn to relish the growth and opportunity that such experiences allow. Don't be blindsided by changes; do your part to create your own disruptions.

What executives put on their desks tells a lot about what they feel is important. Telephone industry executive Ian McNeil stares frequently

> "Life is about storms. . . . Stress, in and of itself, is not the problem. Stress can be a good thing. If you think about the things that created your character, created your ability to fight, and made a difference, in every case, it would be the storms. It's the things that pushed you the most that helped you the most."
>
> —Jim Loehr

> "Prolonged equilibrium dulls the organism's senses and saps its ability to arouse itself appropriately in the face of danger. Survival favors heightened adrenaline levels, wariness, and experimentation. . . . The first rule of life is the first rule of business: Adapt or die!"
> —Richard Pascale

at an unsettling reminder: "Recognize that every 'out front' maneuver you make is going to be lonely. If you feel entirely comfortable, then you're not far enough ahead to do any good. That warm sense of everything going well is usually the body temperature at the center of the herd."

The status quo is not your friend; in a competitive, down economy, the absence of change means death. Those who coast with current best practices may enjoy a period of time where it works. But if you don't reinvent yourself, your competitors will do it for you.

It takes more than vigilant leaders to make change work; it takes vigilant workers who are committed to sustaining a customer-centric company that keeps adapting. Jeff Bezos, the CEO of Amazon.com, talks about a perspective that contributes to the company's success: "We need to be afraid of our customers, because those are the folks who give us money. I remind people every morning we should wake up afraid and use the terror as a motivator. The customers are the folks that at the end of the day are really in control. . . . Customers have a bigger voice online. If we make a customer unhappy, they can tell thousands of people. Likewise, if you make a customer happy, they can also tell thousands of people. With that kind of a megaphone in the hands of every individual customer, you had better be a customer-centric company."

With e-commerce, bad days have a way of expanding in a viral fashion. Today, emotion flies at net speed. Reputations and relationships can be damaged in minutes. Yes, life is difficult for organizations as well.

As a result, excellence has to be earned every single day. The reward is going home satisfied from a hard day's work and the joy of recovery, recreation, and rest. Life is still about playing the bad and the good hands well. So bring on the storms and the stress. But what about life's good hands?

Your Wonderful Life Is Also Filled with Happy Accidents

We should never forget that bad days are only half of the cards we're dealt; we also are given more than our share of good days. A perennial Christmas favorite and movie classic—Frank Capra's *It's a Wonderful Life*—reminds us that during the worst of times, we often forget how precious and important life can be. Jimmy Stewart's character George Bailey—facing a bank run and the imminent failure of his savings and loan—decides that he is worth more to his family dead than alive. Clarence, the incompetent but creative angel charged with bringing him from the brink of suicide, decides to take him on a journey through the Bedford Falls that would have existed if he had not lived. When confronted with many of his life's blessings and the difference he made in the lives of others, George Bailey passionately chooses life.

But, you protest, that's a movie! Okay, so maybe your angel isn't as creative, but the same question remains. When you face challenging times, is your glass half full or half empty? Have you ever tried admitting that it's both? Everyone's life—including your own—has more than its fair share of both bad and good accidents. And while the bad ones get the press, the blessings have a way of passing by unnoticed and unappreciated.

Whether you take time to appreciate them or not, your life has plenty of happy accidents. For starters, you were born in a country you didn't choose and to a mother you didn't get to pick. But if you were born to parents in a developed country, that's a happy accident that positively affected your life in more ways than you can count. Additionally, life has probably given you games you should have lost, but the ball bounced your way. There are those times on the freeway when you didn't switch lanes and missed hitting the car you hadn't seen advancing on the left. There's that missed flight that allowed you to meet that special person or customer. How about that sales call

> "Become a possibilitarian. No matter how dark things seem to be or actually are, raise your sights and see possibilities—always see them, for they're always there."
> —Norman Vincent Peale

you handled poorly—and they bought anyway. Call it fate, good luck, karma, or one of God's blessings; rest assured that life has given you gifts you didn't deserve. As an optimist, be grateful for them. One of the greatest secrets of happiness is gratitude.

Truth #4: This Too Shall Pass

Both good and the bad times will come, and both will eventually pass. Even with the best of teams, a given game's momentum has a way of shifting to the other team. In our competitive, global economy, both the economic booms and the recessions end at some point. Understanding this truth is important in maintaining your sanity, perspective, and focus on what matters most in life.

As Abraham Lincoln struggled with the long and costly Civil War, one of his favorite quotes that fueled both his resolve and his hope was the Middle Eastern truth: "This too shall pass." My mother used to say the same thing, and she was talking about me—"Someday these teenage years will end!" Perhaps as a self-defense mechanism, we tend to overestimate the impact of bad economic periods and underestimate how fast we will be able to bounce back when the good times return. This helps us get busy dealing with the impact of bad recessions and helps us forget them when prosperity returns.

An economist at business periodical *Fast Company* wrote: "Optimism is over. . . . The layoffs, buyouts, and bankruptcies of the past year are starting to look like the good old days. Business sucks to such a degree that unbridled optimism—the kind of wild, harebrained zest to rule the world—is now just a sign that your meds aren't working."

When was that written? If you guessed 2001—right after the 9/11 terrorist attacks and the economic downturn that resulted—then you would be

> "You cannot always choose what happens to you, but you can always choose what happens in you! You cannot change the circumstances that life throws at you, but you can choose how you respond to the circumstances."
>
> —Willie Jolley

right. Within months after that column was written, America was back on its feet and moved into a sustained period of economic growth that lasted through 2007. The media has a way of exaggerating the worst and discounting the best of times.

Parents have a similar tendency to worry about their children and wonder whether they will ever grow out of the problems they face before they enter adulthood. Because of their enduring love and concern, parents through the ages have always had that sense of apprehension. But thankfully, few societies have had to cope with roving gangs of gun-toting, drug-abusing seniors, because life has a way of socializing and training people to become more productive and more socially appropriate to survive. Over the years, to their dismay and wonder, most of those troubled teens end up acting more and more like the parents they swore they would never become. Yes, this too shall pass!

Overall . . . It's a Pretty Good Life

The ebb and flow of the positive and negative in our lives can't be avoided. The great game of business will continue to produce a new set of winners and losers. The market will go up, and it will go down. Your life will have tragic moments and endearing, precious ones as well.

Success is learning how to handle both well. Coach Phil Jackson, the most winning coach in NBA finals history has challenged players and leaders alike to take the middle path: "I got to watch him [Red Holzman, former coach of the New York Knicks] very closely. He talked philosophy with me, and he talked about the importance of staying not too high, not too low and not letting victories or defeats send you tumbling one way or the other. He believed in what was called the middle path."

Never get too engrossed in setbacks, nor too excited about the latest victory. After all, whether as a company or as an individual, you don't want just one good year. You want a sustainable dynasty that finds a way to get beyond any setbacks to win year after year. Coach Jackson never overcoaches or micromanages his players. He lets them play through the tough runs to gain confidence in their own abilities to bounce back. In short, whether leading others or managing yourself, be a perspective leveler. Be humble about success, and don't let overconfidence in the good times set the stage for complacency. Be confident in the face of setbacks. You've bounced back in the past, and you'll do it again.

An engaging cartoon shows a couple staring at a graph of their 50-year marriage that hangs over their family room fireplace. The caption captures the husband's observation to his longtime wife and companion: "Overall, it's been a pretty good marriage."

If you made a similar graph of your life, my guess is that there would be up times and down times. One of life's main challenges lies in learning how to sustain more positive days and bounce back quicker from the tough ones. Think of the practice in major league baseball to pay a .300 hitter more than a .200 hitter. Work to get the best batting average you can get in the game that counts for you! Your attitude in the face of adversity and happy accidents will make a difference in that batting average. As an optimist, you'll know that while you can never control everything that happens to you, you can certainly control your responses.

> "A pessimist is one who makes difficulties of his opportunities and an optimist is one who makes opportunities of his difficulties."
>
> —Harry Truman

Even if you've been on the receiving end of terrible losses, abuse, crimes, or cancer—don't label yourself as a victim. You are a survivor. You control the resilience, resourcefulness, and persistence you demonstrate in the face of any adversity. You also control your initiative and innovation in turning your happy accidents and unexpected opportunities into satisfying achievements. Adversity need not define you; instead, it can refine you.

CHAPTER
3

Your Choice: Victim or Resilient Survivor

"Don't go around saying the world owes you a living. The world owes you nothing. It was here first."

—Mark Twain

There's no question that life is difficult, but the way you respond to those difficulties will determine whether you're a victim or a resilient survivor. That continuing choice has little to do with what happens to you and much to do with how you label its impact on your life. Optimists aren't looking for excuses or searching for people to blame. They're busy finding ways to bounce back and make the best of any setback. Instead of looking back, they're looking forward.

Micron Technology and its subsidiaries manufacture and market semiconductor devices worldwide. CEO Steve Appleton has no room for excuses in driving for the results that

> "The search for someone to blame is always successful."
> —Robert Half

25

mean survival for his company: "I don't believe in being a good loser. It's a ridiculous concept. Maybe it would be a super world if there were no winners and losers. I don't think there has been any time in human history where that was true. That's not the way it is. People in other countries want what we've got, and they're going to go after it. Hey, I'm not going to teach my kids that it's OK to lose. Somebody is going to want their jobs. Somebody is going to want their standard of living. They need to know life isn't fair. Wake up and get used to it."

No matter what life deals you, refuse to label yourself a victim! Depending on what has happened to you, you might find it tempting to label yourself as a victim. But allowing yourself to embrace that label can strip you of the will and the positive attitude you need to overcome the adversities you will continue to encounter. Optimists, by definition, refuse to let what happened to them define or limit their lives.

Truth #5: Be a Resilient Survivor No Matter What You Face

If you are still alive, you are not a victim; you're a survivor. The label you claim for yourself has a direct effect on how you think and act. It also has consequences in terms of how others perceive and respond to you. The word *victim* brings with it an image of continued suffering under the weight of a heavy burden from past experiences that cannot be changed. Addressing yourself as a victim—and having others do the same—produces feelings of helplessness, despondency, and sometimes anger.

The term *survivor*, however, brings to mind someone who endures, lives through the adversity, persists, and bounces back to make progress anyway. To be repeatedly addressed as a strong and resilient survivor encourages feelings of pride

> "The adult child movement, by declaring practically everyone to be a victim of imperfect parenting and therefore eligible for lifelong, self-absorbed irresponsibility, has trivialized real suffering and made psychic invalids of those who once had a bad day."
>
> —Frank Pittman, MD

and personal empowerment. Being a victim is passive; it leaves you feeling powerless, with little faith or hope. Being a survivor is active; it encourages you to regain control of your life and work together with others to rebuild your future. Being a victim creates pity; being a resilient survivor invites respect.

So don't let people call you a victim. Too many seem to treat victimhood not as a temporary problem to be overcome but rather as an identity to be nurtured. Define yourself instead as a resilient survivor and live that definition every day. The best way to overcome adversity is to succeed in spite of it. Victim thinking is a seductive trap that leaves you chained to events that can't be changed.

> "When I grew up, I had physical problems, but my mind worked well. My mother would never let me feel sorry for myself. She just wouldn't allow that. You've got to realize that a situation is only a situation, and you can't lose perspective. You can't let outside circumstances control you. I had an advantage, because I grew up with a handicap. So I think I knew that outside circumstances are just circumstances. I realized that I always had to continue with what I still had left— which was life."
>
> —Tom Denner

The good news, however, is that you have the key to unlock your own chains, and you start with claiming a new label: "I'm a resilient survivor who is ready to get on with my life!" If you want to remain a victim, that is your choice. But if you are ready to change, there are many optimists out there ready to help you do so. We are meant to be masters of our own future, not victims of anyone else's actions or abuse. But to do that, you have to transform your thinking and your habits.

Truth #6: Don't Just Watch Negative News; Get Busy Making Your Own

Hours spent daily watching your television news will do more to add to your depression than to alleviate your feelings of helplessness. So find your own sources to keep you informed about what you need to know, but watch your doses! According to Nielsen Media Research, if you're like other Americans, a television is on somewhere in your house for more than eight hours a day. After all, there are advantages to this form of entertainment. It's the cheapest way to pretend to have people in your home without feeding them. And while you may not intently be paying attention to what's on your television, it still has an effect—and the result often supports your victim thinking.

A local news show producer, frustrated with complaints about how negative media news had become, did a little truth telling of his own: "We have very good data on what the average American wants to watch. Our news has to have 90 percent problems, crimes and catastrophes. If we add 10 percent humor, human interest and good personalities, people will watch our news. That's the nature of the beast. If you lead with a positive story, they'll click their way to another station. I'm embarrassed to even say this, but for every day of the year, we have footage of past deaths and disasters. If there is no current crisis, we can always have anniversaries of old ones!"

Princess Diana will conveniently die every year on cue. The news media is prepared to bring any disaster, political scandal, or graphic crime to your television within minutes. If terrorists and criminals aren't bad enough, we're constantly made aware of the dangerous germs that confront us from every public place and from the air we share on planes. With some welcome exceptions, producers still fill hours and editors fill pages with some of the worst news our world has to offer. The frantic and energizing challenge of delivering "bad" news 24/7 often comes at the expense of our optimism and perceived opportunities. You are likely to find that once you cut your intake of negative news, you will experience a change in attitude. If you are going to continue to watch, actively seek out more stories and programs that uplift you and give you hope in what you can do to better your life.

> "All too often, minority kids never hear about anyone other than athletes. They don't know the living you can make with your mind. When I hear the same thing in black schools as white, kids talking about becoming doctors and lawyers, I know the ghetto will disappear."
> —Rosey Grier

Simpler Times Made for a Powerful People

In ages past, people were far more focused on local news. News of national catastrophes would take days to be covered; international news would take even longer. Since the papers still had to be filled, reporters would look for what they could find. They'd show pictures of Martha's car in a ditch. They'd cover the local churchwomen's group taking casseroles to Martha as she recovered from her injuries. They'd show a community coming together to rebuild a fire-damaged barn.

We were a more powerful people during that time because we could handle the problems we faced. Those local stories and problems still take

> "If you don't like the news, go out and make some of your own."
>
> —Wes Scoop Nisker

place today, but they're seldom covered or they're buried in the back pages of the newspaper. They don't make the headlines or the lead story on the evening news. For far too many years, too many people have settled for being powerless observers. We watch the world around us, transfixed by scandals, wars, and disasters that are beyond our ability to fix, instead of getting involved locally to make a difference where we are. Welcome to learned helplessness and the seeds of victim thinking.

Instead of just following world events, you must begin to invest some of your time in making things happen where you are planted. Don't just read or watch the news; become the news by making a difference, and experience how quickly you will feel like a resilient survivor.

Optimists Still Make a Difference Today

Although resilient survivors are everywhere, they are seldom covered in the news. The United States has always been known for its can-do optimism, and you can still find plenty of examples of that optimism in action today. You can adopt this attitude yourself; find ways to perceive the hardships you face as temporary setbacks rather than as final verdicts.

> "There are many causes to victimization, some direct and some indirect. But these must be seen as hurdles and not excuses! . . . These are simply hurdles to jump, and they can be jumped. . . . A lack of basic education severely limits your life options. . . . No one can stop you from getting educated other than yourself."
>
> —Bill Cosby

Remember, it's what you think and do when things go wrong that determines whether you give up and play victim or get busy as a resilient survivor in overcoming whatever life throws your way. Survivors say to themselves: "I'm going to figure out how to beat this—one way or another!" Victims, on the other hand, lament, "I'll never be able to succeed, so why even bother to try?"

Stop Blaming and Start Helping

Optimists don't waste a lot of time being preoccupied with life's alleged unfairness. Instead, they get busy making things better. You don't have to look too far back in history to find examples of this uniquely American optimism in action. When Hurricane Katrina leveled the Gulf Coast, optimists found a way to create a new beginning one day at a time. Although half of her house was left uninhabitable after a tree crashed through their roof in Covington, Louisiana, Peggy Miranda and her family were still more focused on doing what they could to help others. Peggy confided, "It was healing for us to serve. This is a great opportunity to love on people who you would never love on. . . . It's like sending soldiers back to war. Our men would go out to serve. They'd come back fatigued, beat up and scratched. They rest for a day, eat and then go back."

Charlene Hoover yelled out her car window to a family sitting on the curb outside the Astrodome, "Are ya'll from New Orleans?" When Hasheen Cook replied affirmatively, Charlene said, "Well, we're looking for a family to adopt. Do ya'll need a place to stay?" Members of the Cook family wept with joy. Charlene's husband, Chuck, said, "We had to do this. We couldn't just sit and watch on TV and not do anything."

Michael Bennett—a 43-year-old business owner from Ventura County—joined others making a difference in Baton Rouge. With tears, he said, "Until you've helped someone through a disaster like this, you haven't lived. There's noth-

> "The ultimate measure of a man is not where he stands in moments of comfort and convenience, but where he stands at times of challenge and controversy."
> —Martin Luther King Jr.

ing like helping people." When Michael's neighbors heard he was going to help, they piled food and clothes in his truck. Biloxi *Sun Herald* editor Stan Tiner and his family said prayers together and then did what they could to make a difference. "My plight may be bad, but so many others have it worse. So even if some have lost all of their worldly possessions, they have much for which to give thanks. The statement that has become our mantra is 'I'm still standing.'"

They were just still standing! While some people spent their time and energy complaining about how poorly the government responded to Katrina, these heroes were living examples of resilient survivors who bounced back to help themselves and others in the Gulf Coast reclaim their lives. They certainly may be far poorer on their balance sheet, but they're all much richer in spirit. Don't just applaud them; find a way to join this merry band by making a difference where you can.

The 9/11 Terrorist Attacks Unleashed the Resilient Spirit of a Country

Sometimes disasters come from nature; sometimes they're the result of others' actions. The 9/11 attacks by Islamic terrorists cost thousands of lives and simultaneously assailed the very spirit of those who survived but had to deal with the impact of these violent acts. There is much to learn from average

> "The greatest discovery of my generation is that human beings, by changing the inner attitudes of their minds, can change the outer aspects of their lives."
> —William James

citizens who refused to play the victim and instead reaffirmed their own resilience and inner spirit by rebounding with resolve and determination to keep America strong.

In November 2001, *Business 2.0* and *Fortune* writer Jerry Useem observed: "If this is the first war of the 21st century, then it was also the first war that was visited on the workplace. Home of the cubicle, the busted toner cartridge, and other 'Dilbert' plot conventions, the American office has long been trivialized as a sanctuary of the petty and banal. On September 11th, however it suddenly became anything but. Words and glances passed between colleagues took on life-or-death consequence. Co-workers clasped hands and decided to flee or, in some cases, perish together. . . . Just as the rituals of democracy take on renewed meaning when we're under attack, so too do the rituals of capitalism, however mundane. Now, our work is not only important, but it is now the source of American muscle."

Wall Street is built on hope, and accordingly, the Dow Jones plummeted after the 9/11 attacks. Fear is the coin of the realm for terrorists; they wanted Americans to come to their knees, to become a nation of victims cowering in their homes. After all, when citizens stop the flow of money, they stop the economy. Americans therefore had a choice: to give up or bounce back. Enough Americans made the latter choice, with the support of men and women around the world. The economy rallied. Corporate leaders and workers behaved like warriors. They didn't like what had happened to their country and proclaimed: "We're not going to let anyone pull us under; our economy must thrive, and we'll make sure it does!"

American optimism isn't based on denial or wishful thinking. It stands on a rock-solid history of overcoming obstacles, setbacks, and wars to sustain the American Dream. Americans are practical realists. They want to know the bad news, so they can get busy finding out how to handle it. Hurricane Katrina and the 9/11 terrorist attacks were but

> "Optimism is a duty. The future is open. It is not predetermined. No one can predict it, except by chance. We all contribute to determining it by what we do. We are all equally responsible for its success."
>
> —Karl Popper

two tragic chapters in America's journey. Each event allowed a new generation of Americans to earn the freedoms and opportunities that we so treasure. Americans endured, persisted, and once again showed the world what we're made of. Claim that history as your own history. Be a resilient survivor wherever you are!

Truth #7: Be Patient Active and Risk Thriving in Pursuit of Health

As a member of the advisory board for Cancer Support Community Valley/Ventura, I've seen this organization in action since its inception nearly two decades ago. With sites around the country, Cancer Support Community is dedicated to providing emotional support, education, and hope to people with cancer and their loved ones, free of charge. Through participation in its professionally led support groups, educational workshops, social activities, and stress-reduction classes, cancer patients learn vital skills that enable them to regain control, reduce isolation, and restore hope, regardless of the stage of their cancer. Working in conjunction with professional medical teams, past cancer survivors, and volunteers, patients can help transform this dreaded diagnosis by becoming *patient active* and doing everything they can to fight the disease. Optimistic patients are realists. They don't disregard the mortality statistics; they just do what they can to make their survival more likely. If not, they find ways to affect their quality of life in the days that they have.

With our strong dependence on medical technology, drugs, and treatment protocols, it is all too easy to become a passive patient who relies on

> "This . . . is about living, fighting to recover, and, if possible, recovering. It's about participating in the fight for recovery—being a patient active instead of a passive, hopeless, helpless victim of the illness. It's about hope . . . always hope. In essence it is about the conversion from victim to victor."
>
> —Harold Benjamin, PhD

others to fix the problem. But no matter what the disease or condition, it's important to be patient active in support of your medical treatment plan. The patients with the greatest control over their well-being are the ones who seek out doctors who provide the facts about the medical challenges they face—and let those suffering know what they can do to make a difference in their treatment. Instead of withdrawing, blaming others, or denying the problem, they get busy by becoming part of the solution. They work with their medical team, family, friends, faith community, and support networks to do what they can to become resilient survivors.

California's Kaiser Permanente is another health care organization committed to more than simply treating disease. They've made a commitment to their member community that has become a call to action for everyone in the organization: "We stand for total health!" Whereas most health care providers in our present system are incentivized by patients being sick and needing care, Kaiser Permanente's health care model is built on investing in its members' health. Kaiser VP of Marketing Debbie Cantu says with passion: "All our messages to members are promoting thriving, not just surviving. We are committed to being proactive health advocates on behalf of our members. We don't want them to have to work the system to get care. We want the system to work for them by promoting healthy habits that give them the quality of life they desire. People today don't want health care; they want health!"

And Kaiser is giving people the tools to become patient active by challenging them: "Be Your Own Cause!" While other health care agencies are trying to find the funds to transfer from paper to digital records, 50 percent of Kaiser Permanente's eligible members have already signed on at http://www.kp.org for their personalized health care record titled "My Health Manager!" Its members are learning what it is like to be in control of their own health records. Instead of waiting for government to act, Kaiser Permanente is inventing the future and letting its members experience the benefits now.

Whether you are working with Cancer Support Community, Kaiser Permanente, or like-minded organizations—the message is to take control of your health. No matter where you are in life, or what your health condition or challenge might be, as an optimist, you want to be as self-reliant and healthy as you can be. Be patient active; you just may live long and thrive as long as you live!

Truth #8: No Dream Will Work Unless You Do

Don't kid yourself. Even in the worst of economic times, you'll never run out of opportunities. The world economy thrives on risk and opportunity. The only relevant questions are whether you can endure the setbacks that come your way and whether you can take advantage of the available opportunities. All it takes for the American Dream to work its magic is for you to claim it and translate it into focused action.

Become an entrepreneur. Take your gifts and find a better way to do something people need. Do it cheaper. Do it faster. When you add value and stay in the game, you'll find a way to succeed. Victims have a way of proving how pointless it is to dream by citing the staggering un-

> "People who are achievement oriented feel that they must be in control of their lives. . . . They do not expect to advance by demanding more from 'society,' but by demanding more of themselves."
> —Harold B. Jones, *Personal Character and National Destiny*

employment numbers and how many times their resumes have been rejected. Resilient survivors are out there finding employers who need what they have to offer, or they're creating their own small companies. They stay in the game until they score!

There will always be those who are out of work, are between jobs, or could, for a period of time, be classified as poor. There is a chronic needy population. But the question worth asking is how many of those the government reports as poor actually remain poor over time? The University of Michigan has reported on research that followed large samples of impoverished Americans for decades to assess their progress. Over several decades, results showed that only 1 of 20 poor Americans remained this way. Thirteen of 20 became middle class; 6 become rich as defined by rising to the top 20 percent of American wage earners. Of course, you can argue over whether that's rich, but it certainly isn't poor.

Although there is a small underprivileged population that may not improve, in general, all boats continue to rise—if you're willing to row! There will always be recessions to contend with, and they are hardest on those who have lost jobs and don't have the savings to cushion the tough times. While that is undoubtedly difficult for those experiencing it, your best bet is not victim thinking; it's constructive action. Optimism is infectious. If you don't look out, you may catch it! Dwell on your hopes and your confidence, not your doubts and your fears. Even in the face of new challenges, unseen disasters, and economic trials, you must keep thinking, dreaming, and inventing your future, and you just may become a resilient survivor.

> "The ladder of success is best climbed by stepping on the rungs of opportunity."
> —Ayn Rand, *Atlas Shrugged*

Truth #9: Unleash the Power of Optimistic Stories and Positive Gossip

If you are a leader, it doesn't help to be alone in your optimism. Your challenge is to be contagious. At times, that means becoming a cheerleader, champion, communicator, challenger, change agent, and comic. But in tough times, it all comes down to keeping hope alive. You must both tell the truth about the obstacles your team faces and inspire them to take advantage of the opportunities that lie ahead. One of the best ways to do that is to share heroic stories from the past and present.

Stories turn experiences into narratives, people into heroes, and earned successes into renewed optimism. All of a sudden, optimism is no longer an abstract attitude; it's a message embodied in a team or hero. When people can see optimism in action, it is far more contagious.

The most satisfying stories come out of experience forged through the heat of real-world struggles. The dictionary defines *hero* as a person "distinguished by the performance of extraordinary brave or noble deeds." Since optimism is earned through a track record of overcoming obstacles, find stories about your past heroes and how their optimistic resilience helped the organization turn tough times into a launching pad for growth.

> "Whether you are talking about an organization or a country, stories help us all think about who we are, where we come from, what obstacles we have and must still overcome, and where we are headed. In the right hands such stories can either leave people feeling hopeless and helpless or inspired into purposeful action."
> —Edward O. Welles

To reinforce the 3M culture of innovation with new technical associates, leaders continue to tell "The Post-It Story" to prove that one committed and innovative employee can make a profound difference for the company. But you can't just dwell on the *good old days*; your job is to create the *new good old days*.

So instead of just honoring past heroes, share current stories of optimism in action. After all, the biggest difference between being optimistic and generating optimism is whose stories you get excited about sharing. Capture hope and excellence where you find them, fan the sparks of their enthusiasm by honoring them, and reflect their passion by positively gossiping about their exploits to others who do not yet believe that things can and will be better! The best stories describe both the struggles involved in overcoming obstacles and the hard-fought moments of victory that resulted.

Even in tough economic times, Southwest Airlines seems to continue to fly right. Part of what makes the airline successful is its ability to find, acknowledge, and celebrate the stories of how its people keep the airline soaring. Colleen Barrett, Southwest's president emeritus, treasures her past role as Southwest's resident den mother, the keeper of the flame of excellence. She urged workers to fill out LUV reports every time they had an upbeat story to share. The stories generated were honored and shared. Southwest still celebrates their LUV reports by creating celebrations, tributes, and incentives to keep the unique Southwest persona alive. Who is the den mother in your organization?

To surface stories worth sharing, take the time to ask questions that let people share their successes: What has been working for you? What are you doing differently that's worth bragging about? You can't push or pull people into optimism, but you can catch their optimism in action and brag about it.

> "Our role as leaders is not to catch people doing things wrong but to create an environment in which people can become heroes."
> —Newt Hardie

See your organization as a diamond. By sharing positive stories, you can show its beauty, one facet at a time. Get busy unleashing the power of the story in your organization! Your people deserve to know the rest of the story waiting to be told about your organization. Sharing such stories keeps hope alive in the hearts and minds of your people. Now, do you have any positive gossip to share? Just imagine! Someday, future generations may very well be sharing your stories!

Don't Just Survive . . . Thrive

How does the material in this chapter relate to you? Whether as an individual or as a leader, your attitude and the labels you use to define yourself have consequences. Make the choice today to avoid victim thinking and, instead, seize the day as a contagious, resilient survivor. As long as you are alive, you always have options. Survivors make the best of their available options, while victims whine about how few they have. However, there is never nothing you can do. The only relevant questions are whether a given action will work and whether additional different actions will be required. The choice of whether to be a victim or a resilient survivor is yours. This book is dedicated to helping you make that choice every day until it becomes a self-fulfilling habit. When you are good at doing so, you won't just survive; you will thrive and take others with you!

The Optimistic Power
of Purpose

"It is one of the most beautiful compensations of this life that no one can sincerely try to help another without helping themselves."
—Ralph Waldo Emerson

We now can appreciate that life is difficult—both on and off the job—and that optimists can and do choose to be resilient survivors, not victims. But life is more than a series of disconnected challenges and opportunities. It can provide significant meaning and is best experienced as a journey with a purpose in mind.

A farmer once confided to me, "The problem with our children today is that they are not needed. On the farm every kid was needed, and they learned to deal with life and overcome every obstacle life dealt." Children need to know they are needed. We all need to know we make a difference; we need the power that a sense of purpose can provide.

> "Don't let yourself wake up in three years and say, 'I'm three years older, and I just happened to get here.' Clarify your vision, so that you can grow into it."
>
> —Terri Lonier

Psychologist and author of *Learned Optimism* Martin Seligman added his appreciation for the power that purpose can provide: "Optimism, . . . by itself, cannot provide meaning. Optimism is a tool to help the individual achieve the goals he has set for himself. It is in the choice of the goals themselves that meaning— or emptiness—resides. When learned optimism is coupled with a renewed commitment to the commons, our epidemic of depression and meaninglessness may end." In other words, a positive attitude is a good thing, but it isn't the only thing. Only when it is combined with meaningful goals and supporting actions does optimism really help us get to where we need to be!

Purpose and Optimism Come from a Heart of Service

A powerful purpose can have an impact on all aspects of your life. Nobel Prize–winning medical missionary to Africa Albert Schweitzer knew the power of purpose when he said, "If you truly desire happiness, seek and learn how to serve." Whether you're offering a smile with an encouraging word, taking the time to complete a random act of kindness, or serving a customer on the job—you transform your own optimistic attitude and feelings when you make a difference for others.

> "Everyone has his own specific vocation or mission in life; everyone must carry out a concrete assignment that demands fulfillment. Therein he cannot be replaced, nor can his life be repeated, thus, everyone's task is unique as his specific opportunity."
>
> —Viktor Frankl

Viktor Frankl was a Jewish psychoanalyst and Holocaust survivor who used his analytical skills to understand why some had not lost hope in such a glaringly hopeless situation. In his best-selling book, *Man's Search for Meaning*, Frankl wrote: "We who lived in

concentration camps can remember the men who walked
through the huts comforting
others, giving away their last
piece of bread. They may have

> "Those who have a why to live, can bear with almost any how."
> —Viktor Frankl

been few in number, but they offer sufficient proof that everything can be taken from a man but one thing: the last of the human freedoms—to choose one's attitude in any given set of circumstances, to choose one's own way. And there were always choices to make. Every day, every hour, offered the opportunity to make a decision, a decision which determined whether you would or would not submit to those powers which threatened to rob you of your very self, your inner freedom; which determined whether or not you would become the plaything of circumstance, renouncing freedom and dignity to become molded into the form of the typical inmate. Fundamentally, therefore, a man can, even under such circumstances, decide what shall become of him—mentally and spiritually. He may retain his human dignity even in a concentration camp."

Frankl's words convey a compelling message: that there is a power of purpose that comes in serving others. More people today have the means to live, but few seem to have found their meaning to live. The struggle to find your sense of purpose will pay off in an optimistic attitude, personal satisfaction, and, often, results that make a difference.

Truth #10: Live a Mission That Taps Your Purpose, and Work Ceases to Be Work

Having a compelling purpose can directly affect your work and your organization. After all, you don't just want a job with a good salary and benefits. You want to love what you do, and you want to do your part in making a difference for an organization with a meaningful mission. Ostensibly, serving customers—or the public at large—is what successful organizations are all about. Consistently finding ways to serve others has an added benefit—it makes it easier and more fulfilling for you to keep coming to work every day.

> "I could detect a distinct correlation between this notion of vision and performance. . . . The good ones had a vision. As for the bad ones, it was hard to tell why the people had come to work that morning."
> —Donald Povejsil

Most companies take time to craft a vision and mission, but placing those statements on a wall or in an annual report does little to enliven anyone's sense of purpose. The biggest difference between a vision and a hallucination is the number of people who can see it—and live it! For a mission on the job to make a difference, it must exist and be apparent in your heart, mind, and daily actions. And it helps especially when that mission meaningfully resonates with your own deeper purpose. Successful organizations have torchbearers willing to lead and associates committed to using their skills and experience to deliver on the dream.

Seth Godin describes the impact of leaders with a strong sense of purpose: "Torchbearers . . . are willing to take responsibility for carrying the flame. The biggest chasm in our society has become the gap between people who embrace the torchbearer's responsibility to customers, investors, and companies and those who are just there for the job."

Torchbearers don't accept excuses. They attract others because they care more about moving forward than they do about which route they take. They are pursuing the joy of meaningful achievement driven by an equally strong devotion to duty. These leaders don't give up until they're done. When was the last time you picked up a torch at work that brought you responsibility and satisfaction? Do you see any torches worth picking up on or off the job? Do you see any leaders you are eager to follow?

Instead of settling for people who just want a job, torchbearers want people who share their passion and purpose. Instead of assigning people, there is power in letting teams form around a shared commitment to the project. Maria Dotson, Vice President of Global Clinical Operations at Quintiles Transnational Corporation, has spent much of her career working to develop project management best practices. She does

> "Vision without action is only a dream. Action without vision is just passing the time. Vision with action can change the world."
> —Joel Barker

less assigning and more recruiting for the best people to serve: "When a new project comes in the door, I broadcast it to the organization: 'Who wants to come forward and why?' When people apply, I want to know if there's something special motivating them. If it's a cancer drug, did their grandmother die of cancer? Have they always been eager to work with this particular client?"

> "Especially in troubled times, leaders must be like emotional and intellectual anchors. You must steady the organization and have a passionate belief that what you are doing is important. I never realized how critical that was in times of turbulence. Leadership is about what you do when the going gets tough."
> —C. K. Prahalad

In the same way, today's leaders are riding herd over a never-ending stream of pickup games. They also know the frightening truth: Without people who want to do the job and have the right complementary skills to accomplish it, the project will not be done with the urgency and the quality customers require in today's competitive world economy. Once you have the right people, then, like any good pickup game, make sure the teams have a way to know the score. Then you let them play. A motivated strategic focus, an attitude of fearlessness, a passionate sense of purpose, and a get-it-done-in-whatever-way-that-counts flexibility are what leaders value most in today's pickup players.

Unfortunately, various surveys suggest that as many as a quarter of Americans don't find meaning in what they do on a daily basis. The primary reason they remain in their job is that they can't afford to quit. They're locked into good benefits and a health care plan that they can't afford to lose. This is a bad deal for the organization, and it's bad for those clinging to their jobs.

Truth #11: Risk Becoming the Architect of Your Own Future

Changing this may seem easier said than done; in difficult economic times, people may take a little longer. But in the long run, life is too short to stay in a job that you don't like. So if this describes you—don't settle! You deserve more. Risk becoming the architect of your own future. Even as you continue toiling in your current position, begin looking for ways to find a more meaningful job— one that you can actually enjoy. You may not be able to find your dream occupation right away, but you can find significance and satisfaction by opening new chapters in your life that will get you a lot closer to it. Expand your internal network, and share your career goals. You may just find a pickup game in your current organization that is much more fulfilling.

Writing on intrinsic motivation, Ken Thomas observes: "Self-management is simply the set of steps you go through to apply your intelligence to accomplishing a purpose, . . . but those steps can only be driven by a purpose that is meaningful to you."

So if someone asked you what gives your life meaning, how would you respond? Pretend that you're on an elevator, and you have just one minute to tell another person the truth about your purpose and mission. Can you articulate it? Or are you—like so many others—struggling with the implications of not having an answer?

> "Worse than being blind is to see and have no vision."
> —Helen Keller

After all, you may be saying, "I'm no Martin Luther King Jr.—no Gandhi or Mother Teresa!" But think about it; these individuals didn't immediately begin their lives as the giants they eventually became. Mother Teresa didn't come onto the world stage as a saint. She started humbly by finding one small corner of a broken world and holding the hand of a person in need. They simply did what they felt they were meant to do where they were. Their missions found them as they lived out their lives one choice at a time.

Is there one thing that you feel you are meant or called to do? While this is possible, it's more likely that your life will have many chapters—all of which will be fulfilling in their own way. Be a humble explorer, repeatedly becoming a beginner in new arenas as you keep shaping your life one day at a time. Finding your purpose is too important a goal to come easily, and it's worth every second of the struggle! But don't let finding your grand purpose trap you into purpose paralysis. After all, the very idea of finding one underlying motive on which your entire life value will be based can be intimidating! Take the pressure off by not expecting your stated purpose to be profound or fully developed. Maybe you could start with a general commitment to live life in a meaningful way and to trust that meaning and purpose will most likely shift through the different stages of your life.

You won't find your purpose sitting still; it's in living your life with gusto that your purpose finds you. I respected my father so much that I assumed that if accounting was good enough for him, it was good enough for me. Unfortunately, I soon found that even though the work came easily in my college classes, I didn't enjoy it.

Soon it was psychology that captured my attention and stirred my interest. Through years of graduate school, research, and internships, I looked toward a time when I could start my own practice. I partnered with another psychologist right out of school. It was the right time; I was already used to poverty and had nothing to lose.

Although my work was satisfying, I did not find my current calling until I started speaking to community groups to attract clients. My practice was growing, as was my appreciation of the joy of touching audiences with inspiring content they could use on and off the job.

> "Discovering purpose is like uncovering patterns. If you understand the first chapters of your life, you're in a better position to write the next chapters. We all need to be part of a bigger story."
> —Gregory A. Plotnikoff, MD

After speaking on assertion training to a chamber of commerce group, a businessman asked me to speak to his leadership team. I replied, half joking, "I don't do that. I'm a psychologist. People come to me." He laughed and said the magic words, "We pay speakers."

Money has a way of grabbing your attention when you're poor. I jumped at the opportunity, only to find that I had found my calling. Soon I was speaking more and enjoying doing therapy less. I found a meaningful career that continues to drive my mission and sustains my motivation to this day. My purpose batteries get recharged every time I have the opportunity to speak.

Identifying and Using Your Purpose in Support of a Meaningful Mission

Are you living in support of a mission worthy of your commitment? Do you have a sense of calling that recharges your purpose batteries? There are many things to look for:

- When you're engaged in actions that are aligned with your purpose, you'll feel most alive.
- It will feel life-giving and self-fulfilling.
- Actions will seem to flow naturally from your commitment.
- You'll find yourself looking for opportunities to exercise that purpose and deepen your understanding of what sustains it.

> "Vocation is the place where your deep gladness meets the world's deep need."
> —Frederick Buechner

In many ways, instead of making a rational or even emotional commitment, the right purpose will tend to grab ahold of you!

Okay, are you still struggling with this question? In order to facilitate your journey of discovery, try putting aside the professional and personal masks that we often use to define us. Strip away the letters after your name, your professional and group labels—and even your current position. Instead, let the following criteria guide your discovery:

- What name would you give to the purpose that describes your actions when work doesn't seem like work?
- What excites you about getting up in the morning? What are you looking forward to?
- What part of your organization's mission makes you proud enough to brag about it to others?
- Finish this statement: "I love my job and my life when I get to _____."
- If I had all the money and time in the world, how would I use my talents to serve others?

What stands out in these answers as the purpose that currently drives you? It's time to claim that purpose you've worked to discover and to use it to more consistently energize your daily work and life. Let it change and deepen as your awareness affects your passion for what you do and how you

> "You can only become truly accomplished at something you love. Don't make money your goal. Instead, pursue the things you love doing, and then do them so well that people can't take their eyes off you."
> —Maya Angelou

serve. Don't worry about impressing others. You want your purpose— the one that works for you at this point in your life!

The next question to ask yourself is: Does your purpose fit what you are now doing with your life? Since your calendar is your living creed—do its entries and appointments demonstrate that you are living your purpose on and off the job? After all, what you put in your calendar tends to get done. Start making purposeful commitments that will guide your actions this week.

Consider whether your purpose aligns with your organization's mission and strategic vision. Can you make it fit by adjusting your attitude or your role? Optimism and cynicism are both contagious; your employer deserves your commitment and passion for the work you do! If you can't find alignment and be optimistic about making a difference, start investing time in finding a position that allows you to do just that.

Whether on or off the job, nothing is more motivating than working with others in support of a meaningful mission. Embracing a strong personal calling that enlivens that purpose will allow you to say no to things that aren't worth doing—and to accomplish results you can be proud of.

> "Taking makes me feel like I'm dying. Giving makes me feel like I'm living."
> —Morrie Schwartz

Significant Life Events Shape Our Sense of Purpose

Some tragedies are still emblazoned in our minds. Years later, we can recall where we were when we heard the news about the assassination of President John F. Kennedy, the *Challenger* explosion, and the September 11th terrorist attacks. The Columbine tragedy of April 20, 1999, was one such event. Today, many of the staff working at Columbine High School in 1999 when the shootings occurred have left, but some teachers remain. Five who were students at that time have been drawn back to the school as teachers.

Alise Steiner was a sophomore about to take a math test when violence erupted and the fire alarms went off. She remembers the continued rough times with a succession of suicides in her junior year. But today, she teaches math and coaches girls' lacrosse and cross-country at Columbine High School. "It's like all the roads aligned," Alise said, "and I ended up back at Columbine." Even after being offered a teaching job at a private Christian school, her attachment to Columbine overcame the temptation to move. "I was thinking hard—I was so torn," she said. "But I could not leave. I feel this is where I'm at, and it's meant to be."

Often, our purpose finds us and shapes our mission and our way of making a difference. By helping others cope, we help ourselves. When there was a bomb scare in 2008, one teacher who had gone through the shootings did not want to go to school. A fellow teacher asked her, "Do you want a substitute teacher to comfort your kids on this day?" She went to be with her students. She knew that sharing an optimistic attitude in tough times can be contagious and comforting.

Faith Is a Powerful Source of Purpose and Meaning

Authentic faith-driven missions are a strong source of purpose. I once heard a story wherein a World War II correspondent encountered a nun tending to some horribly wounded and diseased prisoners of war. He said to the nurse, "I wouldn't do that for a million dollars." The nun turned to him and replied, "Neither would I." Purpose gives meaning to even the most difficult tasks.

Faith in what you hold sacred can play a critical role in integrating your life's story around a bigger purpose and plan. It can shape both your sense of calling and your ultimate optimistic view of the future. Believing that God calls you to love your neighbor easily translates into a fulfilling mission of service. Although Freud's early focus on the neurotic influence of religion had an impact on the early thinking of mental health scholars, history shows that religious organizations were often the first to provide compassionate care to vulnerable people. In fact, the first hospitals were church-sponsored and priest-managed. Faith made a difference for believers and those they served.

But only recently has research shown that religious involvement has a powerful and beneficial effect in encouraging hope and meaning. Studies find that believers are more optimistic than nonbelievers and that they regain happiness more quickly after experiencing a crisis.

The power of a community has always been important. What drew early believers to Christianity in the first century was what Keith Miller called the "scent of love." It was the way the community of believers served and lived that pulled people to this little group.

Believing in a loving God where serving others serves God makes for a strong centering purpose. In fact, studies of centenarians, those over 100 years of age who are living healthy and happy lives, are often quick to include spirituality as one key source for their fountain of youth. Although no particular faith was isolated, having a strong belief system is a big factor in maintaining personal vitality.

> "I noticed when you ask the most highly functioning seniors how they are, they always say, 'I feel good . . . thanks to God.' Yet they may be blind and deaf and their bones hurt. . . . The fact that God is in control of their lives relieves any economic, spiritual, or well-being anxiety they might otherwise have. They go through life with the peaceful certitude that someone is looking out for them."
>
> —Dan Buettner

So nurture your beliefs and let them show in your actions and attitude. Instead of making it an argument over religious doctrine, focus on developing a personal love affair with whatever faith drives you and your passionate calling to serve others. As the legendary

UCLA basketball coach John Wooden said in his autobiography, "If I am ever on trial for my faith, I hope there is enough evidence to convict me." Having a strong purpose leaves evidence. Does your purpose show in your actions on and off the job? When it does, one of the by-products is optimism.

Secular Service Also Provides Meaning for Many

Despite the importance that many place on faith, this is not to say that without it, you cannot find a sense of purpose in your life. There are too many instances of purpose-driven nonbelievers to think otherwise.

For example, legendary playwright George Bernard Shaw was clearly passionate—and decidedly secular—in his approach to defining his own purpose: "This is the true joy in life: The being used for a purpose recognized by yourself as a mighty one. . . . Instead of a feverish, selfish little clod of ailments and grievances, complaining that the world will not devote itself to making you happy. I am of the opinion that my life belongs to the whole community, and as long as I live, it is my privilege to do for it what I can. I want to be thoroughly used up when I die, for the harder I work, the more I live. I rejoice in life for its own sake. Life is no brief candle to me—it's sort of a splendid torch which I've got a hold of for the moment and I want to make it burn as brightly as possible before handing it on to future generations."

> "Be led by your dreams, not just pushed by your problems."
> —Roy Williams

Now that is a compelling and passionate purpose worthy of respect. If it resonates with you, let it help you refine your purpose. Shaw's desire to leave a legacy and to hand off his purpose to future generations is shared by many. For you, this might translate into mentoring or coaching others on the job. Off the job, it might give you reason as a parent or grandparent to make an impact on the younger members of your family. If you don't have children of your own, you may be inclined to volunteer with scouting, youth groups, local schools, or Big Brothers/Big Sisters. Finding your purpose leaves evidence for others to see.

Just remember, your purpose will find you if you risk living a life that searches for meaningful ways to serve with the gifts you possess.

A Sense of Purpose Promotes a Hardy Lifestyle and Meaning

If you want added motivation, a powerful purpose may also help you claim a long, healthy life. American psychologist Salvatore Maddi, co-author of *Resilience at Work: How to Succeed No Matter What Life Throws at You*, has extensively studied what makes executives hardy in the face of work-related stress. He found that the healthiest executives shared three characteristics: a feeling of commitment, a sense of control in their lives, and an acceptance of life's stressful moments as challenges rather than threats. This research confirms that having a sense of commitment to a purpose doesn't merely give you meaning; it may well make you more resistant to the impact of stressful living. If you are a hardy professional, another word would capture those same qualities—you are an optimist!

> "Hardy executives are self-confident and have a sense of purpose. They have the knack of making whatever they do feel important."
> —Salvatore Maddi, PhD

So, whether it's sacred or secular, trade your preoccupa- tion with your own daily problems for a centering journey to find your own purpose—your way to use your gifts to make a difference! And take inspiration from the words of Mother Teresa: "Remember this: I can do something you can't do, and you can do something I can't do. But we both have to do it."

When you have faith that your future will make a difference, you'll undoubtedly see the power in your present. Do something today to find and live your purpose—and you'll find the optimism, joy and satisfaction that come along for the ride.

> "The best way to cheer yourself is to try to cheer somebody else up."
> —Mark Twain

CHAPTER 5

Optimists Update Their Gifts into Recyclable Assets

"Today technology can replace whole new industries, so you have to stay flexible. To survive today, you have to be able to walk on quicksand and dance with electrons."

—Frank Ogden

Are you ready to look with fresh eyes at your opportunity landscape? You've already worked at getting a better handle on your purpose. In this chapter, you'll look for a connection between your gifts and current trends that will intersect with that purpose in a meaningful way. You want to put your gifts to work in a way that makes a difference and a living!

In a constantly changing world, it's a lot easier to remain optimistic when you keep turning your gifts into recyclable assets that make a difference where it counts for you—and for those you serve. Today's job market is not the place to be good at something that's no longer needed. So ask yourself: Are you sending resumes for positions that are no longer viable? Is your present career positioned for the past or for the future? Do you have a *Plan B* in place in case you lose your present job? Are you daring to use this time of change as an opportunity to pursue your dream career?

Record-setting UCLA bas-ketball coach John Wooden shares some advice that rings true for every age: "It's what you learn after you know it all

> "Talent is only the start. You must keep working your talent."
> —Irving Berlin

that counts." Don't assume that your education ends the moment you complete college or graduate school. Those who find the most success are those who participate in lifelong learning. Most likely, you will have many varied careers in your lifetime, and many may have nothing to do with your major. If you're lucky, what you learn in college is *how* to learn.

Education has morphed from a K through 12 to a K through 100 phenomenon. People are living much longer; in fact, one of the fastest growing demographics in the United States, in terms of percentage growth, is the 90-100 year range. One study found that 3 percent of those 90-100-year-olds were still working full-time; 1,200 of those were physicians.

Now, I don't know if I would go to a doctor who's 100—"We'll start with blood letting and then move on to something more modern." But seriously, why are so many of these seniors still working? While it's true that some may need the money to make ends meet, for many, it's because of the vitality and meaning their work brings to their lives.

Truth #12: Be a Lifelong Learner by Updating Your Gifts into Recyclable Assets

If you haven't noticed, the time of lifelong employment is over. Your best insurance policy may be to become a lifelong learner and take responsibility for your own short- and long-range career development.

Optimism is one of the natural by-products of productive living. Since you're likely to be living—and therefore working—longer, you

> "In times of rapid change, experience could be your worst enemy."
>
> —J. Paul Getty

must keep developing your gifts into marketable and meaningful skills. If you're not sure how to do that, take heart in the fact that half of what you could be doing in the future hasn't even been invented yet. These are exciting times, and your job is to enjoy the challenge of staying relevant and valuable so that you can capitalize on those changes!

In his book *Future Shock*, Alvin Toffler said: "The illiterate of the future are not those who cannot read or write. They are those who cannot learn, unlearn, and relearn." The hardest part is the *unlearning*. You have to let go of what you're good at in order to learn new skills in areas where you have no idea what you're even doing. And although that can seem threatening, the alternative is worse. If you're already in the obsolete category, you want to surprise your current manager by developing your own recovery program before he or she is forced to do it for you under much less favorable conditions. What's dangerous is to not evolve.

Now, don't worry; working for others is not the only option here. No matter what the current unemployment numbers are, the American Dream isn't dead! Wealth is still out there; it's just moving from one sector to another. As my great uncle Harvey Swanson used to say to me on the farms of Illinois, "It's easiest to ride a horse in the direction it's going." That's a seminar in a sentence. In short, if you master skills that let you capitalize on future trends, you have nothing to fear from the future.

> "In a time of drastic change, it is the learners who inherit the future. The learned usually find themselves equipped to live in a world that no longer exists."
>
> —Eric Hoffer

Ride Trends in the Direction They Are Going

Life is all about riding—instead of resisting—trends. Eco-green jobs are riding a strong horse in a world that fears global warming and supports environmental causes. Whether you agree with such views or not, if you have skills that match your passion to make a difference for our environment—then ride the horse!

While living in California's gold country, celebrated American author Mark Twain advised, "When everybody is out digging for gold, the business to be in is selling shovels." In a gold rush, some strike it rich and others fail, but they all need shovels. What do those mining the future need to find their gold? You can be there to help provide it.

Anthony Mayo, author of *Their Time: The Great Business Leaders of the 20th Century,* shares an observation for our

> "Anything that won't sell, I don't want to invent."
> —Thomas Edison

times: "We discovered that people who were successful over a long period of time were contextually intelligent. They understood the context of their time, how to grow a business, find a new market opportunity and see some possibility others thought was dormant or dying." In these challenging economic times, it's too easy to focus on business that isn't there. When it looks like there are no opportunities, optimists look in a different direction or refocus with fresh eyes. Contextual intelligence suggests that today's treasure maps must change to adjust to the economic and political context for you to have any hope of finding treasure.

A teenager on a job search was tired of going from establishment to establishment and hearing the same message: "We're not hiring right now." He knew he wasn't alone, but it didn't make his hunt any easier. Spotting a handwritten sign in one window reading "Not Hiring," he realized how many managers were just as tired of answering the question as he was of asking it.

On his way home, he passed a sign shop. He stopped, smiled, and placed an order for a sign he was sure people would buy. From that day forward, he had two goals as he entered every establishment—get a job or sell a sign that read "Not Hiring." In fact, he might

> "Find a job that you like so much that you would do it without compensation; then do it so well that people will pay you to continue."
> —Walt Disney

well have added a follow-up message: "Now that you know the innovation I can bring to my work, would you like to reconsider hiring me?"

Use Training as a Strategic Advantage

Organizations can't take advantage of the future without having the people with the right skills to make that happen. Whether they hire people with new skills or promote development within, successful companies address the development of new products or services and new knowledge in an integrated approach. By encouraging everyone to keep learning and hiring for strategic competencies, focused training becomes a powerful tool for inventing a profitable future for all involved.

> "Find your own sweet spot— that intersection of personal passion and corporate need."
> —Craig Steinman

Sometimes the simplest statements can open the biggest vistas into making strategic change work. Stephen R. Covey said it well: "Management is efficiency in climbing the ladder of success; leadership determines whether the ladder is leaning against the right wall."

No one wants to climb the ladder of success to a destination that isn't worth reaching! Whether you're an associate, a manager, a leader, or the CEO, it's everyone's job to make sure that the ladder to success is on the right wall. One thing worse than training people and losing them is not training them and keeping people who aren't prepared for the future you want to create!

Too many former employees share the same statement in their exit interviews: "I'm leaving for a better opportunity." No organization can afford to lose its best people. If you want people who are flexible enough to move to where the action is, let them know where they are going soon enough for them to refocus and retool with the skills needed. To keep your best people, make sure staying in your organization provides more opportunities than leaving!

If your leaders aren't giving you the information you need, take the initiative to let them know you want to be part of your organization's future. Ask your boss, "What's your sense of where the company is going, and what can I do to be part of helping us get there?" Use the magic phrase, "I really want to help make this work."

Are you doing anything now that others in your organization could positively gossip about by the end of the year? We love making a difference, but it starts with taking the risk of adding value to projects that will allow that. Don't wait to be asked. Instead of settling for the status quo, volunteer to be part of a little adventure into unexplored territory that your company wants to claim for the future!

Finally, everyone talks about learning organizations, but they forget that the best organizations value both learning *and* unlearning. Their people must learn new competencies and unlearn habits that constrain them. If you're a leader, take time to share the skills and processes that will have to be left behind to make progress. No one wants to get stuck in the Dead Sea with no outlet when you want to master the whitewater rapids of your organization's uncharted future.

> "Somewhere in the belly of every company, someone is working away in obscurity on the project that 10 years from now everyone will acknowledge as the company's proudest moment. Why isn't that someone you?"
> —Tom Peters

Truth #13: Always Have a Plan B—A "What I Could Do Next" Plan

Whether you stay with the organization you are with or you leave, it is always wise to have options. Uncle Harvey's second piece of advice on the farms of Illinois was equally blunt and timely: "If the horse is dead, get off it!" Stop trying to find a job

> "Gaining an edge in the future depends upon the ability to hone the hyphen—to creatively bundle and re-bundle skills and knowledge. Cross-fertilization occurs when two or more unlikely fields combine. . . . The industries of the future all have hyphens in them: bio-tech, multi-media, eco-production."
> —Kate Kane

with skills that are no longer needed. Today, you either learn new competencies or lose out to those who will. If one door isn't opening, then look for more doors!

Since it is likely that eventually your horse is going to die, always have a *Plan B—A "What I could do next" Plan.* I've added my own horse sense: "Since it's hard to know if your horse is dying, have at least two horses. In fact, in today's world, have a herd." Take every opportunity to develop your interests and gifts into a set of competencies that will continue to add value.

You're Going to Be Forty-five Anyway

One young woman was stressed over how long it would take to get the degree she needed to pursue her dream. She complained, "If I take it one night course at a time, I'll probably be 45 by the time I finish."

Somewhat annoyed by the fact that I had already passed the milestone she considered old, I replied, "Optimistically, you'll be 45 anyway. You're either 45 with a degree or 45 without it. How long have you been thinking about this?"

> "If a man empties his purse into his head, no one can take it away from him. An investment in knowledge always pays the best interest."
> —Ben Franklin

The young woman replied, "Three years." I said with a smile, "You could have been 42!"

Learn from this situation—and don't wait a day longer! At all times, invest 5 percent of your time in your next career or in starting your own business. Look for cross-training opportunities. Volunteer for your organization's strategic projects. Exercise your purpose by donating your time and skills to causes you care about. All will help you turn your interests and gifts into a satisfying new career or your own business start-up. If downsizing is imminent or you hate your job, invest 10 percent of your time. Don't wait for them to get rid of you; begin to establish your own plan for what you will do next. Your optimism and security doesn't come from holding onto the past, but rather in helping to invent the future.

I'm not suggesting that you have to leave your current ca-reer or organization in order to be successful. I am saying that by having more than one op-tion, you have choices. By embracing change and learn-

> "Spend one extra hour every day studying your chosen subject. In five years you will be a national expert in that field."
> —Earl Nightingale

ing strategic skills, you become the gold your organization can't afford to lose while you still have the option to take advantage of new opportunities should they surface or become necessary.

A manager coming back from a seminar on *Making Change Work* was told by one of her longtime nurses, "You need to know I won't be one of your change agents. You see, on the freeway of life, I'm in the slow lane looking for an off-ramp." As you might imagine, it wasn't long before she earned the right to take that off-ramp!

In bad economic times, organizations have to *right size and right-skill.* If you were a corporation, would you invest in you? If not, get busy becoming a recyclable asset.

And if you *do* lose your job, take heart. *USA Today* reporter Del Jones observed about people who had turned layoffs into new opportunities: "Those who lose jobs in recessions can land on their feet, and even thrive. They say being jobless can steel and motivate people to work long and hard hours, teach them to be self-reliant and to distrust safety nets, and to spur them into fields they are passionate about. The result, at least in this instance, is success and content-ment, financially and otherwise."

Years ago, the author Lee Child lost his job in television. The new management decided to change directions and cut

> "When your mind is open, mentors are everywhere."
> —Robert McGarvey

costs, including his job. Lee felt betrayed by his own naiveté. The rules of the game had changed, and he hadn't noticed.

With the support of his family, he decided to become his own boss and take a new path. With an appreciation for which stories connect to readers and with his own rich experiences, he decided to try his hand at writing thriller novels. He introduced a character he could under-stand—Jack Reacher, a man downsized out of the army in the prime of

> "Drucker's Maxims: Pick the future against the past. Focus on opportunity rather than on problems. Choose your own direction rather than climb on the bandwagon. Aim high. Aim for something that will make a difference rather than for something that is 'safe' and easy to do."

his life. Since that fateful day he lost his job, Lee Child has gone on to write numerous international best sellers.

Discussing his career transition, Lee writes: "If you're fired at 40, it's not about hurt and betrayal and fear. It's about opportunity. By that time in your life, you've learned a few things. You've got skills and work habits. You're in charge. . . . Try something. Anything. Sit back, take a breath, believe in yourself, identify your dream, and go for it 110 percent. Trust me, your motivation will never be as strong. And the chance might never come your way again."

Indeed, layoffs and life changes sometimes free you to pursue what you have wanted to do all along. Early in life, many get stuck doing things other people thought was best for their future. At some point, if you are fortunate, you may just have a dream or even a calling that breaks forth with power, purpose, and passion in a way that catches the world off guard. Don't be your own worst enemy in hiding your dream. Instead, be led by it in developing the skills that can deliver that dream!

When Attitude, Skills, and Opportunity Come Together, Mastery and Magic Happen

> "Restlessness is destiny calling."
> —Ian Percy

When Susan Boyle took the stage to audition for *Britain's Got Talent*, the judges and many in the audience snickered and rolled their eyes as this frumpy, middle-aged Scottish church volunteer shared her dream of becoming a professional singer. But when she opened her mouth to sing "I Dreamed a Dream"—a ballad from treasured musical *Les Miserables*—angels soared, jaws dropped, judges let out audible gasps, and hundreds in the audience stood to applaud and roar their approval as she sang her dream into reality. She ended up second in the competition but first in the hearts of many new fans around the world.

On one day in April 2009, Susan's hidden gift and dream exploded onto the world stage. Within hours, YouTube postings of her performance had more than 20 million approving viewers. Her *Britain's Got Talent* videos were the most watched YouTube videos in 2009, attracting more than 120 million viewers worldwide, more than the next top three most-watched YouTube videos combined. Millions were brought to tears merely watching her performance. Many have focused on the need to not judge a book by its cover. That is a valuable lesson, but, more important, you should never let your gifts and your dreams die within you. Never forget that authentic gifts and empowering dreams produce amazing performances when unleashed. Optimism is born when attitude, skills, and opportunity come together at the right time to deliver excellence.

It's amazing to witness someone realize his or her true role in life. Although my son struggled with school and in his early jobs, his drive and his gifts were truly unleashed when he felt called into the ministry. I remember watching, with tears rolling from my eyes, as he delivered his first sermon. It was incredibly clear that he was exactly where he belonged—and was being used for a mighty purpose. I knew that while he might never be rich financially, he is certainly rich where it counts. He gets up every day, ready to learn and serve in a job that he loves. There's nothing better to build authentic optimism than finding your calling.

> "Choose a work you love and you will never have to labor a day in your life."
> —Confucius

Finding a Career That Matches Your Dream

Need help in finding your next career move? Try answering some of these questions:

- What activity makes your heart sing?
- What talents do you have that are still untapped?

- What dreams are unfulfilled?
- What gifts do others repeatedly see in you?
- What training have you always wanted to pursue but have not yet started?
- Looking back, what career choice do you regret *not* making?
- Is it really too late to get the training you need to live your dream?
- What would you do if you knew you would not fail?

Don't worry about the perfect plan, job, or time to start. Just *start!* Once you're in motion, every day will allow course corrections. If your training doesn't live up to your expectations, then make a move. When you find better opportunities beyond what you planned, make a move. Keep looking for what fits you.

Beat Your Impostor Feelings on the Road to Lifelong Learning

> "I am always doing that which I cannot do, in order that I may learn how to do it."
> —Pablo Picasso

But, you might wonder, "What if they find out that I'm just an impostor?" Studies have shown that up to 70 percent of us have *impostor feelings*. In other words, we feel as though we don't have the experience or the skills to meet all the challenges we face. I'm not at all suggesting that you are indeed any kind of impostor. People who know you and your work most likely rate your performance as effective. But inside, you may feel the same way that many others do—"If they ever found out how much I don't know about what I'm doing, I would be in serious trouble!"

The fact is that *no* one knows it all, and the people to worry about are those who *think* they do! In recent years, there *has* been an admittedly alarming increase in the number of things you know nothing about. You may very well own things that you still don't know how to use. If you've lost your manual, your only hope is that you have a young child who will teach you how to use it for the price of a cookie! So you're not alone here. The only places that perfect people exist are in self-help books and training clips. They get to edit out the errors! You live in the real world where real people have real struggles living their dreams and bouncing back from their mistakes on the way to mastery.

Lifelong learning is seldom easy but always exciting. Even when you have a gift and want to learn, you'll make mistakes! But by taking the risk to live your dreams and learn new skills, you'll be on your way to mastery and meaning. There is joy in such a journey and satisfaction when all your work bears fruit. This is all about making the commitment to begin . . . now!

Truth #14: You Become an Old Dog When You Stop Doing New Tricks

While we're tackling excuses, don't feel you're ever too old to live your calling. Everyone talks about eventually being over the hill. Age has a way of making us face signs that are hard to ignore. But even if your older body can't do some of the things it used to do effortlessly, you can still continue to learn. You can still make a dif-

> "Work adds life to your years, and it actually adds years onto your life."
> —Leon Levitt, an 81-year-old machinist trainee

ference. The face in your mirror may not match the playful soul within, and those old people you see at your high school reunion actually went to school with *you*! But life is less about what you've lost and more about what you've got left to give and do.

There was a brief scene in the movie *Finding Neverland* where an admiring patron complimented playwright J. M. Barrie after watching his play *Peter Pan*. She commented on how her departed husband would have appreciated the play: "He would have loved it—the pirates and the Indians. After all, he was just a boy. He was just a boy to the very end."

Instead of sliding graciously into old age, find new ways to live a super second life. After all, as a girl or boy to the very end, you still have a few more hills you want to climb, and no matter your age,

> "The most fun thing about life is that you don't really know. You just let life unfold. Of course, you've got to get in there and make sure you're the one stirring things."
> —Sally Field

you're never really finished. After all, Colonel Sanders started the Kentucky Fried Chicken franchise in his 60s. Today's seniors aren't done dreaming, working, or living. It's been said, "You can't teach an old dog new tricks!" Well, you become an old dog when you *stop* doing new tricks.

Will organizations want old dogs? You bet they will. More and more companies will be looking for well-trained, experienced workers willing to be a contingent workforce who will do contract work on projects as needed. If you want work to supplement your retirement income and increase your motivation and personal satisfaction, try selling your company on keeping your skills current and using you on projects. You can always keep your golf, travel, and other hobbies—and still find ways to keep learning, serving, and earning!

Lifelong education is the antidote to feeling victimized by a world of change. If you want to be optimistic, keep learning and keep turning your gifts into recyclable assets and your dreams into reality. As one wise retiree reflected: "To live life to the fullest, keep learning, keep laughing and keep lovin'! You can change the order, but keep all three!"

CHAPTER

6

Your Health Habits Impact Your Attitude

*"I tried every diet in the book. I tried some that weren't in the book.
I tried eating the book. It tasted better than most of the diets."*
—Dolly Parton

As an optimist, you want a body built to last and a quality of life worth living. By taking care of yourself and being responsible for your health habits, you're more likely to live longer, feel better, and reduce your medical costs. There is also evidence that some health habits have a strong impact on your attitude.

Most reputable health organizations have a consistent list of recommendations: get adequate sleep, limit alcohol consumption, and stop smoking. Two critical health habits on that list are worth addressing here—what you eat and getting enough exercise.

Eat Less and Exercise More

As a nation, we eat way too much. You may be able to get away with it when you're younger and naturally active, but as you age, you are

65

likely to become more sedentary and your metabolism declines. Right at the time that you need less food, you tend to eat too much. More and more young people have weight issues—and the health problems that go with it.

> "He asked me to bring some loose clothing to the gym. If I had any loose clothing, I wouldn't be coming down there."
>
> —Al Walker

Unfortunately—even with all the fitness and diet programs combined—Americans collectively lost a total of one pound last year. Okay, there is no research to prove that. But when you look at our collective girth and the average American diet, it is no wonder that many of us are far from the ideal in health habits.

Perfect diets and perfect exercise plans exist only in infomercials Most of the new and innovative exercise equipment you buy ends up as expensive clothes hangers. Eventually, they are wheeled out to the curb for a garage sale and bought by another well-meaning citizen—who often duplicates the same cycle.

You're probably asking, "Isn't this supposed to be a book about optimism?" Yes, but remember: Optimists are realists. You want to be aware of the practical obstacles you'll have to overcome to make changes. You also want to know why you should even bother to change health habits that you know won't come easy.

Let's start by looking at the advantages of small changes in your health habits. After all, why watch what you eat and exercise daily if it's not worth the effort?

Optimists Want a Body Ready for Action

On average, people are living longer these days. If you're like most, it isn't just the number of years you live that matters to you; it's the quality of those years. You want to be active for as long as possible, which means that you need a body ready for action. The less healthy you are, the fewer choices you have.

Do you want to travel, participate in sports, or live an overall active lifestyle? Well, doing these things when you're overweight and totally out of shape is much more difficult. You don't want to just watch sports when you can participate. You don't want to limit your trips to watching other people's adventures on the Internet; you want to go there yourself.

At 91, my father has already written his obituary. One short sentence ends, "and he died quietly in his sleep." He's already visualized how he wants to go! Reading his premature obit for the first time made the family laugh, but isn't that what we all want? Optimistically, you want to truly live to the last day you are alive.

Of course, you can't control everything that will affect your personal health or longevity. You can, however, control your diet, exercise, and other health habits to make it more likely that you'll be able to live the life you want. There's an added advantage. Even if you face health challenges, serious accidents, or debilitating diseases, when you're in shape, your body is better prepared to overcome any physical challenge that you encounter. If you plan to be *patient active* in working with your medical team to fight for your own recovery, you want a body that's in shape and ready to fight to the last round!

Now, I write this chapter with a healthy dose of humility. My diet has a documented *fudge factor* that includes infrequent but deeply cherished doses of hot fudge, chocolate chip cookies, popcorn at the movies, french fries. . . . Confession is good for the soul, but need I go further?

However, I've found ways to curb my indulgences and increase my positive food choices by keeping these treats

> "I don't diet. I just don't eat as much as I'd like to."
> —Linda Evangelista

out of my home. I'm then forced to go out and find the source of my temptation, which has a way of keeping my doses in check. At home, we prepare tasty but healthy meals with smaller servings to help balance my rushed fast-food purchases as I race to catch a plane to my next speaking engagement.

You don't have to eat perfectly to make a difference in your health and your attitude; the same is true in terms of exercise. I've seen myself run, and I'm not going to win any Olympic medals in track. While some individuals have bodies built for athletic excellence and professional-level competition, most of us have a body that, when healthy, can give us the vitality, strength, and mobility we need to live the life we want.

So whether you like your body or not, there is no replacement. Take care of your body, or it just may not take care of you! Being fit is all about being healthy. You don't need to look like a star athlete or a diet like a vegetarian monk. Okay, aspire to that if you want, but it's more important to develop some consistent exercise and eating habits that you can live with for the long haul.

The Exercise Attitude Connection

> A vigorous five mile walk will do more good for an unhappy but otherwise healthy person than all the medicine and psychology in the world."
> —Paul Dudley White, MD

There is yet another benefit to regular exercise and a sound diet; both can impact your attitude and your activity level. In fact, research shows that exercise can help reduce stress and anxiety, decrease mild depression, and produce a positive emotional effect. Exercise increases the biochemical reactions that increase feel-good chemicals like norepinephrine, serotonin and endogenous opioids, which, I promise, have nothing to do with aliens encountered in *Star Trek!*

Just using our large muscles for something as simple as a good walk is incompatible with maintaining depressive thoughts. Exercise also results in increased energy, improved sleep patterns, and a general feeling of self-accomplishment for sticking to goals and developing new positive habits. In a world where so many things are out of your power, the self-discipline and confidence generated from good health habits will increase your sense of personal control. Optimism is all about taking action; good health habits lead to a body ready for accomplishment.

Even if you're not in shape now, with time, you'll be able to walk or run a couple of miles, take a hike up a hill, or spend an evening dancing or playing basketball—without needing a standby ambulance ready. Then you'll understand why Ralph Waldo Emerson said, "The first wealth is health."

> "The key to cardiovascular fitness is consistency rather than intensity."
> —James Rippe, MD

A private school that I worked with in Hawaii placed strong emphasis on physical fitness. Middle school youths were required to work up to running nine miles before they graduated. If a teen said about any topic in high school, "I can't do that!"—teachers could say, "That's what you said about running nine miles, but you applied yourself, worked up to that distance, and you did it. You can do this the same way!" Now, that's teaching optimism by building a track record of overcoming milestones on the way to success.

It's unlikely that someone is going to require you to run nine miles or force you to eat more healthfully. Your high school coach isn't there blowing any whistles at you, demanding 20 push-ups or sending you on wind sprints down the field. It's your health and your life; it's therefore up to you. This is your chance to get your body working for you.

Truth #15: Eat Smart—Make Progress Not Perfection

The easier place to begin is with your eating habits. You may have seen the bumper sticker that reads, "Life is uncertain; eat dessert first." Don't worry

> "The more you eat, the less flavor; the less you eat, the more flavor."
> —Chinese Proverb

about losing your *fudge factor*. An occasional treat is fine, but don't let it become the norm. You don't have to eliminate every stop to your local fast-food joint—just don't stop every time you go by. It's progress—not perfection—that counts.

Most people are far too worried about what they eat between Christmas and New Year's Day, instead of being concerned about what they eat between New Year's Day and the next Christmas. Building good eating habits is not about having to eat what you hate. It's about learning to love what is good for you. Prepared well, a meal

> "Countless people tell me they would like to eat better, but they don't want to 'give up' tasty food. Rather than thinking about what they can't have, they should think about what they can eat."
>
> —Sybil Stanton

of whole-grain breads, fruits, vegetables, and low-fat meat, poultry, or fish, along with dairy products, can taste fantastic. Need more zing to satisfy your taste buds? There are spices out there that can do the job. Sure, it may take time to develop a taste for healthy foods, but it's well worth the effort. I, for one, used to refuse nonfat milk—none of that blue milk for me. My wife gradually added it to our low-fat milk until it was all nonfat milk. Now, even low-fat milk tastes like cream. Tastes can adjust.

Make small changes. Experiment with new recipes. When you find one that you love, prepare it more often. Make vats of the recipe, and freeze small portions for quick healthy meals. Making changes that last is not about losing food you love; it's about finding healthy food you love as much. You can change your preferences and impact your health.

There is more that you can do to guide your changes. Remember, good and bad habits are both hard to break. Instead of listing any particular diet, consult with your doctor, a registered dietitian, or any reputable nutrition professional.

Truth #16: The Only Good Exercise Plan Is One You Do Consistently

> "People who cannot find time for recreation are obliged sooner or later to find time for illness."
>
> —John Wanamaker

You know that you need to get moving, but what exercise should you choose? When asked if football is good exercise, former Oklahoma football coach Bud Wilkerson replied, "No. In football, there are 22 people on the field in desperate need of rest. And there are 50,000 people in the stands in desperate need of exercise." Don't just be a watcher; be a doer. Exercise doesn't just impact your attitude. Research shows that people who exercise regularly catch fewer colds, maintain their weight more easily, have a higher energy level, and live longer. Not a bad deal, whether you are an optimist or not!

The trick is not in agreeing that exercise is important; that's not a debatable issue any longer. The real goal is to find something you enjoy doing consistently—enough to become a lifelong habit. To be safe and smart, you might want to start by working with a credentialed fitness professional to get the most out of your exercise plan. Here are some habits you can live with:

- Get together with friends who like the same exercise so that on the days when you just don't feel like it, they'll help pull you along.

- If appropriate to your current health status, join a team in a sport you enjoy. Winning and losing together with teammates is an easy way to sneak in increased activity.

- Instead of watching your TV, get a Nintendo Wii. Let your TV take you and your family members through your paces for fun and health.

- Ride your bike or walk to your local store (or to work, if possible) rather than driving your car.

- Take the stairs instead of the elevator, get fewer dings and more exercise by parking your car farther from the store entrance, walk your pets regularly, and, at a minimum, move more, and then move for longer periods of time and at a faster pace.

You'll experience the payoff in attitude and health. You don't have to impress anyone else with your plan or your progress. Just get started by picking something you will do consistently.

Martin Luther used to say, "When you rest, you rust." Exercise is important, but don't forget to partake in some form of relaxation as well. A moment alone, meditation, yoga, or

> "The difference between interest and commitment is I'm interested in losing 15 pounds."
> —Ken Blanchard

prayer can do wonders to recharge your spirit. Every person relaxes differently, so find the method that works best for you. And while we're talking about relaxation, don't forget to get a good night's sleep, which will come more easily once you start exercising on a regular basis. Waking up refreshed has a way of helping you maintain a positive and optimistic attitude.

Take Care of Your Body—It Will Help Take Care of You

Making small changes now in your eating, exercise, and health habits will improve your health and your optimistic attitude now and for years to come. Take care of your body, and it will do a better job of taking care of you.

The lessons in this chapter aren't difficult or complicated. It doesn't provide a specific diet or exercise to follow. There isn't one that will work for everyone. But by taking care of your own body and taking responsibility for your health habits, you're apt to live longer, feel better, and improve your attitude. Make it a habit, and you'll become more optimistic.

> "If I had one wish, just give me health, and I'll get the rest."
> —John Garner

Like everything in this book, becoming optimistic is all about taking action. In fact, that's the focus of the next chapter.

Optimists Embrace Action

"If we listened to our intellect, we'd never have a love affair. We'd never have a friendship. We'd never go into business, because we'd be cynical. Well, that's nonsense. You've got to jump off cliffs all the time to build your wings on the way down."

—Ray Bradbury

earned Optimism author Martin Seligman observed: "Happiness divides into the domains of past, present and future. The past is your feelings of contentment or well-being. It's the life story you tell yourself. Present is what's usually called happiness. It's how you are feeling right now. And future is your optimism."

Making a move today, in the present, is the start of progress. After all, as Will Rogers loved to say: "Even if you're on the right track, you'll get run over if you just sit there." Optimists cultivate a bias for action. You can't change what has happened to you, but you can embrace the action imperative and do what you can to invent a better future—starting immediately. Optimism is all about making a move to turn your worries and concerns into constructive action.

I once had a client who simply refused to act. After a few sessions together, it became clear to me that her past experiences with

> "Isn't it amazing how many people tip-toe cautiously through life hoping to make it safely to death?"
> —Carl E. Hiebert

therapy had provided her with a hiding place from life, one where she had cultivated a vast array of excuses to avoid risk. After experiencing enough of her painful ruminations, I had given her a between-session assignment that required her to risk taking action.

It was a small step, but after a moment's pause, she said with concern, "I'm just not ready. I need a few more sessions to get my head together." I had learned already that humor was effective in breaking her self-defeating responses. I replied with a smile, "Don't go in there. I know what is in your head, and it's not helpful. You'd do better having a vacation with a run-of-the-mill enemy than being alone with your own thoughts for a week."

She laughed. She completed the assignment and was proud of her progress at the next session. She was soon hooked on celebrating her progress instead of avoiding choices. Who has time to over-analyze the past when you are having fun making a difference today!

So ask yourself: Are you hooked on living life to the fullest? The tragedy of life is not how soon it ends, but how long you wait to begin it. To become more optimistic, spend a lot less time ruminating about what has already happened and a lot more time choosing, moving, trying, tasting, experiencing, serving, enjoying . . . living.

Truth #17: Get out of the Rearview Mirror and Move into the Choices out Your Front Window

After all, whether you like it or not, time keeps marching forward with or without your active involvement. It's like a moving vehicle with no brakes. There are no available off-ramps. There's no reverse, and you can't turn the car off. That's why your rearview mirror is smaller than your front window.

Can you imagine driving a vehicle with a huge rearview mirror and a small six-inch opening to guide your driving? That would be one crazy ride, and a dangerous one at that. While you're busy worrying about what's already happened, you'd be likely to hit a tree out the front window. So don't live your life trapped in the rearview mirror! Learn what you can from the past, but concentrate on what you can do now to shape your future.

> "Be quick, but don't hurry. Being quick is a matter of being decisive and knowing where you're going. Quickness is always under your control. Hurrying is frantic and out of control."
> —John Wooden

Your life is lived out the front window—so keep moving and making choices. Every choice you make changes your future ever so slightly. Are you attracted to the mountaintops or the valleys? You pick the terrain, and don't just travel the beaten path others have turned into highways. Take a few back roads. Forge a few trails of your own. The actions you take will generate both successes and failures on your journey. Conrad Hilton observed: "Success seems to be connected with action. Successful people keep moving. They make mistakes, but they don't quit."

You won't want to quit when you see life as an adventure waiting to be experienced. What has happened in the past may limit some of your choices, but the choices that remain are so abundant, you'll never run out of adventure if you seek it.

Truth #18: You Miss 100 Percent of the Shots You Never Take

Hockey great Wayne Gretzky credited one of his early coaches for making him aware of an important truth. After pulling him aside after a difficult loss, the coach said, "You out-skated everyone out there on the ice, but you didn't take a shot on net. Miss some tomorrow night! You miss 100 percent of the shots you never take." Gretzky took the advice and, of course,

> "It often happens that I wake up at night and begin to think of a serious problem and decide that I must tell the Pope about it. Then I wake up completely and remember that I am the Pope."
> —Pope John XXIII

went on to be the most prolific scorer in National Hockey League history.

Mistakes and failures are the price you pay for achieving any success. Michael Jordan didn't make the basketball team in high school until his senior year. Walt Disney was fired from a newspaper job for lack of creativity. Babe Ruth had 51 straight strikeouts the year he hit 60 home runs. Yet every single one of these legendary achievers knew that setbacks and failures were part of the price you paid to play in the game. Thomas Edison is credited with saying, "To have a great idea, have a lot of them." On the way to his historic invention, he found 5,000 ways how not to make a lightbulb, and every one of them was intriguing. Now, that's a history of persistent action.

Innovation requires that you keep generating strategic ideas. Sales success requires that you keep asking for the sale. Leaders do whatever they can to build an environment that fosters motivation and results. Not every idea is implemented. Not every buyer buys. Not every associate will respond to your influence. But not even bothering to try guarantees failure.

> "Do not wait; the time will never be 'just right.' Start where you stand, and work with whatever tools you may have at your command, and better tools will be found as you go along."
> —Napoleon Hill

The Oscar-winning best picture *Chariots of Fire* is more than a movie about runners; it's a tale about what motivates humans to achieve. In this true story of two men competing to bring home medals for Britain from the 1924 Paris Olympics, we learn something about optimism and achievement. Harold Abrahams, played by Ben Cross, was a son of a Lithuanian immigrant and Brit to the core. Ian Charleson played Eric Liddell, a gifted Scot of deep faith and the son of missionaries in China.

Neither man had ever lost a race until the first time these two talented runners competed. Harold's immaturity surfaced when he lost the race with Liddell, and he declared to his fiancée Sybil (played by Alice Krige), "If I can't win, I won't run!" Sybil replied wisely, "If you don't run, you can't win." In spite of scheduling and coaching challenges and strong competition, both men persevered and went on to win Olympic gold.

Most success stories involve failures, perseverance, resourcefulness—and, above all, action. True optimists both lose and win more frequently. Failures don't keep them down for long; they bounce back quickly to get right back in the game. You've doubtlessly had your share of failures and setbacks, but that's the price you pay to lead a life worth living. Just remember: You miss 100 percent of the shots you never take, and you can't possibly win a race that you don't bother to run. Are you ready for a little adventure? Miss a few shots today—but take them!

Truth #19: Life Works Best with the Three P's of Optimism—Position, Perform, and Persist

The only things you truly control are your actions, and some might say even that is in question on Mondays. You do control the Three P's of Optimism—Position, Perform and Persist.

Not every action is worth pursuing. As an optimist, you must learn to *position* your actions where you're more likely to produce meaningful

> "Don't let what you cannot do interfere with what you can do."
> —John Wooden,
> UCLA Basketball Coach

results. It's all about playing in the right game. Let your purpose and mission guide your positioning, and then get busy serving the right people and developing the appropriate gifts to match the challenge the times require.

But finding your focus is only half the battle—you also need to *perform!* Don't rest on your talents; keep working them. Excellence must be earned and reearned every day, so play your best. Keep after the pursuit of quality by actively improving your performance every day in the games that count to you. Be a better professional, leader, spouse, parent, volunteer, citizen, and friend.

Finally, *persist*, because when you think you've arrived with the right positioning and skills, things are already changing again. Customers are ready for the next wave of innovation; new

> "The only man I know who behaves sensibly is my tailor; he takes my measures anew each time he sees me. The rest go on with their old measurements and expect me to fit them."
>
> —George Bernard Shaw

competencies are being required; the global economy is soaring or falling; your children are growing into new challenges. Pretend that you're a tailor, and take your measurements anew at every chance you get. Be ready to reposition before your competitors beat you to it, and remain open to discussions about changing expectations. Adjust your personal development plan to match the opportunities and challenges that emerge.

It's imperative to realize that your job in life isn't to zero in on a stationary target; instead, you must think of yourself as a missile chasing after a moving plane taking evasive actions. Only one thing is certain in a life of never-ending change: You have no excuse for being bored. After all, who wants to be done when you can choose a life of adventure and meaningful discovery?

Control what you can—position, perform, and persist. Make movement matter! Individuals are not the only ones who need to embrace the action imperative. To truly lead organizations into the future requires an equal commitment to action.

> "Act fast. . . . Leaders in a crisis must not lose their rare opportunity to act. The difficulty is that just when decisions are more easily accepted, they're hardest to make. All business decisions are made with incomplete information, and that's especially true in the heat of a crisis. At the same time, the stakes are much higher than usual. Every instinct tells you to decide more slowly than usual, yet it's vital to decide more quickly."
>
> —Geoff Colvin

Truth #20: Act Fast with Focus and Flexibility to Make Change Work

War provides a meaningful laboratory for leadership under stress. Marine General Peter Pace reminds us of an insight all leaders need to take seriously:

"One thing the Marine Corps teaches is that it's better to be doing something than doing nothing. If you stay where you are, you're in the position where your enemy wants you to be. If you start doing something, you are changing the rules of the game." Combat is a verb. It isn't a place. It is an act. Movement matters. You keep asking yourself as a leader, "Now, what are you going to do next?"

Are you a leader of action? Maybe it is time to ask yourself that same question every day—"Well, leader, what are you going to do?" You and your team may not be facing combat, but in these competitive and challenging economic times, you are facing a battle of a different kind. By continuing to move, you keep changing the rules of the game for both your competitors and

> "Too many think inaction is the least risky path. Sometimes action is the most conservative and safest path. Not doing anything is exceedingly dangerous."
> —Fred Smith, FedEx CEO

your customers. It's easiest to take aim at you when you are sitting still, resting on past successes, and coasting on autopilot. To bet on sustaining the past is a losing hand in today's rapidly changing world. Your customers are depending on you to give them a strategic advantage; you won't do that by refining past successes. You get it by helping them invent the future.

Make a commitment to continuous movement; you are more likely to take advantage of changing landscapes and emerging opportunities when you are on the move. Too many wait for stifling task force recommendations, only to find their competitors well on their way to claiming a market share victory because of their quick action. Even if movement requires adjustment and change, you are at least changing the rules of the game, serving your customers, and keeping your competitors guessing.

Ready, Fire, Aim—Feisty Prototypers Win the Day

Complaining that the world is moving too fast is like complaining that rocks are hard. It's true but useless. Your job is to ride the changes worth making!

> "One of the assets I look for in a team or a leader is a bias for action and a willingness to say 'We can do it,' coupled with a solid strategy. The way I interpret it, execution and commitment are absolutely essential to any strategy of initiative in an era too full of plans, processes, and procrastination."
> —Simon Cooper, Ritz-Carlton President and CEO

What we need to invent the future is what Tom Peters calls "feisty prototypers." He cites Stanford researchers who examined 72 projects from 36 companies in Asia, Europe, and the United States. They found that squeezing together and streamlining a rationalized product development process was trounced by the just-do-it, experiential, prototyping approach. With an uncertain market and rapidly changing technology, detailed planning just slows down progress. The winners in a world of constant change start by charting a strategic direction. Then, they refine their strategy by simultaneously trying a number of promising strategies and using frequent tests and aggressive milestones to make the necessary course corrections. That requires fixing all flat tires while you move and getting out of dead ends quickly.

Change leaders are masters of focus. Quick due diligence shouldn't trap you in inaction; it should free you and your team to bravely pursue strategic innovation. There's a distinction between speed and bravery. Organizations evolve the way nature evolves: Bad innovations die, and good innovations survive. Bravery requires leaders and teams to take a chance on themselves and their ideas and be willing to watch them die if they don't produce results. Every improvement is the result of change, but not every change proves to be an improvement worth making. Your job as a leader is to find which changes are worth pursuing as quickly as possible.

> "The plain fact is that no one . . . utterly no one . . . has even an inkling about tomorrow's winners or losers. The good news is that this is good news. If you are unclear about the next step, then there is only one variety of sensible advice: Ready, Fire, Aim."
> —Tom Peters

Milliken is a leading textile company committed to quality, innovation, and change. They have a heritage of getting things done, but done right. Milliken's Gazelle Award reinforces their bias for action. It was built on a lesson learned on the plains of Africa: "Gazelles are the second fastest animal and are capable of quick changes in direction. When a lion wakes up it has one mission, run faster than the slowest and weakest gazelle.

> "The great end of life is not knowledge, but action. What men need is as much knowledge as they can organize into action; give them more, and it may become injurious. Some men are heavy and stupid from undigested learning."
> —Thomas Henry Huxley

When a gazelle wakes up it has one mission, run faster than the fastest lion. When either wakes up, they know one thing—they are going to be running!" That is good advice for all of today's leaders and organizations.

Now Is the Time for Action—Not Perfection

In addition to the Three P's of Optimism, there are also the Four P's of Pessimism—Perfection, Procrastination, Paralysis, and Powerlessness. One prepares you for action; the other results in avoidance and inaction. People who are overly concerned about doing every little thing right may very well wait so long to do anything that they end up feeling powerless—and doing nothing at all. Don't turn a two-week decision about what to do into a doctorate in analysis paralysis. While you do need enough information to organize into action, too much of it merely slows down your progress. Seek different perspectives early, and then make one choice at a time. As Yogi Berra would say, "When you come to a fork in the road, take it."

Remember to take the trap out of achieving excellence by striving for it without waiting for the perfect thought, the perfect action, or the perfect time. You won't even do this perfectly, but that's okay. Neither does anyone else.

Norman Vincent Peale, often called the father of positive

> "You cannot escape the responsibility of tomorrow by evading it today."
> —Abraham Lincoln

> "One of the illusions of life is that the present hour is not the critical, decisive hour. Write it on your heart that every day is the best day of the year."
> —Ralph Waldo Emerson

thinking, knew that any action can help build your confidence when he wrote: "Action is a great restorer and builder of confidence. Inaction is not only the result, but the cause, of fear. Perhaps the action you take will be successful; perhaps different action or adjustments will have to follow. But any action is better than no action at all. So don't wait for trouble to intimidate or paralyze you. Make a move."

When you act, take pride in your progress. Abraham Lincoln had to lead and live in tough times. He shared a reassuring perspective we might all do well to remember: "The best thing about the future is that it comes one day at a time."

Life is all about one day at a time. So today, invest your worry time in constructive action and feel the pride and optimism that purposeful action generates.

CHAPTER
8

Optimists Dispute Catastrophic Thoughts

"People are always blaming their circumstances for what they are. I don't believe in circumstances. The people who get on in this world are the people who get up and look for the circumstances they want, and, if they can't find them, make them."

—George Bernard Shaw

Okay, so you can shape your own circumstance and make your own luck up to a point, but there's no denying that bad luck *does* exist. We've all had our share of unpleasant days; we've all suffered and experienced major disappointments. We've had to deal with the pain of loss as well as the random misery that nature can unleash.

Good employees sometimes lose their jobs through no fault of their own, and even the best sales professionals lose their share of sales from time to time. Hurricanes level some homes while leaving others only feet away completely intact. Illness and accidents can take lives seemingly years too early.

> "Life is tough, but I'm tougher."
> —Andy Rooney

The glass sometimes is more than half empty. In the short run, everything doesn't always happen for the best. Have you had a big enough dose of reality for this chapter? I hope so. Yes, as we discussed in the beginning—life *is* difficult.

But no matter how bad the hand you're dealt in life, you can still strive to make the best of what happens. Optimists have learned to master the mental and emotional inner dialogue that allows you to do just that. Jeffrey Lawrence Benjamin, author of *How to Get What You Want Now*, said it well: "The most important things ever said are the things you've said to yourself." However, what you say to yourself in the face of adversity is not always constructive.

The Heart of the Optimism Technique

Learned Optimism author Martin Seligman confirms how ineffective our self-talk can be: "One often has 'catastrophic thoughts,' feelings that everything is wrong and that nothing is going to change. We teach people to think of these thoughts as if they were being said by some external person whose mission in life is to make them miserable. Then we have them dispute those thoughts, and that's the heart of the optimism technique." In short, your thoughts have the power to make you either more miserable or more optimistic. Depression often involves a difficulty in controlling negative thoughts. Our goal here is to help you shape your own self-talk to maintain a more optimistic attitude—even in the face of adversity.

> "When you are confronted with a situation that is beyond your control, recognize that you still have a choice: you can decide how you will react to it. You can accept it and direct your energies to the areas where you can make an impact."
> —Stephen R. Covey

Martin Seligman also observes: "Positive thinking often involves trying to believe upbeat statements such as, 'Every day, in every way, I'm getting better and better' in the absence of evidence, or even in the face of contrary evidence. Learned optimism, in contrast, is about accuracy. It is how you cope with negative statements that has an effect. Usually the negative beliefs that follow adversity are inaccurate. . . . Learned optimism works not through an unjustifiable positivity about the world but through the power of 'non-negative' thinking."

It's important to grasp that this isn't another book about

> "One of the great discoveries man makes, one of his great surprises, is to find he can do what he was afraid he couldn't do. Most of the bars we beat against are our own. We put them there, and we can take them down."
>
> —Henry Ford

visualizing success, because merely visualizing won't guarantee positive results. Even if 100 sales professionals imagine success with the same client, only one is actually going to *get* the sale. Those who don't get that signature on the bottom line aren't going to be writing a testimonial for that book on visualizing sales success.

Optimism is instead about facing and taking advantage of reality—even unsettling reality. Expecting unrealistic results may actually *increase* your dissatisfaction. Even positive people know they aren't going to win them all; however, your goal is to improve your batting average. You also want to limit your downtime in the face of setbacks and adversity so that you can get back into the game quicker. To an optimist, it's all about resilience and maximizing your results.

Effective salespeople concentrate on and master the art of bouncing back from disappointments, sharpening focus and delivery, and then returning to action as quickly as possible. Effective sales professionals win *and* lose more sales—because they *stay* in the game.

Truth #21: Master the ABCs of Optimistic Self-Talk—Adversity, Beliefs, and Consequences

How do you change the way you talk to yourself about adversity and setbacks? To Seligman, how we see adversity is the critical starting point: "It's a matter of ABC: When we encounter A-ADVERSITY, we react by

> "Nothing splendid has ever been achieved except by those who dared believe that something inside them was superior to circumstances."
>
> —Bruce Barton

> "Don't spend your time on things you can't control. Instead, spend your time thinking about what you can control."
>
> —Benjamin Selekman, Harvard Business School

thinking about it. Our thoughts rapidly congeal into B-BELIEFS. These beliefs may become so habitual we don't even realize we have them unless we stop to focus on them. And they don't just sit there idly; they have C-CONSEQUENCES. The beliefs are the direct causes of what we feel and what we do next. They can spell the difference between dejection and giving up, on the one hand, and well-being and constructive action on the other." By understanding this connection between adversity, belief, and consequence, you can begin to master the ABCs that impact every day of your life.

Adversity can be almost anything frustrating or unpleasant that occurs in your personal or professional life: a flat tire, a public attack by your boss, a relationship breakup, an unexpected large bill, a layoff, or a drastic drop in your stock portfolio. Make this chapter personal and think about the adversities you're facing right now. What about over the past year? Be specific.

Beliefs are how you interpret the adversity. Keep in mind that it's important to separate thoughts from feelings. "I just blew my career," "I'm too old to learn what I need to know," "I'll never find someone to love me again," or "If the market doesn't rebound, I won't be able to afford to retire!" are all *beliefs*. A belief's accuracy can be evaluated and tested over time. Your beliefs are changeable—and they have consequences.

Consequences are the feelings and actions that come as a result of your beliefs; for example, the beliefs just listed might cause you to feel depressed, anxious, angry, or frustrated. You'll often feel more than one of these if the adversity affects many aspects of your life. You'll also be likely to act in some way. You may withdraw from others, send out your resume, seek revenge, call your broker to complain, or even cry your share of tears.

Since the first step in applying the *optimism technique* is to understand what you're currently saying to yourself about the adversities you are facing, let's start there. After all, you can't effectively change your thoughts or reframe your perspective until you've isolated what it is you're saying to yourself that is creating a bigger problem. Use the following space or a piece of paper and write down an actual adversity or problem you are now encountering or continue to struggle with. Putting it in writing will help move your problem from the emotional part of your brain to the part that helps organize and quantify information. By the time you finish analyzing your specific beliefs, feelings, and actions, much of your emotional tension will have been released in the writing exercise.

Be as specific as possible in identifying your adversities, beliefs, feelings and actions:

Adversity:

Beliefs:

Consequences:

Feelings:

Actions:

The Gift of Distraction and Taking Distance

You've put the problem on paper; now, it's time to take a break. As an optimist, you'll learn the gift that comes in distracting your attention from useless rumination and the importance of taking some appropriate distance before tackling difficult challenges. After all, giving in to your nonproductive feelings and counterproductive actions is no way to alter your self-talk habits.

> "Worry is the darkroom where negatives become glossy prints."
>
> —Max Lucado

So before you undertake the challenge of changing how you look at adversity, it's wise to take some time off for another activity. Some people become so trapped in their thinking patterns that they actually employ a simple, physical distraction. Some snap a rubber band around their wrists or say to themselves "stop" every time they start to ruminate ineffectively.

One way to start is to take the piece of paper with your identified problem, fold it, and place it in your pocket or purse. Take a walk, call a fun friend, read an engaging novel, shoot a few baskets, or listen to your favorite music. Participating in an alternative activity allows your mind some perspective and distance. Some problems are better handled after you use that break to calm your emotional and unproductive inner dialogue.

Taking distance doesn't give you permission to duck the problem. On the contrary, it is designed to ensure that you are more likely to come at the problem with a fresh, constructive mind-set. In addition, by postponing worry for even 20 minutes, you're exercising control over it—rather than letting it control you.

Truth #22: Win the Argument with Your Negative Beliefs to Change Your Attitude and Your Actions

Business philosopher Jim Rohn put it well when he said, "You have to stand guard at the door of your mind." Essentially, that means being ready to argue with some of your negative beliefs. If your critical thinking habits aren't helping you get where you want to go, there's no time like the present to take them on. Martin Seligman suggests four ways to make your self-arguments convincing: *evidence, alternatives, implications,* and *usefulness.* I'll add a fifth—*faith.*

Evidence—Only the Facts!

The most convincing way to confront a nonproductive belief is to show that it is *factually incorrect.* After all, optimists are not afraid of the facts, even if they're tough to handle. Facts are your friends—because only by knowing what you are facing can you

> "To ignore the facts does not change the facts."
> —Andy Rooney

actively improve your odds of overcoming it. So don't allow yourself to settle for assumptions that have not been tested.

Optimists find a centering strength in playing detective. Though many readers are probably too young to have heard of *Dragnet*'s Joe Friday, this early television character had one simple statement that defined his approach to solving every crime. When he'd take out his trusty notepad to take down information, he'd caution: "Just the facts, ma'am!"

Play your version of Joe Friday in looking at your own beliefs. A patient receiving test results from a biopsy who hears the word "cancer" may react immediately with a frightening belief—"My God, I'm going to die of cancer!" Doctors must not only treat the disease but also fight the inaccurate beliefs that can work against the patient's chances of recovery. Taking a diagnosis like this well doesn't mean silence or blind acceptance of fate.

> "Optimists, far from protecting their fragile vision of the world, confront trouble head-on, while it is pessimists who bury their heads in the sand of denial. Optimists were more likely to acknowledge the seriousness of the disease, experienced less distress and took more active steps to cope with it. Pessimism was associated with denial and a giving up response."
> —Charles Carver

Whether at that moment or at the next follow-up visit, the *optimist detective* is there with pen and paper in hand, armed with important questions to assess the difficulty of the challenge they face: At what stage did we catch the cancer? How aggressive is it? What is the survival rate? What treatments are best in light of my particular situation? After reading on reputable online sites about some experimental treatments, I want to know if I could be a candidate. What can I do to make it more likely that I will be one of the survivors?

Optimists are realists. An optimistic approach to something devastating—like a cancer diagnosis—does not mean that every patient will beat the disease. Randy Pausch was 47 years old when he died from pancreatic cancer. This inspiring Carnegie Mellon University computer science professor gave his last lecture in September 2007. After stunning the class by confiding, "I have about six

"I feel I had zero control over getting cancer, but I have 100 percent control over how I will respond to dealing with cancer. When life kicks you, let it kick you forward."
—Coach Kay Yow

months to live," he talked about his childhood dreams and what they had taught him about life. It's been said that he was a dying man who taught the world how to live. He said of his struggle with terminal cancer: "Experience is what you get when you didn't get what you wanted. We can't change the cards we are dealt, just the way we play them." The wisdom, passion, and optimistic attitude that he displays in his *YouTube* video and subsequent book, *The Last Lecture*, have become enduring sources of inspiration.

While considering the importance of checking facts when it comes to adversity, remember not to blindly adopt disasters that the media attempts to send your way. Many of those whose job it is to dispense the news try to attract attention from viewers by highlighting the crisis of the week. Don't for a moment assume that because the problem is worldwide that you are next. Your job is to be the optimism detective who looks at the facts, not the isolated examples that inflame panic. Separate the media portrayal of the problem from the actual data of incidence, and invest your worry time in what you can actually *do* something about.

Now, look at the adversity you have isolated. How can you check out the facts associated with the beliefs that are making it hard to deal constructively with the problems? What experts would a detective contact? What sources might give you meaningful information? Could an Internet search do the work for you?

"In the big picture, the world is safer than it has ever been. We're living longer. Do what you can to turn the positive odds in your favor and then enjoy the journey. You only take it once!"
—Simon Briscoe, co-author of *Panicology*

In fact, the mere act of engaging in fact-checking can help you tremendously. You change your focus from ruminating and emotional paralysis to a more productive way of viewing the problem—one that may soon translate into more constructive feelings and actions.

Alternatives—Seek Less Self-Destructive Explanations

Most events have multiple possible causes. Pessimists have a way of latching onto the worst possible explanations for events—the most permanent, pervasive, and personal ones that make bouncing back even more difficult. Optimists, on the other hand, ask: "Is there any less destructive way to look at this or explain what happened?" They expect to uncover causes that can be overcome and that will not necessarily happen again—those that are less permanent, less pervasive, and less personal.

Optimists focus on what can be changed and resist saying "never." When I failed my first test for California licensure as a psychologist, I was confused. I thought I had done well on the exam and was tempted to say to myself, "If I felt I did my best and it still wasn't good enough, I'll never be able to pass that exam." I struggled with my doubts but moved to action when I realized I would have a hard time improving on the next test unless I understood *why* I had failed. Playing detective, I contacted the medical examiners involved. They were sympathetic to my question and sent my inquiry to those involved in grading responses.

Although graders seldom provided feedback, they made an exception in my case. One of the reviewers called with this very valuable information: "As

> "I've never lost a ball game, but I have run out of time on a few occasions."
>
> —Joe Namath

you remember, you had four essays. It was clear to all of us reviewing your exam that you knew the material, but it was also clear that you were in such a hurry that you failed to fully read one of the questions. You gave a wonderful answer to a question we didn't ask. We could give you no credit on that essay."

I therefore found that my reason for failing was changeable, not permanent. It wasn't that I did not know the material; it was simply that I had failed to fully grasp a particular question that had been asked. The following year, I did a better job of fully reading the questions and passed with flying colors.

Optimists look for those rare causes that sometimes make the difference between victory and defeat. Although it was planned well and core samples indicated no problems, a construction project went way over budget because unforeseen soil conditions required extra reinforcement. Your construction team may have a proven track record of success, but sometimes nature throws you a curve. Similarly, when a reporter asked a basketball team's all-star center why his offensive rebounds were down in the game, he replied with a smile, "When the other team makes 72 percent of their shots, there aren't a lot of rebounds for *anyone* to get. It's just one of those games you feel like applauding with their fans. They deserved this one." His optimistic thinking is one of the reasons he's a repeat all-star.

Optimists are ready to accept nonpersonal causes that can explain a disappointing result. It is important to accept responsibility when it is appropriate. But instead of always assuming that something is your fault, be ready to entertain a more favorable explanation. For example, after receiving his first territory, a sales representative was eager to make inroads on some new accounts to impress his boss. After being encouraged to send a proposal to a potentially big customer, he told his boss that he anticipated an order later in the week.

The new rep was disappointed and frustrated when the purchaser called and said that they had decided to go with a different vendor. He thought he had handled the call well and deserved the business; he was quick to talk to his boss about the decision. His boss said with a knowing smile, "He does that with every new rep. His brother-in-law is the other vendor. He just uses your proposal to show his boss that he's open to a competitive bid. As long as he's married, he isn't giving us the business. Don't take every sale personally. It's often not your fault."

That's good advice in facing *any* adversity. Are there any less self-destructive causes involved in the difficulties you're confronting? Does this outlook give you hope for possible future success by eliminating those causes? Always look for alternatives that help you bounce back.

Implications—Realistic Likely Consequences

Don't make any disaster or misfortune worse than it is. Instead of assuming *the worst consequences*, take a realistic look at *the most likely consequences* to your setback.

Former football coach Don Shula had years of experience behind him when he told his young players, "Keep your perspective. Success is not forever, and failure isn't fatal." That's not just good advice for football, but in the game of life as well.

Keep looking for ways to turn your experiences into maturity instead of using them as reasons to give up. It's upsetting when all the old clichés turn out to make too much sense to deny:

- "It's always darkest before the dawn."
- "When life gives you lemons, make lemonade!"
- "This too shall pass."
- "Don't sweat the small stuff. Life and death are big stuff. Everything else is small stuff."

Don't discount clichés simply because they are clichés; after all, they've been around this long because they carry and anchor truths worth remembering.

Before starting his concert, great violinist Itzhak Perlman had moved his polio-crippled body across the stage. He had put down his crutches and picked up his violin. When he began to play, one of the violin strings snapped. He didn't panic, or painstakingly leave the stage to secure a new string; instead, he began to play. Rather than giving in to the belief that it was impossible to play this symphonic work with only three strings, he played with such passion, power, and purity that the audience broke into a standing ovation. He bowed and said to the audience, "Sometimes it is the artist's task to find out how much music you can still make with what you have left."

If the result is not terminal, you've still got a game to play. After all, not getting what you want is sometimes a wonderful stroke of luck that frees you to

> "Living with uncertainty is extremely damaging to your health."
> —Sarah Bulgard

discover something even better. Losing a job is seldom the end of your career unless you let it be. Look back at career moves that were difficult at the time but gave you new opportunities that you now appreciate.

> "If at first you don't succeed, try again. Then quit. There's no use being a damn fool about it."
>
> —W. C. Fields

By helping others keep perspective, you control your own more consistently. One manager learned to help his team frame every so-called disaster with this question: "In five years, will this matter?" The answer was seldom yes. What are the likely consequences you will face from your current setback? Be realistic, and you'll soon be bouncing back.

Usefulness—Will Worry Work?

Worry can exact a price that is sometimes worse than adversity itself. Research has shown that merely *worrying* about an event can be more detrimental to one's health than actually *enduring* the event itself. In fact, two University of Michigan studies followed more than 3,000 employed participants for more than two years. Those who were chronically insecure about losing their jobs reported worse overall health and were more depressed than those who actually *lost* their jobs. Persistent worry takes its toll on your health *and* attitude.

If your negative belief is still stubbornly resisting all efforts to minimize its significance and impact, you might need to ask a very practical question: Will wasting any more time mulling over this situation produce any long-term value? Will prolonged problem solving get you closer to where you ultimately want to go? If not, it's time to be practical. It's time to let it go. Sometimes your goals have changed, and overcoming the problem isn't even relevant anymore. In short, some problems and disasters are worth leaving in the rearview mirror and moving on.

> "It's all about finding the balance between productive and unproductive worrying. Say to yourself, 'Is this worry leading to a to-do-list?' If it doesn't lead to some action on your part today, set it aside."
>
> —Robert J. Leahy

One of my clients had a great sense of humor and a unique way of getting closure on such experiences. After writing out his adversity and fully accepting that nothing could be done, he decided to cremate and bury it. He burned the piece of paper with his notes and then dug a small hole. He took a moment to thank the problem for teaching him some important lessons but confessed that it was time to let it go. He deposited the ashes and then covered them with dirt. As he started to leave, he turned around and said, as if talking to a dog, "Stay!" After that, every time he thought of those *dog days*, all he had to say was "I told you to stay!" and a smile would come to his lips. It simply wasn't worth resurrecting.

Is it time to let go of your adversity? Discover your own creative way of getting this closure in a way that allows that to happen.

Faith—Search for God's Open Door

Any discussion on attitude and beliefs would be incomplete without addressing the role that faith plays in coping with adversity for so many people. Self-reliance is a powerful value

> "I thank God for my handicaps, for, through them, I have found myself, my work, and my God."
> —Helen Keller

and an empowering strategy, but it has its limits. You may find support in a shared faith community and comfort by having faith in God's providence. If you are a religious believer, "In God We Trust" may be more than a slogan on your money. Faith may be a centering belief in your life and may help you cope with life's worst disasters and experiences.

Believers often live with tension that makes room for faith in God and doing their part to work out his will. You can pray to God and claim his providential destiny and still remain willing to be used by God in making a difference for yourself and others. As such, you can find in adversity an experience that brings further clarity to your purpose. Adversity can even open new doors to your calling.

The paradoxical advice most often attributed to St. Ignatius provides a powerful insight: "Pray as if everything depends on God.

> "View each obstacle in life as a little gift. Open it and see what is inside."
> —Mother Teresa

Act as if it depends upon you." This statement highlights the importance of accepting God's will while simultaneously working to live out that will. You do what you can and trust that God will do the rest. Faith like this can lead to inner peace *and* constructive action.

During the 16 years that Scottish missionary David Livingstone spent in Africa, he faced one challenge after another. On nearly 30 occasions, he had been laid low by swamp fever. His left arm was crushed by a lion and hung helplessly at his side. Yet he was never deterred from his mission: "I return without misgiving and with great gladness. For would you like me to tell you what supported me through all the years of exile among people whose language I could not understand, and whose attitude towards me was always uncertain and often hostile? It was this: *'Lo, I am with you always, even unto the end of the world!'* On those words I staked everything, and they never failed!"

Hearing stories of such challenges tends to keep your own adversity in perspective. Faith—in any form—has the tendency to give those who believe constructive principles to hold on to in a difficult world. Use them—and anything else that gives you strength. Seek the support of your faith community; it can give a meaningful perspective to even your worst day. Look at the adversities you are facing—and consider how your faith can provide a fresh perspective that will guide you forward.

Reframe Your Beliefs to Help You Overcome Adversity

> "I've never been one who thought the good Lord should make my life easy; I've just asked Him to make me strong."
> —Eva Bowring

Now that you've effectively countered your nonconstructive beliefs, it's time to shape some new statements that provide a healthier perspective for reframing the problems you're facing. Write these in a way that encourages you to make constructive actions you can embrace.

After repeated efforts to turn an employee around failed, one manager wrote down this destructive belief: "I have no leadership ability." This assertion left him discouraged and reluctant to apply for an open middle-management position he had been encouraged to consider. However, he realized that his self-destructive belief was too sweeping of an indictment in light of his positive evaluation by both his boss and the rest of his team. After further conversations with human resources, he realized that many other managers had experienced similar problems with this same employee.

The manager wrote down a new statement to build a more positive focus: "I'm not the first manager to struggle with this associate. My leadership has been rated as effective by both my boss and my team. Although I do not control his performance, it is my job to do what I can to influence him. Instead of taking his performance personally, I will continue to work with human resources to appropriately counsel and hold him responsible. I'm also prepared to support his positive efforts to change when evident." By affirming his own strengths and continuing to focus on how to deal with the problem effectively, the manager persisted. He began to make noticeable progress in eliciting the employee's gifts in a way that made a difference for him and the team.

You may also find that constructive thinking can result in more positive feelings and purposeful actions. It's time to craft your own statement. After you have reworked your belief and supportive comments, fold your reworked paper and put it in your pocket or purse. Read it daily for a week. If negative thinking patterns recur, pull it out and reread it. Changing how you think often takes repetition, but you'll soon experience its optimistic benefit.

Truth #23: Experience Is What You Do with What Happens to You

Undefeated by a blazing motorcycle accident—and a paralyzing private plane crash four years later—inspirational speaker W.

> "It may be true that life is a grindstone, but it is equally true that whether it grinds us or polishes us is determined alone by the substance of which we are made. . . . That which has proved to be a stumbling block to one individual is a stepping stone to a more courageous soul."
>
> —Cavett Robert

Mitchell has gone on to live an amazing and productive life. He's been a radio broadcaster, a town mayor, an author, and a celebrated professional speaker. The central theme of his message can be summarized in one statement: "It's not what happens to you. It's what you do about it." Optimists around the world keep proving the truth in that statement.

In 1986, following the tragic Space Shuttle *Challenger* disaster, President Ronald Reagan acknowledged the terrible loss by saying, "Today is a day for mourning and remembering. We know we share this pain with all of the people of our country." He went on to provide a perspective that helped reframe the loss and point to the country's need to move forward: "The future doesn't belong to the fainthearted; it belongs to the brave. The *Challenger* crew was pulling us into the future, and we'll continue to follow them. . . . Nothing ends here; our hopes and our journeys continue."

Disasters are not just disasters; they often become the catalyst for the development of significant solutions that pay heavy dividends for years to come. When presenting to a 101 Leaders Institute Summit, speaker and author Jim Cathcart observed that the world faced the Y2K challenge—and the possible computer dysfunctions that threatened to cripple the global economy—with a sense of determination. No one was in charge, yet somehow the world came together to take care of this potential disaster in time. We met the problem, built new competencies, and implemented computer redundancies and backup systems. Then

> "Every crisis builds confidence and competencies for what comes next."
>
> —Jim Cathcart

we all held our breath on New Year's Eve as we watched at the stroke of midnight in Australia to make sure that the lights stayed on!

It was in fact the Y2K challenge that helped create the computer backups that saved the U.S. financial system from total disaster on 9/11. The Twin Towers experience then helped launch Homeland Security, which in turn dealt with future relief efforts. The overwhelming demands that Hurricane Katrina created encouraged the development of new processes for the next disaster. History is nothing more than a compilation of human tragedies and victories earned. It's these experiences that continue to shape human experience and expand human knowledge.

Whether it is the world's economy or your personal corporate journey, optimism fuels progress. Author and speaker Francis Maguire saw his corporate journey as a series of obstacles that became amazing opportunities. He loves to say, "Every time you get hit in the face with an obstacle, look for the gift." As part of Federal Express's leadership team in the early years, Frank shared how an obstacle proved

> "Read stories of courage. They make you wonder how you would have done compared with the hero of the tale, and you get very humble. You start self-querying and fantasizing about your own response, your own reaction. As the psalmist says, 'You become what you behold.' That's why stories of courage take you over. They are such cries of the heart."
>
> —William Ian Miller

to be the need that birthed a company. When the Federal Reserve Bank learned that they needed to get checks to their facilities on the next business day, a small group of entrepreneurs approached the venture capitalists. Two weeks later, they had the money they needed to become the aspirin to the Federal Reserve Bank's headache. They called the new company Federal Express because their mission was getting business checks to the Federal Reserve Bank next day—guaranteed. During their first night in business, FedEx had only 16 packages.

Early efforts to market their services weren't working until a customer at a focus group meeting discovered the key to marketing their struggling brand. Federal Express had tried to sell America on a new kind of airline, but the customer told them the truth they hadn't

> "Optimistic people generally feel that good things will last a long time and will have a beneficial effect on everything they do. And they think that bad things are isolated: They won't last long and won't affect other parts of life."
> —Martin Seligman, PhD

seen: "I don't need another airline. I want my packages delivered absolutely, positively overnight every time."

FedEx became a logistics company that helped organizations accomplish what they needed done faster . . . "absolutely, positively overnight every time!" People love anyone who helps them vault over their obstacles.

So, what are *you* doing to look for the gift in your challenge?

Look for the Gifts in Your Adversity

Your own personal history of overcoming obstacles and taking advantage of the lessons learned is one short chapter in a continuing human story. Nurture your life's story with pride. As an optimist, you, too, can persevere in reframing difficulties and obstacles into new opportunities by taking advantage of Norman Vincent Peale's advice: "Become a possibilitarian. No matter how dark things seem to be or actually are, raise your sights and see possibilities—always see them, for they're always there."

Don't run from hardships; face them! Cultivate positive beliefs and thoughts about what you are capable of doing. Nurture an expectation of success in overcoming what life throws in your path—through good thinking and applied effort. Even in the tough times, look for silver linings.

> "Life is not about waiting for the storms to pass . . . it's about learning to dance in the rain."
> —Vivian Greene

The harder the challenge, the stronger your character can become and the greater your satisfaction will be when you continue to build on your track record of success. By learning to think like an optimist, tough times can become opportunities to reinvent a business, retool your skills, rekindle relationships, find undervalued investment opportunities—and even renew your faith. Albert Einstein put it well: "In the middle of difficulty lies opportunity." May it be so for you!

Optimists Give Thanks for Gratitude

"There is a secret to happiness and it is gratitude. All happy people are grateful, and ungrateful people cannot be happy. We tend to think that it is being unhappy that leads people to complain, but it is truer to say that it is complaining that leads to people becoming unhappy. Become grateful and you will become a much happier person. I try to be happy unless something happens that makes me unhappy, rather than unhappy unless something makes me happy."
—Dennis Prager, *Happiness Is a Serious Problem*

The great game of life presents us with our fair share of both adversity and good fortune. You have bad accidents and happy accidents—things happen to you that you do not and cannot control. In the last chapter, we focused on how optimism can transform the ways in which you handle adversity. In this chapter, we'll discuss how you can enhance a positive outlook by simply becoming more thankful.

We live much of our lives on autopilot. While adversity often gets our attention, the many daily blessings and gifts we experience go by without notice. We seldom take time to even consider the electricity that powers homes and businesses, but when the power is out, we're quickly reminded of how important it is to our lives. Whether it is love or lights, it is absence that makes the heart grow fonder.

> "We need some thanks right now for all the things money can't buy. . . . I'm talking about our kids and grandkids, parents and grandparents, health, faith, a beautiful sunset that doesn't cost a dime and a full life that doesn't depend on the size of your savings account."
>
> —Dennis McCarthy

In short, it's easy to complain about the difficulties and adversity that we face, but far too few of us learn the importance of giving thanks for the many happy accidents and blessings that we experience daily, on and off the job. Those who do are more optimistic and happy.

Roman orator and politician Cicero said centuries ago: "Gratitude is not only the greatest of all virtues, but the parent of all the others." Whether it comes as a result of our faith traditions or simply commonsense life experience—optimists learn to appreciate the power and the healthy perspective that an awareness of our many blessings can provide.

Holocaust survivor and *Man's Search for Meaning* author Viktor Frankl realized the power of reflecting on one's blessings in the midst of his Holocaust experience. During a predawn march to work on laying railroad tracks, another prisoner wondered out loud about the fate of their wives. The young doctor began to think about his own wife and realized that simply by thinking

> "In the hospital in 'Nam, I learned something. Real miracles have to do with your perceptions being made finer. They don't have to do with God coming down in a lightning bolt or guys like me walking again. What they have to do with is how you perceive the ordinary things around you."
>
> —Anonymous partially paralyzed Vietnam veteran

> "When we choose not to focus on what is missing from our lives but are grateful for the abundance that's present . . . we experience heaven on earth."
> —Sarah Breathnach

of her in this way, she was present within him. Frankl later wrote: "The salvation of man is through love and in love. I understood how a man who has nothing left in this world still may know bliss, be it only for a brief moment, in the contemplation of his beloved."

But how do gratitude and a sense of thanksgiving help sustain a positive, optimistic attitude? As we've already discussed, life is difficult, with adversity and disappointments built in. Expecting that everything will go well is not healthy; in fact, unrealistic expectations are a sure road to unhappiness and disappointment. But failing to appreciate the best in life is equally unhealthy.

Avoid Pits People and the Complain Game

It used to be when you asked a person, "How are you doing?" They'd most likely reply, "Great!" However, with today's growing cultural preoccupation with feelings and self-disclosure, complaining is far more accepted. Together with years of programming by a media focused on bringing you the worst up-to-the-minute disasters, problems, and crimes, it's hard not to internalize that same negative scanning. Most news sources today take advantage of that very preoccupation. Members of the media are more than happy to have you use your cell phone or camera to capture crisis video to headline their evening news, which only feeds our own negative addiction.

Do you know any *Pits People*? Those are the people with whom every conversation involves some kind of complaining. They simply

> "Ingratitude is always a form of weakness. I have never known a man of real ability to be ungrateful."
> —Goethe

cannot see the positive aspect of anything—their personal lives, their professional lives, or society overall. "The economy is the pits; this company is the pits. In fact, you're the pits!" After 30 minutes with a Pits Person, everyone's morale is sagging.

So don't get stuck playing the Complain Game; you simply cannot do that and expect to be more optimistic. Start some new habits. Try responding in a more thankful or upbeat way during daily conversations. People will ask you, "How's it going?" Simply answer, "I'm just blessed out!" After returning from Vietnam, POW survivor and speaker Capt. Charles Plumb's standard reply became an enthusiastic "I'm living the dream!" Spread a few smiles and watch attitudes lift. Even if it doesn't help the outlook of others, it will certainly improve yours! When you begin to look for reasons to celebrate your day, you'll find that there are plenty.

What can you do about the *Pits People* in your world? They control their comments and their attitude, but sometimes a gentle and respectful comment shared privately can make a difference. Some negative comments are necessary in business and in life, because hidden problems can become big problems. Let these negative people know that your goal is not to eliminate appropriate criticism; you'd just like them to consider adjusting their doses. After all, constant complaining isn't welcomed on or off the job. Request that they try interjecting a few more compliments about what's working well, so that others know they are part of the team. We listen to people who can tell the truth about what's working and what isn't.

> "Our goal is to hold a 48-hour marathon of good news. This is our Christmas gift to show that Colombia can send a positive message."
>
> —Carlos Santa

People and cultures can change, and even the media can occasionally help with this. For example, Reuters reported that Radio Deportes de Caracol—a Colombian radio station in the northwestern city of Medellín—had given a positive gift to an area famous as the center of the country's cocaine trade. The station dedicated itself to delivering two days of nonstop Christmas glad tidings in an effort to show that there is more to Colombia than bad news about war, violence, and drugs. In an effort to win a place in the *Guinness Book of Records*, some 15 journalists read more than 3,500 dispatches highlighting positive sports news, good corporate results, and other upbeat stories. The feedback from listeners was so positive that the station created a daily good news hour.

You don't have to have your own radio station to make a difference. Try talking about good news in the hallways of your organization, and think about what you would highlight in your own *good news* hour.

Truth #24: Turn Happy Accidents into Tomorrow's Innovations

> "Smart? It's not about being smart. It's about being able to recognize when you do something accidentally that in hindsight looks smart."
> —Nick Reed, Paragon Biomedical CEO

Sometimes the best innovations are simply a consequence of happy accidents. In fact, the economic hall of fame is full of companies that in searching for an improved product were blindsided by an unexpected opportunity they almost missed.

Creator of the 3M fabric protector Scotchguard Patsy Sherman was the sixth woman inducted into the national Inventors Hall of Fame. Although initially hired as a temporary employee, her discovery had a way of extending that job for another 40 years. Her journey of discovery is proof that appreciating happy accidents is at the core of innovation. Sherman asserts: "Anybody can be an inventor. It has absolutely nothing to do with how much education or how many degrees you have after your name. It's a mind-set. When an inventor sees something unusual or something that is a disappointing result, they don't just throw it out and start over. They say, 'Hey, what happened here? Why did it happen? What does it mean? What might it be good for?'"

Many of the world's greatest discoveries—such as penicillin and the vulcanization of rubber—came about strictly by accident. However, somebody was keeping their eyes open and their brain in gear. These inventors gratefully rode their accidents into history on a course that still has an impact today.

The path to success does not necessarily follow a straight line. It's like a winding river, and like water, it eventually finds its course. Being smart means developing the mental flexibility and the eye to recognize and seize opportunities that appear in the flow. The best innovators are always looking for new gems within the open cracks in seemingly dead ends. They like dabbling in what-if games with life, and they seldom follow the shortest paths. Instead, they take time for excursions into tangents and activities that others just race by.

You most likely loved the process of discovery as a child. Maybe it is time to reclaim some of the joy so that you, too, can take advantage of the happy accidents that happen on your journey. Keep your eyes open and your brain in gear; be grateful for the gems you find.

Truth #25: Hope for More, but Never Be Thrown by Less

As an optimist, you can hope for more out of life, but don't be thrown when you receive less. Don't expect things to automatically go well; instead, be pleased and thankful when

> "Joy is what happens to us when we allow ourselves to recognize how good things really are."
> —Marianne Williamson

they do. Just as your optimism has grown from a track record of overcoming the obstacles you've faced, your positive attitude matures when you can acknowledge and appreciate the experiences, people, and things that you value most.

As Dr. Joyce Brothers suggests: "Count up every single thing—large and small—that makes your life worthwhile, including your own innate talents. . . . When you quantify these things, gratitude—the mighty river to happiness—begins its journey through your soul." Now, that is a powerful picture of the kinds of things that genuine gratitude can produce! Remaining appreciative will keep your frustrations and setbacks in perspective. By taking the time to collect joy, you will learn that stressful worry and grateful thoughts are incompatible.

> "My office is in the unit where the babies and mommies are brought together for the first time. Every day, I walk by the newborn nursery and see families gathered around smiling and happy. They're not thinking about what's going on in the world. They're thinking about that brand-new baby."
> —Kathleen Alfe, Northridge Hospital Medical Center

So, instead of just focusing on the biggest hurdles on your to-do-list, start your day by taking a few minutes to actually count your blessings. What are you most thankful for today? Be specific, and try listing at least five things.

Two teens built a thriving business selling T-shirts with the positive message "Life is good!" They've had trouble keeping the T-shirts in stock. The media may make a living bringing you the worst, but the people making things happen in the world don't have time to watch. They're too busy inventing a future they want to live in and enjoying every step of the journey.

Live Simply and Focus on What You Have

Demanding more and more possessions and money in order to become happy seldom has the effect of actually creating the happiness you desire. Far too many people spend years gathering more things to fit into increasingly bigger houses, only to spend their later years getting rid of things and craving simplicity and satisfying relationships. Why wait? Claim a little more simplicity now; avoid the wasted cost and stressful aggravation involved in competing for who can own the most toys and the biggest mansion.

> "The real beginning of being happy is having gratitude. That's where I live. I'm just grateful for what I have. I'm not vying for other things. I don't need to do this. I don't need to have that. I think it is the way I was raised."
> —Cameron Diaz

Writing commentary from Kentucky in the early years of our country, Francis Johnson wrote: "If we fasten our attention on what we have, rather than on what we lack, a very little wealth is sufficient." You'd certainly rather be rich than poor, but riches won't always bring an optimistic attitude or satisfaction with your position in life. The rich still worry—their concerns simply involve more expensive toys.

When our son traveled with other teenagers on his first service mission to Mexico, he came home with a surprising observation. He had expected before he left that he would find children living in poverty to be unhappy. But as he watched these young people entertain themselves with makeshift toys and watched teens play on dirt fields, he saw more smiles, joy, and laughter than he did with teens from home. Just as he observed, your attitude can overcome almost any circumstance in order to find all the joy that is needed. Simple pleasures are seldom expensive, and appreciating them costs you nothing. In fact, this book has an entire chapter on developing simple activities that can break the momentum of a bad day and reset your attitude to positive.

Truth #26: Rejoice in the Gift of Every Day

Maybe there's a reason that so many different faiths encourage a spirit of gratefulness. Giving thanks to God is, for example, very much a part of the Jewish faith. The Mizmor L'todah, a psalm of thanksgiving (Psalm 100), was originally sung as believers brought their thanksgiving offering to the Jerusalem Temple. Since then, it's been incorporated into the introductory praises leading up to the main part of morning prayers.

> "When you arise in the morning, give thanks for the light and for your life, for your strength. Give thanks for your food and for the joy of living. If you see no reason for giving thanks, the fault lies only in yourself."
>
> —Tecumseh

Why do they start the day this way? Because every day—without even realizing it—each of us benefits from countless miracles. The believer's mission in this world is to see the blessings, divine acts of kindness, and miracles that surround them and to respond by serving with gladness. Jewish believers therefore pray not just to give thanks

> "O Lord, who lends me life, lend me a heart replete with thankfulness."
> —William Shakespeare

to the Holy One, but as a reminder of the necessity to serve with joy. That means daily miracles from God above and daily service from believers below.

That same spirit of thanksgiving is evident in the Christian faith. The Apostle Paul, writing to Christians in Philippi, wrote: "Rejoice in the Lord always. I will say it again: Rejoice! Let your gentleness be evident to all. The Lord is near. Do not be anxious about anything, but in everything, by prayer and petition, with thanksgiving, present your requests to God. And the peace of God, which transcends understanding, will guard your hearts and your minds."

I've developed a habit that centers me on a path of gratitude. Before I start my 30 minutes on the cross-trainer equipment, I consciously repeat the sentiments expressed in Psalm 118:24—"This is the day the Lord has made. Let us rejoice and be glad in it." While I exercise, I focus on the many things that I am grateful for. You may want to try the same thing as you exercise!

Faith may not be the answer for everyone, but hope and optimism seldom exist in a vacuum. Many find them by being part of and in serving within a community. Successful actor Michael J. Fox tells the powerful story about his journey living with Parkinson's disease in a book that he called *Always Looking Up*. Fox has learned to accept what fate has brought him, but that has not eliminated his choices or his commitment to remain optimistic. During an interview on an ABC special about his illness, Michael shared what his particular situation had taught him about life: "The answer had very little to do with protection and everything to do with perspective. The only unavailable choice was whether or not to have Parkinson's. Everything else was up to me. I could concentrate on the loss or just get on with life and maybe see if the holes started filling in for themselves."

> "Most people are as happy as they make up their minds to be."
> —Abraham Lincoln

Even without faith, gratitude impacts the one who gives thanks and those who are thanked.

Michael J. Fox is bringing his optimism and hope to communities and readers throughout the world. He may not address his gratitude to God, but he certainly is still making a difference. And you can do the same yourself.

> "Since I am not sure of the address to send my gratitude, I put it out there with everything I do."
> —Michael J. Fox

Truth #27: Be Grateful for the People Who Make the Ride Worthwhile

If you've ever lost—or came close to losing—someone you love, you know what matters most. You've had the opportunity to realize that it's your loved ones, not your luxuries that truly count. Are you taking time to let others know how much you appreciate them? Don't wait for going-away parties or memorial eulogies to express your gratitude.

June Solberg, who later with her husband, Dick, was sent to Germany to assist with post–World War II recovery, often told the story of a turning point in her life. During difficult economic times as a young couple, June and her husband struggled to make ends meet and provide for their two very young children. Walking back to her apartment on a cold winter evening, she clasped her two children on each arm. While wondering where the next dollar would come from, she was met on the snow-covered sidewalk by a smiling stranger. He paused for a moment, knelt down to look at her two children, and said, "Oh my, but you are rich."

Solberg thanked the stranger for his kind words

> "I used to ask my students, 'How many of you have sent a handwritten thank-you note in the last year?' Less than 10 percent could say they had. Gratitude is everything. Somebody once asked me if cancer had changed my views on life, and I said, 'Not really. I've always believed every day is a gift, but now I'm looking for where to send the thank-you note.'"
> —Randy Pausch

"What amazing gifts the new year brings! An entire year's worth of wonderful opportunities, given to us one sunrise at a time. Many of the moments ahead will be marvelously disguised as ordinary days, but each one of us has the chance to make something extraordinary out of them. Each new day is a blank page in the diary of your life. The secret of success is in turning that diary into the best story you possibly can."

—Douglas Pagels

and walked the rest of the way home with tears running down her face. She recognized that she was indeed rich in what mattered most—her husband's love, her faith, and her treasured children.

If you are rich in relationships, as Solberg was, express your appreciation often. Developing your sense of gratitude won't just help you and your attitude; it will allow you to reinforce the power of community and acknowledge the importance of others. Expressing gratitude is all about stopping the flow and letting people know how much you value them and what they have done.

A few months before his father's death, John Craig visited him at his law office in Wabash Valley, Indiana. While waiting for his father to finish with a client, John was called into the office. The client was a man known to the family for years—a prosperous, immigrant dairyman. Though John was aware that his father had handled a large and costly legal transaction for this man, he wasn't sure why he was brought into the conversation.

His father pointed at his son John and spoke firmly, "That is the reason!" His father turned back to his client and continued, "My friend, when that man (nodding toward his son) was a baby during the height of the depression, you delivered a bottle of milk to my door every morning. I couldn't pay for it. You never asked. No, my dear friend, there will be no fee owed to me in this case. That debt was retired years ago."

Can you imagine the impact of that message on all involved? Who do you need to thank on and off the job? Put it on your to-do list now!

Handling What Comes Your Way and Making Things Go Your Way

You can increase your chances of happiness and optimism by choosing to be thankful. Count your blessings more than your problems. Instead of dwelling on what ought to be, look for the happy accidents that have provided blessings you couldn't have expected. As Albert Einstein so wisely observed, "There are only two ways to live your life. One is as though nothing is a miracle. The other is as if everything is."

You've learned that optimism is all about handling what comes your way, but it's also about actively doing your part to make things go your way. So, as we turn to focus on how you manage yourself and your actions, you can be thankful for the exciting adventure that lies ahead as you work to invent a better future—one day at a time.

> "Gratitude unlocks the fullness of life. It turns what we have into enough, and more. It turns denial into acceptance, chaos into order, and confusion into clarity. I can turn a meal into a feast, a house into a home, and a stranger into a friend. Gratitude makes sense of our past, brings peace for today, and creates a vision for tomorrow."
>
> —Melody Beattie

CHAPTER 10

Optimists Provide Constructive Self-Criticism

"The only man who never made a mistake is the man who never does anything."

—Theodore Roosevelt

Not only can you expect to experience your share of adversity and good fortune in your life, but also you will most certainly earn your share of both successes and failures. We all make mistakes; that is a given. But optimists learn to turn those mistakes into learning opportunities that point the way to eventual success. So, how do optimists handle the mistakes that are a natural part of every person's life?

"A life spent in making mistakes is not only more honorable but more useful than a life spent doing nothing."

—George Bernard Shaw

Truth #28: The More Mistakes You Make, the Quicker You Learn

Children live on a steady diet of mistakes. You can't learn to walk without falling down or to speak without mispronouncing and misusing words. It's not possible to build a learning culture if people are afraid of making a mistake; they'll go into hiding instead of learning.

Those people born before the era of frequent PC use can vividly recall the first time they touched a computer. They didn't want people to watch as they tentatively typed on the keys. They were somewhat frightened, even worried, that if they touched the wrong key, Burbank might disappear! Younger generations, however, seem to have no such fear; they are experimenting, rebooting, experimenting again—taking learning to the edge and back again. By failing, they learn faster.

Fear of failure is something that we tend to learn in school; we become hesitant to raise our hands and give a wrong or stupid answer. The fear of success often hits later in life after years of achievement. The higher you go in the organization, the further you have to fall and the more people you take with you. In both cases, anxiety about making a mistake is a significant problem in a world where we face constant change. Progress today is regularly the result of rapid, often chaotic, change and the myriad of risk takers and innovators who make it happen. Too many Americans get an F where it counts the most: They fail to fail.

> "If I had known what I know now, I would have made the same mistakes sooner."
> —Robert Half

That's precisely why business consultant Michael Gelb wrote in *Training* magazine: "I think organizations should change the name of the training department to the 'department of constructive mistake-making.' If you're not making mistakes, you're not learning anything valuable." Leaders' willingness to be transparent about their own failures and mistakes can go a long way toward creating a culture that capitalizes on failures instead of hiding them. No leader can know it

> "A vital ingredient of success is occasional failure. Decision making is a prime responsibility of those in top positions, and their batting average between right ones and wrong ones must be high. . . . Apparently it is not a long leap from being right most of the time to the assumption that one is right all the time. . . . A big shot who has never laid an egg—in his opinion—is in the position of a hen under a similar handicap, about to be made a meal of."
> —Malcolm S. Forbes

all. That's why you have people on your team who know more than you do, and it's why you are wise to listen to them. Admitting failures makes you approachable to your biggest asset—your people.

Start by affirming the value of mistakes in setting the stage for success. Striving to produce failure-proof performance is often done at the expense of necessary progress. Business consultant and author Tom Peters reminds us: "Mistakes are not the spice of life. Mistakes are life. Failure is the only precursor of success." Playing to win in the great game of business is guaranteed to produce many fouls and missed goals. It's one of the prices you pay for competing; it's the same with all facets of your life. The more missteps you make as a parent, a salesperson, a manager, or a partner—the quicker you learn.

BusinessWeek Online contributor Ira Sager writes about what sets the Silicon Valley apart: "Failure is O.K. Push all levels of management to try new ideas. Let ideas incubate. Learn to live with creative chaos. Be your own toughest competitor. Don't stick with your starters too long. Spread the wealth broadly. Grab market share at all cost. Stay at the cutting edge by investing in startups. In the end it comes down to an ill-defined, yet critical ingredient: culture. You have to change the way you do business. And remember the first item: Failure is O.K."

Resilience and persistence consistently pay off. If you get out of the game because you make a mistake, you can't win. As one soccer

> "If you want to succeed, double your failure rate."
> —Thomas J. Watson Sr.

coach drilled into his young players, "It's not how many times you fall; it's how quickly you get back up!" The way in which you talk to yourself when you make a mistake doesn't only impact your attitude and self-confidence; it can determine how quickly you rebound and get back in the game.

Your Worst Critic May Be Sitting in Your Seat

> "No matter what our achievements might be, we think well of ourselves only in rare moments. We need people to bear witness against our inner judge, who keeps book on our shortcomings and transgressions. We need to convince us that we are not as bad as we think we are."
>
> —Eric Hoffer

Unfortunately, the way you privately evaluate yourself is most likely making matters even worse. As most people are, you are probably far more critical of your own behavior than you are of anyone else's. Such negative self-evaluations can affect your optimism and your performance on and off the job.

One way to view self-confidence is to see it as an inference you make from your own private self-evaluations. It's estimated that you assess some aspect of your performance between 300 to 400 times a day. You often break the flow of the day's activities—if only for a moment—to mentally evaluate your own performance.

Unfortunately, most of this self-analysis tends to be unfavorable. For the average person, 80 percent of internal dialogue regarding their own performance tends to be negative, and only 20 percent is positive. With that kind of critic on board all day long, you might be treated better if you spent time with your enemies!

We'll leave positive self-support for our next chapter; however, our tendency to major in self-criticism is too glaring to ignore. Do those numbers seem outrageous—80 percent negative? Do a little reality testing on yourself. How often do you appraise your own personal and professional actions as less than satisfactory? Would you accept that a good mistake is easily worth 45 minutes of self-whipping interspersed over a three-day period? You've

> "I am always with myself, and it is I who am my tormentor."
>
> —Leo Tolstoy

> "Let's face it. Everyone fails so much these days. You can't let it intimidate you. What I tell people, and try to tell myself, is: The only way you truly fail in this day and age is to stop trying altogether."
> —Stephen Covey

heard yourself: "That was stupid. I can't believe I said that. And they were all watching me. They're probably talking about me right now over dinner!"

And as if that's not bad enough, you have a very efficient filer in the back of your brain. Every time you call yourself a name, he goes back to check the evidence. Can you hear him? "Just a minute, boss. Let me check your 'stupid' file. Why, yes, you are stupid. In fact, you're getting worse. This reminds me of the time you. . . ."

Most of us are good at making ourselves feel worse—not better—about our mistakes and failures. But as an optimist, you can change that.

Majoring in Self-Criticism Leaves You Needing the Support of Others

As research suggests, most of us are four times as negative as positive when speaking to ourselves. However, we are publicly more likely to present ourselves as being 95 percent effective and admit making an occasional mistake to appear human. There's nothing wrong with putting your best foot forward. After all, you clean your house before you invite neighbors to come over, and you try to dress nicely for dates and job interviews. We all do the same with the image we try to convey to our customers and our colleagues. Thankfully, only you know the worst about yourself.

Unfortunately, when you compare what only you know about yourself with everyone else's public image, you lose, badly. You may even fear that people will discover the truth about you and withhold their approval. After all, when you are preoccupied with your faults, you seek 80 percent support from others just to break even with your 80 percent self-criticism! You search for loved ones, associates, and bosses who will affirm you and make up for your own self-esteem deficit.

Respected speech coach Ron Arden shared an insight from legendary actress Jessica Tandy, one that we all ought to appreciate: "Understandably, every human seeks some expression of approval. But, in our eagerness to please and be pleased with ourselves, we choose too often to hear the

> "By recalling those inglorious, ineffective events of yesterday, our energy is sapped for facing the demands of today. Rehearsing those wrongs, now forgiven by grace, derails and demoralizes us. There are few joy stealers more insidious than past memories that haunt our minds. . . . Forget the past!"
>
> —Charles Swindoll

applause rather than the suggestions for further improvement of our work or ourselves. Throughout my career, the following thought by Constantin Stanislavsky has served as a guide: 'Young actors fear your admirers! Learn in time, from your first steps, to hear, understand and love the cruel truth about yourselves. Find out who can tell you the truth and talk of your art only with those who can tell you the truth.'"

Approving applause can often seem shallow, short-lived, and sometimes undeserved to an actor. It's what the audience says as the people leave the theater that often contains the truth actors need to hear. You want and need to have discerning, independent people who are assertive enough to confront you when you need it. But when you require the approval of others, they control your confidence. By withholding that approval, they leave you feeling less effective and less confident. At a time when you want to be more active and assertive on and off the job, this need often leaves you more dependent instead.

There are days when no one will support you, no matter what your leading role—manager, actor, parent, or president. As a sales professional, there are days no one will even answer the phone, much less buy your product. Being dependent on the approval of employees, your children, or anyone else is no way to live life. To fight this need, start by judging yourself as you would others you care about. When you do that well, you just may be able to listen to the criticism you need to hear from others.

Truth #29: Love Yourself as You Do Your Loved Ones, Neighbors, and Colleagues

Religious principles challenge you to love your neighbor as yourself, but heaven help your neighbors if you talked to them as you talk to yourself. "You did what? You're so stupid! Did anyone see you? They saw you! Do they know I know you? I mean it reminds me of the time you. . . . You're getting worse!"

> "The brilliant moves we occasionally make would not have been possible without prior dumb ones."
> —Stanley Goldstein

Who needs neighbors or colleagues like that! If you talk to an employee the way you talk to yourself, he could file a grievance and win. It's time to find a new way to speak to yourself about the mistakes and failures you have made. Start by treating yourself like you treat those you care about. Just as you would forgive them, forgive yourself and make room for your mistakes as valued learning opportunities that help you grow.

As Confucius said, "Our greatest glory is not in never falling but in rising every time we fall." Or as one particularly insightful manager put it to her team, "Mistakes are clear evidence that someone out there is trying to do something."

Mistakes are always going to be made; your challenge is to figure out how to be self-critical without verbally abusing yourself. Start by looking at self-criticism as *course correction data* that helps you get back on track to achieve your goals. Every time you wander off course, this feedback allows you to refocus on your target. The purpose of feedback ought not to be self-conviction or blaming; rather, it should be to make you more effective tomorrow in reaching your goals.

You know the importance of forgiving others; it's time to get better at forgiving yourself. Almost every mistake is part of a learning process. They're seldom terminal and always essential for any lively, forward-looking organization. As former NBA basketball player and coach Pat Riley says, "There are no failures, just results. Now get busy doing what you can to make your results better." Now, that is good advice.

Truth #30: When Self-Critical, Avoid General Labels and Focus on Specific Feedback

Instead of using general labels like *stupid* or *rude* to describe yourself, use specific, detailed descriptions. What exactly did you do that you feel you did not handle well? Remember, it's easier to admit that you made a mistake than to admit you are one. While you probably wouldn't describe yourself as a generally rude person, you've certainly had moments you aren't proud of. I've had my own share of those experiences on the freeways of Los Angeles. I know that my driving wasn't appreciated; the other driver didn't wave with all his fingers. Over the years, however, those instances have been far less frequent.

You can always learn important life lessons by looking in your rearview mirror, but continuing to stare at it is never wise. Crashing out the front window just makes your mistake a lot more expensive. Look back just long enough to learn. Memorize this important question to help control your focus: What did you specifically do that contributed to the problem or failure? And don't beat yourself up over things you couldn't have controlled or didn't cause. Although you may not be pleased with the result, you'll be hard-pressed to identify anything you did that contributed to the failure. While you of course want to take responsibility for your errors, don't take responsibility you don't deserve. In some situations, you simply don't deserve criticism; you

> "Notice the difference between what happens when a man says to himself, 'I have failed three times,' and what happens when he says, 'I am a failure.'"
> —S. I. Hayakawa

deserve a pat on the back for your heroic efforts in the face of otherwise frustrating circumstances. And when you can't get a pat on the back any other way, then give yourself one!

There may, of course, be many situations in which you can clearly identify specific mistakes you made that contributed to the problem or poor results. But it's time to leave any verbal self-abuse or replays of similar past failures to the pessimists in our midst. Instead, opt to do what optimists do—a little problem solving out the front window.

Truth #31: Claim Optimism by Making Your Future Work

When reporters asked former IBM CEO Lou Gerstner to look back at the most important decision he had made, he responded honestly and wisely: "I've been working so hard here and focusing on the future, I haven't had time to think about it. To contemplate . . . on the hills and valleys of history is not on my agenda. I want us to keep running, to keep moving ahead. Some may feel that because the wind is now at our back, it's time to coast. They are allowed a five-minute celebration; then it's time to get back to work." The moral? If you're going to reflect on past decisions—the good ones and the mistakes—don't take too long. There's too much to do in improving your situation today.

Professional golfing legend Tiger Woods is also known for his future-focused approach: "People want to compare my performance to the past, and I'm trying to get better in the future, not the past." Woods seems to win far more tournaments than he loses and is consistently close to taking the trophy almost every time he plays.

> "A man should never be ashamed to admit that he has been in the wrong, which is but saying, in other words, that he is wiser today than he was yesterday."
>
> —Jonathan Swift

Yet, with all the victories and great moments in his career, he continues to focus on improving. Even at the top of his game, Woods changed his swing and paid the price as he waited for it to produce results. Why? He knew it would help him score even better in the future. Top performers don't bask in reliving the past; they keep raising their own bar! They don't want to settle for a good year; they want to sustain a dynasty year after year.

While you are unlikely to ever match Tiger's golf prowess, you can claim his future-focused attitude for your own life. Professionalism is not about coasting or resting on laurels; it's about lifelong learning and the pursuit of excellence. You earn it one day at a time, every day. A mistake is just a problem in need of a solution.

It's time to put this message together into a script you can use to give yourself constructive feedback. After identifying your own specific mistake, focus on the future by asking two important questions:

- What specifically can and will you do to rectify the problem?
- How would you handle the same situation next time?

First, take responsibility by asking what you specifically can and will do to rectify the problem. If any constructive action or apology could help fix the problem or heal a relationship—do it. If you didn't do the right thing for an on-going relationship at the time, nothing should stop you from doing that now. Taking responsibility for your own errors is always the right thing to do.

> "It's called 'attention to detail'! Some of the best lessons are when you get something wrong and learn from it."
> —David Nelms, CEO of Discover Financial

There is a myth of spontaneity that implies that if you didn't handle a situation correctly at the time it occurred, there's no point in bringing it up again. But spontaneity is overrated. We've all watched too many movies where actors always say the right thing at the right moment. Why? They have a script!

Real life is different, of course, but when a conversation is not going well, wouldn't it be wonderful if you could say: "Cut! Let's take this scene from the top . . . and this time let's adjust our lines!" We don't get to go back for retakes; we live life in real time with no dress rehearsals. We make mistakes both by being too spontaneous and by not saying anything at all. Take responsibility for both, and take the initiative to offer an apology when appropriate.

However, you don't want to take this personal responsibility to an extreme. After all, an apology is simply not practical in some situations. If you inappropriately cut someone off on the freeway, it's not wise or a good use of time to go back to that place and wait for that driver to appear again so that you can say you're sorry. Sometimes you just have to let the past go and let what you've learned benefit others in the future.

> "People want to hear apologies. Next, they want you to fix the problem, to clean up the mess or make sure it never happens again."
>
> —Bill Benoit

There is an added benefit to being easy to reach when you've made a mistake. Being a problem solver rather than a problem evader is a sure way to build strong personal and professional relationships. When you take responsibility for your mistakes, you are more likely to have people join in when you celebrate your victories. As we've previously stated, hidden mistakes can become very big mistakes. What really makes mistakes expensive is failing to admit them right away. Unfortunately, too many business cultures discourage leaders and associates from admitting mistakes. Instead, they hide mistakes and play the blame game. Similarly, many parents feel that it undermines their authority to acknowledge to their children that they handled a situation poorly.

Don't let that happen in your organization or your family. Everyone would learn so much more from their mistakes if they weren't so busy denying that they made them or blaming others.

As one executive said to his leaders, "You have the right to make a mistake. You don't have the right to cover your ass over that mistake." By publicly modeling appropriate self-criticism, you can help build a culture where it is safe to surface errors quickly.

Make It Safe to Surface Problems Quickly by Doing It Yourself First

We are entering an accountability age in which most people abhor leaders who say one thing and do another. In today's world, it is always right and prudent to take responsibility for errors and communicate problems as soon as possible. Don't wait for *20/20* or *60 Minutes* to come to your door to ask why you didn't act. The best leaders don't wait for crises to force action; they initiate action in pursuit of strategic and ethical change. Learn to take responsibility and apologize when appropriate, but even more important, solve problems instead of attempting to dodge them. One way to do so is to make sure that others feel safe and comfortable bringing up any problem. As one woman executive said, "They have to be able to tell me my baby is ugly—even when I don't want to see it!"

> "We all make mistakes. But what really makes mistakes expensive is not admitting them right away. Business culture teaches us never to admit to our mistakes but to bury them instead or to blame someone else."
> —Katie Delahaye Paine, CEO of KDPaine & Partners LLC

One particular CEO approached this in an interesting way by putting $100 on the table with his top executives. He shared a costly mistake he had made and what he learned from the mistake. He then offered a challenge: $100 for the one person who could top his mistake. Learning from mistakes became an important part of their corporate culture.

In Ann Arbor, Michigan, executives compete for the Golden Egg Award for the most notable errors made by company presidents. At Graphic Controls Corporation in Cherry Hill, New Jersey, the management invites others to tour their facility. They don't just showcase their benchmark

> "As strange as it may sound, the work of execution is actually all about failure. So celebrate it! Bronze an oversized screw, and award it each week to the project-team who made the 'best screwup of the week.'"
> —Tom Peters

achievements; they reveal some of the warts as well. They find that visitors can often provide new ideas they need to explore.

Are you making it safe to admit and confront problems in your organization? Don't force your people to wait until a problem spirals out of control. Learn to ask frequently, "Are you aware of any *red flags* we ought to be concerned about?" And if there are—listen!

Don't Just Admit Your Mistakes—Learn from Them

Finally, and most important, don't just admit mistakes; learn from them as well. Former MarketWatch CEO Larry Kramer is now a senior advisor at Polaris Ventures, a life sciences venture capital firm. He has an interesting perspective on picking his team: "I like hiring people who have at least one failure on their resume. It's a character-building experience and a reminder of how things can be worse. It's kind of like people who have lived through a war and those who have not." Kramer realizes that times of disappointment and failure compel us to search for anchors to help us recover and carry on with renewed strength and resolve. True optimism is born of struggle, and Kramer likes to extract that struggle by asking, "Tell me about a disappointment or failure you have had that taught you an important lesson." Candor in the face of failure shows that people can benefit and learn from the past and that they have no illusions about whether problems that do occur can be overcome. Being open to learn from your errors helps prove this to yourself and others.

So learn from every mistake by asking yourself a centering question: How would you handle a similar situation next time? In fact, if you want to spend more time in constructive self-criticism, then this is where to invest it. Setting the stage for improving your performance in the future is always a worthy use of your time. If you struggle with being able to turn your internal comments into constructive problem solving, then try these two time-tested strategies. Use a valued colleague or friend as a sounding board to talk through your self-criticism.

If that is impractical—or there is no one available—write out your self-criticism. Writing can be quite a therapeutic process when used to appropriately channel self-criticism into a problem-solving strategy. People used to have time for diaries and more conversations with friends. These days, we don't appear to have time for either. As a result, we spend more time in therapy with professionals whom we've sworn to confidentiality. This is often a good investment. You may feel better after a few sessions, but it may be less costly and perhaps as effective to first start making more time available for friends and writing in your journal.

So start now. Use this appropriate self-criticism script and begin writing.

Appropriate Self-Criticism:

To understand your role, what did you specifically do that contributed to the problem or failure?

To take responsibility, what specifically can and will you do to rectify the problem?

To learn, how would you handle a similar situation next time?

Mistakes Are Tough but Essential Teachers

Using our mistakes to learn can be an incredibly tough process. Life often gives you a surprise quiz and a failing grade before you even get to learn the lesson. So when your mistakes cost you and your organization, make sure you don't double the price by losing the lesson. Being overly self-critical forces you to waste time hiding errors and seeking affirmations that could have been invested in inventing your future. Hopefully, this chapter has given you assurance that you are not alone. It's nice to know that we all make mistakes and have a tendency to major in self-criticism.

Thankfully, it doesn't need to remain that way. You can manage yourself the way you would want to be managed by others. Self-confidence doesn't

> "The brick walls are not there to keep us out; the brick walls are there to give us a chance to show how badly we want something."
>
> —Randy Pausch

come from an absence of self-criticism but from a realistic balance of learning from our errors and celebrating our victories.

Welcome to the challenge of turning your mistakes into stepping stones for future growth and success. Now, it's time to learn how to major in support by catching yourself being effective. Sometimes you amaze even yourself. As an optimist, it's time you celebrate those moments!

> "To look back all the time is boring. Excitement lies in tomorrow."
> —Natalie Makarova

Managing Your Own Motivation Means Catching Yourself Being Effective

"I wish I would have followed my instincts earlier in my career rather than looking for others' approval. While it's easy for people to be their greatest critics, it took me years to become my own best advocate."
—Ellen Langas Campbell, President of NouSoma
Communications

C onstructive self-criticism is an important part of life, but so is self-support. Mistakes help you learn what not to do. Acknowledging your successes allows you to reinforce what's already working.

So instead of repeatedly focusing on what's going wrong, take the optimistic approach and concentrate more intently on your own positives. Take

"To be encouraged look at how far you have come. To be discouraged look at how far you have to go."
—Mark Sanborn

> "Calm self-confidence is as far from conceit as the desire to earn a decent living is remote from greed."
> —Channing Pollock

time every day to examine what you've done that has contributed to your achievements—both on and off the job. After all, a big part of maintaining a healthy, optimistic perspective in challenging times is managing your own motivation. This requires that you *catch yourself being effective*. You've learned the importance of nurturing gratitude for the happy accidents that happen—those things that you don't control but can and should appreciate. It is all the more important to appreciate what you do control—the actions that you initiate.

As we discussed in the last chapter, self-feedback research finds that our internal evaluations tend to be 80 percent negative and 20 percent positive. You may now have a better understanding of how you can focus your negative self-evaluations, but how can you do a better job of celebrating your triumphs?

Needing the Support of Others Leaves You Dependent Instead of Confident

As much as you appreciate the support of others, you don't want to completely depend on their approval in order to make decisions and take action. You want to enjoy the positive comments from an appreciative boss or loved one, not falter because of its absence.

In *The One Minute Manager*, author Ken Blanchard asserts that for managers to be perceived as supportive, they need a four-to-one positive to negative contact ratio—that's four positive messages for every one criticism. That fits! When you make four

> "They cannot take away our self-respect if we do not give it to them."
> —Gandhi

critical self-evaluations for every complimentary one, you need some positive feedback from an appreciative boss just to break even. Unfortunately, few managers are that positive. Most compliments come at going-away parties or in eulogies when you die. And the same often occurs in your personal relationships. In fact, one of the few times in life you will receive 80 percent support is when you're initially dating a new person, because that's essentially the sales phase of your relationship. When you're just getting to know a new roman-tic partner, both parties tend be on their best behavior.

After several years of marriage, however, those "I love you" comments and sweet nothings tend to decrease. As one golden oldie said of his wife, "I told her I loved her when we got married, and if I ever changed my mind, I'd let her know." It certainly would be wise for bosses and spouses to be a lot more appreciative, but it's not especially healthy to expect that kind of support.

Never let yourself rely that heavily on others' approval—no matter how much they profess to love or support you. While you, of course, may value and appre-ciate those comments, don't allow yourself to become emo-tionally dependent. Face an unsettling reality—you're stuck

> "It takes half your life before you discover life is a do-it-yourself project."
> —Napoleon Hill

with you! Your motivation ultimately is your job. You're the only person who's with you 24/7, so it's time you learn to increase your frequency of appropriate self-support.

But don't worry. Help is on the way.

Truth #32: When You Cannot Get a Compliment Any Other Way, Give Yourself One

Mark Twain had some excellent advice: "An occasional compliment is necessary to keep up one's self-respect. . . . When you cannot get a compliment any other way, pay yourself one." Twain's words encourage us once again to treat ourselves as we treat people we care about. You shouldn't take yourself for granted any more than you would undervalue an associate, friend, or loved one. And while this is easy to state, very few people actually live it. To build a strong and realistic self-confidence,

> "Rather than giving people an inflated view of themselves, we need to give them concrete reasons to feel good about themselves."
> —Martin Seligman, PhD

you must develop a habit of recognizing your own commendable actions on a daily basis. This isn't about feeding a big ego; it's about becoming aware of your strengths as well as your mistakes. You may be winning and truly not know it—unless you're keeping score of your own effectiveness.

Unfortunately, it's far too easy to take yourself for granted. The reason is simply that you're around yourself all the time. In fact, if you find that you aren't, as a psychologist, I'd suggest that you need more than this book can provide. But in all seriousness, spending every waking moment with yourself comes with a cost—namely, the familiarity that causes you to miss so much of what you do. Your own skills and accomplishments are like the pictures you hang on the wall. You enjoy them for a time, but after two weeks of walking by them, you don't even see them anymore. They become part of your gray zone of unobserved treasures—those things you possess but no longer experience or appreciate. You see them when you move or when new guests point them out when they visit. That's actually why you have guests—they show you your home!

Don't hide your achievements in that gray zone of hidden treasures. Cultivate your confidence by scheduling time to appreciate yourself in your daily routine.

What's Working for You?

When I was 17, my first and best manager—a man by the name of Jack Nichols—asked me a question that has impacted my confidence and my life ever since. Every week, this construction supervisor took a 15-minute walk with each of his eight employees. The question he asked on every one of those walks was as simple as it was unsettling: "What's working for you?"

Even when I was a teen, my supervisor expected to learn from me. I was surprised by his question on our first walk together. While I had been privileged to learn from good parents and excellent teachers, none had ever asked me that question. I felt like responding, "Have you forgotten what it's like to be a teenager? We don't know anything. In fact, talk to my mother. She knows I don't know anything and might give you an excuse note!"

Near the end of our first walk, Jack informed me that he was going to ask me that question every Friday. As a good student, I'd already learned to figure out how teachers construct tests and to use that to guide my study habits. If the teacher used the text, their lectures, or both, I'd focus my study for the test accordingly. My supervisor made it similarly clear—I was going to have a quiz every week, and he wasn't giving me any of the answers. I had to come up with my own innovation every week. If nothing worked by Thursday, I had a mission—something has to work today, because he's going to ask that stupid question tomorrow! And every Friday, I had an answer. Twice, the team even implemented my suggestions.

Jack Nichols helped nurture my confidence at a time I needed it most, and he didn't do it by providing empty praise to a young teenager. He did it by asking a weekly question that forced me earn his respect. He expected me to make a difference, and I did.

Use Jack's question to guide your own self-motivation strategy. And don't just accidentally notice the ways in which you're effective; use a calendar or journal to keep track of and record everything you do that works. One manager made a habit of ending his work day by sending an e-mail to himself to document his daily accomplishments. When it arrived, he would save each of them in an e-mail folder to review when he needed a lift or to use to document his effectiveness at his own evaluation.

Whatever way you catch yourself being effective, before ending your day, force yourself to identify and write down at least one thing you did that you handled well. Focus on what stood out in your own performance. Just being aware of the fact that you have to make this daily entry will compel you to make each day significant. Make your entries short and specific, but write them every day until it becomes a habit.

Your Self-Support Strategy

What have you done today that has worked for you? Record every day a specific reference in your calendar, journal or e-mail to yourself.

There are many benefits to developing this habit. If you've ever struggled to think of specific examples of your own work or value, your documented entries will give you all the evidence you need. If you're having a bad day, nothing is more uplifting than scanning through some of your recent accomplishments.

Self-Confidence Is Not Self-Delusion

> "Act in ways that will cause you to respect yourself. Self-love is unconditional. Self-respect is something you earn yourself. Self-esteem will come later out of self-respect."
> —Dennis Prager

Effective self-motivation is one thing, but appropriate confidence is not built on self-delusion. It seems nowadays that we're flooded with advice on how to overcome feelings of inferiority. But if you haven't noticed, everybody is less proficient in some areas. Acknowledging one's natural limits is a healthful and realistic attitude. Success comes when you can accept your limitations and capitalize on your strengths. Nobody can be exceptional at everything—a simple fact that too many success mavens fail to acknowledge. In fact, very often, feelings of inadequacy eventually arise after hearing that we're good at everything—and then coming face-to-face with reality.

Psychologists Harold Stevenson and James Stigler tested the academic skills of elementary school students in the United States, China, Japan, and Taiwan. Although the Asian students outperformed the Americans, the U.S. students felt better about themselves and their work. They had somehow managed to combine high self-esteem with poor work—perhaps from the abundance of recognition for just showing up. The lesson we can learn from this is that we must care enough to be honest in our self-evaluations. We have to earn our own respect by acknowledging what we truly do well.

Sustainable and realistic self-confidence will always be built on accurate assessments of yourself. It requires you to discover your strengths and develop

> "You can only become truly accomplished at something you love. Don't make money your goal. Instead, pursue the things you love doing, and then do them so well that people can't take their eyes off you."
> —Maya Angelou

them in a way that brings satisfaction and makes a difference. It's even better when someone is willing to reward you for the value you provide. When you're good at something that others want and/or need—and you love doing it—you're on your way to a satisfying life. Keep developing and acknowledging your greatest gifts, and you will be more optimistic.

Humility Is Strength with Gentleness

You don't have to leave your faith out of your efforts to build a stronger self-confidence. One of the greatest acts of faith is to transfer God's love for you into a realistic faith in yourself. If you believe that you were created with gifts and a purpose to use those gifts, using them in a meaningful way—and becoming aware that you're doing so—allows you to reinforce your faith and to serve God.

A study by Rebecca Nolan of Louisiana State University at Shreveport found that the more religiously involved eighth graders were, the higher their self-esteem was. Spending time hearing about God's love may soften some of the self-critical doubts that come from constant peer comparison. After all, many of us are still just teenagers with older skin; faith can be helpful for self-affirmation at any age.

But, you might wonder, what about the importance of humility? *Humility* can be defined as "strength with

> "Know your strength. The most important thing is to know what you're good at."
> —Peter Drucker

gentleness." The truly humble know their strengths but go beyond that to affirm others' gifts as well.

Truth #33: Lead in a Way That Instills Confidence in Others

Former SAS CEO Jan Carlzon reminds us all of the importance of building others' confidence: "People aren't born with self-confidence. Even the most self-confident people can be broken. Self-confidence comes from success, experience, and the organization's environment. The leader's most important role is to instill confidence in people. They must dare to take risks and responsibility. You must back them up if they make mistakes."

With empowerment comes responsibility. As a result, some workers would rather stick to their job descriptions than take on new responsibilities that risk visible failure. Few want to be empowered if failure means being next in line for losing one's job. It is also true that leaders generally don't empower workers they don't trust.

> "The greatest good you can do for another is not just to share your riches, but to reveal to him his own."
> —Benjamin Disraeli

The challenge is for workers to develop confidence while managers gain that needed trust. When that happens, workers want to be empowered, and managers want to empower them to do as much as they can.

To accomplish this with your team, set clear boundaries for authorized decision making and expand those boundaries as your worker's self-assurance grows. Provide the resources and responsibility your people need to succeed, and take time to notice and acknowledge their effectiveness. By doing so, you'll build their confidence and gain trust in their performance.

Make sure your people also know that the challenge of taking on new projects in unexplored territory can occasionally lead to wrong turns and dead ends. Even though they do the best they can, good results sometimes remain elusive. Encourage the heroic efforts they make in support of strategic change. If all you recognize are successes, your employees will soon begin to limit their work to what they know will produce safe results. You'll soon hear a familiar reply: "It's not in my job description."

> "Every person I work with knows something better than I. My job is to listen long enough to find it and use it."
> —Jack Nichols

Affirming others doesn't threaten your own self-worth; it confirms it. Only those bosses, parents, and partners who are self-confident have the ego strength to watch others succeed. It's those who are not confident who must steal the credit to prop up their own inadequate self-worth.

Whether your confidence is strengthened by faith, appropriate self-support, or both, never forget to extend the gift of cultivating positive self-support to others with whom you interact, work, and live. As a leader, you may want to add a little positive reporting to your staff meetings, e-mail, and phone exchanges or your one-on-one walks. Join my first manager, Jack Nichols, in asking others: "What's working for you?" Don't just do it once, or they'll probably think that you're trying something you read in a book. Instead, make it a repetitive habit. Consistently asking that question will help others build a stronger sense of self-worth—and all will learn in the process.

When you're truly confident, you aren't threatened by others' admirable attributes; you're inspired by their strengths in action. After all, their success doesn't take away from yours. They just give you another reason to celebrate life and the gifts each person brings to the party!

Care about How You View Yourself

We've learned that while it's important to value the feedback of others, it's imperative to value your own. Teddy Roosevelt shared the same sentiment when he said, "I care not what others think of what I do, but I care very much about

> "There's no limit to what a man can do or where he can go if he doesn't mind who gets the credit."
> —Ronald Reagan

> "Remember always that you have not only the right to be an individual, you have an obligation to be one. You cannot make any useful contribution in life unless you do this."
> —Eleanor Roosevelt

what I think of what I do! That is character!" And that kind of character takes an optimist willing to major in self-support.

When you cultivate a strong belief in your own capabilities, you will think, feel, and behave differently from those who are overly critical of their own potential. People who have persistent self-doubts shy away from difficult tasks; they tend to have low aspirations and a wavering commitment to even the goals they've chosen to pursue. As an optimist who has earned confidence, you will have the drive to seek and achieve challenging goals both on and off the job. You'll have earned the resilience needed to overcome the obstacles you encounter on the way to success.

Be the person you were meant to be, and manage your own motivation to make that possible. Remember, nothing is more affirming and effective in gaining a realistic self-confidence than a healthy dose of accurate self-recognition.

> "Many people feel paralyzed by their lack of control over life. What can you do about it? For one thing, focus on all the things you do control. In doing so, you take control over your life and begin to lead your life, rather than letting life lead you."
> —Mark Sanborn

So, what's working for you? In fact, what did you do this week that's worth celebrating with others? Now, document what you did and go celebrate!

CHAPTER
12

Simple Pleasures: The Optimist's Wild Card

"Is not life a hundred times too short for us to bore ourselves?"
—Friedrich Nietzsche

While meditating in the chapel at the La Casa de Maria Retreat Center in Santa Barbara, California, my eyes caught a Zen saying on the wall: "After ecstasy—the laundry." I laughed out loud. There was wisdom in those few words, but I wasn't sure what it was. Was it that we appreciate the joy of ecstasy but somehow forget the hard work involved in making it possible? Was it that there is as much joy in doing laundry as in a mountaintop experience? Maybe it wasn't even meant as wisdom. Could it be that it was some Zen master's to-do-list? I came to realize that, for me, there can be as much personal satisfaction in some simple activities

> "Enjoy pleasures, but let them be your own, and then you will taste them."
> —Lord Chesterton

139

and chores as there is in many grand and expensive experiences. Both are part of life. When asked why I don't pay someone else to do my gardening, I have a simple answer: My gardening gives me satisfaction. Why would I pay someone to take over an activity that I enjoy doing?

Life deals you a number of wild cards that, when played well, can give you an optimism advantage. With this chapter's wild card, there is another benefit; you are entitled to designate what is wild. After all, the pastimes in which you find simple pleasure aren't necessarily the same for others. The trick is finding what it is in your world that can transform a bad day and bring you back to a positive mind-set. So what activities bring you joy, peace, or even a moment's relief? If you can't think of any, then you have some work to do!

> "I have five kids, 10 and under. If I can make them smile, or better yet, laugh, I become just about the most positive man alive."
>
> —John J. Serrano

Most of us have heard kids complain, "There's nothing to do!" Faced with bins of toys, a garage full of sporting equipment, and video games galore, they can still make a claim of utter boredom. I've seen some of those children grow up to be adults who keep sharing a version of the same complaint: "Nothing interests me!" Do you look into a mirror at a person like that?

Truth #34: Engage in Simple Pleasures That Impact Your Attitude

Far too many people keep trying to find new ways to improve the quality of their lives while neglecting the simple pleasures they already know bring them joy. Don't be one of these people. Recognize that your world is full of simple pleasures and that the variety of interests and experiences you can have only expands as you age. No matter how much money you have, you still have the freedom and the opportunity to exercise countless choices in what you can do.

Simple pleasures are just that—uncomplicated, unpretentious experiences that affect your attitude and feelings. In these complex and stressful times, the desire for simplicity is becoming more and more preferred—and even essential.

> "You can't have it all, but when you know what's important, you don't want it all anyway."
> —Mark Sanborn

Watching people buy increasingly larger homes early on—only to see them move to smaller homes, and eventually even apartments, later in life—made me realize an important truth. Even when you win the rat race, you're still sapped by having to collect, pay for, and manage all your stuff, not to mention finding a place to store it all. Buying bigger, better, faster may help the economy, but it burdens you with possessions you have to take care of.

Simple Pleasures Are Simple and Often Inexpensive

As I already discussed previously, my son Sean went on a mission trip to Mexico several years ago and arrived home marveling at the happiness of the children he met. They had none of the possessions he treasured, but they were happy to play with a discarded hubcap and a stick to keep it rolling. Instead of piling up unused toy treasures, these children used their imagination to foster shared joy. What can one say to such an observation other than that simple, shared pleasures clearly don't have to cost a lot of money!

Though a singular reflection made by one person, Sean's observation actually matches empirical survey data on cultural happiness. Studies have shown that 63 percent of Mexican adults (almost two-thirds!) claimed to be "very happy" or "completely happy"—despite the fact that most live above subsistence level but are still poorer than residents of either the United States or Europe. French citizens have three times the purchasing power of Mexican citizens; however, recent happiness surveys indicated that only 35 percent of French citizens surveyed said they were very or completely

> "You can never get enough of what you really don't need."
> —Eric Hoffer

happy. How, you might wonder, can this possibly be? The answer has to do with what psychologists call "adaptation" and what economists refer to as the "hedonic treadmill." In short, people tend to psychologically adapt to their circumstances—including their financial conditions—very quickly. An increase in income becomes the new normal; therefore, living the good life then requires more things than you currently possess in order to be very happy.

> "The more things you own, the more things own you."
> —Mark Sanborn

Even with challenging economic times, Americans have, on average, become richer over the past three decades. But the inconvenient truth is that while national income has doubled, the percentage of Americans in the same happiness study who said that they were "very happy" has remained virtually unchanged at 31 percent.

The size of one's boat doesn't always translate into a difference in one's joy or happiness scale. As I paddled a small canoe through a row of expensive yachts in Balboa, California, one man smiled down at me from his fancy yacht and asked, "Do you want to trade?" I laughed. He continued, "I spend more of my Saturdays cleaning this thing than enjoying it! Somehow your canoe looks a lot easier to enjoy!"

Okay, I don't really think he would have traded, and I don't think my son would have changed places with any of the children he saw playing in Mexico. But the truth behind both encounters is worth repeating: Amassing possessions will never be as important as experiencing the truly enjoyable pleasures in life. He who dies with the most toys still dies. Knowing you can make choices that give you pleasure helps you claim—and sustain—your own optimism advantage.

Simple Pleasures Often Find You

Maybe it's something as simple as taking a walk in the park, reading an engaging novel at the library, listening to your favorite music, going to a good movie, petting your dog or stroking your cat, or engaging in a relaxing conversation with a neighbor. All are simple pleasures that can put you in touch with what you enjoy most about life. These types of experiences

> "One benefit of having cancer is that it may teach you how to enjoy one day at a time."
> —Harold Benjamin, PhD

often surface in the midst of challenging circumstances, when life seems to naturally show you what most uplifts your spirits. Such experiences can actually change habits and strengthen your appreciation for community and the simple blessings life provides.

When faced with the inconvenience of extended power outages following Hurricane Katrina, person after person reported a common reaction. For the first few days, they focused on what they didn't have—no TV, no lights, no microwave. But as the days passed, families spent more time outside. Creative games surfaced, and new community relationships were nurtured. Neighbors who never saw one another be came valued friends. The loss of modern-day conveniences opened the door to a long-lost community lifestyle that was far more satisfying and affirming. You may enjoy watching TV, but that TV won't be there to watch over you during the tough times. Engaged neighbors care; they are there for you, as you are for them.

Taking Nature for a Ride on the Wild Side

As young psychologists, my colleagues and I developed COPE Wilderness Workshops—a program that combined wilderness survival training with assertiveness training by the campfire. We'd teach participants how to survive both in the woods of the Sierras— and when facing the wild beasts of Los Angeles back home.

Unfortunately, we were forced to stop the workshops because lawyers told us how much we could lose if someone didn't survive. The liability insurance coverage cost more than the revenue the programs produced. All who participated survived, but the program didn't.

> "May you live all the days of your life."
> —Jonathan Swift

> "Walk on a rainbow trail; walk on a trail of song, and all about you will be beauty. There is a way out of every dark mist, over a rainbow trail."
> —Navajo Song

However, since the COPE Wilderness Workshops, I've had a fallback plan that I find very reassuring. If my wife and I ever lost our home and jobs, we could grab our backpacks and head for the hills, spending each night at a different lake, living off the land, and sleeping under a star-studded sky. Simply knowing how little you need to survive gives you confidence that you can handle whatever life throws your way and still maintain a high-quality life worth living. Any wilderness is teeming with simple pleasures just waiting to be experienced. My wife, however, is not so sure about the wild animals who might see us as a simple pleasure worth eating.

Needlepoint and Other Therapeutic Pleasures

Earlier in my life—and early in our marriage—my wife and I faced many challenges. I started our company right out of graduate school. I figured, why not? We were already used to poverty; we had nothing to lose. However, this also meant that discretionary money was nonexistent. If you wanted something, you looked for ways to make it—or improve it—yourself.

For instance, we bought an antique (translation: old) upright piano. The bench was worn and needed a fresh needlepoint cover to give it new life. Thankfully, my wife's grandmother had given her an unfinished needlepoint project that would fit perfectly. She was not as enthused as I was about completing the project, so I volunteered to get instructions at a local craft store.

Long before NFL football Hall of Famer Rosey Grier took up the craft, I added my needles, cover, and thread into a side pocket on my briefcase. I'd pull it out on the plane or while waiting for boarding. The looks—and occasional comments—from men and women alike made it a fun conversation piece. And even more surprising was the simple pleasure needlepoint provided. I discovered a secret that most men never realize; these mindless finger movements are actually therapeutic. Lost in sheer methodical repetition settles you, like a slow run through a park without the sweating. And there's the added benefit of actually having something to show for your therapy. That needlepoint is still in our living room, and now you know the rest of the story.

Since those early days, I've taken time to experience other crafts, like making stained glass windows and quilting. Maybe

> "No pleasure endures unseasoned by variety."
> —Publilius Syrus

it's in my genes. At various stages of his life, my father took up woodworking, carving, silver jewelry, coin collecting, mosaics, and other crafts. They brought him joy as well as an endless supply of treasured gifts to bestow upon others. He engaged in all of his hobbies with a passion that brought him both a mental recess and satisfaction.

Simple pleasures like these can be incredibly therapeutic. When Diana Harberts's husband died at age 61, she was left with a hurting heart and a closet full of his clothes—a constant reminder of her loss. A longtime quilter who used this art form to preserve memories, Diana decided to make a quilt of some of her husband's favorite garments to provide a touching way to keep his memories close to her and their daughter, Joanna. The front of the quilt was more formal, with his clothes and ties from work; the back was more casual, with knit shirts and pullovers.

Diana's daughter, Joanna, sleeps with the quilt. Since she used to give back rubs to her father, rubbing the fabric on the quilt was like rubbing him. The quilt has not only been comforting to the family; so many other people requested similar quilts that Diana started a home business that she's named One More Hug. She encourages people not to wash the clothes before giving them to her, because family members often value the smell and perfume that remains in the fabric.

What kinds of activities are therapeutic for you? What hobbies take you away from life's stress and bring you peace and pleasure? As an adventurous soul, what additional experiences are you willing to try?

Truth #35: Find the Music That Makes Your Soul and Attitude Sing

> "Birds sing after a storm. Why shouldn't we?"
> —Rose Fitzgerald Kennedy

In a world of iPods, iPhones, and other fancy audio equipment, more and more people are experiencing the power of music. As radio talk show host Dennis Prager loves to say, "The only research I respect is research that supports what common sense has long before affirmed." You don't need elaborate studies to tell you that music is one of life's gifts and that listening to your favorite songs is one of the simple pleasures that makes the ride worthwhile.

What music would be on your playlist? How are you using it to impact your attitude? You know what music works for you, so your job is to find and then experience the right tunes at the moments in your life when you need them the most. The good news for music lovers everywhere is that songs have never been more accessible and easier to enjoy. Take advantage of your musical wild card when your optimism needs a momentary lift. Instead of having your blood pressure rise as you listen to your daily dose of negative news, try tuning in your favorite music station—and watch that blood pressure drop.

Truth #36: Turn the Love of a Pet into a Health Break and Attitude Boost

Nancy, a local volunteer, spends many Saturdays taking her therapy dog Sadie to hospitals in Southern California. After hours of ongoing training, they bring smiles and joy to bed-bound patients who come alive as their hands reach out to pet Sadie. Such animal-assisted therapy volunteers have been shown to improve patient attitudes and promote health.

> "After silence, that which comes nearest to expressing the inexpressible is music."
> —Aldous Huxley

Of course, you don't have to share your pets with others

to reap their countless benefits. Most pet owners rave about the joys of sharing their homes and lives with an animal—whether that pet is a cocker spaniel, a calico cat, or a chameleon. And even beyond the pleasure they bring is the mental health boost these nonhuman companions can provide on even

> "We all crave affection, but sometimes we find we have difficulty obtaining it from other people. Companion animals provide friendship, constancy and love. They're always there, always happy to see you."
> —Dr. John Wedderburn

the worst of days. There's nothing like a pet's unconditional love to warm your heart and lower your blood pressure.

Admittedly, pets of all kinds can be costly; they demand time, care, attention, and extra planning. There are vet bills to consider, along with those early morning and late night obligatory dog walks. But a host of research studies have shown that pets can be helpful in treating the mentally ill, revitalizing the elderly, motivating the disabled, relieving the lonely, and giving a renewed sense of purpose to the grieving.

If your living situation won't allow it or you can't afford the expense, don't worry. Even offering to take a neighbor's dog on a walk can significantly boost your mood. A Swedish study revealed that people who walked a dog experienced an improvement in the quality of interaction with others. Sixty-three percent of dog owners surveyed said their pets had added to their opportunities to talk to people, and 57 percent said their dogs had "made them friends."

Unlike usually unpredictable people, pets don't talk back, are consistently welcoming, and love being loved. They give people a living being to care for that makes them feel needed and wanted. While physical contact with other human beings can come with a host of questions and issues, most pets crave touch and will gladly fill this most primitive and basic need.

After a devastating 1995 earthquake in Kobe, Japan, thousands of people had to be housed in halls and gymnasiums. Rules barring animals from public buildings were lifted, and people were allowed to bring their pets. "It was an eye-opening experience for everyone," says Dr. Gen Kato, president of the Japanese Animal Hospital Association. "People who had pets were clearly more happy and coped better with the disaster."

Additional studies indicate that people over age 65 who own pets made up to 30 percent fewer visits to doctors than those who had no pet. Pets may very well be one of your best attitude-adjusting simple pleasures. If you ever needed an excuse to get yourself a pet—now you have one.

Truth #37: Reading Opens You to New Worlds and Provides a Mental Recess

> "The only way to improve your life is through the books you read and the people you meet."
> —Charlie "Tremendous" Jones

Books are essentially treasures waiting to be found. However, in this world of cyberspace and high-definition TVs, many are trading time with a good read for a flashy multimedia experience that makes cultivating an imagination less necessary. You've no doubt heard people say of many a movie: "The book was better." With a book, there's no condensed dialogue, no actors who don't fit the characters, and no sets that diminish the impact of the story. Why? The amazingly personal and rich stage of your mind is always more vibrant than any movie or TV program can provide.

While a visit to the movies provides two to three hours of entertainment, picking up a novel, finding a chapter, and re-entering the world of a story you love provides an almost endless amount of joy. Such an escape provides a stress break that can work wonders in putting your life and your own challenges in perspective.

If optimism is born by claiming your history of overcoming obstacles, then nonfiction biographies afford both a distraction from daily pressure and the inspiration to meet the challenges that men and women of history have already overcome. History often repeats itself. We learn what to avoid, how to persevere, and how to succeed by learning from both common and famous people who have left a legacy worth reading.

What books do you enjoy? Which ones help you maintain a positive attitude?

You Don't Remember Days—You Remember Moments

Centenarians don't need scientific data to prove that happiness in old age has more to do with attitude than health. They've learned that develop-

> "The genius of life is to be able to take childhood into old age."
>
> —George Burns

ing effective lifestyle habits can last you a lifetime—a long lifetime. A plethora of research indicates that a positive attitude—combined with healthy living choices—can take aging well beyond average life expectancy. One study conducted by the U.S. National Institute on Aging focused on regions where people live significantly longer. One of the findings that they isolated was the importance of curiosity, play, and hobbies. Healthy centenarians keep up with their world and their interests. Finding new hobbies and pastimes may be part of the map for finding that elusive fountain of youth.

The list of possible activities is as extensive and diverse as the number of people reading this book. But whatever you pick, satisfying hobbies will provide an oasis-like experience in the deserts of your daily life—a few moments of escape from a monotonous or stressful day. Such activities will help you achieve balance between your busy life and your personal interests. Many people continue to find sports—both playing and watching—to be an enjoyable distraction. Playing provides the added advantage of building team relationships and integrating a little exercise into your daily routine.

Certainly, your choices of simple pleasures are far greater. Play a musical instrument by yourself or with others, go to a local park or beach, collect almost anything, cook zany food recipes and make others eat the results, do your own gardening, join in a little fun dancing, paint landscapes, play solitaire or poker with friends, or take photos of anything that interests you. Actually, life is so great that, with a little imagination, you can make a hobby out of the most insignificant thing, and it will still help you become more optimistic.

The Power of a List of Memories

During one of my many presentations to health care teams on optimism, a nurse shared a story of hope and inspiration that has stayed with me for years. The names of the characters and the hospital have left me, but the inspiration remains.

> "Somebody should tell us, right at the start of our lives, that we are dying. Then we might live life to the limit, every minute of every day. Do it! I say. Whatever you want to do, do it now! There are only so many tomorrows."
>
> —Michael Landon

A terminally ill young boy left the hospital to be at home for his last days. He was often groggy from the heavy doses of morphine that he took to relieve the pain. Handing a note to his hospice nurse was one of his last lucid moments. With a smile and an enthusiasm he had not demonstrated in days, he told the nurse, "Give this letter to my parents when I am gone. You will know when the time is right." She asked what was in the letter, and the boy replied, "It's a list of all the fun moments we had. The times we laughed and couldn't stop."

He shared the time the family went to a party dressed as the guys in the Fruit of the Loom underwear ad. On the way to the party, the police pulled his father over for speeding. The officer could hardly stop laughing when he saw the family outfits. He let them go with a warning: "The next time you race off to join a salad bar, take it slower."

Later that night, the nurse read his list of memories peppered with humorous anecdotes. At the end was a note to his parents that said: "I know that you are sad that I'm going away, but don't forget this stuff. Don't remember me sick; remember us laughing."

It's been said, "You don't remember days; you remember moments." At today's hectic pace, it's far too easy to forget to savor the small pleasures while we make bigger plans. You may not be able to change or even number your days, but you can always change your moments. What simple pleasures are you willing to make part of your optimistic lifestyle? Hopefully, continuing to read the rest of this book will be one of them.

CHAPTER 13

Humor Is the Joker in the Hand of Life

"Everybody has used the expression, 'Someday we'll laugh about this.' My question is, why wait?"

—Joel Goodman

Jan was in her early 90s and still finding her way around New York City. When her car stalled at a bridge toll booth, she was unable to restart her engine. Knowing nothing about cars, she put up her hood to a chorus of honks from the irritated drivers behind her. Smiling at the man in the first car, she slowly walked to his door and knocked on the window. "I'm 93 years old, and I don't know anything about cars. Optimistically, if we're going to move, somebody is going to have to help me start my car. Why don't you go work on my car, and I'll take over the honking."

> "The human race has only one really effective weapon, and that's laughter. The moment it arises, all our hardness yields, all our irritations and resentments slip away, and a sunny spirit takes their place."
> —Mark Twain

When she told her newest 89-year-old boyfriend about her humorous exchange, he reminded her that she was probably too old to be driving in New York. She responded with smile, "You better be careful. I've buried everyone who ever told me to act my age."

Talk about wild cards! There is no better card to play in life than the joker. Humor has a way of making even a poor hand a winner. And even if you don't win, you have a heck of a lot more fun while losing.

Renowned psychiatrist Eric Berne was once asked to define a healthy person. He replied: "Healthy people go 'Yes,' 'No,' and 'Whoopee!' Unhealthy people go 'Yes, but,' 'No, but,' and 'No whoopee!'" Giving way to laughter is one of the best ways to turn any moment into instant "Whoopee!" It also has a way of bringing other people along for the ride.

Man's Search for Meaning author Viktor Frankl called laughter "the currency of hope" and a surefire way to cultivate the optimism advantage. Frankl wrote: "An outsider may be astonished to hear that one could find a sense of humor in a concentration camp. . . . Humor was another of the soul's weapons in the fight for self-preservation. . . . It can afford an aloofness and an ability to rise above any situation, even if only for a few seconds."

> "Humor is the healthy way of feeling a 'distance' between one's self and the problem, a way of standing off and looking at one's problem with perspective."
>
> —Rollo May

Frankl's fellow inmates survived daily by inventing one amusing story to tell others. At night, they would gather to laugh together. If humor works in a situation as dire as a concentration camp, it can certainly help you cope with just about any circumstance you will ever have to face.

Truth #38: Use Humor as an Ever-Present Stress Breaker You Control

One of the most compelling uses of humor is its value in reducing the stress of our crazy world. Laughter is a nonfattening,

> "Worry knocked at the door, but hearing laughter, it hurried away."
> —Ben Franklin

contagious, pleasant tranquilizer that doesn't have any major side effects. It can help people live longer, healthier lives and recover more quickly from stress-related illnesses. Humor provides the counterbalance to life's more somber moments. It's your inner upper, your mental recess, your ever-present safety valve, and one of the most effective stress breaks you will ever find.

After one couple managed to escape a raging California fire with nothing but their lives, the husband confided to a reporter, "We'll be fine. We've lost our home, but we've got the clothes on our back. We've had to start over before, and we can do it again." The reporter was confused as the man's wife began to laugh and even more perplexed as the husband joined in. The wife—aware that the reporter was unsure of how to proceed in the live, on-scene broadcast—said to the camera, "My husband is right. We had to leave so fast, all we do have is the clothes on our back. Neither one of us have underwear!"

Even the cameraman had trouble keeping the image steady as the crew burst into laughter. Everyone watching was left with the sense that this couple was going to survive their personal catastrophe just fine. In fact, the woman's humorous comment turned a typical disaster news report into much-needed humor therapy for all those facing the loss of their own property. The reporter ended the coverage with the line, "Looks like I'm the only one here with underwear. Back to you in the studio!" Who would bet against this optimistic couple's ability to bounce back quickly from their loss?

Author and professor Norman Cousins observed the following during his own struggle with cancer: "Laughter interrupts the panic cycle of an illness." While it may not be a cure for cancer, there is

> "Warning: Laughter may be hazardous to your illness."
> —Nurses for Laughter

some clinical evidence that laughter mobilizes the human body's defenses and reduces pain. Apparently, humankind has been aware of humor's value for some time. The ancient Greeks included a visit to the "home of comedians" in their healing centers as part of their *therapeia* process.

In his book *From Victim to Victor: For Cancer Patients and Their Families*, Harold Benjamin shared the insightful comment of one cancer patient at Cancer Support Community, "I know laughter is good for me. I don't know if it is helping me get better, but it makes me feel better—not only mentally but physically as well—and it takes my mind off my own situation.

> "Humor gives us the freedom to act. Patients can be so paralyzed by conflicts and self-imposed restrictions that they forget they are free to act to change their circumstances."
> —Dr. Weeled A. Salameh

Life and its pleasures have become very real to me and I know just how important it is to enjoy each enjoyable minute. So when something strikes me as laughable, I laugh. I want to be conscious of every joyful part of life."

And if you still need more scientific proof of this, research supports a direct correlation between laughter and levels of cat-echolamines in the blood, triggering the release of endorphins in our brain. Endorphins are one of nature's built-in painkillers, and they are what incites the feeling of pleasure that occurs after a good workout session or a hearty laugh. Humor isn't just fun; it actually is healthy for you.

Additionally, a variety of muscles are activated when you laugh. When you stop laughing, those muscles relax. Because muscle tension tends to magnify pain, many people suffering painful conditions can often benefit greatly from a healthy dose of laughter.

If you are someone who doubts the value of humor in medicine, you are not alone. The late columnist Art Buchwald once reacted to an American Medical Association article on the importance of laughter by writing his own humorous letter to the editor: "There is still a lot of work to be done before the Food and Drug Administration will permit it to be used in large doses. Many unanswered questions remain: if laughter is good for your health, why don't doctors ever laugh when they are with their patients? Is it possible to transplant a sense of humor? If it is so good as a medicine, why doesn't Medicare pay for it?"

Maybe we ought to change the adage to say, "It only hurts when you don't laugh!" Even in the face of serious disease, patients are able to make choices. Someone who's diagnosed with terminal cancer can fight for life or usher in an early funeral. Think of the attitude difference in these two comments: "I don't think I'm going to last much longer" versus "Life is terminal. If I'm going to die soon, I'm going to have fun with every moment I have left." Who would you bet on living longer?

Not All Humor Works to Produce Optimism

"Some people can make others laugh at others, some with others. Does your humor isolate or bring together?"
—Norman Cousins

Unfortunately, many have forgotten the value of humor in making us more resilient during this age of constant change and uncertainty. Far too many people walk around looking like they're in pain. You know the ones; instead of leaving their cars *in park*, they leave their faces *in park*. Don't let that be you! Let there be smiles, laughter, and joy, and let it begin with you.

It is true, however, that not all humor works; some creates laughter at the expense of others. So keep your humor positive and life enhancing; leave sarcasm and jokes that make fun of others out of your repertoire. Even if you don't offend everyone, chances are that you will offend someone. If in doubt, leave questionable humor out. After all, you don't need negative humor when there is so much positive humor available every day.

Laurence Peter said it best: "Realize that a sense of humor is deeper than laughter and more satisfying than comedy and delivers more rewards than merely being entertaining. A sense of humor sees the fun in everyday experiences. It is more important to have fun than it is to be funny."

Translation: Leave room for laughter every day, and always be ready to invite humor into your life. Great humor is warmer than scripted jokes because it connects to our shared funny

> "A jest's prosperity lies in the ear of him that hears it, never in the tongue of him that makes it."
> —Shakespeare

experiences both on and off the job. You aren't laughing at anyone; you are laughing with them. Natural humor is there if you have eyes to see, enjoy, and share it with others.

Truth #39: Take Your Life and Work Seriously, but Take Yourself Lightly

The safest target for your humor will always be yourself. If you can learn to laugh at your errors, the world will laugh with you—not at you. Only the self-confident can admit their mistakes. Laughing at your own errors will help you let go of mistakes and rebound quicker to get back into the game, and that's what optimism is all about.

We all like to be with people who are comfortable in their own skin—pimples, warts, receding hairlines, and all. It's usually a good rule of thumb to take your work and life seriously but yourself—and your problems—a bit more lightly. Just remember, if you laugh at yourself before others do, you win. Self-deprecating humor is therapeutic and attractive to others.

Bill Cosby knew the value of a humorous perspective when he observed: "You can turn painful situations around through laughter. If you can find humor in anything, even poverty, you can survive it." We've discussed plenty of examples of this: the children in Mexico my son met on his mission trip, the California couple who managed to joke on camera moments after their home was destroyed by a fire, and the countless cancer patients who used their humor to battle their disease. It truly seems that happiness and optimism are more a matter of your internal attitude than any external realities.

> "A person without a sense of humor is like a wagon without springs—jolted by every pebble in the road."
> —Henry Ward Beecher

Teams Work Better with Humor as a Social Lubricant and Attitude Adjuster

Working with others can naturally create some friction—as well as ample opportunities for you to use humor to diffuse this tension. The amount of negative stress that your team experiences in any situation will usually vary according to the ways that members perceive that circumstance. The same situation can create panic in one person and generate laughter from another. Well-placed humor can break the urgency cycle and create a drastically different and less stressful perception for the whole team. It also has the potential to promote some pretty constructive problem solving. Since humor and creativity are highly correlated, use it whenever you can. Instead of being consumed with crises, learn to roll good-naturedly with what life gives you. If you have friends or associates who—at the most opportune moment in a shared crisis have a way of saying something so bizarre that everyone laughs—give them free reign to work their magic whenever they can.

During one of my presentations, for example, two health care leaders laughed a little too hard when I discussed the use of humor in minimizing conflict. When challenged, they shared a story of how humor helped turn around their strained relationship. The director of nursing hadn't been pleased with some of the changes that the new administrator was putting into place. After a particularly frustrating conversation in his office, she had exploded. For fear of saying something she would regret, she stopped mid-sentence and stormed out of the office.

Later in the day, she turned a corner and saw the administrator approaching down the hall. Rather than turn around or face him, she decided to enter the next available door.

> "Stay out of fun's way. If you are a structured funster, don't get so caught up in orchestrating other people's merriment that you become oblivious or resentful of outbreaks of actual fun that may occur naturally, in the wild, as it were. . . . Don't push too hard."
>
> —Jack Gordon

It was a closet. Hoping that he would not know it was a closet, she closed herself into the small dark space. Listening intently from inside the closet, she waited until she heard no footsteps. Slowly, she started to open the door. Suddenly, it was thrust open by the administrator who said with a smile: "Do you enjoy it in there?"

She grabbed the administrator's suit coat and said in panic, "Don't you dare tell anyone I was in there . . ." He started laughing, saying, "I won't. I promise." She soon realized that she hadn't merely threatened him; she had almost lifted her boss off the floor! His disarming laughter proved contagious, and she soon blushed and joined in.

From that moment forward, every time their disagreements needed a humor break, he'd just look at her and smile.

> "Laughter is the shortest distance between two people."
> —Victor Borge

She would move her lips silently in a clear message—"Don't you dare!"

Shared laughter has a way of moving people beyond the adversity and into problem solving with a fresh—and much more manageable—perspective. Why cry when you can laugh? Why get stuck in a cloud of worry when you can get busy coping with the problem after a good laugh?

There is a reason that sales professionals often have a good supply of humorous stories. Humor works; people like doing business with people who bring them joy and make them smile. Frustrated with his inability to get an appointment with a critical customer, one sales representative delivered a homing pigeon with a note to the prospect's office that read, "If you'd like to know more about our product, throw our representative out the window!" Another salesperson, before catching a flight back home, bought a $500,000 flight policy naming a reluctant prospect as the beneficiary. He sent it to the prospect with a handwritten note: "Last time I left your office without an appointment, I bought this policy. I wanted you to know my last thoughts were of you and what you are missing by not meeting with me!" He got an appointment with him the next time he came to town.

Laughter—and cynicism—are equally contagious. Which would you prefer to give to others? You know the answer; we love to be around those who radiate joy. People consistently rate a sense of humor as one of the most valued attributes of friends, loved ones, and associates. Though what's on the outside might diminish with age, the spark of joyful humor that you carry with you is a hard light to put out.

Truth #40: Cultivate Humorous One-Liners That Invite Laughter into Your Life

It doesn't take much to unleash the humor advantage. While speaking at a youth leadership conference at a major university, I mentioned how one-liners can help reframe even your worst day. A month later, a letter arrived from a young woman thanking me for what has become one of her favorite quotes: "Some days you're the bug; some days the windshield!"

You can give the gift of a humorous perspective as well, simply by using a few memorized one-liners that invite a change in perspective. They're urgency breakers that can transform even life's most frustrating moments. Do any of these statements work for you? What might you add to the list?

"This life is a test. It is only a test. If it had been a real life, I would have been given instructions on where to go and what to do."

"Is this some hidden video show?"

"Where's my mother? She usually takes care of days like this!"

"Are we having fun yet?"

"This may be the worst day of my life. Then again, I've only kept statistics since 1995."

"Did you ever have a day when you felt like a fire hydrant and everyone you met was a dog?"

One-liners that work provide ready statements that any team or family member can use to bring humorous relief to others.

Such declarations have a way of reminding others that laughter is a handy joker to add to any of life's bad hands—on and off the job.

But don't stop with memorizing a few one-liners. Welcome to the challenge of making humor work for you.

Developing Your Sense of Humor Takes Work

You may not be known for your sense of humor and may even wonder whether it's possible for you to cultivate one. But if you act happy, you will feel happier, and if you work at developing your sense of humor, you will find all the laughter you need.

No two people have the same sense of humor. You must start by recognizing what makes you laugh and then put more of whatever that is in your life. Open a humor file in your computer and type in your best stories, quotes, or jokes. Collecting these tidbits will stimulate your own memories of both personal and professional humorous encounters. Just add them to your file as you find them.

Lifting or borrowing humor created by others that is entertaining helps you develop a sense of wit that works specifically for you. Soon, enjoying the humor of others will allow you to generate your own spontaneous, humorous contributions

> "A day without laughter is a day wasted."
> —Charlie Chaplin

to life. Others may soon say, "What happened to you? Are you on something? Did you get a humor bone transplant?" Just reply, "I'm learning to bring a little more humor into my life. Join me!"

After an 85-year-old woman was evacuated to an community shelter during a Santa Barbara fire, she helped others in the gym cope with the cramped conditions by saying with a smile, "In 85 years, I've never been able to go to summer camp. Isn't this a blessing?" One's perspective can change in an instant with one simple dose of humor.

Truth #41: Stretch Your Humor Muscles Daily

Keep copies of your favorite comedies or TV shows and watch them when you need a lift. Buy the ones that you want to watch over and over again; rent those that people say are worth watching. Keep a col-

> "Have fun at what you do. It will be reflected in your work. No one likes a grump except another grump!"
> —Bill Swanson, Raytheon CEO

lection of your favorite cartoons and funny pictures; have one at the office and one at home. The comics you collect tell you more about your family and job than any description could provide, because we have a tendency to laugh at cartoons, pictures, and stories that remind us of our shared experiences. Your organization doesn't just have a serious culture; it has a humor history worth treasuring.

Send occasional humor messages to whatever online networks you frequent. It's the short funny videos on YouTube and the humorous comments on your favorite social network that get the most attention. They are positively viral; you just can't help but smile. YouTube has an almost unlimited and ever-growing collection of short videos capturing the lighter side of life. When you begin sharing humor you enjoy with others, you can create a lighthearted network that everyone will appreciate.

In these stressful times on the job, suggest putting up a humor board or laugh spot in your employee lounge. Something like this is an ongoing reminder to keep humor working. Breaks will take on a new dimension—one that's creative, stress reducing, and enlivening. Encourage people to get involved by adding their own pieces to the humorous collections.

Promote creativity by displaying cartoons with no captions and let associates make their own. Post memo bloopers and funny stories from the Internet. With imagination and frequent pruning, you just may harvest an untapped supply of new cartoons, anecdotes, and sayings for your humor collection. What would you want to include in order to increase your team's laughter quotient?

Of course, it's vital to monitor the contributions to remove any comments or material that might be offensive or inappropriate. Let people know that this is designed to cultivate positive humor. In that same vein, don't get mad; get funny! Try sharing humorous incidents instead of negative gossip when you talk to coworkers. Take time to initiate and discuss humor over dinner at home. The more you look for amusement, the more you're apt to find. Always be ready to say, "That's funny!"

Keep Your Optimism Laced with Laughter

Many of your best memories are laced with laughter, so promise yourself that you'll have more fun in your life and you will become more optimistic. Keep an air of playfulness in everything you do, and take time to laugh and smile daily. After all, when God created Adam and Eve and they ate that apple, he took back the apartment with a view, gave them a baby, and made them work. Then—to keep the whole thing from falling apart—he granted them a sense of humor as a ready sidekick to help them survive.

> "He that is of a merry heart hath a continual feast."
> —Proverbs 15:15

Let me close this chapter with a wise motto from Russ Walden, a successful company president: "If you aren't having fun in your work, fix the problem before it becomes serious; ask for help if you need it. If you can't fix it and won't ask for help, please go away before you spoil the fun for the rest of us." That's good advice.

He who laughs . . . lasts! That's worth remembering as you journey through these uncertain and changing times. Now, let there be laughter, and let it start with you.

CHAPTER

14

Build an Optimistic Network that Works

"Thank you Lord for the success of my friends and the fewness of my enemies! May all my friends achieve their fondest dreams."
—Ben Franklin's Morning Prayer

There is one final—and very important—wild card that needs to be played. If you want to be optimistic, spend more time with other optimistic people willing to encourage and support you.

"One's attitude is a lot about the people you hang around with. When you lie with dogs, you get fleas. Some people bring you down; others bring you up. I've learned to spend more time with people who bring me up."
—Gary McGinnis

In the words of legendary American author Mark Twain: "Keep away from people who try to belittle your ambitions. Small people always do that, but the really great make you feel that you, too, can become great."

The company you keep can pull you up or bring you down, so pick your friends, mentors, and colleagues wisely. You know the difference people can make in your life. Spend more time with those who do.

Truth #42: Thank the People Who Have Helped and Encouraged You

Let Your Life Speak author Parker Palmer reminds us: "Some teachers shine a light that allows growth to flourish, while others cast a shadow under which seedlings die." You know the bosses and teachers you're glad you no longer have to deal with. You also know which ones made you better.

Fred Rogers, former host of the children's television show *Mister Rogers' Neighborhood*, was a frequent and popular speaker. Every time he spoke, he'd ask those attending to pause for a minute of silence to think about all those people who helped them become who they are. Maybe it would be a supportive boss, a challenging teacher, a loving grandparent, or an eccentric neighbor. But it was always that moment of silence that they would thank him for.

> "At times our own light goes out and is rekindled by a spark from another person. Each of us has cause to think with deep gratitude of those who have lighted the flame within us."
> —Albert Schweitzer

Do the same for yourself as you read this book. Who would you think of in this moment of silence? Who are your private everyday cheerleaders and mentors whose presence, acceptance, and availability made the difference at critical turns in your life? Sometimes they fan the flame within you and ignite a spark that transforms your gifts into a career dream. Or maybe they deliver a heartfelt compliment that makes you feel valued. Perhaps it's even their unspoken support—their mere presence during times of both trouble and happiness—that means the most. In some way, they believed in you, perhaps even before you believed in yourself.

If special people come to mind, don't just appreciate them; take the time to actually go and thank them. If you can't think of anyone, you've got some effort you'll need to invest to make your *net work*. It's time for you to seek out a few more supportive people who believe in you and encourage the best in you.

Truth #43: Put Your Calendar Where Your Priorities Are

Professional catalyst and speaker Toni Newman wanted to find an innovative way to let people know that she was on vacation and would not be checking her messages until her return. When you called her office you heard: "If you get this message, please be aware that I am being held hostage by two wonderful children under the age of six. They have hidden my Blackberry and my cell phone. They have locked me out of my office and away from my computer. The red light on my phone blinks helplessly but alas, I am forbidden to check my messages. Their demands are simple. Two weeks of my undivided attention. If I obey, I will be allowed to return to my office on Monday, August 1st. I look forward to reconnecting with you then."

The response to her message was phenomenal, and it also ended up being a wonderful marketing tool. It differentiated Newman from the norm and showed her clients that striking a balance between one's personal and professional life can be a fun and profitable way to live. In a world where far too many of us are checking our Blackberry, iPhone, or wireless Internet connection every chance we get, it's time to discover that everyone needs some time to disconnect and just breathe a bit slower.

Although everyone talks a good game about achieving

> "The greatest discovery I've made is that if I were to be hit and killed by a big truck today, I'd be replaced at work tomorrow. But I'll never be replaced at home. I'd be missed there forever. Stop giving your family the leftovers of yourself. Remind yourself that a wider path to success is out there, one that is wide enough for family, friends, and fun."
>
> —Jeff Conley

balance in life, it's obviously much easier said than done. Most of our professional lives are focused on making critical appointments, achieving business goals, attending important meetings, and completing tasks in time for demanding deadlines. Personal relationships and gatherings tend to be relegated to "let's get together soon" promises. Unfortunately, soon never seems to get into your calendar, and work conveniently expands to fill your available time. But it doesn't have to be that way and shouldn't be that way, if you want to be more optimistic.

Making time for your family and friends is essential to maintaining a positive outlook, especially in these challenging times, when there are countless reasons to do so. If you don't find some sort of happy medium between your personal and professional lives, you actually risk

> "The trouble with the rat race is that even if you win, you're still a rat."
>
> —Lily Tomlin

losing your vitality on the job. You need more than work relationships; you need people you can have fun with, caring friends, faith communities, and individuals who embrace similar hobbies and enjoy the same kind of entertainment as you. Spending time with your energy-boosting relationships can do wonders to improve your attitude and rejuvenate your motivation on and off the job.

But how do you make it a habit to find this kind of balance? Affiliated partner of venture capital firm Kleiner Perkins Caufield & Byers Vinod Khosla knows the importance of metrics in measuring company priorities. As a leader, he's also aware of how vital deadlines, stretch goals, and weekly monitoring of progress are. Khosla has applied those same tools to his personal commitments: "People also need to place metrics around their priorities. I track how many times I get home in time to have dinner with my family; my assistant reports the exact number to me each month. My goal is to be home for dinner at least 25 nights a month." Do you measure anything like this? What might you find if you did?

If you don't think that keeping metrics would work for you, try a different approach. Your calendar is your creed; it shows what really matters to you. What you schedule, you do. So start by making a few dates with the friends and family who matter most. Buy a few tickets and get those events in your calendar. Don't worry; when you've paid good money for theater, concert, or sporting event tickets, you'll find a way to get everything done so that you can go. When you already have tickets, you'll plan for your on-time exit by getting important things done early. If coworkers come in and start to waste your time, you'll end the conversation quickly. You'll remind your boss, "I've got tickets. I have to leave at four." In short, you know what you do when you have tickets; you leave on time!

In fact, we'd like to have tickets every day and be willing to give them up when job demands truly require it. Count time at your son's soccer, coffee with friends, or a night out with your spouse as tickets. It's time you commit to your work and your life. When you live with both passion and commitment, you'll be more optimistic and significantly healthier—both mentally and physically.

Good Relationships Promote Health, Happiness, and Optimism

Carnegie-Mellon University researcher Sheldon Cohen summed up his research by saying, "Someone who works, has a family and goes bowling with a group has an edge on a person whose life is work. With each added relationship you have, the less likely you are to become ill." While this doesn't necessarily mean that you have to go bowling, you do need to do more than work. Few people want the phrase "I finished everything on my to-do-list!" written on their tombstones. Treat the investments of your time and your team members' time as carefully and respectfully as you do your financial investments.

> "A crucial strategy is to stay connected to friends and relatives. Find emotional support. Loneliness is a major stressor that can heighten every other problem."
> —Barbara Basler

Unfortunately, the people with whom you most want to spend time are people you have to schedule time to even see. The people you want to see least, on the other hand, have a knack of finding you wherever you are. As a wise senior citizen suggested, "Pretend your life has a dance card, and fill it every day with people who make your days dance to the music of life!"

What dates do you need to make? What tickets do you need to buy?

Truth #44: Avoid Pits People and Worrywarts!

We introduced you to *Pits People* in Chapter 9 on gratitude. Whenever you ask them how they are, they reply with a steady stream of complaints. Any attempt at countering their negativity results in a "yes, but" and further evidence of how impossible it is to overcome life's challenges because of what they face. They play hopeless, and they want you to play hope. When you do, they can shoot down your suggestions to avoid personal responsibility and any kind of constructive action. Don't just walk away from these people; run away.

Not all families and friends are created equal; some are supportive, and others are not. If you find yourself faced with a family that isn't particularly supportive of you, work to create your own family of encouragers. This doesn't have to include anyone to whom you're related; it can simply be a collection of people you are close to who consistently provide you with the encouragement you need. Similarly, if your friends spend time awfulizing or trapping you in the rearview mirror by ruminating about things you can't control or change, start to build some new friendships.

Overcoming the Odds author Emmy Werner wrote about the importance of establishing and cultivating a supportive community. She explains: "In an extensive study of resilience, researchers . . . tracked 505 children from early childhood to age 40. Almost a third came from homes troubled by poverty, alcoholism, divorce and other obstacles. Yet, in spite of these obstacles, the majority of this 'high-risk' group overcame their hardships. What made the difference? The resilient kids possessed hope, determination and a strong sense of

> "Sometimes people need new friends—people who will problem-solve with them and not indulge in 'tit-for-tat' worrying sessions."
> —Susan Holen-Hoeksema

community and religious faith. Plus, they were able to cultivate emotional support from outside their troubled families. All these factors helped them improve themselves and their lives." In short, the people we surround ourselves with really do make a difference in our lives.

For example, women are more likely to have a good network of friends. But are they the right friends? Some women keep you focused on the problems; others encourage you to bounce back stronger. Susan Nolen-Hoeksema, psychologist and author of *Women Who Think Too Much*, shared her research findings: "Women fall into what I call 'endless analysis of the past, present and future.' If they're upset, they tend to call friends who hold a magnifying glass to every little angle. At the first sign of problems men head out for a game of pickup basketball or other distractions. 'Later,' they say. So who is better off? There's a downside to stewing over life's issues. It amplifies sadness, makes problems harder and alienates others. Women are twice as likely as men to develop depression. But women who act more like men—distracting themselves first and then plotting solutions—have the same depression rate as men."

Now, before I get flooded with letters from my readers, men can certainly learn a few things from women as well. Many men will talk to no one when they are hurting and, instead, tend to rely solely on themselves. They won't tell a soul that anything is amiss until after they have handled their own problems. And those men who do talk about their problems often prefer to talk with women rather than their male friends. In fact, most married men claim their best friend is their spouse. Men could take a cue from women and spend some time developing friendships with other males who care, listen, and encourage timely problem solving without threatening their relationship. Both genders find it easier to be optimistic when they have friends who support and encourage them.

Truth #45: Fill Your Village with People Who Make a Difference

Always remember that no matter how dysfunctional your past or current relationships were or are, you can build a supportive community that helps you move out of the rearview mirror of your life and into inventing a more optimistic future.

> "None of us is as smart as all of us."
>
> —Satchel Paige

But where do you begin in building a strong and satisfying community?

Most people count on their spouse or partner for the lion's share of their emotional support. Obviously, working to maintain such a relationship with a spouse is important and ought to be evident in your calendar commitments. But there are dangers in depending too much on one person.

Barbara Ehrenreich talked about this concern in a magazine article for *Time:* "Today, a spouse is expected to be not only a co-provider and mate, but a co-parent, financial partner, romantic love object, best friend, fitness advisor, home repair-person and scintillating companion through the wasteland of Sunday afternoon. This is more than any one spouse can provide. What we lack is not 'values' but the old-fashioned neighborhood or community. Once people found companionship among their old high school buddies and got help with child-raising from grandparents and aunts. Marriages lasted because less was expected of them. If you wanted a bridge partner or plumber or confidant, you had a whole village to choose from. Today we don't marry a person, i.e., a flawed and limited human being; we attempt to marry a village."

Sometimes you can depend on a spouse or significant other too much. Don't expect your partner to fill every role, especially those better filled by others. Men used to have time at the tavern; women would gather with other women. This time apart served important functions that are now either politically incorrect or squeezed out of our busy schedules.

There's More to Connection Than Cyberspace

The majority of Americans have a committed partner or loving family, work relationships, and a commute between the two. But there is very little sense of caring on the freeways.

> "The ability to sell, explain, persuade, organize, motivate, and lead others still holds first place. Making things happen still requires the ability to make people like you, respect you, listen to you, and want to connect to you. And by connect, I mean connect personally, not digitally. The human connection will always, always, always outrank the digital connection as a get-ahead skill."
>
> —Karl Albrecht

In fact, loneliness in the midst of millions of people may become the real disease of our age. More and more people live, work, and play alone in their individual, digitized worlds. We are insulated and often obsessed with our personalized iPods, computer games, BlackBerries, and HDTVs. Outside our cyberspace social networks, it's no longer clear where we connect to real people. Too many people belong to nothing: no community groups, no faith assemblies, no service groups, no sport teams. They settle for texting a few tweets of 140 words or less, but they don't get many touches.

Are you squirming while reading this? If something happened to your partner or your job, what relationships would be there for you? Would your network provide the support and the opportunities you need in today's changing, stressful world? How alone—or connected—are you?

Coming to Grips with Your Own Relationship Deficits

Author, executive, and speaker Harvey Mackay shared an early life lesson: "My father handed me a Rolodex when I was 18 and said, 'Every person you meet for the rest of your life goes into this. You add a little something about them on the back of the card—family, hobbies, et cetera. And you cultivate that Rolodex like a garden.'" Today, that Rolodex has been traded in for a contact management database, but the need to cultivate your contacts like a garden remains.

It's time for you to take all of your relationships seriously. No single person can fill all the needs you have to support your optimistic future, so think of people in your network who meet these various needs. If you notice holes, identify any who might be able to make up your personal support team, your vital village.

People Who Care. Who are the nurturers who listen, encourage, support, acknowledge, and emotionally support you?

People Who Confront. Who are the truth tellers in your life who care enough to confront you privately when you need to make changes?

People with Expertise. Who are the experts you value most on the job, in your profession, and in your areas of interest who help you learn what you need or want to know?

People with Social Contacts. Who are the critical hub people who know a vast array of the people you need to know to achieve your goals on and off the job?

People to Play with. Who are the people who share your passion and make time to join you in enjoying your interests, hobbies, and activities?

People Who Feed Your Need for Community. Who are your soul mates, the ones who share your beliefs and nurture your common values?

You've read the questions, so where are your most significant needs? Who do you value that you haven't been in contact with for months? It's time to make a few dates in your calendar and a few calls to people who can fill your network holes. And don't do this for the sole purpose of finding encouraging, positive people—unless you're ready to support

them in the same way that you want to be supported. It's been said that many go out to find a friend and find no one, while others go out to be a good friend and find friends everywhere. When you make a conscious effort to nurture positive bonds within your relationships—both

> "Happiness is like a stampede. . . . Each happy friend boosts your own chances of being happy by 9 percent. Having grumpy friends decreases it by about 7 percent."
> —Nicholas Christakis & James Fowler

on and off the job—you can expect to see your *net work* for you. If you believe people are the biggest resource you can have, then make sure it shows in your calendar—and your actions.

Networking with Integrity Makes Relationships Work

Good relationships are built on the premise that we give as much as we receive. Don't expect to have others be part of your vital village unless you are willing to be a contributor to theirs. American founding father and patriot Benjamin Franklin confided in his autobiography, "Always ask people for favors. People will ask you to return them. That is how one painstakingly con-

> "Other things being equal, people do business with people they like. Other things not being equal, people still do business with people they like."
>
> —Mark McCormack

structs free exchange, which is the basis of all public and private business—one polite request at a time." Franklin was a precocious young inventor and networker and—given his place in history—clearly knew a thing or two about fostering rich relationships with others. He put his words into practice when, as a young man, he asked to borrow a book from the governor of Pennsylvania. Franklin credited that interaction as the networking request that truly launched his publishing career.

The value that lies in this kind of exchange is no different today. The nature of change is fluid and dynamic, and it requires the synergy that comes from extended associations and strategic alliances both in and outside your organization. It's the master bridge builders that have the most influence. They make relationships work by taking the time to share information, give and ask for feedback, and compliment those who deserve recognition.

Ogilvy Public Relations Worldwide CEO Pam Alexander knows the importance of making her network work: "The new economy is not just about the exchange of information; it's about the exchange of relationships. If you can cultivate relationships with thought leaders in your industry, you can reach their network of relationships. To build trust, invest in your relationships constantly. . . . By nurturing your personal relationships to help people excel, you build exponential impact in the marketplace. Ultimately, their success is your success."

> "One of our people was just promoted to run marketing for a major division. Somebody said, 'We lost Lee.' We didn't lose Lee. We gained a whole division."
>
> —John Patrick

Sales are similarly built on the development of such connections. Salespeople know the importance of putting deposits into a relationship bank account; while such deposits do not guarantee a sale, the bridges they establish provide the builder with the opportunity to be heard. Remember the following: *The less authority you have, the more you are in sales, and your influence is a function of how well you can sell your ideas and build commitment to a shared goal.* In an age of cross-functional teams and partnership collaboration, bridge building and relationships are more important than ever before.

Of course, people don't need to report to you to be valued members of your network. By helping your colleagues develop and grasp new opportunities when they are ready, you will be remembered and valued for a lifetime. As a result, your strategic alumni can be one of your biggest assets in building support.

Don't limit your connections solely to those with whom you work. Today's best catalysts are hub people, those who use the power of empowered networks. They know how to find, connect with, and utilize loose networks of the people whose involvement they need to make things happen. They are connected—digitally and personally. It's not enough to merely be a connector. Catalysts aren't above helping where they are needed, no matter how insignificant the role. That kind of support forges strong emotional bonds with people on the ground and builds an extensive trust account that comes in handy in the midst of changing times.

> "What do catalysts do? They accelerate growth and effectiveness by increasing the trust and connectivity of the networks they inhabit."
>
> —John Robb, Global Guerillas Blog

Who you come to know does make a vital difference. It always has, and it always will. So be known for networking with integrity. Give as much as—if not more than—you receive, and you will have valid reasons to be optimistic. So ask yourself (and follow through on it!): What can you do this week to extend your relationships and make a few more positive deposits in the ones you have?

Truth #46: Renew and Revitalize Your Most Valued Relationships

Now, before you start adding new people, don't forget to keep the friends and loved ones you already have. A manager from India made an observation at one of my presentations about relationships that has stuck with me for years. He confided, "In India, marriages are arranged. We start without love and know we must work to bring love to our life together. In the West, you work hard looking for love, and when you find it, you assume that it will last without having to work. Love takes work to keep the flame alive wherever you live."

This man's assertion doesn't just apply to the bond between spouses. His insight speaks to the need of not just finding relationships initially, but recognizing the need to renew and revitalize those valued connections as well. Relationships of any kind take work to initiate and maintain. You can't simply put esteemed associations on autopilot and expect them to continue to grow without any effort. Most won't burn out; they'll rust out for want of attention.

So keep cultivating the unexpected in the relationships that matter most to you. Whether you do so through word or action, find ways to show caring and support. Remember: Relationships are like deposit systems; you can't expect to make withdrawals unless you make a few deposits.

> "There is only one thing better than making a new friend, and that is keeping an old one."
> —Elmer Letterman

I know a father who was an assistant coach for his son's baseball team. To the team, his signature baseball cap was the good luck charm that carried them into their playoff winning streak. When his company requested him to make a trip to New York for a critical customer presentation, he knew that it would cause him to miss a pivotal game. He came up with an acceptable compromise that required him to take a picture of him wearing his lucky hat at the time the game was scheduled to begin.

He had anticipated no problem in doing this, but as the designated time approached, his meeting was still tied up in tight negotiations. Overcoming his own reluctance and concern about how his colleagues would react to his request, he stopped the proceedings, explained the situation, and asked the customer to take a picture of him next to the clock. He kept his promise, his son's team won the game, and his client was so touched by his commitment to his son that the negotiations ended favorably and quickly. Making relationships count makes for some memorable experiences—and some equally strong bonds.

Be the kind of friend or associate who catches others being effective. Don't just think it; express it. Take the time to recognize and formally acknowledge people who make a difference. Be ready to give more than your share of credit to others and take more than your share of

> "Two are better than one. . . . If one falls down, his friend can help him up."
> —Ecclesiastes 4:9–10

blame. As successful businessperson Mary Kay used to say, "Imagine every person you meet has on his chest a sign that reads, 'Make Me Feel Important.'" Now, act that way!

Listening is one of the most important relationship skills that you can develop. Of course, it's easy to listen when you are dating someone new or trying to impress a potential customer. The trick, however, is to learn how to listen anew to those you already value and know well. Don't lock others into who they have been. Listen with fresh ears to your established customers and to the seniors, boomers, Gen Xers, and millennials who inhabit your life. Show more interest and make more effort toward being an encouraging listener committed to helping them become what they can be. Never limit yourself to the digital connections available through social networking. Nothing beats a call or a face-to-face coffee break to get caught up and replenish your relationship account.

Use Relationships as an Optimism Advantage

"We are all tied together in a single garment of destiny, caught in an inescapable network of mutuality. Whatever affects one directly affects all indirectly. . . . I can never be all that I ought to be until you are all you ought to be. And you can never be what you ought to be until I am what I ought to be."
—Martin Luther King Jr.

Whoever you bring into your network, remember to pick people who believe in you. When you do, you will soon find that you believe more in yourself.

Your positive network makes for the final wild card in your deck. Play it, and you'll have more of the optimism you need to make your life's journey worth living—and that's one heck of an optimism advantage!

CHAPTER 15

How to Become Optimistic in Life . . . By Really Trying

"Life is what we make it. Always has been, always will be."
—Grandma Moses

Your future optimism depends on many things, but it mostly depends on *you*. There isn't one particular silver bullet that will make you the practical optimist you want to become. Someone who exhibits excellence in action isn't just behaving this way after reading a book on the topic and trying it for the first time. Serious learners cultivate personal change, and mastery is the result of sustained dedication and focused application.

Change is about personal accountability and choices. So what are you going to do

> "At a certain point there are more yesterdays than tomorrows. So, I plan on spending all my tomorrows very carefully and appreciating every one of them."
> —Chris Gardner

with the insights you learned here to make the optimism advantage work for you? Here's a summary of some of the key points about optimism for you to consider:

- No matter what has happened to you, you're not a victim. You are a survivor with choices about how you can respond to the hands you've been dealt.

- Have a purpose worthy of your commitment to make your choices and actions meaningful and compelling.

- Choose lifelong learning as your ticket to renewal and revitalized opportunity at any age.

- Take care of your body and maintain good health habits, and your body will do a better job of taking care of you.

- Cultivate a bias for action that gets you out of the rearview mirror and into making a move.

- Turn adversity into opportunities by replacing your negative beliefs and refocusing your feelings, attitudes, and actions.

- Become more grateful by being thankful for what life gives you and by never being thrown by less.

- Care enough about yourself to confront your own mistakes in the same way that you would challenge a loved one to learn from their errors.

- Catch yourself being effective daily instead of depending on the approval of others.

- Choose to enjoy life's simple pleasures to impact your attitude and rekindle your optimism.

- Take your life and work seriously and yourself lightly; your sense of humor can become an ever-present stress breaker that you control.

- And finally, create your own village of support and encouragement by building and renewing an optimistic network that works for you!

You Want More Than Insights—You Want Changes That Last

Whenever you read a book or come back from a conference or training experience, your friends, family, and coworkers expect you to act bizarre for at least three days. They're anticipating a list of New Year's resolution-type goals, a renewed sense of enthusiasm, and a plethora of changes to take place. They're betting, however, on these

> "The biggest person standing in your way is you. Others can stop you temporarily—you are the only one who can do it permanently."
>
> —Zig Ziglar

changes being short-term. They don't expect them to last, and they assume that you'll revert back to the same old way you've always done things. They've seen it before, and they are sure they'll see it again.

It's not surprising that such expectations exist; research suggests that relapse rates—and our tendency to return to old habits—can be as high as 90 percent. Even when you value the content you've learned, the scorecard could read: "Happy Face Testimonials 10 vs. Life Changes 1."

Don't let that happen with this book. Don't put this on a shelf until you've isolated your *Keepers*—the key points that you've found most valuable and worth applying in your daily life.

Find the learning nuggets that are critical to ensuring your personal change. Most notes you take at training events usually go in files or piles; even the books you read often end up collecting dust on a shelf somewhere. Unfortunately, 85 to 95 percent of this material will never be looked at or read again. What we know about learning and change is very clear: Without focused review, you're unlikely to retain the information or change your habits.

At the beginning of this book, I asked you to devour the content. I suggested that you underline or highlight and make notes in the margins. Some of the truths you skimmed and left unmarked because they didn't connect with your life experience. That's fine; every person is different, and some insights won't be relevant unless your

> "If you don't know where you are going, you'll end up somewhere else."
> —Yogi Berra

life presents a need to learn them. Some of the things that you highlighted are things you already do—insights you've already mastered. While that's affirming, it's important to move ahead to isolate additional changes you need to make now.

Truth #47: Making Changes That Last Is All about Focusing Your Goals

So while the experience of reading this book is still fresh, take time to review the material you highlighted and the notes you wrote in the margin. If an insight is a *Keeper* you want—and need—to focus on to improve, use a blank piece of paper to capture a phrase that will consistently remind you of that insight. Keep your entries short and legible without long explanations, and be sure to indicate the page of the insight's source for review. Don't write down things you already do; just record those you believe are worth remembering.

No matter how many pieces of information you isolate, you'll want to identify no more than three content *Keepers* to begin working on now. The more goals you give yourself at any given time, the less likely you are to do any of them well. By limiting your focus to only three goals, you'll probably see progress where it counts. Once you hone in on the material that resonates most, you'll want to translate those insights into personal development goals to guide your focus. Make these objectives as specific as possible. It's best if you can actually keep score or show evidence of progress.

> "The most difficult shift is moving passion into practice. We all need an action initiative. Stop the head nodding and do something! Focused action beats brilliance."
> —Mark Sanborn

But how do you decide which goals to seek first? Start by focusing on the ones that help fulfill your mission or purpose *and* that you're most motivated to change. If you still have trouble, give precedence to the goals that will have the most impact on your life on *and* off the job. If you're going to make personal changes, make

> "By failing to prepare, you are preparing to fail."
> —Benjamin Franklin

it worth the effort for you and your organization.

Don't worry about making your list perfect. You don't need flawless goals; you just need to trust your ability to concentrate on bringing the ones you've picked to fruition. You can change your goals, of course, but having a clear focus worthy of your efforts will go a long way toward getting you moving.

Translate your top three content KEEPERS into three specific goals:

1.

2.

3.

Use Your Calendar to Support Change

Use your calendar as a tool to remind yourself of your commitments. After all, it's important to keep your personal goals visible and at the top of your mind once you've taken the vital step of making them. And similar to your personal dates and professional meetings, *there is no better reminder than your existing calendar system*, because you have to process calendar changes daily. Having your goals visible makes it much easier to keep your focus.

No matter what system you decide to employ, make your three key goals immediately noticeable every time you open your calendar. Some use a small Post-It to move their goals around on a daily basis; others make them evident in computerized to-do lists or online calendars. But wherever you put them, make yourself reread your three goals each day before you look at your daily schedule. This will put you on your way to *claiming your optimism advantage and making changes that last!*

> "Most people don't need to be taught. They need to be reminded."
> —C. S. Lewis

Be a pride builder for you—*and* your team. Jon R. Katzenbach—author of *Why Pride Matters More Than Money*—knows what it takes to build pride in your team: "Always have your compass set on pride. . . . Where motivation is concerned, the journey is more important than the destination. It is more important for people to be proud of what they are doing every day than it is for them to be proud of reaching a major goal. That's why it's crucial to celebrate the 'steps' as much as the 'landings.' The best pride builders are masters at spotting and recognizing the small achievements that will instill pride in their people."

Although money is often short in difficult times, nothing should stop you from developing pride and confidence in yourself and your teammates. Major victories may be few and far between, but daily heroic efforts are seldom noticed—and need to be. As you read in the chapter on catching yourself being effective, don't forget to end your day by recording one successful step you've taken to further your targeted goals. When you record—and see—your own progress, you are more likely to create momentum for change. Don't forget to use your time with others to acknowledge what's working. Take time to let everyone feel the pride of progress!

Move from Focus to Stepped Progress

Although it's vital for you to have a clear change focus, it's also necessary to build in realistic, stepped progress. Take a hard look at the steps you need to take to achieve your goals. You learned to drive because it was a long way to walk, but you didn't start driving at the Indianapolis 500. You started in a deserted parking lot. Do the same with any goal-driven change; begin with small, easy steps to cultivate your successes without risking major failure. Think in terms of steps, not miles. With this in mind, establish your first step for each targeted goal. Pick a short-term

> "Start by doing what's necessary, then what's possible and suddenly you are doing the impossible."
> —St. Francis of Assisi

target date for accomplishing those first steps. Remember, these don't have to be big steps. Big steps create unnecessary obstacles. You don't want to intimidate yourself or give

> "Habit is habit, and not to be flung out of the window by any man, but to be coaxed down the stairs one step at a time."
> —Mark Twain

yourself any excuses to procrastinate further. You want something you will actually *do* soon—and successfully.

For example, to develop a habit of regular exercise, one woman made the commitment to get into her jogging suit every morning—whether she ran or not. On most mornings, getting dressed was enough to get her out the door and around the block. By having a minimum commitment daily, she was soon chalking up the miles.

Many swear by the insights provided by FlyLady, a self-proclaimed home executive turned clutter consultant. One inertia-breaking suggestion she has made is something she calls the "5-minute Room Rescue." You set a kitchen timer for five minutes and then rush to the dirtiest room in your house—the one no guests ever see. As the timer ticks down, you start clearing a path. When it buzzes, you can stop tidying up with a clear conscience. You get started by scaling down the goal to just five minutes. FlyLady realizes that changes seldom arrive in big, miraculous undertakings; they come in small steps. And you don't have to limit her kitchen timer approach to clearing a path in your house; you can use it to make progress on *any* of your goals. Once you've invested five minutes of your time, you may find yourself working longer. Doing more than you planned makes you more likely to take your next step. While expansive, long-term goals may sound impressive, it's better to give yourself the right to break those enduring goals into a number of smaller victories that you actually accomplish.

Former all-star catcher Mike Piazza was known for his long-ball hitting, but he learned the importance of *trying easy*. He warned: "The minute you think about hitting a home run is when you *don't*. . . . Sometimes you

> "We cannot do everything at once, but we can do something at once."
> —Calvin Coolidge

over try. You have to 'try easy,' not 'try hard.' Hitting a home run is an effortless exertion of everything coming together and meeting at one energy. It comes from being focused, and not forced." So take a cue from Piazza and focus on realistic goals; don't attempt to force unrealistic change. Use stepped progress, and you'll soon be *changing easy*.

Involve Your Buddies, Bosses, and Cheerleaders

It's nice to have a focus, a reminder system, and identified first steps, but every effort for personal change comes much more easily with a good dose of support from your partners, buddies, bosses, and resident cheerleaders. It's easier to cheat when it comes to privately held goals, because no one knows you are working on them. Making early commitments to your energy boosters will increase your likelihood for personal change.

You already know your energy boosters. They're the people who encourage you, who love to celebrate your accomplishments with you. Go beyond telling them about your goals; ask for their help in achieving them. Let them know that you expect change to be difficult, and ask them to alert you if they see your old habits creep back into your life. Arrange to take them with you to celebrate pre-established milestones in your change effort. Every once in a while, enjoy a standing ovation from your friends and colleagues.

Now, who would you add to your energy boosting support group? Depending on your goals, don't be afraid to consider asking one from your personal life and another from your professional network.

Build Your Support Group for Your Changes

Who will best encourage and support your change efforts?

Identify Names:

1. _____

2. _____

Truth #48: Use the Rehearsal Studio of Your Mind to Support Positive Change

Another constructive component for reaching your objectives is practicing visual imagery. Even if you can't use

> "The man who has no imagination has no wings."
> —Muhammad Ali

your new skills to make progress every day, you can begin using the rehearsal studio of your mind to reinforce your desired changes. You've heard people say, "Imagine that!" Using your imagination positively in mental rehearsal can and does make change easier. You can start visualizing by focusing beyond your goal and distinctly imagining how you will think and feel as the new *optimistic* you in specific situations. Expand the image in your mind to cement the positive benefits and the likely opportunities it will create. Imagining colleagues responding positively to your optimistic comments about new strategic initiatives can be rewarding in and of itself.

Golf great Phil Mickelson's coach Dave Pelz provides a valuable warning when it comes to effective practice: "Having the right device but using it incorrectly is worse than no practice. Practice does not make perfect; practice makes permanent. And if you practice as poorly as most golfers do, then you will be a permanent bad golfer." In short, *whether you are visualizing or actually engaging in your practice, learn it fully and correctly from the beginning.*

To develop habits that are worth keeping, you can learn best from those you respect. If you know others who have effectively made similar changes, try borrowing images from your observations about how those changes have worked for them. Never stand in awe of others; instead, use their examples to model and inspire your own growth. After all, if they can improve, so can you.

You can also use your visualization skills to imagine how you would positively handle obstacles you may face. Identify likely problems, develop a positive strategy to handle them, and then imagine yourself successfully applying that strategy. Since you are writing the script and get to do as many retakes as you desire, *never leave*

> "If you don't control your mind, somebody else will."
> —John Alston

> "I discovered one more limitation that would last only as long as I let it."
> —W. Mitchell

a visualization practice session without imagining handling the situation well. You want to build confidence to overcome obstacles, not fear of facing them.

Bounce Back Quickly from Lapses with Resolve and Determination

Don't forget to treat yourself well on the downside of your change journey. Along with your progress will undoubtedly come occasional setbacks and errors. Bad habits and negative beliefs often don't give up without a fight. Remember that you aren't experiencing these impediments because you're a slow learner, but because you're a serious student. Lapses are a part of any significant change, and it's your responses to those lapses that count most. Your job is to turn momentary failures into opportunities to bounce back even stronger.

Legendary actress Mary Pickford wrote this timeless advice: "Today is a new day. You will get out of it just what you put into it. If you have made mistakes, even serious mistakes, there is always another chance for you. And supposing you have tried and failed again and again, you may have a fresh start any moment you choose, for this thing that we call 'failure' is not the falling down, but the staying down." Merely getting back up quickly is a huge step in moving beyond these obstacles.

If you need motivation, think back to all the times in your life that you've turned setbacks into stepping stones. It's easy to forget how some of the most positive outcomes in your life came about as the result of some of your most difficult experiences. Since optimism comes from a track record of recovering from defeat and finding new

> "Many of life's failures are people who did not realize how close they were to success when they gave up."
> —Thomas Edison

ways to win, you must keep reminding yourself that you are a resilient survivor. Victims look for someone or something to blame; optimists keep seeking out the silver linings, new pathways, and open doors that become visible when you really look for them. While learning can often be three steps forward and two steps back, progress builds as we keep climbing that mountain. Never overlook the importance of confronting your own mistakes the way you would talk to someone you care about and are trying to encourage. You've survived tough setbacks before; you will again.

While it's essential to keep past mistakes and lapses from stopping you, it's equally vital to avoid overburdening yourself with unrealistic future expectations. General manager of the NBA's Orlando Magic Pat Williams doesn't let the past—or the future—interfere with his desire to make a difference in the present. Williams writes: "We all have three blocks of time in our life: yesterday, today and tomorrow. I think more problems with worry are caused by focusing on yesterday and tomorrow. We can learn from yesterday, but we must not get stuck living back there. The other block of time is tomorrow. Too many people worry about what might happen ten years from now, and it stops them from doing things today."

Take Williams's words to heart, and never let the weight of your future expectations discourage your progress today. Don't carry the full burden of your future now; get on with the challenge of making progress in inventing your future one day at a time.

> "If you have built castles in the air, your work need not be lost; that is where they should be. Now, put the foundations under them."
> —Henry David Thoreau

Truth #49: Nurture New Learning in Support of Your Change Goals

Of course, there's more to sustaining change than simply having a focus. You must document your progress in turning your setbacks into stepping stones for personal transformation. Every new change you make requires additional learning to deepen your understanding,

> "I'm simply suggesting that whether you stay with this company or go to another one, the person who sees a career as one of perpetual investment in education stands a lot better chance of surviving in today's world. Education is the only defense."
>
> —Tom Peters

fortify your beliefs, and strengthen your emerging habits and attitudes.

You've had years of experiences to cement old habits; accordingly, you need more than a single lesson or book to develop the depth and ideas needed to sustain your desired changes. It's the same as being able to take just one shower and feel refreshed; it doesn't mean you won't need another one tomorrow. Use your goals to bring focus to your commitment to lifelong learning. Look online or in bookstores for material that will allow you to support the changes you are trying to make. I've included a list of resources at the end of this book for that very reason; you want the best mental ammunition available. But don't merely read these books and articles; really investigate them with an eye toward isolating more insights worth memorizing.

People today seem increasingly obsessed with the prospect of finding something *new*. They want the newest book on optimism or the hottest seminar on corporate cultures. But novelty can be a shallow temptress, where substance gives way to flashy packaging

> "I've been guided in my work by the notion that older is often better. If an idea has been around for a few thousand years, it's been submitted to many tests— which is a good indicator that it might have some real merit. We're fixated on newness, which often misleads us into elevating novelty over substance."
>
> —Debahish Chatterjee

and creative PR. Yes, some new perspectives will produce tangible insights, and the results are there to prove it. But throw out established truths and wisdom with the greatest of caution.

Even the most time-honored wisdom, however, must be refreshed and reformulated for every new age. New examples must be found to prove enduring truths; new stories worthy of legend need to be told to show how that wisdom is still working. However, the longer we live, the more we find that even some of the newest and boldest innovations remind us of ideas that have been heard or tried before. The Bible, for example, has been providing fresh yet lasting insights for centuries.

Nineteenth-century authors and orators on positive thinking also ring true to many of today's challenges. Fellow speaker and historian of positive thinking Danny Cox has said: "Open a book by Elbert Hubbard, Samuel Smiles or Orison Swett Marden and read one page. I dare you not to be touched by the enduring insights you read." One of Marden's books from 1907 was titled *The Optimistic Life* and is still available in paperback. Truth has a way of coming back in a new wardrobe. Instead of asking what have you learned that is new, ask yourself what truths are still worth affirming that can accelerate your progress.

Share these timeless lessons with others. Although you may have resented some of your parents' lectures when you were a youth, you often find yourself sharing your version with your own children. Those messages are laced with timeless certainty.

> "Don't avoid the clichés. They are clichés because they work."
> —George Lucas

Clichés have power when they become shared wisdom that is valued by all members of your team; they become treasured statements that anchor your organization's culture. They don't have to be explained, just repeated when necessary. What are your favorite clichés or sayings that unlock wisdom you want to remember—and can't afford to forget?

You don't just want to collect great quotes and catchy phrases; you want them in the front of your mind and ready when you need them. If you like listening to CDs, your iPod, or another MP3 player, try recording your own collection for playback. Start by recording your *Keepers* from this and other valued books. To make listening more enjoyable, break up the quotes and content by inserting one of your favorite inspirational songs. By listening to your *Keeper* messages weekly—as you commute or take a break—you'll soon memorize them and make them available whenever you need to motivate yourself or others.

If you want more material, you don't have to go far to find a fresh motivational shower with an optimistic focus. If you are enjoying this book, you will benefit by visiting the *Optimism Advantage Blog* at http://www.optimismadvantage.com. You'll find timely quotes, informative videos, stimulating commentary, and even an occasional humor break to keep you learning and laughing your way to an optimistic attitude. Those who visit the site will also be invited to share their comments and discuss what works in sustaining their own optimism advantage.

If taking time to read a blog doesn't fit your lifestyle or schedule, try signing up for *Dr. Paulson's Daily Dose of Optimism* at http://www.terrypaulson.com/optimismdaily. This will allow you to receive an inspirational message that will support your optimism advantage every day for a year. The short, free message will arrive every day at the same time you signed up to receive it. You don't have to read it every day, but it will always be there when you need an inner upper.

Try a Dose of Inspiring Stories of Courage and Change

Whether it's reading the latest version of *Chicken Soup* for any particular soul or a current best seller about an admirable recovery

> "Technology is the campfire around which we tell our stories."
> —Laurie Anderson

or deed, a good dose of inspirational stories can do wonders to boost your own courage and motivation. Such stories remind us of what is possible. Finding such inspiring mental ammunition is easier than ever. Former CNN daytime anchor Daryn Kagan lost her contract in January 2006, an event that allowed her to reinvent herself and her career. Kagan took her newly discovered free time and developed a web site devoted to telling inspirational stories. Visit and you'll find a centerpiece story of the day, as well as an archive of dozens more. Her mission is to "show the world what's possible," and her book *What's Possible* does just that. Reading inspirational stories has a very positive by-product; it's really hard to keep having a bad day once you've heard stories of others who have turned significant hardships around.

William Ian Miller, author of *The Mystery of Courage*, talked about the importance of using stories to inspire courage: "Read stories of courage. They make you wonder how you would have done compared with the hero of the tale. . . . You get very humble. You start self-querying and fantasizing about your own response, your own reaction. As the psalmist says, 'You become what you behold.' That's why stories of courage take you over. They are such cries of the heart."

Courage is a character trait we aspire to possess, but how we can foster it remains somewhat elusive. For centuries, leaders have used tales of legendary courage to motivate others to emulate heroes and heroines. In a world preoccupied with measurement systems, processes, and best practices, we shouldn't forget the power that stories have to energize and inspire. Don't just read them; look for stories being acted out in your life and the lives of others you know. What characters you know have exhibited courage and fortitude in overcoming adversity? Who had the courage to confront unethical behavior and challenge others to do what was right *before* it resulted in headlines? Who was bold enough to champion change before it was popular? If you want more courage, find a few more stories worth sharing.

Don't Forget to Reward and Celebrate Your Own Progress

Most people usually forget to take the time to enjoy their own progress. After all, you don't often lose sleep thinking about how great your day was. But it's time we make these efforts pay off in a tangible way, and your self-reward options are limited only by your imagination. Go to a

> "The nice thing about teamwork is that you always have others on your side."
> —Margaret Carty

movie or sporting event, buy a brand new book or movie, or take time to call a friend or colleague whose conversation and company you enjoy. Only you know which rewards you enjoy the most. Many may very well be some of the simple pleasures you isolated earlier. When you earn them, you will enjoy them even more.

> "The best part of waking up . . . is not the coffee."
> —Frank Bucaro

If you call a friend as a reward for progress, tell them why you're getting in touch: "I want you to know that calling you is my reward!" They will probably reply, "A reward for what?"—which will give you the opportunity to share your accomplishments. Not only will they encourage your progress; they are apt to be quite flattered that you have chosen *their* company as a way to treat yourself. Expect a heavy dose of reinforcement for your growth in becoming more optimistic. Remember that optimism is contagious, and this is one of the best ways to spread it among those you value most.

The best part of life isn't the coffee you drink; it's enjoying the company of those with whom you are drinking the coffee. Don't just compensate yourself for progress; let your support team join in the fun. And since the journey to change is never fully complete, don't wait until you have arrived to celebrate early successes along the way. Take time to commemorate your achievements with your energizing buddies, bosses, and cheerleaders who are there to support your change goals. People always love an excuse to party, and your progress will give everyone all the excuses they need.

Fellow speaker and former radio reporter Suzie Humphreys once told her friends that she deserved her own surprise party. They all assumed that she was kidding—until each one received an invitation that had instructions for where to park so she wouldn't be suspicious, who would take her for dinner so she would be out of the home, and when to arrive so that no one would spoil the surprise. She even instructed her guests that instead of buying "trashy trinkets," they should pool all their money to get one nice gift. When Humphreys entered her home at the designated time, her friends all jumped out and yelled, "Surprise!" She replied with a knowing smile, "You guys! I am so surprised! You shouldn't have!"

Don't be afraid to let *your* imagination guide your celebrations with your encouragers. Whether it's your own surprise party, a simple lunch, shared coffee, doughnuts, or tofu substitutes, once you've set your date to celebrate, fun is on the way. Make sure you share the obstacles you've had to overcome and thank those attending for their part in making progress possible. If your change goals involve your work, make one of your support group choices your boss. If your goals have a potential impact on your organization and team, you want your boss to know what they are. By making a clear statement of what you have learned, you force your boss

> "Success is best when it is shared. You will be left with an empty feeling if you hit the finish line alone."
> —Howard Schultz, Starbucks CEO

to listen anew to how you're changing, how it can make a difference, and what you need in the way of his or her support.

Whole Foods CEO John Mackey has established a unique way to end his meetings with encouragement: "People nurse petty grievances in day-to-day life. That's why we've been ending meetings with voluntary appreciations for 20 years. It's a chance for people to say nice things about one another, and the appreciations tend to break down barriers." Building a habit of ending a meeting with shared statements of appreciation may seem forced, but it works in building a habit worth continuing. Don't expect a torrent of compliments the first time you try this; some may think it's corny and refuse to participate. But stick with it. With volunteer appreciation on your meeting agenda, you'll have all the material you need to positively gossip your way to a strong culture of pride. Add it to your agenda this week, and watch it make a difference for any team.

Truth #50: Never Give Up on Becoming the Optimistic Person You Want to Be

Change rarely comes in the form of instant gratification. However, if you're like most people, you want success yesterday. Television has

exposed most of us to more than a million incredibly unrealistic 30- to 60-second solutions. These ads teach us to expect immediate rewards and results, but life teaches us that real solutions take work, persistence,

> "The reason a lot of people do not recognize opportunity is because it usually goes around wearing overalls looking like hard work."
> —Thomas A. Edison

and time. As has been said, "Motivation is when your dreams put on work clothes." This is not a time to slack on claiming your optimism advantage; it's the time to push for the summit on the horizon.

If your changes are worth making, it's worth persevering to find a way to achieve them. Norman Vincent Peale had a plaque on his

> "Don't give up at half-time. Concentrate on winning the second half."
>
> —Coach Bear Bryant

wall that read: "Anybody Can Quit!" But you're not just anybody, and it's always too soon for you to quit if your mission and goals are important enough.

Be patient but persistent. You don't know which day and which step will put your goals within reach. Imagine that you're making the blows to break through a stone wall to reach your goals. Social reformer Jacob Riis described a century ago what it takes to make change work: "When nothing seems to help, I go and look at a stonecutter hammering away at his rock, perhaps a hundred times without as much as a crack showing in it. Yet at the hundred and first blow it will split in two, and I know it was not that blow that did it, but all that had gone before."

When it seems like you're not making progress, keep your perspective. Your next blow for change may produce the breakthrough you are looking for.

Marathoners and Tour de France racers will tell you that a race's hardest parts—the uphill stages—are where victories are truly assured. When recessions end, when the roads level off, and when the world seems full of promise, your position in the great game of life will depend on how skillfully you managed the tough times—how you optimistically persisted to make change work.

Make Every Day Count to Become the Best You Can Be

Woody Allen has famously claimed, "Half of life is showing up!" The other half, of course, is doing something with the day once you *do* show up. In fact, do something *positive* every day. Although it doesn't have to be a big thing, you must do more than show up. Life is best taken one day at a time, no matter what the change. The most important changes have to be earned and earned again every single day. Don't waste any of them.

Making progress isn't about comparing yourself to others or being limited to what has worked in the past; it's about working to be the best you can be today. The natural tendency is to compare

> "On our track to success, we have to fight the tendency to look at others and see how far they've come. The only thing that counts is how we use the potential we possess and that we run our race to the best of our abilities."
> —Dennis Waitley and
> Reni L. Witt

yourself to others you respect. In some areas, they will easily outperform you. In your strengths, you may very well outperform them. But if you keep judging yourself based on the best in every area, you will always feel discouraged. Trophies may have one day motivated your performance, but most now gather dust on mantels or in attic boxes. As an optimist, get busy controlling what you can where it counts.

Popular leadership author Jim Collins makes a case for practical flexibility: "Applying persistence not to an idea but to a company, and willingly changing the ideas until you find some combination that works, is an enormously powerful way to go about an entrepreneurial adventure." An organization that attempts to deliver an inflexible vision—or a person who confidently persists to achieve a fixed goal—may *sound* good, but these are seldom the approaches to success that work in a rapidly changing world. If they fail to achieve their vision or goal, does it mean that they were not focused enough, didn't want it badly enough, or maybe—just maybe—they were in the wrong game?

Persistence—in both organizations and individuals—is an asset only when it adds a key component—a flexible destination. As we have learned, no matter how nice the horse, if the horse is dead—you better get off it. As an organization, persist in riding any horse that will keep you moving to profitable and meaningful destinations. As an indi-

> "There is no such thing in anyone's life as an unimportant day."
> —Alexander Woollcott

"Consult not your fears but your hopes and dreams. Think not about your frustrations, but about your unfulfilled potential. Concern yourself not with what you tried and failed in, but with what is still possible for you to do."

—Pope John XXIII

vidual, don't fall in love with one goal. Instead, fall in love with doing whatever it takes to advance your journey and claim your optimism advantage. Be flexible, realistic, and practical. Focus on your mission, your goals, your best, your choices, and your progress. Use every day, because every day matters.

Let me end with the prayer we began with:

"God grant me the serenity to accept the things I cannot change, the courage to change the things I can, and the wisdom to know the difference."

—Reinhold Niebuhr

Let it be so!

RESOURCES

Aspinwall, Lisa and Staudinger, Ursula. A Psychology of Human Strengths, American Psychological Association, 2002.

Bender, Peter Urs. Leadership from Within, Stoddart, Third Edition, 1997.

Benjamin, Harold. From Victim to Victor for Cancer Patients and Their Families, Penguin, 1995.

Blanchard, Ken, Hutson, Don and Willis, Ethan. The One Minute Entrepreneur, Broadway Business, 2008.

Briscoe, Simon and Aldersey-Williams, Hugh. Panicology, Skyhorse Publishing, 2009.

Buckingham, Marcus and Clifton, Donald. Now, Discover Your Strengths, Free Press, 2001.

Burns, David. Feeling Good, Quill/Harper-Collins Publishers, 2000.

Cameron, Kim S. Making the Impossible Possible, Berrett Koehler, 2006.

Clance, Pauline. The Impostor Phenomenon: Overcoming the Fear that Haunts Your Success, Peachtree Publishers, 1985.

Cosby, Bill and Poussaint, Alvin. Come on People: On the Path from Victims to Victors, Thomas Nelson, 2007.

Cousins, Norman. The Healing Heart: Antidotes to Panic and Helplessness, Avon Books, 1984.

Diener, Ed and Diswas-Diener, Robert. Happiness: Unlocking the Mysteries of Psychological Wealth, John Wiley & Sons, Inc., Blackwell, 2008.

Fast, Julie and Preston, John. Get It Done When You're Depressed, Alpha Books, 2008.

Frankl, Viktor. Man's Search for Meaning, Beacon Press, 2006.

Fredrickson, Barbara. Positivity: Top-Notch Research Reveals the 3 to 1 Ratio That Will Change Your Life, Three Rivers Press, 2009.

Gilbert, Dan. Stumbling on Happiness, Vintage, 2007.

Greengard, Samuel. *AARP Crash Course in Finding the Work You Love: The Essential Guide to Reinventing Your Life*, AARP Books/Sterling, 2008.

Jolley, Willie. *A Setback Is a Setup for a Comeback*, St. Martin's Press, 2000.

Jolley, Willie. *Turn Setbacks into Greenbacks: 7 Secrets for Going Up in Down Times*, John Wiley & Sons, Inc., 2010.

Kagen, Daryn. *What's Possible!* Meredith Books, 2008.

Leahy, Robert. *The Worry Cure: Seven Steps to Stop Worry from Stopping You*, Three Rivers Press, 2006.

Leider, Richard. *Something to Live For: Finding Your Way in the Second Half of Life*, Barrett-Koehler, 2008.

Lucado, Max. *Fearless: Imagine Your Life without Fear*, Thomas Nelson, 2009.

Lyubomirsky.Sonja. *The How of Happiness*, Penguin Press, 2008.

Maddi, Salvatore and Khoshaba, Deborah. *Resilience at Work: How to Succeed No Matter What Life Throws at You*, AMACOM, 2005.

Maurer, Robert. *One Small Step Can Change Your Life: The Kaizen Way*, Workman Publishing Company, 2004.

McKibben, Bill. *Deep Economy: The Wealth of Communities and the Durable Future*, Times Books, 2007.

Nielsen, Doug. *Take Life by the Helm: Proven Strategies for Gaining Control*, DNC Publishing, 2009.

Miller, William Ian. *The Mystery of Courage*, Harvard University Press. 2002.

Nolen-Hoeksema, Susan. *Women Who Think Too Much*. Henry Holt & Co., 2004.

Norem, Julie. *The Positive Power of Negative Thinking: Using Defensive Pessimism to Harness Anxiety and Perform at Your Peak*, Perseus Books Group, 2002.

Palmer, Parker. *Let Your Life Speak*, Jossey-Bass Publishers, 2000.

Paulson, Terry. *They Shoot Managers Don't They?* Ten Speed Press, 1991.

Paulson, Terry. *Leadership Truths One Story at a Time*, Amber Eagle Press, 2006.

Paulson, Terry. *Making Humor Work*, Crisp Publications, 1989.

Pollay, David. *Beware of Garbage Trucks: The Law of the Garbage Truck*, Sterling Publishing, 2010.

Prager, Dennis. *Happiness Is a Serious Problem*, Regan Books, 1998.

Putnam, Robert. *Bowling Alone: The Collapse and Revival of American Community*, Simon and Schuster, 2001.

Reivich, Karen and Shatte, Andrew. *The Resilience Factor: 7 Keys to Finding Your Inner Strength and Overcoming Life's Hurdles*, Broadway, 2003.

Sanborn, Mark. *You Don't Need a Title to Be a Leader*, Waterbrook Press, 2006.

Seligman, Martin. *Authentic Happiness: Using the New Positive Psychology to Realize Your Potential for Lasting Fulfillment*, Free Press, 2004.

Seligman, Martin. *Learned Optimism*, Vintage, 2006.

Seligman, Martin. *The Optimistic Child: A Proven Program to Safeguard Children Against Depression and Build Lifelong Resilience*, Mariner Books, 2007.

Seligman, Martin. *What You Can Change and What You Can't*, Vintage, 2007.

Sykes, Charles. *50 Rules Kids Won't Learn in School*, St. Martin's Press, 2007.

Thomas, Kenneth. *Intrinsic Motivation at Work: Building Energy and Commitment*, Barrett-Koehler Publishers, 2000.

Tiberius, Valerie. *The Reflective Life: Living Wisely with Our Limits*. Oxford University Press, 2008.

Williams, Mark, Teasdale, John, Segal, Zindel and Kabat-Zinn, Jon. *The Mindful Way through Depression*, The Guilford Press, 2007.

Zinger, Jim. *Life Enrichment through Self Hypnosis*, Hypmovation Training Institute, 1998.

INDEX

ABOUT THE AUTHOR

Terry Paulson is a PhD psychologist, honored professional speaker, national columnist, and celebrated author. He brings knowledge, humor, and a refreshingly unique approach to every presentation and book he writes. With over 30 years of experience in conducting practical programs on optimism and change for such companies as IBM, 3M, Boston Scientific, HBO, KPMG, Kaiser Permanente, Sony, Starbucks, Verizon, Wal-Mart, and hundreds of hospitals, universities, and associations, Dr. Paulson helps organizations, leaders, and teams *make change work*!

He's the author of the popular books: *They Shoot Managers Don't They*; *Making Humor Work*; *and Leadership Truths One Story at a Time*. He is a "Distinguished Faculty Member" for the Institute for Management Studies and a past president of both the National Speakers Association and the Global Speakers Federation. He's been inducted as a lifetime member of NSA's CPAE Speakers Hall of Fame, along with Ronald Reagan, Colin Powell, and Norman Vincent Peale, an honor given to less than 200 speakers worldwide.

Terry's tasteful humor and down-to-earth insights have earned him a deserved reputation as one of the nation's best authors and keynote speakers. That's why *Business Digest* calls him "the Will Rogers of management consultants."

Visit www.terrypaulson.com to learn more about Dr. Paulson. Share your comments at www.OptimismAdvantage.com.

—Terry L. Paulson, PhD, CSP, CPAE,
Paulson and Associates, Inc. Agoura Hills, CA
(800)-521-6172 • (818)-991-5110

M

COMMITTEE ON PUBLIC ADMINISTRATION

SOCIAL SCIENCE RESEARCH COUNCIL

Studies in Administration: Volume VI

THE ADMINISTRATION OF
OLD AGE ASSISTANCE

PUBLICATIONS OF THE
COMMITTEE ON PUBLIC ADMINISTRATION
SOCIAL SCIENCE RESEARCH COUNCIL

Studies in Administration

The Administration of Federal Grants to States, by V. O. Key, Jr., 1937

The Works Progress Administration in New York City, by John D. Millett, 1937

The Administration of Canadian Conditional Grants: A Study in Dominion-Provincial Relationships, by Luella Gettys, 1938

The Administration of an N. R. A. Code: A Case Study of the Men's Clothing Industry, by Robert H. Connery, with a Foreword by Lindsay Rogers, 1938

Public Employment Service in the United States, by Raymond C. Atkinson, Louise C. Odencrantz, and Ben Deming, 1938

The Administration of Old Age Assistance, by Robert T. Lansdale, Elizabeth Long, Agnes Leisy, and Byron T. Hipple, 1939

Monographs

Unemployment Compensation Administration in Wisconsin and New Hampshire, by Walter Matscheck, 1936 [Public Administration Service No. 52]

The Administration of Old Age Assistance in Three States, by Robert T. Lansdale and others, 1936 [Public Administration Service No. 53]

The Administration of Unemployment Compensation Benefits in Wisconsin, July 1, 1936, to June 30, 1937, by Walter Matscheck and R. C. Atkinson, 1937 [Public Administration Service No. 58]

Films as an Aid in Training Public Employees, by John E. Devine, 1937

Research in Administrative Law—Scope and Method, by Oliver P. Field, 1937

The Administration of Public Tort Liability in Los Angeles, 1934-38, by Leon T. David, and John F. Feldmeier, 1939

Monographs on City Manager Government, by Harold A. Stone, Don K. Price, and Kathryn H. Stone:

San Diego, Cal., 1939 [Public Administration Service No. Sp. 7]
Janesville, Wis., 1939 [Public Administration Service No. Sp. 8]
Charlotte, N. C., 1939 [Public Administration Service No. Sp. 9]
Fredericksburg, Va., 1939 [Public Administration Service No. Sp. 10]

THE
ADMINISTRATION OF
OLD AGE ASSISTANCE

By

ROBERT T. LANSDALE

ELIZABETH LONG

AGNES LEISY

BYRON T. HIPPLE

*Published for the
Committee on Public Administration of the
Social Science Research Council by*

PUBLIC ADMINISTRATION SERVICE

CHICAGO: 1939

PRINTED IN THE U. S. A.
BY R. R. DONNELLEY & SONS COMPANY,
CHICAGO, AND CRAWFORDSVILLE, INDIANA

FOREWORD

THIS VOLUME is the product of one of a series of studies initiated by the Committee on Public Administration in 1936, dealing with the administration of the emerging social security program. Students of social insurance and public welfare had studied and written about the content of the program and the problems of the unemployed and the aged, but the administrative aspects were relatively neglected. The Committee on Public Administration, foreseeing the importance of administration to the future of the program, undertook this series of studies, of which that dealing with administration of old age assistance is one of the most important. At the time of the enactment of the federal Social Security Act in 1935, only a few states had had any substantial experience in the administration of old age assistance, and a majority of states had no experience whatever. It was anticipated that within a few years the total expenditure for this purpose would exceed five-hundred million dollars annually.

For this study the Committee was fortunate to obtain the leadership of Robert T. Lansdale, whose experience as administrator and researcher both in welfare work and public administration fitted him peculiarly for this task. With him were associated Elizabeth Long, who had had experience both in social research and public and private welfare administration; Agnes Leisy, who contributed her expert knowledge of statistics and records; and Byron T. Hipple, who had been on the staff of the Governor's Commission on Unemployment Relief in New York.

After they had visited Massachusetts, New York, and New Jersey, three states with the greatest experience in old age assistance administration prior to the enactment of the federal Act, this staff prepared an interim report, "The Administration of Old Age Assistance in Three States." This was published as a monograph in the Public Administration Service series, in order to make immediately available to state officials and others some of the results of the study. The staff subsequently visited nine additional states; throughout their study they were in close touch with the federal offices concerned with the program.

The series of studies sponsored by the Committee on Public Administration, of which this volume is one product, included, first, an analysis of the experience of other federal agencies in administering grants-in-aid

v

to states, by V. O. Key; of Canadian experience with conditional grants by the Dominion to the provinces, by Luella Gettys; and of British administration of central grants to localities, by Norman Chester. The administrative problems of the employment service, as an essential tool of a social security program, were studied by Raymond C. Atkinson, Louise C. Odencrantz, and Ben Deming. Developments in unemployment compensation administration have been observed and studied for several years by Mr. Atkinson and Walter Matscheck, first under the auspices of this Committee, later under those of the Committee on Social Security of the Social Science Research Council. Mr. Matscheck also studied the nexus of employment exchanges and unemployment compensation offices in Great Britain: those in Germany were observed by Robert Frase. The publications which the Committee has sponsored, resulting from these studies, are listed elsewhere in this volume. In addition, the Social Security Board reproduced for limited circulation Mr. Matscheck's report on Great Britain and Mr. Frase's report on Germany; Mr. Chester's study will be published by the University of Manchester Press in England.

Two statements should be made about the responsibility for the present volume. First, while the Social Science Research Council has made available the funds with which the study has been conducted, neither directly nor through its Committee on Public Administration has it reviewed the findings of the study in the sense of approving or disapproving them. The responsibility for the statements of fact and opinion, as with all studies under the auspices of the Council, rests with the authors. Secondly, the three co-authors who have, since the completion of the study, joined the staff of the Social Security Board, Miss Long, Miss Leisy, and Mr. Hipple, wish it clearly understood that the statements attributable to them in this report are based upon work done before their connection with the Board and in no way represent or reflect the views of the Board.

JOSEPH P. HARRIS,
Director of Research

AUTHORS' PREFACE

THE WIDESPREAD establishment of state systems of old age assistance administration has been one of the outstanding phenomena in the history of public relief in this country. Twenty years ago there was but a single old age assistance law in effect—that of Alaska. Ten years ago only seven old age assistance statutes were operative. By December, 1934, under the provisions of twenty-seven state and territorial laws, some 236,000 old people were being cared for through public old age assistance at an approximate annual cost of $32,000,000. For the month of January, 1939, the federal Social Security Board reports that approximately 1,800,000 aged received $35,000,000. Every state in the Union, as well as the District of Columbia and the territories of Alaska and Hawaii, now has an old age assistance program and receives federal aid in support of it.

As all the states that have adopted plans have discovered, the problem of providing aid for the aged involves much more than passing a law and appropriating public moneys for those who need assistance. A program of this nature requires machinery for its execution and leadership to make the machinery work. Those eligible for benefits under the law must be selected from among the applicants and the degree of their need determined. The available funds must properly be distributed to those found to be eligible. The state must assure itself that recipients of assistance receive just and adequate treatment. The achievement of these objectives is the administrative task in old age assistance.

In this study an attempt has been made to discover the best practice achieved to date in the administration of old age assistance and to describe and analyze this experience for the benefit of those who are responsible for planning or administering state and local programs. Ideally, such a study would include a review of the operation of the old age assistance programs in all the states that have plans under way. Practically, with the limitations of time and funds available for the project, a selection of states had to be made. At the outset of this inquiry it was decided that it was better to study a small number of states intensively than to try to cover a large number more superficially. Twelve states were chosen: California, Colorado, Connecticut, Florida, Indiana, Iowa, Massachusetts, Mississippi, New Jersey, New York, Washington, and Wisconsin.

Two alternatives were open to the staff in selecting the states to be observed. Ordinarily their choice would be an attempt to present a fair cross section of existing practice—good and bad. The alternative was to select states in which it could be anticipated that reasonably sound administrative practice would be found. The latter alternative was followed because the principal objective was to find and analyze successful experience rather than to appraise the degree of efficiency achieved in the country as a whole. The following were the major criteria used in determining the states to be studied: evidence of effectiveness of plan in operation; length of time that the program had been in operation; uniqueness of the administrative plan; location of the state. No single factor was used in any selection; nor did all four factors direct the choice of any one of the states.

In each of the states studied, the primary visit was to the state office. After consultation with state officials, visits were made to local offices within the state. An attempt was made to select local offices in which reasonably good practice prevailed, including at least one rural unit, one local jurisdiction that included a small-sized or medium-sized city, and the largest operating unit in the state. Altogether, sixty-one local offices were visited in the twelve states. In addition, many studies and reports on local operation within these states were placed at the disposal of the staff. In New York State, the detailed studies of the Governor's Commission on Unemployment Relief on the operation of old age assistance in twenty-two local districts were made available.

Some attempt has been made to keep in touch with the development of old age assistance administration in the states not visited. For the most part, however, material on these states has not been used in this report except for incidental reference, since second-hand reports on state operation and procedures cannot fairly be weighed against first-hand material.

Three of the states, Massachusetts, New Jersey, and New York, were studied in April, May, and June, 1936, and a preliminary report on their administration of old age assistance was issued in the fall of 1936.[1] The other nine states were subsequently observed—the field work terminating in 1937.

During the period of this study striking changes occurred in the administration of old age assistance: federal grants-in-aid were first made available to many states, and most state legislatures were either

[1] See Robert T. Lansdale and Associates, *The Administration of Old Age Assistance in Three States* (Chicago: Public Administration Service, 1936).

initiating or revising old age assistance legislation. Of no state could it be said at the time observed that the old age assistance program had reached a stage that might be considered static, or about which it might be said, with some assurance, that a pattern of administration had been adopted that would remain intact for any length of time. As a matter of fact, change and experimentation are two of the major features observable in old age assistance administration in the United States at the present time.

Three states were studied before the receipt of federal funds; in nine of the twelve states, including these three, new legislation had recently been passed or was subsequently adopted that radically affected either the program, the plan of administration, or both. Some may insist that the authors of a study of this nature should keep abreast of all changes made in the states studied so that the final material would be current. The changes, however, have been so far-reaching and so numerous that an inquiry in even as few as twelve states would never be finished were an attempt made to keep up to date on all the major developments and changes. Consequently it has been necessary to consider the operation of the state systems as they were at the time of the visits. An effort has been made, nevertheless, to keep track of the developments in these states, and references to changes occurring after the staff visits have been made, either in the text or in footnotes.

The aim of this study has been to evaluate principles of administration; hence, exact current details of any individual plan are not essential. No complete standardization of old age assistance administration has been achieved as yet, and, with the variety of local and state conditions and of political patterns, it is unlikely that any one system of administration will ever completely fit the needs of all states. No attempt has been made, therefore, to give a complete picture of any one state system from beginning to end. The report has been organized topically, and state material is brought in only illustratively. A complete state plan is interesting as an exhibit, but its value to any other state is dubious. On the other hand, methods that have been tried in a group of states are exceedingly important at this stage.

Readers who anticipate finding in this book an exposé of corrupt conditions in the administration of public aid to the aged will be disappointed. Although the instability, crudity, and partisan political coloring of some of the old age assistance plans in the country may not be denied, the constructive purposes of this study would not be served by denunciation and sensational charges. The aim of this enterprise has rather been to record and analyze material from the administrative experience in the states which will be useful to public officials responsible for planning and administering old age assistance.[2]

The first section of the report is devoted to a discussion of organization, general administration, and executive control. Although it is recognized that any schematic consideration of public welfare administration suffers from the artificiality of classification of activity required for description, the subsequent sections of the report discuss under a series of appropriate headings those activities which seem to the writers to be the main components of a public assistance program. The first of these topics is the administration of the social service activities, which includes the direct relationships of the agency to the individual. The activities considered next are the financial aspects of the program, including financing of the program, budgeting, disbursement of funds, accounting, and the control of financial procedures by central or overhead agencies. The final part of the report includes chapters on personnel activities, fair hearings and appeals, and the place of boards in the management of agencies.

The specific staff assignments for the writing of this report have been as follows: Part I, Mr. Lansdale; Part II, Miss Long; and Part III, Mr. Hipple. All members of the staff, however, have participated both in making the field studies and in analyzing and collating the data.

In preparing this report the staff became acutely aware of the paucity of material on the methods and principles of public welfare administration. For example, no standard definition could be found for so basic a term as "application." Even the nomenclature for procedures and for staff positions is still far from standardization. The lack of established principles and of accepted terminology has greatly complicated the task of analyzing the processes of administration. It has compelled the authors at some points to discuss basic processes in considerable detail, and at others to advance tentative conclusions that may appear to some readers to be beyond the scope of an inquiry into the administration of only a single type of assistance.

The staff received generous and hearty cooperation from all the officials—local, state, and federal—from whom assistance was sought. In addition, many individuals have helped at various points in the

---

[2] The authors recognize the importance of calling public attention to the abuses which have occurred in old age assistance administration, but regard this as a different task from theirs and one more effectively performed through journals of opinion or other periodicals. See, for example, Beulah Amidon, "Sooner Security," *Survey Graphic,* April, 1938, and John T. Flynn, "Dear Pensioner," *Collier's Weekly,* April 16, 1938.

enterprise from early planning to final editing. In fact, so many have contributed to this volume that it is impossible to single out any few for specific mention. The staff can only hope that this final product is sufficiently worth while that those who helped to make it possible will feel recompensed for their time and efforts. The staff, of course, bears the sole responsibility for the form and content of this study.

ROBERT T. LANSDALE

CONTENTS

COMMITTEE ON PUBLIC ADMINISTRATION
OF THE
SOCIAL SCIENCE RESEARCH COUNCIL

MEMBERS OF THE COMMITTEE

LOUIS BROWNLOW, *Chairman,* Public Administration Clearing House
WILLIAM ANDERSON, University of Minnesota
JOHN DICKINSON, University of Pennsylvania
ROWLAND EGGER, Director of the Budget, Virginia
LUTHER H. GULICK, Institute of Public Administration
LEWIS MERIAM, The Brookings Institution
LINDSAY ROGERS, Columbia University
LEONARD D. WHITE, University of Chicago
JOHN H. WILLIAMS, Harvard University
GEORGE F. YANTIS, House of Representatives, Olympia, Washington

CHARLES S. ASCHER, *Secretary,* 306 East 35th Street, New York
JOSEPH P. HARRIS, *Director of Research,* Transportation Building, 17th and H Streets, Washington, D. C.

CONSTITUENT ORGANIZATIONS OF THE
SOCIAL SCIENCE RESEARCH COUNCIL

AMERICAN ANTHROPOLOGICAL ASSOCIATION
AMERICAN ECONOMIC ASSOCIATION
AMERICAN HISTORICAL ASSOCIATION
AMERICAN POLITICAL SCIENCE ASSOCIATION
AMERICAN PSYCHOLOGICAL ASSOCIATION
AMERICAN SOCIOLOGICAL SOCIETY
AMERICAN STATISTICAL ASSOCIATION

ROBERT T. CRANE, *Executive Director of the Council*

PART I
General Administration and Organization

CHAPTER I

THE ORGANIZATION AND FUNCTION OF THE FEDERAL SOCIAL SECURITY BOARD

THE CARE OF the dependent aged has become a part of a national plan of economic security; it is no longer a matter left entirely to the initiative of the individual states or, within the states, to the option of the localities. Through the Social Security Act of 1935 the provision of federal funds to match state and local expenditures for assistance to the aged has in itself been a stimulus to the development of state programs. Furthermore, although the federal Social Security Board has no statutory authority to promote state plans of assistance to the aged, by implication it is responsible to do everything in its power to see that the states adopt and maintain such plans in order that care may be available to the aged throughout the United States. Because of the important position now occupied by the Board in relation to state old age assistance operations, an analysis of the administration by states of aid to the aged must be made against a background of the federal activity. Hence, although this study is concerned primarily with state and local administration, the reader must be made aware, at the beginning, of the structure of the federal agency and of the general nature of its activities in dealing with the states.[1]

ORGANIZATION OF THE FEDERAL SOCIAL SECURITY BOARD

The Social Security Board is responsible for a diversified program, the elements of which are linked together by the bond of a common purpose—security against certain hazards of modern industrial life. Its three main functions are: the direct operation of the federal old age insurance program, the administration of federal aid for unemployment compensation, and the administration of federal grants for public assistance.

The administration of federal old age insurance is by far the most

[1] The effect of the federal Act and of the Board's administration of it on specific areas of old age administration, such as social service activities, financial activities, personnel control, etc., appears in the discussion of those topics.

3

extensive activity of the Board; administratively it overshadows the other functions in terms of funds involved, personnel employed, and the magnitude of the operations required to execute the program. This vast social insurance scheme is the only direct operation for which the Board is responsible. To administer this program, the Board has established branch offices throughout the United States. These operating units are directly responsible, through a line organization, to the Bureau of Old Age Insurance in Washington. In carrying out this program the Board does not deal with states and need not even consider state lines in its administration unless it finds it expedient to do so. Since agricultural employees are not eligible for these benefits, the area of activity of the old age insurance program is proportionately greater in industrial states than in agricultural states.[2]

As for the second function, the Social Security Board does not itself administer unemployment insurance benefits; it is responsible for the supervision of unemployment compensation plans in those states which are organized to render this service and whose plans have been approved. In this field the Board supervises, with one exception, different state agencies from those with which it deals on public assistance matters.[3]

The public assistance responsibilities of the Board involve the supervision of approved state plans of administration of old age assistance, aid to dependent children, and aid to the blind. As in unemployment compensation, the federal function in public assistance is indirect or supervisory; the Board does not engage in the direct rendering of assistance.

Administratively the Board is responsible for three separate and distinct programs. Ultimately the old age insurance program will have a direct effect on the administration of old age assistance, but the processes involved in old age assistance and old age insurance administration are so different that the local management of the two programs by the same agency is almost inconceivable. It is also important to stress that one of the Board's functions is a direct line activity, while in the other two fields its function is the supervision of the operation of state plans.

By law, the administrative responsibility for the federal program is

[2] See Social Security Board, "Press Release," March 16, 1937 (mimeographed), showing the number of registrations in various states.

[3] From 1937 to 1939 there was one exception, the Department of Social Security of the state of Washington, which is responsible for the administration of employment offices and of unemployment compensation, as well as the state public assistance services. Since this Department was established after the field work for this study was completed, its operation has not been observed in this inquiry; by legislation adopted in February, 1939, the unemployment compensation administration was vested in an independent agency.

lodged in a board of three salaried members appointed by the President of the United States for overlapping terms of six years. The Board established the position of executive director as its chief executive officer, but has itself retained considerable responsibility for the details of operation. The management of its diverse functions is centralized in a single channel of control and coordination which flows through the executive director to the Board. The main subdivisions of the organization are called bureaus, three of which are classified by the Board as operating bureaus, and five, as service bureaus. The operating bureaus are: the Bureau of Federal Old Age Insurance, the Bureau of Unemployment Compensation, and the Bureau of Public Assistance. The service bureaus include the General Counsel's Office, the Bureau of Research and Statistics, the Bureau of Accounts and Audits, the Bureau of Business Management, and the Informational Service.

The Bureau of Public Assistance is the only operating bureau that is directly involved in the administration of grants to states for old age assistance. Its functions have thus been described:[4]

> The Bureau of Public Assistance is responsible for the administration of grants to States for old-age assistance (under title I), aid to dependent children (under title IV), and aid to the blind (under title X). It recommends to the Board the approval of State plans for the three types of aid which satisfy the requirements of the act. It exercises a continuous supervision over the operation of State plans through its review prior to recommendations to the Board for the certification of grants. The Bureau of Public Assistance is also called upon by States which have not as yet submitted plans for advice with respect to the preparation of such plans. When requested, it consults with the States concerning technical problems involved in the administration of public assistance; to this end it develops general procedures and standards.

Although it appears from this description that this Bureau bears the main responsibility for the administration of public assistance grants, some of the service bureaus, in addition to their other activities, play an important part in the relationship with the states in this field. The Office of the General Counsel "reviews State legislation submitted to the Board for approval under the Social Security Act and assists States, at their request, in their preparation or amendment of State legislation for assistance to the aged, to dependent children, and to the blind."[5] The Bureau of Research and Statistics "establishes systems of statistical re-

[4] *First Annual Report of the Social Security Board* (1936), pp. 3-4.
[5] *Ibid.*, p. 4.

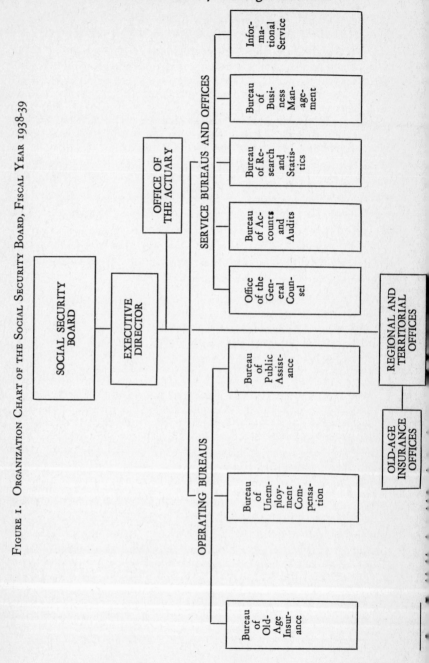

FIGURE I. ORGANIZATION CHART OF THE SOCIAL SECURITY BOARD, FISCAL YEAR 1938-39

porting to provide current information on the various aspects of the social security program."[6] The Bureau of Accounts and Audits[7]

> assists States, when requested, with the initial establishment of procedures for the accounting and reporting of funds allotted by the Federal Government. . . . This Bureau also makes audits of payments by the States to individuals receiving public assistance in order to determine, first, the cost of administration of the public-assistance titles; second, the conformity of payments to the requirements of the Social Security Act; and, third, the share of the cost of benefit payments and of administrative expenses borne by the State.

Clearly these service bureaus are expected to conduct an essential part of the supervisory program.

The supervisory program of the Board respecting public assistance therefore involves the operation of at least four coordinate bureaus of the central organization. Since the heads of these bureaus report independently to the executive director, that official, rather than the head of the Bureau of Public Assistance, is responsible for the coordination of the total supervisory program in this field. The executive director has a similar coordinating function for unemployment compensation; but in the administration of old age insurance, he has a coordinating function that is quite different, since the activities of the service bureaus in this direct operation are distinctly facilitative and secondary, while in public assistance and unemployment compensation they are primary.

The organization of the field staff of the Social Security Board is briefly described as follows:[8]

> In conformity with the Board's policy of decentralizing its activities and its relationships with the several State governments, regional offices have been established in 12 accessible centers. Each office is in the charge of a regional director who is the official representative of the Board within the region and is responsible to the executive director.
>
> These regional offices provide requisite services to cooperating States, coordinate activities of the Board located within their respective regional areas, and furnish information to individuals affected by the Social Security Act. To insure the efficient administration of State plans for public assistance and of State unemployment compensation laws and to aid States requesting such service in setting up plans of administration, the Board maintains in each regional office a regional attorney and a staff of statisticians and experts in public assistance, unemployment compensation, and old-age benefits.

[6] *Ibid.*, p. 4.
[7] *Ibid.*, p. 5.
[8] *Ibid.*, p. 5.

The regional office is set up as a counterpart of the central office in Washington, with representatives of the operating bureaus and of the service bureaus on an equal footing. Presumably, also, the regional director, like the executive director, is the coordinator of the program as a whole and also of the program within any one of the three lines of operation. In direct dealings with a state on public assistance administration, the regional director in theory must coordinate the activities of the representatives of the Bureaus of Public Assistance, Research and Statistics, Accounts and Audits, and of the General Counsel's Office. At the same time, the regional director is in direct charge of the federal old age insurance program; he also coordinates the supervisory activities in unemployment compensation.[9]

FEDERAL INFLUENCE ON THE DEVELOPMENT AND MAINTENANCE OF STATE OLD AGE ASSISTANCE PLANS

Early in 1935, after the President's Committee on Economic Security had submitted its report and while the federal security legislation was under consideration, several members of the staff of the Committee undertook the task of advising states that were seeking help in reshaping their laws to conform with the anticipated federal legislation. For this purpose the staff of the Committee on Economic Security prepared a suggested state old age assistance law which was sent to those states requesting advice.

The Social Security Board was appointed on August 14, 1935. States immediately began to clamor for advice on legislation and administration, but the Board had no adequate staff to assist them since a filibuster in the United States Senate had choked off the appropriation bill that accompanied the Social Security Act. As an emergency measure the Board commenced work with personnel and funds made available by other federal agencies. A skeleton staff for the Bureau of Public Assistance was assembled during the first few months, but it was too small to cope with the requests from the states. The American Public Welfare Association, a national organization operating in the field of public welfare which had been advising states on public welfare legislation, stepped in to assist the Board. In November, 1935, this organization issued model state bills for old age assistance and other categories of relief included under the Act.[10]

[9] The original conception of the regional director's relationship to old age insurance was a supervisory one, but in practice he has become a direct administrative official.

[10] American Public Welfare Association, *Suggested State Legislation for Social Security,* November 15, 1935.

Early in 1936 the Bureau of Public Assistance was organized on a permanent basis with both a central office and a field staff. During the first years one of its most important enterprises has been the task of consulting with the states when they are developing new assistance legislation or reconsidering existing statutes. The regional representatives of the Bureau of Public Assistance have been made available to the states as consultants on both legislation and administrative plans, although they have been careful to indicate that their position is an advisory one. This type of field service is a useful aid to the states, for it means that a person is at hand who can advise on the content of proposed legislation and speak unofficially of its conformity to federal requirements.

Once an old age assistance law has been adopted, the state plan of administration must be approved by the Social Security Board before the state is qualified for federal grants. The review and approval of these plans potentially offers an effective medium by which the Board can influence the organization of the state old age assistance programs. To facilitate the process of reviewing state plans, the Board has provided a schedule of instructions for the advance submittal of a description of the state plan of administration, which requires that the state set forth in detail evidence to show that the state plan conforms to the specifications of the Social Security Act.

In general, the material called for consists of the state laws establishing the authority of the state and local agencies; the administrative regulations prepared by the state agency in further application of the law; and the administrative machinery set up to carry out the law and the regulations. That part of the plan schedule now in use concerned with organization and administration asks first for a detailed analysis of the state agency itself, including a description of the state board or commission; the functional organization of the state agency; the organization of the various divisions within the state department; and the arrangements for field service. The next section calls for a description of the local administration, including the organization of the local departments of public welfare and the membership and powers of local boards. The third section requires a complete description of the state supervisory program under headings such as rules and regulations, field supervision, reports, personnel, and complaints. Other parts of the plan schedule call for descriptions of the social service, financial, and recording procedures.

It has been the recent practice to have the public assistance representatives and other field personnel of the Board assist the states in drawing up the description of the state plan. After the statement has been prepared by the state officials, it is submitted to the Board for approval. Within the Board, at least four different bureaus scrutinize the plan for its conformity to the Social Security Act; there may be considerable correspondence between the Board and the state during the review process. After the plan has been approved, the state is required to notify the Board of any significant changes. Major modifications must presumably have federal approval, and if the state assistance law is drastically amended, a new plan must be submitted.

The state plan gives the Board a document which, if properly drawn up, should afford a complete picture of the state's program of old age assistance administration. After its formal approval, the Board's supervision of the operation of the state program may be built around this plan. In effect, the Board possesses an official prospectus from the state in terms of which the actual performance in the state may be gauged. The use of state plans as a fulcrum for the federal supervisory program has not been altogether successful. In the first place, the Board has had to experiment with the material and data to be required in the statement of the plan. The requirements have been completely revised in the light of the early experience; they are now much more specific and much more inclusive. Prior to the revision, some states had regarded the description of plans as a routine requirement and had not amplified the material sufficiently to give the Board a detailed picture of their proposed system of operation. Other states, particularly those undertaking the administration of old age assistance for the first time, used the submission of the plan as a means of setting forth what they hoped to do or, in some instances, what they thought they were expected to do; thus the state plan amounted to a promise of future achievement, which was not always fulfilled.

The Board has at times treated the state plans with undue formality. They are reviewed in the Washington office by the various bureaus, some of whose members are either not conversant with the field of public welfare administration or have no firsthand knowledge of the individual states and their particular requirements. Consequently, this review has often been focused upon minutiae in the plan rather than upon its more fundamental provisions. As a result, some states have been compelled to satisfy the Board on many minor points before securing final approval, whereas other state plans that contained basic flaws have apparently been approved without careful scrutiny.[11]

[11] The contrast of treatment was noted in two neighboring states. In one, although

Some uneven treatment is inevitable in a new agency: federal bureaus in which subordinates of the central office, rather than officials in close touch with field conditions, take the major part in determining official action frequently tend to be formalistic. The responsibility for the major recommendations to the Board regarding the state plan should reside with the field-staff members who supervise a particular state—as has been the recent tendency in the Board's policy. These officials are in a position to understand local arrangements and local attitudes, and the language of the plan will have more significance to them than it can possibly have to workers in the Washington office who are not in touch with field conditions. Furthermore, since the field representatives are required to determine that the state plan is adhered to once it has official sanction, they should be primarily responsible for the interpretation and review of the plan prior to its approval by the Board.

The staff of the Board has labored under a handicap in that the Board has promulgated no formal policies regarding state plans of administration and has issued no interpretations of the requirements set forth in the Act. The Board wisely refrained from enunciating any standards during the early months of its operation, since time was required to became acquainted with the problems in order to determine the most acceptable practice. Three years have elapsed; this should have been ample time for experimentation, but at this writing[12] no formal rules have appeared. In the absence of specific regulations, the staff members must rely upon memoranda and instructions in advising the states on matters of policy.

The state plan, furthermore, has the inherent shortcomings of any formalized administrative document. Many of the old age assistance agencies are still in process of development; to describe the complete program at any one time is difficult enough in itself, and to keep the plan current is an even greater task. To be effective, state programs must be dynamic: they must be adjusted from time to time in the light of experience and new circumstances. There is danger that the requirement of a formal plan may become an instrument of reaction and that

---

a state official had spent much time in Washington explaining the plan of administration (there was no field representative available to the state at the time), the state was compelled at the eleventh hour to furnish considerable supplementary detail on its proposed plan of operation, including formal certifications on minor points by state officials after the plan had substantially been approved. In the other, a document basic to the plan was accepted by the Board without question, although it did not bear the official sanction of the state welfare board and appeared to have been prepared merely to get the plan approved.

[12] December, 1938.

constructive modifications may be challenged simply because they are a departure from the "approved" plan. On the other hand, the plan cannot be permitted to become such an adjustable document that it becomes useless as a device for federal control activities. To tread a path between these two extremes requires rare administrative statesmanship.

POWER OF THE BOARD OVER STATE ADMINISTRATION

One of the problems in the relationship of the Board to the states is the limitation of the formal authority of the federal agency over state administration to approval or disapproval of state plans. Legally, there appears to be no intermediate step. Once the Board has approved the plan it stands until modified by the state, or until it has been formally disapproved in accordance with the procedure specified in the Social Security Act:[13]

> In the case of any State plan for old-age assistance which has been approved by the Board, if the Board, after reasonable notice and opportunity for hearing to the State agency administering or supervising the administration of such plan, finds—
> (1) that the plan has been so changed as to impose any age, residence, or citizenship requirement prohibited by section 2(b), or that in the administration of the plan any such prohibited requirement is imposed, with the knowledge of such State agency, in a substantial number of cases; or
> (2) that in the administration of the plan there is a failure to comply substantially with any provision required by section 2(a) to be included in the plan;
> the Board shall notify such State agency that further payments will not be made to the State until the Board is satisfied that such prohibited requirement is no longer so imposed, and that there is no longer any such failure to comply. Until it is so satisfied it shall make no further certification to the Secretary of the Treasury with respect to such State.

When federal funds first became available, the Board decided that it would be advantageous to the program as a whole to approve as many plans as possible at the outset, even though some were admittedly imperfect. The Board stated its position as follows:[14]

[13] 49 *Stat. L.* 622, chap. 531, Title I, sec. 4. The Board has power to refuse federal funds for individual grants of assistance made by the state in violation of the eligibility provisions of the Act. The exercise of this authority is largely negative in its effect, since it does not reach back to the factors in the administration that produced the illegal expenditure. For further discussion of this point, see chap. 14.

[14] *First Annual Report of the Social Security Board* (1936), p. 11. One critic has charged that other factors actuated the Board. See Abraham Epstein, "Killing Old Age Security with Kindness," *Harper's Magazine,* July, 1937, pp. 182-92.

State legislatures and administrative officers have been confronted with the difficult task of enacting legislation, formulating plans, and setting up machinery. Laboring under great obstacles, they have made a notable achievement in getting the program under way. The Board has sought to render every possible assistance to the States. It has realized that the immediate necessity for aiding the needy outweighed considerations of administrative nicety. Smoother operation and more highly perfected plans will follow further experience of the Board and of the States.

Fortunately many states have been compelled to resubmit plans because their statutes have been amended to such an extent that the existing plan was no longer effective. Even when there have been significant administrative changes in the state program, the Board has been able to require that a new plan be drawn up. No mechanism for a periodic resubmission of state plans has been devised, however, so that many plans which have been given the official stamp of approval fall short of the Board's ideal of effectiveness. Improvement in operation under these plans requires patient supervision, with the threat of complete withdrawal of funds—an extreme step—as the only weapon of authority.

Naturally the Board has been hesitant to take the drastic step of complete withdrawal of federal funds involved in disapproval of the state plan when states are not providing satisfactory administration, both because this action is likely to cause suffering among the dependent aged—since most states do not have funds available to carry on the program without the federal money—and because it marks the failure of a cooperative administrative effort. The first use of the withdrawal power was made in July, 1937, when the Board, after a public hearing, decided to suspend federal aid to the state of Illinois "until such time as the administration of the old-age assistance plan in that State substantially complies with the requirements of State and Federal laws." [15] Subsequently federal funds have been withdrawn from the states of Oklahoma and Ohio. In another instance, the scheduling of a formal hearing was sufficient to bring about the reform of a state's administration of old age assistance. The results of these actions upon the Board's relationships with other states have not been observed, but it is reported that they have strengthened the federal staff's efforts to secure more satisfactory administration elsewhere.

Even though in a strict sense the Board's power over state administra-

---

[15] Social Security Board, "Press Release," July 30, 1937 (mimeographed). Federal funds were restored a month later when the Board was convinced that substantial changes had been made to bring the state administration into conformity with the Act.

tion is explicitly limited to complete approval or complete disapproval of state plans, no reasonable person would deny that it has an implicit obligation to obtain the best possible use of the federal funds invested in old age assistance administration. The degree of the implied responsibility is heightened by the extent of federal financial participation—that is, by the fact that the federal government bears approximately half the state and local expenditures for aid to the aged. Furthermore, an approved state plan must provide "methods of administration . . . necessary for the efficient operation of the plan." So the Board must assure itself that the methods adopted result in efficient operation. The Board has recognized this obligation by organizing a field service to carry on a program of supervision of the operation of the state plans. The contribution of the field staff to the improvement of the organization and operation of the state plans has been extensive. Much of its constructive work has been effected so deftly and skilfully that it would be difficult to isolate the federal suggestion from the state action.[16]

The results to be expected from a field service, apart from the individual strengths and weaknesses of members of the staff, cannot fully be realized from the present plan of field-service organization. The Board plan of organization as it stands is not conducive to an integrated approach to the administrative problems of the states; it creates confusion within a state by the diffusion of authority inherent in the arrangement. The principal representative of the Social Security Board in each region is the regional director. His primary responsibility is for the direct activity of the Board, namely, the federal old age insurance program, but, in addition, he is responsible for the coordination and direction of the two supervisory programs. This combination of duties assumes that the regional director is not only a capable administrator of a direct operation but is also an expert in state relations and in the administrative problems faced by states in three types of public assistance and in unemployment compensation. It also assumes that he can give the time required for the fulfilment of all these duties. Few of the regional directors are able to function effectively in all these capacities; yet for the supervision of public assistance programs the results are almost equally bad if the regional director refrains from participation or if he asserts his prerogative and directs the supervisory relationships with the states.

To comprehend this dilemma, one must again envisage the arms of

[16] The federal activities in technical aspects of old age assistance administration are discussed under appropriate headings throughout the report.

the Board's field staff which directly affect the administration of public assistance in a single state. Aside from the regional director, at least four bureaus maintain field representatives to deal directly with the states on public assistance matters: the Bureau of Public Assistance, the Bureau of Accounts and Audits, the Bureau of Research and Statistics, and the General Counsel's Office. Even when the regional director abstains from leadership in the program of supervision, the state agency still finds itself subject to suggestions from four different sources, and frequently the advice received from one source is in conflict with that from another. But when the regional director attempts to direct and coordinate the supervisory activities of the field staff, the results are no more satisfactory because he usually does not have the time, the knowledge, or the particular skill required for this task.

Steps have been taken to obviate some of the difficulties arising from the present plan of field-staff organization. Through agreement of the two bureau directors involved, the representatives of the Bureau of Public Assistance and of the Bureau of Research and Statistics have worked together in advising the states not only on technical problems but also on matters of organization. For practical purposes in most regions the representatives of the Bureau of Public Assistance have assumed the leadership of the field program in the public assistance area. Although this leadership has been recognized to a degree by the orders of the Board, it is still informal. Any official action by the public assistance representative which needs to bring to play in a single state the total supervisory program of the Board, still requires an intricate series of interbureau and field-to-office communications, as well as separate orders from at least three bureau directors, the executive director, and the regional director.[17]

Agreements and orders have helped to simplify interstaff relationships, but coordination of the federal supervisory program is still based more upon personal relationships than upon official sanction. The results of this situation, noted in the states to date, are that the state official must deal with several semi-independent representatives on different phases of a single state program; and that there is no one federal person

---

[17] The Bureau of Accounts and Audits at the time of this survey had not fully accepted the relationship of its field auditors either to the regional director or to the field representatives of the other bureaus. It was found that the regional auditor was almost never available in the regional office for consultation with the other representatives on state problems but was invariably in one of the states with an audit group. The activities of the Bureau of Accounts and Audits within the purview of this study have been focused largely upon a detailed audit of the state and local operations with little attention devoted to assisting the states in developing adequate financial procedures.

in the field whom the state director can consult with any degree of finality regarding the entire program for which he is responsible. Although some of the representatives of the Bureau of Public Assistance may not have had the experience to qualify them to pass on all administrative matters, the fact that their position is *officially* coordinate with the representatives of the Bureau of Research and Statistics, of the Bureau of Accounts and Audits, and of the General Counsel's Office makes it impossible for them, no matter how well qualified, to exert their full influence upon the management problem in the states.

The Social Security Board has established a pattern of organization which is not only ill adapted to its own purposes but one which state agencies administering grants to localities may attempt to emulate. Dr. V. O. Key, Jr., author of a recent volume on the administration of federal grants to states,[18] has pointed out in an unpublished manuscript a basic fault that appears in the organization of a few of the federal grant-administering agencies. To quote Dr. Key:

> When specialization in the federal organization is required, the question arises what principle shall be followed in making the necessary division of labor. It is believed that in a few cases some of the difficulty has been due to the fact that the practices applicable to operating departments have been applied without much thought to the federal grant-administering agency. For an operating agency a division of labor may be worked out between "line" and "staff" functions, the "line" divisions consisting of those units of the organization concerned with actual operations; and the "staff" divisions, those concerned with the overhead services of personnel, accounting, research, etc. The application of the same principle to the division of labor within a grant-administering agency, however, tends to create a multiheaded agency to deal with the states, with consequent lack of coordination. The function of supervision, or the conduct of federal-state relations, dictates internal divisions of labor on a different principle from that required when the function is direct operation.

This fundamental misconception of function explains the chief difficulty in the present organization of the Board. Responsibility for all the supervisory activities relating to state public assistance administration—reporting, auditing, legal advice, social service, and administrative supervision—must be placed in the Bureau of Public Assistance before the Board can be fully effective in its responsibility for the development and maintenance of state plans of old age assistance administration.

[18] V. O. Key, Jr., *The Administration of Federal Grants to States* (Chicago: Public Administration Service, 1937). This work will be found illuminating on some of the administrative and organizational problems of federal agencies that make grants to states.

CHAPTER 2

THE DIVISION OF ACTIVITIES BETWEEN STATE AND LOCAL AGENCIES

THE PROVISIONS of the states for the administrative organization of programs for the care of the aged appear on the surface to be fairly uniform, but are found upon closer analysis to present many subtle variations. In establishing state plans, the legislatures have been confronted with two fundamental administrative questions: With the state participating financially in old age assistance, how shall the administrative activities be distributed between the state and local subdivisions? And, to what degree shall the administration of old age assistance be integrated with other state welfare services and with other local welfare services?

The answers to these questions have determined the administrative pattern in particular states; that the conclusions have differed from state to state—frequently for sound reasons—accounts for the present lack of uniformity of state plans of administration. An examination of administrative organization must be made in terms of these fundamental questions.

THE EXPANSION OF STATE PARTICIPATION

Most of the earliest state old age assistance laws established plans under which the state did not participate either financially or administratively and which were operative only if the county so elected. The first system providing for state participation was established by Wisconsin in 1925, and the second, by California in 1929. From 1930 on, the proportion of state plans involving either state financial participation or state administrative participation grew gradually, and by December, 1933, sixteen state old age assistance laws provided for state participation.

Both the philosophy and the practical considerations which led to the adoption of a plan of joint state and local administration of old age assistance in New York—one of the pioneer plans of this type—are preserved in the report of the New York State Commission on Old Age Security, which investigated the problem of care of the aged in that state, and whose recommendations were embodied with only minor changes in the old age assistance law of the state.[1] The reasoning of this Commission may be paraphrased as follows:

> Exclusive state operation would entail the establishment of a large agency duplicating many of the activities of local departments. The cost, delay, and possible effects on local organization were all factors cited against this proposition. Under exclusive local operation there was the possibility that the law might be ignored, that poor-relief concepts of an illiberal nature might obtain, and that state funds, if any state aid were provided, might be wasted. Protection against the dangers of exclusive local operation may be secured by extensive state supervision. A plan of joint state-local administration does not disturb the development of a unified local program of social welfare, does not cause a duplication and confusion of agencies in the localities, yet retains in the state sufficient authority to produce uniform enforcement of the act throughout the state.

The federal Social Security Act specifies that in order to receive federal grants, a state plan of old age assistance administration must, among other requisites, provide for state financial participation and for "the establishment or designation of a single State agency to administer the plan, or provide for the establishment or designation of a single State agency to supervise the administration of the plan." [2] In consequence, both state financial and administrative participation are today provided for in the old age assistance laws of all forty-eight states. With such participation universally achieved in this country, it is desirable to examine its results in terms of the allocation of administrative activities to the two levels of government. The ratio of state funds to local funds used in the program is only a contributing factor to the assignment of operating activities and not, as might commonly be supposed, the sole determinant.[3] The assignment of administrative activities has usually been defined by statute or by administrative regulation; in some instances, however, it has merely evolved from practice.

The fundamental problem in setting up a state plan of administration is to assign the operating activities so that adequate service may be given to eligible aged and that economical administration may be secured. Ac-

---

[1] *Old Age Security,* Report of the New York State Commission, 1930, pp. 18-20.

[2] *49 Stat. L.* 622, chap. 531, Title I, sec. 2(a).

[3] Many of the state old age assistance laws recently adopted or amended assign more complete control to the state agency than that involved in joint state-local administration, and place the major share of the financial cost of the program upon the state. The reasons for state assumption of more complete administrative and financial responsibility vary from state to state. The degrees of state financial participation and the effect upon administration are discussed in chap. 11.

cording to a commonly accepted classification, two basic methods of distribution of activities have been developed in the states: a plan locally administered but state supervised; and a state-operated system. In the former, the operating activities are usually allocated by law to subdivisions of the state, and a state agency is designated to supervise the program. In the latter, the major administrative responsibility for the direct execution of the program is assigned to a state agency. In the selection of states for this survey, a proportionate sample of each system was included. Of the twelve states surveyed, seven were in the first category: California, Colorado, Indiana, Massachusetts, New Jersey, New York, and Wisconsin. The other five states studied, Connecticut, Florida, Iowa, Mississippi, and Washington, had state-operated systems.

Close observation of these plans has revealed that this classification is superficial and not particularly illuminating. The fact is that the degree of centralization has no consistent relationship to the proportion of funds supplied by the state and the locality. In all the plans studied, some degree of local participation in administration was discovered, and, likewise, most of the state agencies were found to have assumed some direct operating activities. A common administrative problem of all the states is the question of the degree of decentralization that is desirable within the program; and, since all the plans have been at least partially decentralized, the states are faced with the problem of the proper relationship between the supervisory or state agency and the operating or local agencies.

ADMINISTRATIVE ACTIVITIES OF AN OLD AGE ASSISTANCE PROGRAM

A delineation of the principal administrative activities is required before their allocation to states and localities may be considered. The function of a public old age assistance agency is to grant assistance to eligible applicants in accordance with legal provisions. The systematic execution of this program requires the following principal administrative activities, which are common to the operation of any public assistance program:[4]

Social service activities, which involve direct relationship with applicants for and recipients of assistance, and, in general, include the receiving and the investigation of applications, the determination of

[4]The administrative activities are discussed in their technical aspects in subsequent chapters; the emphasis here is upon the distribution of responsibility between state and local agencies.

eligibility and the calculation of degree of need, and, finally, the maintenance of continuing relationship with the recipients.

Fiscal activities, including disbursement of funds, accounting, auditing, financial planning, and the maintenance of budgetary control.

Reporting and recording, which involve keeping detailed records of
the program for administrative, control, and planning purposes.

Personnel management, involving recruitment and selection of staff
and the management of employees.

Miscellaneous activities, including office management, legal counsel,
research and planning, information, and public relations.

ASSIGNMENT OF SOCIAL SERVICE ACTIVITIES

Experience has demonstrated that to be effective the direct relationships with the applicants for, and recipients of, aid must be carried on
in proximity to the persons served. The reasons for this are apparent.
Applicants must be interviewed and their social and economic conditions investigated. The investigation entails considerable consultation
with other persons in the community acquainted with the applicant
and his circumstances and, in addition, requires searching of many
community records. Many of these steps must be repeated in the subsequent reinvestigations required by most states. Furthermore, some
continuous contact with recipients must be provided in order that their
emergency needs may be cared for and changes in their circumstances
noted, such as death, removal from the community, and loss or gain
of income.

The social service activities are entirely assigned to a local agency or
a branch office in all the states studied except three—Iowa, Washington,
and Connecticut. Before these exceptions are discussed, it is well to see
what the procedure is in the majority of the states. The applicant applies
to a local agency, where his application is received by the social service
department. An investigation of the applicant's eligibility and need is
made; then a determinative recommendation, based upon the findings,
is made by the social service department, first, on eligibility, and second,
if this is affirmative, on the size of grant.[5]

In Iowa and Washington the local agency actually goes through these
steps, but its recommendations carry little weight. A report is sent to
the state office for final authorization. The state agency, before making
the authorization, repeats some of the steps already taken by the local

---

[5] The *authorization* of the grant—that is, the administrative decision—is, strictly speaking, an executive, not a social service, activity. For a detailed discussion of the nature and
processes involved in the decision on and authorization of grants of assistance see chaps.
5 and 9.

agency, and, using its own formula, recalculates the size of the grant.[6] Administratively the dual performance of this activity is indefensible. If the state possesses some superior device for determining the amount of assistance needed by eligible applicants, why should it bother to have the local workers go through the motions of making calculations of need according to another method? Many local workers in these states (and in both states the local workers are paid by the state!) were found to be either discouraged or cynical. Furthermore, in both states, the local workers are compelled to explain to local citizens obvious inequities caused by the calculation in a distant state office; but the state officials need only answer protests about grants by letters in which they hide behind the assumed accuracy of a mechanical system.[7]

Connecticut has divided the social service activities between the local agencies and the state. Under its plan, the local public welfare department is responsible for receiving applications and investigating three points in the eligibility requirements: age, residence, and citizenship. The application is then passed on to the state agency, which assigns a worker to complete the investigation.[8] The old age assistance director in this state has pointed out the difficulties of this plan:[9]

> Many of our problems arise from the fact that our law provides for a dual responsibility in investigation between the towns and the state. Although the responsibility for final decision and action is placed upon the state, the chief executive authority of the town or his appointee must receive and investigate all applications and forward them with his record of investigation and his recommendations to the Bureau. The State Bureau reviews the same and grants an award if the applicant is eligible. Regulations place responsibility upon the towns for determining proof of age, citizenship and residence; the other factors of eligibility are established or checked by the Bureau. The state organization has no control over the appointment of the local officials nor does it exercise any right of supervision over the personnel in the towns. As a result, we have many varieties of organizations in the towns resulting in little uniformity of interpretation and a great deal of confusion and misunderstanding among the applicants.
>
> In the smaller towns, for instance, the local official does not, as a rule,

[6] The technical weaknesses of the formula method are discussed in chap. 6.

[7] It should be noted that in 1937 Washington abandoned central administration and allocated all the social service activities to local agencies.

[8] The local agency also makes a recommendation on the size of the grant, but this is usually not based upon detailed knowledge of the applicant's circumstances except when he has previously been a recipient of another type of relief from the local agency.

[9] Edward H. Reeves, "Problems of Old Age Security Administration in Connecticut," in *Social Security, 1937*, pp. 50-51.

delegate the responsibility for receiving applications but does the work himself. Recommendations from this source are likely to be based upon subjective facts with little substantiating information and the amounts recommended are all too frequently for the maximum. The local officials of some towns delegate the full responsibility to an appointee who is seldom a person with previous experience in this type of work. Some officials have delegated responsibility to an appointee, who in turn refers the applications to the local welfare department, but retain the power of recommendation. In other towns the appointee has a special staff of investigators who may or may not have had previous experience in social work. In a comparatively few towns, the officials have placed the supervisor in charge of relief and given him complete responsibility.

The effects of these diverse methods of approach can readily be seen: (1) They result in duplication of effort. (2) Action on cases is delayed. (3) Applicants may be visited by two or three workers before final action is taken. (4) Recommendations are made by the towns after a cursory investigation, which are often found to be unjustified, with the result that final action taken by the Bureau necessarily differs from the original recommendation by the town.

The split responsibility in the Connecticut plan is a striking example of the present confusion of state and local functions in public assistance which exists in many parts of the country. The responsibility for the dualism in this instance rests squarely with the state legislature, which provided in the old age assistance law that:[10]

Sec. 7. Application for old age assistance shall be made to the chief executive authority, or his appointee, of the town in which the applicant resides. . . . Upon application so made the chief executive authority, or his appointee, shall, without delay, *thoroughly investigate such application* and shall, within thirty days after the application has been made, forward such application, with the record of the investigation thereon and with recommendations as to its disposition, to the bureau of old age assistance.

Sec. 8. The bureau, upon receipt of an application for an award, *shall investigate* the same and shall grant an award, etc.

Statutory language of this sort is, of course, subject to interpretation. The department in this state has experimented with a simplification by delegating its responsibility for investigation of applications to some of the larger local welfare departments whose administrative competence has been demonstrated. But the department remains without power to secure adequate standards of administration in the local public welfare offices; therefore, in the greater part of the state, the duplication of

[10] Connecticut, *Public Acts,* 1935, chap. 110. (Italics added.)

activity is apt to continue until the legislature establishes a more radical reorganization of the state welfare system.[11]

When the direct social service activities have been allocated to a local agency or a branch office, the state agency retains the function of supervising these activities. The degree of state control is expressed in the state law and in the supplementary rules and regulations of the state agency. The law and the regulations affect the performance in two ways: by defining the results to be obtained—that is, eligibility requirements and limitations on the amount of assistance; and by prescribing how the results are to be accomplished—that is, the methods of administration. Enforcement of the law and regulations is carried out by the state agency, with major emphasis either upon checking the results through a review of the action taken on individual cases by the local agency, or upon supervision of the methods of operation.

The effectiveness of these two philosophies of state supervision will be discussed in detail in the section on social service activities. It is sufficient to note here that supervision of the methods of operation tends to strengthen the performance in the local agencies, whereas major attention to case review may result in a subtle substitution of state activity for local responsibility. A local agency of any considerable size ordinarily provides within its own organization a case supervisor whose chief responsibility is to review the action of staff workers before final administrative action is taken. When the state also reviews the individual cases, it means a double review, state and local, or else the local agency comes to rely upon the state for a determinative case review. Both results have been observed. In one large local office, for example, the local supervisor and the state field supervisor sat in the same room independently reviewing the same cases. Some local agencies have so arranged the timing of their payment of grants that a person does not receive his first check until the state has reviewed the case. This shifting of supervisory responsibility has frequently been found to result in relieving the local agency of the necessity of making an unfavorable decision when there is local pressure to accept an individual. As one local official expressed it, "I like this system of the state passing on cases. When the local politicians put the heat on me to approve someone for old age relief who isn't eligible, I pass the buck for refusal to the state."

Ordinarily, the state's review of cases accepted by the local agency consists merely of scrutinizing the documents in each case, but in one state a complete reinvestigation of the eligibility of applicants is made

---

[11] For further discussion of this point, see chap. 3.

by a state worker. In some parts of the state this has resulted in a complete duplication by the state of the local investigation—an expensive operation which does not yield a proportionate return. In small or poorly organized local districts, however, the local agency frequently does not bother, or cannot afford, to make an adequate investigation of its own; in reality the state worker performs the social service activities for these local agencies even though they take final administrative action. In this state, local responsibility for relief is so entrenched politically that the legislature has apparently not dared to establish a system that will assure satisfactory local administration; hence this illogical and expensive plan of duplicate investigation has been resorted to as a means of ensuring that state funds are properly expended.

ASSIGNMENT OF FISCAL ACTIVITIES

The assignment of responsibility for financial activities in the state plans has usually followed upon the decision on the method of financing the program. Two principal patterns appear: (1) When the localities contribute to the cost of the program, they disburse the funds for assistance in the first instance and receive the state's share in an allotment made either before or after the local expenditure. The recipients of aid receive their allowances in the form of checks prepared by the local agencies. The accounts of these transactions are kept locally. The expenditures are usually audited by some local authority. Accounts of the state's contributions to localities are kept by the state agency. It also makes an audit of the total funds expended by the local agencies which is entirely separate from any local audit. (2) When the state bears the entire financial burden, disbursement of funds is made by the state agency; that is, recipients of aid receive their allowances in checks from the state. Under this centralized plan, accounting and auditing are conducted solely on the state level, usually in accordance with the procedures used for all types of state expenditures.

A single exception to each of these patterns has been observed. In Florida, only limited funds were made available by the state for old age assistance; in fact, the amount was so nominal that no program could have been inaugurated without additional money. In order to have the benefit of federal funds, however, the counties were requested to contribute sufficient sums of money to provide for a program. Each county appropriated money in proportion to its estimated population of needy aged, but instead of expending the funds directly, the counties turned the money over to the state agency, which used it for the care of the aged within each county. An accounting was rendered to each county of the use made of its appropriation; if they so desired, the county officials were informed currently of the local residents who had been placed on the assistance rolls. Otherwise, no authority was exerted by the county over the funds granted to the state. Since this plan was in operation only nine months, it did not bear the test of time, but novel though it was, it worked.

The exception to the second pattern is the Colorado plan in which the entire cost of assistance is borne by the state, but the funds are granted to the county agencies for expenditure in accordance with their estimates. (The counties, in this plan, bear half of the administrative costs.) Administratively, no essential difference is found between this plan and those in which the county bears a share of the assistance costs. In this instance, the state pays 100 per cent of the assistance costs rather than a smaller fixed percentage.

The centralization of financial operations in the state-financed systems has presented problems revolving around the disbursement of individual assistance grants. Central check writing presents an opportunity for mechanical efficiency through the use of check-writing and check-mailing equipment, which small units cannot afford. In order to operate effectively, however, the procedures must be sufficiently sensitive and flexible to absorb changes in authorization of grants almost up to the time of check mailing. Although an old age assistance roll is more constant than most relief lists, it is nevertheless subject to considerable adjustment because of death, change of address, suspension of grant, cancellation of authorization, or change in the size of grants. The experience with centralized disbursing has not been altogether successful.[12] In two states decentralization of the disbursing activities has been sought as a means of avoiding the issuance of too many incorrect checks. In one instance this consisted of assigning the distribution of checks to the local agencies for examination immediately prior to distribution; thus any checks requiring change could be withheld at this direct point of contact with the recipients. Another state agency attempted to set up regional disbursing offices of a type found practical when the state was expending federal funds in the unemployment relief program. But the welfare department was prevented from executing this plan because the state disbursing official who issued the checks claimed that legally he could have only one office in the state and that at the state capitol.

In one locally administered plan much of the local accounting is

[12] See chap 13.

centralized in the state office, which has extensive mechanical equipment. Local expenditures are recorded on punch cards which are sent to the state office where the bookkeeping operation is performed mechanically, and the local agency is subsequently furnished with statements of its accounts. Some officials in this state believe that it would be possible for the state agency to take over disbursing for the local agencies through the use of mechanical equipment, though this plan has not seriously been advanced.

REPORTING AND RECORDING

In administrative control and planning, it is necessary to keep accurate statistical records of the volume of work handled by the local agencies and by the state as a whole. These records must be kept currently, and if they are to be influential in the determination of policy, they must be compiled to show trends of the work in considerable detail. The basic data are derived both from the social service and from the financial activities. Gathering and compilation, however, are two separate steps. When all basic social and financial case records are maintained in the state office, the statistical work is also centralized there; that is, a unit in the state office gathers and compiles the data for both the local agencies and the state as a whole. When the basic data are kept in the local agency or are divided between it and the state agency, the question arises: who shall take the basic data from the administrative records and who shall compile the data thus obtained?

The allocation of the responsibility for gathering the basic data is usually made on practical grounds. In one state, for example, many of the local agencies are so small that they do not employ even a part-time worker to perform the functions of the agency, and the work is done by elected officials as a side line to their main occupation of farming, storekeeping, etc. Obviously, no consistently reliable data may be expected from such units; the state must send out workers to collect the material if it wishes to have records that are even reasonably satisfactory. Another state has felt from the outset of the program that it could obtain more reliable basic facts by having a specialized staff travel around the state to gather data in the local offices.[13] The practice most frequently followed, however, is to leave the collection of the data to the local units, the state agency furnishing detailed instructions on the manner of gathering the material. Satisfactory results under this system are achieved only

---

[13] These state workers happen to be employees of a coordinate state welfare agency, and the same person is in charge of the statistical work in both agencies.

when the state agency can furnish direct field service to the local units in addition to formal instructions.

Only the largest local agencies assume responsibility for the compilation of their own data because this activity requires a technical staff which smaller units cannot afford. Most of these large agencies were already engaged in the compilation of some type of relief statistics prior to the inauguration of the state plan of old age assistance. In small units the purposes of local control and planning appear to be equally well served whether the local agency compiles its own data or whether the state provides the compilation for the local unit.

The centralization or decentralization of reporting activities is not an important administrative question in itself. Adequate results in this field are more significant than the observation of the niceties of jurisdictional authority. One word of caution, however, must be added: the statistical activities in the field of old age assistance should be so administered that they contribute to the development of more adequate records for the entire field of public assistance. Integration of old age assistance recording with other public welfare statistics should not be regarded as an unselfish gesture of the old age assistance administration: the planning of care for the aged is intimately tied up with the developments in other welfare fields.

PERSONNEL MANAGEMENT ACTIVITIES

When the state has delegated some of the operating activities to local agencies or to branch offices, it may delegate selection of the local workers to the subordinate unit; or it may delegate the power of appointment but limit or control the selection in varying degrees; or it may retain the appointing power itself, but prescribe, or have prescribed, limitations on its own freedom of selection.[14] Salaries of local workers either are entirely a matter of local determination, or are determined locally within certain limits set by the state, or are fixed exclusively by the state.

Five of the states observed leave the selection of employees entirely to local agencies.[15] The quality of selection in these states therefore depends entirely upon the traditions and standards of government in the political subdivisions. In four of these states civil service systems exist in at least some of the local units. When these are effective, they exert a positive

[14] This discussion is concerned primarily with the employees who perform direct activities in the local agencies or the branch offices, and the limitations on selection of the central state staff are not considered.

[15] One of these states has recently brought the local agencies under a merit system operated jointly by the state welfare department and another state agency.

influence upon the quality of local personnel. In four of the five states the locality determines the rate of pay of all employees. In the fifth, the salary of the county directors is prescribed by the state law, but the compensation of subordinate staff members is fixed locally.

In five of the states visited, selections are made locally but in accordance with a state-operated merit, certification, or examination system.[16] Although the effectiveness of these plans of state control of appointments varies, they all represent a definite limitation upon the local appointing authority. The state either sets the local salaries or prescribes a scheme of salary grades within which the salaries are to be kept. It is significant that in two of the five states the state pays the entire salary of the local employees; in two, half the local salaries; and in the fifth, the state agency passes on to the counties the total federal grant for administration, which, in effect, is a state contribution to local administrative costs since most state agencies retain at least half this sum.[17]

In the two remaining states, local workers are selected by the state office and are assigned to the local agencies. The state fixes their compensation in accordance with an established salary scale. Regard for local sentiment, however, affects the selection in both states. In one, it is the practice to assign workers to the counties in which they live. In the other, all clerical employees are local residents, and, other things being equal, an attempt is made to assign local residents to social service or administrative positions.[18] Both these states have voluntarily set up standards of qualifications to govern their own selection of local workers, though one of the states has not rigidly adhered to them.

MISCELLANEOUS ACTIVITIES

Several additional activities may be mentioned briefly which, although not universal, represent a significant problem of division of labor between state and local agencies.

The services of the city or county attorney are ordinarily available to the local welfare agency. Such an attorney, however, may not be well versed in welfare matters, or may be too busy to handle the detailed questions arising in the administration of public assistance in the locality. A few local agencies responsible for old age assistance, therefore, have

[16] These merit systems are discussed in chap. 15.

[17] See discussion of this point in chap. 12.

[18] Practically all the employees in the largest local office in this state are local residents. This may be attributable to the fact that many trained and experienced persons were available in that community.

employed their own legal counsel with or without the advice of the city or county attorney. One state attorney general has ruled that a county welfare department could hire its own attorney, if it had the funds to do so. Many state agencies have arranged that competent legal service be available not only for their own administrative needs but also for the benefit of the local agencies. Since most controversial matters in old age assistance involve the interpretation of state laws, the state is the natural agency to supply legal service, which is usually provided by special arrangement with the state attorney general or by a person on the staff of the state welfare department who is acceptable professionally to the attorney general. In one state which made no provision for such service local agencies were observed to be at a loss to know where to turn for counsel, particularly when the legal service in their own county was not competent to interpret state statutes. Some local units, however, occasionally pit their own legal talent against that of the state.[19]

Few local agencies are large enough or sufficiently well financed to be able to embrace any considerable research or planning activities. In fact, only a small number of state welfare departments have been able to afford, or have seen the value of, a research program. In several instances research activities have been joint projects conducted by a state agency in cooperation with a local agency or vice versa. The potentialities of joint action in this area have not fully been realized.[20]

Only the largest local agencies are able to engage in any formal informational program. Several large urban welfare departments issue printed annual reports of their work, and some of them assign a staff member to prepare material for the press, for public addresses, and for radio talks. Most state departments have developed some publicity activities; a few have engaged in extensive state-wide programs. Two state agencies furnish local units with material which may be useful for local educational work, such as press releases, and data for talks. A member of the central staff of one of these state departments meets with the local boards periodically to help them develop programs of interpretation within their jurisdictions. These state agencies regard the education of the public on the problems and progress of the old age assistance

[19] One county agency decided that an unemployed person over sixty-five who was able-bodied and had previously been employed was the responsibility of the state unemployment relief agency and was not eligible for old age assistance. This agency through the county attorney was trying to convince the state attorney general, without consulting the state old age assistance agency, of the correctness of its position.

[20] Federal leadership in the research field may prove a stimulus to more effort on the state level in the future.

program as a joint state-local responsibility. In contrast, some of the state departments issue bulletins and reports for public circulation which glorify the state's performance and almost completely ignore the participation of the local communities.

★   ★   ★

State participation in public assistance administration has raised many new administrative problems, one of the most perplexing of which is the division of responsibility between state and local agencies. Many of the newer programs are still in transition, but it is quite clear that no standardized plan applicable to all states is evolving. The most wholesome aspect of the present stage of development is that states are attempting to meet their own peculiar circumstances. Despite the many variations in form and method, however, one guiding principle emerges from the experience to date: service to needy human beings which is both adequate and flexible cannot be attained through operations that are prescribed in minute detail by a distant central office.

CHAPTER 3

THE RELATIONSHIP OF OLD AGE
ASSISTANCE TO OTHER STATE AND
LOCAL WELFARE SERVICES

EARLY EFFORTS to establish systems of old age assistance were made
at a time when local public relief was in ill repute. Before the depression, local public poor-relief administration was characterized
in most states by the niggardliness of the amounts of aid given, by the
fact that relief was generally given in kind, by the incompetence of the
officials responsible for its administration, and by the stigma attached
to the recipient of public aid. The reform of public outdoor relief administration was under way in some sections of the country prior to the
depression, but, for the most part, the system was thoroughly entrenched
as an activity of the smallest units of government, and it appeared to
many to be unregenerate.

It is not surprising to find that the advocates of old age assistance programs in this period were zealous in their attempts to establish plans
that were completely divorced from established systems of poor-relief
administration. The so-called "model bill" of the Fraternal Order of
Eagles, drawn up late in 1921 and still sponsored by this organization,
provides for a state old age pension commission and for county old age
pension boards, neither of which has any official connection with other
state or local welfare activities.[1] The New York Commission on Old
Age Security reported to the legislature in 1930 that, although the
tendency in the state plans adopted up to that time had been to graft
the assistance plan upon some existing body, "in most cases, with the possible exception of California, the endeavor has been to select an organization which is to a great extent dissociated from all other relief activities.
The desire has been to separate, through a distinction in administration,

[1] "This [model bill] was drafted by Past Grand Worthy President Frank E. Herring,
William J. Brennan, and Michael O. Burns in cooperation with Dr. John B. Andrews,
Secretary of the American Association for Labor Legislation, and Professor Joseph P.
Chamberlain of Columbia University, both authorities in welfare legislation." *The Eagle
Magazine*, XXIII (June, 1935), 13.

the old age assistance plan from the poor relief distributed by the county." [2]

The vast relief burden that states and localities had to assume from 1930 on, because of widespread unemployment conditions, showed the glaring weaknesses in the existing welfare machinery. Most states were compelled to establish emergency agencies to handle unemployment relief, and public opinion was aroused to the need for replacing a seventeenth-century poor-relief system with a program adapted to present-day economic and social conditions. The reform of public welfare administration, which had slowly been gaining force in the 1920's, acquired great momentum in the 1930's. Most states that were adopting or revamping old age assistance programs in this latter decade were also reorganizing both their state and local systems of public welfare administration. Although many advocates of old age assistance were still insisting that the aged would receive better care if their interests were entrusted to state and local agencies organized for the care of the aged only, state legislatures began to give less heed to this phase of their appeal. For one thing, the protest of this group against the humiliating effects of poor relief looked backward rather than forward. Had not vast numbers of citizens been receiving public relief in a most respectable form and in amounts frequently more generous than were proposed for the aged? Furthermore, other special classes were seeking separate systems of administration for their needs and few legislators could be shown the wisdom of independent establishments to care for the aged, widows, the blind, veterans, and the unemployed. Although few states have completely integrated their welfare service, most of them have moved toward some combination of assistance services on both state and local levels. According to the Division of Research of the Works Progress Administration,[3] by July 1, 1938, forty-four state old age assistance programs were being administered or supervised by a state agency responsible for at least three different types of assistance.[4]

The degree of administrative coordination of the old age assistance program with other public welfare functions on both state and local levels is highly important for a consideration of the administrative organization of the program. When only this one type of assistance is administered, the organization problem is much simpler than when

[2] *Old Age Security*, Report of the New York State Commission, 1930, p. 228.

[3] Hereafter cited in the text as W.P.A.

[4] Works Progress Administration, Division of Social Research, "State Public Welfare Administration" (manuscript of forthcoming publication).

three or more public welfare functions are administered by the same agency. The twelve states visited provide ample illustration of varying degrees of organic relationship between the administration of old age assistance and of other welfare functions.[5] Three different situations appear: States in which the organization of old age assistance has been set up on both the state and local levels administratively removed from all other welfare activities; states in which the responsibility for old age assistance has been grafted onto existing welfare machinery, both on the state and local levels; and states in which old age assistance either on the state or the local level or both has been made a part of the responsibility of new welfare agencies established for the purpose of administering more than a single type of aid.

ORGANIZATION OF OLD AGE ASSISTANCE, SEPARATE FROM OTHER WELFARE FUNCTIONS

The Iowa law of 1934 provided for a state old age assistance commission with no organic relationship to any other state welfare activity or agency. The legislature evidently intended that the administration of old age assistance on the state level should be separate from all other welfare programs.[6] Provision was also made for county old age assistance boards as separate and distinct entities, although the statute recognized, to a degree at least, the problem of working relationships with other local welfare bodies. For one thing, the law required that one of the three members of the county old age assistance board be the county overseer of the poor, ex officio. It also stated that "The [county] board in its discretion may arrange with other public or private relief departments or agencies to use one or more of their investigators who meet the required qualifications." [7] Thus the state and local old age assistance

[5] The fact that an agency is responsible for the administration of several public welfare functions is no assurance per se that there is any real integration of services on the operating level. The concern at this point is with the opportunity for coordination of public assistance administration presented in the assignment of functions made by the state laws.

[6] A new welfare act was passed in Iowa in 1937 which provided for the integration of the administration of old age assistance with the management of several other welfare programs.

[7] *Code of Iowa*, 1935, chap. 266-f1, sec. 5296-f7. The state attorney general was apparently of an unqualified opinion about the intent of the law regarding separation of county old age assistance administration from other local welfare activities. The following summary of his opinion appears in the Iowa Old Age Assistance Commission, *Handbook for County Old Age Assistance Boards and Investigators*, 1934, p. 52:

"Q. Can the work of the county old age assistance boards be conducted in connection with the emergency relief, county welfare work, widows' pensions, blind pensions, etc.? May the board use the same quarters as [the] several poor funds of the county?"

units in this state had, at the time of this survey, only a single program to administer; therefore the basic organizational problem was simple.

OLD AGE ASSISTANCE GRAFTED UPON THE EXISTING WELFARE STRUCTURE

In four of the states studied—California, Connecticut, Massachusetts, and New York—the legislature assigned the new function of old age assistance to an existing state welfare agency and to established local agencies.[8] At the time of the enactment of its old age assistance law, each of these states had already centered the principal noninstitutional welfare functions in a single state welfare agency which had had some years of successful performance.[9] All had long established local welfare agencies, but two of the systems could not be called successful by present-day standards. The assignment of old age assistance to the state welfare department in these states added a new activity to an agency already engaged in a variety of welfare enterprises. In all four states the responsibility for the new program was lodged in a unit created for the purpose and called the "old age assistance division" or "bureau."

These states present different situations respecting local agencies. California had previously centered its local welfare functions in the county. The only conceivable alternative to establishing old age assistance apart from all other welfare activities in this state was to attach it to the existing welfare unit; this was done. As a result, the California county became one of the earliest examples of the complete integration of a highly differentiated welfare program in a local unit larger than the town or city.[10]

The town system of home relief continues in the majority of counties

---

"A. No. The legislature set up county boards entirely apart from any other relief agency. The time and *place* of meeting will be set by the old age assistance commission."

The Commission, pursuant to this opinion, ruled that "The [county] board shall select a place for meeting, but under no circumstances shall said place of meeting be in connection with the place, room, or office of the county overseer of the poor, county welfare workers, city or county charities, or any other charity or benevolent organization." (*Ibid.*, p. 47.)

[8] Were only the state level considered, New Jersey would be included in this list. Since the old age assistance law in this state made mandatory the establishment of a new county welfare mechanism, New Jersey is considered under the third classification.

[9] For a brief history of state departments in Massachusetts and New York, see Robert T. Lansdale and Associates, *The Administration of Old Age Assistance in Three States* (1936). For a history of the California state department, see Frances Cahn and Valeska Bary, *Welfare Activities of Federal, State, and Local Governments in California, 1850-1934* (1936).

[10] The county in California is not, in all instances, sufficiently populous to afford a satisfactory welfare program. Alpine County with a population of 241 is an example of a county too small to support any extensive governmental services.

in New York State despite many efforts to unseat it; but the role of the town has lost much of its earlier importance. All new types of public assistance introduced by legislation in the last two decades have ignored the town as a unit of administration, and the general public welfare law of 1929 strengthened the county's hand in all public welfare matters. The county public welfare district was selected as the principal local unit for old age assistance administration; thus the trend toward consolidation of local welfare activities in the county was furthered. The state public welfare law of New York also contains provisions for certain city public welfare districts which have the powers of a county public welfare district. In addition, the old age assistance legislation makes it optional for other cities to administer old age assistance independently of the county. Altogether there are eighty-six local units of old age assistance administration in this state.[11]

Massachusetts and Connecticut present an interesting contrast since in both states the traditional local unit of welfare administration is the town, which is frequently too small to provide modern governmental services. Massachusetts has apparently never considered it possible to depart from this long established local welfare agency, although adherence to it means that 355 units of government administer outdoor relief, old age assistance, and mothers' aid. Welfare services are maintained on this level at the cost of inadequate local service and of a highly complex and expensive system of state supervision. The astonishing thing is that, although there have been numerous revisions of the old age assistance law in recent years in Massachusetts, there has been no effort to establish a larger operating unit. Connecticut, faced with a similar situation, has set up a state system of old age assistance administration in which local coordination is attempted by having the local welfare officer receive applications from the aged and make certain preliminary investigations. Although the Connecticut plan presents certain difficulties, which have been pointed out above, it avoids the administrative complications of supervising the work of 153 towns and cities and of entrusting the care of the aged to small, unequipped local units.[12]

---

[11] There are fifty-seven county public welfare districts in New York State and six city public welfare districts. In addition, twenty-two cities and one town which has the powers of a city administer old age assistance. See Elsie M. Bond, *Public Relief in New York State* (1938).

[12] Other New England states faced with an entrenched town system have assigned important operating activities of old age assistance to a state agency.

OLD AGE ASSISTANCE AS A FUNCTION OF NEWLY CREATED WELFARE AGENCIES

In Colorado, Florida, Indiana, Mississippi, New Jersey, and Washington, the welfare structure has been revamped either on the state level, the local level, or both. The necessity for organizing a system of old age assistance has been one of the important factors in bringing about a new administrative plan in these states. The changes on the local level have followed a somewhat similar trend, but there has been a marked difference on the state level.

New Jersey has a well organized state welfare department; the responsibility for the care of the aged was assigned to this agency under circumstances similar to those in the four states mentioned in the preceding category. Indiana and Florida had state welfare departments with limited functions prior to the depression. Although they received the heritage of the old departments, the new agencies created in these states in 1936 and 1935, respectively, represented a complete revamping of the organization and the addition of new functions. In Colorado, Mississippi, and Washington there was no state welfare department of any importance prior to the depression; consequently new mechanisms were established when the present assistance program was inaugurated.

It is significant that four of the state departments in this group are responsible for at least the three types of public assistance provided in the federal Social Security Act in addition to other welfare programs. The exceptions are the Florida and Mississippi departments, but both were organized with the thought that they would be responsible for other types of aid established as the finances of the state permitted.[13]

The new units for local welfare administration in these states have the same public assistance functions as their respective state agency; thus they, likewise, are multifunctional. In all six states an entirely new local organization was provided which differed from established local patterns of welfare administration. In Colorado, Indiana, Mississippi, and New Jersey, by statute, and in Washington, by administrative order, new county welfare organizations were established to provide for coordinated administration of public assistance. The Florida law not only provided for coordinated local administration but also established

---

[13] At the time of the staff visit, both state agencies were responsible for functions other than old age assistance. Mississippi administered federal surplus commodities; Florida, in addition to commodity distribution, conducted a child welfare program and handled the certification for the various federal work programs. Florida made funds available for aid to dependent children and for blind assistance in June, 1937; these functions were subsequently assigned to the state welfare department.

new areas of local administration. These areas are districts, defined in the law, which may include from one to ten counties.

Wisconsin has achieved a consolidation only of the administration of the three types of aid under the federal Social Security Act in the new machinery which it has established. The early old age assistance law was administered in the county by the county judge, and limited state supervision was provided by the Board of Control—a state agency which, although primarily responsible for the administration of state institutions, was nevertheless a consolidated state welfare department. When new state plans of administration of old age assistance, aid to dependent children, and blind assistance were established in 1936 there was a disagreement over the assignment of these functions on both state and local levels. There was some pressure to establish them as a part of a new state welfare department to include the unemployment relief program, but an effort was also made to keep old age assistance—regarded as a "pension" program—separate from "relief activities." The compromise arrived at was a new state agency, the State Pension Department, which was made responsible for the administration of the three federally aided assistance programs. As a result, the state has three state welfare agencies: the Board of Control, the Department of Public Welfare, and the State Pension Department.[14]

On the local level, Wisconsin has more patterns of administrative organization for old age assistance than were found in other states. There are three principal types of county welfare units: the consolidated county welfare department, which includes general relief as well as old age assistance, aid to dependent children, and aid to the blind; the county pension department, responsible in most instances for old age assistance, aid to dependent children, and aid to the blind; and the county judge plan, under which that official administers one or more of the special types of assistance.[15]

[14] Legally, the Department of Public Welfare is under the State Industrial Commission, which has some indirect control over the State Pension Department, but actually no coordination in activity appears to result from this affiliation.

[15] A commission appointed by the governor recommended a coordinated plan of welfare administration for both the state and the counties. In a special session in 1937, the legislature provided for a State Department of Mental Hygiene and a State Department of Correction to take over some of the functions of the State Board of Control. In November, 1938, the governor established by executive order the State Department of Social Adjustment, to which he transferred the functions of the State Pension Department, the Department of Public Welfare, and certain noninstitutional services of the Board of Control. See "Public Welfare in Wisconsin: Preliminary Recommendations and Report of the Citizens' Committee on Public Welfare," February, 1937 (mimeographed), and Benjamin Glassberg, "Wisconsin's Increasing Public Welfare Agencies," *The Compass*, XIX (1938), 3-7.

★   ★   ★

As shown in this sample of states, the trend in the United States is toward the integration of welfare programs on both the state and local levels. In terms of service, there is no evidence that the aged suffer from this movement toward consolidation. The treatment of beneficiaries is dependent more upon public opinion, liberality of laws, adequate appropriations, and quality of personnel. In terms of administration, integration of welfare machinery presents more complex problems of organization and operation, which will be discussed in succeeding chapters.

CHAPTER 4

STATE AGENCIES: FUNCTION AND ORGANIZATION

THE PRINCIPAL FUNCTIONS of the state agency in old age assistance administration are to see that the program is in effect throughout the state and that the operating units maintain a satisfactory standard of service to the aged. In some of the earliest state laws, state participation in public assistance programs appears to have been conceived of primarily as financial aid to localities, with state activity correspondingly limited to control of local expenditures.[1] Recent state legislation, adopted to conform with the requirements of the Social Security Act, gives the state agency a role of leadership in public assistance that has shifted the emphasis of state participation from negative control to positive leadership. State supervisory efforts in particular areas, such as social service, finance, and personnel, form an important part of the state's program and receive due attention in subsequent chapters. But the central problem of administration toward which all state activities are directed is the establishment and maintenance of an effective state-wide program of old age assistance.

THE FUNCTION OF THE STATE AGENCY

The Social Security Act requires that an approved plan of old age assistance be in effect uniformly in the state, and that if it involves local administration it be mandatory upon the local units. The state law, to meet this condition, must contain mandatory provisions and must place the responsibility for enforcement of such requirements upon the state old age assistance agency. Some states have attempted to simplify compliance with this federal requirement by adopting state plans of administration so that state coverage may be effected by the establishment of branch offices throughout the state. Even in these state-operated plans, there must be some participation by local units if the plan is to be in effect universally. The required local participation in most plans

[1] For an extreme example, see Martha A. Chickering, "An Early Experiment in State Aid to the Aged, California, 1883-1895," *Social Service Review*, March, 1938, pp. 41-50.

involves the establishment and operation of an agency to perform the duties assigned to the locality by law or regulation.

State Help in Initial Organization

The formal organization of a local old age assistance unit, or of a welfare agency responsible for old age assistance, usually entails three steps. The first is legislative; ordinarily it means either the adoption of an amendment to the charter or the passage of an ordinance. The second, which gives reality to the legislative step, is the provision of funds for the operation of the agency. The third is the appointment of the executive authority for the local agency, whether this be a board or a single executive. Once these formal steps have been taken, the local organization is ready to begin its work.

Several state agencies observed took an active part in the formal organization of the local operating agencies. The state department in Wisconsin worked out with the state association of boards of county commissioners a model ordinance to be used by the counties as a basis for action in establishing county agencies. Subsequently the state officials reviewed the ordinance passed in each county. In Indiana, where new county welfare departments were to be established to succeed to some of the duties of other county officials, the law provided that[2]

> Notwithstanding the taking effect of this act, the several officers, agencies, and boards of any counties whose duties are transferred by this act to the county department of public welfare shall continue to discharge the respective duties which they were discharging at the time of the taking effect of this act, until the state department of public welfare shall certify, in writing, to the board of commissioners of any such county, that the county department of public welfare is organized, as prescribed in this act, and is prepared to assume the duties assigned to it by the provisions of this act.

This proviso was used as the sanction for requiring from each county a formal statement showing that it was organized and had met the qualifications set by the state agency. A form was prepared by the state for use by the county in submitting its statement of organization. When this statement was received from a county it was reviewed by the central state staff and submitted to the state board for approval. The approval was expressed in a formal document submitted to the county board of commissioners as a certification that the county department of welfare had been organized in accordance with the state welfare act and was "pre-

[2]Indiana, *Acts,* spec. sess. 1936, chap. 3, sec. 120.

pared to assume the duties assigned to it by the provisions of this act." [3] The effect of these two plans of reviewing the formal organizational procedure was limited, since in neither case was the action recurrent. Nevertheless, both represented a noteworthy attempt to obtain a sound organizational basis for the county work.

Several state departments have been of assistance to the local agencies in getting the program under way once the necessary legislative steps have been taken. In New Jersey, which organized its old age assistance program prior to the Social Security Act, assistance to the localities in the establishment of their work was the major activity of the state staff in the early days. New instrumentalities were organized in the counties for the administration of old age assistance. Only a small sum of money was provided by the legislature for a state staff; hence the state agency was faced with the question of determining the phases of the supervisory program to which it should devote its limited services. The state agency decided that the most important thing to be done was to establish good local organizations, and this was made the first line of attack by the state staff. In making this decision the state officials were conscious that such emphasis would mean less attention to other supervisory activities, but they felt that sound local organization would insure a substantial beginning of a successful program. The first state director described his experience as follows:

> We made it a point to attend the first called meeting of each county board, which usually took place at the county court house. When I arrived at the place of meeting I usually found a group of people sitting around a table who seemed to be acquainted with one another but who didn't seem to have much of an idea why they were there. First I would introduce myself as from the state department and explain that I was there to help them to organize. This approach was immediately appreciated since the people seemed puzzled about how to get started. We told them what officers they should elect, suggested a temporary secretary, and assisted them in other initial formalities. Having thus established an advisory relationship at the start, most of the boards immediately sought our advice on selecting a staff, and we were able subsequently to keep in close terms with them.

The state department in Florida assigned state staff members to attend the first meetings of each district welfare board. In fact, the state commissioner made it his personal responsibility to be present at the first meeting whenever he could and to assign a member of the field staff

[3] All the counties in this state had been so certified within three months after the passage of the welfare act.

to attend subsequent meetings in order that the agencies might get under way effectively.[4] At the beginning of the program in Colorado, the state department arranged two-day district meetings at specified points throughout the state for the county officials who were to be in charge of the program. The state director and a group of his technical assistants made the rounds of these meetings. The first day was devoted to a discussion, led by the director, of the state law and of the requirements to be fulfilled by the county organizations. The second day was turned over to the technical assistants, who in small group conferences worked out detailed procedures with the local representatives.

The value of these early contacts is shown by the attitude of the local agencies toward the state department. In the three states mentioned, most of the local units were, at the outset, led to look upon the state agency as a sponsor and an advisor rather than as a hostile body that was attempting to coerce them. Having established this type of relationship, the state agency was in a much more effective position later to bring about changes and improvements in the local programs.

Continuing Services to Local Agencies

Many of the state agencies observed have taken some responsibility for continuing organizational services to the local agencies, though in some states this type of activity has almost totally been neglected. Only one or two states, however, can be singled out as having any well developed service to the local departments on general administration. Since this area of supervisory activity is so frequently slighted, it is desirable to discuss various activities observed in this field.

Several states have made a practice of assigning state staff members to meet with the local boards at periodic intervals. In three instances the chief executive officer of the department or of the old age assistance bureau was giving a great amount of time to this activity. In one of these, the state commissioner had made two trips over the state, visiting the county departments; local officials were enthusiastic because he had met with them to learn about their problems at first hand and to explain to them the requirements of the state agency. Other state departments required their social service field staff to meet as frequently as possible with the local boards, or, in the absence of boards, to offer to assist the executive with his administrative problems.

A requirement that local boards submit their monthly minutes to the

[4] New Jersey and Florida have a comparatively small number of local units to deal with. Ordinarily the field staff would be responsible for local relations of this sort.

state agency has, in several instances, proved an effective tool in state supervision of the functioning of the local organization. In one state the minutes are circulated among the principal state officers so that they may keep track of what the county boards are doing. Frequently the minutes show the need for a special field visit. Another state has set up detailed requirements for the content and form of the county board minutes, which are reviewed carefully by the field staff.

A few state agencies have attempted to provide a survey service to the counties. Unfortunately most state staffs have been too busy in the initial organization of the program and the detailed actions involved to give much time to this type of work. Undoubtedly surveys that give the state a chance to participate with the locality in a complete review of the entire program provide a means of appraisal of the total local operation which can be secured in no other way.[5]

One state that reimburses the locality for part of its administrative costs has required the local agencies annually to submit a "plan of administration" for approval. This requirement has been used by some alert field-staff members as an opportunity to advise the locality on needed changes in its organization. The state regulations in another state require that the organization plan of the local agency be submitted in writing to the state department for approval, and, although not uniformly enforced, this provision has been used by the state agency as a means of bringing about a reorganization of the old age assistance work in several local districts.

A number of states have provided either for meetings of the entire group of local boards and executives or for district meetings of these local officials at which administrative questions are discussed. Although these meetings are sometimes poorly organized, ordinarily they present a medium for discussion of administrative questions that do not arise in the day-by-day control activities of the state department. They also serve as a means both for localities to air grievances and for the state to secure practical suggestions for the improvement of its own procedures.

Discipline of Localities

In the majority of systems observed where some degree of local ad-

[5] The Bureau of Public Assistance of the Social Security Board is using a device called the "administrative study" for making a complete appraisal of the effectiveness of the operation of a state program. A special staff is now maintained in the Bureau for this purpose. Unfortunately the Board has been compelled to use this staff to make investigations of state operations in several instances, and this has accentuated the inspectorial as opposed to the constructive aim of the administrative study.

ministration is maintained the state supervisory program is limited to a scrutiny of individual acts of the local units. State disciplinary action is confined to the withholding of sanction of specific action taken by the local body, such as the state's refusal to reimburse for an individual case approved for a grant in the locality, or, in those states where the state reimburses for a part of the administrative expenditures, the refusal of the state to pay its share of the salary of an individual whose qualifications do not meet the state requirements.

Most of the states visited apparently have no specific power to demand a complete reorganization of a local agency. The Indiana law is the only one noted definitely authorizing the state department to take drastic action in the event of general noncompliance by the county with the state law or regulations. The provisions for discipline in this statute are:[6]

> In administering any funds appropriated or made available to the state department for welfare purposes, the state department shall:
> (a) Require as a condition for receiving grants-in-aid that the county shall bear such proportion of the total expense of furnishing aid as is fixed by the law relating to such assistance.
> (b) Withhold any grant-in-aid to any county if the laws providing such grant-in-aid and the minimum standards prescribed by the state department thereunder are not complied with.
>
> * * * *
>
> If, in the opinion of the state board, the duties, functions and activities prescribed in this act are not performed in compliance with the provisions of this act and in accordance with the rules and regulations prescribed by the state department, as provided in this act, the state board may, after five days' notice in writing to the county board order the removal of such [county] director. The order of removal so issued shall be certified to the county board and to the auditor of the county or counties affected. Upon receipt of such order of removal, the county board shall thereupon remove such director and appoint a successor, and, upon its failure so to do, within ten days after the receipt of such order of removal, such office shall become vacant. If the county board shall fail or refuse to appoint a successor within thirty days after such removal, or if a vacancy occurring for any other cause shall not be filled within thirty days, the state board shall appoint a county director and the director so appointed shall serve at the pleasure of the state board.

Whether other state statutes could be interpreted as giving the state power to insist upon local administrative efficiency is a matter that only

[6] Indiana, *Acts,* spec. sess. 1936, chap. 3, secs. 6, 20. At the time of the staff visit, the state department in Indiana had not taken action under either of these clauses, but the law had been in effect only seven months.

the courts could decide. An instance of disciplinary action occurred in New York State prior to the receipt of federal funds. The state department withheld the entire amount of a six months' reimbursement to a large district for the following stated reasons: the district was behind in handling applications; the ratio of cases to investigators was too high; and the organization was unsatisfactory. Only when assurance was received that these shortcomings would be corrected was the money due the locality released. In another state, at the time of the staff visit, a check for quarterly reimbursement to a county was being held in the state office because the state officials were not satisfied with the county's administration of the law.

Unfortunately the Social Security Board has made disciplinary action of this type difficult through a literal interpretation of the provision of the Social Security Act that the state plan must be in effect throughout the state. As the states now understand the Board's policy, they would not be able to carry through a threat of withholding state reimbursement to a local agency to effect compliance with the state law because, if the program were in consequence suspended in a local agency, the state plan would not be in effect in all local units and would cease to have federal approval.

If the state agency under such circumstances had the power to take over and operate the local program when the county authorities were unable to provide satisfactory administration, this conflict with federal requirements would not arise. So far as is known, however, no supervisory state agency (with the exception of the Department of Social Security of Washington State) has the authority in an emergency to operate and finance a local program.[7] Although it presents some difficulties, some such provision should be included in the state law if real state control is to be assured. A saving clause of this sort not only gives the state agency the possibility of insuring that the state program will be in effect throughout the state in order to meet the technical requirements of the Board, but it also means that innocent and helpless beneficiaries of aid will not suffer through malfeasance of local officials. One difficulty, of course, is inherent in the state's use of such authority. Some

[7] In May, 1938, the Department of Social Security of Washington assumed administration of assistance in King County under authority provided in 1937: "It shall be the duty of the director of social security to fully inform the board of county commissioners of the requirements of the Federal government to require full compliance with such regulations, and in the event of noncompliance, in order to prevent interruption of Federal aid to other counties of the state, to take over administration of public assistance in the county until such compliance has been effected." (Washington, *Laws*, 1937, chap. 180, sec. 6.)

local units might be so callous and penurious that they would prefer to have the state take over the local program. It is doubtful whether this would be the point of view in many localities, but if it were, the state would find itself in a position of pauperizing some of the counties.

Since federal funds for administration are granted without restriction on their distribution by the state, provided only that they are used for administration or assistance, these funds might conceivably be used for disciplinary purposes. So far, the states have used little imagination in applying these funds, most of them having taken the line of least resistance and apportioned the money first between the state and the localities and then among the localities in accordance with their expenditures for assistance. With specific authorization in the state law, the state agency might use the federal administrative grant as a discretionary fund that could be used to assist localities in need of extra financial help, or as a bonus that would be withheld from localities refusing to comply with the major requirements of the state law.[8]

Staff Responsibility for Administrative Supervision

The continuing relationship between the state agency and the local operating units requires a conscious focusing of state staff efforts upon the central problems of local administration. This responsibility in the state office usually rests with the chief executive of the department or with a major subordinate such as the head of the bureau of public assistance, depending upon the size of the state agency, the number of welfare activities for which it is responsible, and the type of organization plan. On the whole, the state agencies have achieved a more satisfactory plan of central responsibility for local relations than has the Social Security Board. This is no doubt partly due to the greater experience of most state officials in dealing with subordinate units of government and also to the greater facility of state executives for keeping in close touch with the local executives merely because states are smaller.

Few of the states observed have officially recognized that the duties

[8]One ingenious suggestion for discipline of nonconforming local agencies was made by the governor of a western state at an early conference of state officials held by the Social Security Board. Although, so far as is known, this scheme has not been tried and would require legislative authorization before any state could experiment with it, it has some elements of common sense which recommend it. This governor proposed that if a state wished to discipline a county by withdrawing state aid, the state should be empowered to place the responsibility for the old age assistance program thus curtailed in one of the adjacent counties. This would mean that old age assistance for the defaulting county would be administered by a neighboring county. The governor suggested that no county would be willing to tolerate for long the management of its relief activities by a rival county and would quickly mend its ways.

of the field staff should include supervision of the total local operation. Where this responsibility has been recognized, the social service field staff is usually made responsible for such field efforts in the absence of employees specifically designated for this purpose. The social service field staffs in five states observed are concerned to some degree with local administration in addition to the supervision of those activities which would strictly be defined as social service. In these instances the social service field staffs are not engaged in the routine review of large numbers of individual cases; their time can accordingly be devoted to more constructive supervisory efforts.

With the development of specialized field staffs for auditing and reporting, in addition to the social service staff, the state agencies are facing a problem of coordinating the field force so that the relations of the state to the local agencies may be centered through a single channel. Most states cannot afford a separate administrative field staff in addition to the specialized representatives. To meet this problem, Indiana and Wisconsin have been developing the social service staff as an administrative field staff. This has meant that in appointing field representatives they have endeavored to select employees who are not only competent in technical aspects of social service but who have also had some experience in administration.[9]

The important objective is the establishment of a main line of relationship between the state agency and the operating units. This may be achieved by the designation of the social service staff as the administrative field staff, if it consists of properly qualified employees. Technical staffs may then work in the localities on matters of finance, statistics, or special social service problems. The findings of these staffs, however, must be interpreted to the local administrator by the administrative field staff. If the problem to be discussed is of such a technical nature that the administrative representative cannot handle it adequately, the specialized field person should present his findings to the local administrator with the full knowledge and consent of the administrative field worker; the latter official should have the opportunity to be on hand when the presentation is made if he believes his participation is desirable.

No instances have been discovered of confusion arising in local jurisdictions from conflicting instructions of different representatives of the

[9] The new plan of operation in New York State decentralizes state supervision through district offices. The head of the district office is responsible for the total relations of the state department with the local agencies in his district on all aspects of the program.

state agency, comparable to those caused in the states by uncoordinated federal representatives. This is not necessarily to the credit of the states studied because, for one thing, the states had not at the time of this study developed extensive specialized field services. Field auditing, for example, had only recently gone into effect in the few states that had undertaken this activity. With the refinement and extension of the state field services, the problem of coordination of these activities will be a matter for major concern in state administration if the state agencies are to achieve an effective and productive plan for maintaining good local administration of old age assistance.

INTERNAL ORGANIZATION OF STATE AGENCIES

The state welfare agencies supervising old age assistance administration vary from the simple department responsible for a single program to complex, multifunctional departments. The problem of internal organization will be considered first under the following headings representing the principal administrative activities of state agencies relating to old age assistance: social service activities, fiscal activities, research and statistical services, and personnel activities. Since the state agency is primarily responsible for the supervision of the local operation, the problem of administrative coordination is complex, for financial, reporting, and personnel activities are as much a part of the total supervisory effort as is the social service activity. Consequently, detailed consideration will be given to the patterns developed in the organization of state agencies to obtain coordinated administration and to the problem of field-staff organization.

Social Service Activities

The form of organization of the state social service staff is determined in part by the nature of the duties of these workers. In the majority of states visited, the state agency is confronted with the task of reviewing a large number of individual cases either because the authorization of all grants is made in the state office or because the principal method of control employed by the state is the scrutiny of all cases approved for a grant by the local agencies. The magnitude of this reviewing job and the fact that it entails specialized, routine work have apparently led to the segregation of the social service activities affecting old age assistance in a unit in the state office independent of other social service activities of the agency. It usually follows that the social service field staff also operates only in the field of old age assistance.

In the states that do not review or act upon individual cases in the state office, a generalized social service staff is found which supervises local operations in several types of assistance. The central social service staff is engaged in the preparation of manuals and instructions to provide the basis for better operation in the localities. Likewise, the field staff is more concerned with organization and administrative matters in the local agencies than with the action taken on individual cases. The primary concern of the members of the field staff is to develop good local administration, but they are expected to give some attention to sample individual cases as a means of directing the work of the local units along more constructive lines. Specialists in problems of the aged, the blind, children, etc., may supplement the work of the generalized staff.

Financial Activities

Financial activities of the state agencies serve two distinct purposes. In one group are those activities involved in the administration of the agency itself—the facilitative services[10] of the state department. These include budget preparation, appropriation accounting, bookkeeping, pay-roll preparation, etc. The other activities are those directly concerned with the administration of the old age assistance program or other assistance programs in which the state participates financially. In the state plans in which disbursement of assistance is made locally, these latter fiscal activities consist chiefly of the control measures used to insure the authenticity of the claim for reimbursement made by the local agencies. When disbursement is made from the state office, they include the operations performed in the payment of individual assistance grants.

The financial activities that are a part of the internal management of the agency are not essentially different from those in any public agency. But the control of state reimbursement to localities for grants of assistance and the direct state disbursement of assistance grants are financial problems peculiar to all forms of public assistance in which the state participates. The facilitative activities will not be considered in detail in this study; the discussion of financial problems will largely be focused upon the fiscal procedures required for the assistance program. In the discussion of the organization of the financial staff of the state

---

[10] "Institutional services" is the term used more commonly to describe this class of activities, but in the field of public welfare administration the term "institutional" used in this sense is confused with the function of institutional management. See W. F. Willoughby, *Principles of Public Administration*, pp. 45-46.

agency, however, the relationship of the two spheres of financial activity must be considered.

Two principal patterns of organization of financial activities are found within the state agencies. In one plan all financial activities of the department, both the facilitative and those of the assistance program, are carried on by the same division; under the other plan the financial procedures of old age assistance are detached from the facilitating activities and are made part of the responsibility of the old age assistance division or of a general public assistance division.

A central finance unit is usually found in the type of state agency that has as its principal function the administration of the state's share in old age assistance or in several public assistance programs. The preponderant fiscal activities in an agency of this type are those involved in the assistance programs. The fiscal services required in the operation of the agency itself are sufficiently simple that they may be provided by the same unit that handles the financial aspects of the assistance programs without interfering with this primary operation.

The financial activities relating to old age assistance are generally placed in an old age assistance division or in a public assistance division in the state agencies that have more complex and diversified financial problems. The New Jersey Department of Institutions and Agencies, for example, is responsible for the administration of state welfare institutions as well as for participation in the financing of three types of public assistance. The specialized fiscal problems in these operations are sufficiently different that they may be separated, and, so far as old age assistance is concerned, decentralization of fiscal responsibility to the bureau of old age assistance has made possible a close integration of the review of cases and the financial audit of claims. The central division of audits and accounts in this department maintains general oversight of the fiscal operations in the various bureaus and institutions and also is responsible for the internal financial management of the department itself.

The problem of financial administration in the Connecticut Department of Public Welfare is complex because in old age assistance, disbursement of individual grants is made from the state office while other public assistance programs are operated on a reimbursement plan. The advantages of decentralization of fiscal activities to the bureau of old age assistance in this state are readily apparent since the final authorization of grants and the issuance of checks must be closely related. The Massachusetts Department of Public Welfare, which is responsible for a diversified program, has placed the responsibility for all reimbursement of localities for various types of public assistance in the finance section of the division of aid and relief, of which the bureau of old age assistance is one unit. Other types of fiscal activity are assigned to the respective functional divisions of the department.

Only four of the state departments—California, Colorado, Indiana, and Wisconsin—had a field-auditing service at the time of the staff visit. In most of the other states observed the supervision over local assistance expenditures is limited to an audit of local claims, which is made in the state office.[11] In Colorado, field auditors, who are expected to make an inspection of the books of every county department, work out from the state auditor's office, although they are paid by the Department of Public Welfare and are under its general supervision. In the other three states the field auditors are employees of the welfare department.[12]

Statistical and Research Services

All the states studied except three have established a central-staff unit for both the statistical and the research program, the director of which is responsible to the head of the department. In these states the principal research activities are carried on as a direct activity of this central division. Two plans are followed, however, for the gathering and compilation of statistical data. In five of the state agencies all the statistical work is done directly in the central division. In contrast, in four state departments the basic statistical tabulations for old age assistance are made in the bureau of old age assistance but under the general supervision of the director of the central division of research and statistics. Both plans seem to be satisfactory arrangements under the circumstances in which they are used, though the effectiveness of the decentralized system appears to depend upon the amount and the intensity of the supervision given by the director of the central division. When the detailed recording is removed from his immediate supervision, the director is sometimes inclined to be less troubled about the details of its operation and to become engrossed in more fascinating problems of exploratory research to the detriment of the compilation of basic data. The decentralized plan appears to insure better integration of reporting with the other supervisory activities in old age assistance.

[11] See chap. 14.
[12] The New York State Department of Social Welfare is not included in this list. This Department formerly conducted the audit of local claims in the state office but, under a new plan, field audits are made by representatives of the State Comptroller's Office.

Personnel Activities

Personnel activities of the state agencies are of two types. In the first place, there is the personnel work involved in the management of the central state staff. In addition, some of the states maintain a program of personnel control as a part of the supervision of the local agencies.

In none of the states studied is there a major personnel unit for personnel management in the central state agency alone. Usually these management activities are conducted within the central finance unit or directly within the commissioner's office. In Wisconsin the personnel activities are performed almost entirely by the central state personnel agency. An unusual program is found in Indiana, where the state welfare department, in conjunction with the state unemployment compensation division, operates a personnel agency that serves both state departments. Although it has some responsibility to the two state departments, the personnel agency maintains a semi-independent status, which is desirable under the circumstances. By recent amendment of the law, its scope has been extended to include the appointment of some county welfare employees.

Two state agencies have considered the problem of local personnel sufficiently important to maintain a personnel service in the state office. In Washington State, where all local employees were state appointed, a member of the commissioner's immediate staff was responsible for all personnel records, appointment procedures, and pay-roll approvals; and the professional side of recruitment and training was handled by the assistant director of the department, who was, in a sense, the head of social service activities. The responsibility for the operation of the merit system in Florida, under which all employees of the district boards must qualify, was originally in the hands of a personnel officer on the central staff. This position was later placed in the bureau of public assistance of the department.[13]

EXECUTIVE CONTROL AND ADMINISTRATIVE COORDINATION

Important as is each of the administrative activities, they are subordinate to the most vital problem of state agency administration: the channeling of all these activities into executive action. The organization

[13] The New York State Department of Social Welfare has added a personnel officer to its staff under its reorganized plan of operation. The personnel unit in this plan is responsible for both departmental personnel matters and for supervisory activities relating to local personnel.

chart represents a formalized conception of the plan to effect coordinated executive action; but it must be remembered that organization charts, useful as they are, do not determine the efficiency of an agency's operation; they represent only a basic arrangement of the staff of a department. The test of administration is found in the vision and ability of the personnel working within the scheme or organization and in the capacity of the chief executive to make the administration of the agency a dynamic rather than a routine mechanical operation.

Central-Staff Organization

The lines of effort that must be brought together for executive action

FIGURE 2. ORGANIZATION OF UNIFUNCTIONAL AGENCY

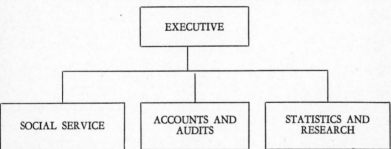

are most clearly seen in a state department responsible only for old age assistance.[14] The function of a state agency in old age assistance is the conduct of relationships with local agencies or branch offices to insure that the state law and state regulations are adhered to so that those eligible for the benefits of the program are adequately served. The supervisory program is broken down into specialized activities, but the head of the agency is responsible for the total operation and keeps its direction focused upon the main objectives of the program. The simple organization plan in the unifunctional agency is based on the pattern illustrated by Figure 2.

When the state agency is responsible for the administration of two or more programs of public assistance, the task of coordination in executive control immediately becomes twofold. Administrative integration must be achieved not only among the supervisory activities within each pro-

[14] For purposes of analyzing the organization of the state agency as a whole, the problems of the state agency which supervises local activities will be considered primarily, since this is the method of administration used in most state plans. By reference to previous material the reader may adapt the principles drawn in this chapter to state plans having centralized operations.

gram of public assistance (intraprogram) but also among the two or more programs (interprogram). Unaided, the chief executive cannot readily maintain both intraprogram and interprogram coordination for two or more types of public assistance; consequently mechanisms of integration must be worked out at a level below the director. This need has led to the development of two patterns of organization, one of which secures interprogram coordination on the staff level, leaving to the executive the problem of intraprogram coordination. This, for convenience, may be called the "generalized plan." The "categorical" scheme reverses this plan: on the staff level, coordination within each program is maintained, and the executive is responsible for the coordination of the total programs.

FIGURE 3. GENERALIZED ORGANIZATION OF A MULTIFUNCTIONAL AGENCY

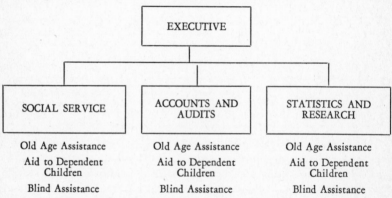

The generalized plan, illustrated by Figure 3, provides for the organization of the staff according to technical fields of work. The same group of social workers supervises old age assistance, aid to dependent children, and blind assistance, and keeps them integrated within their share of the total supervisory program. Likewise, one group of auditors handles the financial control of all three aids. The executive in this plan has the primary responsibility to see that a balance is maintained among the various lines or fields of supervision. This plan is used most by state agencies, such as those in Wisconsin, Florida, and Colorado,[15] that have relatively few, if any, functions aside from public assistance activities. It requires much more detailed attention of the executive than does the

---

[15] It is also the general pattern followed in the Indiana organization except that some integration of services on a secondary level has been provided by placing financial and statistical activities and several other administrative services under a single subexecutive.

categorical plan not only because the problems of intraprogram coordination are subtle but also because lack of integration among the
fields of state activity has more violent repercussions upon local administrative officers. For example, the line of division of jurisdiction
between social service supervision and the financial audit is not always
clearly established, and if a local agency receives conflicting instructions
from different representatives of the state agency on the same issue, the
local authorities are confused and the state loses prestige.

FIGURE 4.   CATEGORICAL ORGANIZATION OF A MULTIFUNCTIONAL AGENCY

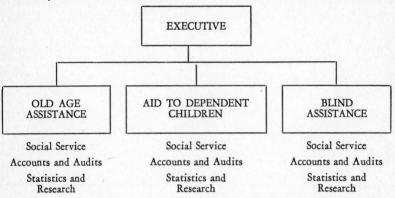

The categorical plan, shown in Figure 4, is employed with local modifications in the state departments of New Jersey and Connecticut, which
are large agencies responsible for a number or a variety of welfare functions.[16] It provides a subunit for each special type of public assistance.
The intraprogram coordination is handled by the head of the functional
division, who serves as a subexecutive, and the interprogram coordination is the responsibility of the chief executive officer. The main draw-
backs to this plan are that these units are likely to become too self-
sufficient; that duplication of specialized staff services frequently occurs;
and that both state and local welfare planning tend to become concerned
with particular categories rather than with the assistance program as a
whole.[17]

A modification of these two patterns appears in an organization which

[16] This plan was also followed in New York State prior to the 1937 reorganization.

[17] It is also significant that the states organized according to this pattern operate under
a number of public assistance laws which are less uniform in their administrative provisions than are the statutes in the states which have more recently adopted programs
of special aid, or which have recently amended their laws to obtain the uniformity which
the former states lack.

is illustrated by Figure 5. This plan provides categorical social service supervision and generalized financial and statistical services. Since neither interprogram nor intraprogram coordination is completely achieved at an administrative level below that of the chief executive of the department, a heavy burden is thrown upon that official. The California Department, which is organized in this fashion, has attempted to lighten the load of the executive by establishing the position of "administrator of social security program" to provide administrative coordination for the public assistance programs receiving federal aid. This device has not worked well, partly because the responsibility of this official was never clearly analyzed, nor were his duties clearly specified.

FIGURE 5.   PARTLY CATEGORICAL AND PARTLY GENERALIZED ORGANIZATION
OF A MULTIFUNCTIONAL AGENCY

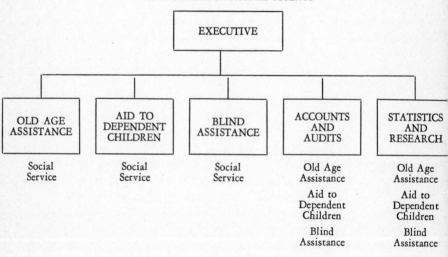

The organization of public assistance in Massachusetts resembles the pattern represented by Figure 5, but with an important difference. Under the chief executive of the Department of Public Welfare is a subexecutive in charge of the public assistance work of the Department. Within the public assistance division (known as the Division of Aid and Relief) are categorical units for social service supervision and a generalized unit of accounting and auditing. Thus the chief executive, relieved of the responsibility for coordination in this area, has as his major job the administrative coordination of public assistance with the other functions of the department.

Field-Staff Organization

The field staff is the state agency's most important link with the operating units. The scope of activity of the field staff is determined by the conception which the state agency has of its supervisory responsibility. Many of the states studied regard their function as primarily that of protecting state funds from misuse by the local units. Where this negative approach predominates, the field staff gives its major attention to detailed review of action taken by the operating unit on individual cases. In other states, however, the major emphasis of the field staff has come to be placed upon the improvement of local administration.

A supervisory program that aims to improve local administration should ideally encompass the entire group of activities involved. Most states, however, have been unable to afford separate field employees for social service, finance, statistics, and general administration. All states observed that provide some field service have specialists in social service activities supervising the local units. Field-audit service has been developed in some of the states. No state observed had a field staff to supervise local reporting and recording, but in several instances the statistician in the state office advised the localities through the social service field staff.

In addition to social service supervision, some of the state field workers, employed primarily for social service supervision, give advice and assistance to the local districts on the organization and operation of the agency. This is, in fact, the major activity of the field staff in five of the states visited. Some field workers in two other states render incidental service of this nature to the localities, but it is not officially recognized as a part of their duties. This type of supervisory activity is performed by the central old age assistance staff in New Jersey, and in three other states central-staff members give advice on organization matters to the local units, supplementing the work of the field staff.

Two states that employ field auditors—Indiana and Wisconsin—recognize that in order to avoid confusion in the local agencies it is desirable to establish some precedence of one arm of the field staff over the other. These two state agencies are attempting to develop as the basic administrative field staff a group of workers who are not only technically proficient in social service matters but also competent to advise the counties on administrative problems. Consequently, the auditors are expected to defer to these workers on matters arising locally which have administrative implications.

When both the state and local agencies are responsible for more than one public assistance program, the state department must decide whether it will have specialized field workers representing each type of aid or whether it will employ generalized workers to represent the total assistance program of the state in dealing with local agencies. The newer welfare departments that have organized a central bureau of public assistance have uniformly adopted the plan of having generalized field workers perform the supervisory functions for the total assistance program. This has reduced to a minimum the number of state representatives with whom the local welfare official has to deal. The antithesis of this system, however, is seen in the Massachusetts department. Even though the public assistance activities have been grouped together in a central division—the Division of Aid and Relief—each bureau within that division has its own field representatives. Thus the local welfare director deals with separate state representatives on matters pertaining to old age assistance, aid to dependent children, and unsettled general-relief cases. The California department, which, as indicated above, has achieved only a limited coordination of old age assistance, aid to dependent children, and aid to the blind in the state office, is developing a unified field service by which a single worker visiting the county will represent all three programs.

All the states having a field staff face the problem how best to cover the state with the number of field workers that they are able to employ. Most of the states have adopted a territorial plan. A region composed of a group of counties is assigned to each worker. These regions are selected on the basis of such factors as total population, relief population, natural areas formed by common economic interests, and ease of transportation, but no organized field offices are maintained.

The Massachusetts plan of field-staff assignment is based primarily upon the concept that the chief function of these workers is to review or reinvestigate cases; therefore the territory of the worker is so arranged that he will be responsible for about seven hundred cases. In the rural areas some allowance is made for time consumed in travel so that the case load may be proportionately lighter. For the large cities this plan results in an arrangement that divides the city among several state workers, no one of whom is responsible for the total relations of the state agency with the city department. For example, when the work was observed, the city of Worcester was divided between two workers, and the city of Boston, among eight.[18] The territory of each state worker in these cities bears no relationship to the administrative organization of

[18] Some of the workers also covered small towns adjoining the large city.

the city staff. This demonstrates that the Massachusetts supervisory plan is chiefly concerned with the negative control of the social audit and that little attention is paid to problems of local administration.

Most plans of field-staff organization observed provide for covering the entire state with a fairly uniform pattern of services, but a few states have recognized that the largest city in the state presents a special problem of supervision. Frequently the large city has a quality of administration equal or superior to that of the state agency, and intensive supervision by the state is a duplication of high-grade supervision performed within the unit itself. Even where its performance is not high-grade, the large urban unit has problems of staff organization and administration that are quite different from those in smaller agencies. Examples of flexible service to urban units may be cited. The state of Washington, under its original plan, had one large metropolitan unit—King County (Seattle). The state department avoided the problem of duplicating local supervisory work by naming the chief supervisor of the King County organization as the state field supervisor for this and a small adjoining county; the plan appears to have worked satisfactorily. The Indiana Department assigns a single state worker to supervise Marion County (Indianapolis), the largest county in the state. The Colorado department has omitted Denver from its regular field territory, and the head of the bureau of public assistance assumes direct responsibility for this, the largest local unit in the state.[19]

★   ★   ★

The state welfare agency today bears the main responsibility for the effectiveness of public assistance programs. In view of the limited experience of public welfare officials with the supervisory approach inherent in the responsibility to see that a program of public assistance is well administered by subordinate local units throughout a state, considerable progress has been made in developing effective organizations. In observing the experience in old age assistance, however, one is struck by the fact that too much attention is still being given to minutiae of control rather than to constructive supervision. Most state agencies can well afford to re-examine their basic structure and procedures to see whether they are directing their efforts along the simplest lines of helping the local units to give adequate service to the aged.

[19] In New York State the new plan of field organization provides a separate area office to supervise all state welfare activities for New York City alone.

CHAPTER 5

LOCAL AGENCIES: FUNCTION AND ORGANIZATION

THE MAIN FUNCTION of the local or operating agency in old age assistance administration is the authorization and payment of grants of aid to eligible applicants. Executive authority in local agencies is assigned by law either to a board, a single executive, or a combination of board and executive. Regardless of the degree of authority of the boards where they exist, a paid officer was found in all agencies observed who bore major executive responsibility. It is desirable, however, to discuss the function and organization of local agencies without taking the boards into consideration, in order to visualize clearly the processes involved.[1]

THE FUNCTION OF LOCAL AGENCIES

The operating agency in old age assistance is ordinarily a unit of local government, though in three states observed payment of assistance is made from the state office, with some of the operating activities carried on by local units.[2] Whether the operating unit is a local agency or a branch of a state agency has little effect upon the principles involved in action on individual cases, though it affects considerably the processes that lead up to administrative action.[3]

The exact nature of the decision in individual old age assistance cases is often obscured by the fact that in large-scale operation it is necessary to reduce administrative processes to the simplest possible routine in order to get the work done. Its true nature is also often lost sight of because administrators frequently delegate the bulk of the responsibility for individual case action to a case-work supervisor who, in turn, may pass responsibility to subordinate supervisors. Despite the variety of practices, executive responsibility is clear cut and definite and must be

---

[1] The part played by boards in old age assistance administration is discussed in chap. 17.
[2] See chap. 2.
[3] These processes form the major part of the discussion of Part II.

sharply distinguished from the technical and facilitative phases of operation if sound administration is to be achieved.

The decision on individual cases occurs after the executive authority has received the results of the investigation of an application for old age assistance from the social worker or the social service department. The report of the investigation usually contains a determinative recommendation on eligibility, and, if that is affirmative, a recommendation on the size of the grant needed. The executive's function is to act upon the recommendations. He makes his decision by considering the recommendations in terms of the policies of the agency, the state laws and regulations, and the availability of funds for assistance. When he has made the decision, the executive bears the responsibility for the action taken. If a supervisory agency or the applicant questions the decision, the executive is the one who must defend it.

Obviously the executive officer of a large agency cannot and should not pass in detail upon every case. To expedite the work he delegates part or all of this responsibility to trained subordinates; if such delegation is properly made, the subordinates are equipped with clear statements of policy to govern their executive action. Policy in this sense is the expression of executive decision on a case or a class of cases which has been so formulated that it may subsequently be applied in similar cases without individual reference to the executive.

The administration of old age assistance is so circumscribed by laws and regulations that if the facts have been gathered and interpreted satisfactorily, the scope of administrative discretion in individual cases is ordinarily limited. In most cases appearing for decision the major task of the executive is to see that a completed investigation has been made and that the facts disclosed by it have correctly been interpreted. A review of this type can usually be made for the executive by a casework supervisor, who is able at the same time to use the results of the review to guide the staff in subsequent investigations.

Despite the multiplicity of regulations on procedure and action in the operating agency, new circumstances constantly arise for which no precedent or regulation exists. For example, the establishment of the federal works program in 1935 raised a new set of problems about eligibility. Were W.P.A. earnings to be regarded as wages covering the requirements of all members of a household including an aged spouse or parent? Most states eventually set up rules on W.P.A. employment but in the meantime the local executive was compelled to decide cases involving W.P.A. wages.

The distinct nature of the executive decision is brought into sharp relief when the funds of the operating agency are too limited to meet the local share of assistance costs. When funds are adequate to grant eligible applicants the required amount of assistance, the recommendations for individual grants made by the social service division are usually determinative in their effect. When the financial resources are less than the sum needed, the executive authority must determine what modifications are to be made both in the acceptance of new applicants and in the revision of grants previously authorized. The manner in which executive decision comes into play under these circumstances is illustrated in one community visited. The local appropriating body had failed to grant an additional sum of money needed both to carry the list of recipients already granted assistance and to provide for the acceptance of new applicants. To meet the shortage, a special staff was assigned to review large numbers of cases to see whether the grant of assistance might be adjusted downward. Each case recommended for reduction received an individual executive review. This procedure proved so time consuming, however, that it was abandoned, and uniform cuts in grants were decided upon for all recipients of more than a certain amount of aid. Even this wholesale plan of reduction was accompanied by the administrative review of selected cases in which it was felt that the lower amount of relief would cause a severe hardship. Whether the grants were reduced individually or in groups, an executive decision was made that arrived at an amount of assistance representing a compromise between the budgetary needs of the aged person as determined by social investigation and the amount that could be granted in view of the total sum made available.[4]

In his responsibility to see that approved grants are made available to the recipient at the earliest possible date, the executive officer has a coordinating function to perform which involves bringing into play the entire mechanism of the agency. In a small operating unit this presents no great problem since staff relationships are simple and direct, and the load of work is usually not heavy enough in itself to cause delay. In large organizations, however, there is frequently considerable delay in putting a decision into action—that is, in getting a check to an applicant who has been declared eligible—merely because of the complexity of administrative procedures or because services within the agency are not properly geared. In one large agency there was a minimum delay of

[4]The alternatives facing an operating unit when funds are limited are discussed in detail in chap. 9.

from three to six weeks from the time when a decision was made on a case until the first check was received by the applicant. This delay was attributable partly to the inadequacy of clerical staff to prepare the records on the cases and partly to the use of hand methods in the disbursement process. Although a larger staff and better equipment would have eliminated some of the gap between decision and payment, it was obvious to an observer that the disbursing staff was more concerned about the minutiae of its own job than the social effects of delay in payment. It was also clear that more attention by the executive to coordination of the administrative efforts would have eliminated much of the delay.

Ignorance of the philosophy or of the techniques either of social service administration or of financial administration is likely to make the executive the victim of the aggressiveness of one or the other staff group. Thus, in the above-mentioned instance, financial procedures dominated the administration to the detriment of the beneficiaries of the program largely because the executive was not well enough informed on fiscal matters to be able to speed up the activities of a meticulous accounting staff through simplification of the procedures. A peculiar psychological attitude often appears in the executive who knows one phase of administration well and is ignorant of the others. Instead of giving the weight of his authority to the side of the program that he knows best, he is apt to be controlled unconsciously by those elements of administration that he does not fully comprehend. For example, an executive who is highly skilled in the social service aspects of the program and has little knowledge of the financial procedures is frequently overimpressed by the requirements of his fiscal assistants. Since he does not understand accounting and disbursing procedures, he permits the demands of the financial department to stand unchallenged and thus allows the program to be dominated by considerations which are primarily restrictive.[5] Likewise, an executive without social service train-

---

[5] This is a problem met in other fields of management as the following quotation indicates: "Of course, the reason that many accounting departments have assumed responsibility closely akin to the functions of command lies largely in the fact that altogether too many, one might say the great majority of, operating executives know so little about accounting, accounts, and statistics that they are unable to use accounting and statistical data properly to make operating decisions. Failure so to do almost inevitably leads a major executive to rely too much on the judgment as well as the analytical ability of his accounting department and too often operating executives discover that the situation which has thus arisen offers them a beautiful alibi for operating inefficiency." W. J. Donald, "Essentials of Large Scale Organization," in *Handbook of Business Administration* (1937), p. 1505.

ing or experience may, through his ignorance, permit the social service department to dominate the other phases of management.[6]

In order to effect a productive working plan between the social service staff and the accounting staff the executive must recognize the fundamental conflict between the two groups. The social service staff is close to the needs of the beneficiaries of the program; hence the importance of prompt payment of assistance is real to them. The fiscal officers are more keenly aware of the necessity for keeping exact records of all transactions and of preserving complete accountability; quite naturally they see the performance of the steps in the disbursing process as the principal desideratum. Effective executive control is attained when a proper balance is maintained between these two forces—when benefits are made available to those in need with the maximum speed possible within the procedures required by the financial regulations. No formula can be stated to guide the executive in arriving at this administrative balance. He achieves it through the use of imagination and skill tempered by knowledge of the processes involved both on the social service and the financial side of the agency. The executive must be fundamentally equipped with an understanding and zeal to care for the needs of the aged but at the same time he must be aware that he is an accountable public official.[7]

THE INTERNAL ORGANIZATION OF LOCAL AGENCIES

In all the states studied, at least one operating activity is always carried on at the local level, the maintenance of direct relationship with applicants for and recipients of aid. In addition there may or may not be other administrative operations. Also, the local agency is usually responsible for the administration, in whole or in part, of other welfare services. Thus, the problem of organization of the typical local agency involves the alignment of staff for several administrative activities and usually for several welfare functions.

Organization becomes a significant problem only when the local agency carries on different welfare functions or is responsible for a sufficiently large case load to require a corps of workers. Obviously, no plan of organization is needed in small local units when one worker performs all the duties of the agency. Organization in a one-man agency

[6] In one county the director had permitted the case-work supervisor to dictate the selection and assignment of persons performing fiscal and office management duties for which a coordinate division head was in reality responsible.

[7] The procedures involved in the decision on individual cases are discussed in chap. 9.

consists largely of self-organization—that is, management by the individual of his own time so that the proper balance is given to his various responsibilities.

The organization for the execution of the social service program, the arrangement of the other administrative activities to facilitate its operation, and the provision for executive coordination and control are the principal organizational problems of local agencies. Although the structure varies somewhat among the local agencies studied, certain general patterns prevail. These principal problems are considered in the order mentioned.

Social Service Activities

If the local agency is responsible only for old age assistance, the objectives of the organization of the social service division are chiefly those of arranging for staff supervision, making the proper integration of the activities of consultants and auxiliary workers, and providing for an equitable distribution of the work. Before these topics are discussed, however, problems of organization peculiar to local agencies responsible also for other types of assistance will be examined.[8]

A convenient method of staff organization for a variety of assistance programs is to employ generalized workers[9] to be responsible for all types of assistance. The organization then becomes one of deploying the workers to cover the territory assigned to the operating unit. Under this plan, staff organization becomes largely a problem of distribution of workers to meet population and geographic requirements. Only one supervisor is needed for the smaller agencies, and a series of unit or junior supervisors, in the larger ones. The principal argument for the generalized staff is that it provides better and more economical service to the beneficiaries. Its use is becoming more and more common, particularly in smaller communities. For the most part agencies in large metropolitan counties or large cities have not used this type of staff organization. The claim is usually made that the advantages of a generalized plan are more than offset by the difficulty of training a large

[8] The functions of an operating unit in public welfare divide themselves on the basis of method of treatment into two principal groups: institutional care, and direct service to individuals. Since this report is primarily concerned with old age assistance, which falls into the latter category, only incidental attention will be given to institutional programs.

[9] By generalized worker is meant a social case worker who is responsible for more than one type of public assistance. In contrast, a specialized worker is one responsible for only a single type (or category) of assistance.

number of workers in the special requirements and regulations of several types of aid.[10]

King County (Seattle), Washington, with a population of approximately 464,000 (1930), is the largest unit observed with a generalized staff responsible for several categories of assistance including care of the aged. One set of case workers, grouped under supervisors in district offices, is responsible for all relations with applicants and recipients. The same scheme prevails in El Paso County (Colorado Springs), Colorado, with a population of about 50,000 (1930), where a staff of fourteen workers, working from a central office under a single supervisor, is responsible for general relief, old age assistance, aid to dependent children, and blind assistance. The staff of the district boards of social welfare in Florida are organized on a generalized basis. The typical plan of staff organization in the districts is to assign a worker to each county and to place a unit supervisor over a group of these workers, the unit supervisors reporting to a chief supervisor or to the district director if no chief supervisor is employed.

The grouping of the social service staff of a local public assistance agency may be made on the basis of the types of individuals served— that is, in terms of the special techniques or special information needed to deal with various groups in the population. On this principle a public assistance staff may be subdivided to serve any of the following six groups, or several of them in combination, depending on the functions included in the agency's program: aged, blind, children, veterans, the unemployed, or the residual dependents. This use of a specialized staff is sometimes known as categorical administration.

An example of complete categorical administration of public assistance is found in Oneida County, New York, where there is a social service division handling home relief (general relief); an old age assistance division; a child welfare division handling mothers' aid; and a single worker handling blind assistance. In the Department of Public Welfare of Boston, Massachusetts, units are maintained to handle mothers' aid, dependent aid (general relief), and old age assistance. The Marion County (Indianapolis), Indiana, Department of Public Welfare has

[10] The New York City Department of Welfare established one district on the generalized plan in September, 1937; although the intention to extend this to other districts in the city was announced at the time, no other districts had been placed on a generalized basis by December, 1938. The authors of this report will be condemned alike by the proponents and opponents of noncategorical administration for not declaring positively for or against the plan. An objective evaluation of categorical and noncategorical administration needs badly to be made but such an evaluation was beyond the scope of this study. Satisfactory provision for the aged was found under both systems—and unsatisfactory care likewise.

one unit handling aid to dependent children; one, assistance to the blind; and one, old age assistance. Public assistance in the New York City Department of Public Welfare is administered through separate units responsible for old age assistance, veteran relief, blind relief, and home relief.[11]

Several examples of combinations may be cited. In the social service division of the Los Angeles County Department of Charities, indigent relief and aid to dependent children are in one unit; blind assistance and old age assistance are grouped together in a coordinate unit known as the adult state-aid section. In one Wisconsin county, old age assistance and blind assistance are grouped together, but aid to dependent children is carried by the general-relief staff. Another county department in this state has one section for aid to dependent children only, and one that handles aid for the aged and the blind.

The organization of the local social service staff may be affected by provisions of the state law. For example, the Massachusetts statute requires that there be a separate bureau of old age assistance within the local board of public welfare. Although the law is not uniformly adhered to throughout the state, nevertheless it is responsible in some instances for the establishment within the local welfare department of a special division of the staff for old age assistance only. A separate bureau is not required by statute for aid to dependent children; this function is usually handled in connection with general relief in the Massachusetts towns and cities.

Some counties which include a large city and a surrounding rural area have worked out a combination of a specialized staff for the city and a generalized staff for the rural districts. A department of this type is found in San Diego County, California. This arrangement is justified by the director on the grounds that an urban organization works better with specialized workers, while generalized workers serve a scattered territory more satisfactorily.

SUPERVISION AND COORDINATION OF THE SOCIAL SERVICE STAFF.[12] In the smallest agencies the executive also acts as supervisor; this type of position may be classed as the director-supervisor. This official performs the executive duties in the agency and at the same time gives some time to the supervision of the case-work staff. As soon as the administrative duties of the head of the operating agency are sufficient to absorb the

---

[11] See page 66, n. 10.

[12] The concern here is primarily with the control and coordinating functions of supervision rather than the technical phases of supervisory activity.

major amount of his time, a separate supervisor is needed to coordinate and direct the activities of the social work staff. This supervisor, working under the director, heads the social service division.

If a specialized staff is used, it is desirable to have supervision for each of the major groupings of the staff, and the coordination of the several programs becomes important. The activities of the supervisors may be coordinated by the executive of the department; or he may find it necessary, especially in a large agency, to have a chief supervisor in charge of all the social service activities. The use of a central supervisor of a group of programs is best shown in the Boston Department of Public Welfare, in which each of the three specialized social service divisions has its own head supervisor; but the supervisors are all under a single director of social service. One two-county unit in the state of Washington has specialized workers; but a single supervisor, working under the director, is responsible for the supervision of all programs in both counties.

Some agencies have not worked out any well-planned system of central coordination of the supervision of social service activities. In three welfare departments visited, separate supervisors are maintained for the separate units in the department, without a central or head supervisor.[13] In one county observed, general relief is under a single supervisor; but old age assistance and blind relief, which are in a unit together, are under the direct supervision of the executive, as are also the other activities of the department, such as veteran relief. In one large county agency there are three main staff units, each of which theoretically has its own supervisor. Actually, however, a member of the governing board of the county department acts as supervisor and reviewer for the work of two of these units.

CONSULTANTS AND AUXILIARY WORKERS. In larger operating units it is frequently found desirable to employ consultants to advise on particular problems of the assistance program, who are usually from the following fields: medical care, insurance, property, employment, and home economics. Ordinarily they advise the staff workers on difficult cases or special aspects of cases, though occasionally they may engage in direct activities, such as carrying a limited case load.[14]

Besides the consultants, auxiliary workers or groups of auxiliary

[13] A senior supervisor in one of these departments, however, who is responsible for the general-relief division, maintains some technical direction over the old age program.

[14] Some agencies that use a generalized staff employ special supervisors in child welfare, old age assistance, and care of the blind, who are called consultants but who possess more administrative authority than the consultants discussed here.

workers are employed in large staffs to perform a segment of the total job of the social service staff. For example, the social service staff is required to examine public records to verify items on the applicants' claims to eligibility. In a large agency this particular phase of investigation may be assigned to a group of workers who do nothing but search records. They become specialists in one aspect of the total process in order to conserve staff time and to do this specific task more effectively. An isolated trip to a public record room is time consuming, but when auxiliary workers do this task a large number of cases may be cleared at one time. The outside agency whose records are being searched prefers to deal with a few representatives of the welfare department and to have the searching made at stated intervals by persons familiar with their procedures rather than to have a constant stream of inquiries coming from a large number of workers. Auxiliary workers are used to verify employment information, residence data, and other documentary evidence; to handle complaints; and to prepare material for use in court action.[15]

Although the consultants are ordinarily recognized as a definite part of the social service staff, the auxiliary workers are not uniformly so considered. The confusion arises from the fact that the nature of the duties of some auxiliary workers is clerical and routine. It is not necessary, for example, to have trained social workers to consult property records. Persons of intelligence and some degree of technical knowledge may easily be trained for this job. Yet all these steps must be recognized as a basic part of the direct service of the agency if they are to be placed properly in the organization scheme. This is seen clearly only when the nature of the activities of the auxiliary workers is thoroughly understood as a part of the total process of relationship of the agency with the applicant for or recipient of aid. If auxiliary workers are used, they should be responsible directly to the head of the social service division in order that their activities may be supervised and their work integrated with the main investigational procedures. Of course, if the local agency has a diversified program, including institutional management as well as public assistance functions, units of auxiliary workers may be set up to serve both the institutions and the public assistance programs.

The Denver Bureau of Public Welfare employs specialists in insurance, employment, and property, and other legal matters, who serve

---

[15] The use of members of the social service staff to act as intake workers is different from the employment of auxiliary workers, for intake is here a special assignment of the social workers. See discussion of intake procedures in chap. 7.

on the staff of the director. The Boston Department has had at various times specialists on real estate, insurance, medical social service, and home economics serving on the staff of the director of social service. In these two agencies, the auxiliary workers serve three different programs of public assistance.[16] The division of old age assistance in the New York City Department of Public Welfare is large enough in itself to afford its own specialized services. These include a property and estates unit and a medical care unit. The welfare departments in Los Angeles and Milwaukee counties, which are examples of large county units responsible for institutional as well as for public assistance programs, have a variety of special services.[17] In the Los Angeles Department special services are provided for property, insurance, medical care, boarding homes, and employment. Most of these are organized as staff units under an assistant to the director of the Department.

In some agencies the auxiliary workers are grouped with the office management activities of the department. For example, in one large county the following special services appear under the direction of the office manager of the department: insurance, collateral, intercounty investigation, and death claims. Thus they are aligned with such units as "records and files," "clerical and stenographic correspondence," and "janitorial service." This grouping of the auxiliary and special services with the housekeeping and facilitative activities fails to recognize that the former are an integral part of the functional program of the agency, and removes them from the control of those responsible for the execution of the social service program.

Facilitative Services

The function of a local public welfare agency is to render assistance or direct service to individuals. All the secondary activities of the operating unit—those devised to make the rendering of assistance possible—are considered to be the facilitative services[18] of that unit; they include financial activities, office management, personnel administration, and record keeping.

FINANCIAL ACTIVITIES. The principal financial activities of the local agencies are: the disbursement of funds or the preparation of assistance

[16] One advantage of having several types of assistance in a single local agency is that these programs may profit by the central services which a larger unit can afford.

[17] The old age assistance unit in Milwaukee County is primarily under the county judge, but it is able to profit from the central services of the county welfare department through a joint administrative relationship that has been developed.

[18] See page 49, n. 10, for the use of this term.

rolls, the accounting for expenditures, financial planning, budgetary control, the preparation of state and federal claims for reimbursement, and the preparation of administrative pay rolls.[19] As previously indicated, some of the states conduct the fiscal activities in the state office. In only seven of the twelve states studied—California, Colorado, Indiana, Massachusetts, New Jersey, New York, and Wisconsin—are major financial activities found in the local agency; hence this discussion will largely be concerned with the local agencies in these states.

The fiscal unit in the local welfare department is usually organized under a finance director with subdivisions grouped either in accordance with the types of activity—accounting, disbursement, etc.—or in accordance with the major parts of the service program. The former is the more common arrangement. In a few operating units, however, the financial activities are decentralized: there is a fiscal unit within each of the several main divisions of the service program. This is ordinarily found if the program is highly diversified and includes institutional management as well as public assistance activities.

The Los Angeles County Department of Charities includes the following major functions, each of which is organized as a major division of the department: a county general hospital, a county tuberculosis hospital, a large county institution for the aged and chronically ill, an "outside medical relief" program, and a social service division which handles the various types of public assistance for which the department is responsible. The financial administrative problems of these various activities are quite different; this fact has led to the decentralization of the fiscal activities. For example, a business management unit has been set up in the social service division to handle accounting, preparation of relief rolls, and of state and federal claims, thus making the financial service immediately available to the needs of the public assistance program. Central departmental control is provided by staff assistants to the superintendent of charities who oversee all the financial work of the Department. One of the central-staff officers, at the time of this survey, was devoting himself to perfecting the mechanism of handling the state-federal claims in the business management unit of the social service division. These central-staff members also, from time to time, make studies of administrative methods and procedures.

[19] Most local units bear a close relationship on the financial side with the fiscal agents of the city or county in which the operating unit is located. The financial department of the welfare agency may perform some of these activities in preparation for final action by the fiscal official of the unit of government, or may even be acting as his agent in most of this activity.

OFFICE MANAGEMENT. Activities frequently found in public welfare departments falling under this classification are: management of the stenographic force, operation of central files, handling of routine correspondence, procurement, plant maintenance and telephone, telegraph, and mail management. In the smallest agencies these activities are limited in scope and may all be performed by the director's secretary. As the agency increases in size, however, the full-time services of an office manager are usually needed, and in the largest agencies subdivisions are required for most of the separate types of activities.

In these large agencies two plans of organization are found. The first provides for a large business management department, divided usually into two sections, one concerned with the financial program of the organization, the other, with office management. Under the second plan two separate divisions are organized; one is devoted to office management and one to fiscal management, with the heads of the two units reporting directly to the executive of the agency. No dogmatic conclusion can be made in favor of either plan purely on the basis of organizational principles; both seem to work.

In some agencies, the office management and financial activities have been added to the department by a process of accretion without regard to their integration with established divisions. A person is placed in charge of files, for example, and filing is immediately made an independent section. Another person is placed in charge of the stenographic pool, which becomes a unit. The result is a congeries of small semi-independent sections which provide facilitative services for the agency with no unity of action among them and no central control. An example is found in one county agency with an office manager who also acts as assistant director of the department, under whom are gathered units with the following titles: clerical and stenographic, accounts, correspondence, janitors, death claims, records and files, collateral, insurance, intercounty investigation, and complaints. One city welfare department maintains fourteen semi-independent units to handle financial and office management activities, several of the units consisting of a single employee. These two examples, of course, represent the antithesis of organization.

PERSONNEL ADMINISTRATION. Only the largest local agencies have found it necessary to maintain a specific personnel unit. The personnel activities are separated into two distinct categories: the operating and mechanical procedures of personnel management, including appointment, attendance, efficiency records, etc.; and recruitment and training of professional staff. Ordinarily, the former are lodged in a separate unit with other central-staff services, and the responsibility for recruiting and training the social work staff is assigned to the social service department. In other words, this latter phase of personnel is treated as a part of professional staff supervision.

RECORD KEEPING AND STATISTICS. The function of the record-keeping service is to collect, arrange, and issue data for planning, control, and information purposes. The basic data used are derived both from the social service and from the financial sides of the program; thus the activity falls between the two, although in smaller units one person is generally responsible for both types of recording and statistics. In large units the service statistics are usually compiled by a record clerk either in the social service division or in a central-staff unit. He also prepares reports which combine service and financial statistics, although in a few places this work is the responsibility of the financial division. One of the local agencies visited, however, has a statistical unit which is separate from both finance and social service, the chief statistician reporting to the head of the department. With the growing recognition of the usefulness of social statistics, this latter pattern will probably be adopted by other local welfare departments.

ADMINISTRATIVE COORDINATION

In a local public welfare agency two of the principal internal duties of the chief administrative officer are to take executive action and to coordinate the program. In a unifunctional agency these two duties become one; that is, executive control consists primarily of preserving a proper relationship between the social service activities and the facilitative units which implement the program. The executive's job is to see not only that the facilitating units are aiding the service side of the organization but also that those persons responsible for the social service activities of the agency are giving due regard to the administrative requirements. The simple pattern for the unifunctional agency is that of an executive with two lieutenants: one responsible for the social service activities, the other, for the facilitative activities.

In more complex local agencies the organizational problems differ considerably. The program may be so diversified that it is necessary to have a number of major units. This is always true when the agency is responsible for institutional management as well as for direct services to individuals. Here the executive task is twofold. The director must see to it that the various programs are well managed and that the facilitative services are implementing but not dominating the operations. Furthermore, he must be sure that the several programs are coordinated so that the best possible service is given without an overlapping of activities. An effective administrative pattern to fit these circumstances is to have a subexecutive in charge of each of the main functional groups (usually each institution and the public assistance program), with one or two main staff assistants responsible for the facilitative services.

Large local agencies responsible for the administration of several types of public assistance, but not including institutions, usually organize social service activities in categorical divisions and center the business management activities under a single department head. Unless there is a subexecutive or supervisor to coordinate these different social service programs, the burden of responsibility for coordination and professional leadership rests upon the executive. The device used in Boston of having a social service director coordinate and direct the three units of social service program appears to be a satisfactory arrangement which releases the chief administrative officer for broader executive tasks. In the San Diego County Department a deputy immediately under the director is responsible for the executive coordination of the service programs. In the New York City Department of Public Welfare the commissioner delegates considerable executive responsibility for separate programs to his deputy commissioners. Little attempt is made to coordinate these programs on the service level, but financial, personnel, and office management units provide central operating control.

The effects of lack of coordination in a local welfare agency's program are felt chiefly by the beneficiaries, who may receive unsatisfactory service as a result of faulty operation. The taxpayer, too, may suffer, since uncoordinated services are usually more expensive than the same services properly integrated. The problem of maintaining a balance among administrative activities should not be an involved matter on the local level. The function of the assistance agency is quite clearly that of making benefits available to eligible applicants, and the operations of the facilitative services must be shaped to that end.

PART II
The Administration of the Social Service Program

CHAPTER 6

ELIGIBILITY REQUIREMENTS

Activities of old age assistance agencies that involve direct contact with, and service to, old age assistance applicants and recipients are herein classified as "social service activities." [1] They include selecting eligible applicants, determining the extent of their need for assistance, re-examining eligibility of recipients, and rendering other services that may be considered necessary or desirable.[2] The supervision of these activities on the federal, state, or local level is also included in the social service program.

The clearest presentation of this program can be made by outlining the flow of work through the usual channels from the first contact of the agency with the applicant to the final one with the recipient, and any later procedures, such as those involved in the payment of funeral costs and the settlement of claims against the recipient's estate. The discussion of application procedures, with which the social service activities normally begin, will be preceded by a review of eligibility requirements, since their nature largely influences subsequent procedures.

FEDERAL PROVISIONS

The Social Security Act does not, strictly speaking, impose any eligibility requirements upon applicants. It does, however, place limitations upon the eligibility requirements of states that share in federal

[1] The term "applicant" as used in this report means a person who either has applied or who plans to apply for old age assistance. A "recipient" is an individual who is receiving old age assistance; this term is also used to refer to a former recipient who has died while on the active assistance rolls. There is no generally acceptable term that includes both applicants and recipients. The word "client" commonly used by social agencies is occasionally employed in this report and, when used, it means any person—applicant or recipient—for whom the agency is attempting to provide assistance or service.

[2] A few state agencies do not recognize these activities as coming within the field of social work, but there seems to be no other generally accepted descriptive term. The indefinite term "service" used in the earlier report (see Robert T. Lansdale and Associates, *op. cit.*) has been discarded since the majority of agencies now use, or at least accept, the term "social service," which, therefore, has a generally acceptable and recognized connotation. It will also be apparent in the discussion that the activities so described are in fact social work in that they utilize the special skills of the trained social worker.

funds. Apparently the chief purpose of some of the limitations is to prevent too severe specifications by states rather than to restrict the eligibility of applicants; they are, on the whole, more liberal than those imposed by states prior to the federal Act. The federal eligibility provisions may be said, therefore, to be outside limits for the guidance of states in setting up plans that qualify for federal aid. A state plan may not require longer residence in the state than five years out of the past nine, with one continuous year immediately preceding date of application; or establish a citizenship requirement that excludes a citizen of the United States. Nor may an age requirement higher than sixty-five be approved, except that a seventy-year minimum may be adopted and remain in force until January 1, 1940. It is a further restriction on the age qualification that federal funds will be allowed only for payments made "with respect to each individual who at the time of such expenditure is 65 years of age or older."

The Act also limits state action by denying reimbursement for payments made for a recipient who is "an inmate of a public institution." Need as a prerequisite for receiving old age assistance is mentioned only in the first paragraph of the Act: "For the purpose of enabling each state to furnish financial assistance, as far as practicable under the conditions in such State, to aged needy individuals. . ."; but no definition of "needy" is given.

STATE REQUIREMENTS

In contrast with the federal Act the state laws are usually specific, since the states are responsible for the actual operation of the program. Although the federal Act allows considerable latitude, conformance with it has tended to produce uniformity in state legislation, especially in the age requirement, for in this respect the Act allows the least deviation for states receiving federal grants. Tendency toward uniformity is also noticeable in the residence and citizenship requirements, both of which are usually just within the limits of the federal Act. Another factor that has encouraged uniformity has been the use of model laws. States also copied from each other. New York, because it was one of the first states to establish a mandatory plan with partial state financing, was followed by several states.

Age

The state systems antedating the federal Act usually placed the minimum age limit at seventy years. The states had had little experience and proceeded cautiously. Less opposition to the program might be expected with the age limit at seventy rather than at sixty-five because seventy was generally regarded as the normal age for old age dependence (the Biblical three score and ten), and then, too, a program with a seventy-year limit would be less expensive owing to the high death rate in the upper-age groups. As public demand for old age assistance has brought increasing pressure on state legislatures to broaden the program, the age limit has been lowered to sixty-five.[3] The sixty-five-year provision of the Social Security Act has probably been a potent factor in its establishment as the minimum in state laws; but that minimum in the Act was doubtless itself the result, as well as the cause, of an increasingly liberal public opinion on a suitable minimum age. Pressure to lower the age limit still further is apparent. Colorado has already reduced its limit to sixty years.[4] Other states have provided for lowering the age to sixty if the federal government should decide to share the expense of grants to that age. Several congressional bills in recent sessions have provided for lowering the age limit to sixty; and numerous state bills have also provided that minimum; a few have gone even lower.

While lowering the age limit from seventy to sixty-five greatly increases the number of eligibles, it is difficult to ascertain just how much it has increased the number of recipients. Frequently other changes in state laws have been made simultaneously; hence the resulting increase cannot be credited entirely to the lowering of the age qualification.[5] California made an analysis of increases resulting from modifications of its state old age assistance law, projecting these changes to guide fiscal authorities in planning for the next biennium.[6] The expectation was that the change in the age limit in 1936 would of itself result in doubling the number of recipients by the end of 1939. Statisticians in other states have estimated that lowering the age limit from seventy to sixty-five would likewise double the case load. Administrative officials in New York State expected that similarly lowering the age limit in

[3] When Indiana lowered its age limit from seventy to sixty-five years on July 1, 1938, only three states, Missouri, New Hampshire, and Pennsylvania, still had age limits above sixty-five years. See U. S. Social Security Board, *Characteristics of State Plans for Old-Age Assistance,* June 30, 1938.

[4] Assistance costs for the age group sixty to sixty-five years are borne by state funds since the Act does not allow federal matching of such expenditures.

[5] An increase in the funds available and changes in administrative procedures also affect the acceptance of recipients and hence the gross case-load figures.

[6] Budget for the Biennium, July 1, 1937, to June 30, 1939, chart, p. 15.

that state in October, 1936, would increase their load 85 per cent, but the increase apparently exceeded the estimate.[7]

Although there has been pressure to lower the age limit below sixty-five, there is, on the whole, less dissatisfaction with this requirement than with most of the others. The idea is generally accepted that there must be a lower age limit for an old age assistance program, and sixty-five has been recognized as a reasonably low minimum. Few of the foreign programs studied by the President's Committee on Economic Security had age limits below sixty-five.[8]

The age requirement is perhaps the simplest of all the eligibility requirements to administer. The chief difficulties in putting it into effect have been caused by lack of documentary proof. Birth records are available for this purpose in only a few states; other satisfactory proof is difficult to find as well as to evaluate.

Residence

Residence requirements usually involve residence both in the state and in the local subdivision. In the beginning, when few plans were in operation, it was believed to be necessary that a state protect its assistance funds by making it difficult for needy and aged residents of other states to move in for the purpose of obtaining old age assistance. Although greater uniformity has tended to remove the incentive in most instances, such migration is still a threat to states whose grants are markedly more generous than those of other states. The states that advertise their healthful climates are particularly concerned lest they attract many elderly people for whom they may shortly need to provide

[7] Complete data on the increase in the total case load are not available, but for the year July 1, 1935, to June 30, 1936, the total number of applications approved was 12,928, while in the following year the number was 42,756. Even though other changes were made in the law, it is obvious that the chief factor was the lowering of the age limit, since, of the 42,756 applications approved, 25,272 were received from persons in the age group sixty-five to seventy, although persons of this group were eligible only from October, 1936, to June, 1937. During this period, however, 58.9 per cent of all applications received were from persons sixty-five to seventy. (Figures for 1936-37 were furnished by Bureau of Research and Statistics, Division of Public Assistance of the Social Security Board; and for 1935-36, from *Seventieth Annual Report of the State Board of Social Welfare of New York*, pp. 38 ff.)

[8] Table 40 facing page 184 of *Social Security in America* (summary of the Staff Reports to the Committee on Economic Security, published by the Social Security Board, 1937) shows that in 1933 eight of thirteen foreign countries which reported data on their noncontributory pensions had minimum age limits at sixty-five or above, the most common being seventy years. Two of those with a lower limit had a minimum age of sixty-five for men and sixty for women. Age limits were lower in several instances if the applicant was incapacitated. Only three countries, Uruguay, Greenland, Iceland, had age limits definitely and uniformly below sixty-five. In the United States sixty-five is the federal minimum age for old age insurance as well as for old age assistance.

assistance and so tend to be strict in establishing and enforcing residence requirements. Local units that contribute funds for old age assistance usually wish to limit their expenditures to bona fide residents of their communities lest differentials in assistance attract "outlanders."

Since under the Social Security Act states sharing in federal funds may not require a period of residence longer than five out of the past nine years, with one year of continuous residence immediately preceding application, the great majority of states adhere to this maximum. The analysis of the characteristics of state plans prepared by the Bureau of Public Assistance early in 1937 showed that of forty-two plans, thirty-seven followed closely the residence limitations of the Act.[9] Six other states allowed one year additional in which to qualify (five out of ten), but only one state, Arkansas, had as low a residence requirement as one year—a period which had been customary for general-relief purposes in many states prior to the Social Security Act. The provisions of the Act seem, therefore, to have led to the establishment of requirements more liberal than those of former old age assistance programs but distinctly higher in many states than for other types of aid.[10]

Although the federal Act does not mention local residence requirements it indirectly affects them. If local units establish requirements that exclude persons who meet state requirements, the state must either step in and provide for such persons or risk abrogation of the state plan by failure to conform with the Act. The representatives of the Bureau of Public Assistance have advised against restrictive residence requirements, state or local, when their advice has been sought on legislation and state plans. The Bureau has also insisted that state plans provide for eligible persons having state residence whether or not they can establish residence in any local subdivision of the state. Interstate agreements that will help obviate the difficulties arising from state residence restrictions have also been advised.

States have an incentive for keeping local requirements in conformity with those of the state when there is local financial participation; for by this means they avoid having to provide wholly for a large number of needy persons without local residence.[11] If the state furnishes all funds

[9] U. S. Social Security Board, *Characteristics of State Plans for Old-Age Assistance*, April 1, 1937.

[10] Colorado has established a residence requirement of thirty-five continuous years of residence" for applicants sixty years old but under sixty-five, for whom federal matching cannot be obtained, and who, because of age, would not be eligible for old age assistance in other states.

[11] These are often called "unsettled cases" if eligibility for local aid depends on hav-

the question of residence assumes less importance since the purpose of local restrictions is chiefly that of limiting local expenditures for aid to those having a claim on the locality through residence. Thus the requirements of the Act have tended, on the whole, to reduce emphasis on local residence.[12]

Citizenship

States sharing in federal funds may not exclude a citizen of the United States. Prior to the Social Security Act, many states with old age assistance programs required applicants to be native born or citizens of the United States for a specified period. States that receive federal aid have been obliged to eliminate these provisions; most of them now merely require the applicant to be a citizen. Three states grant old age assistance to noncitizens if they have been residents of the United States for a long period (fifteen, twenty, and twenty-five years); seventeen have no stipulation about citizenship.[13] Its absence simplifies the establishment of eligibility since citizenship is often difficult to prove, especially for those who have derived it from others (husbands or parents). It is also advantageous to the state, if aged aliens must be supported, to have the support provided through old age assistance that is federally aided rather than through general relief for which no federal reimbursement can be obtained.

Although great hue and cry are frequently raised over aliens on relief, many applicants of foreign birth are old and respected members of their communities, who have long been accepted as such by their native-born neighbors. Many have voted unchallenged for years, have exercised other rights of citizenship, and have regarded themselves as American citizens. A number have confidently believed themselves to be citizens until investigation revealed unknown or long forgotten facts of birth and parentage showing that American citizenship had never been established. When such persons, who have done much to build up the communities in which they live, are denied assistance, their native-born neighbors feel that the denials are unfair and unjust; a community sentiment in favor of more liberal provisions thus develops. Several

---

ing local "settlement." They are sometimes called "state cases" if the state assumes the cost of care for persons otherwise eligible for aid and having state but not local residence or "settlement."

[12] Local residence requirements usually conform with those established for other types of aid and most commonly call for residence of one year.

[13] U. S. Social Security Board, *Characteristics of State Plans for Old-Age Assistance,* June 30, 1938.

states have removed some of the restrictions on citizenship in their old age assistance laws.

Need and Its Determination

Need is the most troublesome factor that enters into the determination of eligibility. Although it is perhaps the most important single factor, it is the most difficult to define and to measure. Unlike age, residence, and citizenship requirements, which are fairly simple and may easily be defined or limited, need is always relative and complex, and the standards for measuring it must be flexible and take into account a number of variables. Even the physiological basis of need—provision for food and bodily warmth supplied by clothing and shelter—is not easy to determine since allowance must be made for differences in health, physical activity, ability to assimilate food, and other individual variations. Moreover, need cannot be regarded as wholly physiological; hence social needs must be considered. Furthermore, to determine what may be called "net need," the cost of supplying essential physiological and social needs must be ascertained, adding another variable—namely, cost in terms of the current local price level; this cost, moreover, must be calculated in relation to income. Income may be in cash or in goods and services, the value of which is often difficult to ascertain; it may also be regarded as potential rather than actual. Nonincome-bearing property and ability and willingness of relatives to support are examples of potential income.

Determination of the degree of need serves two purposes: it provides a basis for deciding on the eligibility of the applicant, and for establishing the amount of the grant to be made to eligibles. Although this chapter is primarily concerned with eligibility, it is impossible to separate wholly the two objectives of the need-determining process.

THE BUDGETARY METHOD OF NEED DETERMINATION. The typical method of determining need is the budgetary method. The correct use of a budget requires first of all that the agency adopt a basic standard or content of living. State laws do not attempt to define the standard except in general terms, such as "a reasonable subsistence compatible with decency and health." [14] A state agency must decide what quality and quantity of goods are necessary to maintain such a content of living for a given period of time; for persons with varying needs, expert help will be required to determine this standard and to translate it into

---

[14] See Washington, *Laws*, 1935, Chap. 182, sec. 3 (b), and Mississippi, *Laws*, 1936, H.B. 381, sec. 10 (d). A number of other states have similar provisions.

monetary terms by studying the cost of the required goods and services in terms of the prices in various sections of the state.

The discovery, evaluation, and economical utilization of the varied resources also require skill.[15] The staff of experts for this purpose comprises social workers and home economists trained in this special field. On the basis of the study of quantity, quality, and cost, a schedule, or "budget guide," is set up to be used by the less skilled staff members under the direction of the expert supervisory staff. Application of the budgetary schedule, sometimes called a "standard budget" or "family budget," requires that both needs and resources of each applicant be studied. His needs are estimated for a stated period of time under expert supervision, with the help of the established budget schedule, and always in consultation with the client himself. For convenience the estimated needs are set down on the needs, or expenditures, side of an especially prepared budget sheet. On the opposite side are noted the resources, which have also been studied carefully, including income estimated for the same period as that used for entries on the needs side. After the data are thus assembled the needs are balanced carefully against the resources. If the calculations show that a surplus exists, the applicant is presumed to be ineligible. If a deficit is discovered the applicant is eligible, and the amount of the deficit measures his need and constitutes the basis for the award.

A properly established budget schedule based on a decent but practical standard of living reviewed by intelligent workers can be fair and equitable for clients and economical of agency funds. It can be more generous than a less careful method by making every dollar count to the fullest extent in comfort and security for the client. Unfortunately the method is not always so used. Budget schedules have been set up without relation to a defensible living standard; sometimes they have been used as a means of forcing upon the needy a standard of living unjustifiable in terms of health and decency of living. A good standard has also sometimes proved devastating in the hands of inexpert workers. The method thus applied or misapplied has produced dissatisfaction and resentment charged to the method rather than to its misuse. The fact that the budgetary method has for a long time been associated with relief administration has also made it somewhat opprobrious. At best it is

---

[15] The economic use of resources may not appear at first to be a part of the budgetary process. If proper utilization is not understood, however, evaluation is impossible. "Value for use" is the best criterion. Helping applicants utilize their resources to the fullest extent can and should be a natural development, a service which if offered on a free and self-respecting basis can be utilized by clients with no loss of independence.

not a simple method; but, on the other hand, the factors to be evaluated are not themselves simple.

OTHER METHODS OF NEED DETERMINATION. Although the budgetary method has been adopted in most states, the adequacy of its procedures is frequently questionable. The Bureau of Public Assistance of the Social Security Board recommends this method and has offered expert consultation in setting up suitable procedures; nevertheless, there is great unevenness in its administration. In several states it has been rejected, in part at least. Various substitutes have been attempted directed toward finding a simpler method that could be applied without expert guidance or by "business methods" or common sense; a method that would be removed from taint of charity; a method that would ensure more generous treatment of applicants than methods associated with poor relief. These methods are efforts to establish a quasi-pension system rather than a relief or public assistance program. Their effects on eligibility requirements will be discussed, but first it seems advisable to trace briefly the influences that have produced these modifications.

At present the strongest influence in the direction of generosity is the organized pension movement. In some states groups of pension advocates are politically powerful and, in others, potentially so. In some respects their influence is reinforced by other groups whose members share the fundamental philosophy of the pension groups even though not attracted either by the specious economic theories or the appeal to the self-interest of the elderly. This philosophy briefly stated is that the citizen ordinarily contributes to the upbuilding of the community in his productive years and deserves as a matter of right a share in the community surplus when those years are over. The ideal of social justice is reinforced by other ideas and attitudes. The traditional religious ideal of charity—the obligation of the more fortunate to care as generously as possible for the poor and needy and especially the helpless— is not without influence toward liberality. Ordinary human sympathy and a degree of sentimentality tend to reinforce the religious ideal. The public has also become more familiar with the unreasonable restrictions of many of the old poor laws and consequently more impatient with the results of the attempts to apply them to the new poor of the present industrial era, especially those whose need was caused by the recent depression.

Resistance to budgeting and advocacy of other methods, as noted above, are not always motivated by a desire for generous treatment of recipients. Advocates of schemes believed to require only common sense or business methods are sometimes influenced largely by the distrust of the ordinary man for the expert. A budget is a recognized business method, but because in its application to individual families it also requires the special skill of the home economist and the social worker, it is an object of suspicion to the poorly informed.

USE OF INCOME DEDUCTION AND FORMULAS. The methods used to simplify need determination usually do not eliminate the necessity for individual differentiation, but, in general, they attempt to limit the area of discretion and flexibility. The most common method is some form of what, for convenience, is here called "income deduction." A figure is selected as a standard or norm for income to provide for all needs. It is usually arbitrary and is often set at $30 a month, not because study of costs indicates that a satisfactory living can be provided for that amount, but chiefly because this is the maximum that will be matched by the federal government. Whatever amount is selected as the norm is used as the base, and any income received is deducted from this amount. The difference represents the deficit that must be supplied by the grant.

The application of this method might be simple if needs were uniform and if all variation occurred on the income or resource side of the budget. In order to compensate the rigid value assigned by these agencies to the need or cost side and to bring the result into some sort of approximation to individual requirements, states adopting the income-deduction method are compelled to manipulate arbitrarily the resource items. This they do by assigning values to selected resource items, particularly those involving a consideration of cost, and by allowing exemption of these items in whole or in part. For example, earned income, into which cost usually enters, may be exempted up to a certain figure.[16]

Income deduction plus income exemption may result in the payment of what is practically a flat grant to all recipients and hence in virtual nullification of the requirement that the grant be determined in accordance with need. This plan (income exemption), advocated for the purpose of providing more generously for the aged and actually costing the state more in the gross amount, tends to discriminate in favor of

---

[16] Costs that commonly enter into earned income are increased need of food, including lunches bought or carried; clothing, warmer or better in appearance than would be needed only at home; carfare or other transportation costs; union dues; tools and other special equipment or materials; and recreation and other social needs. A scientific standard budget would make allowance on the expenditure side for such items in accordance with the circumstances of worker and job.

the least needy—those with income and resources. Those without resources or income may or may not receive more than they would under
a more flexible plan so long as the state resources are sufficient to pay
the full amount contemplated. If a shortage of funds develops under
such a plan and cuts are made either on a percentage or a flat-deduction
basis, the neediest will suffer most because the deduction will be made
on their gross income, whereas for those with other income the cut
will be made only on that part of their total income represented by the
grant.

Perhaps the effect on income exemption can best be seen if illustrated
by two hypothetical cases. The state in this instance is assumed to grant
a maximum of $30 with an exemption of $15 for earned income. Two
hypothetical applicants apply and both fulfil all other eligibility requirements and claim to be needy. The first man is in good health and is
able to earn $15 per month as janitor of a church. He has some extra
expenses for clothing, tools, cleaning supplies, etc., but these amount to
less than $2 per month. The second man is unable to work and is in
constant need of expensive medical care which costs at least $12 per
month. The state grants $30 to each applicant since both are without
income except for the $15 per month earnings of the first applicant,
which are exempted. The second man whose needs are greater has
a total gross income of only $30. If he pays for needed medical care
his net income for other living expenses is $18. The first man, on the
other hand, has a gross income of $45; his expenses outside of normal
living costs are only $2 and his net income for living expenses is $43
(grant $30 plus exempted income of $15 less expenses of employment
$2).

The inequitable effect of such a system is still more serious if the
state, because of a shortage of funds, is unable to pay the maximum
amount to all applicants and a decision is made to cut all grants 10 per
cent. The first recipient will still have $40, a loss on his net income for
living expenses of just under 7 per cent, while the second, whose income
for living expenses has been reduced by nearly 17 per cent, now has only
$15 for this purpose.[17]

The attempt to translate needs and costs into income terms has in
some states led to the development of more or less complicated formulas

[17] The result would be the same if a straight cut of $3 in all grants were made. But
if a straight deduction of $5 were made, the percentage reduction in income available
for living would be respectively 12 and 28 per cent. Although these two cases are
wholly imaginary, the conditions described are by no means impossible or even unlikely. Such a system can hardly fail to produce inequitable results.

88 The Administration of Old Age Assistance

for computing individual grants. The so-called "rating mill" used in Iowa, the most complex of these formulas, is too intricate to explain fully in brief compass. In general it operates on the assumption that the state maximum, $25, must be taken as a norm and that deductions should be made and credits allowed for varying individual or community resources or deficiencies. The values assigned to these resources or deficiencies are calculated on numerical scales established for each item usually without sufficient research or sound technical advice.[18] The scales are applied to the data in the case record by a group of clerical workers or raters in the state office, each of whom applies the scale covering one item and sets down what he judges to be its numerical value in the individual case. These items are then computed according to a predetermined schedule or formula of deductions and credits; the result is presumed to represent the extent of need and forms the basis for a recommendation to the state board on the amount of the grant. Elaborate computation of unsound or distorted data gives no assurance of "mathematical justice" and may be especially unjust because its complexity is impressive and discourages questioning of results by disappointed applicants and their friends.[19]

The desire to find a system that will provide generously for the aged without humiliating restrictions and will avoid expensive administrative procedures is commendable. Experiments in this field should be made with certain cautions: they should be regarded as tentative and not become too early crystallized by enactment into law or inclusion in state constitutions before their validity has been tested. Every effort should be made to safeguard those whose needs are greatest rather than those whose needs are least. Results should be studied carefully and checked against those obtained by other methods. Enthusiasm for an untried and unsound but plausible method can result in its being firmly intrenched and stoutly defended by deluded advocates long before its value in practice can be determined. Better understanding and more effective use of older methods are also worth considering. Whatever methods are attempted must, of course, be evaluated for their administrative efficiency as well as for the extent to which they promote the comfort and security of the needy aged.

[18] The values in the scale for physical condition, for instance, were established without medical advice, and the standards for the application of the scale to specific diseases, defects, or ailments were set up by an office clerk.

[19] For a fuller discussion of the inadequacies of the Iowa rating system see editorial comment, "Pseudo-Science versus Sound Administrative Procedures," *Social Service Review*, XII (September, 1938), 499.

Need and Income Limitations

In some states an established maximum for income constitutes practically a separate eligibility requirement. If the law specifies a maximum, an applicant, regardless of his need, must be excluded if he has an income equal to or greater than the specified figure. In other states income is mentioned only in connection with the maximum grant or in defining need and then only in general terms. In these states the law provides that an applicant may be excluded if he has an income "sufficient to support himself in decency and in health." When income is related to the maximum grant in the state law and when, as usual, the maximum grant is $30, the law usually provides that the amount granted "shall not *when added to income* exceed $30." [20]

An income maximum appears to be a simple method of eliminating quickly those persons who have income sufficient for their needs. It is not, however, so simple as at first appears. To apply it the term "income" must first be defined. Often when income is mentioned in the law, what it means or how it is to be determined is not specified; furthermore some state agencies have not resolved the issue by regulation.

Income for the past year may be taken as the income to which an established maximum or other limitations apply. The use of this base has some advantages. It covers a long enough period to eliminate minor, temporary, or seasonal variations, but if the applicant's present income is much more or much less, the decision will be made with little relation to the applicant's actual or present need. An attempt to arrive at present income involves the difficulty of deciding what is "present." A short period, such as a week or a month, is not necessarily typical; yet a longer period would cover the past or a future time. The grant is, of course, made for the future. Old age assistance is seldom payable immediately. The income that the applicant will have when he receives his grant is an important item in arriving at the amount of the grant; it is also perhaps the most important consideration in determining eligibility. The difficulty is to forecast future income. For this purpose the average income of the preceding quarter may be a guide, but no designated period can safely be adopted and rigidly observed. Certainly it is unwise to attempt definition of this sort in the state law.

[20] Strangely enough the statement in the law bears little relation to the method of determining need used by the state. Several states with this sort of legal wording use a budgetary system rather than the income-deduction method. These latter use the income maximum only as a means of eliminating applications at intake. To those applicants whose income is less than the maximum the budgetary method of determining need is applied.

Net instead of gross income may be considered when income deduction is the method used for determining need. A small business may produce gross income well above the maximum allowance, yet the actual profits to the owner may be small. What items may legitimately be counted as necessary business expenses must be decided upon in order to arrive at an estimate of the net income. Rental income often involves determining net income after deductions for repairs, insurance, taxes, interest on mortgages, and other carrying costs, as well as the amount to be considered the owner's rent if he occupies one of the units. A budgetary system does not attempt to calculate net income for each different source of income, but itemizes the gross income on the income side of the budgetary statement and the necessary costs on the needs or expenditure side.

Rigid policies on income are hard to apply when income is irregular or uncertain. Few old age assistance applicants are able to earn regular wages. Relatives and friends sometimes contribute gifts of unpredictable amount and frequency, which may represent a considerable part of the applicant's yearly support. To count all such gifts as part of income, if the income-deduction method is rigidly applied, may result not only in penalizing the applicant unfairly but also in discouraging further gifts. In one state the practice is to calculate income largely on the basis of the past year and to allow the applicant to deduct $100 for occasional income or gifts. It is not always easy to decide what income shall be counted in this category, but probably no solution would be simple. The probabilities of continuance of the income would also seem to require exploration since future rather than past income is the important consideration in determining need.

A problem closely related to irregular and uncertain income is income in kind. Applicants may be paid for their services or may be given gifts of food, clothing, or fuel. Rent may likewise be provided or may be furnished in return for janitorial or other service. It is extremely difficult to value such income in monetary terms, yet if income in kind is ignored, applicants whose income is in cash may justly claim that they are being treated less generously than those with income in kind. As in gross and net income, this problem presents less difficulty if a budgetary system is used rather than income deduction. The budget schedule contains guidance for estimating the items constituting an acceptable standard of living. The estimate will be entered on the needs or expenditure side and a corresponding item, in whole or in part as the circumstances warrant, on the income side.

To estimate farm and garden income is especially hard since it involves most of the problems already discussed about income. The seasonal variation in income makes the farmer's earning hard to calculate on a shorter period than a year. The selection of an appropriate period is as difficult as for any other type of income. The net amount is apt to be both irregular and uncertain and much of it is "in kind." Most of these difficulties will be encountered whether the applicant is an owner, a tenant, or a share cropper.

Farm income presents another difficulty, but one not confined entirely to farm income—the problem of shared or split income. Many applicants are members of families and share in a family income to which they may or may not contribute by their labor. This problem involves also the legal obligation of relatives to support dependent relatives. Income in kind and family income present many complexities whatever system of determining need is used. In general, income deduction as usually practiced appears to be better adapted to an individual cash economy. Presumably it would be possible under such a system to establish a content of living defined wholly in terms of income. If this were done, however, the results would be identical with those achieved by the budgetary method and the process itself not greatly different. Moreover, the elaborate definitions of income required by such a plan would eliminate from income deduction the feature which its advocates consider its chief advantage—its simplicity.[21] Individualization of need can be achieved only by individualized consideration of all important factors; and, whether one approaches the problem directly or indirectly, the inherent complexities cannot be both ignored and encompassed. If simplicity is insisted upon, inequality of treatment must be accepted. If equitable treatment is a paramount consideration, a system that ignores important individual differences must be discarded.

Most states using an income-deduction or formula method of determining need ignore community resources as income; yet an applicant who lives in a community in which, for instance, good medical care is available to needy persons without cost is relatively better off than one who must pay for such service. One of the states visited worked out a rating scale for the localities in that state; but the differentials in the scale adopted were based on the financial condition of the localities

[21] Undoubtedly proponents of these schemes have in some instances hoped they were procuring more generous treatment for recipients. Generosity to the less needy may even be attained; but if generosity to those whose need is greatest is desired, raising the maximum, or removing it entirely, and increasing appropriations appear likely to be far more effective.

rather than on the availability of community services directly benefiting applicants. Financial and employment conditions in his community are not often of direct significance to an old age assistance applicant; but they may have an indirect importance through their effect on the ability of relatives to provide support, and, perhaps, on the ability of local agencies to provide supplemental relief or service. It is difficult, however, to discover criteria for rating communities according to the free services they provide; and if their resources do not affect in a fairly direct way the income of the applicant, a rating that credits him with resources merely because he lives in a favorably equipped community really penalizes him. Individual determination of the availability of resources to each applicant appears to be the only way in which differentials can be calculated and allowance made for them.

Need and Property Restrictions

The attempt to isolate and to legislate on one type of resource does not necessarily simplify the problem of determining need. To deal with property by means of rigid restrictions has not been much more successful than have similar efforts respecting income. Property requirements have, in general, been more numerous, detailed, and restrictive than those about income. They have, moreover, often been applied as separate eligibility requirements rather than as an integral part of need determination. Consequently, in most agencies visited neither clients nor administrators were satisfied with the results.

The most common requirement declares ineligible any applicant who has disposed of property in order to make himself eligible for assistance. This restriction is usually in the state law itself. Its main purpose is to avoid the shifting of responsibility for support from relatives to the state; in effect it also strengthens other property requirements, especially the one that the recipient shall reimburse the state for the assistance provided. Restriction on prior disposition is sometimes limited to a definite period preceding application. The most common period is five years. In some states any sale or other disposal of property by the applicant within the proscribed period is assumed to have been "for the purpose of rendering himself eligible for old age assistance." In others, no presumption is established, and the agency must attempt to determine in each case whether fraud or evasion has been attempted.

The interpretation of this provision has, on the whole, been fairly reasonable. For instance, the *Iowa Handbook* instructs its workers: "A bona fide transfer for a sufficient and proper consideration and a proper and frugal use of the proceeds since that time should not bar the granting of a pension under the terms of this section." [22] Obviously individualized consideration is necessary for a decision on this requirement, which thus appears to be no short cut to the establishment of eligibility. In fact, it might be noted that even the investigation required—the searching of property transfers for a five-year period—is time-consuming and expensive. Consequently, most agencies make such search only when evidence comes to light indicating that the applicant has disposed of his property prior to application. In short, agencies generally individualize both investigation and decision. Even though this provision is usually administered fairly, it has possibilities of oppressive use if the applicant is one who has aroused prejudice in the community.

Next to provisions on prior disposition of property, property maximums are probably the kind of restriction most commonly found. Establishment of a property maximum for eligibles, like the income maximum, has a certain value in making possible quick elimination of applicants whose property holdings exceed the requirement. The agency thus saves the cost of detailed inquiry into the applicant's needs and resources and also spares the ineligible applicant a detailed questioning. If these ends are gained the rule is justifiable. Unfortunately the application of a property maximum is not so simple as it appears in theory.

Administration of a property maximum requires that the term "property" be defined. In some states real estate and personal property are lumped together and a single property maximum is established for both. In most states with maximums, one maximum is set for real estate and another, usually smaller, for personal property. In some instances personal property includes every sort of movable property of any value; in others, cash or other supposedly liquid assets, such as stocks and bonds, mortgages, bank accounts, and similar items, are the only ones included. Insurance is often singled out for special treatment; household goods may be exempt or may have a special maximum; and one state establishes a maximum for household goods and heirlooms. In real estate a distinction is frequently made between property owned and occupied as a homestead and other real estate. In both real and personal property requirements a distinction may be made between productive and nonproductive property.[23]

[22] See Iowa State Old Age Assistance Commission, *Handbook for Old Age Assistance,* 1934, p. 25.

[23] In some states nonproductive property is assumed to be productive, in some instances at 5 per cent of its value—an arbitrary and largely fictitious valuation.

To apply a property maximum it is necessary to determine how property will be valued for this purpose. In the valuation of real estate the assessed valuation for tax purposes is generally accepted as a standard. It is less satisfactory in some states than in others, but it is usually the best standard available. Individual appraisal by experts, even if they were readily available, would be prohibitively expensive. Assessed valuation is apt to be more consistent than one based on the guesses of workers inexperienced in this technical field. An attempt is generally made to use equity rather than gross value as a basis for applying the maximum. State instructions to local agencies, however, have not always been so clear as they should be, and some variations in practice exist. Questions arise about valuation when there is joint ownership. It is not always safe to assume, as some agencies do, that joint ownership involves equal sharing. Fairness dictates that the share of each applicant be determined individually before the maximum is applied. Sometimes a special maximum is set for property owned jointly by husband and wife.[24]

Standards for valuing some forms of personal property are even more difficult to establish than are those for real estate. Tax valuations are not helpful for valuing personal property. Listed stocks and bonds present no problem, but often the value of unlisted stocks, deposits in closed banks, and other miscellaneous items is not ascertainable. Insurance, although much less complex than many other items, is not so simple as is sometimes assumed, for the face value of the policy may be the potential value but it is not the actual or cash value that is usually applied to other items. Hence, a special maximum is sometimes established for insurance.

In old age assistance, property requirements appear to be restrictive, although their original purpose may have been to insure some liberality in the treatment of old people while at the same time protecting the interests of the state. It has already been noted that the tradition of poor-law administration and sometimes actually its practice have required public aid to be given only to paupers or to persons entirely without resources; old age assistance laws, however, were designed to take care of persons above the level of absolute destitution. On this point the Wisconsin Pension Department has made a clear presentation of what it judges to be the object of the framers of the state law: "The intent of the old age assistance law is to assist not only those persons who

[24] In Iowa, for example, the real-estate maximum for one person is $2,000, but for combined real-estate holdings of husband and wife it is $3,000.

are absolutely destitute, but also those persons who have property which cannot be readily converted into cash without undue hardship and loss." [25]

The maximums set forth in the laws of other states were doubtless intended not so much to restrict eligibility as to guide or compel administrators of old age assistance laws to allow applicants to retain their property if its value was not excessive. Thus there is a liberal aspect even to the use of the lien upon the applicant's property. It allows the administrator to accept applications that he might otherwise be compelled to reject. Without a lien provision a rigid property maximum or an adverse local public opinion may compel the administrator to reject the application of a person with property holdings, which, though having a high valuation, are temporarily nonproductive and unsalable. Such an applicant may be totally without income or other means of obtaining cash and be needy even though not destitute. He might be glad to surrender his property in return for assistance but be unable to find a purchaser or anyone to lend him cash for living expenses with the property as security.

That requirements for surrender of property, or the full control of property, occasionally work more beneficially than is sometimes believed does not constitute a recommendation to establish such procedures. There are undoubtedly better ways of protecting the interests of applicant and agency than the elaborate property requirements of many states. It is particularly unwise to have such requirements in the law, for they are difficult to change even when proved unsatisfactory.

Usually, however, the requirement that an applicant sign a lien agreement is the most difficult eligibility requirement for him to accept. The status of being a property owner may be important to him, and signing a lien seems to put him in danger of losing it. Often the savings that have gone into property have meant sacrifices, justified only by a belief that ownership of property would make his future more secure. Signing a lien seems to surrender the protection which he fears may later be needed more greatly than at present—difficult as his situation may be. Many old couples, too, have made sacrifices to save for their children's future security. It is not easy for them to give up this objective. A little present comfort seems hardly worth the sacrifice. The children, too, may object to having their parents' property jeopardized. Several instances are reported in which children preferred to continue the struggle to

---

[25] Wisconsin, State Pension Department, *Social Security Laws of Wisconsin Relating to Blind Pensions, Aid to Dependent Children, Old Age Assistance,* 1936, p. 20.

provide for eligible parents, without public assistance, to the point of depriving themselves and their children not only of reasonable opportunities but also of necessities rather than to give up future rights in their parents' homestead.

Much of the applicant's objection to the lien is based on misunderstanding. To many people the signing of an official paper relating to their property is equivalent to its immediate loss, with no hope of eventual recovery. Actually the lien required by old age assistance regulations is little more than a promise to repay whatever assistance is advanced, secured by the property owned. The law may forbid the enforcement of the lien during the lifetime of the applicant or so long as the property is occupied by surviving wife or minor children.[26] The lien is sometimes only a second- or third-class claim against the estate. It may usually be liquidated by payment of the total amount of assistance advanced or by other settlement satisfactory to the agency.[27] In some states little attempt is made to enforce liens, yet the lien is a legal claim which seems to threaten the client's future and is undoubtedly a cloud on the title until released.[28]

An "agreement to reimburse," used in some states in place of a lien, is sometimes more acceptable to applicants although its effect is about the same as that of a lien. Immediate conveyance of property by deed or similar instrument is not commonly used for real estate. When immediate conveyance of real estate is asked, it is usually required only for property not used by the applicant as a residence. The lien may be automatic; that is, the signing of the application form authorizes the placing of a lien, the confirmation of which is made by sending to the responsible local official a copy of the notice of award. Often, however, the property forms are entirely separate and bring the transfer issue more definitely before the applicant, making it less likely that he will unintentionally authorize conveyance. One large metropolitan agency requires the presence of a relative to whom the nature of the transaction can be explained before accepting the applicant's signature.

Assignment of insurance policies with surrender of the policy may be required if the applicant's assets, including the insurance, are above

---

[26] This latter provision, though made to liberalize treatment of dependents, may have objectionable consequences if the agency is without authority to release the lien: it has the effect of compelling occupancy of the home by the surviving dependent even though some other living arrangement might be preferable.

[27] A provision for release or compromise of a lien at the discretion of the agency is particularly important.

[28] For a discussion of objections to liens in connection with recoveries see chap. 10.

the maximum allowed. In a few state laws the adjustment of insurance is limited by special restrictions, but ordinarily assignment can easily be made. The same emotional resistance to assignment of insurance is sometimes met that is encountered in signing liens on real estate. In both instances one factor often complicates the situation: the interests of others may be involved with those of the recipient. If a relative who is the beneficiary has been paying the premiums he feels that he should be given consideration. Perhaps there has previously been a virtual assignment of the policy to this relative, although it may be difficult to prove. In such cases an agreement to take care of the applicant's funeral expenses is frequently obtained from the relative and the case accepted on that basis.[29] Sometimes if the amount of insurance exceeds the maximum, the applicant is asked not to assign the excess but to reduce the face amount of the policy in accordance with the insurance maximum. On the whole, insurance appears to be handled even more arbitrarily than real estate, probably because the relationship of these resources to the total problem of need determination is a technical area which has not been explored carefully and expertly.

States vary greatly in the maximum amounts set for different kinds of property. It is difficult to judge what factors induce a state to set the real-estate maximum. Sometimes there is apparently a connection between this maximum and the amount allowed as an exemption from judgment or levy for debt on other liability; sometimes it appears to be arbitrary. In some states the amount is specified by law; in others, by the agency. The latter method allows greater flexibility and hence permits some experimentation; it does not, however, always insure flexibility.[30] The establishment of maximum amounts, especially those for personal property, is often left to the local units. Whether a lien on, or the surrender of, property should be required of all applicants within the unit may also be decided by the unit. Thus even within a state these eligibility requirements may vary from one county to another.

[29] Agencies providing burial expenses for recipients who die leaving no estate and who have no relatives able to provide burial thus guard their funds from a future expenditure of this sort.

[30] The real-estate maximum that had thus been established in one state was found to be so low ($2,000) that an obviously needy applicant would be excluded. Instead of raising its maximum, which the state officials recognized to be too low, the state agency advised the local unit to allow the needy applicant to deed his property to his ineligible spouse and thus render himself eligible. This recommendation was made although an applicant in that state became ineligible if he transferred or assigned property within five years immediately prior to application in order to make himself eligible. This is an extreme example, but it illustrates the inconsistency common in the administration of property requirements.

The amount of personal property that an applicant may retain is frequently determined by the amount usually spent for funeral expenses in the community. It is generally recognized by administrative officials that applicants should be allowed to retain sufficient funds, if they have them, to assure decent burial; and maximums for cash assets or insurance resources are usually set at such a figure as to provide sufficient funds for a funeral that meets the social requirements of the local community; amounts of $300 to $500 are common practice.[31]

A few agencies allow retention of funds for medical and other emergency needs and for other items that the agency cannot supply from public funds. A real consideration of future needs when the budget is set up allows sensible planning of this sort. A small sum which the applicant feels is truly his and which at the same time he feels no need to conceal is a means of sustaining his morale, and, as a part of the joint plan of applicant and worker, helps to establish a sound relationship between applicant and agency. Security for the applicant and sensible and kindly but economical administration seem to be achieved. This result can, however, be attained whether or not a definite maximum for personal property is set. The absence of legal or regulatory provision would not usually preclude such an arrangement as a normal phase of the budgeting or planning process.

Need and Support of Relatives

In many ways support of relatives is the most difficult of all questions of eligibility. Nearly all states require that an applicant to be eligible must have no legally responsible relative able to provide for his support.[32] Responsibility of relatives' support is usually defined elsewhere in the statutes than in the old age assistance law; it varies from state to state. In all states children are included in the list of relatives responsible for support. Such responsibility, however, cannot always be enforced against married daughters because sons-in-law are exempt from liability. Parents are also responsible for children; in one state

[31] In most states provision is made from state or local funds (frequently the former) for burial of old age recipients leaving insufficient funds for this purpose and whose relatives are unable to provide burial expenses. The amount allowed is less than that allowed the recipient in cash or insurance for this purpose; $100 or $150 are commonly allowed from state funds. If provided from local funds the amount tends to be lower ($50 to $100 commonly). A few states make no provision for burial of old age assistance cases. These expenditures are not reimbursable from federal funds.

[32] A relative is supposed to contribute toward the support of a dependent for whose care he is liable to the extent of his ability, whether his means permit him to provide total or only partial support.

assistance was actually denied to an aged applicant on the grounds that her mother had sufficient means to provide for her. Grandchildren, particularly males, are sometimes required to support, especially if there are no children able to do so. Spouses are usually required to support each other. Support may also be required of other relatives if none of nearer relationship is able to assist and if they have means.

Generally speaking, the law places no obligation upon the old age assistance unit to aid the aged applicant to obtain assistance if relatives are able but unwilling to support him. Hence, the application may simply be rejected and the applicant left to gain support as best he may. A few state laws permit the acceptance of the application and place upon the agency responsibility for recovering the amount of assistance advanced from the legally liable relative. Other old age assistance units, although not legally responsible for obtaining support, undertake to assist the applicant in working out some kind of arrangement with relatives able but unwilling to help; or they may only go so far as to refer the rejected applicant to a social agency equipped to deal with such problems.

No easy solution to the problem of relatives' support has been found. Although the law may specify the classes of relatives who are responsible, there is no simple way either of determining the relative's ability to contribute or of compelling him to contribute regularly. Determination of ability to support if rigidly applied would require a detailed and searching study of the relative's resources and of his other obligations. Action for nonsupport usually entails fine or imprisonment, neither of which will assure support of the aged applicant. Even if public opinion supports drastic action of this sort against nonsupporting relatives, the results are far from satisfactory.[33] Relatives beyond the jurisdiction of the court can seldom be prosecuted, especially if they live across a state line and extradition proceedings are necessary. A court order directing payment of a stated sum at regular intervals does not necessarily bring in the money. Occasionally court action or threat of action may obtain results, but generally it is ineffective in providing support.

The purpose of eligibility requirements pertaining to relatives' support should be that of obtaining as large a contribution from relatives as they are able to make in view of their other important obligations. Nothing is gained by collecting support for an applicant if it deprives

[33] Several agencies reported reluctance of courts to take such cases, and when undertaken convictions were seldom obtained.

the relative's children or other dependents of necessities or reduces the relative's resources to a point that will make it impossible for him to provide for his own old age or for other future needs.

The difficulties of administering these requirements seem to arise from two causes. First, many administrators without experience in social work problems, especially the complex problems of family relationships, start out with a naïve confidence in legal machinery and compulsion as a means of handling a problem whose solution requires an individualized approach, such as that used by a skilled family case worker. Support can actually be obtained only when relatives are able and willing to contribute. The extent of ability to support can be learned only by adequate but tactful inquiry. Such an inquiry can also serve as a means of interpreting the needs of the applicant, the policies and objectives of the program—misunderstanding of which often contributes to the relatives' unwillingness to aid—and the obligations of the individual as a member of the applicant's family and as a citizen of the community. The most ingenious questionnaire and the most elaborate affidavit form will not produce this result.

The second cause of difficulties is the conflicting opinions about family obligations. Unquestionably the mores involved are changing. There is no general agreement on the obligation of the younger generation to the older. The duty of a son to support his parents would not have been questioned in an earlier day, even though such support deprived his own children of an opportunity for an adequate education. Now many people doubt whether the state gains any advantage in compelling support of the aged if the young are thus deprived of education necessary to make them useful, self-supporting citizens. On the other hand, the citizens of our communities are not now willing to assume support of the aged from public funds while well-to-do relatives are able to provide it without lowering their own standard of living below the usual standard of that community.

Communities are generally not ready to dispense with at least a moral obligation of responsible relatives to support dependent relatives. Nominal requirements must probably be retained. On the other hand, most communities are unwilling to support a rigorous legalistic and punitive enforcement of these provisions, and if they were sympathetic the methods themselves would in the end defeat rather than further the purpose of the agencies using them. Public opinion will not support prosecution of relatives, nor will it generally approve rejection of needy applicants because the agency believes relatives have means, if such rejection results in suffering by the denied applicant or in an undue burden on a relative whose ability to support has been overestimated. Administrators are, in short, compelled to use case-work methods; thus, the success of their efforts will depend on the case-work skill of their staffs.

Occasionally an applicant has entered into a more or less formal agreement for support with an individual or corporation (including a public body). Sometimes it is obtained in consideration of property transferred to the one promising support; or, it may be in the nature of a pension for services rendered. Some state laws provide that assistance be denied if any person or corporation is liable for support however the liability was originally established. In some instances this requirement has been sensibly and liberally construed; in others hardship has resulted. If the person (or corporation) is unable to furnish the promised support owing to altered circumstances, the aged applicant is helpless if such a requirement is enforced with extreme rigor. The requirement, however, may be a protection to old age assistance funds from persons or corporations desiring to free themselves of a burden. In cases of inability to carry out the agreement it has sometimes been possible to obtain a return of the property previously deeded or to make some other adjustment which avoids two extremes: that of freeing the individual (or corporation) from its obligation without penalty, and that of penalizing the aged applicant for the failure of the other party to carry out his obligations.

Institutions and Eligibility

The old age assistance program was established primarily to aid needy old people in their own homes. The President's Committee on Economic Security made the following statement about noncontributory old age pensions: "Old-age pensions are recognized the world over as the best means of providing for old people who are dependent upon the public for support and who do not need institutional care." [34] The Social Security Act makes no statement about need of institutional care or residence in a private institution, but provides that a state with an approved plan may claim reimbursement for an otherwise eligible

---

[34] *The Report to the President* (1935), p. 26. A stronger and somewhat more specific statement is found in *Social Security in America*, p. 189: "In entering upon an exposition of proposals for old-age security, it should be asserted that the 'poorhouse' or 'almshouse' method of providing for all aged dependents has been rejected by thinking opinion as both wasteful and inhumane. Noninstitutional assistance for those who are not in need of institutional care has become an accepted standard of decent provision for the dependent aged."

recipient who "is not an inmate of a public institution." States may therefore allow or prohibit, as they choose, assistance to persons in private institutions or to those needing institutional care, and receive federal reimbursements for such cases. Although states necessarily comply with the provisions of the Act in denying aid to inmates of public institutions, they vary in their provisions regarding private institutions and need of institutional care. A few that originally prohibited aid to inmates of private institutions now permit it.

Forbidding payment of old age assistance to inmates of public institutions probably has two main objectives: namely, to enable and encourage the beneficiaries who are able, and desire to do so, to live outside institutions; and to maintain the identity of purpose of public appropriations rather than to allow the assistance program to subsidize institutions. Unfortunately, the Social Security Board and many of the states did not foresee the difficulties that would arise through a narrow interpretation of terms. The federal Act does not define either "inmate" or "public institution." [35]

The framers of the laws in several states did not sufficiently take into consideration the effect on administration of a rigid prohibition of assistance to inmates of institutions, with no provision for advance grants or for an interim or grace period in which the applicant might leave the institution and establish living arrangements outside. Inmates of institutions, especially institutions for the care of the aged poor, seldom have either cash or credit to obtain accommodations outside. A few state laws permit inmates to file an application and receive an award while still in the institution if they leave before the first payment is received. If advance grants are made and if the agency can notify the applicant when his first check may be expected, it is sometimes possible for the applicant to leave with his check in his hand.

Although one purpose of some state laws was to clear institutions of able-bodied old people who could live outside, the laws were framed in a way that denies aid to such persons. There seems to be no reason why provision should not be made for at least one payment to an eligible applicant while still in the institution. Certainly it was not the intention of the federal Act to deny assistance to otherwise eligible persons who could live outside. Nor was it probably the purpose of most drafters of state legislation; but the law has had the effect of denying assistance to many persons forced by circumstances to reside in institutions although not in need of custodial care.

[35] See chap. 10.

Some state laws provide for denial of assistance to persons "in need of institutional care," even though the applicant is not, at the time of application, an inmate of an institution. Apparently this requirement was adopted to force acceptance of institutional care upon applicants who appeared apt to benefit by it or unable to maintain themselves properly without special care. It may also have been thought necessary to discourage relatives from keeping at home patients whose mental condition might make them dangerous. Obviously this provision is one that can be used unfairly and even oppressively if proper standards and sufficient controls are not established.

Ordinarily the need of institutional care is largely a matter of medical judgment. This eligibility requirement might be applicable when need for institutional care is the result of physical or mental difficulties making it impossible for the applicant to care for himself and requiring his segregation either to improve his condition or to protect himself or others from his irresponsible behavior. Social factors, however, may enter into the decision where the patient may best be cared for.

If the patient is afflicted with an infectious disease or suffers from a mental disorder that may make him dangerous a medical diagnosis may be sufficient. Most states have laws prescribing procedure in such cases, which, as a matter of fact, usually do not constitute problems for the old age assistance administrator. The mild or borderline cases more often come to his attention. Here the decision depends less on the patient's condition than on the facilities for his care outside the institution. If the applicant's home is suitably equipped and a relative is able and willing to care for him, home care may be satisfactory and even preferable for a bedridden or mildly demented patient who would otherwise require institutional care. A careful investigation of available facilities is necessary, however, in order to arrive at a satisfactory decision.

Decisions on need for institutional care made without careful investigation or medical and social judgment are too often determined by subjective factors. Local prejudices often result in denials or discontinuances on moralistic grounds. An applicant who drinks occasionally or who keeps a dirty house or who is untidy and unclean in person may be judged to be "better off at the county home" and denied assistance even though he is otherwise eligible, able to look after his essential needs, and not dangerous to others. Some applications have been rejected because of supposed need of institutional care although no appropriate institution was available; and no responsibility was assumed for seeing that the applicant's need was met in some other way.

Moralistic Provisions

Some eligibility requirements are frankly directed toward selecting applicants who are "worthy" or "deserving." Some are undoubtedly an expression of the idea that old age assistance is a new kind of public aid more respectable than ordinary poor relief, with which are associated such odious terms as "pauper," "indigent relief," or "public charity." The public still likes to believe that it is possible to give assistance on the basis of rewarding the deserving and ignoring the undeserving. A difficulty in attempting to separate the two groups is the establishment of criteria for their differentiation. Generally, those old age assistance laws attempting to provide for selection of "worthy" applicants forbid giving assistance to one or more of the following groups: (1) Persons who have been confined to a penal or correctional institution, or, more commonly, who have been convicted of a felony within a specified period of time. In one state persons on probation are excluded regardless of the seriousness of their offense. (2) Persons who have deserted or failed to support a spouse or minor children within a specified number of years. (3) Persons who have been vagrants, tramps, or beggars within a stated period. (4) Persons guilty of intoxication or handling liquor or narcotic drugs.

These requirements can be enforced without much difficulty in states that provide reasonably adequately for general relief. The applicant denied old age assistance can thus be cared for. Otherwise pressure to make exceptions is sure to be felt. If the law is not definite and specific, decisions cannot be sustained when the applicant appeals. A general term, such as "deserving," or "a record of decency and self-respect," requires a subjective judgment by the administrator which is difficult to make fairly and, even when so made, is almost impossible to defend if the applicant and his friends do not agree. An adverse decision is never readily accepted, and one that reflects on character is most likely to be resented. When the law is specific, denial of such an application must usually be based on the facts of the applicant's past conduct; denial may appear even to the moralists to be unfair if his present conduct is exemplary. In fact, criticism will be heard in the community whether the town drunkard or "black sheep" of good family is accepted or denied.

The experience of states administering moralistic requirements fails to justify any arguments for their retention. There is no evidence that excluding persons whose conduct has been unconventional results in their sudden transformation. The deterrent effect on prospective applicants is doubtful. Moreover, the requirements of "worthiness" rather than objective standards of need are unsatisfactory criteria for a public assistance program and often result in injustice to needy applicants. The representatives of the Bureau of Public Assistance have advised against their inclusion in state laws, but not always with the desired result. Once such a provision gets into the law it is difficult to eliminate. Presumably the federal auditors take exception to evidence of violation of such requirements of state plans but, on the whole, it is believed that they do not look for such evidence quite so carefully as for other kinds.[36]

Miscellaneous Requirements

A few other eligibility restrictions are found in state laws. In Iowa and Connecticut, where the program was supported by a per capita tax, state laws made payment of the tax a condition of eligibility. In Iowa the applicant who had failed for three years to pay the required tax became permanently ineligible.[37] In Connecticut public officials could abate the tax of persons too poor to pay.[38] In Iowa loans made by local officials or private agencies to applicants that were to be repaid out of the first assistance check enabled some applicants to qualify by permitting them to pay up back taxes, but if the applicant lived in a community where public officials or private agencies were unwilling to donate or lend money for this purpose his application was denied. Thus eligibility might depend on the circumstance of geographical location and not on the qualifications of the applicant.

In Mississippi an applicant must not be contributing to "the support of any able-bodied person over the age of eighteen years other than husband or wife." [39] The purpose of this provision is to prevent adult children from taking advantage of the recipient by coming home to be supported by him. In practice little attention is paid to this requirement. It is regarded as a threat or weapon to be invoked for the recipient's protection rather than as a limitation on eligibility. The grants in this state are so small as to make it seem impossible that any grant could be stretched to cover the needs of an additional person.

---

[36] Theoretically federal auditors must determine whether expenditures are made "in accordance with the approved state plan." Since the state law is a part of the state plan, the acceptance by the Security Board of a state plan that includes a state law with a provision the Board disapproves places it in the position of enforcing requirements that it would prefer to see eliminated.

[37] The poll tax in Iowa was eliminated in 1937.

[38] Connecticut, *Public Acts,* 1935, chap. 110, sec. 1 (g).

[39] Mississippi, *Laws,* 1936, H.B. 381, sec. 10 (g).

One of the most troublesome of the miscellaneous requirements is the one that the applicant shall not be in receipt of public assistance from any other source; medical care, however, is frequently excepted. It is desirable to prevent duplication among public agencies, but it can be done by more constructive methods than legal restrictions on this sort of supplementation. Even when grants are reasonably adequate, individual recipients are overtaken by emergencies, and some require additional aid because of special needs that cannot be met even when the maximum grant is allowed. If no contingent fund is provided to meet these special demands the recipient must either suffer or give up his grant and have recourse to general relief or to some other source of funds.

Signature and Oath

A number of states require that the applicant's signature be attested on oath. This requirement has received criticism out of all proportion to its significance. Critics have asserted that it was a return to the hated pauper's oath of an earlier day, although they are unable to produce an example of such an oath or evidence that it actually was ever used. Objection has been directed, in fact, toward the oath itself, which is unimportant, rather than toward the purpose which the oath (or affidavit) is expected to serve and toward the administrative methods used in carrying out these purposes. An oath is sometimes attached to an application chiefly to prevent fraud and incidentally also to make unnecessary an investigation of the application. These purposes appear to be based on false assumptions. It is a naïve though persistent belief that requiring the attachment of an oath to the document in which claims are set forth will prevent false statements by persons seeking benefits of one sort or another. The inclusion of threats of severe penalties for perjury or misstatement is supposed to be an additional assurance of truthful statements. In practice the only persons who will be impressed are the conscientious and the timid, neither of whom is likely to make a wilful misstatement if only a simple signature is required. Applicants who are both bold and unscrupulous are those most likely to constitute a problem; they are not apt to be deterred by an oath or by threat of penalties for perjury.[40]

The assumption that truthful statements in the application blank will

---

[40] The agency has a responsibility for assuring itself that the applicant understands the nature of the penalties imposed for false statement and all the responsibilities he undertakes in affixing his signature.

eliminate the necessity of investigation of the application is almost equally naïve. The purpose of an investigation is not merely to check the accuracy of the applicant's statements, although that is incidental to a complete investigation. Actually few people make deliberate misstatements, and if detecting falsehoods were the chief purpose of an investigation of eligibility the value of an extensive (and expensive) one might indeed be questioned. The real purpose is to obtain all the data necessary to determine an applicant's eligibility, and to interpret and evaluate the facts in accordance with the administrative requirements of the program. No application blank can possibly supply all the data needed for all the situations that may be presented, although it may and should provide clues; nor can any blank yet devised insure that the queries made thereon shall not be, in some instances, ambiguous and that the most conscientious answers may not sometimes be mistaken or incomplete.

Another purpose of an affidavit attached to an application is to authorize the agency to take certain action on the application. Ordinarily the signing of an application, whether or not an oath is attached, must be regarded by the agency as an authorization to proceed with an investigation of the applicant's eligibility and to decide the amount of award if eligibility is established. It should, however, be clear to both parties to what is, in effect, an agreement just what it involves. The applicant is entitled to know in a general way the area of the proposed investigation, the facts to be obtained, and the methods to be used in obtaining them. If banks, insurance companies, hospitals, physicians, relatives, and other personal and confidential sources are to be consulted, the applicant has a right to know and to give his consent with a full understanding of the meaning of his signature on the authorizing form. For this reason some agencies prefer to use a separate form for authorizing consultation of those persons and agencies that are in a confidential relation to the applicant.[41]

If an applicant is asked to make any commitments about property he must clearly understand what he is doing. He should not be permitted to authorize the placement of a lien on his property or sign an agreement to reimburse from his estate all the assistance that may be given, under the impression that he is applying for a pension. The presence or absence of an affidavit is not the important consideration. The responsibility of the agency is to assure itself before any papers are signed

[41] For further discussion of reasons for separate authorization see chap. 7.

that the applicant and any other persons whose interests are involved fully understand what rights are being surrendered. The desirability of requiring surrender of property is another issue discussed earlier. Surrender of property usually requires an attested signature (oath or affidavit), but the presence of an oath on the application blank does not necessarily mean that an agreement about property is required. If it is the surrender of property to which the critic objects, modification of property requirements is more likely to result if he directs his criticisms specifically toward them rather than toward the relatively harmless affidavit used only to attest a signature.

Although many applicants object to signing a lien agreement or otherwise involving their property, there is no evidence that they object to the oath or affidavit used by some states. Affidavits are required in signing a variety of other official papers, and most applicants find nothing derogatory in the requirement of an oath on their old age assistance applications.

In one respect the requirement of an oath may be undesirable. It may be unduly burdensome if it causes applicants to travel considerable distance, to wait a long time, or to pay a notary's fee. Of the twelve states observed, eight require some form of oath, but in three of these, employees of the local old age assistance units are legally authorized to receive the oaths either by blanket or specific action of the governing board. Thus, applications can be taken in the home, in the office of the local agency, or wherever convenient, and no fee is necessary. New York and Washington do not require an affidavit but rather the applicant's signature to a statement that he is "fully informed of the contents of this application and knows that making false statements or misrepresentations constitutes a violation of the law, with penalties fixed therefor." One witness to the signature is required, unless the signature is by mark, in which event Washington requires that there be two witnesses. Massachusetts has the same requirements except that the applicant's statement is still simpler: "This application is made under penalties of perjury." Florida merely requires the applicant's signature and asks for witnesses only when the applicant must sign by mark.

★　★　★

It should now be fairly evident that while the Social Security Act and the requirements of the Social Security Board place some restriction on the old age assistance program, the important details of administration are, nevertheless, largely in the hands of the states. While the kinds of eligibility requirements are limited by the Act, the selection of those to be adopted and the method of administering them are matters solely of state discretion. Only the general scope of the administration of these requirements has here been set forth. The details of their application will be elaborated in succeeding chapters.

CHAPTER 7

APPLICATION AND INTAKE PROCEDURES

THE TERM "application" is used variously to indicate the request
or claim for assistance, the procedure by which this request is
made, and the official record of the request. It is not important
for the present discussion that a precise definition be adhered to if the
various steps in the application process are kept clearly in mind and,
furthermore, if the official recognition or reception of the claim by
the agency is regarded as the significant step.[1] Under a strict definition,
only those requests that have officially been received by the agency are
"applications."

ADMINISTRATIVE RESPONSIBILITY FOR APPLICATION PROCEDURES

The responsibility for establishing the policies and procedures by
which application for old age assistance is made rests with the states.
The federal Act furnishes no guidance in determining what an application is and how it shall be handled.[2] The Social Security Board has
prescribed no form and issued no requirements for handling applications, although an outline of application procedure and a copy of all
forms prescribed by a state must be included in the material submitted
to the Board as part of the outline of the state plan of administration to
be approved if federal funds are obtained.[3]

[1] Official recognition or reception of the applicant is sometimes called "acceptance of
the application." The term "acceptance," however, is frequently understood to mean
"approval" as opposed to "rejection" of the application. It is therefore avoided in this
report, and "reception of the application" is substituted.

[2] The term "application" is mentioned only once in Title I of the Security Act. Section
2 (b) (2) uses the term incidentally in connection with residence requirements: "Any
residence requirement which excludes any resident of the State who has resided therein
five years during the nine years immediately preceding the application and has resided
therein continuously for one year immediately preceding the application; . . . " In an
early section, 2 (a) (4), the Act speaks of a "claim for old-age assistance" as follows:
". . . provide for granting to any individual, whose claim for old age assistance is denied,
an opportunity for a fair hearing before such agency; . . . " Nowhere in the Act is
"application" or "claim" defined.

[3] The field staff of the Bureau of Public Assistance has advised states informally regarding forms and procedures. A special consultant on forms in the Division of Standards

Opportunity to Apply

The requirement of the Act that the state plan "shall be in effect in all political subdivisions of the State" presumably imposes upon the state agency the responsibility for seeing that opportunity to apply is available therein to persons who may be eligible. State agencies appear, at least for the most part, to assume that they have a definite responsibility for making this opportunity reasonably accessible to applicants and to inform applicants of eligibility requirements and of their right to make application. The tasks involved in the application process become largely the responsibility of the local agency, although the state retains some supervision and control over them.

The responsibility to provide opportunity to apply involves somewhat different problems when the program is wholly state financed than when there is local financial participation. In the former instance, the state agency has, presumably, full responsibility for the establishment of local offices handling applications. Theoretically, the state could establish as many local offices as it saw fit and locate them wherever convenient. In practice, however, this freedom is somewhat limited. It is necessary to have the offices accessible to the applicants who cannot afford to spend money to make long journeys and who may be too feeble to travel even if they have means to do so. Failure to make opportunity to apply at convenient offices is almost equivalent to denying aid.

For the sake of justice, as well as to meet the provision that the program must be "in effect in all political subdivisions," the state agency is compelled either to establish units of its own in each subdivision or to induce the local officials to assume some responsibility for application activities. In most states the responsibility of these officials is fixed by law. In Connecticut, for instance, where the town is the local unit, the chief administrative official of the town is made legally responsible to provide facilities for filing applications. The completed applications are forwarded to the state, and all other contacts with the applicant are handled by state workers operating through district offices. County officials in other state-operated systems are induced to supply at least some essentials—office space, equipment, or supplies—even when they are not expected to assume responsibility for carrying on any of the actual application procedures.

---

and Procedures has been available to the field staff for special technical advice on the make-up and use of application blanks and other forms. Certain statistical forms and uniform procedures have been prescribed by the Bureau of Research and Statistics and consultant service has also been provided in this area.

In locally operated, state-supervised systems, the supplying of facilities and the carrying out of all procedures are, naturally, the responsibility of the local unit. Responsibility for furnishing information to the public about application procedures is usually more or less divided. The state agency tends to handle information of state-wide interest and of general application, while the local units undertake to inform communities of the existence of local facilities, their location, office hours, and special requirements. Some state agencies have also recognized the value of assisting local units in disseminating information; a few, however, when presenting the program to the public, have really hampered local units by overemphasizing state activities and ignoring those of the local unit.

Uniform Procedures

Since old age assistance programs are state-wide they must in general provide, as Social Security Board representatives have repeatedly urged, for similar treatment of persons in similar circumstances. Uniform application procedures throughout the state appear to be necessary toward this end. If procedures are to be uniform, however, the state agency must assume responsibility for establishing them. This has generally been done. A blank form on which the necessary data are to be recorded is adopted by the state agency and furnished directly or prescribed as a model for local agencies. In either event the form is mandatory. Other subsidiary forms may also be prescribed. The distribution of blanks may be controlled by the state or delegated. The best practice seems to be for the state to hold each locality responsibile for this activity within its jurisdiction and to refer to the local agency all inquiries about the filing of an application. Uniform procedures for receiving, handling, recording, and counting applications are also outlined by state agencies.

Other Supervisory Methods

Although the state agency administering or supervising a program must delegate to local units a considerable measure of responsibility for application activities, it cannot relinquish final responsibility for maintaining a satisfactory standard of administration of these activities throughout the state. Hence it cannot stop merely with providing opportunity to apply and presenting standard forms and uniform procedures: it must exercise general supervision and establish suitable controls over local performance. To accomplish this end, state agencies usually depend chiefly on two methods: review of the case records, including the application and supporting documents, either in the state office or in the field; and supervision of staff through a qualified field staff.[4]

INTAKE

The first part of the application process carried on by the local units is sometimes known as "intake." This generally includes: (1) reception of persons who believe themselves eligible for assistance; (2) answering inquiries about eligibility requirements and other provisions of the law; (3) assisting applicants to complete the application blank; (4) administering the oath, if one is required; (5) assisting applicants to obtain documentary proof of eligibility, when such proof is required prior to application; (6) explaining property provisions to the applicant and to relatives whose presence may be required because their interests are involved; and (7) clearing the way, by explanation to the applicant, for the full investigation which must follow official receipt of the application and thus, so far as possible, forestalling the possibility of misunderstanding and antagonism.

Public Information

The tasks involved in intake are definitely affected by the state of public opinion in the community—the amount of information that the public has about the program, as well as the general attitude toward it. It is unfortunate that the value of public information about eligibility requirements and application facilities is so often underrated by administrators. Fear of the demoralizing effect of public relief seems in some instances to deter them from taking any action to popularize a public assistance program by a campaign of public information. Others assert that through the so-called "grapevine" or activities of "pension agitators" the public, and especially the aged in the community, are fully informed on assistance matters. Often, however, the same administrators complain of the number of ineligible applicants who besiege the local office and the difficulty experienced by the agency through misunderstanding. If the public is fully informed about eligibility requirements, the agency is saved much trouble and expense since fewer ineligibles apply. Both state and local agencies must carry on public information

[4] In some states an applicant may ask for a fair hearing if the decision on his application is long delayed. This provision, while doubtless intended to control delay, whether occurring before or after reception of the application, is more effective in curtailing subsequent delay. Hence, fair hearing is not included among the methods chiefly used for controlling local action on applications. For further discussion see chap. 16.

activities; but best results seem to be obtained when the state agency takes advantage of its special opportunities for disseminating information, as well as for consultation in the field, and uses these facilities not only in its own special activities but also makes them available to the local units.

State agencies have access to state-wide publicity media and often have contact with representatives of press associations that maintain offices in capital cities to keep in touch with state official news. Some state agencies also have access to radio broadcasting facilities. Nearly always they have frequent opportunities to appear before meetings of state-wide groups and to meet and confer with representatives of large organizations and associations whose understanding of, and cooperation in, the program are needed. They, oftener than local agencies, have skilled help in planning programs, preparing copy, and in maintaining relations with representatives of the various media through which material is disseminated. State agencies with such equipment have found a number of ways to aid the local units besides the indirect help from the use of state-wide media.

Special articles have been prepared adaptable for use in local newspapers; informative leaflets and pamphlets have been made available for distribution to prospective applicants and to other interested individuals and groups. Bulletins have been issued containing suggestions and instructions which have assisted local directors to select and prepare their material so as to fit it into the general state program of public education. The provision of service of this sort through personal consultation was a plan employed successfully in one of the states visited, and as a method appears to be more promising than those used by public information representatives who ignore the local agencies in planning their programs.[5]

Public information has a special relation to intake. If prospective applicants understand the function of the agency and the limitations of the program and have some knowledge of eligibility requirements and their proof, the agency's intake job is much more easily and speedily performed. Those who apply are better prepared to accept the necessary procedures; some of them may even have assembled much of the data needed for proving their eligibility, which the agency would otherwise be compelled to have its workers search out or to aid the applicants in obtaining.

---

[5] Care must be taken to channel consultation through the regular field service in order to avoid disrupting the established lines of supervisory responsibility.

Quarters

In arranging for the reception of applicants and others seeking information, an agency needs suitable office space. At the time the field visits were made many local agencies had unsatisfactory quarters. The program in many states had been in operation only a few months, and often the agency had been compelled to receive applications before there had been time to find and equip desirable quarters. In some communities office space was not available, and in others limited funds for administrative purposes made it impossible to rent or lease sufficient and suitable space and to equip it adequately. In the locally operated program provision of space, equipment, and supplies was the responsibility of local officials; and often even in state-operated plans no responsibility for office quarters and equipment for local representatives was assumed by the state agency. In large cities offices were generally found in old warehouses or loft buildings, often spread over several floors and served by antiquated elevators originally intended for freight, or by stairways too long or too steep and often poorly lighted. In some instances these buildings were isolated and not easily accessible.[6] Few branch or district offices of a local agency were established to provide more accessible and less crowded reception facilities.[7]

In the small communities the headquarters of the old age assistance agencies were most frequently located in county courthouses (town halls in New England). A program only recently added to the county's list of activities had, as a rule, to take what was left in the way of space, whether or not suitable in size, location, or equipment. Often the agency was compelled to share the quarters of other officials. An agency in Indiana shared two small basement rooms with the county surveyor's staff; an Iowa unit used a small hall-like room concealed behind the county recorder's office. One Mississippi unit shared with representatives of two other programs the county commissioners' boardroom from which the workers were necessarily barred on board-meeting days; another used the county law library for the director's office, the upstairs

[6]The dangers of heavy traffic might seem to make a downtown office less desirable than one removed somewhat from the center of the city. Downtown traffic under the control of well placed traffic signals may, however, be less dangerous than the lighter but less well supervised traffic of a suburban area or traffic hampered by narrow streets, loading operations, and the heavy trucks that infest a wholesale district.

[7]Even when old age assistance was handled by a local agency having branch offices for the administration of general relief or other programs they were often not utilized in old age assistance administration. The reason for this was apparently the desire to prevent old age assistance from being contaminated by the taint of relief, but the result was sometimes discomfort and inconvenience for the applicant.

hall for the clerk's desk, and the county courtroom for a waiting room when court was not in session and the halls or the courthouse square when it was. When no space in the courthouse was available, quarters in other publicly owned buildings were obtained; old storerooms or former residences were sometimes utilized.

Some agencies arranged to take applications at designated spots where regular daily office hours were maintained. In other areas scheduled office hours were held at such places at less frequent intervals. A few agencies were assisted by volunteer workers or board members who used their own homes or local public buildings, stores, banks, and lodgerooms as application headquarters. In at least one instance a worker parked her car at a crossing of two highways on certain days and used either her car or the shade of a tree as her interviewing room. Most of these arrangements, however, were temporary: after the initial period of the program applications have normally been received only at agency headquarters. State-operated systems acting through district (multi-county) rather than county offices usually found it necessary to have some sort of intake facilities in each county in the district. These have usually been continued beyond the initial period.

Offices were not only inconveniently located geographically but were also often physically inaccessible. A single long flight of stairs may be a real obstacle to a feeble or physically handicapped person. An effort was generally made to procure ground-floor rooms if possible. Elevators are not provided in most small courthouses, and, even where they are, they may seem a formidable barrier to an old person unfamiliar with them. If stairs could not be avoided, most agencies tried to make special arrangements for applicants unable to make the climb. Home visits, which must always be resorted to for bedfast or housebound applicants, had to be arranged also for many less severely handicapped. Sometimes officials in first-floor offices offered temporary space for special interviews. One worker reported that she held many interviews in cars parked around the courthouse square. Clerks in first-floor offices often cooperated by watching for handicapped applicants and by acting as their messengers in notifying the agency of their plight.

Reception

Suitable reception facilities should include pleasant and comfortable waiting space and courteous and speedy attention. In very few units were these requirements fulfilled; many agencies had no waiting rooms. Applicants whose needs could not be served immediately were often compelled to stand about in halls and corridors or on stairways. Oftener, perhaps, they waited in rooms used for other purposes, where they were troubled by noise and confusion and where they interfered with privacy needed for interviewing other applicants. Poor reception facilities also impeded prompt service. In a city office where large numbers of applicants must be handled one or more attendants are necessary. Sometimes the same waiting room must serve other programs or categories; usually it must also serve miscellaneous agency callers and recipients who have come to interview their visitors (case workers) to make inquiry of some sort or to request some special attention. A person should be available who can answer inquiries, take messages, make appointments, and handle the routing of those who are to be interviewed. If many persons are to be handled, several receptionists may be needed. Other attendants may also be required to serve as ushers, couriers, or messengers.

Agencies generally recognize that the frail health of many applicants makes them peculiarly susceptible to fatigue. The agencies visited generally made an effort to avoid long periods of waiting. On the other hand, the appointment system, often used in scheduling intake interviews for applicants for general relief, is recognized by agencies to be unsatisfactory for handling applicants for old age assistance. Old people may find the trip to the office too fatiguing to be repeated within a day or so; and those who are unable to make the trip alone must depend upon a friend or relative who might be unwilling or unable to make a second trip. Although office interviews are generally preferred for the initial interview, it is often possible to set a date for a home visit if an office interview cannot be arranged immediately. Sometimes a short interview will be sufficient to determine whether the applicant is eligible and, if not, to direct him elsewhere; or, if probably eligible, to obtain enough information to allow clearance in the social service exchange prior to the home visit.

In small offices less formality is necessary, but it is just as important that the individual applicant be met pleasantly and aided in transacting his business with the agency. When applicants appear at infrequent intervals, an agency is inclined to overlook the need of making suitable provision for them. If the staff consists of only two or three persons the office clerk will usually greet most callers. When the reception of callers, including applicants, is one of the duties of a clerk, the local director should see that the clerk is as well instructed in this function as he is in his routine clerical duties. It is quite as important a task and one that clerical workers do not always perform satisfactorily.

The point at which the duties of receptionist and interviewer are divided is not always clear cut. The receptionist must actually hold a sort of preliminary interview. It is necessary for him to learn enough about the business of each caller to determine what the next step should be. A person who inquires about eligibility requirements does not necessarily become an applicant. If the age limit for old age assistance is sixty-five, it is unnecessary to refer to an intake interviewer a person of sixty-four years who asks about eligibility requirements and who understands at once why he is not eligible.[8]

An inquirer who is not fully satisfied with the answers given him, or who is not obviously ineligible, usually needs a fuller explanation than a receptionist can give him and should be referred to an interviewer whose knowledge or experience exceeds the receptionist's. Often the intake staff is expected to note recipients' changes of address and to see that a report of them is transmitted to the visitor to whom the case is assigned and to the central file. Responsibility for such routine activities as tracing lost checks may also be delegated to intake staff. Most of these duties can be performed by receptionists under the general direction of the intake supervisor. In general, however, tasks that cannot be despatched without extended interviewing cannot be handled successfully by a receptionist: his job by its very nature precludes his offering the applicant the privacy, continuity, and undivided attention necessary to successful interviewing.

The task of receiving applicants, answering their inquiries, and aiding them in preparing the formal application has a public relations aspect that agencies cannot afford to ignore. The way in which contacts with applicants and their friends are handled determines, to a large extent, their future attitude toward the program. Visitors to the agency who find a reasonably comfortable waiting room and who are treated courteously by the workers will have a vastly different attitude toward the program from those whose experience may be unpleasant. Many agencies are aware of this fact and make an effort to organize their intake activities so as to create good will in the community and particularly to win the cooperation of applicants.

Clearance

Before an applicant is referred to an interviewer it is usually desirable to learn whether he has previously been known to the agency. Often

---

[8]One large agency tallied such inquiries but did not obtain names or other identifying data. Many agencies kept no record whatever of such contacts.

the time of both applicant and interviewer can be saved if the information in a previous record is made available at once. Hence the receptionist customarily obtains enough identifying information from the applicant to clear his name through agency files.[9]

In large city agencies the inquiry is often cleared at this stage with the files of the social service exchange. This is usually a preliminary clearance, often made by telephone, followed by a written confirmation and perhaps by an additional, fuller report following the intake interview or the home visit. In small communities without such exchanges, it is sometimes customary to clear with the agency handling general relief or with one or more other agencies. Such clearance may be handled by telephone, personal conference, or by the use of lists. In some instances the files of the local public assistance unit are so arranged that they may be used as a local clearing house. It takes a little more time and effort to combine clearing data with other material on the individual cards, but the value of the service thus obtained may far outweigh the cost. A few social service exchanges, such as the Boston Central Index, operate on a state-wide basis, but this practice is not yet general.[10]

State agencies may also use their files for clearance. Some duplication between counties is discovered in this way, but most of the state files are not so set up as to be effective for other clearance purposes. On the whole, since clearance seems likely to be most useful at the local level, state agencies might well place emphasis on developing local facilities. State clearance can probably best be handled by interexchange clearance through well developed local exchanges.[11]

The Application Form

It may seem that the application form or blank should be discussed with recording procedures; yet the use of the blank has so close a relation to other procedures, especially to the intake interview, that it is

[9] If a previous record is discovered it is usually called from the files and placed on the interviewer's desk with the other information obtained by the reception clerk.

[10] Although the state agency in Massachusetts clears all applications outside Boston with the Boston Central Index, it does not send the report to the local agencies; thus no use of its reports is made by intake workers outside the city of Boston. The local agency in Boston handles its own clearance directly with the Index and uses the Index reports in the intake section as well as in its investigation tasks.

[11] State agencies requiring a report of local clearance on the investigation report do not always take the trouble to see that local agencies understand what is meant by the request. Use of reports received from the exchange rather than mere registration should be emphasized; this use can only be made clear by personal explanation if untrained workers are not familiar with facilities of exchanges.

desirable to give some attention at this point to the content of the form.

Although some states do not insist upon a formal, signed application of persons asking general assistance, such a blank is almost universally prescribed in the three categorical programs that are the responsibility of the Bureau of Public Assistance of the Board. Both the content and the form of the application blank used vary, however. Some of them are simple and limited in content; others are comprehensive and detailed; many are, in fact, needlessly elaborate.

The purpose of an application blank is primarily to record evidence that an applicant has on his own responsibility and in the belief that he is eligible made a formal request for assistance. To make such evidence valid and significant the applicant must be identified. The amount of identifying information required by state blanks varies greatly. Usually the full name, address, and age are sufficient. The spouse's name is frequently included and may be desirable to clinch identification, especially when a case number is not used. Provision is made, however, for including case numbers on the form since they are generally used. Names of other relatives are requested on some blanks but should be unnecessary.[12]

It is desirable to have on the blank a brief statement of the eligibility requirements in order that the applicant may know what they are before he makes a claim of eligibility. The statement of the eligibility requirements usually follows the wording of the state statute. If the wording is technical, it may be necessary to simplify it and restate the requirements in language comprehensible to the ordinary applicant. Besides the statement that he believes himself to be eligible, the applicant's signature may be all that is necessary to complete the application. Provision must be made, however, for witnesses if the applicant must sign by mark.[13] If an oath is required by state law, this must be attached. If penalties for false statement are provided, or if any penalty or obligation is imposed upon the applicant in signing the application, these should be stated clearly so that the applicant may be aware of all the obligations

[12] All identifying information required for clearance in a social service exchange need not be put on the application form. The complete case record should contain all needed data, and if unmistakable connection between the application and the full case record can be established the application blank itself need not carry items which are significant to the handling of the case but not essential to the validity of the application document. The case number is commonly used for this purpose, but if the number of cases is small and the duplication of names infrequent, even this method of connecting the two is not necessary.

[13] The signatures of two witnesses identified by their addresses are usually necessary, though only one may be required by the state law to attest a signature by mark.

he undertakes when he affixes his signature to the application form. A statement that the applicant understands his right to a fair hearing if a decision satisfactory to him is not made in a reasonable time may be added.

Many states have cumbered their applications with needless items. In the beginning these states evidently expected that it would be possible to have the applicant set forth on the application blank all the facts necessary to establish eligibility, and that when such a comprehensive statement was accompanied by an oath the task of investigation would, in most instances, be completed. In some localities the idea still lingers that a sworn statement is all that should be required for a satisfactory determination of eligibility. In most states, however, it has come to be recognized that no application blank can possibly be entirely self-acting. Many misunderstandings and consequent errors and omissions are sure to occur. Agencies have thus learned from experience that it is better to use a simple, easily comprehended application form and supplement it with a careful explanatory interview followed by the assembling of whatever factual data are needed to establish eligibility.

A number of agencies include in the application blank a statement that the applicant is willing to furnish all information necessary to establish his eligibility and that he authorizes others having information about his eligibility to furnish the required facts to any duly authorized representative of the agency. This sort of statement is often helpful in the investigative process and is necessary in some states because of state laws or the policies of groups which must be consulted. If such a statement is needed it is best, however, to use a separate form that the investigator can carry into the field to be shown to informants who may require it. The application itself is too valuable a document to be carried about in the worker's pocket or brief case unless several signed copies are available.[14] A simple form containing the necessary authorization can be signed when the signature is affixed to other documents.

The Intake Interview

One of the most important objectives of the intake interview is the interpretation of the program to the applicant. Many applicants come to the agency with definite preconceptions about the program—often

[14] A simple separate form may be cheaper, as well as more convenient, than additional copies of the application blank. The applicant may also prefer not to have the statements made on the application revealed to everyone who might need to see the authorization.

mistaken ones. The one most commonly encountered is that old age assistance is a pension, payable to all who have reached a certain age regardless of their need for it. The general use of the word "pension" in newspapers and conversation tends to reinforce the notion that the aid given is, in fact, a pension rather than a type of relief. Applicants, especially those whose resources make them ineligible, are often reluctant to give up the idea of a pension and accept that of assistance on a need basis; intake workers have a difficult task to perform in convincing such applicants that no pension, as such, is available. It is usually impossible to proceed satisfactorily with the application until the applicant has a reasonably clear idea of the objectives and the limitations of the program. It is important that he also understand the eligibility requirements other than need, although they present fewer difficulties.

The intake interviewer has an especial responsibility to see that provisions for placing liens on real estate and assignment of other items of property are understood before the application is signed and any necessary supporting documents executed. A few agencies require the presence of at least one close relative—usually a son or daughter if the applicant has children. The responsibility of relatives for providing support should also be explained at intake, for this is another matter on which misunderstanding frequently arises. Although this point usually needs to be covered again in the home interview, all discussion of it should not be postponed until that time. The right to a fair hearing should also be reviewed during the intake interview.

A number of states have found it useful to have a small printed or mimeographed pamphlet prepared and issued to prospective applicants containing the eligibility requirements and a brief explanation of each. Some of these are prepared in simple question-and-answer form with a short nontechnical explanation of the answers if the reasons for them are not immediately obvious. One enterprising local director during a few weeks after applications were first accepted ran a column in the newspaper of widest circulation in his jurisdiction, in which he daily propounded and answered one or more questions most commonly asked of his intake interviewers. Public meetings, newspaper articles, and other methods of informing the public about the program and especially eligibility requirements were all generally employed. The use of volunteer help in preliminary interviewing when the program was initiated—especially when an effort was made to select volunteers carefully and to see that they were themselves correctly informed—also helped to overcome misunderstandings and thus to reduce eventually those encountered by the intake interviewers.

Some state laws definitely place upon the applicant responsibility for presenting proof of his eligibility. In the absence of this requirement, agencies may recognize the value of having the applicant participate in the task of proving eligibility. Many applicants, of course, are physically or mentally incapable of taking any active part in this process; the intake interviewer must judge the extent to which it is wise for the applicant to assume this responsibility. On this point the *Visitors' Manual,* issued by the Wisconsin Pension Department, instructs its workers as follows: "While the applicant, or his relatives, may assist in the actual investigation process by securing proof of age, residence, etc., care should be exercised not to place a burden on the applicant greater than he is capable of assuming."

The intake interviewer usually assists the applicant in completing the application blank. Even though it is made as simple as possible, the blank may look rather formidable to a person unfamiliar with forms and unaccustomed to expressing himself in writing however simple. In a few local units visited, however, it was a definite policy not to help the applicant with his application blank on the theory that this undermined his sense of responsibility for the statements made on it. Most agencies, however, prefer to help if the applicant wishes; many discourage applicants from attempting to complete the application by themselves on the theory that errors are thus avoided and much time and trouble saved both applicant and agency. It appears to be good policy to offer assistance freely and to encourage the applicant to make use of it. If he prefers to take the application home with him for study and for consultation with his family, friends, and advisers, he should be permitted to do so. When he makes out his own application the agency may still have an opportunity to review the blank both before and after the applicant has made his entries; thus the agency gains the chief advantages of having the form completed by the worker—namely, being sure that the applicant fully understands the program as well as the blank itself to insure accurate entries. Several interviews may sometimes be necessary before the application is completed.

Agencies usually prefer to have the application made out in the office. Often the home offers unsatisfactory facilities both for privacy in interviewing and for writing. If copies must be furnished to the state office it is a decided advantage to use the typewriter and thus make the necessary duplicate. The typewriter also provides a more legible copy, as a rule, than is possible if entries are made by hand. In the matter of copies it may be noted that in no instance observed was a copy of the application furnished to the applicant himself. From his point of view, however, the application is an important document and may be especially so if the decision is adverse or delayed.[15]

When the applicant is bedfast or housebound, agencies must send a worker to prepare the blank at the home. A portable typewriter is sometimes used, but if this is not practicable the application may be taken in longhand. Sometimes longhand entries are later copied on the typewriter for the use of the state office. Some state agencies required that the original be submitted to the state office and also that the blank be filled in on the typewriter. Some local agencies met these requirements by making a longhand original and obtaining the applicant's signature on a second blank form onto which the longhand entries were later copied. Sometimes only notes of the applicant's wishes were made by the worker and later transferred to an application on which the applicant's signature had been affixed; and no complete original made in his presence and approved by him was actually prepared. Under satisfactory practice an original copy should be prepared which should either be read by the applicant if he is able to read, or be read to him and approved by him before he signs it. The signing of applications in blank should likewise be avoided, and applicants should be encouraged to ask for copies of all important documents that they sign, including the application blank itself.

The extent to which agencies administering old age assistance attempt to screen out eligibles at intake varies. It is obviously foolish to insist on regarding as an application every inquiry that comes to the agency. Many inquiries are made merely to confirm the inquirer's own impression that he is ineligible. It is evident, however, that the method of handling the interpretation of the requirements may affect applicants' decisions. A timid applicant can easily be discouraged from applying even though his eligibility is no more doubtful than that of a more determined applicant. Workers handling intake should therefore be persons of good judgment, skilful in drawing out shy, inarticulate applicants whose interests might be overlooked by an unskilful or impatient interviewer. On the other hand, it seems useless to accept an application from one who is obviously ineligible.

[15] Both the date and the nature of the entries on the blank may be important to the applicant who appeals for a fair hearing on the grounds either of long delay or of an unfavorable decision.

Considerable expense to the agency is usually involved in putting an application through all the processes of acceptance, investigation, disposition, and the accompanying recording. Investigation may involve expense and trouble likewise to persons and agencies outside the old age assistance agency itself. Moreover, the mere acceptance by the agency of the completed application form often raises the hopes of the applicant and makes all the harder for him the final denial. Nevertheless, refusal to accept an application is, in effect, a denial of assistance, and theoretically, at least, denials should be made only by persons with whom responsibility for making final decisions rests.

Because of the dangers involved in delegating any considerable amount of responsibility for decisions to the intake interviewers, agencies have sometimes made regulations designed to establish definite control over such decisions. In most agencies intake workers are not permitted to refuse or deny any applications unless the applicant himself fully concurs in the decision. Some agencies allow intake interviewers to eliminate applicants whose ineligibility relates to any of the definite or absolute factors, such as age.[16] But applications of persons whose resources appear to make them ineligible will be received by the agency and put through the routine by which the decision on award and amount of grant is made.

Relation of Intake and Investigation

In some agencies a separate intake staff handles all contacts until the application is signed—even home visits when these are necessary. Usually, however, cases requiring home visits are referred immediately to the visiting (investigating) staff without passing through the intake department. In some instances the intake staff performs a considerable part of the investigation. In one large city visited all eligibility requirements that could be established by search of public documents either locally or by correspondence with other localities were handled by the intake staff; cases were referred to the visiting staff only when a home visit or reference call (other than to a source of public records) became necessary. In this city all eligibility requirements except need were covered by the intake staff; and even respecting need, verification of property holdings and other financial matters were handled by that staff. If the applicant owned property, one relative at least would be asked to come to the office before the application was signed. Theoretically, all that was left to the visiting staff was to make a home visit and report of living conditions; complete the proof of residence; visit any relatives believed to be able, willing, and legally liable to support; work out a budget; and make the final recommendation on acceptance and amount of the grant, or denial.

The procedure followed when an applicant makes a reapplication is generally much the same as for original applications. Agencies frequently require a new application, and the intake interviewer must usually, in that event, give as much assistance in completing the blank as if the application were new. If the original application was denied, the reason for denial will need to be reviewed. If circumstances have not changed since the denial but the applicant is not satisfied with the previous decision, the interviewer may advise him to institute a request for a fair hearing rather than to file a reapplication.[17]

Another sort of reapplication problem is encountered at intake if the state law forbids reapplication within a given period (usually six months to a year). If the applicant asks to reapply within the period specified, the interviewer must explain the impossibility of granting his request. If the applicant reapplying is a former recipient whose grant has been suspended, the procedure may be simpler since some agencies do not require the filing of a new application in such cases. Inquiry is made about removal of the condition that caused the suspension; and, if the reason is easily established, the interviewer may aid the applicant in obtaining the necessary proof before the case is referred to the visitor for a home visit and reconsideration of need. If, on the other hand, the applicant's circumstances appear to be little altered by the suspension and its removal, and especially if the period has been short, reconsideration of need may be deferred until the regular period for reconsideration has elapsed.

Some agencies reassign the case immediately to the former visitor for a home visit and recommendation regarding reestablishment of the grant without a full intake interview. Whichever procedure means least delay and uncertainty for the applicant would seem the best; but agency organization and legal regulations are so varied that it is not possible to say precisely which method will produce that result.[18]

Still another problem arising at intake is the determination of the category for which the applicant will be accepted if he is apparently eligible for more than one. Applicants who are both aged and blind, for instance, may be eligible under two programs; but, since the Security

[17] For further discussion of complaint and fair-hearing procedures see chap. 16.
[18] For further discussion on the subject of reapplication procedure see chap. 9.

Act and most state laws forbid payment of blind aid to recipients of old age assistance, a choice must be made. In some agencies a definite rule may be adopted requiring that one or the other be given precedence regardless of the wishes of the applicant; in others, the decision is left to the applicant.

Some agencies wishing to place the emphasis of blind aid on the constructive aspects of the program, remedial work, such as restoration of vision and vocational education rather than relief or pension, prefer to put the aged blind on the old age assistance rolls. In locally operated plans a differential between the two programs in the amount of state reimbursement may lead the local agencies to prefer one or the other.[19] If the choice is left to the applicants they are apt to be influenced by differentials in eligibility requirements that seem to make one program or the other more favorable to their interests. If one program requires liens on property, for instance, and the other does not, applicants with property will often prefer the program (usually aid to the blind) not having the requirement.

Differentials between programs resulting from eligibility requirements, amount of state reimbursement, or the size of grants are likely to be less justifiable. Some state agencies appear to need to review this aspect of their programs and to work out their policies more thoughtfully. If state agencies fail to establish policies governing choice of categories, the local agency should do so in order to maintain a fair and consistent policy at intake. Whether choice is left to the applicant or not, intake interviewers will need to explain the policy adopted when applicants eligible for more than one program apply.

RECORDING PROCEDURES

In order to make a preliminary clearance prior to the intake interview, the receptionist may write the necessary identifying information on a plain piece of paper or a simple form which is transmitted to the interviewer with the report from the agency files and the social service exchange.[20] If the applicant has not previously been known to the agency, a card containing identifying data should immediately be placed in the master file or agency index.

[19] If one program is entirely state supported and the other requires local support, local officials are likely to have a decided preference for putting cases on the state-supported program and thus conserve local funds.

[20] In larger agencies the slip will be transmitted by tube or messenger to files and possibly also to the exchange; otherwise clearance with the exchange will usually be made by telephone from the file room. In smaller agencies the receptionist may handle clearance by consulting the files and possibly also by telephoning the exchange.

The Master File

The master file should contain a card for every case known to the agency and should indicate where the record of contacts with the case is to be found. A simple card designed only to identify the client and locate the record is best.[21] Some agencies have attempted to record alterations in the amount of the grant and other administrative changes better adapted to other records. The cards should be filed alphabetically and if, as is customary, a numbering system is used in filing case records, the case number should appear on the index card.[22] A single file should be used so that there will be only one place to look when clearing.[23]

The Case Record

Some agencies use the application form as a face sheet placed on top of the case record for reference purposes. Others use a report of first interview form at the head of their permanent case record. Various combinations of application, report of first interview, and report of investigation were observed in the field. Increasingly, however, agencies are turning to the simpler form of case record used for many years by case-working agencies. Even some of those agencies most anxious to have old age assistance different from older types of aid are discarding their earlier, complex methods in favor of a simple record. It is made up like the typical case record and consists of a face sheet containing important reference data, and, as needed, of plain sheets of paper, known as "history sheets," on which to record chronologically notes

[21] Usually a four-by-six-inch card is most satisfactory because of the necessity of providing sufficient space for recording changes of address (usually essential for identifying purposes). Many agencies use a three-by-five-inch card, but these are often too small to provide enough space for changes (especially address) and are entirely too small if the agency wishes to use its files as a social service exchange.

[22] Alphabetical filing includes the various systems of phonetic filing necessary where numbers are large, especially in communities in which names of varied nationalities are common.

[23] Some agencies set up a separate card file for active and inactive cases. This is both unnecessary and undesirable. If the card is properly arranged, space will be provided to designate the assignment of cases, with the date; transfer of case to another district or worker, with date; and the closing (also any reopenings), likewise with date. Agencies sometimes hold cards for pending applications in a separate file and while less objectionable than division into active and inactive sections, separate files for pending cases tend to increase errors as well as make necessary search in two files when a new inquiry must be cleared. A temporary (duplicate) pending card or slip is sometimes used to keep track of pending cases and thus the main file is, as it should be, a complete index. If the application is never received, a report of contacts is usually worth recording, and, if brief, may be written on the reverse side of the card. (Case records pending or active should usually be kept in a readily accessible file preferably in alphabetical order, by districts or by workers, and not filed with the closed cases in the main file, which are usually filed in numerical order.)

of later contacts; they are attached to the face sheet by a paper fastener.

Official forms are sometimes fastened to face sheets and history sheets but are often kept in a separate group in the same folder. Correspondence is filed either with history sheets or in a separate group in the case folder (or envelope). Forms more closely related to history forms, such as budget sheets, resource sheets, insurance forms, etc., are usually filed with the history sheets. The face sheet is often printed on heavy paper or light cardboard in order to withstand the hard wear it receives as the top sheet of the case history. Agencies often find it convenient to print the same items on lighter paper for temporary use of intake interviewers.

The intake worker in conducting the interview usually uses the application blank as a starting point; but, as other facts useful in the investigation are elicited, these are recorded in pencil on the temporary face sheet. At the end of the interview this sheet can be checked quickly to see that all needed facts are recorded. Later, notes of additional and supplementary data obtained in the interview are dictated for inclusion in the case history, and the entries on the temporary face sheet are typed on the permanent face sheet. The temporary form (intake work sheet) can then be destroyed.[24] The case record is now a permanent working record.

The reason for the adoption of this form of case record is the great economy that results from recording facts as soon as they are learned in order to avoid repetition of the same steps by the investigator who begins where the intake interviewer leaves off. Even if the same interviewer carries the case a few steps farther before turning it over to the visiting staff, notes are necessary because it is impossible for a worker who is seeing applicants in rapid succession to remember all the necessary details of each case. There is also the danger that the worker may resign, become ill, or die, and thus all the work previously done might need to be repeated.

Receiving and Recording the Formal Application

After the application is completed it is numbered; this number,[25] the

---

[24] In large agencies, especially those with district offices, the intake work sheet is often kept at the district for immediate use, while the case record is sent to the central office for indexing and numbering. Some agencies also keep the intake work sheet, if the applicant fails to complete his application, as a permanent record to be filed pending future inquiry and perhaps later application.

[25] The case number is an individual number, which is kept permanently as a means of identifying the case to which it is assigned. One state agency uses a separate series for applications (application number) and assigns the case number only after an award is made

date, and certain identifying information are recorded in a journal kept for this purpose. The date recorded in the journal marks the official date of application, which may be important in later activities.[26] It furnishes an official, chronological record of applications received and is useful as a source for compiling statistics on the basis of which the activities of an agency can be studied and compared for different periods and also contrasted with the activities of other agencies.

When the official reception and recording of the application take place in the state office, the local unit usually keeps an unofficial record which duplicates the official journal in the state office. Local units have found it indispensable for keeping track of applications sent to the state office, and, when they were sent, for recording what action is later taken and for compiling reports of local activities.

The counting of applications presents some difficulties because of differences in practice relating to when the application is completed. Simple applications can usually be completed in one or two interviews when proof of eligibility and other items are unnecessary. When most of the investigation is made before the application is completed, applications are kept pending for a long time, and the number of applications officially received by the agency is much less owing to the number of eliminations during the process of investigation by death, withdrawal, or denial. The point at which an inquiry becomes an application and an application a case varies from state to state and sometimes from agency to agency within a state.[27]

(pension number). This duplicate system seems to have no advantage and has the disadvantage of complicating recording more than the immediate assignment of the permanent case number which is the procedure followed by other states. The case number in centralized systems is sometimes assigned in a single series to each case as it reaches the state office. More often, however, composite numbers identifying the locality where filed, as well as the case, are used. The most common method is to range the counties in alphabetical order and number them and use this county number as the first part of the case number. Each county has a separate series of numbers beginning with one. This serial county number is attached by means of a dash to the number designating the county. In some instances a letter is also used to designate the category. The category letter may precede the county number or be interposed between the county designation and the county serial number. Thus No. 22-O-175 would be used for the one-hundred-seventy-fifth application for old age assistance in the county that is twenty-second in alphabetical order in the state. Since the field study was completed, a number of agencies handling several categories have adopted a household numbering system in place of individual case numbers. No household system was in use in the twelve states during the period of the field study.

[26] It may be the basic date for establishing a period within which the agency must make its investigation and reach a decision. Wisconsin, for instance, allows an applicant to appeal if he does not secure action on his application within a period of ninety days.

[27] See chap. 9.

SUPERVISION OF APPLICATION PROCEDURES

The responsibility of the state for establishing standards and for prescribing uniform procedures has already been pointed out. The state law itself may prescribe some of these procedures. It often specifies that an oath must be attached to the application blank and prescribes the qualifications of the person who must attest it.[28] It may even specify items to be included in the application blank, such as a statement describing income and property holdings, but usually these details are left to the rule-making authority of the state agency. Methods of supervision may also be specified in the law, and the state agency may have no discretion in deciding whether to require the local units to send the completed application blanks to the state office. If the state agency is required by law or chooses to have a central review of case records, the original application blank, or a copy of it, must be forwarded to the state office. Even when the review of case records is decentralized, state agencies sometimes require that local units submit copies of application blanks.[29]

The nature and extent of the review of applications varies from state to state. In states with strongly centralized plans, closer scrutiny tends to be given than in decentralized systems, but the kind of review in the former states, although more intense, is narrower in scope. The completed applications are closely inspected by a clerk or checker, who customarily notes such matters as whether all blank spaces have been filled in; whether the applicant's signature or witnessed mark is affixed; whether it has been countersigned by a properly authorized official; whether the oath is properly executed; and whether required supporting documents, liens, and assignments have been executed and attached in due form. Any apparent errors or omissions are occasion for correspondence with the local unit and return of the blank for correction if the error is deemed to be serious. Frequently this correspondence goes directly from the checking unit to the local unit, without any thought of the desirability of routing it through the field staff; if the checking unit is not a part of the social service staff—as it often is not—the social service division neither sees the application nor receives copies of the correspondence. Thus, one of the most important of the social service

---

[28] It may provide that the oath be administered before a notary or other designated official, or it may provide some method of authorizing members of the staffs of state and local agencies to administer oaths.

[29] Completed applications were required by the state agency in both Indiana and Wisconsin, although review of cases was decentralized in those two states.

functions is, to a considerable extent, removed from the supervision of the social service division, and the field staff, supposedly responsible for contacts with the local unit, has neither knowledge of, nor control over, this avenue of contact with the local unit.[30]

Supervision through centralized checking without relation to the field staff is probably the least effective method of improving intake procedures. The better procedure is to have state field representatives review case records, including applications, in the local office, where mistakes can be discussed with local supervisors and the method of handling applicants can be observed. In this way undesirable practices can be corrected and improved methods suggested.

Local supervision of intake is even more important in many ways than state supervision. The amount and kind of local supervision varies from unit to unit. In large city agencies with well staffed intake departments, special intake supervisors are usually employed. In the majority of agencies, however, intake supervision is handled by the supervisor who handles other case supervision. Occasionally checkers are used, but they are less likely to be divorced from case-work supervision than are state checkers and, being subordinated to it, are less apt to be obstructive of other and better supervisory methods. They were observed only in large agencies, but their usefulness appeared to be questionable. Application, whether in large or small units, should be reviewed by an informed and discerning supervisor who is in a position to bring about correction of fundamental errors revealed by inspection.

When decisions are made at intake, their review is not different from similar action taken after a case has been transferred to the visiting staff. Disposition of cases and review of decisions will therefore be considered in later chapters. Similarly, no attempt has here been made to discuss methods of investigation, although intake workers in many agencies perform a considerable amount of investigation.

[30] Not all states requiring submission of applications to the state handle them in this way. In Indiana at the time of the field visit the clerk who inspected applications was officially attached to the Public Assistance Division and reported to the administrative assistant to the director of the Division, although she had her desk in the Division of Business Management in order to be near the general files. Incorrect or incomplete forms were returned to the county by the clerk with a brief letter on printed form requesting correction. Reports of these corrections were made to the field staff; thus persistent errors in the application from any county came to the attention of the person whose responsibility it was to discover the cause of error and correct it.

CHAPTER 8

INVESTIGATION AND DECISION

AFTER THE COMPLETION of an application and its presentation to the agency, the social study or investigation is made. Investigation and decision are often regarded as separate processes, or at least as distinct steps in a single process, but in practice they are inextricably mingled. Hence they are treated together in this chapter. The supervision of investigation and review of decisions by supervising officials or agencies are likewise considered together.

ADMINISTRATIVE RESPONSIBILITY

Whether the final decision on eligibility is made locally or in the state office, the investigation must be carried on locally. The client is the primary source of information regarding his eligibility, and most of the factual data relating to it are found in the local community. The Social Security Act does not mention investigation as such, though it provides that payments made only to persons who meet specified eligibility requirements can be matched with federal funds. The method of determining such eligibility, however, is left entirely to the states. Most state laws provide for investigation by the local unit.

In investigative methods and procedures there is in practice little difference between state-operated systems and those locally operated but state supervised. In making investigations the state agencies have invariably found it necessary to maintain local offices and local investigative staffs. Such differences in investigative methods and results as were noted related more to the competence of staff and to adequacy of equipment and supervision than to differences in administrative responsibility between state and local levels of government.

The location of administrative responsibility for decision and for supervision, unlike responsibility for investigation, varies from state to state. In locally operated systems the local unit is responsible for the administrative or determinative decision in each case; but if every decision is reviewed by the state agency, and reimbursement of a considerable part of each authorized expenditure is made by it, the local agency may become so dependent on state decisions as to make them in effect determinative. Local agencies with limited funds and sensitive to political attack on the grounds of extravagance are fearful of losing state reimbursement; some of them even defer final decision until the state agency has approved. The repressive effect on local initiative may not apply merely to grants or to high grants only: denials or grants lower than the state might consider desirable may also be controlled, since a state recommendation for a grant or for an increase in amount, backed by the fair-hearing provision, gives dissatisfied clients a weapon by means of which the local agency can be forced to accept the state's recommendation.

In state-operated systems responsibility for making final decisions naturally rests with the state agency, but in some programs local workers and advisory boards make recommendations which are given considerable weight; review of them differs only in degree from state review in some of the locally operated systems. For example, in Mississippi, decisions (or, more accurately, recommendations) made by local boards on prior recommendation of the local workers (state-paid but local residents in all instances) are all reviewed in the state office. In general they are approved after a cursory inspection unless the local worker indicates disagreement with the board, in which event more careful scrutiny is given to the report and recommendation. If the board's recommendation is not supported by the state decision, the worker's may be, and the decision will still be largely a local one. Nevertheless, the state agency has final authority; the local representative and board are not empowered to change the state's decision and have no funds to make payments if the state's decision is to refuse or curtail a recommended grant.[1] The close relation of decision and supervision in these centralized programs is evident.

INTERVIEWS WITH THE APPLICANT

In general the methods of social investigation in old age assistance are similar to those used for many years by public and private case-work agencies. The chief differences lie in the special eligibility requirements of old age assistance and in the necessity for submitting evidence to meet the requirements of a more detailed audit than has usually been made of general relief and other welfare programs.

[1] In a locally operated system the local unit has legal authority to give aid and may do so when the state disapproves the decision if it is willing to forego state reimbursement; but the local agency may find it inexpedient to exercise this right. While legal responsibility varies, the practical results may be the same in both systems.

The First Interview

The investigation begins with the first interview with the applicant and is ordinarily held in connection with the filing of the application. Several interviews may be necessary before the application is completed. If they are conducted by a special intake worker (interviewer) a report of the interview will be included in the record before the case is turned over to the home visitor for further action. If the case has been cleared with the local social service exchange (central index) and a listing of the individual or his family has been discovered, a report containing names of agencies that have known the applicant and the dates of their registration will be included in the report from the exchange. Sometimes a brief summary of the contacts of these agencies with the applicant will have been obtained by the intake worker; but, if not, the visitor will ordinarily find it worth while to follow up these registrations since they are apt to be a fruitful source of data. If no exchange exists, clearance with the central file or register of agencies that the applicant may have consulted may be desirable.

The Home Visit

Most agencies customarily require a minimum of one home visit as prerequisite to a satisfactory investigation. The applicant can be seen in his normal environment, where he is more at ease, as a rule, than in the unfamiliar atmosphere of the office. Thus he may talk more freely and give the worker a better understanding of his circumstances, as well as clues leading to the establishment of his eligibility. The applicant himself may possess most of the necessary data; if so, he can present them to the visitor who can then discuss with him their possible inadequacies and also work out with him an agreement for filling the gaps. Sometimes other members of the household can assist in gathering proof or can offer suggestions; this is one of the great advantages of the home visit.

At times the home visit may prove unsatisfactory. Applicants who live in institutions, boarding or rooming houses, or with relatives or others who are unsympathetic may feel more at ease elsewhere. It is usually desirable, however, that the visitor see the home surroundings. Sometimes it is possible to make special arrangements for greater privacy in the home if that is the chief problem; otherwise it may be desirable to hold interviews at the agency office or in some other place, such as the home of a friendly relative or of an old friend, or in a settlement house, parish house, or other convenient place.

Purpose and Content of Early Interviews

Wherever the early interviews are held, there should be an effort to make clear to the applicant the purpose of the investigation and, so far as possible, to stimulate his interest in the process of establishing his eligibility. Any services the agency may be able to provide should be freely offered, but there should be no prying into other matters. Whatever facts are needed the applicant is usually willing to reveal if he understands their necessity, and he should know what sources the agency plans to consult. If he objects to any of them his wishes should be respected, although the agency, through the visitor, must aid him in understanding to what extent the elimination of one or more sources is apt to jeopardize the establishment of his claim. It is also the visitor's responsibility to inform the applicant of his right to a fair hearing. Since the establishment of liens or surrender of property often involve the rights of relatives, the visitor should see that they, too, understand the requirements.[2] If the mentality of the applicant is uncertain, consultation with responsible relatives is important whether property rights are involved or not. If a guardian has been appointed, all action must be taken with his knowledge and consent.

Discretion must be used in determining the length of interviews. Old persons, especially those in frail health, may easily become tired from the effort to recall needed facts. Hence several interviews may be necessary. A later interview, when the worker is satisfied that he has sufficient facts to make a decision, may be particularly helpful. The data gathered can be reviewed, and existing gaps in the evidence can often be filled. Predecision interviews are helpful if the decision seems likely to be unfavorable. Then, too, the applicant has a final opportunity to present additional facts; if he cannot do so, the reasons why his application cannot be given favorable consideration can be pointed out. Furthermore, an interview of this sort offers an excellent opportunity for explaining the fair-hearing procedure. If the decision appears likely to be favorable, a post-decision interview may serve as well.

METHODS OF FACILITATING INVESTIGATION

Since determination of eligibility is a function of primary importance to the agency, every effort should be made to facilitate the work of the

---

[2] The intake interviewer has presumably already discussed property requirements with the applicant and perhaps also with relatives. Office interviews, however, are often subject to special limitations that may have made understanding of these matters impossible. Hence the visitor is responsible for their clarification.

staff engaged in this task. One of the first essentials is to ensure understanding of the eligibility requirements by the workers who apply them. Various formal and informal methods have been used for this purpose. In several states, state or regional meetings were held during the initial period in which the law, the rules and regulations, and the necessary procedures for establishing eligibility were explained to the groups assembled. In some instances the local directors only were invited to attend these meetings; in others, directors and their staffs were present; in still others, board members or local officials were also invited. One state has held annually a series of regional institutes, followed by a competitive examination, which all prospective applicants for county positions were compelled to attend if they wished to be appointed.

In some states the larger agencies held institutes or training courses at which the law and both state and local rules, regulations, and procedures were explained. Some state agencies issued special bulletins, pamphlets, or manuals and handbooks for the use of local workers. As time has elapsed less emphasis has been given to emergent measures. Training of new visitors is carried on informally by the supervisory staff or is made part of a more formalized in-service training program. Manuals of information for instruction of visitors are now more generally available and superior in quality to those of the early period. On the whole, however, the development of the staff's knowledge and skill is the result of constructive supervision by qualified local and state supervisory personnel.

Information on Sources of Verification

State and local agencies have found it worth while to furnish their investigative staffs with some guidance in discovering sources of verification. Some states issue lists of the kinds of documents that are considered satisfactory proof of age.[3] California includes such a list in the law itself, but more often these lists are found in state rules and regulations or in manuals or other material prepared for staff use.

The difficulty with a simple listing of documents is that it fails to recognize the differences in the degree of validity of each. Iowa meets this problem partly by issuing two lists. The first includes documents of unqualified validity, any one of which is considered sufficient; the second names the kinds of documents considered valid but less con-

[3]Some also list the kinds of documents acceptable as proof of residence and citizenship, but lists for proof of age are more common. The discussion herein of the determination of validity applies to these other lists as well.

clusive. If it is impossible to obtain any of the items included in the first list, any two from the second will be accepted as adequate proof. Some states attempt to list the kinds of documents in the order of their validity, but this method presents difficulties; for, in the first place, several documents may be of about the same validity but a great gap may occur between them and the next group; and, in the second place, the same kinds of documents may vary tremendously in validity. For example, a birth record made at the time of, or shortly after, birth is quite different from a so-called "delayed birth record" made on the simple (or sworn) statement of the applicant or other interested person. Likewise the name of a document does not necessarily help workers who are untrained in social investigation to locate the documents listed or to judge their adequacy.

In view of their emphasis on documentary evidence, it is surprising that so few states have taken a keen interest in assisting their local units to locate and make use of existing documents. It is possible for a state agency to render useful service to the local units by obtaining and passing on to them information about the availability of local as well as state records. The Wisconsin Pension Department compiled, for its *Visitors' Manual,* a brief "History of County Records." For each county, information is furnished of the date from which records of birth, marriage, and citizenship are available. Dates are also furnished for state and federal census and school records, with additional information about these records. Census records are not always found in the same office in each county; hence the office having custody of them is listed for each county. The existence and the completeness of school records, which vary from county to county, are indicated on the list by "yes," "no," and "fair." In addition to the above items issued in the form of a table or check list, some descriptive information is furnished to aid both in discovering and evaluating local records. Wisconsin has also established cooperation with the State Bureau of Vital Statistics. Through this Bureau the existence was discovered of old census records in the custody of the State Historical Library and Secretary of State's Office and certified statements of the census record were made available through a special after-hours searching service provided by two expert clerks from the staff of the Bureau.[4]

---

[4] Funds were not available in the beginning to provide this service free of charge; whether they have since been provided has not been learned. Certified copies of birth records already on file in the Bureau itself are furnished free to old age assistance applicants though the regular fee is fifty cents. In return the county agencies aid informally in the Bureau's campaign to obtain complete registration of all persons born in

At the time of the staff visit in Florida, service was provided through a cooperative arrangement with the W.P.A. State Archives and Historical Records Survey. Such surveys have been carried on in other states, but in many instances the state old age assistance agency was apparently unaware of their possible utility.[5] The Bureau of Public Assistance through its field representatives has supplied state agencies with some information about the use of the records of federal agencies including the Bureau of the Census and the Naturalization Service. Classified lists of official and unofficial sources of verification have also been furnished. Some large local agencies have been ingenious in discovering sources of information and have made the results available to their investigative staff.

Cooperative Arrangements with Other Departments and Agencies

Cooperative arrangements with other state departments, such as those made by Wisconsin, are a means by which some states have provided useful service to their local units. Several other states have obtained special service from their state bureaus of vital statistics and from state libraries. Similar cooperation with state institutions and with private agencies and associations operating on a state-wide basis has been instituted and has proved useful. If the state does not take the initiative in working out such relationships, local units are left to work them out individually and to develop their own procedures. Those that fail to discover such resources will spend more time in the process than if standard procedures had been worked out at one time for the group. Competent local administrators, however, have discovered the value of developing local cooperation even when the state has been negligent in the matter.

Some agencies had made special arrangements with their local registrars of vital statistics for verification of, or current information on, deaths of persons over sixty-five. Special arrangements were made for obtaining information from hospitals—especially public hospitals— social and health agencies, postmasters, registrars of deeds, assessors, county treasurers, and other public officials, from undertakers, physicians, employers, banks, life insurance companies, lodges, labor unions, and other groups.

---

the state even though the "delayed certificates," recognized by the Bureau of Vital Statistics, are not recognized as valid proof of age by the old age assistance administration.

[5] The Florida project was perhaps more vigorously prosecuted than some of the others. Excellent results were attained there despite paucity of good record material and difficulties peculiar to the region.

Provision of Forms

Forms suitably designed and accompanied by instructions may also aid the visitor; others may prove a handicap. Some agencies have developed forms for making inquiries of banks, for instance. Such a form worked out in cooperation with the banks in the agency's jurisdiction may prove a great timesaver. The worker fills in the items which the bank must have in order to locate the account and identify the customer. If the rules of the bank require a signed release from the customer, this can be included. In response the agency receives in writing the data it requires. Similar blanks have been found useful in making inquiries of life insurance companies, building and loan agencies, employers, and former employers. Inquiry blanks, however, have limitations and dangers. They may be relied upon exclusively although in some instances a personal call would be more satisfactory. The use of printed forms as a method of consulting relatives is particularly deplorable, for in terms of results it is usually an entire waste of agency time; it often prevents the agency from gaining the desired cooperation because the relative, having made a premature statement, is reluctant to alter it. Furthermore, the relative who wishes later to change his statement is in danger of appearing to have perjured himself in his earlier declaration.

In some of the agencies visited the number of forms appeared to be needlessly large. Many were developed for other administrative purposes, but inquiry forms can also be multiplied uselessly and hamper rather than help the worker. In several agencies much of the workers' time was spent filling in forms, often duplicating material already available. The case records as a result tended to be a confused mass of forms from which it was difficult to arrive at an understanding of the client's circumstances. Agencies should not adopt a form without first ascertaining that its purpose is essential; next, that the form really serves that purpose; and finally, that a plain sheet of paper would not serve equally well. Periodically forms should be reviewed, and those no longer needed should be eliminated; unnecessarily complex ones should be simplified.

The forms used for recording the investigation may, like other forms, aid or hinder the worker. In the older programs a detailed questionnaire was adopted, which was widely copied by other states, although these are now being discarded in favor of the more flexible type of record already described. There were probably several reasons for adopting the rigid questionnaire. In the first place, in all the earlier old age assistance plans the social audit was the method of supervision, and it virtually demanded a rigid form that could be inspected rapidly.[6] In the second place, the agencies recognized that investigations would generally be made by inexperienced and often unsupervised workers who would not know how to obtain or to record social data if the forms used did not specifically indicate what was required. Finally, in some instances, there is evidence that agencies expected the applicant himself to insert the answers to the questions on the blank, possibly without the aid of the agency.

Many agencies are now finding that the disadvantages of the rigid form outweigh its advantages. Although the questionnaire may be better adapted to the use of inexperienced workers, it is hampering to skilled case workers.[7] If cases were all alike the questionnaire type would be more suitable, but spacing which has been devised for the typical case may be totally unsuited to those cases that deviate. It is quite unsatisfactory for records that are to be used over a long period and that need space for adding current data to keep the case up to date. Incidentally, the questionnaire type is generally more expensive because of the printing cost. Many of those seen were also awkward to file because the necessity for attaching later reports was apparently not considered in planning the arrangement of items.

The most satisfactory of the more rigid types consisted of separate forms for the application, first interview (or applicant's statement), and report of investigation. Thus it was possible for the reader to know the source of the statements recorded and to arrive at some evaluation of their validity. When items are properly arranged, it is also possible to attach history sheets and other additions to the record. Even the more flexible face-sheet, history-sheet type of record can develop many of the faults of the rigid type through the use of a multiplicity of subsidiary forms or detailed outlines and schedules for dictation.[8]

[6] For definition of social audit see earlier report of the survey staff, Robert T. Lansdale and Associates, *op. cit.,* p. 30.

[7] The supervisory staff of the Indiana Department of Public Welfare reported that untrained workers who had used a more flexible type of recording in their prior experience in unemployment relief thought that the more rigid and detailed form had certain values for untrained and inexperienced visitors.

[8] The question is sometimes raised why records are necessary at all. It is obvious, however, that the agency must be able to prove that it has given assistance only to eligibles and that records must be prepared and maintained in which the facts regarding eligibility, including continuing eligibility, are set forth. It is also fairly obvious that both agency and applicant would suffer loss if the visitor who had not recorded the facts obtained should be removed by death, illness, transfer, or resignation before a decision had been reached. Repetition of all the work done and consequent delay and expense would be entailed. Supervision and planning would also be hampered if case records were eliminated.

Bulletins, Manuals, Notebooks, and Kits

In the beginning most agencies depended largely on bulletins as a means of informing their staffs on matters of general interest to the agency. Bulletins are especially adapted to furnishing quickly information of immediate concern to large numbers of agencies, branch offices, or workers. They are generally less speedy than telegraphed or telephoned instructions but are less liable to error in transmission and, being in writing, they have value as a permanent and valid record.

The New Jersey state agency was quick to realize the advantage of making bulletins useful to county agencies. Each bulletin issued dealt with only one subject. All of them were numbered and classified, and instructions were given for indexing and inserting them in a loose-leaf note book. When these instructions were followed, the local agencies had a working manual of state policies and procedures that served effectively through the early period.

For permanent use in instructing local agencies, most states have found the bulletin method less satisfactory. Often bulletins contain information of only temporary interest and include more than one subject; frequently they must be prepared hurriedly. The order in which they are received is chronological rather than logical by subjects covered; thus items tend to be dispersed and may be hard to unify and comprehend. A number of states have now reworked much of the bulletin material into well written manuals containing copies of pertinent laws, rules and regulations, agency policies, procedural instructions, copies of forms and accompanying instructions, and material on sources of information and cooperation. These are usually in loose-leaf form to permit insertion of new and amended sheets. They are generally written for local agencies and usually include instructions in administrative, financial, and statistical procedures, as well as in social service.

A few local agencies developed manuals for the use of their staffs when the states failed to do so. It is advantageous to the workers to have local and state policies, rules and regulations, and procedural instructions on any subject combined for reference purposes, but state agencies have not always seen fit to arrange their manuals to allow insertion of local material. A few of the earlier ones were not loose leaf, and revision of those that were has not always been speedy. Despite these common faults, they are a useful device for aiding both state and local staffs in understanding and in performing their various tasks.

A few agencies furnish notebooks or special field kits for workers. A notebook is essential for visitors, for few if any could remember all the detailed information about each case. Investigations are not usually made one by one; thus a worker may have twenty or thirty in process at one time, besides being responsible for revisits to a still larger number. Visits are grouped in neighborhoods to save time, and calls on sources are likewise combined for the same reason. A briefcase or kit in which the worker can carry a supply of the forms that he is likely to need while in the field and a notebook with a sheet for each family are minimum essentials. Some notebook sheets are printed for convenience in recording the more significant permanent facts about each case and are provided with space for recording notes of facts needed or obtained when a visit is made; and at times plain sheets are used. Day sheets are also frequently supplied for recording dates of visits and notes that will aid the worker when he dictates his report for the permanent record.

Office Equipment and Clerical Assistance

Lack of suitable waiting rooms and proper privacy unquestionably affect unfavorably the investigative process. Failure to obtain needed information at intake makes the work of the home visitor more difficult. This fact was generally recognized by visitors and supervisors.[9]

Office quarters in a number of the agencies visited were so crowded that it was impossible to assemble the entire staff at one time. The office hours of the visiting staff were accordingly staggered. In these agencies and in some others field workers did not have individual desks and were compelled to assemble anew on each return to the office the supplies and equipment needed for their office work. Desks when supplied were often old, battered, uncomfortable, and inconvenient. Chairs were at a premium. If a worker left his chair to go to another part of the office, he frequently had to hunt for another on his return. If a caller appeared the worker stood, or sat on desk, file, or other piece of furniture. Ventilation, heating, and lighting were often bad. Basement rooms were frequently used and were generally hard to heat and often impossible to ventilate. Washrooms and other facilities for the workers were unsatisfactory, and rest rooms were exceptional. Lack of privacy for supervisory conferences often interfered with proper direction of the staff.

The amount of clerical help for the staff varied greatly. In some agencies workers were expected to do all their own clerical work, including the typing of case records, field notes, reports, and letters. Workers

[9] An untrained but observant supervisor in one of the larger agencies remarked: "Any failures or mistakes at intake seem to carry through the whole case."

who must perform these tasks in addition to those of a visitor will usually not do both equally well. Efficiency and economy of operation are usually increased by hiring clerks and stenographers for clerical work and allowing workers selected for their aptitude, training, or skill in social service tasks full time for these latter activities.

Transportation

Another mistaken economy is limiting beyond a reasonable figure the funds allowed for transportation for the visiting staff. The area to be covered and accessibility to public conveyances affect the amount and kind of transportation needed. If the population is concentrated and the districts small, some of the visitors may be able to cover their districts on foot. Even in a very large city the concentration of cases varies greatly; some districts must inevitably be too large and cases too scattered to cover without recourse to some means of transportation. Even when applicants live close together the investigator often finds that his investigations carry him far afield. A few agencies furnish automobiles for the use of their workers. Streetcar, bus, and subway fare may be provided for workers whose districts can be reached by common carriers. The most common transportation provision is an allowance to workers for their privately owned cars. A definite cost per mile may be set by the agency and paid to the worker on the basis of a report of the number of miles actually travelled. Other agencies pay gas and oil, or only gas, on a mileage basis. The commonest method of payment is flat rate per month, usually included in the salary check. Sometimes the flat rate is set after a study of the probable cost to the worker and rechecked occasionally as prices and other factors change. More often it is set arbitrarily with little consideration of the actual cost or of the variation in needs for transportation among workers.

A flat rate has the advantage of requiring less auditing than a detailed mileage expense account and of causing the worker less trouble in record keeping; but it is difficult to calculate equitably. For the agency it has also the disadvantage of putting a premium on keeping mileage low by postponing visits or using telephone, letter, inquiry blank, or office interview when a home visit would be preferable. The workers sometimes suffer because transportation is a vulnerable spot for economy when agency funds are limited. A decrease in transportation allowance without corresponding reduction of territory or case load often results in a lowering of the standard of work and amounts to a reduction in salary for the worker. If the latter is the intention, it seems fairer to make the reduction directly instead of using this subterfuge. Reducing a flat allowance far below the actual cost of necessary travel tends to penalize the most conscientious and faithful workers and often, in the end, to lower their morale. The reasonable cost of necessary transportation is a responsibility of the agency and should not be shifted to the shoulders of the visiting staff.[10]

ORGANIZATION OF THE SOCIAL SERVICE STAFF

Number and Kind of Workers

The first problem about staff that a new agency faces is how many and what kind of workers will be needed to carry on its social service activities. The chief factor in determining the number is the case load—the number of cases to be handled per worker. The probable future case load of a public assistance agency is not easy to determine, although planning should be somewhat in advance of actual requirements. If the work of the agency is limited to old age assistance, the number of persons over sixty-five living in the jurisdiction may give some rough idea of the number for which plans must be made. This number is, however, only a rough guide, for a large number of aged persons will be ineligible and will not apply. It is, of course, difficult to determine how many will be eligible, but a number of both ineligible and eligible persons will apply and will thus require intake and perhaps investigative service.

The rate at which applications are received, as well as the total number of applications, has an important influence on the number of staff workers required, since new cases usually take more time per case than older cases. The extent of the differential doubtless varies among agencies, but most of them have no definite idea of what it may be. The New York City agency in 1935 made a study of its cases, using the number of interviews per case as a rough indication of the difference in the amount of time required. This study showed that interviews for new cases averaged 9.2 per case; for reconsiderations, 5.5 per case; for formal reinvestigations, 3.3 per case; for service cases (usually illness, death, eviction or some other emergency), 4.6 per case. Whether the proportion in the number of visits to the different groups would be the same in another agency or at another time in the same agency is not known. Moreover, a visit may not be the best unit to measure such differentials, for visits themselves take varying amounts of time.

[10] Consultant service is another means of aiding investigation, but since it is closely related to supervision it is discussed in that connection. See below, pp. 153. ff.

Many administrators probably have little idea of the time required to complete an initial investigation to a point that justifies a decision on eligibility. In Indiana the Marion County (Indianapolis) Department of Public Welfare had made some study of this subject prior to the visit of the survey staff. The results indicated that a competent worker with the best of luck could seldom complete more than five new cases per week even though he had no other responsibilities and everything was done to facilitate his efforts. An average of twenty new cases per month was considered a good monthly output for workers handling just new cases and receiving new assignments only as fast as they were able to take them. The experience of other agencies that had given any consideration to the subject seemed to check with that of Indianapolis. The number of new cases that could be completed in a month would be less in many agencies where clients were less accessible and facilitating services less adequate. Other factors, such as the number and kind of eligibility requirements, and the standards of work exacted of the staff in relation to number and kind of sources consulted, and completeness of data, would also alter the figure. The training, experience, and general competence of the workers must also be considered.

An agency may administer one or more types of aid and use the same visitors for all programs. Differentials are often assumed to exist between various programs in the amount of time required per case, although few data are available. The Bureau of Public Assistance of the Social Security Board, while recognizing that many differentials between agencies influence the number of cases that can be carried efficiently by one worker, suggests a maximum of 100 cases per worker in an undifferentiated load; no more than twenty new applications per month for a worker with no other responsibilities; and no more than ten new cases per month with continuing responsibility for fifty cases. These maximums are intended for experienced workers. For beginners still needing intensive supervision and workers with responsibility for special services, a maximum of forty-five cases is suggested. The maximums appear to be moderate if a reasonably good job is to be done. In many of the agencies visited, case loads were far higher; but it was evident that the quality of work was unsatisfactory.

The amount of clerical assistance furnished to the visiting staff varied greatly in the agencies visited. In a number of small agencies no clerical help at all was available. The Bureau of Public Assistance suggests one clerical worker for every three visitors; this figure seems reasonable for large agencies at least. In a local agency with only one or two visitors a clerk is as necessary as if the staff were larger, especially if the case load is high. He can usually perform varied duties, such as preparation of pay rolls, filing, etc., and need not spend full time in recording the case data. If no clerical help is provided, the director in a one-man agency must assume these duties in addition to those of administrator and visitor, and the number of cases he can carry must correspondingly be reduced if a satisfactory level of work is to be maintained. Usually, the absence of a clerk also makes it necessary to close the office while the director is in the field; thus the problem of receiving applications is often complicated.

In small local agencies case-work supervision is usually handled by the director. In larger agencies his administrative duties are greater and make it impossible for him to carry other responsibilities. Often, too, a director of a larger agency has special qualifications for administrative work but may not be so well qualified for the task of supervising the visiting staff. The exact point at which a supervisor should be added must therefore depend upon the qualifications of the director and the amount of time he can spare from his other duties. Usually one supervisor should not attempt to supervise more than ten visitors. In some larger agencies, visitors are directed by supervisors who are in turn supervised by a general case supervisor or by a group of more mature and experienced supervisors working under a departmental director. Sometimes these supervisors also carry a considerable amount of administrative responsibility. Only a few agencies are large enough, however, to require a supervisory hierarchy of this sort.

Auxiliary workers, sometimes called "investigators," as distinguished from home visitors or case workers employed by the same agency, were found in some local units.[11] In some agencies they were used only for searching records; in others they were grouped in special departments and assigned to specified phases of the visitor's job, such as investigation of real estate, insurance, or other property, or to check employment

[11] Many local agencies apply the term "investigator" to all workers who perform any sort of social service tasks involving field work or office interviewing and who rank below the grade of supervisor; others use "investigator" for beginners or for untrained social service personnel, and the terms "junior" and "senior case worker" or "junior" and "senior visitor" for trained or experienced visitors; others use "junior visitor" for beginners, and "senior visitor" for trained or experienced workers; and a few use "investigator" for a worker who searches records and makes field contacts with various sources of verification but who makes no contacts with clients. There was little standardization of terms at the time the survey visits were made. In this section the author has generally used the term "investigator" or "investigative staff" to include all social service staff, except clerical, below the grade of supervisor, including the intake interviewers. The term "visitor" is used to indicate local workers (investigators) whose duties take them into the field.

records, or to maintain liaison with employment departments of large industrial establishments and with public employment offices.

Some of the specialization observed in the agencies visited seemed of rather doubtful value. Centralization of record searching and other consultation with outside agencies and government departments may be necessary if the volume of inquiries is so large as to be burdensome to the agencies from whom data are sought. Moreover, familiarity with certain records and with cooperating agencies may both speed and smooth the process of getting needed data. On the other hand, the task of coordinating inquiries and reports and routing them to and from visitors and auxiliary workers may consume an undue amount of time and effort.

Segmentation of the visitors' task may also tend to undermine their sense of responsibility for the total job, especially if the coordination of activities is not well handled. Frequently too much specialization results in the overlooking of valuable clues. It is not always possible to foresee what items may reveal useful facts. For instance, a worker would not ordinarily find any value in obtaining names of the witnesses to a marriage and thus would not include this item in the request for search. Yet familiarity with the case might result in thus recognizing unexpected connections. The witness might turn out to be a relative not previously recognized as such or the name might recall to the worker a suggestion that this person previously mentioned by the applicant would through interest and long acquaintance be a good source of much needed data.

If auxiliary or specialized workers are departmentalized in the organization they often tend to institutionalize their function, building up needlessly elaborate forms and procedures and pursuing their activities as primary rather than as facilitative services. They also tend to overemphasize the extent and value of such special skill as they have acquired and, on the basis of their claims to expertness, infringe upon the supervisory function.

Assignment of Work

When two or more workers are engaged in the process of investigation, some method of dividing the work must be devised. Division may be made partly on a functional basis, but the usual process is a case-by-case assignment. The worker having a case assigned to him assumes responsibility for following through all the procedures that are necessary until administrative action is taken.

Several methods of assignment are used. The most common is the geographical, in which the area is divided into districts and all cases living in a district are assigned to one worker. Districts are arranged so that the case loads will as nearly as possible entail an equal amount of work. A thinly settled or inaccessible district requires the worker to spend more time in transportation and so reduces the number of cases that he can handle as compared with the number a worker in an area of concentrated population may handle.[12] Since old age assistance is given in accordance with need, applicants tend to be concentrated in relatively poor sections and to be more scattered in well-to-do neighborhoods. Such factors as these make it impossible to have districts equal in area if case loads are to be comparable. Considerable study is sometimes necessary to map out satisfactory districts. Transportation facilities need to be taken into consideration, and if district offices are used the location of suitable and convenient quarters may affect the determination of district boundaries.

When the case load grows and a new visitor or visitors must be added, a redrawing of district lines is necessary to relieve workers of excessive loads and to provide a district for the new worker. To avoid the necessity for radical changes of this sort, agencies in cities of dense population sometimes set up large districts to which several workers are assigned.

These large districts may be divided into subdistricts to each of which a visitor is assigned; sometimes the visitors work at large throughout the district. It is somewhat easier to increase or decrease the visiting staff when necessary under this plan without disturbing the whole district plan of the agency. Workers-at-large or floaters are sometimes employed and are assigned temporarily to overloaded districts.

Other methods of assignment are occasionally found. When the agency is so small that only two workers are necessary, each may take cases in rotation or as other applications are disposed of.[13] If one worker also carries administrative responsibility for the agency, he is usually unable to carry so large a load as the other. More flexibility is generally possible

---

[12] This is not invariably true. One agency discovered that in its jurisdiction the suburban areas where cases were widely scattered took no more time than downtown districts with concentrated populations. The explanation appears to lie in the fact that collateral sources in this suburban area were less dispersed. Applicants in the suburban area lived near friends, relatives, and other sources of information whom the visitors needed to consult. The applicants in the downtown area, on the other hand, were often in rooming houses rather than with or near relatives; they had moved more frequently and were less well known in their immediate neighborhood. Collateral or reference calls might, therefore, be spread through widely separated neighborhoods.

[13] In one large agency visited, cases were assigned to the visitors in rotation in the order in which applications were received and without regard to the location of the applicant. The plan appeared to work uneconomically.

in a small agency than in a large one, but even in small agencies geographical districting is frequently found to be more satisfactory as the basic method although it may not be adhered to so rigidly as in a large agency.

Assignment in accordance with the problem presented by the case and with reference to the special skill of the worker to whom it is assigned is not common in old age assistance. This functional assignment is best adapted to, and most frequently found in, agencies emphasizing treatment of a variety of problems. The old age assistance program in most states is still new, and up to this point its emphasis has been on investigation of eligibility. It is possible that old age cases present greater uniformity than do general-relief cases, for instance, and that functional assignment may be less useful in old age assistance agencies. A few old age assistance agencies located in large cities assign responsibility for handling cases referred to them for local investigation by out-of-town agencies to a special worker. A few have special Negro case loads. Assignment of cases in agencies handling two or more public assistance programs, or a combination of categorical programs and general relief, may be made on the basis of the type of assistance for which the applicant has applied; or the type of assistance involved may be ignored and assignment made on some other basis.

Not infrequently combinations of methods are found. Cases may be assigned to large districts on a geographical basis, but assigned to workers within the large district on a rotating basis. Functional assignment, on the other hand, is usually supplementary to a district or geographical plan. The number of cases requiring special treatment is always relatively small, and other methods must be used for assigning the large number of cases presenting no special problems. Categorical and geographical assignment may be combined.

In some agencies the visitors are expected to carry the same cases through continuing or emergent care and formal reconsideration or other follow-up. Others require that the visitor surrender the case when the investigation has reached a point that will justify a recommendation on eligibility and the record is ready for submission to the designated administrative authority for official approval. Closing cases thus at the time of decision is satisfactory for those that are disapproved, for it removes from the active file of case records those with whom the agency plans no further contacts.[14] When the agency approves a grant, how-

[14] Cases that are denied may be reopened at a later date when changes in the applicants' circumstances make them eligible; denied cases may also require further con-

ever, it assumes responsibility for assuring itself of continued eligibility and for providing whatever service to recipients its program calls for. It must, therefore, prepare for periodic contacts with recipients whether the state law requires formal reconsideration or not. It is advantageous to both recipient and agency, as a rule, to have the worker handle cases with which he is already familiar, and thus the reassignment of approved cases to another worker is wasteful.

SUPERVISION OF INVESTIGATION

Workers investigating eligibility must know sources of information, their location, how to consult them, and how to judge their validity. They must be skilful in interviewing both applicants and informants. Other case-work skills are essential to the satisfactory handling of the many problems bearing on need determination, including relatives' support, property ownership, and institutional care. Workers are required to deal with facts in specialized fields, such as industry, medicine, family (or home), economics, property, and, most difficult of all, perhaps, that of personal and family relationships. Thus it is evident that workers, especially those who are untrained and inexperienced, need considerable guidance in collecting the data on which eligibility can be determined.

Adaptation to Varying Needs of Local Units

Individualized teaching and personal demonstration are a necessary supplement to the written material provided for workers. In small local agencies the size of the job often does not justify the expense of a full-time trained supervisor, and even if it did there are not enough trained case-work supervisors to supply such a demand. In some states the state agency has recognized a responsibility for giving special supervisory aid to such units. An effort is made to visit them more frequently than better equipped units, to stay longer, and to supply additional instructive material especially suited to the needs of the local workers. Training courses, institutes, and regional or state conferences are sometimes arranged. Opportunities may be provided to visit better equipped units and observe their methods. Special consideration is given to opportunities for educational leave for the more promising workers.

In somewhat larger units the supervisory service may still require

---

sideration in relation to appeal for fair hearing; the number of reopenings and denials is usually small, however, and ordinarily the agency may reasonably expect denied applicants to assume responsibility for initiating future contacts after it has fully informed them of their rights.

supplementation, but the approach of the state field worker must usually be different. In several instances observed, this need for a different approach was not fully comprehended by the state field workers. If the local unit has a case supervisor, supervision of the visiting staff by the state field worker must be done through and not around the supervisor if the quality of work in the unit is to be improved. If the local supervisor is hopelessly incompetent, the only remedy is removal. Undercutting will not help the situation, and if the state worker is not in a position to do anything about replacement with a better qualified person, his only alternative is still to do what he can through the supervisor. Even when the supervisor has some competence and is teachable and willing to learn, state field workers are not always careful about avoiding undercutting. It is often temptingly easier to go directly to a visitor for correction of an error made by the visitor rather than to teach the supervisor a method of supervision that will reduce the number of errors; but the results are often disastrous. Staff morale is disrupted; the visitors lose confidence in the supervisor; the supervisor loses confidence in himself; and, in the end, the unit may be worse off than it would have been if the state worker had stayed away.[15]

The state field worker likewise must beware of undercutting the director by dealing with the case supervisor on administrative matters which should be the concern of the director. If administrative matters must be discussed with the supervisor, the discussion should be carried on in a joint conference with director and supervisor. Often, however, it is better to handle all administrative matters entirely through the director; in any event, his responsibility in administrative matters should never be ignored. Neither of these cautions implies that the state field worker should not be alert in observing and attempting to appraise without comment the work of subordinate workers in the local unit. When, where, and to whom a comment about the work of any staff member is to be made is a matter calling for a state field representative's utmost discretion.

Supervision in a large local agency with well qualified case supervisors presents a still different problem to the state staff. Sometimes the local supervisor is a better trained and more competent person than the state field representative assigned to the area. The state worker in such a situation sometimes feels at a disadvantage and is apt to react either by attempting to become authoritative or by avoiding contacts

[15] See Josephine Brown, *Field Work with Public Welfare Agencies* (Chicago: American Public Welfare Association), pp. 4-5.

with the supervisor and even with the agency. Local supervisors of large agencies may also assume that they are in a special class and that the state staff has nothing to give them. Such attitudes are obstructive. Large city units should recognize the danger that confronts them of becoming isolated from the rest of the state and thus insular, narrow minded, and self-satisfied. They should—and some of them do—recognize the value of contacts with other units both directly in conferences and indirectly through the state staff.

The problems in large and small units are different; nevertheless each can learn from the other. State representatives recognizing this fact need feel no embarrassment in approaching a large unit. They may be surprised, in fact, to find the city staff more receptive than they had expected. If the large agency staff has the use of special facilities that the state lacks, it may be willing to share them with the state office or with other units. Often large agencies have opportunities for experimenting and would make the results available if the state were interested in developing a cooperative relationship with them. In states in which there are several large units the state staff may find some value in arranging for exchange of experience between them. While there is some danger of building up a cleavage between large and small units, this can be somewhat offset by district or state conferences in which an effort is made to develop programs or projects which will promote interchange between large and small units.[16]

Use of Consultants

Special consultants are usually necessary either at the state or local level. Consultants may be required on medical care, on legal problems, on family economics, in connection with special services, and for training personnel.[17] Usually consultation service must be provided by the state, although large city agencies may have sufficient work to justify the employment of either part- or full-time consultants. Consultants carry on a great variety of tasks, bear varied titles, and are diversely organized in relation to the work of the visiting staff. One of their most important tasks is to assist the agency to establish what the staff of the Bureau of Public Assistance of the Social Security Board calls "standards of assistance," which are standards established by the agency as a

---

[16] The writer is inclined to be skeptical of the plan adopted by some agencies of assigning to a large agency a worker who has no responsibility for supervising other local units. Such a worker soon loses his perspective and has little to give either the state office or the unit he supervises.

[17] For a discussion of the use of training consultants see chap. 15.

means of determining need of applicants and amounts of individual grants. In this connection the duties of a state consultant, as the Bureau sees them, are as follows:

CONSULTANT, STANDARDS OF ASSISTANCE—DUTIES

Under the general supervision of the director of social work:

To develop a quantity-quality budget of requirements of individuals of different ages, conditions, and activity that may be used in determining the adequacy of individual resources in relation to assistance that may be made available;

To check periodically the cost of purchasing the basic requirements in selected communities of the State, or to approve schedules of costs established by the local unit for adoption as a basic budget;

To develop procedures to be used in analysis and evaluation of resources and to prescribe methods to be used in determining effect of resources on the eligibility of the individual;

To develop and supervise the use of forms for obtaining and recording factual data in relation to the financial needs and resources of the individual applicant;

To develop and supervise the use of special facilities available to the local units for conservation and adjustment of insurance and analysis of real and personal property, as such service may be most economically made available on a State-wide basis;

To provide, by arrangement with the field staff, for periodic review of practices in the local units for promotion of a better understanding of the nature and purpose of State standards of assistance and for elimination of variations in treatment on the basis of local prejudice or the investigator's individual standards of essentials;

To cooperate with other State, Federal and private agencies, such as the Departments of Education, Departments of Agriculture, Works Progress Administration, Parent-Teachers Association for the development of educational programs;

To provide direct consultation at the request of the local units on problems relating to special nutritional needs, household management and family budgeting where those services are desired by recipients of assistance;

To prepare educational and informational material for distribution among recipients of public assistance to aid them in making best use of their assistance grants.

The State Field Staff

In draft material prepared by the Bureau of Public Assistance, the duties of the state field representative are described as follows:

STATE FIELD REPRESENTATIVE—DUTIES

Under immediate supervision of the director of field staff:

To interpret Federal and State requirements relating to local practice;

To make available to local units guidance and consultation on problems within the community;

To share with local communities experiences of other communities and give practical advice on the every day problems of administration;

To establish effective working relationships between the State agency and the local community, reporting to the State on local progress and performance, and stimulating coordination of effort to promote the intelligent use of State facilities by arranging for technical consultation with representatives from all bureaus or divisions of the State office;

To review periodically a substantial sampling of case records in the local unit, and, where the size of staff or special circumstances do not permit the employment of a trained supervisor by the local unit, to supervise the activities of the local investigators relating to investigation and service;

To participate in periodic evaluation of performance of local staff;

To provide the State agency with comprehensive and current reports on local progress and development;

To review and approve routinely in the local unit authorizations for disbursement in the name of the State agency where the State plan provides for the approval of individual applications by the State agency;

To interpret to the State agency the special circumstances in the local unit warranting or necessitating adoptions of policy;

To stimulate and participate in local experimental projects;

To represent and act in the name of the State agency in conducting fair hearings where this function of the State agency is exercised in the local unit.

This statement stresses the administrative aspects of the job, although the special responsibility for supervision of the social service activities is also included. It is not always easy, however, to find persons qualified to handle the many complex problems of administration requiring the attention of field representatives, and, at the same time, to furnish consultation on the details of the social service program. In a few states it was assumed that administrative skill and experience only were required, or that such skill was so important as to be preferable to skill and experience in social case work. The results observed did not commend the agency's decision. Best results were seen where field representatives were selected who had experience in the administration of social work programs, particularly in public welfare.

CASE DECISIONS: DETERMINATION, SUPERVISION, AND REVIEW

After the application is received by the agency it technically remains pending until official decision has been made. The method of arriving at decisions and authorizing grants varies in different states and even among agencies within a state. Because the approval of cases carries with it the necessity for authorization of disbursement, it is commonly regarded as the more important decision and tends to be given more attention. In relation to the objectives of the program—security for aged applicants—the control of denials seems equally important.

Inseparability of Investigation and Decision

Investigation of, and decision on, eligibility and extent of need are not always recognized as practically inseparable processes. Although discretion and judgment enter largely into the final process they must actually be employed at every step. Each bit of information or verification gained must be added to what has gone before and must be evaluated in itself and in relation to what has preceded. Conflicting evidence usually means that not all the facts have been unearthed; when all important discrepancies have been cleared the decision is to a large extent made. Supervision of investigation is usually a process of helping the worker to find, assemble, and evaluate evidence, but, as already explained, evaluation is applied to each new bit of evidence if a logical and economical scheme of inquiry is followed. An accumulation of a mass of miscellaneous data to be sorted and evaluated at the end of the process is a wasteful and often a useless activity, for there is no certainty that a decision will be possible at the end. If a just decision is to be made it must be related to the facts in the case and must grow out of them. The visitor and supervisor must therefore participate in the decision. In fact, by making the investigation they determine what the decision is to be. If a decision is made which does not fit the facts it is faulty. If poor judgment of worker and supervisor has operated throughout the process, it cannot be fully corrected by imposing a superior judgment at the end.

Failure to recognize the connection between investigation and decision accounts for many of the varied and peculiar methods adopted to control decisions. Legislators and administrators unfamiliar with the problems of public welfare administration and unacquainted with methods of social inquiry into determination of need and of the interrelation of investigation and decision have attempted to establish control over expenditure through control of decisions.

In agencies in which the virtual inseparability of investigation and decision is recognized, the visitor, in consultation with the supervisor, who has, perhaps, already reviewed some of the evidence when directing the worker toward suitable lines of inquiry, prepares a report and makes a formal recommendation. In this process the evidence is given a final review, and if any gaps are noted additional facts are sought. In the final report, all items of eligibility are covered, and the facts to support the decision are duly marshalled.[18] The report is initialed or signed by the visitor and approved by the supervisor. If the supervisor is empowered to authorize the grant, he signs the authorization document; the next step is official notification to the disbursing official by transmitting to him the authorization forms legally authenticated.[19]

The procedure described is a simplified one. Many variations and elaborations of preparing reports, of review approval, and of grant authorization were observed. In highly centralized systems, approval by state as well as of local officials is required, but simpler reports may be used if the state representative makes his review in the local rather than in the state office.[20]

Decisions in Local Agencies

In most of the agencies visited in which local approval of the decision only was required the director's approval was necessary. His signature is required on the ground that he is responsible for all disbursement and must, therefore, authorize all grants. In small agencies the director usually acts as case supervisor and thus reviews the entire investigation

---

[18] The formal report may actually be brief, but the case record must contain the supporting data carefully arranged and fully recorded.

[19] Notification of the applicant, of the state agency, and of any others specified to receive notification is also a part of this step. See chap. 9.

[20] If reviews are made in district offices of the state the procedure is the same as when the records are sent to a central state office. It is only when the review is made locally that simple reports are possible, for then the case record itself can be reviewed, and it is unnecessary to repeat the data on that record in a special report.

and participates in it at various steps. Through his direct participation and his acquaintance with sources of information and often with applicants, he is able to supplement the record by a considerable amount of firsthand knowledge.

In larger agencies the task of directing and overseeing the work of the visitors is delegated to one or more supervisors. When the director of a large agency reviews decisions he must depend upon the written record supplemented by oral questioning of supervisor or visitor, and thus may, and usually does, participate very little in the decision. From the point of view of sound administration it is, on the whole, not desirable that he should share actively in all decisions. In very large agencies it would be impossible for him to do so, and even in most smaller ones he could not take part in all decisions unless he gave full time to this one task; and if he did he would be not only neglecting other important duties but also duplicating to a large extent the work of the case supervisor.

The director needs to know the trend of decisions and to share in the decision of difficult and puzzling cases, especially those not covered by state or local policies or those in which established policies are operating unsatisfactorily. He is technically responsible for every decision, but his methods of control over decisions are: selection and general direction of the staff; interpretation to the staff of local, state, and federal policies and procedures; development of local policies and procedures for guiding the staff; and general oversight of all activities of the unit. He has authority to intervene and actually to make the decision, but if he is wise he does not do so often. Once a function is delegated it is necessary to respect the integrity of that responsibility in the subordinate to whom it has been allocated. If the director lacks confidence in the subordinate, he should find out why. If the cause seems to be incompetence the available remedies are to remove the worker, to narrow his scope of responsibility, or to transfer him to a more suitable task. Workers to whom responsibility for decision is delegated should clearly understand the limits of their responsibility and be trained to respect them. In general the executive must also respect the limits he himself has set up, if his administration is to run smoothly.

The responsibility of a local board for delegating authority to make decisions is much the same as that of the director. The difficulties may be somewhat accentuated for various reasons. The law or the specific rules of the state department may seem to prohibit delegation of this responsibility to the director, and thus the board may feel that it must make an individual decision in each case even though the volume of work prohibits their doing so. Prior approval of the director is usually required, but if the board is inexperienced in administration it may feel uneasy about accepting the authorization of a director as a valid discharge of its responsibility for individual decision. Even when the number of cases is small enough to allow a few minutes' attention to each, individual decision by a board is seldom satisfactory. As already stated, decision cannot be divorced from investigation, but board members are seldom experienced in the making of social investigations; even if they were, it would usually be impractical for them to attempt an intensive supervisory review of the investigation and thus to duplicate the work of the director or supervisor.

A board may come nearer to exercising a satisfactory supervisory function in one-man agencies with small case loads than in large agencies. Even though members are not skilled they often have sources of information in the community and may have personal knowledge of the case. Such information, however, is often more useful in the early stages of the investigation than at the point of decision.[21] Unless the number of cases is small, the board can seldom take the time to consider every case, and thus it actually must delegate responsibility for part of the decisions. When authority is delegated, whether by board or executive, the extent of delegation should be determined and the established limits carefully maintained.

When the case load requires the services of more than one worker, individual approval cannot usually be given satisfactorily by a board. If the board attempts to review all cases the review will take more time than the board can or will give and will be so cursory as to have little value. If it is unwilling to accept the director's recommendation, the board must make an investigation for itself and thus duplicate the work of the visitor; or it must read the case record or a special report of the investigation or question the visitor or supervisor and thus infringe on the responsibility of the director.

Both boards and directors have been puzzled over the meaning of their responsibility for decision and have attempted in various ways to work out a satisfactory method of handling it. Some of the methods have already been suggested. It is impossible to cover all those used, but it may be worth while to outline a few. Both boards and executives have resorted to committees, some of which are made up of board

[21] The workers in small agencies often use board members as sources of information prior to decision, just as they use other public officials.

members only; others of board and executive; and still others of some combination of board, executive, and staff. Sometimes the decision of the reviewing committee is final. More often it must have official approval from board, or executive, or both; but this approval tends to be a rubber-stamp type of action on the committee's recommendations.

In a few agencies, hearings were held at which the applicant and worker might both be required to be present. The decision might be made by the administrative official, by the board, or by a committee. The applicant was permitted to bring friends or relatives and to present any information in his possession. If county judges are responsible for the administration of old age assistance, they are apt to prefer this method. In one agency where the decision was made by a committee after such a hearing, it was argued that the method helped future relations of visitor and applicant, for the visitor presumably appeared as the applicant's advocate while the judicial action was taken by the committee. Where the clients seldom appear before a committee, they generally know only from the visitor's statement that he has fully represented them. Consequently it is questionable whether the visitor can or should avoid full responsibility for the decision.

Observation of the proceedings in several hearings in a judge-administered program, supplemented by the reading of case records, did not commend the hearing as a method of reaching a decision. Applicants were required to be present if physically able and were expected to bring with them one or more of the relatives legally liable for their support. Although the survey staff was assured that all hearings were held in chambers, the room used had all the appearance of a court-room, with raised dais for the judge and tables for the supervisors who presented the cases. Even though the judge conducted the hearing in a friendly manner, the procedure was obviously an ordeal for the applicants and their families. No doorkeeper was on duty to make sure that curiosity seekers or casual visitors did not slip in. No separate waiting space was provided; thus the first cases could be overheard by applicants whose hearings came later.

The recommendation of the supervisor had previously been worked out with the visitor in conference.[22] The judge was also furnished with

---

[22] In cases in which a denial or other unfavorable action was being recommended, the applicant might also have been invited to a preliminary conference. If he could produce additional facts they would be utilized; otherwise he could be prepared for an unfavorable outcome and thus avoid argument and delay in the courtroom. It is not certain whether concern for the client or fear of the judge's displeasure was the paramount consideration in adopting this predecision review procedure.

a report of the investigation, which he generally used as a basis for questioning the applicant. New facts were seldom brought out, and the decision usually followed the staff recommendation. The time occupied in hearings had greatly delayed accession of cases with no apparent advantage.[23]

The most satisfactory procedure in agencies in which decision is made locally is generally as follows: The case is assigned to the visitor, usually on a geographical basis, by the person responsible for direct supervision of the visitor. A record is made of the assignment, and a date may be set for submission of report and recommendation with some sort of tickler arrangement for follow-up on or before that date. If the visitor is new or the investigation presents difficulties, several preliminary conferences between visitor and supervisor may be held; but if no difficulties are encountered and the visitor is ready to report on or before the specified date, the case record is submitted to the supervisor with all dictation written up and with a tentative report or suggested recommendation. If he approves the recommendation, he so indicates on the authorization form.

Usually the supervisor reviews the record or report in conference with the worker. If the worker's report appears inadequate, the supervisor may suggest further investigation or improvements in the method of presentation. When both supervisor and visitor are satisfied, the recommendation is submitted to the official (or board)[24] having final authority for decision. If the supervisor in conference with the visitor finds that the situation of the applicant is such that established policies seem inapplicable, doubtful, or unsatisfactory, he withholds recommendation or makes it tentative pending a conference with the director. The conference may be oral and informal; or a special detailed report may be presented. Similarly, special reports may be prepared for cases to which the administrative authority has agreed to give special consideration.[25]

[23] It is possible that the unusually accurate recording of sources of information in the case records of this agency was a direct result of the necessity for having an impregnable case in court; but even this was rather offset by a corresponding and undue dependence on personal affidavits containing statements of little value although giving an appearance of legal conformity.

[24] If the final decision is not made by the local director, the recommendation is submitted to him and by him to the board.

[25] In one large urban county the director submits routine reports on classified lists for all cases in which no question of policy has arisen and in addition prepares a special docket of cases which seem inadequately covered by established policies or that involve the question of obligation to support of an elected or appointive public official related to the applicant.

The determinative authority usually reserves the right to question any case presented but prefers to pass routinely on those not needing special attention.[26] Lists may be classified as new approvals, reinstatements, increases, decreases, discontinuances, and denials. Passing these cases by a rubber-stamp procedure saves time for cases requiring reconsideration, or the application of new policies, or special consideration to enable the administrative authority to assume responsibility for decisions that might affect the prestige of the local agency.[27]

State Decision

Difficulties of local agencies in arriving at determinative decisions in individual cases are intensified when such decisions are the responsibility of the state agency. Separation of decision from investigation is inevitable if the decision is made in the state office since all investigations are made locally. Relationship of decision to investigation tends, under these conditions, to become dislocated and time consuming. The problem of making a large number of decisions is greatly increased when decisions for an entire state are centralized in the state office. Even in the smaller states individual consideration of each case is practically impossible. The state agency is thus forced either to decentralize the process in whole or in part or to find short cuts to speed it up. No important, satisfactory short cuts in meeting these problems were observed in the states visited. Partial decentralization was observed chiefly in a tendency to accept uncritically recommendations of local boards or directors in denied cases while ignoring their recommendations on approved cases.

The short cuts commonly used have to do mostly with records. A decision made in the state office is necessarily on the basis of a special report or duplicate record submitted to the state office. It is presumed that decisions can be made more rapidly if a detailed report is submitted whenever a decision is necessary. These reports may be short cuts for the state staff but at the same time exceedingly burdensome to the local staff; and they result in the development of case records that are a mass of reports containing repetitious matter rather than the selective, cumu-

---

[26] It is sometimes assumed that the administrative authority should pass on individual cases because funds may be inadequate to meet the needs of all. Such a situation should, however, be met by formulation of general policies to which individual decisions will be adjusted rather than by individual decisions not controlled by policy considerations. For discussion of the problem of insufficient funds see chap. 9.

[27] Backing and support can also be afforded to some extent by an advisory board without administrative authority. For fuller discussion of the function of boards see chap. 17.

lative data that make a case record an effective instrument. Because state decision assumes that a complete and consistent report is all that is needed in making a suitable decision, effort is directed toward obtaining reports that show no discrepancies and are assumed, therefore, to be accurate. This tendency to regard the report as paramount has encouraged the use of, and dependence on, the work of checkers, formulas, and other mechanical aids.

State Review of Decisions

Theoretically state review does not relieve local units of responsibility for their decisions, but actually it may do so to a considerable extent. If the local agency makes only a tentative decision pending review, or if after review it invariably alters its decision to conform to that of the state, the results are the same as if the original decision had been made by the state. The fact that the local agency is not legally compelled to follow these courses does not affect the immediate results. Agencies reviewing all local decisions in the state office are forced to the dependence on recorded data characteristic of state decision. Checkers are sometimes used. Decisions may be, and perhaps more often are, confined to accepted cases, since the theory of state review is that of determining the validity of the state's contribution to the local expenditure. As in state decision, the process of review tends to absorb the supervisory effort of the state office and thus to deprive local workers of the more constructive supervision that might be given them.

When state review is decentralized, the reviewing is done in the local offices directly from the local case records. Although decentralization obviates some of the worst features of review, it still requires undue effort in routine reading of records, with concentration on results in terms of detailed factual data rather than on methods.

Concern with details and a tendency toward approval of stereotyped records that show no obvious discrepancies, even though they may be inaccurate, are inherent in the method and are intensified if the reviewer is unskilled in the process of investigation and case-work supervision. If, on the other hand, the worker is thus skilled, the routine examination of cases is wasteful of that skill. All cases, all workers, all agencies are treated alike, for there is no time for individualization although the need of supervision is varied in amount and kind. Some agencies have recognized the advantages of more flexible methods, either from the beginning or after some experience with the complete social audit. The staff of the Bureau of Public Assistance has advocated selective review coupled with other supervisory methods, and the more progressive agencies are in accord with this advice. They recognize that the state field representatives must, if they are to do effective work, individualize the units and adapt their supervisory methods to the requirements of each unit. Occasionally a unit may profit by a complete review of all its decisions in a given period. In most instances, however, a sample review coupled with other firsthand knowledge of agency and staff will furnish all necessary leads for discovering the fundamental strengths and weaknesses in the organization and operation of the local agency and for suggesting to an alert state field supervisor the direction of his efforts toward improvement.

CHAPTER 9

DISPOSITION OF CASES

THE DISPOSITION OF applications for old age assistance has already been outlined. The process is sufficiently important, however, to merit more detailed discussion. Moreover, it is desirable to give attention to related problems connected with action taken on cases already on the rolls, cases that require readjustment, and cases of re-application after rejection or discontinuance. There are at least eight possible dispositions[1] of these cases, but, for purposes of discussion, they may be grouped under three general classifications: withdrawals, approvals and denials, and reconsideration of cases previously granted assistance.

That every application, whether formal or informal, should be disposed of by some fairly definite procedure seems such an essential requirement of sound administration that it should be unnecessary to mention it. Observations in the field, however, revealed so many violations in this respect that it is necessary to emphasize the importance of establishing and adhering to definite procedures. In a number of local agencies, completed and partly completed applications were carelessly left lying about or were filed away in a seldom used drawer and apparently forgotten. In only a few agencies were adequate procedures systematically followed.

Failure to act on an application is tantamount to rejection. Some state laws recognize this fact and provide that if an application is not acted upon within a specified period, usually thirty to sixty days, the applicant may appeal to the state agency for a fair hearing. In the absence of such a requirement, state agencies have sometimes adopted regulations similarly requiring local units to act promptly on all

[1] These are: 1. Withdrawal of a tentative request for assistance before actually making out the required application form. 2. Withdrawal after filing formal application but before presentation of case for administrative decision. 3. Acceptance and approval of an application or a reapplication previously withdrawn or rejected. 4. Denial or rejection of a new application or of a reapplication previously withdrawn or rejected. 5. Modification of an established grant (raising or lowering the amount). 6. Suspension of a grant (temporary). 7. Discontinuance of a grant (final). 8. Restoration, renewal, or reinstatement of a suspended grant or of a discontinued grant not requiring formal reapplication.

applications. Unfortunately such laws and regulations do not provide an adequate remedy. Local units that wish to do so can easily evade the intention of these provisions by postponing completion of the application or postdating it; thus the delay is not apparent on mere inspection of the application. Unless the applicant can prove that his application has been pending longer than the date on it indicates, appeal will not be an effective weapon. Furthermore, appeal does not sufficiently protect the applicant against undue delay since its effectiveness depends upon the applicant's being fully informed of his legal rights. Well informed and aggressive applicants, who ordinarily are the ones to make use of the appeal weapon, are not those who would be most likely to suffer from the dilatory action of the local agency. There is another reason why appeal to the state agency may be ineffective: lack of prompt action may be due to the dilatory practices or the cumbersome methods of the state agency itself.[2] In the end the conclusion must be that the best way to ensure protection of applicants is through improved administration from the state agency down.

WITHDRAWALS

An agency could probably dispose of every application or reapplication by adopting a policy of counting as formal applications all inquiries about eligibility; requiring that every application (or reapplication) be followed up carefully by an investigation; submitting every application (or reapplication) to the administrative authority for decision; and making decisions on all applications or reapplications either approvals (grants) or rejections. No agency observed in the field was following so comprehensive a procedure. All were disposing of some cases by withdrawal, but practices varied widely as to the cases which might well be so disposed of and as to the procedures to be followed in utilizing this method.

General Use of Method

Withdrawal is a satisfactory method of disposing of an application in several instances. If an applicant has been given complete information about eligibility requirements and is fully satisfied that he cannot meet

[2] The delays observed in the field appeared to be the result of varied factors, most common among which were: the rush of new applications at the initiation of the program; poorly trained, inexperienced, and overloaded staffs; poor supervision, state and local; insufficient equipment, supplies, and service, including allowance for transportation; poor organization of work; and other administrative failures. Carelessness and indifference were seldom encountered.

them, there seems to be no reason why he should not be permitted to withdraw his application. Withdrawal may also be used if an applicant, although not obviously ineligible, is indifferent or refuses to prosecute his claim further. Some agencies handle these cases as rejections; others, especially those having elaborate procedures for presenting cases for administrative decision, prefer to establish a voluntary withdrawal procedure. Some applicants, eligible at the time of application, become ineligible through change of circumstances before the investigation is completed. Such cases are often handled as withdrawals. Cases in which death removes an applicant may also be counted as withdrawals.

Some agencies operate under state laws that prohibit the applicant whose application has been denied from reapplying within a specified time—usually six months or one year.[3] In these states, agencies frequently resort to withdrawal to avoid penalizing an applicant who, though ineligible at the time of application, appears likely to meet the requirements within the specified period. Unfortunately changes in an applicant's circumstances, especially those relating to need, cannot always be predicted. A sounder method of meeting this problem is to repeal the prohibition against reapplication.[4]

The Need of Controls

General policies governing acceptance of applications affect withdrawals. Most old age assistance agencies place upon the applicant major responsibility for making his own application. This policy is undoubtedly sound; the chief difficulties of applying it come from its

[3] None of the officials in the states having such laws seemed to know why this provision had been included in the state law. It was in one or more of the draft bills used by states in preparing their legislation; thus it was included in the state acts, unfortunately, without much attention to its purpose and probable results. An applicant who is uncertain or mistaken about the date of his birth or who is not well informed about age requirements may apply a few months too early. If the agency rejects him he cannot reapply after he becomes eligible until the time specified in the law has elapsed. An applicant rejected because his son is able to support him cannot reapply within the interdicted period even if his son loses his job, becomes ill, or dies.

[4] As noted by several workers, this prohibition makes it easier to obtain withdrawals, but it is doubtful whether this is a real advantage. Genuinely voluntary withdrawals may be preferable to a rejection because of the more favorable reaction of applicants and community. It is questionable, however, whether a withdrawal induced by the fear of losing the opportunity to reapply is a truly voluntary withdrawal. Moreover, it should be noted that the applicant who is not fully satisfied that the agency's judgment on his eligibility is correct may lose his right to appeal that decision and request a fair hearing from the state agency if he withdraws his application. If the state law limits appeals to rejected applicants—as it does in several states—the applicant must risk the possibility of later penalty on reapplication in order to retain his present right to request a fair hearing. Even if the state law is liberal in appeals, the applicant who has withdrawn his application is in a peculiar position regarding a request for a fair hearing.

too narrow interpretation by the agencies. Although the decision to apply for old age assistance lies with the applicant, the agency, nevertheless, has an obligation to see that the applicant is sufficiently well informed that he will not jeopardize his interests; furthermore, it should be able to demonstrate that it has met this obligation should the question arise. Consequently, the administrator of a local old age assistance agency must recognize the importance of establishing adequate controls over the handling of all withdrawals, including tentative applications.[5]

Methods of Control

The administrator of a local unit who desires to maintain control over withdrawal procedures must depend on two methods: supervision and recording. A record should be made of every inquiry; if the applicant fails to return or to take any further action toward filing a formal application, his inquiry should be followed up and effort should be made to see that he is supplied with all needed information and service. The records of these inquiries should be so kept that they may be checked at regular intervals and submitted to a supervisory review or otherwise disposed of. In this way the administrator may be assured that the agency has overlooked no opportunity to help the applicant make a suitable presentation of his claims of eligibility. Some agencies, as a final safeguard, when the other efforts have failed, use a special notice which is mailed to the potential applicant informing him that, if he manifests no interest before a certain date, his inquiry will be given no further attention.[6] At the end of the time specified the tentative application is, with the approval of the supervisor, counted as withdrawn.

Some agencies attempt to obtain a signed withdrawal form from all applicants who withdraw a pending application or who fail to follow up an incomplete application or inquiry. The agency should be sure that the applicant really wishes to withdraw and to record in the case

[5] Applicants are not always clear about what constitutes an application and what obligations an agency assumes when it accepts an application. In one Wisconsin county, the county judge turned over to the local old age assistance unit when it was organized a list of potential applicants. Later, criticism of the agency arose because of its failure to take action on the cases of several persons who believed that by giving their names to the judge they had made application. The fault was not with the agency, for the list furnished by the judge was itself incomplete, but the incident illustrates the attitude toward application of most communities and makes apparent the importance of careful attention to tentative applications and inquiries.

[6] It should be noted that this is merely a final step to be used only when other methods of reaching the applicant and getting a definite response from him have failed.

record not only the fact of withdrawal but the reason for it. It should not be necessary to insist on the applicant's making formal withdrawal and to place upon him responsibility for the agency's action on his application. After the supervisor has approved of a withdrawal, the record of all contacts with the applicant is filed in a permanent file established for such cases, and no further attention is given to it unless the applicant renews his inquiry.

The death of an applicant frequently intervenes before presentation of his case for decision. When this happens it is desirable to record some proof of death. A death certificate is adequate, but other evidence may serve and be not only cheaper but more easily obtained. A newspaper clipping, if the item sufficiently identifies the applicant, attached to the record, specifying the name and date of the paper or the oral statement of a responsible person (relative or other person who has personal knowledge of the applicant's death), recorded in the case record should suffice. Rumor and hearsay evidence should not be accepted as final proof, but may give clues helpful in ascertaining the facts.

Frequently, too, an applicant leaves the community before a decision is rendered; it is then often difficult to obtain information about him, but every effort should be made to do so. It may even be desirable to communicate with an agency in the community to which he has moved, especially if it appears that he has gone merely to stay with relatives and if his new place of abode is not in another state. Procedure in removal cases is largely a matter of case-work judgment and should normally be determined by the visitor in conference with the supervisor.

The administrative principles pertaining to withdrawals are not greatly different whether the application is formal or informal, although agencies tend to formalize the procedure for completed applications. A number of large agencies maintain a tickler or other semi-automatic system of checking up on applications that have not been presented for administrative review or decision within a specified period after their assignment to the worker. This procedure is useful in keeping control over applications and seeing that suitable disposition is made of them. An agency maintaining a large intake office usually arranges for a similar check of inquiries to see that progress is being made in completing applications and disposing of pre-application inquiries. The smaller agencies and sometimes even large ones are likely to be less careful and exacting in their follow-up of inquiries and the recording of the disposition than of formal applications.[7] The procedure need not be elaborate, but it should provide for periodic check of all pending cases and for supervisory review before final action.

APPROVALS AND DENIALS

The procedure followed in disposing of a new case has already been covered in some detail.[8] It may be identical for cases previously withdrawn, denied, or discontinued. A case in which an application has previously been withdrawn is usually treated like a new case except that the agency should have some information, recorded at the time of the previous contact, which may still have significance and may thus shorten the investigation. If the case was previously denied by the agency, much information will usually be on file; hence the investigation may be largely one of bringing the data up to date. Particular scrutiny is usually given to the factors on which the previous denial was based so that the agency can be sure that they have been modified sufficiently to justify a change in the original decision. If new facts are presented they must be evaluated in relation to facts previously learned. The restoration of a discontinued grant may follow much the same process; but, because the problems involved are so closely allied to those of the modification of an existing grant, it seems appropriate to consider them in that connection.

Methods of Handling Approvals and Denials

Although the handling of a case that is finally denied is almost identical with that of approved cases, fundamental differences are apparent. An approved case must be accompanied by an authorization for the expenditure of a specified amount from the public treasury. For this reason approved applications are given special scrutiny. The legal safeguards of public expenditures tend to ensure the exercise of some degree of control over the approval of cases.[9] On the other hand, rejections,

[7] The state and federal governments require the local agencies to keep account of their applications for statistical purposes. This requirement undoubtedly influences the attitude of the agencies toward such recording. If the state does not require recording of inquiries they are not likely to be regarded as important by the local agencies although, as indicated above, the client and the community may not distinguish between the two.

[8] See chaps. 7 and 8.

[9] The emotional reaction connected with money transactions, especially the transfer of money which the taxpayer regards as essentially his to another who offers no tangible value in return, is not easy to demonstrate to the uninformed. Undoubtedly it has been a factor in many persistent beliefs which appear to have little basis in fact such, for instance, as the belief that the unemployed generally prefer relief to jobs, despite repeated demonstrations to the contrary. Again the likewise persistent belief that relief

which may involve denial of individual rights but do not result in payments from the public treasury, are regarded as less important.[10]

The preponderant emphasis on approvals is indicated by the extent to which state supervision is directed toward approved cases. In several states whose method of supervision is largely the review of individual case decisions, rejected cases are ignored unless an appeal or some special issue raised by workers in the local agency, by the individual applicant, or by other interested persons brings them to the attention of the state agency.[11]

The state's attention to approved cases tends to be focused on expenditure aspects. Care is taken to see that expenditures are authorized only for eligible applicants and are not excessive. There is less concern about seeing that the amounts recommended are in proportion to need and adequate to meet it. Apparently it is assumed that a dissatisfied applicant can be depended upon to press his own case. This is not a safe assumption about either denials or inadequate grants; but the statutes generally appear to give more recognition to the rights of the rejected applicant to protection than to the rights of the applicant whose grant is inadequate. The federal Act and several state laws provide methods of appeal for applicants "whose claim for old age assistance is denied," but fail to provide specifically the right of fair hearing for one who believes that his grant is unduly small. Wisconsin met this situation through an opinion of the State Attorney General, who interpreted

---

rolls are full of so-called "chiselers," regardless of evidence that such persons are numerically negligible. For other examples see Herman M. Somers, "Ten Delusions in Need of Relief," *Survey Graphic,* February, 1938. These fears do much harm, but they have, nevertheless, the effect of focusing attention on careful expenditure of public funds for assistance.

[10] The right of a citizen to relief at public expense is not fully recognized, but the Social Security Act and the state laws that conform with it seem to establish the right of an eligible applicant to some measure, at least, of security at public expense. The provision of the federal Act that an applicant whose application is denied must be granted a fair hearing by the state agency appears to indicate that the applicant is recognized to have certain rights to relief, since his right to a grant is thereby assumed to be capable of adjudication by the state agency.

[11] In one state, which is usually classed as state-operated, all approved cases submitted by county units are reviewed; and, if accepted, the amount of the grant is recalculated in each case by an elaborate system; but rejected cases receive only cursory attention. Another state agency, also state operated, although using a less elaborate method of recalculating grants of cases recommended for approval by local workers, likewise largely ignores decisions on cases recommended for disapproval. In a third state, one classed as locally operated and state supervised, cases submitted by local units as approved are completely reinvestigated, but no consideration whatever is given to rejected cases unless the applicant appeals. A fourth state, which uses central review of decisions, ignores all rejections unless the cases are appealed or other action is taken by the applicant or by the local agency.

an unduly low grant as a "partial denial" and allowed the recipient thereof to appeal to the State Pension Department for a fair hearing.[12]

The survey staff obtained figures on the number and amounts of individual grants from eleven of the twelve states visited. In the main such figures were available for the local units; and when tabulated and charted they revealed variations significant both for supervision and for future planning.[13] Figures indicating the number and incidence of rejections were not generally available. Although analysis of reasons for rejection should be useful in understanding and evaluating a program, such analyses were not being made.[14] State agencies, however, were beginning to recognize the need for analyzing rejections; several agencies were planning to obtain the required data from the local units.

It is possible that if more attention had been given to reasons for rejection, modifications of the program—especially of restrictive eligibility requirements not necessary for compliance with the federal Act—might have been made in some states. The shortsighted policy of one state is clearly presented in the report of the survey of the administration of relief in Newark, New Jersey, made by Conrad Van Hyning for the Newark Citizens' Advisory Committee in October, 1937.[15] In studying cases under the care of the Newark Department of Public Welfare—the public relief agency administering general relief—the survey staff found 778 cases in which the head of the household was sixty-five years of age and over. Of this number 357 were not eligible for old age assistance owing to their inability to prove American citizenship. The federal Act contains no limitations on matching state funds granted to noncitizens otherwise eligible for old age assistance, but the New Jersey law limits old age assistance to citizens. As the Newark report states,

> If relief is to be given to needy non-citizens over sixty-five from public funds, a point about which there seems to be and hardly could be any difference of opinion from a humane point of view, then it would be

[12] See chap. 16.

[13] The tabulation of these figures in Indiana, for instance, revealed the failure of certain counties to reinvestigate and absorb in the new program recipients taken over from the former (old age pension) program. This discovery made it possible for the state office to direct supervision toward stimulation of the lagging counties.

[14] The social data card supplied by the Bureau of Research and Statistics of the Social Security Board as a means of gathering current statistics of the social characteristics of applicants for old age assistance provides space and lists items which would allow a state to make an analysis of the reasons for rejection, but states are not required to submit these data to the Board.

[15] *Survey of the Administration of Relief of the Newark Department of Public Welfare,* The Newark Citizens' Advisory Committee, October, 1937.

to the interest of the State to have the Federal Government share in the cost and to have these aged cared for as well as possible.

If states were more aware of what their restrictive requirements cost them in loss of funds which the federal government stands ready to supply, more of them would have liberalized their requirements by now.

What other facts study of reasons for rejection would reveal it is impossible to foresee fully.[16] Undoubtedly states would find differences in the methods of their local units in handling rejections which should be known and evaluated both for supervision and program-building purposes.

Responsibility for Denied Applicants

The extent to which local units assume responsibility for needy persons whose applications must be denied or discontinued varies greatly from state to state and from community to community. Some local agencies visited apparently felt no concern about this matter; others made considerable effort to see that such cases were referred to another agency that might be able to assume responsibility; or lacking the resources of other agencies the old age assistance unit itself might attempt to develop resources to meet the contingency. In a few local units the director seemed to feel a genuine concern, but he and his staff were too ill informed and inept to give the rejected applicant the kind of service he required.

The attitude of the local unit toward these problems appears to be influenced by the state policy. If the state is indifferent or actually discourages assumption of responsibility for denied cases, local policies are apt to be different from those in a state that encourages interest in the problems and that gives advice and help. A state that feels no responsibility for applicants except to see that eligibles receive grants is less apt to suggest to its local units the assumption of responsibility for denied applicants than a state that regards the program as essentially one of special relief.

Local units are also influenced in their attitudes by the extent to which they are responsible for other forms of assistance—especially general relief. Even if other relief programs are in different departments or office suites, their existence seems to make old age assistance workers more aware that the problem of need requires the attention of public welfare officials whether or not the needy person is eligible for the form

---

[16] For a discussion of the special problems involved in denials due to insufficient funds see below, pp. 182 ff.

of assistance he seeks. Even when the connection with a general-relief program is not official but is close physically or in cooperative relationships of any kind, there seems to be a carry-over that increases the interest and activity of the old age assistance unit. If the program is directed or greatly influenced by persons with social work training and experience, the responsibility for doing something about rejected applicants appears to be increased.

Notifications

Whether the action taken on an application is favorable or unfavorable, it is generally agreed that the applicant should be informed of the decision. The procedures followed in notification vary considerably. Some state agencies prescribe a special form; others leave the method to the local unit. A few states issue formal "certificates of award" to all accepted applicants, sometimes for a definite period at the end of which the applicant is required to reapply if he wishes the award to be continued. Usually, however, the award is for an indefinite period and remains in force so long as the applicant continues to meet eligibility requirements.[17]

The notice of award usually specifies the amount of the grant and its effective date. It may also inform the applicant of the right to appeal if he is dissatisfied, sometimes including further instructions about his rights and obligations. This latter information is more satisfactorily transmitted in a separate letter or pamphlet, often supplemented by a personal interview.[18] Some agencies hold the first check for personal delivery and send a visitor to explain in detail about the program and especially to give instructions about endorsement of checks. This seems a desirable procedure: fewer checks are incorrectly endorsed and many other difficulties and misunderstandings are avoided.

Notifying applicants of rejection is equally important, especially in relation to fair hearing, since in several states request for a hearing must be made within a specified period following the decision. The notice usually gives the date of, and reasons for, the decision and explains the provisions for a fair hearing. A few states fail to include

[17] If the applicant remains eligible on the basis of need but the degree of his need changes, the grant will continue but its amount will be changed.

[18] Several agencies have prepared pamphlets written in simple and clear language, explaining payment procedures and setting forth the rights and obligations of the recipient of assistance. The Connecticut pamphlet, *Instructions and Information for Beneficiaries of Old Age Assistance in Connecticut*, issued in 1937, is exceptionally well organized and written.

the latter provisions; they are, nevertheless, overlooking an obligation to the applicant.

Many agencies consider that it is even more important to interview rejected than accepted applicants and make greater effort to interview such persons promptly after a decision has been made. Some of the wisest administrators are aware that careful interviewing and full explanation from the beginning prepare the way for the final decision, which, when made, is thus not a surprise to the applicant. As already indicated, many applicants whose eligibility is doubtful prefer to withdraw; hence those that are finally rejected should ordinarily be borderline cases, in which the applicant knows that the decision will be close and is prepared for its being unfavorable; or cases in which the applicant cannot be convinced of his ineligibility although he is also prepared for an unfavorable decision.

When final administrative action on a case is taken, it may be desirable that the agency notify another agency, or perhaps an interested individual, of the decision.[19] If a private citizen, a public official, or the representative of another agency refers an applicant to the old age assistance unit, especially if the interested person has undertaken some responsibility for helping the applicant complete his claim for old age assistance, it is a courtesy to inform that person of the action taken. Thus if his cooperation is won, the sponsor, upon whose opinion the applicant usually relies, may aid in gaining the applicant's acceptance of the decision. In only one state were formal notifications of this type made with any degree of regularity.

When the local unit makes the final decision on applications it may be required to notify the state office of its action on each case. This procedure is customary if the state employs the complete social audit as its chief method of supervision, and keeps a duplicate case record at the state office. The record forms prescribed or furnished by the state usually include a special section for recording the decision.[20] If duplicate records are not kept at the state office, notification on separate individual forms for each case may not be required. If grants are disbursed centrally, the disbursing office must have official authorization on each case in order to make payments; but even these authorizations may be made by lists or pay rolls certified by the administrative officials. Changes in the amount of the grant may likewise be made by individual notices,

[19] This procedure may be desirable in final action on withdrawals as well as on awards and rejections.

[20] This section is usually appended to the "Report of Investigation."

by list, or pay roll.[21] It is unnecessary that the state have reports of local action on each case if the program is entirely decentralized, since the state takes no action on individual cases except complaints or requests for fair hearing.[22]

If the decision is made centrally, however, it is always desirable that the state notify the local unit promptly of any action on an individual case. If the state agency's decision does not follow the recommendation of the local unit the reasons for the difference should be explained.[23] Supplementation of the written notification of the applicant by a personal interview may not be possible in every case, but the local unit should always render this service when it is needed. In order to interpret a decision the local unit must not only know what the decision is but must understand its basis.[24]

RECONSIDERATION OF GRANTS

The task of administering an old age assistance program would be less complicated if eligibility of applicants could be determined once and for all. Unfortunately for simplicity of administration, the condition of human beings, including recipients of old age assistance, seldom

[21] The state may require that the pay roll be classified to show new cases, reinstatements, suspensions, discontinuances, or may simply accept the grant list with amounts and status (if any change) opposite each name.

[22] The state needs reports on the disposition of cases for statistical purposes. The Bureau of Research and Statistics of the Social Security Board devised a report for this purpose (called Social Data Card—Old Age Assistance, R. S. 201). Early in 1939 the Board decided to require centralization of eligibility reports in the state office. Suggestions were made about the form, and states were advised that the form adopted should be submitted for approval as part of the state plan of administration. Some states had already adopted a form which, if acceptable to both the Bureau of Public Assistance and the Bureau of Accounts and Audits, could be approved. In order to keep eligibility data current, it is necessary that local units report to the state office the disposition of each case and any change in status of cases on assistance rolls, as well as the results of periodical reconsiderations of eligibility.

[23] Central decision is not recommended as a desirable procedure, but where it exists its disadvantages can be mitigated if the local unit is encouraged to function as fully as possible within its legal scope.

[24] One state agency in which the pension idea was strongly intrenched feared that its workers might attempt too much supervision of the recipients; hence it instructed the local unit to avoid not only suggesting what expenditures the grant was expected to cover but also any explanation of how the amount of the grant was calculated. This was probably a needless caution; for, since the local workers themselves had never received an explanation of the method by which the state office made its calculations, they could not well explain the method to the grantee. The purpose of this restriction was to give the recipient entire freedom in spending his grant, but its effect on recipients was not so favorable as the state official who had promulgated it had hoped. The state agency's lack of frankness was a grievance shared by workers and recipients alike and was conducive neither to good state-local relations nor to agency-recipient relations.

remains static. Applicants accepted as eligible may become ineligible through altered circumstances.[25] Under some state plans changes in residence, such as remaining out of the state beyond a prescribed period, cause loss of eligibility.[26] A recipient who enters an institution or who requires institutional care may likewise become ineligible.[27]

Changes in financial status most frequently affect eligibility. Recipients may acquire additional income through increased employment, inheritance of income-bearing property, or increased returns from property; or they may acquire cash or other capital by inheritance or from other sources; and thus they may be able to support themselves for a considerable period. Relatives legally responsible but unable, at the time of investigation, to provide for a recipient may become able to do so through increased employment opportunities, improved health, or some other factor. On the other hand, the financial condition of a recipient may deteriorate through loss of income or other resources and needs may increase owing to failing health or other reason; and thus a grant which was adequate when made may, in a few months, become inadequate.[28]

Periodic reconsideration or reinvestigation of the cases on the rolls of an old age assistance agency is necessary if the agency is to make payments only to those who are eligible and in amounts suited to their needs. If the agency assumes no responsibility other than that of paying grants to qualified applicants, it still cannot avoid the necessity of revisiting applicants from time to time. Several factors influence the setting of the time for the revisit. It is sometimes possible to judge the probable stability of a recipient's circumstances on the basis of facts learned during the investigation. The recipient himself may know of an impending change that may call for an early reconsideration of his case. The accessibility of a recipient's home may also be a determining factor. When snow and ice, floods, or muddy roads seem likely to interfere with visits, it may be wise to take these factors into consideration. It may also save agency time to schedule all revisits in one locality so that they can be made on one trip. Economy of operation also makes it

[25] Persons whose applications have been denied owing to ineligibility may become eligible, but these cases are classed, for purposes of this discussion, as "reapplications" and are not included under "reconsiderations," which are here limited to reconsideration of cases of recipients.

[26] A state plan will not be approved that contains provisions causing recipients to lose eligibility merely by moving from one county to another within the state.

[27] The handling of suspended and discontinued grants is discussed below, pp. 181.

[28] Readjustments may also be necessary if eligibility requirements are changed, or if more or less money is available for paying grants.

desirable to relate scheduled and emergency visits.[29] As nearly as possible the desirable time for a revisit should be determined when the first supervisory review is made and should then be scheduled according to the calendar or tickler system of the agency.

It is advisable that the recipient be informed of the agency's plans for revisits. Usually it is neither possible nor necessary that he know precisely when a revisit will be made, but he should know why and approximately when. This information may be given in a pamphlet. Oral instructions about revisits may well be given during the interview following notification. The recipient needs to understand his obligations to furnish information about current changes in his resources; he should also be informed of his right to request a reconsideration of his case if his circumstances change or if he is dissatisfied with the amount of his grant; and he should be acquainted with the general nature of whatever special services the agency offers.

Periodic Reviews in Centralized Systems

In centralized programs the state usually determines the frequency of reinvestigations[30] and prescribes a special form on which the local agency is expected to report its findings. These reports are reviewed in much the same way as the original reports of investigation. If the state requires reinvestigation every six months the first report is due in the sixth month after the case was accepted, and a new report is required each six months thereafter so long as the recipient's name remains on the rolls.[31] Usually the items included in the reinvestigation report duplicate those on the original report. Such duplication is wasteful of time both in preparing and in reviewing the report. Presumably these detailed reinvestigation blanks are adopted in the hope of forcing the local staff to make a thorough review of all the circumstances set forth in previous reports. In actual practice the effect is quite the opposite.

---

[29] The desirability of districting visits and revisits instead of assigning revisits to a second worker has been covered in an earlier report: Lansdale and Associates, *op. cit.,* pp. 55-56. See also chap. 8.

[30] Six months is the most common requirement in both centralized and decentralized programs, although it may vary from one month to one year. In the initial period when the intake of cases was abnormally high, many agencies were unable to plan revisits oftener than twice a year and keep up with the investigation of new cases.

[31] In the early period of a program the rigidity of this requirement is troublesome because the first cases are often accepted within a short period after the program is put in operation; thus the reinvestigation reports of a large proportion of the case load are due at about the same time. Some of the state agencies have recognized the need to stagger the reinvestigations and have allowed the local unit some freedom in rearranging the due dates for the cases accepted at the initiation of the program.

Because the task of preparing reinvestigation reports is so burdensome to the overworked local staff, the practice is to copy as much as possible directly from the original investigation record and to spend less time in actual checking of the facts than when a simpler report is required.[32]

It is possible that state agencies adopted a detailed report form because they wished each report to be complete in itself in order to save the time of state reviewers who would thus be able to make their reviews directly from the current reports. The result, however, is a set of duplicate case records, unduly cumbersome and expensive; and because they are necessarily repetitive and lacking in continuity, they are poorly adapted to one of their chief purposes—supervision and improvement of the methods of the local investigative staff. It is doubtful, too, whether much time is saved by the state staff since, when errors are discovered, the state reviewer must sift a great mass of material in order to find the data on a single questionable item.

Only good local administration, including adequate case supervision, can really assure satisfactory supervision of continuing grants. Mechanical methods and remote control do not suffice. They are too easily evaded if the local staff is not conscientious; nor is a conscientious but untrained and inept staff helped by such procedures; moreover, an able staff is impeded by them. So long as centralization is maintained, distance and the large number of cases in proportion to the number of state reviewers will force the central agency to depend upon mechanized reporting procedures, and just so long will the local units be handicapped rather than improved and developed by state supervision.

Periodic Reviews in Decentralized Systems

In decentralized systems reinvestigation procedure is much less rigid than in centralized programs. No formal report is usually required, and state review of all cases is not attempted. Reviews can be made directly from the current case records, and thus the necessity of preparing an elaborate report is obviated. A reconsideration involves an interview with the applicant, preferably in his home, as well as a rechecking of the items of the budget if any changes in needs or resources have occurred since the previous visit. The supervisor may supply workers with

[32] In several instances it was noted that items of the original report were copied even though the worker was obviously aware that the situation had changed sufficiently to make the original entries inapplicable. The preparation of a reinvestigation report had in fact become so mechanical that the worker tended not to relate the items of the report to his actual current knowledge of the recipient's circumstances.

an outline of the facts to be checked, but this may be flexible in form. Its adaptation to the individual case may be suggested in conference between worker and supervisor before and after the recipient is visited, and more specific guidance can be given less experienced workers about the follow up and rechecking of information which may be needed in verification or elaboration of the data obtained directly from the recipient. If the reinvestigation reveals no change in circumstances, and the supervisor is satisfied on reviewing the record and conferring with the worker that no change has taken place and no further service is needed, the case may be held in abeyance until the reinvestigation period has again elapsed[33] or until the recipient or someone on his behalf requests the attention of the agency.

Decision and Notification

Whenever a reinvestigation reveals the need for a discontinuance or for a reconsideration of the amount of the grant, the procedure should generally follow that established for the determination of the original grant. The worker's recommendation supported by adequate data is submitted in the usual manner to the administrative authority for decision. If the amount is changed, authorization must be sent to the disbursing official; likewise the recipient must be notified of the change in amount and its effective date. Discontinuances, except death cases, require similar handling. When the amount has not been changed it may still be necessary to notify the disbursing office of continuing eligibility if the state law requires periodical reinvestigation.[34]

---

[33] Whether the program is centralized or decentralized the supervisory authority needs to have some sort of tickler or calendar arrangement by means of which attention will be called to the case in sufficient time to complete the reinvestigation before the reinvestigation period has expired. Reinvestigation should not be required, however, of cases that have had an interim review. If an emergency arises which calls for interim review the calendar or tickler should be changed to date the next reinvestigation from the interim review rather than from the previous investigation or reinvestigation. Many centralized programs are needlessly rigid in maintaining dates for periodic review. If the state agency were willing to accept reports of interim contacts made before the expiration of the prescribed period in lieu of the regularly scheduled reports and to reschedule with the new date as the base for the beginning of the next period, local agencies would be encouraged to report such interim contacts, and the state case record would more often be complete and up to date. Simpler report requirements would also encourage reporting of facts learned in interim contacts. It is the belief of the author that duplicate case records in the state office are unnecessary, but if there is any value in having them it is greatly enhanced by reporting methods that keep the data they are supposed to contain complete and current.

[34] Agencies that use a combined authorization and certificate or report of eligibility which they file at the disbursing point usually have a special notification form on which changes in eligibility, amount of grant, or continuing eligibility are reported whenever a change is noted or a reconsideration of eligibility is undertaken. The general adaptation

Discontinuances and Suspensions

Although there is little uniformity of terminology among agencies administering old age assistance, unconditional termination of a grant is usually called a "discontinuance" and a temporary or limited discontinuance (conditional termination) a "suspension." Restoration of a discontinued grant generally requires reapplication and the completion of the whole procedure involved in making a new grant; restoration of a suspended grant merely requires that the agency have assurance that the conditions of the suspension have been met. The suspension may be either for a definite or indefinite period.[35] Its purpose is to provide greater flexibility in handling the changing needs of recipients. There is little question about the need for flexibility. If reinstatement is slow, recipients may be reluctant to take any action that would render them temporarily ineligible for aid even though it might otherwise benefit them. At the time of the field visits persons receiving care in public hospitals were, in some states, regarded as inmates of public institutions and denied assistance.[36] Temporary resources may make a grant unnecessary so long as the resource is available; and, if assurance can be given that the grant will be resumed without too much difficulty, recipients are encouraged to take advantage of all such opportunities, often with benefit to themselves as well as to the public treasury.

The crux of the difficulty in a termination of this kind is not discontinuance but reinstatement. On the other hand, there seems to be no reason for establishing a special procedure for reinstatements, since it is almost equally important that the agency be able to place new cases on the rolls with reasonable speed. In some agencies, it is possible in an emergent situation to place an applicant's name on the pay roll within forty-eight hours after the investigation is completed and the recom-

---

of centralized reports of eligibility now required by the Social Security Board will make the use of notifications of change of status necessary for all agencies.

[35] In several agencies a procedure of holding checks was used in lieu of suspension— or was called "suspension." Sometimes it is necessary to hold a check returned by the post office as undeliverable, but such checks should not be held beyond the next pay period. There seems to be no other reason why checks should ever be held. If the recipient is eligible the check should be delivered to him as soon as possible; if he is ineligible the issuance of checks should be stopped. If the agency is in doubt about the recipient's eligibility it should resolve the doubt immediately; it should usually assume the burden of proof and continue the grant until the doubt can be cleared. If the doubt seems a certainty the agency should discontinue the grant with due notification, a procedure much fairer to the recipient than holding the check, since he can upon discontinuance invoke the fair-hearing procedure, if he wishes. A drawer full of checks, such as was seen in one state office, seems inexcusably bad practice both socially and financially, even though the checks might eventually be released or cancelled.

[36] See chap. 10.

mendation for approval is made. Such speed is seldom necessary, but if it is possible in some agencies there appears to be no valid reason why in other states it should take a minimum of two weeks (and a maximum of six weeks) to get an approved case on the assistance rolls. Flexibility is needed, but it should be provided not through methods that short-cut necessary controls and thus endanger client rights or public funds, but rather through revision of the regular procedures so that client needs will be served. That the necessary flexibility can be attained has already been demonstrated.[37]

Discontinuance owing to death requires prompt notification of the disbursing official so that payments will be stopped at once. The proof of death need be no different from that suggested in withdrawal cases. The adequacy of the proof should be determined by supervisory review, and a report may be submitted to the administrative authority for final approval and recording as official action. Death cases are sometimes handled with less formality than are other reconsiderations. The agency may not require, for instance, that such cases be presented to the local board even though the board is theoretically responsible for all official action on grants. If they are presented they are usually passed as routine. It may be necessary to notify special departments or officials with re-sponsibility for following through recovery procedures if the decedent owned property. State agencies may also require special reports from local agencies in death cases if either payment or reimbursement of funeral expenses is allowed.[38]

Voluntary discontinuances are handled in the same manner as with-drawals. A signed statement of the reason for discontinuance is some-times used but is not necessary. The reason for discontinuance should be clearly presented in the case record. As in any other alteration of eligibility status the disbursing official must be notified promptly. The agency may require presentation of voluntary discontinuances to the administrative authority for official sanction. To avoid misunderstand-ing, formal notification should also go to the recipient.

DISPOSITION OF CASES WHEN FUNDS ARE INADEQUATE

In some of the states visited, appropriations were insufficient to pay grants to all eligibles on an acceptable standard, and old age assistance agencies were forced to modify their programs. Modifications are un-

---

[37] For a discussion of the financial procedures involved see chap. 13.

[38] For a discussion of the procedures involved in burial provisions and property ad-justments see chap. 10.

satisfactory makeshifts, since no real substitute can be found for adequate funds. In choosing which alternatives to accept, the administrative authority must carefully evaluate them and consider both their immediate and ultimate effects. The agency must face the fact that any change in the program tending to prolong the stringency rather than to relieve or eliminate it will probably be harmful in the end. A method alleviating immediate pressures on the agency but tending to conceal from appropriating bodies and taxpayers the evil effects of deficient appropriations may be particularly tempting but none the less dangerous. The responsibility for presenting the needs of the program is no less important than the responsibility for administering available funds fairly, economically, and as constructively as possible.

Reduction of Grants or of Case Load

When funds are insufficient to cover known needs, the agency must either limit the number of recipients or reduce the amount of individual grants. Whichever alternative it chooses, the agency must face other problems. If the decision is to limit numbers, the next question is how? Shall it be done by one or more of the following methods: stopping intake entirely and, if so, for how long; limiting intake and, if so, by what method—chronological or selective waiting lists, and, if the latter, by what means of selection; reducing present case load and, if so, by what process of elimination?

The possible complications in each of these methods are considerable. There is also the problem of the eliminated eligibles: how can they be cared for if they are needy, and what can the state do if they appeal? Facing such obvious difficulties it is not strange that agencies decide to limit amounts rather than to control case load. If present grants are reduced, how shall it be done: by horizontal cuts of an agreed amount; by percentage cuts; or by some sort of graduated system favoring the more needy? Whatever alternative is selected, still further problems arise in deciding the method of application. But the greatest objection to the spread-thin plan as opposed to the limitation of load is not the immediate problem it creates but its long-time effect, and this, as noted above, is the most important consideration of all.

One reason why the reduction of individual grants is tempting to a harassed administrator is that it tends to decrease pressure on the agency. A recipient of a small amount is less apt to complain, appeal, or rally political or other support to his aid than is an applicant whose claim has been denied or a recipient whose grant has been discontinued. Recipients may all receive a mere pittance, and thus no single eligible person really attains security from want; and though the program may be, in reference to its objective, a total failure, yet, so long as each eligible person receives something, most of them will not complain lest they lose that; and since all receive little, few can complain that others are more favored.

This absence of complaint and pressure appears advantageous to the agency; considering the ultimate effect on the program, however, absence of pressure is one of the great disadvantages of the method since the real needs of the program are thus hidden from view. The public in general and more especially the political leaders who control the source of funds are, on the whole, unaware of the failure of the program; if some inklings do come to them they are often inclined to blame the agency for its niggardly policy or its inefficient administration rather than to recognize that the real cause of difficulty is inadequate funds. Appropriations are unlikely to be increased if no pressure is exerted and if the administering agency is ineffective or unpopular. Thus, instead of removing the cause of failure in the program, the spread-thin method tends to perpetuate it.

In another insidious way the spread-thin method tends to be self-perpetuating and its ill effects cumulative. In the first place, low grants conduce to relaxation of intake procedures. When each recipient receives a very small sum the agency tends to be more lenient in applying eligibility standards in general and especially those relating to need. If only one or two dollars are to be given, it seems wasteful to spend five dollars' worth of administrative service in determining eligibility. Relaxation of intake scrutiny invites more applicants; acceptances increase both absolutely and relatively, and denials decline. With more recipients on the rolls and no, or slight, increases in funds, the money available must be spread thinner and thinner. At the same time administration though often poorer in quality rises in proportionate cost. This seemingly high administrative cost when grants are distressingly low may easily become a target for popular or political attack; in consequence administrative funds may be further curtailed. Progressively poorer administration is the inevitable outcome, while the program becomes in essence a dole, granted to all who apply, and eating up public funds though serving no constructive purpose.[39]

[39] This whole picture may appear exaggerated, but evidence of the tendency to self-perpetuation of a spread-thin policy with accompanying disintegration of the program was only too apparent in at least one state studied.

Adapting Program to Inadequate Budget

Generalization, of course, has its limitations in a discussion of methods for meeting the problem of inadequate funds constructively. States vary greatly in their laws and customs and usually adapt methods to their individual needs. If lack of funds is likely to be of short duration, the simplest and least destructive procedure is probably that of stopping intake temporarily and holding applications in chronological order to be investigated as soon as there is prospect of more funds. Stopping intake, however, is a temporary expedient that cannot be prolonged for more than a few weeks. It may not even be possible if the state requires that all applications be investigated promptly and acted upon within a specified time. It is possible simply to keep a list of inquiries and to take no applications; but applicants do not always distinguish between an application and an inquiry and thus are likely to feel as much aggrieved over the agency's inaction as if an application had been filed. This method also sacrifices the applicants' right to appeal if the state law permits appeal for failure to act on an application.

A still less desirable alternative is that of refusing applications and keeping no list even of inquiries; this would place on applicants the entire responsibility for later application and might mean a long series of fruitless returns by them—a procedure that seems unfair to them and time-consuming to the agency. It also deprives the agency of facts about the total problem, though facts are its most dependable weapon in the fight for adequate funds.

WAITING LISTS. Whether intake is temporarily stopped or is controlled to slow down accession of cases to the number that can be cared for by the funds on hand, the agency must face the problem of waiting lists.[40] If a chronological method only is used the agency needs merely to proceed to the next name on the list when more funds become available. This simplifies procedure greatly in comparison with selective methods, but it ignores differentials in the urgency of need of those on the waiting list. Hence chronological selection is possible only when the stringent period is short or when other resources are available to applicants.

The agency that must select from a waiting list on the basis of need faces a number of difficulties. It must first determine need. In other

[40]Under some state laws, it is questionable whether an old age assistance agency can legally establish a waiting list of eligibles. The law may require the agency to accept applications from all who believe themselves to be eligible and may require prompt action on all applications received. The agency must, under such conditions, either adopt new eligibility regulations which will produce more eliminations and spread assistance thinner, or amend the state law.

words, it must investigate all cases on the waiting list and devise a fair method of selection and yet keep the number sufficient to absorb funds as fast as, but no faster than, they are available. Theoretically this plan seems fair and reasonable, but from a practical standpoint it presents problems. Although, as already pointed out, it is desirable that applications be investigated promptly, there is no great advantage in promptness if cases must remain pending for a long time.

One of the disadvantages of investigating the entire waiting list is the administrative expense. A waiting list, especially one made up from a group with a high mortality rate, continually shifts. The time spent in investigating such cases has been in a sense wasted as it would not have been under a chronological system. If the waiting list is long, repeated investigations may be necessary because, as noted earlier, there is no finality about an investigation. An agency ready to add cases to its grant list may find that those classed as most needy have not been seen for six months or a year. Under such circumstances it is obliged to recheck the question of need and other doubtful or changeable factors of eligibility as it periodically rechecks cases already on the rolls.[41] Repeated reinvestigations prior to acceptance are not only expensive, but are also extremely irritating to many applicants who naturally expect results from the agency's activity.[42]

RAISING ELIGIBILITY STANDARDS. In effect, selection of cases from a waiting list on the basis of need implies setting a new and higher standard of need for this preliminary selection. Theoretically it should be possible to investigate all cases promptly, determine their budgetary deficits, and rank them in order, placing those with the largest deficits at the top.

Such a procedure encounters practical difficulties. From day to day the number of changes in the waiting list is considerable; and from month to month, still greater. The attempt to use such a method of ranking over any considerable period of time would in reality result in an attempt to apply a shifting standard of need. If the number of applicants with maximum deficits is large one month, an agency might find, for instance, that it could take on only persons whose budgetary deficit was twenty dollars or more; while for the preceding month, when those with maximum deficits were fewer, it could take cases with a deficit as low as

[41]One state with a long waiting list has sometimes found it necessary to investigate waiting cases three or four times before their names are reached.

[42]Any method of selection from the waiting list according to need is apt to be hard to explain. If imperfectly understood it is especially likely to cause dissatisfaction to those it excludes.

eighteen dollars. It is obvious that such a shifting standard would be impractical. In addition, the budgets of all waiting applicants would require frequent checking and, even so, inequalities would be unavoidable. Consequently agencies attempting selection on the basis of need have usually sought methods of selection conducive to more stable results.

Agencies attempting to keep within a too meager appropriation often find it difficult, if not impossible, to apply a secondary standard of need at intake only. Although it is desirable so far as possible to leave undisturbed the case load which has already been accepted, this cannot always be done. The available funds may not be sufficient even to cover the needs of those already on the rolls. Under such circumstances the agency is compelled to find some method of reducing either the case load or the amount paid to individual recipients. Preferably, the method adopted should eliminate the least needy rather than spread an inadequate fund over all persons receiving assistance. Usually the method adopted for the accepted case load will be more satisfactory if the same standard can be applied at intake, since differentials between new and old grants can thus be avoided.

ESTABLISHMENT OF MINIMUMS. Establishment of minimums has sometimes been a useful method of eliminating the least needy, although it is not popular. A minimum can be applied to the calculated budgetary deficit that most states require the local unit to determine for each case investigated. It has the further advantage of being easily applicable as a guide in the elimination of applicants as well as in reconsidering the present case load. The operation of a minimum standard is simple. If a minimum of five dollars is agreed upon, any applicant whose budgetary deficit is that sum or less is eliminated. Thus the minimum method easily eliminates the less needy. Administrators are often tempted to cut large grants or to make a percentage cut in all; both procedures penalize the neediest cases—those with greatest needs and least resources. The establishment of a minimum has the opposite effect: it eliminates those who require the smallest grants either because their resources are greater or their individual needs (or both) are less than those of others. It has one further advantage over a mere cutting of grants: it reduces the administrative expense of handling so many more cases, including the cost of clerical, financial, and social service. The reason the method is not more popular is that it involves actual denial or discontinuance of all cases affected, with the result that the agencies are besieged with complaints, appeals, and other pressures. To avoid this situation, agencies prefer all too often to penalize the more helpless cases—those receiving the maximum grant.[43]

MISCELLANEOUS METHODS. Criteria selected by states to determine relative need of those on waiting lists vary.[44] Some states have assumed that persons on general-relief rolls when the old age assistance program was started were likely to be needier than those who had managed without public aid; hence preference in selection was given to such cases. On the other hand, in a state where funds for general relief were more adequate than those provided for old age assistance, relief cases were assumed to be better cared for than the so-called "borderline need" cases, and those on general relief were thus discriminated against. If a program of old age pensions was in operation prior to the old age assistance program, it was usually assumed that the beneficiaries of that system were needy and should have preference over new applicants.[45] It is sometimes assumed that applicants without children or other legally liable relatives are more needy than those with relatives. Although this assumption is one of doubtful general validity it was found in use in a number of local units. Some institutional cases though eligible have been excluded on the ground that they were already receiving essential care and that, since funds were limited, old age assistance grants should be reserved primarily for those needing care in their homes.

When the state law is general rather than specific, and the rule-making authority of the state agency is consequently extensive, it may be possible to cut down case load through raising eligibility requirements by state regulation. It may be possible, for instance, to lower the maximum property requirement for eligibility. Income maximums can likewise

[43] It is well recognized that although the budget deficit gives a practical index to need, there is likely to be a slight differential favorable to individuals with low deficits. Persons with high deficits usually have either unusual needs or a total absence of resources and usually both. If at the top (maximum), such persons can seldom either reduce their needs or increase their resources. Persons with good health and some resources can sometimes augment their resources by part-time employment. They may also be able to practice economies in living that would be impossible for a sick or handicapped person. Those receiving the maximum amount may be prevented by the maximum from receiving the full amount which they need because the maximum grant does not cover their budget deficit, whereas those with lower deficits might have them fully covered. This situation is not uncommon and is another good reason for not assuming that a recipient with a high grant is necessarily best able to absorb a cut.

[44] "Waiting list" is used in this instance to include groups known to be needy and presumably eligible even though not formally included in an actual list.

[45] Undoubtedly political considerations entered into this assumption, for in some instances the old age assistance program could not have been adopted if assurance had not been given that these old cases would have preference over others if they met the eligibility requirements of the new program.

be lowered. Moralistic requirements might conceivably be added although the tendency is away from such criteria.[46] State raising of eligibility requirements is somewhat curtailed by the federal Act. A state might assume that need would tend to be affected by advancing age and consequently adopt a higher age limit. States sharing in federal reimbursement may not, however, increase their age limit beyond seventy years and may not keep it at that level after January 1, 1940;[47] nor can they raise residence and citizenship requirements above the maximums allowed in the Social Security Act. The state might, of course, amend the law to restrict case load, but most legislation has been rather in the direction of liberalization of the program. Lack of funds has been the chief restricting force, although it is presumably temporary; hence flexible rules and regulations are better adapted to emergent conditions.

Whatever methods are selected to meet an inadequate budget should be adapted to the needs of state and agency and be as constructive as circumstances permit. Expedients should be recognized as such, dispensed with as soon as practicable, and never be allowed to become a cycle of undesirable, permanent procedures.

[46] No moralistic requirements added for the purpose of reducing case load were noted; but it was apparent that in some jurisdictions the need to keep case load down had a tendency to encourage continued application of these requirements that might otherwise have been repealed or have become inoperative.

[47] One state circumvents this provision by assigning an arbitrary value to each year of age beyond sixty-five as one of the factors in the rating formula which is its method of selecting cases from the waiting list. To what extent this operates to select the older cases was not learned.

CHAPTER 10

MISCELLANEOUS ACTIVITIES

CONTACTS WITH recipients, as already indicated, do not end with grant authorizations. In addition to the periodic reconsiderations necessary regarding changes in eligibility and extent of need,[1] other contacts may be required in connection with grant payments, such as nonreceipt, loss, or destruction of a check, improper endorsement, or inability to endorse a check owing to illness, disablement, or the development of mental incapacity. Then, too, a final reconsideration of the case is usually necessary when the recipient dies, especially if the state defrays all or part of burial costs, or if it attempts to recover all or part of assistance costs from the decedent's estate.[2]

Furthermore, many conditions not directly connected with payment of grants bring requests for service and demands for attention. Many of the aged turn to the old age assistance agency when unexpected difficulty overtakes them or when their ordinary troubles seem unusually burdensome. Conversations overheard in agency waiting rooms, letters to agencies, interviews recorded in case records, and informal reports of visitors, directors, and others all bear witness to the need and to the opportunity for service to recipients.

The public, too, seems to regard the old age assistance agency as responsible in some measure for meeting emergent and other special needs of recipients. If an aged recipient falls ill, or becomes helpless and has no one to care for him, or is burned or flooded out of his home with no place to go, the agency is sure to have a deluge of telephone and personal calls. In most communities these callers will not be satisfied with a mere statement that "the monthly check was mailed yesterday." The need for some sort of action exists, and the agency cannot afford to be indifferent even though it would prefer not to accept responsibility for the social and personal problems of recipients. When it does not meet these needs itself, the agency must call on other local agencies

[1] See chap. 9.
[2] Reconsideration may also be necessary in connection with requests for fair hearing. See chap. 16.

equipped to render the needed service if it wishes to retain public support.[3]

These problems, briefly outlined, that call for continuing service, and the methods of handling them warrant discussion in some detail.

MEDICAL CARE

One of the most urgent and frequently recurring needs coming to the attention of old age assistance agencies is that of medical care. The morbidity rate is high among the old and is likely to be particularly high among the needy aged.[4] Theoretically it should be possible to budget health needs, but actually the inclusion of an item for health care in the grant has provided only a partial solution.

Illness is unpredictable in its incidence, as well as in its duration and probable cost. It is predictable only in the long run and for a large group. Even if it were possible to determine accurately the future health needs of each recipient and allow a sufficient amount each month to cover the annual cost, the agency would have no assurance that the recipient would always reserve the sum to pay the cost of such care when the need arose. If, however, the agency holds the money in a pooled fund and makes direct payment to the physician, nurse, hospital, or druggist who supplies medical service or supplies, it cannot receive payment from federal funds, since matching is allowed only for direct money payments to the aged. Health care must, nevertheless, be provided for the aged if the objective of the program is attained.

It is not always necessary for the old age assistance agency to supply medical care directly. Although other forms of public assistance may be denied to recipients, medical and surgical care are commonly exempted from this prohibition. If the community provides medical facilities in hospital, clinic, and bedside care, it may not be necessary for the agency itself to supply health care from its own funds. Since such care is seldom

[3] Sometimes the request for service arises not so much from concern for the recipient as concern for public funds which the complainant feels are being wasted because the recipient drinks or otherwise spends his grant unwisely. The task here is only indirectly a service to the recipient—that of interpreting his behavior to the complainant and giving the latter an explanation why an old age assistance unit or other agency administering public or private aid cannot hope to give such aid on a merit basis but must confine itself to payment on the basis of determined need.

[4] The recent national health survey shows that the disability rate (annual days of disability per person) rises with age. In the age group under fifteen years it is estimated that the rate is 6.0; for the group fifteen to sixty-four years, 9.1; and for those over sixty-five, 32.6—more than three times the rate for all ages (9.8). See National Health Survey, *Preliminary Reports* (Sickness and Medical Care Series), Bull. No. 1, 1935-36. In Bulletin No. 2, the survey shows an illness rate rising in inverse proportion to the income of the groups studied.

available, old age assistance agencies have generally had to find ways of filling some, at least, of the gaps in the general community program. Various methods are in use. It would take more space than is here available to describe these methods, but some of the usual procedures may be indicated.

No local unit studied attempted to meet the problem wholly by inclusion of medical care in the grant, but allowance could be, and often was, made for predictable items. A small allowance may be made for supplying the home medicine chest with ordinary household remedies and first-aid supplies just as recurring personal needs, such as haircuts, may be provided for by the ordinary budgeting process. Other items may be included in the grant. A diabetic may have a regular need for insulin, which under proper medical advice may be predicted with sufficient certainty to permit its being budgeted. Similarly, provision may be made for other chronic conditions. Although the budgetable needs are a small proportion of the total, for items that can thus be handled this is a satisfactory method; and the agency has the advantage of federal reimbursement of such expenditures.

Before the issue of federal matching became important in the older programs, payment directly to the vendor [5] was the usual method of meeting emergent health problems. There is nothing to prevent an agency's continuing the practice if it is willing to forego federal reimbursement; and in some instances the practice has been continued, although usually an effort is made to include in the grant an amount to cover predictable needs. Agencies have generally preferred this system because it conserves the amount to be spent for medical care in a single fund under the control of the agency, which may use it for emergencies.

The agency is often regarded by recipient and community as being responsible for meeting emergencies, yet if funds are dissipated in individual grants they cannot be mobilized for such needs. Various expedients have been tried for retaining the advantages of the central fund without losing federal matching. Some agencies increased the recipient's grant and issued the increase in a separate check. The agency was then able to put pressure on the recipient to endorse the check over to the vendor. A few agencies tried the expedient of making checks out jointly to recipient and vendor, but this plan did not meet with federal approval since under the Social Security Act payments must be "money payments to aged individuals." Moreover, the Act limits matching pay-

[5] "Vendor" is here used for convenience to indicate the person or agency furnishing service or supplies.

ments to half the total sums expended for old age assistance "not counting so much of such expenditure with respect to any individual for any month as exceeds $30." This provision rules out federal reimbursement for medical care for recipients whose regular grant without medical care amounts to $30 per month.

In few, if any, states are funds sufficient to provide all medical care. Ordinarily the old age assistance agency depends upon supplementation from public and private sources. The medical care program then usually involves cooperative relationships with other agencies. Some agencies employ physicians, nurses, and medical social workers under whose direction the problems of cooperative care are worked out.[6] At the time of the field study visiting housekeepers and nurses were often supplied through projects worked out with the W.P.A. One of the most interesting of these was the carefully planned New York City program, in which results were watched and reported with equal care.[7] Westchester County, New York, has had a particularly interesting experience in the use of a consulting physician attached to its staff.[8] The Boston Department of Public Welfare at the time of the visit employed a medical social worker who served as a staff consultant and was available to staff members of the old age assistance division.

State agencies, perhaps because they are so far removed from the emergent pressures that fall upon the local unit, have been slower than local units to recognize the problem and to make a constructive effort to meet it. Consultative service furnished to local units in planning local programs of medical care and the working out of agreements and other cooperative arrangements with state-wide health agencies are helpful to local units.

THE USE OF INSTITUTIONS AND BOARDING HOMES

The problems involved in suspending or discontinuing a grant when a recipient enters a hospital and in reinstating it when he leaves have

[6] In some local agencies physicians render direct service to recipients, but usually such service is limited. It is usually part-time, and agencies recognize that more is gained in using such service for consultative purposes—to build up a suitable program—than would be possible if direct service to a few recipients were attempted and the general program of medical care for the whole group neglected.

[7] A mimeographed report, "Study and Demonstration of Home Care of Recipients of Old Age Assistance," was prepared by Arthur D. Baird, Managing Project Supervisor, Project Number 165-97-799 (7025-1085), U. S. Works Progress Administration for the City of New York, and issued July 1, 1937.

[8] Westchester County was not included in the survey although one staff member made a brief visit to this unit, and another member consulted with the Westchester staff.

already been outlined.[9] The continuing services to applicants or recipients, arising from difficulties over institutional care, merit special
attention. In states prohibiting residence in private as well as public
institutions, a hospital patient was usually regarded as "an inmate of
an institution"; and thus he became automatically ineligible as soon as
he entered the hospital. If the prohibition extended only to public
institutions, the agency was free when the hospital was under private
auspices to adjust the grant in accordance with the recipient's actual
needs and thus permit him to pay his rent and to meet other expenses
that continued while he was in the hospital; but if the only or the best
available hospital was under public auspices no satisfactory arrangement was usually possible. Sometimes the old age assistance agencies
were able to call on other agencies for supplementation; or they might,
if the spouse were eligible, increase the spouse's grant to make up the
deficit; or they might increase the recipient's grant after he left the
hospital to allow him to catch up with obligations that accumulated
during his absence. These methods are usually makeshifts of limited
efficacy; and, although they helped in individual cases to mitigate the
unfortunate severity of the prohibition, they did not meet the problem
satisfactorily.

Flexibility is important for satisfactory adjustment, but something
additional is needed in this instance: definition of terms. At the time of
the field study only two of the states visited, Connecticut and Indiana,
had adopted definition of the terms "public institution," "private institution," and "inmate"; nor had the Social Security Board at that time
defined its policies in this respect. Consequently, administration of the
requirement pertaining to institutions and institutional care varied
greatly not only from state to state but within a state. Some local
agencies made every effort possible to aid inmates of institutions who
appeared to be otherwise eligible for assistance, and who were desirous
of leaving the institution, to find accommodations outside. Other
agencies took no such responsibility. Some agencies even gave inmates
of institutions no opportunity whatsoever to apply for old age assistance.
One agency visited had received applications from inmates of a county
home but had acted only on those of applicants who had made their own
arrangements to leave the home and had thereafter reapplied. In the
meantime the original applications had been held without any investigation and presumably without the knowledge of the state agency, which
was responsible for the decision on all applications in the state.

[9] See chap. 9.

Since the field visits many states have defined the terms "inmate" and "institution," by law or by regulation, to permit hospitalization in public and private hospitals for short periods without discontinuance of the grant when the recipient has expenses that continue during his absence. The Social Security Board has advised states so to define the terms, and the federal auditors do not take exception to payments made under such circumstances. The period of residence is limited—usually to ninety days—although in some states it may be prolonged under specified conditions.

Some agencies were concerned with the problem of boarding homes. To differentiate between them and institutions was not always simple. Difficulties were also noted when the state had insufficient power of inspection, licensing, and control over boarding homes, leaving the way open for exploitation of recipients by unscrupulous boarding-home managers. When a state has authority to license, it seems wise to require recipients to live only in licensed homes. On the positive side, the development of good homes and satisfactory cooperative arrangements between the agency and the managers of such homes appeared to promise opportunities for care of recipients. Many old persons need partial or even complete care yet are happier in the more homelike atmosphere of a well managed boarding home than they would be in an institution. Sometimes a boarding home may also be preferable to the home of a relative. One agency visited had taken the initiative to encourage a few unemployed nurses to establish boarding homes for aged clients. Obviously a great many possibilities, as well as a great many problems, are involved, but this subject must be left for development by other students of the problems of old age assistance administration.

FOLLOW-UP OF CHANGES OF ADDRESS

Frequent moving of recipients occasions more follow-up service than would ordinarily take place. Besides recognizing the necessity of having the recipient's correct address, most agencies like to assure themselves that he has not entered an institution or left the jurisdiction. Agencies that assume an obligation to see that an applicant is receiving suitable care will also need to ascertain the conditions under which he is living at the new address. Sometimes a visit there reveals resources that had not been discovered in the original investigation, such as relatives who are willing and able to give partial or complete care, or the ownership of property, or newly acquired resources, such as an inheritance, award, or gift. Agencies have, therefore, generally found it advisable to have a thorough reinvestigation made whenever a recipient has moved.[10] The problem of keeping track of recipients is sometimes difficult. Although recipients may be instructed to keep the agency informed of changes in address, they often fail to do so; occasionally they wish to evade the attention of the agency. To prevent this latter possibility, agencies sometimes instruct the post office not to forward letters having the agency's return address printed on them.[11] When checks are returned the agency may attempt to locate the recipient by sending a visitor to the former address or to the homes of relatives or friends, who may be able to furnish the new address. If the recipient cannot be located the check may be held until the next pay period, after which payments should be discontinued until the recipient is found and his circumstances reexamined. Agencies with some recipients who move very frequently have resorted to holding their checks at the agency office and have required the recipients to call for them. Although this procedure is generally undesirable, it seems unavoidable in some instances; agencies should not extend the practice unnecessarily.

Practices regarding change of residence from one jurisdiction to another within a state vary widely from state to state. The procedure is generally somewhat simpler in the centralized than in the decentralized programs.

Whether the program is centralized or not, transfer of a recipient from one jurisdiction to another requires procedures that should be uniform and therefore established by the state.[12] Both units involved in a recipient's move need to be notified;[13] the one to which the recipient

[10] If the recipient makes a practice of moving more or less regularly from the home of one relative to that of another and all the homes on his itinerary have been seen, it is not always necessary to revisit every time he moves and certainly not necessary to make a complete reinvestigation on every such occasion.

[11] Sometimes the envelope used for mailing checks contains instructions not to forward; or the agency may merely have an informal agreement with postal officials about forwarding. A combination of printed instructions and agreement is most effective. In one state with central disbursing and with instructions not to forward printed on all envelopes containing checks, one local unit had still further cooperation from the local postmaster: instructions were issued to postmen to deliver the envelopes containing checks personally to all recipients—a service, except for the signature of the recipient, equal to that of registered mail.

[12] State regulations governing procedures for interunit cooperation should also cover such things as correspondence and exchange of service in connection with investigations and reinvestigations.

[13] It is important that recipients be instructed to notify the agency of intention to move whether within the jurisdiction or outside it. Agencies sometimes require the recipient to obtain permission to move even within the state; and, if residence requirements are in effect, this may be necessary in order to assure the recipient that the second unit will be willing to accept him and to assume payment of his grant promptly. It is often desir-

moves must be given sufficient information to administer intelligently whatever continuing service is customarily available. This information is usually provided either by transfer of the complete record or by submission of a full report.[14] When the necessary procedure is set up and adhered to, no hiatus in grant payments should occur.

When a recipient wishes to visit outside the state, the problems are more complicated than intrastate moving. Some state regulations forbid such visiting, usually by declaring ineligible a recipient who leaves the state. Nevertheless, a recipient may need to go to another state. He may have relatives there who are able and willing to give partial or complete care; some special kind of needed medical care may not be available in his own state; the climate of another state may be more favorable; and many other reasons may operate to make the change advantageous.[15] It is not impossible to have such problems covered by interstate agreements permitting some flexibility. Few interstate agreements were in effect at the time of the field visits, but interstate problems were apparent.[16]

Interstate agreements may well include provisions for exchange of

able, too, to assure accommodations where the recipient plans to move. Such a requirement may thus be a protection to the recipient, but it should not be employed as a means of asserting authority over him under threat of losing his grant—as sometimes happens.

[14] It is desirable for the unit from which the recipient moves to retain skeleton information, at least. Identifying data, a record of when assistance was given and in what amount, and the disposition of the case (date of transfer and the unit to which transferred) constitute the essential items. When a duplicate case record is on file at the state office still other duplication ought surely to be avoided so far as possible. If, however, the recipient moves or appears likely to move frequently between the two jurisdictions, duplicate case records in the files of the two (or more) units may in the end be the simplest solution. The record in each can be kept reasonably complete by reports covering the intervals of absence prepared and forwarded by each agency to the other when the recipient moves from one to the other.

[15] State borders are artificial lines; and, at the periphery of a state, a recipient's relatives are often scattered in communities on both sides of the line; and, at the junction of several state borders, they may actually be in three or four states although distant only a few miles from the recipient and from each other. Several instances were noted of persons moving about among relatives in two or three states.

[16] Some local agencies were making unreasonable requests of other states, such as demanding frequent and apparently pointless visits to relatives in connection with reinvestigations. At times the inquiring agency requested documents and other information but sometimes included with the request insufficient information to make identification of documents possible, and often gave so little indication of the proposed use of the requested data as to render intelligent service impossible. The completion of elaborate report forms in duplicate might be asked. Some states were even mailing long and complicated forms to relatives, who could not understand them and hence took them to the old age assistance office in their own community for completion. It was amazing to discover that several states whose local units were asking this sort of help directly or indirectly were themselves refusing to answer reasonable requests from other states, on the excuse that they could not spare the time to attend to out-of-state inquiries.

services and information about investigations, reinvestigations, and transfer of cases. Such agreements can be most satisfactorily worked out by the welfare departments in the two states rather than by local units along the border.[17] Ordinarily requests for service should be cleared through the central agencies so that some idea can be gained of the volume and nature of service asked and rendered. In this way the state agencies will be able to plan more realistically for future needs.

INTERAGENCY COOPERATION

Cooperation of old age assistance units with other agencies and organized groups requires the adoption of definite policies, as well as methods for carrying them into effect.[18] In these matters the state agency has an opportunity to exert leadership. On the state level, it has a special responsibility not only to initiate programs and gain the interest of state-wide (or national or regional) agencies operating in the field in which cooperation is needed but also to negotiate and promulgate the agreements. As a part of its supervisory service, the state agency is in a position to advise and assist local units in the development of local opportunities for cooperative effort.

Various kinds of cooperation were observed in the states visited. Perhaps because the program was so new in many states, the accomplishments were not extensive. Cooperative arrangements with state bureaus of vital statistics were found in only a few states. Several agreements were noted with state associations of morticians about provisions for burial. Some state agencies had arranged with large insurance companies

---

[17] The border units will need most to operate under such agreements and may have valuable and practical suggestions to make with regard to the content of such agreements. Negotiations are much simpler if only two agencies take part in working out the agreement. Each must, of course, be responsible for putting its part of the joint agreement into effect and in living up to whatever promises are made on its own account and in behalf of local units. Terms of the agreement may need to be made effective in each state by legislation or by state regulation, followed up by the necessary supervision and such other methods of control as may be called for.

[18] The development of a program of medical care of old age assistance recipients requires cooperative agreements with various organized groups, which may include state and local professional groups (medical, dental, nursing, and pharmaceutical associations), hospital associations and individual hospitals, state and local departments of health, state-wide voluntary health and welfare associations and agencies, and local organizations of related objectives and functions. It may require adoption of definite policies of eligibility for care and mutual safeguarding of records and information; agreement on standards of care, the adoption of fee schedules and mileage rates, and also the adoption of forms, methods, and procedures for initiating and discontinuing care, for proper authorization, for the submission and approval of bills, for payments to vendors, for reimbursement of expenditures by the state, when such expenditures are reimbursable, for miscellaneous accounting and statistical purposes, and for interagency reporting.

and other insurance groups for furnishing information and making adjustments in the insurance problems of recipients; a number were making available to their local units information about the cooperative service offered by the Life Insurance Adjustment Bureau.[19] Agreements with medical associations, state and local, were also found. Cooperation with other state departments was found less often than might be expected.[20] Even within the welfare department itself cooperation and coordination of activities were often far from satisfactory.[21]

Whether general relief is administered by the same state or local agency, it is important to have satisfactory cooperative relationships between that program and old age assistance. The more limited the latter program, the more important is such cooperation, since the needs of old age recipients are not stereotyped; and, when the program is rigid, there must be supplementation from an agency that operates more flexibly if the recipients' needs are not neglected. Even if direct supplementation is impossible, there may still be need for cooperative agreements supported by suitable policies and procedures for handling the joint cases that inevitably occur and for referral of cases from one agency to the other.[22] Problems of cooperation with other categories are similar, although joint cases and referrals are generally fewer than in general relief.

In general, local agencies have gone farther than state agencies in working out cooperative relationships. It is in the local communities

[19] The Life Insurance Adjustment Bureau, 450 Seventh Avenue, New York City, represents three large insurance companies and offers advisory service to social agencies in the adjustment of the insurance plans of any client who owns a policy in one of the three companies; it furnishes upon request general guidance and advice in insurance matters to social agencies. The head of the Bureau is the former executive of a private social agency. The service is free and noncommercial; many public and private social agencies use it. The Bureau's Pamphlet, *Life Insurance: A Handbook for Social Workers,* may be had upon request.

[20] It was surprising to find generally so little cooperation with state universities, with agricultural extension work, home economics departments, sociology, social research and social administration activities.

[21] In a few instances there was rivalry with other programs. In several states workers from different bureaus and divisions of the welfare department supervised the same local county units, not infrequently giving contrary advice and inevitably placing upon the local unit responsibility for coordination of the programs—a responsibility which the state itself should assume. In some states there was recognition of responsibility for such coordination on the state level and a genuine effort to meet it. For further discussion of state agency coordination see chap. 4.

[22] As has previously been noted, state laws may forbid supplementation. It is undoubtedly desirable that each program carry its own load if results in proportion to effort and expense are ever to be judged. It is evident, however, that if the state is to fulfil its obligation of meeting need and assuring even a reasonable degree of security to its dependent groups it must provide for flexibility either by making each program flexible or by allowing the more flexible programs to supplement the rigid ones.

that activities requiring cooperation generally take place; thus local agencies naturally feel a more direct concern. This fact, however, does not relieve the state agency of its responsibility for initiating and developing cooperation needed on the state level or for assisting local units in their own cooperative efforts. If one general agreement could be made for the whole state with a state department, it is wasteful to require each local unit to work out an individual relationship with that department. Sometimes satisfactory cooperation between two agencies operating locally is impossible because the state policies of the two agencies, which the local units cannot modify, stand in the way. Under such circumstances local cooperation can become operative only if one or both state agencies alter their policies. Often this can best be done by a conference of the state agencies.[23] With stronger state leadership local cooperation could advance much faster.

PROMOTION OF OCCUPATIONAL AND VOCATIONAL OPPORTUNITIES

Contentment of the aged may be increased and health often improved if they are afforded opportunity for useful and satisfying occupations. The response of recipients to the few sporadic efforts that have already been attempted show that there is a real need in this field. Many are shut in by physical ailments; others, though not disabled, have withdrawn from contact with other people, not because they no longer desire such contact, but rather because they have grown fearful that they are no longer acceptable socially. Some, compelled by illness or lack of resources, have drawn back from former church connections and participation in other activities once enjoyed and now do not know how to rebuild their lost social life. Many, through the necessity of living with their children, have moved from communities where they were once well known to new towns or neighborhoods.

In many respects need for social contacts and for interesting occupations is not greatly different whether the recipients live in the Mississippi Delta or in the slums of a city like New York. In the Delta region prior to the visit of the staff, one of the more resourceful workers had in-

---

[23] Several examples were noted of effective local cooperation despite state-agency inertia or antagonism. In at least two states there was antagonism between directors or staffs of the old age assistance and general-relief agencies, and local units were either openly or tacitly urged to ignore the other program. Fortunately these antagonisms seldom carried over to the local units, and local workers because of their real need to get together in the interests of their clients managed to cooperate fairly well despite the barriers raised by the attitudes of the state agencies.

terested several recipients in reviving handicraft skills and had arranged for the results to be shown in a special exhibit at the local county fair. In New York City a special exhibit of treasures (heirlooms, articles of beauty and interest saved from more prosperous days or manufactured for the occasion by revival of almost forgotten skills) was arranged and displayed at one of the settlement houses. Both these opportunities for recognition and appreciation of possessions and skills brought response in increased interest and in satisfaction of the participants. Other parallels between activity and response in widely different areas could be cited.[24] The conclusion of all those acquainted with the facts is that a field for real service exists here, although in the press of getting programs organized little has been done to meet this need.[25]

FRIENDLY VISITING

A few agencies have seen in the need for service beyond that which their own limited staff could offer a need for reviving volunteer service of the type known as "friendly visiting." The state of Washington has developed a friendly visiting program more extensively than any other state. Despite the strength of the pension idea in that state, there has been a recognition that not all needs can be met by a money payment. Hence an attempt has been made to supplement the work of the regular visiting staff with selected volunteer service.[26] Agencies in other states have used volunteers, though none so extensively. As the organization period is completed and time can be spent on the selection and development of suitable volunteers, more activity of this sort may be undertaken.

ADJUSTMENT IN DEATH CASES

As previously suggested, various administrative problems may arise when the recipient dies, especially if burial funds must be provided or if property adjustments must be made. The death of a recipient, therefore, usually calls for a final reconsideration of the case. The Social

[24] Arrangements for church attendance, invitations to attend parties at institutions (private homes for the aged, etc.) and other opportunities for social contact seemed to give great pleasure to many of the aged. Contacts with their visitor in home or agency office and often those of clients with each other in agency waiting rooms are obviously social pleasures to not a few of the aged.

[25] Some workers believe that the rapid growth of the Townsend movement and of other similar groups operating through local clubs and associations has largely been due to the fact that these clubs have met a real need of social activity for the aged.

[26] See Charles F. Ernst, "The Use of Friendly Visiting," *Proceedings of the National Conference of Social Work*, 1937, pp. 517-22.

Security Act includes no reference to burial, but most states make some provision for defraying burial costs.

Property also has a direct relation to the provision made for burial. Much of the concern of applicants over their property is related to their fear of not being able to provide themselves with suitable burial. Their savings, whether insurance, cash, or other assets, have been accumulated and retained with this objective. Doubtless it is also this consideration that has influenced old age assistance agencies to allow the retention of an amount of insurance, cash, or other liquid assets frequently equal to the amount allowed for burial. If it must provide burial when the recipient dies without assets, the state is interested in conserving by means of assignments, liens, or other controls a sufficient amount of the recipient's assets to meet burial costs. The agency also finds that unless burial is provided, applicants are more reluctant to sign liens or conveyances in favor of the agency. It is also notable that burial costs are usually a first claim against property when the time comes for settlement.

Provision for burial, if made from old age assistance funds, may be entirely from state or local funds, or from local funds with partial (or total) reimbursement by the state. Standards may be set by the state, as they always are if funds are provided directly by it. If local funds only or joint state and local funds are used, the state may still control the amount either absolutely or within specified limits.[27] The amounts allowed may be set by state law or by state or local regulation. The state (or local) requirements may limit not only the total amount but also the items that may be included and the amounts that may be spent for specific items, such as casket, lot, or marker.[28] Special allowance may sometimes be made if it is necessary to transport the body a long distance; or supplementation may be allowed for this purpose or for an unusually expensive lot.

The state often requires detailed reports in death cases. It must have the necessary data for accounting of burial expenditures if burial funds are supplied from state funds; and it may require additional reporting of property items if they are involved. If the program is centralized, a special report may be needed to complete the case record even if burial expenses are not furnished by the state. If the disbursing is done centrally

[27] The state office sets a maximum. Ordinarily public funds for burial are provided only when the recipient leaves no estate or when the estate is insufficient to provide burial; and supplementation may or may not be allowed.

[28] In New York City masses for the dead are allowed for Catholic decedents, and a special grave marker prized by Jewish families is allowed if the decedent is Jewish.

the local unit must notify the state agency to discontinue payment. The remaining chief responsibility of the state agency is for interpretation of burial policies to state organizations of morticians and other groups, whose cooperation is needed or who may have a special interest in the requirements established, and to the general public. The state agency also has its usual responsibility for supervision of local procedures.

The operating unit must ordinarily undertake the responsibility for contacts with the family and with the undertaker who handles the burial. It must also be responsible for seeing that the local morticians' organization is informed of state and local regulations and for interpretation of burial policies and procedures to other agencies and to the public within its jurisdiction. It is responsible for instructing the family or undertaker in the preparation of claims for reimbursement from the public treasury, and if payments are made from the funds of the local agency it must handle the details of payment and accounting. The local unit must also prepare and forward whatever state reports are required and must notify the local disbursing office to discontinue the grant if grants are disbursed locally. The local units are usually responsible for initiating recovery proceedings and other property procedures.

Public funds for burial are not always requested by the decedent's family; hence the agency may not be informed immediately of the recipient's death. To ensure prompt notification, a number of local agencies have arranged with the local registrar of vital statistics to receive reports of all deaths of persons over sixty-five. In a large agency these reports are cleared through the file and the appropriate worker is notified. A number of agencies depend largely on inspection of death notices published in local newspapers; and small rural agencies often depend on informal reports reaching the workers as they move about the community if the family itself does not report promptly. In some of the larger cities arrangements have been made with public hospitals to receive reports of all admissions, discharges, transfers, and deaths. These notifications are often particularly helpful since they may be received more quickly than are reports from the registrar of vital statistics.[29] Agencies may also arrange to be notified of wills probated and of property transfers. They may also procure the cooperation of insurance companies in notifying them when payment of an insurance policy is requested by the beneficiary of the recipient's insurance.

---

[29] The reports of deaths to the registrar are often made by the undertaker handling the burial. They may be required before the burial permit is issued, but even so they may be a day or so later than the hospital discharge reports.

The policy of visiting the family when a death occurs varies greatly among agencies. Some visit promptly and offer to assist in making funeral arrangements and to render other services. Others visit only when family, neighbors, or friends request assistance. Still others vary their procedure to suit the individual case, visiting to be sure that a responsible person is available to take charge if relatives or friends cannot be counted upon; and visiting, also, if relations with the family have been close because of recent service rendered by the agency. A few agencies visit only when property adjustments are necessary, waiting usually until after the burial has taken place.[30] The visiting policy of other agencies depends on the family's means for meeting burial costs. If the family is believed to have sufficient funds, no visit is made unless the family or friends request help; but if the decedent and his family are known to be without resources a visit is made in order to explain procedures for arranging burial at public expense.

THE HANDLING OF PROPERTY

The problems involved in the handling of property are varied and complicated. To cover the subject with any degree of completeness would require not only a much more intensive and extensive study than it was possible for the survey staff to make but also an additional report. At the time of the field visits many agencies had not had time to set up their methods and procedures; and few of them had had sufficient experience to evaluate the results of the methods they had adopted. A great deal of interest at the time centered around the relation of property to eligibility and intake. Comments have already been made on some of these matters. Additional problems of continuing service pertain to the conservation of property, to adjustment of property at the time of death, and to other recovery procedures.

As previously noted, not all states require surrender of property, although nearly all have some means of recovery in case of fraud.[31] If the old age assistance law does not mention recovery in fraud cases it may still be possible to take action under more general statutes. Few fraud cases have been instituted, however, although threat or even fear without threat has often been effective in stimulating voluntary recoveries. Several agencies reported that in a number of cases and in

---

[30] In one state the local unit is required to have a representative present at the funeral if the state pays burial costs, in order to determine whether the service is in accordance with the bill later submitted by the undertaker.

[31] Some states have a provision for punitive double recovery (twice the value of the assistance advanced) in fraud cases.

amounts recovered, voluntary recoveries far exceeded those obtained from legal action. In a few of these cases assistance had been obtained illegally and legal action might have been taken; in the majority, however, voluntary recoveries were made either when the family acquired additional resources or when relatives decided that they would rather retain title to the property even though to do so meant sacrifice of present comforts—and often of necessities—than to have the property go to the state.[32]

Under popular misconception property means real estate only. Accordingly, in connection with mortgage, lien, and assignment procedures, there has been much wailing about the injustice of requiring the applicant to "sign away his rights to his little home." As a matter of fact, real estate, though presenting troublesome problems in administration, appears to be a minor source of the total sum received in the recovery process.[33] In most instances, whether the applicant executes a quitclaim deed, a mortgage, or other lien, he still retains life-use of his home, and often the right of use is retained so long as his spouse or other dependents continue to occupy it. Thus if the agency eventually obtains a return from the sale of the home of any of the money expended on behalf of the recipient, it is apt to be long after the recipient's death. In perhaps the majority of instances it might be more economical for the agency to surrender its right immediately rather than to continue to administer or to maintain some sort of supervision over its interests in the home for a long period.

Whatever procedure is used in establishing a lien or other claim, the agency should have authority to release it under adequate safeguards without payment or with only partial payment.[34] Difficulty arises if freedom to compromise claims is not allowed. In other words, there should always be authority to release or to compromise claims against a recipient's estate if by so doing the public interest is better served.

[32] Some states apparently value the property requirement chiefly for its deterrent effect. They stress the requirement in their literature and at intake and willingly accept voluntary repayment, but make no effort to recover through the courts.

[33] Unfortunately few reliable, complete, and well analyzed figures were obtainable, but such figures as were available unmistakably showed insurance to be the major source of recovery. Other personal property, cash in banks (frozen or liquid), stocks and bonds, and similar property appeared to rank ahead of real estate as sources of recoveries.

[34] Claims are sometimes established only when assistance is discontinued owing to the ineligibility or the death of the recipient. These claims may not directly control the property during the recipient's lifetime. If, however, they are accompanied, as they frequently are, by legal prohibition of alienation of property while receiving assistance, the effect of the procedure is much the same as that resulting from the establishing of a lien. It is more complicated in operation because it requires frequent checking of property transfers to guard against alienation.

As pointed out in connection with eligibility,[35] provisions for lien or for provisional or absolute surrender of property instead of being invariably harsh in their effect on applicants may really be benign. The agency may often be much more liberal in accepting applicants who own property than it could be without such provisions. A low property limitation, on the other hand, by excluding really needy applicants may cause much more suffering than do lien provisions. Compelling immediate sale and use of resources during a period of depressed prices may be disadvantageous both to the applicant and the agency.[36]

Satisfactory administration of surrendered property is, however, not a simple matter; it requires expert and specialized service. A knowledge of market conditions, values of real estate, stocks, bonds, and mortgages is necessary. Insurance values and special procedures must be known. The management of rental and other income-bearing property may be involved. Expensive accounting procedures are generally required. It is evident that only where the volume of property is sufficient to justify the employment of experts can the kind of administration that seems necessary be supplied.[37]

A large department with a special corps of workers presents problems inherent in size and in specialization. The chief difficulty is in relating the work of the special staff to the regular work of the agency.[38]

[35] See chap. 6.

[36] Mr. Benjamin Glassberg, Superintendent, Department of Outdoor Relief, Milwaukee County, Wisconsin, has given a clear presentation of the advantages of a flexible policy about assets of applicants. See "A Relief Agency Plays the Market," *Midmonthly Survey,* September, 1937, pp. 282-83.

[37] The question of the cost of administration in proportion to gain ought to be studied carefully. Some agencies showed much pride in the accretion of value of the property supervised by an elaborately organized property division and also of the recoveries obtained. In most instances it appeared that although the amounts looked large in the totals reported, had the total costs of the elaborate property operations been charged against the sums which would have been lost had no property division been in operation the balance might not have been favorable.

[38] Other investigators studying the administration of public assistance and observing the work of special units have noted results similar to those observed by the survey staff. In a study made by the American Public Welfare Association in 1938 the following statement appears: "In the larger agencies special departments were found that consisted of a special person or group of persons whose sole function was to search for documentary evidence of age, marriage, divorce, property, etc. This device served a useful purpose when properly integrated with the social worker's function of determining eligibility. However, where isolated from the social service division, resource workers tended to pile up mechanical operations around search for property, and to impose their decisions as to liquidation of assets, eligibility, etc., without knowing the whole picture and without reference to proper budget and social considerations for the client situation. When the resource department personnel tended to proceed on a legalistic or punitive basis, they distorted the purposes for which the public assistance laws were passed. Appraisal of resources of the clients was, obviously, when properly handled, an in-

Property is, in its most important aspects, a part of the social service activities of the agency. An attempt to deal with one part of the client's budget as if it were a separate entity has a tendency to warp the whole budget plan and to confuse client and visitor rather than to aid them. In the units observed, visitors were not given help in understanding the problems of property and in relating them to the other problems in a client's total situation. Rather they were made to feel that property was something mysterious and difficult and should be kept separate and apart. They might be expected to supply information to the property division, but they were often given no idea why the facts requested were needed or what plans were made for the client's property on the basis of the facts supplied. Clients were confused by the necessity of dealing with two representatives of the agency whose relationship was not clear and who, on occasion, gave him conflicting advice and information because each was only partially informed.

Specialists tend to develop a vested interest in their specialty. Thus property divisions are eager to develop their own division and to show results in terms of cash collected even though the cost of collection may exceed the amounts collected. The emphasis should not be on cash returns but on conservation of clients' rights of ownership and on the prevention of unnecessary dependency. Some collections were made from recipients' estates; thus dependent heirs were left penniless and compelled to apply immediately for public assistance—a futile and often destructive proceeding. Enthusiasm for showing large returns in cash also seems to blind some agencies to the fact that the large cash returns may be the result of poor investigation of property resources and poor budgeting methods which are in turn the direct result of the attempt to deal with property as a separate entity.

Satisfactory agency policy about property would seem to call for instructions of the visiting staff in good investigative procedures including the investigation of property, and in sound budgeting of resources. It is better to plan to discover such resources early and utilize them constructively rather than to count later on collecting amounts which might not have been expended if the visiting staff had had sufficient skill in investigation and budgeting. If the state agency has available a consultant on standards of assistance, property should be a part of his re-

---

separable part of determining the amount of relief or assistance need by a given client; it was, therefore, a normal part of the social worker's function. In difficult cases, special technical advice, such as that needed for real estate questions and insurance problems, was sought by social workers." See *American Public Welfare: A Public Welfare Job Study* (Chicago: American Public Welfare Association, 1938), pp. 35-36.

sponsibility. Standards for the evaluation and wise use of resources may thus be established along with other items of the standard budget. For example, standards of housing, relating both to owned and rented property, are important in determining the shelter item of the budget. Standards of housing are developed in much the same way as are food and clothing standards, and can be handled by a consultant on standards of assistance who is trained in both social work and family economics. If special knowledge of real estate values and of legal requirements is needed to supplement the other fields, this can usually be obtained from experts in these fields.[39]

CASE-WORK SERVICE

Nothing has been said, up to this point, about the need of the aged for case-work service. This is not additional—another procedure added to all those that the administration of any form of public assistance entails; rather it is a method of using these procedures in constructive ways to serve the client. The social service staff needs to be qualified to do this if its work is to be effective. The skills required in dealing with the aged, however, are not greatly different from those used in dealing with other groups. "But here," as Gordon Hamilton says, "case work must be just as discriminating as elsewhere." [40] No stereotyped methods for dealing with the aged can be prescribed. Again, according to Miss Hamilton,[41] "an imaginative approach, a differentiated program, and the attitude of seeing old people as individuals and not as a category, and of working *with* them and in response to their expressed needs and wishes rather than *for* them" are necessary to make case work with the aged "sensitive, sensible, and acceptable to a discriminating clientele."

[39] In many agencies the property division is not manned by experts but by a staff that has acquired on the job whatever special knowledge its members have. They are sometimes less qualified in education and experience than are the members of the visiting staff.

[40] "Case Work in Old Age Assistance," *The Family,* February, 1938.

[41] *Ibid.* Some of the special problems of case work with the aged are indicated by Miss Hamilton. The Family Welfare Association of America has recently published a brief pamphlet, "Mental Hygiene in Old Age," in which still others are discussed. The literature on the subject is not abundant but is developing. The Family Welfare Association of America has available a list of references on the care of the aged, which may be obtained by writing to that agency at 130 East 22nd Street, New York City.

PART III
The Administration of Fiscal Activities

CHAPTER 11

PROBLEMS IN FINANCING THE OLD AGE ASSISTANCE PROGRAM

TABLE 1 INDICATES that within the past few years public expenditures for old age assistance have increased phenomenally and become a major fiscal problem for every state. Indeed, in a number of far western states, where the old age pension movement has been unusually strong, expenditures for this purpose have assumed such proportions that it has been necessary to curtail other activities. Some states are spending considerably more for this one form of aid than for all other relief activities; a few are actually spending about as much for old age assistance as for all other state activities combined.

TABLE 1. OLD AGE ASSISTANCE EXPENDITURES, 1930-37

Calendar Year	Amount
1930	$ 2,138,441
1931	16,234,989
1932	25,051,177
1933	26,167,117
1934	32,379,993
1935	65,001,664
1936 [a]	136,122,498
1937	310,872,850

SOURCE: Data for 1930-35 from *Monthly Labor Review*, XLIII (October, 1936); for 1936, from *Second Annual Report of the Social Security Board* (1937); for 1937, from *Tabular Summary of Statistics of Public Assistance under the Social Security Act for the Calendar Year 1937*, Social Security Board, Bureau of Research and Statistics, Bureau Report No. 1.

[a] Covers eleven months only: February through December.

In this chapter we shall not attempt to review the adequacy or inadequacy of the several states' old age assistance programs or their effect upon state and local finances; nor shall we undertake to discuss the tax aspects of old age assistance. Though highly important, these problems relate to policy rather than to administration and hence fall outside the scope of this study. This chapter deals particularly with questions of finance which bear more or less directly upon administration; only incidentally does it touch upon the broader field of public finance.

FEDERAL AID

The Social Security Act established a national policy of federal aid for old age assistance. By committing the government to paying 50 per cent of total state expenditures (not to exceed fifteen dollars a month per recipient), the law imposed upon the federal government a heavy obligation which, within a few years, was expected to reach nearly a half-billion dollars annually—more than all previous non-emergency federal-aid grants combined. By the terms of the Act the federal government undertook to match state payments for old age assistance (as well as aid to dependent children and the blind) dollar for dollar within the specified limitation per recipient, instead of making a definite appropriation to be distributed among the states. Under this powerful stimulus, the states that had not already enacted old age assistance laws hastened to do so, and states with such legislation on their statute books made more liberal provisions and appropriated more adequate funds. With the approval of the Virginia plan in 1938 every state in the Union had qualified for federal aid.

To qualify for federal aid, state old age assistance plans must meet the conditions of the federal Act and are subject to periodic review and approval by the Social Security Board. A discussion of the detailed provisions of the federal Act and of the supervision exercised by the federal agency over the states appears in pervious chapters.

Federal grants to the states are made quarterly in advance, on estimates submitted by the states. In computing the quarterly grant, balances or deficits from preceding grants are taken into consideration. No uniformity could be detected in the method by which the federal fund was transmitted to local units, in the states observed, that provided for local financial support and local administration. In some states the grant was forwarded in advance of disbursement, and provision was made for its custody and expenditure. In others, the fund was retained by the states and handled as a supplement to state moneys being used in turn to reimburse the localities. Ordinarily federal grants received by the local government were deposited as a special fund with the county treasurer or other local fiscal officer, and in some instances with local welfare agencies. As a general rule, it would seem preferable to utilize the regular fiscal officers and to carry out the normal financial procedures applicable to other state and local funds in order to avoid duplication of organization and effort and to safeguard against loose financial practices.

In addition to the basic grant for assistance which must be matched by the state, the federal government makes a further grant—5 per cent of the basic grant—which need not be matched and which may be used either for administrative expenses or for old age assistance. In the states visited that administered old age assistance directly, this fund was expended for administration, frequently being lumped with state administrative funds and losing its identity. Where administration was left to local units, the use of this grant varied. Some states turned the sum over entirely to the local units, with or without restrictions on its use. Wisconsin required that it be kept as a separate fund and used only for administrative purposes. Indiana stipulated that no county was entitled to receive from this source a sum greater than that actually spent for administration. A number of states divided the fund between the state agency and the localities. Colorado retained the entire amount for state administration, though the plan was administered by the localities. Another state, which exercised supervision over the local units, turned half the grant over to them, retaining the remainder for its own administration. It would appear that the amount retained by the state agency in each instance was out of proportion to its administrative task.

It is appropriate for the federal government to bear part of the cost of administration. The grant for this purpose is not designed to cover all administrative expenses, or even one-half, but is merely to aid the states and localities. Since the federal government bears approximately half the total cost of old age assistance, it is necessarily concerned with the quality of administration. Inadequate administrative funds lead to weak administration, to unsatisfactory investigation and follow-up of applicants, and to excessive total costs. Unfortunately the Social Security Act makes no requirement whatever concerning state administrative standards and the use of these funds. It is not sufficient merely to turn over the administrative grant for the states to use entirely at their discretion without federal authority to review its use. The history of grants-in-aid in this country, as well as abroad, indicates the unwisdom of unconditional grants.

The weakness of the law is indicated by the wide variation among states in their use of federal money for administration and in the failure of the states generally to exercise adequate supervision over its expenditure. Because of the differences in state plans and in the problems of administration from state to state, it might be difficult to specify in the law detailed, uniformly applicable standards. Instead it would be advisable to provide that grants for administration be subject to the approval of the Social Security Board, thereby providing a salutary safeguard and establishing some assurance of reasonably satisfactory administration by the states. Even without such amendment of the Social Security Act, the Board might undertake to encourage more constructive use of administrative grants and the establishment of appropriate regulations by state authorities. Without any specific sanction in the Act, the Board so far has been unwilling to advise how the grants be spent.

STATE FINANCIAL SUPPORT

The Social Security Act requires that states receiving federal aid make a financial contribution to the old age assistance plan. The purpose of this provision is to assure that the state, which is entrusted with the responsibility of supervising the local units under a state-local plan, have a financial stake in the system. The congressional policy was to limit federal supervision to the states. If a state plan is locally administered the state must exercise surveillance over the localities. Prior to the Act the trend was definitely toward state aid to localities for their assistance programs. Now, with federal aid, all the states provide some financial support of the program, and many have gone a step further and assumed complete fiscal responsibility.

Of the twelve states surveyed, five—Colorado, Iowa, Connecticut, Mississippi, and Washington—provided for state financing. Iowa and Washington now require some local support. Six of the states studied followed a joint plan, with the following percentage division of costs in 1936:

	State	Local Unit
New York	25	25
Massachusetts	33⅓	16⅔
New Jersey	37½	12½
Indiana	30	20
Wisconsin	30	20
California	25	25

These percentages, however, are subject to qualification. Expenditures in excess of thirty dollars per month for any individual were, in some states, borne by the locality; medical care, burial expenses, and other unusual costs were frequently carried by the local unit, sometimes with state aid. Even where the program was classified as state financed, the local governments frequently provided a variety of supplementary services for old age recipients and thus bore a portion of the total cost of the program.

Although the relative merits of state operation and of local administration with state supervision are discussed elsewhere, some observations

TABLE 2. AVERAGE GRANTS PER RECIPIENT IN SELECTED COUNTIES IN
WISCONSIN AND IOWA, 1936

Month	Wisconsin Average	Barron County	Dane County	Milwaukee County	Wood County
February	$16.96	$16.34	$20.71	$22.49	$18.58
March	17.14	16.10	20.93	23.68	19.22
April	17.39	16.08	20.78	23.53	16.87
May	17.64	15.94	20.63	23.71	18.49
June	17.74	16.08	20.67	22.92	18.43
July	18.10	16.17	20.72	24.97	17.97
August	18.13	16.27	20.82	24.40	17.93
September	18.29	16.53	20.91	24.19	17.91
October	18.50	16.78	20.96	24.26	17.84
November	18.72	16.84	21.10	24.76	17.98
December	18.84	16.89	21.24	24.93	18.01

Month	Iowa Average	DesMoines County	Henry County	Mahaska County	Polk County	Wapello County
February	$14.28	a	a	a	a	a
March	14.42	a	a	a	a	a
April	14.39	a	a	a	a	a
May	14.56	a	a	a	a	a
June	14.54	a	a	a	a	a
July	14.55	a	a	a	a	a
August	14.53	a	a	a	a	a
September	14.58	$15.25	$14.38	$14.50	$15.30	$15.20
October	14.64	15.34	14.54	14.55	15.42	15.24
November	14.64	15.33	14.48	14.58	15.42	15.30
December	14.69	15.32	14.52	14.72	15.43	15.32

a Data by counties not available.

may be made here on the financing of the program. State-financed and -administered programs tend to a uniformity of operation throughout the state. Assistance policies formulated in accordance with the funds available from state sources are applied with little variation among sections of the state. If ample funds are available, the standards of assistance will be high. But if funds are insufficient, standards will be low or the program will be limited to an incomplete coverage of the needy aged. Changes of state financial policy toward old age assistance will have immediate effects on the whole program. Jointly administered and financed state-local programs, on the other hand, frequently show wide variation in standards of assistance within a state. This situation is generally attributable to differences in local financial resources and in local attitudes toward the program. The more progressive localities set a high standard of administration and of grant policy that serves as an example for other localities.

Table 2 shows the level maintained in the Iowa state-administered and -financed program in 1936 in urban and rural counties and the standard maintained in Wisconsin in that year although the state did not contribute its full share of assistance costs during the first six months of the year. The counties selected were those visited by the staff.

Exclusive state financing has been opposed on the ground that it would lead to excessive centralization and take the program out of the hands of the localities. Actual experience, however, does not appear to bear out the contention. Several state-financed programs have been as effectively decentralized as jointly financed programs in other states. The amount of state control does not automatically vary with the amount of state contribution. In any event, it is the kind of state supervision and the wisdom with which it is exercised that really matter.

STATE REVENUES FOR OLD AGE ASSISTANCE

Unlike other relief programs, whose beneficiaries may become self-supporting as economic conditions improve, the establishment of an old age assistance program generally imposes a continuing obligation. Old age assistance grants are seldom reduced or discontinued except upon the death of the recipient. The total amount of expenditures does not decrease appreciably in periods of prosperity as for other forms of relief. In hard times, when governmental revenues are apt to be impaired, increases in the number of applicants may be expected. At such times it is difficult to decrease commitments for old age assistance since this can be accomplished only by reducing amounts of individual benefits or by removing recipients from assistance rolls. Reduction of benefits does not compensate for the hardships imposed on the needy aged or for the obvious disfavor this action would bring to the administration. Removing recipients from the assistance rolls does not eliminate public responsibility of providing adequate care for the needy. Consequently, a sound financial basis is necessary to meet the constant or increasing expenditures for an old age assistance program.[1]

Several states have enacted mandatory statutory provisions giving a

[1] Although the financing of any new state activity is obviously interwoven with the total state fiscal structure, it is not within the scope of this study to consider state tax programs. Specific reference to revenue sources for old age assistance is made only where there are special funds with earmarked revenues.

preferred position to this form of public assistance and specifying minimum amounts to be received by eligible applicants. The California law, for example, provides that "The amount of aid to which any applicant shall be entitled shall be when added to the income of the applicant from all other sources, thirty-five dollars per month." [2] By constitutional amendment Colorado provided for assistance to the aged under such liberal conditions as seriously to jeopardize all other state activities. Aside from statutory provisions, the popular appeal of this form of assistance and pressure by potentially benefited groups have affected the administrative attitude. Such pressure, if effective, may place as great a burden on state revenues as any legal mandate to liberalize assistance policies.

Of the states covered in this study, specific revenues were earmarked for old age assistance in Colorado, Connecticut, Massachusetts, and formerly in New Jersey and Iowa.[3] Per capita or poll taxes earmarked for this purpose were adopted a few years ago by several states, but were abandoned by most of them, including Massachusetts and Iowa, because they operated unsatisfactorily and failed to provide sufficient funds. In Connecticut—one of the few states to retain this type of tax—the assessment was levied upon each municipality, which was then held responsible for its collection and payment. If the tax was not collected, the municipalities raised the levy from other sources.

Students of taxation have deplored the per capita tax as regressive, difficult to collect, and relatively unproductive. It was adopted by a number of states at the inception of old age assistance legislation under the mistaken assumption that there was some relation between the payment of a per capita tax and the receipt of old age assistance. Massachusetts, which formerly used an earmarked per capita tax for old age assistance, replaced it with receipts from liquor taxes. In Colorado a state public welfare fund was established to provide financial support for the welfare programs of the state including old age assistance. The fund consisted of revenues from the state sales tax, portions of the liquor tax, and other miscellaneous taxes. The law originally stipulated an allocation of 50 per cent of the fund for old age assistance, but by constitutional amendment in 1936 this was raised to about 85 per cent.[4]

---

[2] California, *Statutes,* Ex. Sess., 1936, chap. 7.

[3] New Jersey originally provided a special old age assistance fund supported by inheritance taxes. After the first year of operation this provision was suspended, and allotments from the state emergency relief administration were made available. Subsequently the state's share of assistance has been provided from the general fund.

[4] This amendment provided for minimum pensions of forty-five dollars per month

The earmarking of revenues for special purposes is seldom desirable. It can be justified only if there is a direct relationship between revenue and need. There are no revenues that bear such relationship to old age assistance. If the earmarked revenues are large, they may result in unduly liberal grants while other governmental activities are starved; if insufficient, the program will, of course, be handicapped. Several states discontinued earmarking special revenues for old age assistance when they proved inadequate, but only after considerable suffering by needy applicants and recipients.

The state's share of assistance costs was financed from general-fund revenues in the remaining states covered by this survey—California, Indiana, Mississippi, New Jersey, New York, Washington, and Wisconsin. Definite appropriations for the fiscal year were made by the legislatures in all these states except California. There the act provided for a continuing authorization of the expenditure of state funds to the maximum amount legally permitted for each case under the state-aid provision of the act. This was interpreted to make the state's share of old age assistance costs a direct charge against available state general funds without recurring appropriations.

The provision for old age assistance out of the state's general fund is sound policy. The amounts appropriated will presumably bear a direct relation to the needs of the program and will not be subject to the wide fluctuation of earmarked revenues. Thus a more consistent state program can be established.

STATE APPROPRIATIONS FOR ADMINISTRATIVE COSTS

State administrative expenditures are relatively small where old age assistance is administered by the localities and the state activity is confined to supervision. Where the program is administered by the state agency, state administrative costs are necessarily higher. Two methods of state appropriation are generally used: specific appropriations for administration, and percentage appropriations either of the total expenditure for old age assistance or of the state appropriation. The former practice was followed in four of the states surveyed—California,

and contained a "jack-pot" provision whereby an annual distribution of unexpended moneys in the fund was to be made among the recipients of pensions. The amendment cannot be nullified by repeal of supporting taxes since a safeguarding provision requires equivalent substitution of revenues for any taxes withdrawn. By lowering the eligible age limit, however, the amendment defeated the purpose for which it was framed: the increased number of beneficiaries proved to be more than could be taken care of by available funds.

New York, New Jersey, and Massachusetts—the states with the longest experience in administering old age assistance. In Colorado the state welfare department was allowed not more than 5 per cent of the public welfare fund. In Washington the state agency was allotted up to 5 per cent of total expenditures; and in Mississippi, no more than 10 per cent. In Washington and Mississippi the program was state administered; in Colorado, locally administered. In Connecticut and Iowa state agencies had no specific appropriation or limitation on administrative expenditures, but could expend whatever amounts they deemed necessary from state appropriations for old age assistance, subject to the approval of the comptroller. States that had a special fund for old age assistance customarily used it to pay administrative expenses. In other states administrative costs were paid out of the general fund.

Making a percentage appropriation for administrative expenses or limiting administrative expenses to an arbitrary percentage is unsound. On the surface an appropriation of a fixed percentage of the total expenditure may appear to be reasonable and conducive to economical administration. Actually, the total expenditure bears an uncertain relation to the task of administration. The expense of administration does not necessarily vary with the amount of the grant and may be greater to handle a small grant than a large one. It may cost more to investigate a case in which a grant is denied than one in which it is allowed. The ratio of administrative expense to total outlay may be much higher in one community than in another. Then, too, during its early years a program will cost more because of the high proportion of new applications to be investigated. If average grants are, say, thirty dollars per month, a fixed appropriation of 5 per cent allows $1.50 per month for administration; but if the grants average ten dollars per month, only fifty cents per month would be provided.

If the percentage appropriation is higher than necessary, it is a positive inducement to extravagant administrative expenditure and sometimes unnecessary services; if inadequate to provide necessary administrative services, the funds on hand will have to be supplemented by other available means. An attempt to enforce effective and economical administration through arbitrary percentage limitations often leads to ineffective and inefficient administration or to attempts to evade restrictions by obtaining other support. In Mississippi and Washington, where the percentage appropriation proved inadequate, it became necessary to utilize other relief funds, and Mississippi's program was greatly handicapped by lack of sufficient funds for administration.

It is unfortunate that the federal appropriation for administration is fixed at 5 per cent of the federal grant, for this has led many states to assume wrongly that 5 per cent of the total cost is a fair standard and hence to incorporate it in their law. Doubtless the Act should be amended to provide that the federal government bear a definite proportion of the cost of administration, subject to the Social Security Board's regulation and approval. This would do away with an arbitrary 5 per cent limitation and would establish more adequate safeguards of the expenditure of federal funds.

LOCAL CONTRIBUTIONS

When local funds have been required for the old age assistance program, they have usually been supplied from general revenues of the local governmental unit. Special provision, however, is made for the local cost in several states. In California, although local practice varied, several units made separate tax levies for welfare purposes. In Indiana there was a separate levy for welfare activities, and the county appropriating authority had little discretion in passing upon the amounts requested by the county welfare agency. Appeal to state authorities for review of appropriations could be made by the local or state assistance agency if the funds were deemed insufficient. In New Jersey the county welfare boards were semiautonomous, and the local governing body was required by law to appropriate the amounts requested by the board. County welfare boards, which were viewed by other local authorities as creatures of the state, were to form the nucleus of an integrated local welfare administration. But their effectiveness for this purpose may be injured somewhat by their preferred and somewhat isolated financial position, which has engendered an unfavorable local attitude.

Under the Social Security Act, old age assistance programs must be in operation throughout the state and, if partially supported by local units of government, must be mandatory upon them. By this requirement federal aid may be cut off if a single local unit does not make the required appropriation. In that event the state may proceed with legal action against the local officials. So far as is known there have been no cases of this kind. The real problem arises not through the failure of the local authorities to make any appropriation but through inability to provide adequately for their needy aged. Federal and state funds are conditioned upon the local contribution, and if the locality cannot provide the necessary funds, the program breaks down. In many if not most states, some local governmental units—generally counties—are so poverty stricken as to be unable to raise even the small percentage of old age assistance costs required of them by state law. Consequently the needy aged within their boundaries are inadequately cared for. Some form of equalization of state aid to take care of the very poor communities is obviously necessary. The easiest way to side-step the issue of equalization is state assumption of total costs. This blanket leveling of the financial burden may, however, not be the best method of solving the problem, particularly if local participation in the administration of the program is desired.

State aid for old age assistance has been so closely tied up with formulas for grants in a fixed ratio to assistance expenditures that there has been little or no exploration of other methods of distributing aid. Some experimentation should be worth while with revised state-aid formulas to compensate for variations in the ability of local units of government to pay. To devise and administer a formula for distributing state aid according to relative local financial ability, however, will be difficult until some criteria have been established of measuring the ability of governmental units to pay. The Wisconsin emergency relief administration has had a study made of the relative financial conditions of counties. A scale was prepared ranking all counties in their relative positions. On the basis of their rating, the allocation of relief funds was brought somewhat into line with local needs.

Indiana, under its emergency relief administration, had a contingency fund for the purpose of underwriting stranded localities, but the need was never deemed sufficient to require its use. Now the state welfare agency desires a similar fund to protect the state plan by grants to local units whose resources may be inadequate to permit participation. Another state emergency relief agency, during its period of operation, was able to fix by regulation the rate of reimbursement to local units. Indiana has adopted the preventive measure of establishing a special finance unit in the state welfare department with the responsibility of observing county fiscal conditions. If the financial standing of a county seems endangered, the staff of this unit is available to offer advice which may help restore the affairs of the county to a sound basis.

State-financed programs have been much concerned about the means of assuring necessary local contribution to the old age assistance program, but have accorded less attention to coverage. Insufficient funds for such a program may actually limit coverage more than one locality's deficiency in a jointly financed state-local program. In several state-financed programs, as those in Iowa, Mississippi, and Washington, grants have been withheld from applicants because of insufficient funds. A state administering and financing its own program may by thin distribution of funds obscure deficient coverage. All sections of the state may share in these grants but the extent to which the problem of aged indigency is met may be negligible. Under the provisions of the Social Security Act, however, the program must be in effect in all administrative subdivisions of the state. If certain coverage requirements are enforced for jointly financed state-local programs, it is only reasonable that similar examination be given to the actual coverage of state-administered and -financed programs. In either case the criterion should be more than the bare requirement that the program be "in effect" in all political subdivisions of a state.

CHAPTER 12

BUDGETING AND CONTROL OF EXPENDITURES

THE CLOSE relationship of an agency's administrative policy to its funds makes budgeting a major executive responsibility. The following pages discuss budgeting of grants-in-aid and the estimation and control of expenditures for old age assistance; but the preparation of estimates of administrative costs and control of administrative expenditures receive only brief reference, since they are problems common to most governmental agencies.

RESPONSIBILITY FOR BUDGETING AND BUDGET CONTROL

The old age assistance authority's responsibility for the budget is not confined to estimating expenditures; its duties also include operating the program within available funds. Sometimes it must revise its estimate and adjust its assistance standards because of restricted operating revenue. Adjustments can be determined only by the executive who is responsible for administration of the agency. The operating budget constitutes a financial interpretation of operating policies and program determined by the executive authority.

The significance of budgeting and budget control as a direct function of the executive authority is not always fully appreciated. In several states the board that is the legal head of the state welfare department gives but cursory attention to the budget. One state welfare board delegates this responsibility to the director of the department; another gives the budget only brief consideration before it is submitted to the state budget director and subsequently receives quarterly reports on it only as a routine formality. Some boards, however, appreciate the value of taking action on the budget and the opportunity it gives to review and discuss program plans and policies. In New Jersey members of the State Board of Control are usually present at both executive and legislative budget hearings to lend support to the representations of the commissioner.

223

Preparation of budget estimates and the maintenance of current financial control require detailed work to which the executive can give only general supervision and direction. Responsibility for much of this work, therefore, often devolves upon the financial staff of the assistance agency, with the staff chief acting as budget officer. This pattern is followed in the state agencies observed in California, Indiana, New Jersey, and Wisconsin. Similarly, the finance officers of divisions in state welfare departments where financial administration is partially decentralized often act as budget officers for their respective sections, e.g., the chief accountant in the Connecticut Bureau of Old Age Assistance and the assistant director in charge of finance in the Massachusetts Division of Aid and Relief (of which Division the Bureau of Old Age Assistance is a part).

When the finance officer of an agency acts as budget officer, his budgetary activities must not be confused with his administrative duties as head of a division, wherein he usually enjoys a certain amount of administrative freedom in handling matters of operative detail clearly within his division. As budget officer, however, he is acting as staff assistant to the executive on matters affecting the entire agency and should constantly confer with the executive.

Budgeting and the maintenance of the budget plan are frequently regarded merely as financial functions with which, next to the executive, the fiscal staff is primarily concerned. The budget and its execution, however, are matters of concern to all divisions of the agency. A budget committee, composed of the agency's division heads under the chairmanship of the executive, or possibly of the budget officer, to discuss the financial program and its effects on the various divisions' activities can give valuable advice on matters requiring executive decision. Such a group might aid in coordinating division policies and preventing any one division's unduly influencing the executive on budgetary questions.

Local assistance agencies generally recognize the executive responsibility for budget preparation. The smaller agencies, lacking staff specialization, require the executive to assume this function personally, whereas the larger often delegate responsibility for budgeting and financial control to the chief finance officer. Furthermore, local administrative and advisory boards take much greater interest in budget activities than do most state welfare boards and are at times, in whole or in part, composed of members of the local governing body. Directors of the local agencies often receive valuable assistance from such members, since they are in a position to interpret intelligently the agency's needs when its budget is being considered by the local appropriating authority.

The executive of the local assistance agency is also generally responsible for budget control, but in actual practice it is in many instances divided among several local authorities. For example, a finance committee of the board of supervisors in Dane County, Wisconsin, meets with the director of the county pension department at occasional intervals to discuss the financial condition of the program. In Barron County funds for the local assistance agency are appropriated subject to release by the executive committee of the board of supervisors. The county auditor or county clerk often keeps the assistance agency's appropriation accounts and thus may participate in its budgetary affairs.[1]

BUDGETING EXPENDITURES FOR ASSISTANCE

Local agencies must determine how much local money will be needed for old age assistance programs locally financed and administered with state supervision and grants-in-aid, as in California, Indiana, Massachusetts, New Jersey, New York, and Wisconsin.[2] The first step in formulating estimates of assistance costs is to determine the standard of assistance and methods of granting it. In several states standards of assistance have been established by legislation, which sets a fixed amount of assistance to be granted, allowing deductions for income and other personal resources. In other states, however, aid is granted largely without regard to relative needs of individuals as determined by investigation. In some instances this practice has resulted from a deliberate policy; in others, it is caused by inadequate funds for the initial period of operation. A state desiring to remedy this condition must determine the amount of the deficiency. Adequate case records can supply this information. If these are not available a sampling of the case load will yield data on grant deficiencies. For an agency that has been granting assistance on the basis of an applicant's actual needs, past expenditures will, of course, provide the foundation for estimates of future assistance costs.

When estimating an increased case load, the local agency should familiarize itself with application statistics not only within its own jurisdiction but in similar localities in the state to ascertain probable future need. The number of removals from the assistance rolls, through death

[1] See discussion of expenditure control, p. 232.

[2] When the operating agency is the state agency, as in Connecticut and, to a lesser degree, in Iowa and Washington, where all administrative responsibility is concentrated in the state agency although local offices are maintained for investigations, the problems are sufficiently similar to those of a local agency that discussion of local budgeting may suffice to include these programs.

or other circumstances, can be calculated with reasonable accuracy, and must be subtracted from the potential increase. The average cost of additions to the rolls will in normal periods probably parallel the average amount granted to current recipients, if assistance has been given in accordance with the applicants' actual needs. Where this policy is followed, studies indicate that the amounts granted will follow a normal curve of distribution. Consequently, the aid given to future applicants will probably be distributed similarly, if the same standards of determining need govern the agency's policy.

If a locality receives state and federal grants-in-aid for assistance, estimates of these anticipated reimbursements are needed in preparing the local revenue program. Since both state and federal aid are usually granted in a fixed proportion to local assistance expenditures, estimating these receipts is for the most part not difficult. If assistance is granted to individuals who do not meet the eligibility requirements of state and federal laws, or in amounts exceeding the maximum for which state and federal aid is allowed, anticipating expenditures is more complex, since excess charges must be borne entirely by local funds. In some instances state aid may be permitted in whole or in part on grants for which federal aid may not be claimed. Adjustments in the amounts which may be expected from state and federal sources must, therefore, be computed, but it is doubtful that they will affect the local budget seriously except in large units. Where the number of cases not meeting state or federal requirements and data on expenditures in such cases are available, computing net estimates of state and federal receipts should not be difficult.

Local budget estimates are affected by the state's method of paying the state and federal share of the costs of the program. If the policy is reimbursement of the local agency rather than payment in advance, a working capital must be provided, and its amount will be influenced by the frequency of reimbursement. In some instances the local authority must allow for advance payment of the federal share and reimbursement of the state contribution. Such a system complicates the preparation of estimates and causes unnecessary confusion in records.

A local agency maintaining an efficient unit to handle financial data and service statistics should have little difficulty in formulating budget estimates of assistance costs. Recording and reporting procedures for state public assistance programs are being developed under the leadership of the Bureau of Research and Statistics of the federal Social Security Board. In turn, many local agencies are now preparing current statistical reports and compiling service data, both of which were heretofore unavailable. Their maximum use for administrative purposes, such as budget preparation, has not yet been realized. Local informational resources are generally adequate for budget purposes if supplemented by data on state assistance trends and adequate guidance in their interpretation.

A state agency that grants aid to local agencies on a percentage basis faces the problem of estimating total assistance costs so that it can compute its share. A direct relationship exists between the amounts estimated by localities for assistance costs and the sums that must be appropriated from state funds. This makes the planning of state expenditures for grants-in-aid a problem of greater complexity than computing the probable cost in a specific locality for a given period.

In estimating the amount of grants-in-aid for old age assistance, a state agency is concerned not only with the probable cost of assistance but with the amount of the local agencies' share. Furthermore, if several local agencies determine upon a more liberal standard of assistance, additional state aid will be required. State estimates of total assistance costs based on past experience do not allow for changes in local assistance policies and may prove inadequate. Nevertheless, some state agencies have only recently correlated the budgeting of state funds with local budgeting, and many still rely on the data available in the state office in computing future assistance costs.

In Indiana and New Jersey the state welfare departments require reports from local agencies of the amounts budgeted for old age assistance, as well as work sheets and incidental calculations. Local estimates furnish the basis for determining the amount of aid. The work sheets permit the state agency to make any adjustments in its own estimates owing to inadequate or excessive local estimates.

In Colorado and Mississippi, where old age assistance programs are locally administered but state financed, the state specifies the amount to be spent for old age assistance;[3] but the responsibility for its administration and for maintaining the program rests upon the local units. Therefore they should participate in budgeting activities of the state. The local agencies in Colorado submit monthly estimates of requirements, which, in effect, constitute budgets of assistance expenditures. In Mississippi, however, local agencies operate under budgets prepared solely by the state agency. That actual conditions and the localities' needs may be taken into account, either the local units should submit estimates

[3] In Colorado, only assistance costs are paid in full from state funds.

to the state for the period of anticipated expenditures or the state should submit estimates for each locality to amend or approve.

If state assistance costs are financed from special revenue and expenditure funds, as in Colorado, Connecticut, Iowa, and Massachusetts, expenditures are necessarily limited to the funds available.[4] Here the state assistance agencies have continuing authority to spend for assistance purposes and do not have to submit budget estimates of assistance costs in order to obtain financial support. Budgeting of assistance may thus be ignored with no immediate consequences if the special-fund revenues are plentiful. But, neither financial conditions nor expenditures under assistance programs are static. Hence it appears desirable to have not only estimates of expenditures for each fiscal period but estimates of potential revenues as well, so that if anticipated revenues fall short of expected expenditures the fact may be known sufficiently in advance to permit the revision of budgets.

In budgeting state assistance costs some consideration must be given to anticipated federal receipts. The federal government will match grants up to thirty dollars a month if the state meets its requirements, and the amount of federal aid may readily be computed from estimates of total assistance expenditures. There may, however, be certain grants to individuals which do not comply with federal conditions, for which no aid will be received, or grants in excess of thirty dollars per month. These must be deducted from estimated federal reimbursements. This problem may be overcome by adequate service statistics on the condition of persons to whom assistance is being or may be given and by comprehensive financial data, including, for example, the amounts expended for assistance in previous periods, classified according to the number of individual grants above and below thirty dollars per month, the total amount, and the distribution and amounts of grants over thirty dollars.

BUDGETING ADMINISTRATIVE EXPENDITURES

An old age assistance program is predominantly a service program. Thus it follows that a large portion of administrative costs is for personnel. Determination of staff needs is, therefore, the major budgeting problem in handling administrative funds. A minimum amount of equipment is necessary, but additions and replacements are comparatively negligible. Furthermore, materials, supplies, current charges, rentals, and maintenance expenses are generally predictable from past operations. In determining adequate personnel requirements, the ad-

[4] See chap. 11.

ministrator must have a clear conception of what is to be accomplished. He must recognize that a program which includes not only the granting of money, but supplementary services as well, requires a larger staff and personnel of higher caliber than a program exclusively preoccupied with determining eligibility and need. At present, there are varying standards of proper ratio of staff to work load—a term which in itself is subject to various interpretations—making the task of planning personnel needs difficult. A few regulations have been established as a guide for administrators, such as the New York State Board of Social Welfare's ratio of one investigator to 150 cases.[5] But a standard satisfactory to one locality will not necessarily be applicable to all. Each local agency must study and analyze its own needs and set forth guiding principles accordingly. In the meantime administrative costs will be decided largely by rule of thumb.

A convenient but misleading scale for gauging costs has been developed to measure the effectiveness of administration by determining the ratio of administrative expense to total outlay. There is a popular notion, for example, that if administrative costs do not exceed 10 per cent of total expenditures for both administration and assistance, the administration is *ipso facto* efficient. The fallacy of this measure is obvious to persons who know the work. Such a rating actually places a premium upon the expenditure of funds for assistance rather than upon the conservation of public funds through investigation of applications by local agencies and through constructive supervision of local activities by state agencies. Yet attempts thus to legislate administrative economy were witnessed in Mississippi and Washington. Administrative expenditures were legally limited in Washington[6] to 5 per cent of total expenditures; in Mississippi,[7] to 10 per cent. With only a small appropriation available for assistance in Mississippi the grants were

[5] Regulating the ratio of cases per worker is difficult. Many agencies carry on other assistance programs and their workers carry case loads of families receiving assistance for two or more such programs. Old age assistance cases are assumed to take less time than those where aid is granted to dependent children, for instance; but the exact differential between the two is not easily determined. Even when the agency administers only old age assistance there are differentials. New cases take more time per case than do those whose eligibility has already been established. The Marion County, Indiana (Indianapolis), agency at the time of the field visit estimated that one worker with responsibility for only new cases could not, on an average, complete more than five cases per week. The public assistance staff of the Social Security Board has informally suggested a ratio of 100 cases per worker when the worker assumes no responsibility for new cases, or fifty cases with responsibility for investigating ten new cases per month, or twenty new cases with no responsibility for continuing service.

[6] *Laws,* 1935, chap. 182. This provision was repealed in 1937.

[7] *Laws,* 1936, chap. 175, sec. 26.

low and administrative costs proportionately high. In Washington the fact that old age assistance administration was a part of the operations of a large department afforded the use of staff charged to other programs for assistance purposes.

If the costs of administration are to be defended both before appropriating authorities and the public, the costs must be presented in the light of work done. For this purpose the cost per case offers an approach to a more intelligent interpretation of administrative expenses. But even this method means little without defining a "case" and without analysis of the work being done. The development of criteria for measuring administrative costs, based on work units, appears to be the prerequisite of sound administrative planning.[8]

The requirements of a state supervisory agency appear to be more intangible than those of a local agency, since the latter administers assistance to applicants, whose number, and therefore the extent of the task, may reasonably be estimated. The supervisory task of a state agency, which may extend from financial audits of local accounts through social service supervision of local personnel to the certification and approval of local employees' qualifications, has infinite ramifications. To determine the need for, and extent of, various types of supervision is the responsibility of the administrator of the state agency. In budgeting his administrative needs, little past experience is available to guide him. Perhaps greater emphasis is frequently placed on time-honored supervisory activities, such as auditing, than is justified by the results. Analysis of supervisory activities and appraisal of the effectiveness of present methods are prerequisite to an intelligent approach to the problem of determining requests for administrative funds. A state newly entering into a program of public assistance, for example, might well demand greater emphasis on in-service training activities than a state with a long history of public welfare administration.

STATE PARTICIPATION IN LOCAL BUDGETING

To aid so far as possible in the development and use of service statistics and financial data should obviously be a state agency's initial step in assisting local agencies to budget. Some state agencies, however, believe in doing the work for the local agencies rather than attempting to foster local development. If this attitude obtains, it is useless to continue

---

[8]In this connection see Anne E. Geddes, *Papers on Relief Statistics, Number Two,* Joint Committee on Relief Statistics of The American Public Welfare Association and The American Statistical Association, April, 1938.

the fiction of local operation under state supervision. Local agencies generally gather a great deal of statistical data for their reports to the state, but the meaning of these data and their usefulness to the local agencies has not been adequately emphasized by most states. In a few, however, aid in relating statistical data to administrative problems is given by the state staff, particularly its field representatives. Since the state agency often has trained personnel, and since its statistical data cover the entire state, it is the logical source of information on assistance trends.

In Indiana and New Jersey the state agency is legally empowered to review local budgets prior to local appropriations. The authorization in New Jersey was made only recently and was preceded by a period of voluntary cooperation between the state and local agencies, during which the state agency prepared financial and service data as a basis for the local agencies' budget estimates. The present law requires local agencies to submit these estimates to the state for review. In both Indiana and New Jersey, budget work sheets, prepared by the state agency and sent to the local agencies, contain detailed instructions for preparing the financial plan for both administrative and assistance needs. The New Jersey agency transmits with the budget work sheet a tentative estimate of the locality's assistance needs computed from statistical data in the state office. In Indiana, a specialized county finance unit of the Public Welfare Department's Division of General Administration has been established to carry on much of the technical work. Local agencies' budgets are reviewed by a committee comprising the heads of the assistance and administrative divisions of the state agency and the chief of the county finance unit. Approval is a matter of official action and record by the Indiana State Welfare Board.

State review of local welfare budgets may affect action of local appropriating bodies more in New Jersey than in Indiana. Apparently the local appropriating body in New Jersey is not permitted to revise the estimates submitted by the local welfare agency after approval by the state. In Indiana the local authorities in making budgetary appropriations are also limited by the law and the state attorney general's interpretation of it. An additional safeguard to protect the program, however, is included in the Indiana law: county welfare agencies may appeal adverse action on the budget by local appropriating authorities to the State Tax Commission. The state welfare agency also has the right to initiate an appeal from local budgetary action that may jeopardize the local assistance program. This right, however, is limited to appealing adverse actions on assistance items only. In 1936 the state agency initiated six appeals, four of which were adjusted before hearing; decisions on the other two were favorable to the state agency.

In both New Jersey and Indiana the local assistance programs are financed by separate tax levies. Local agencies, consequently, have the additional problem of computing a levy sufficient to meet budget estimates. Determining the reserves necessary to compensate for delinquencies and to provide working funds prior to tax collections is a problem that a local assistance agency is generally not equipped to meet; the provision of aid from the state staff specialists is undoubtedly a fortunate solution. In Indiana the county finance unit of the state agency has proved of great help both to the state agency and to local agencies. Staff members of this unit frequently appear at county budget hearings to present the state's case when its agency has revised local assistance estimates.

EXPENDITURE CONTROL

The problem of expenditure control is faced by all spending agencies. It is important to bear in mind the relationship between demand for assistance and the sum appropriated. Assistance grants must be limited to the available funds. Need is a relative term susceptible of widely variable interpretations, but always determined by legal and administrative regulations. Expenditure control, to be effective, must be exercised at the point where commitments are incurred. Consequently, budget control becomes a coordinate responsibility of the official authorized to determine and make grants. In the states [9] where grant authorization lies with localities the responsibility for budgetary control of assistance expenditures rests primarily on the local assistance agency; where grant determination and authorization are centrally performed,[10] it falls on the state administrator.

Although budget control is a function of the executive, this duty may, of course, be delegated to subordinate officials under his general supervision, just as the determination and authorization of grants may be delegated. In New York City, for example, where grants are authorized by the chiefs of three district units, monthly allotments are made to each unit, and the financial division maintains general control over them. Information on the current status of the appropriation and ex-

[9] California, Colorado, Indiana, Massachusetts, Mississippi, New Jersey, New York, and Wisconsin.

[10] Connecticut, Iowa, and Washington.

penditure accounts of the agency is a prerequisite to control. State assistance agencies administering a centralized program carry on such a large volume of work that their accounting is largely performed in a specialized bureau. But when local agencies administer assistance, the accounting may be carried on by the assistance agency itself, or by a local fiscal officer, such as a county comptroller, auditor, or clerk. If local funds are used in the assistance program, this fiscal officer inevitably functions in a supervisory capacity. Sometimes he keeps general control accounts, with the assistance agency maintaining its own detailed records of operations; or he may maintain all accounting records.

Local assistance administrators must have adequate accounting information and this need has been recognized by several state supervisory agencies. In Wisconsin, for example, at the time that local pension departments were established, the State Pension Department requested the State Budget Director and his staff to assist in establishing a uniform accounting system for the county assistance programs. Supplementary service has since been given by the field staff of the State Pension Department's financial division. The Indiana Department of Public Welfare has a system for reporting the outlay of county assistance agencies. Itemized monthly expenditures of the local agencies are sent to the state office, where they are analyzed and classified and a summary report returned to the local agency. This procedure assures that local assistance agencies have a monthly statement of commitments classified in accordance with appropriation schedules.

Given the data from which to appraise the financial condition of the assistance agency, there remains the problem of keeping the assistance program within the budget. The program, predicated on need as a primary factor in determining expenditures, cannot be equitably controlled by limiting expenditures in advance to so many units per week or per month—as might be done in purchasing or construction operations where expenditures are made for items comparatively exact and predictable. Actual control of assistance expenditures resides in the agency's policies on eligibility requirements, within the general limits established by law. An upward revision of the budgetary estimate is possible when an adequate appropriation balance exists. If it be near the close of the fiscal year, there may be a sufficient balance to carry on normal operations for the remaining period without revising social service policies. When an unexpected influx of applicants occurs earlier in the fiscal year, established social service policies are sometimes maintained in the hope that subsequent demands will decrease, thus balancing earlier expenditures. Sometimes it is inexpedient to change the internal budget program. In that event a supplementary appropriation may be obtained to meet unusual demands on the assistance agency. There is no doubt that most assistance programs endeavor so far as possible to adjust budgetary policies to the demand for assistance, to keep established eligibility and social service policies intact.

Some change in these policies is necessary, however, when funds are very low and positive control of further commitments is essential. Not to accept additional applications is, of course, a possible expedient; but short of this, a less drastic measure would be to retard the intake process. Applications may be accepted in the order taken or in the order of need. Equally effective may be the raising of eligibility requirements for new applicants. But if these stricter rules are applied without reinvestigating the eligibility of current recipients, the change in policy is unjust to new applicants.

A method similar to raising initial eligibility requirements, but more equitable because it affects the total case load, is the establishment of a minimum level of grants eliminating those whose net need is slight. By this method the agency may determine, for example, to pay no grants when the need of the applicant amounts to less than five dollars per month. The reverse policy may be established by setting a maximum level of grants, regardless of need. The latter policy, however, penalizes those of greatest need, while those whose need is comparatively negligible continue to receive their full grants. A flat-rate cut is similarly inequitable. The fairest method would be to reconsider all awards individually; but this is so time consuming that it is seldom used.

SPECIAL PROBLEMS IN STATE-FINANCED PROGRAMS

State assistance agencies administering centralized programs have problems similar to those of local assistance agencies. In the Iowa and Washington [11] plans, however, the county is regarded as the appropriate unit for some social service activities, and county offices are maintained even though grant authorization is a function of the state. Consequently, these state agencies have found it necessary to recognize the counties by apportioning expenditures among them. Budget control in these state agencies requires not only control over total commitments but adjustment of expenditures in accordance with predetermined county quotas.

[11] The Washington old age assistance program is here treated as observed in 1936.

In Iowa and Washington unobligated assistance funds are apportioned to the counties according to specially developed formulas. One quota scheme is based on three factors: the relative number of unpaid eligible applications on file in each county; the relative number of applicants whose eligibility has not yet been determined; and the relative number of potentially eligible aged population in the county. Where a quota system has been applied, selection of applicants is made according to relative need. This need is established by a somewhat mechanistic scheme and the formula has proved so complicated that adjustment of quotas to compensate for changing conditions has been ignored. The other more equitable formula is based on the relative population of eligible age by counties, modified by classifying applicants according to year of application, so that those who have received no aid for the longest period may be considered first.

The state agency must establish budget control over local expenditures when the assistance programs are financed by the state but administered by the localities. To this end, the Colorado and Mississippi state agencies periodically fix allotments limiting the total amount expendable by each local agency. In Colorado allotments are advanced monthly in cash; but in Mississippi centralized disbursing of assistance grants necessitates only the monthly advance of credit allotments. Colorado had adequate state funds to permit allotments to county agencies in accordance with estimates of actual needs. Mississippi, however, with severely limited state funds, determines allotments by the relative population of the localities. This procedure, based on a fixed formula, is extremely simple. Local agencies are told the amount of their allotment, to continue until further notice, and are responsible for keeping assistance authorizations within that sum. Since each monthly relief roll is prepared in the state office where all disbursement is centralized, the total for each locality is charged against its allotment. A computation of the monthly balance or overdraft, as the case may be, accompanies a copy of the relief roll to the local agency. If a local agency repeatedly overdraws, the state office may notify it to restrict authorizations; otherwise the state office takes no positive action.

The needs basis for distributing state funds to localities in Colorado offers a much more equitable method of allotment than flat apportionment. Estimates of needs, submitted monthly in advance to the state office by the local agencies, contain information on the previous month's expenditures, the number aided, the net amount of assistance, the amount for burials, various receipts, and balance on hand at close of month. From these data the state agency prepares allotments and adjusts prior commitments. The state auditor is then authorized to issue checks to the county treasurers for the funds allotted, and these are deposited in the local old age assistance fund. Since balances or deficits in local funds are considered in making monthly allotments, the obligation of large amounts of state funds in unexpended local balances is eliminated.

Under a plan whereby the state and the localities share costs on a fixed percentage basis, commitment of state funds is largely controlled by the amount of assistance authorized by local units within the limits prescribed by state laws and regulations. In Massachusetts, with adequate funds for state aid, no attempt has been made currently to record commitments against state funds for assistance. Obligations against state funds are not known until annual claims for state aid are received.[12] Budget control of funds for state aid in Indiana, New Jersey, New York, and Wisconsin exists through monthly local-agency reports of assistance expenditures. The following statement[13] illustrates the liberal attitude which obtains in California toward these grants-in-aid, although the plan precludes positive control of local expenditures for assistance, a fixed portion of which is chargeable to state funds.

> Payments to minor civil divisions represent charges against the state government which are beyond executive control. They are fixed charges, either written into the Constitution by action of the people, or written into the Statutes by actions of previous State Legislatures, and are, therefore, not subject to executive control.

STATE REVIEW OF INDIVIDUAL GRANTS

State control of local assistance commitments in Massachusetts, California, New York, New Jersey, Wisconsin, and Indiana lies primarily in the audit,[14] although the audit of local assistance grants ostensibly serves, on the whole, a much broader purpose than the limitation of commitments against state-aid funds.[15] Retrenchment in state budgets in New York in 1933 required close supervision of local grants. A letter to local commissioners of public welfare outlined the

---

[12] Quarterly reports of local expenditures are now being received for purposes of federal reporting.

[13] State of California, *Budget for the Biennium*, July 1, 1937, to June 30, 1939, II, iii.

[14] The federal Social Security Board also uses the audit as its primary means of control of assistance expenditures by the states.

[15] The intensive development of the social audit in Massachusetts, New York, New Jersey, and California, for example, permits a strict enforcement of eligibility requirements by the state agency.

items of eligibility and limitations on grants to be given particular attention, including the responsibility and ability of children and grandchildren to contribute support, the application of a budget schedule, and the fullest use of individual property and assets to minimize the need for public aid.[16] Doubtless these suggestions were closely followed by the state in reviewing individual cases of assistance recipients.[17]

The intensive social audit of individual cases as a method of budgetary control by the state is impractical. The cost, rigidity, and negative character of this method in contrast to broader and more positive forms of supervisory control are arguments against it.[18] In totally state-financed programs this method alone would obviously not suffice to meet budgetary restrictions, since exceptions could not be charged back in full against local funds as is possible when local contributions are made to the program. In Mississippi the social audit is used as a means of budget control, but it is a pre-audit rather than a post-audit—as in New York, New Jersey, California, and Massachusetts[19]—and control of the extent of local obligations is also maintained through allotments. The adoption of an allotment system in connection with proportionate reimbursement might be advisable if state aid is limited. The Wisconsin old age assistance law alone recognizes this contingency and makes provision for meeting it. If the amounts available for state aid are insufficient, the Secretary of State is empowered to prorate available funds among the localities without advance notification to the counties. This situation has arisen, and state aid was prorated, but the state-aid deficiencies were subsequently paid in full.

[16] Letter to commissioners of public welfare from Division of Old Age Security, New York State Department of Social Welfare, January 9, 1933.

[17] The case-audit procedure has been greatly modified in Wisconsin and Indiana to the extent of cursory review in the state office of applications and test checks in the field to assure general compliance with state eligibility and grant requirements. Broader supervision has replaced reliance on this method of control.

[18] For a more detailed discussion of the social audit see chap. 14.

[19] In several of these states local administrators have taken advantage of state case review to obtain state approval of individual cases and therefore of reimbursement in advance of granting assistance; this procedure, in effect, amounts to pre-auditing.

CHAPTER 13

DISBURSEMENT OF ASSISTANCE GRANTS

THE DISBURSING process consists of preparing assistance warrants or checks, distributing them to recipients, and maintaining records of expenditures. Authorization of payments, the preliminary to disbursement, has already been treated. Discussion here will be limited to the procedures involved in making payments to assistance beneficiaries.

ADMINISTRATIVE RESPONSIBILITY FOR DISBURSEMENT

Two major patterns of disbursement appear in the state plans observed. The centralized system, where the function is carried on at one point for the entire state, is employed in Washington,[1] Iowa, Connecticut, Florida, and Mississippi. The decentralized plan, in which payment is handled by each local operating unit,[2] is utilized by Massachusetts, New York, New Jersey, Wisconsin, Indiana, California, and Colorado.

Usually those officials charged with disbursing funds for general government in an administrative area handle social security grants. For example, the state comptroller performs this function in Iowa for the Old Age Assistance Commission; the county comptroller, in Oneida County, New York; the city auditor, in the city of Springfield, Massachusetts; and the town clerks, in small towns of Massachusetts. The old age assistance agency's share of operations varies not only among states with centralized systems but also in states where disbursement is decentralized. The local agency may merely authorize grants, as in Milwaukee County, Wisconsin; it may prepare the warrants and perform many of the operations for the county disbursing officer, as in Los Angeles County, California; or it may itself carry on the total process, as in New York City.

---

[1] As of 1936.
[2] Partial centralization of the disbursing operation at several points for different sections of a state is possible, although none of the state plans observed utilized this method.

The handling of local disbursing operations by fiscal authorities, such as the county clerk, auditor, or comptroller, is satisfactory so long as the volume of work is small; with increasing volume, however, division of functions between the assistance agency and the financial authority may be impracticable. With increasing work the disbursing authority may, for his own convenience, advance the date on which preparation of warrants begins, thus shortening the time during which new authorizations may be made effective within the payment period. For example, one county auditor required the authorized assistance roll on the tenth of the month for payments due the first of the following month. Consequently, an applicant approved for assistance after that date was compelled to wait until the second following month for his first grant. Many agencies with adequate staff and equipment prepare assistance warrants for the disbursing officer in order to speed up the process and extend the time during which new authorizations may be made effective for each payment period.

In a few instances the volume of disbursements has led to special procedures, as in New York City and Boston.[3] In metropolitan local governments the functions of the fiscal office are generally so extensive that disbursement for an activity such as old age assistance is excessively burdensome. Hence by its decentralization to the assistance agency the local fiscal authorities are relieved of the pressure of large-volume disbursement; their work is thus reduced to the issuance of, and accounting for, one warrant periodically rather than thousands.

The handling of disbursing operations by the assistance agency, however, does not of itself guarantee better service. The procedures of one unit disbursing assistance from an imprest fund have become so inflexible that a new grant or change in grant frequently requires two months to become effective. The extent to which decentralization is desirable depends, of course, on the volume of work normally handled by the local fiscal authority and the staff and equipment available. The old age assistance agency may have greater resources of staff and equipment than the local auditor or comptroller, and hence may better be able to carry on this work. There appears to be no guiding rule, and the practices observed seem, in each instance, to be dictated by individual considerations.

In three of the five states studied where assistance disbursement is

---

[3] Although the old age assistance load in Boston does not compare in volume with that of New York City, the Boston Welfare Department handled general relief and mothers' aid which, with old age assistance, account for large-volume disbursing operations.

carried on centrally—Connecticut, Florida, and Mississippi—the state agency disburses directly from its own accounts. The Washington State Welfare Department, as required by law, prepares warrants and keeps accounts, but the state auditor signs all the warrants. In Iowa the assistance agency keeps the detailed disbursement accounts, but the state comptroller prepares and signs the warrants. The allocation of disbursement activity to the state welfare agency is specified by law in Connecticut, Mississippi, and Washington; it is apparently an administrative arrangement in Iowa and Florida.

DISBURSEMENT POLICIES

Since the Social Security Act defines old age assistance as money payments to aged individuals, to be eligible for federal reimbursement assistance grants must necessarily be given in cash or by check,[4] and most states so provide. Prior to the Act many state plans permitted "voucher" relief or relief "in kind" to aged individuals for certain items, and granted state funds in aid of these payments as well as in aid of cash grants. Relief for which voucher or in-kind grants usually replaced cash assistance in these plans was special or seasonal, such as fuel supplies, medicine, and medical care, and occasionally shelter. Voucher or in-kind assistance for such items has some justification. Attempts to budget emergency needs have not been wholly satisfactory since both amount and occurrence are unpredictable. There is also assurance that in voucher payments for these special items recipients actually receive the services authorized and do not divert the funds to other uses. Finally, the mechanics involved in issuing special assistance by voucher or directly in kind are not governed by the necessity of adhering to the normal grant date and grant procedures.

The frequency, commencement, termination, and period of grants may be prescribed by law or by regulation. The common payment period is the month, although one state agency pays weekly for the state as a whole; one large city made weekly payments for some time. The relative merits of the weekly, semimonthly, or monthly payment periods are matters of social policy. Certainly the monthly payment simplifies the work of disbursement. With adequate procedures and the necessary equipment, however, payments may be adjusted to meet whatever period seems socially desirable.

To simplify disbursing and accounting operations, some states do

---

[4] Since no payments in cash have been encountered, the term "check" will be used throughout to cover all types of money payments.

not pay for part of a month, but commence grants for the first full month after official approval of an application. Partial monthly grants add to the work involved in disbursing where mechanical equipment is used,[5] and special adjustments have to be made for a single partial payment; this additional work is not so great, however, that grant-payment policies need be changed. Partial monthly payment at the time of the first grant is most equitable to the recipient. Hence some states compute grants from the date of official award.

Assistance may be given at the beginning or at the end of the disbursing period; but payment in advance generally yields the recipient a full grant sooner. Furthermore, payment is received in the month of death under an advance-grant plan, whereas none is generally made under the second system. Consequently, advance payment of assistance seems socially more desirable.

DISBURSEMENT PROCEDURES

No matter what agency makes the disbursements, to be effective the system must be capable of ready adjustment to changes, additions, and cessations of grants. Ordinary disbursement procedures may be suitable for the payment of most grants, but they may be too inflexible to care for necessary changes. If cancellations or reductions of grants are not expedited, the agency will have to seek recovery of the amounts improperly paid. When customary disbursing procedures do not serve these requirements effectively, some decentralization of the work to the assistance agency may be advisable.

To take care of new grants and changes during the check preparation period, some agencies keep supplemental assistance rolls; the checks to cover these grants are made out after the completion of routine checks. To facilitate smooth operation under this plan, most of the check writing can be completed prior to the deadline.

When the volume of disbursements is large, staggering payments is a time-saving device. In Connecticut, where payments are made weekly, the load is distributed over a five-day schedule by town groupings. This plan eliminates peak loads and slack periods and makes for smoother operation. It is surprising that so few agencies with problems of large-volume disbursing use stagger systems to equalize the burden. Geographical division of the load is possible, although it has some objectionable features: movement of recipients from one district to another periodically requires adjustments of records and files as well

[5] See below, p. 242.

as of the total work load. The division of the load, however, may be made alphabetically by recipients rather than by territory. Of course, any plan for even distribution of the load may be thrown out of adjustment by gross changes in the recipient roll; but the elimination of recurrent periods of overwork and stress in large agencies is important and warrants experimentation to determine a practicable method of distributing payments over several dates.

Manual methods of disbursing assistance grants are justifiable in small agencies. If the volume of grants increases considerably, however, the use of mechanical aids, such as addressing, accounting, and check-writing machines, saves staff time and lengthens the period during which new grants and changes in grant can be put into effect. When to install partial or total mechanical disbursing equipment depends upon the agency. Economy may be achieved if disbursement reports are adapted to machine performance, and if the equipment is also used for statistical operations.

At times, the advantages of mechanical installations may be offset by antiquated procedures. In one large county the assistance agency installed machines to speed up the preparation of warrants, but the county auditor insisted upon numbering warrants by hand and signing them in his own office, thus partially nullifying the advantages of mechanical equipment. In one state agency where check writing is centralized and done mechanically, a ruling of the state attorney general requires all checks to be signed by hand. This task consumes most of the disbursing officer's time. Since it is probably easier to forge a written signature than one machine stamped, such procedural delays seem unnecessary.

Pressure is sometimes exerted to reduce the frequency and number of changes in grants so that mechanical procedures will not be disturbed. The commissioner of one state agency disbursing for the localities suggested that "since we are making [addressing machine] . . . plates of all names sent in on the April pay roll, I trust that the amount given these people will be fixed as you wish to carry them for some time, so that we will not have to make new plates every month." This restrictive attitude is, of course, not the fault of mechanical equipment, but a misconception of the purposes it is to serve.

DELIVERY OF PAYMENTS

Checks are usually mailed to recipients. In Mississippi, however, personal delivery is made because of the inadequate mail facilities in rural areas and the high rate of illiteracy among recipients. Personal delivery gives more assurance that the beneficiary gets the check, but it is time consuming. The same advantage might be gained by requiring recipients to call for payments at local offices, but the hardship to aged beneficiaries living at a distance makes it inadvisable.

Mailing of warrants or checks does not entail much added labor if the addresses of recipients are on the warrants and window envelopes and metering machines are used, but mailing does call for current information on address changes. Conversely, change of location of recipients will be discovered automatically by printing instructions on the envelope not to forward the warrant. When checks are prepared outside, they are frequently returned to the assistance agency for distribution. Although this procedure may seem wasteful when centralized mailing facilities are available for all governmental agencies in the administrative area, it gives the assistance agency an opportunity to make last-minute changes in address and to withdraw warrants where grants have been suspended or canceled during the preparation period.

RECORDS

The data required for disbursing assistance grants vary with disbursement systems, but several basic records are required under all. The authorization is the formal record of the agency empowering the disbursing officer to pay a specified amount to a designated recipient. An assistance roll of all recipients and the amounts to be received is generally prepared by the assistance agency before each payment period. Actually, this roll is a recapitulation of currently effective authorizations for the disbursing officer's convenience in preparing warrants or checks. It also serves as the voucher register of warrants issued, although in some mechanical systems copies of the warrants or checks serve this purpose.

A ledger record of payments to individuals is generally maintained, although the voucher register is sometimes considered sufficient. The usefulness of individual records of payments varies with the complexity of the old age assistance plan. If payments are charged to localities in which the recipients have legal residence or settlement, individual records of payments, and receipts on account of such payments, by or for other localities is necessary. Likewise, it is desirable to have an individual record of payments against which to compute and credit recoveries or refunds and cancellations of assistance. One state agency listed the following reasons why local agencies should keep a ledger record of individual payments:

1. All payments to one individual can be determined from one record.

2. Counties charging payments to other counties will have a record to determine charges.

3. Amounts due from estates (of deceased recipients) may be readily computed.

4. In the event of fraud most courts will accept these records as prima-facie evidence of payment.

These records of individual payments are frequently maintained by the assistance agency but they may be kept by central disbursing and accounting authorities in conjunction with the assistance disbursement. Since individual records of payments are required by the assistance agency for daily reference, duplication of effort may be eliminated if the accounts are maintained solely by that agency.

Because disbursement is generally carried on outside the assistance agency, record-keeping complications often result. If the volume of grants is small, the keeping of detailed records and accounts by the fiscal authority is logical and offers no great problem. As the number of grants increases, the assistance agency is required to keep more accounts and records for its own administrative and reporting operations, and the record keeping of the central fiscal authority becomes burdensome. Duplication of work and records is always expensive, and when two agencies attempt to maintain similar records, additional staff and procedures are necessary to insure accuracy. By a proper division of labor between the assistance agency and the fiscal office needless duplication may be eliminated in the keeping of accounts.

Maintenance of adequate control accounts by the disbursing official offers a protection to the disbursement of funds. By building up predetermined totals from basic documents authorizing new grants, increases, decreases, and cancellations of grants, he can periodically check the amount of the assistance roll. Maintenance of detailed case accounts by the disbursing officer seems unnecessary if they are adequately controlled by the assistance agency.

CENTRALIZED AND LOCAL DISBURSEMENT

Although disbursement is one of the direct or operating activities of old age assistance administration, preparation of assistance checks or warrants does not require direct contact with recipients. Consequently, it can occur at some point remote from the local agency. Preparation and distribution of large numbers of warrants at recurrent intervals are processes which lend themselves to routine or mechanical treatment. Especially is this true when the amount and destination of most payments remain static.

Under these conditions centralized disbursement for a number of local assistance agencies offers certain advantages. Foremost among these is the specialization permitted by a large volume of work—a specialization of both staff and equipment that the disbursing jobs for local areas would not ordinarily justify. Centralization reduces the number of activities for which the locality is responsible and accordingly simplifies local management problems. Where funds are supplied from state and federal sources with little or no local financial participation, there is a tendency toward centralization. Four[6] of the five states without local financial participation in assistance funds disburse centrally. When the custody of all funds for assistance is initially entrusted to the state, central disbursement eliminates fund transfers to the many localities and consequent multiplication of the accounting and supervisory financial activities necessary under local disbursement.

The economies and other advantages of centralization, however, must be weighed against the social requirements of the old age assistance program. The beneficiaries, whatever procedures are followed, expect their grants at current intervals. If living costs rise and the grants are correspondingly increased, this change should be quickly effective. Similarly, other adjustments, such as changes in address, must not be unduly delayed. With removal of disbursement to a central point, the advantages in operating procedures may be offset by decreased service.

Remote operation of disbursement is only as effective as the speed with which communication about adjustments in the grant list can be made from the most inaccessible locality. In Connecticut it is possible to maintain a central disbursing system of weekly payments in which a grant authorized one week is paid the following week or sooner. Yet even here difficulty is encountered in keeping central records abreast of changes in address and cancellations.

A large volume of operations in a centralized disbursement system demands a meticulous development of procedures to insure smooth operation and to reduce procedural errors that take time to adjust by

[6]Connecticut, Iowa, Mississippi, and Washington. Colorado disburses locally, although no assistance funds are supplied by the counties. Florida, at the time of this study, also disbursed old age assistance centrally, but the nonfederal portion was contributed entirely by the counties of the state.

correspondence. Consequently the disbursement activity may be made an end in itself rather than a service to the local agencies through an effort to keep grant changes at a minimum to prevent undue disturbance of the state agency's routine.

Disbursement of assistance by the localities does not preclude their enjoying specialization of staff and equipment. When local disbursing offices expend funds on the authorization of the assistance agency, there is of course specialization of staff. Varying degrees of mechanization in warrant preparation are also found in local systems, depending upon the volume of work. In some large local agencies, such as the departments of public welfare of Boston and New York City, specialization of staff and equipment exceeds that of many of the states observed.

If the local agencies are responsible for determining grants, centralized payment relieves the agency of financial transactions and relationships that are otherwise necessary whether the local agencies disburse directly or through other local officials. Nevertheless, a local agency usually finds it necessary and desirable to maintain case-expenditure accounts for reference purposes even though disbursement is centralized. Consequently, the amount of effort saved by centralization is not so great as might appear from casual consideration of central versus local disbursement. The majority of financial reports and records is continued regardless of centralization or localization of the payment process; but the destination of the records and reports is changed. Cash transactions are largely eliminated by centralization, as well as much auditing work necessary to verify local expenditures when disbursements are decentralized. Nevertheless, individual transactions continue, and the remoteness of central disbursing is a factor to contend with. To correct a single mistake under a centralized system requires much correspondence, whereas under a local system personal contact can effect adjustments at once and thus partially compensate for the procedural weakness that often prevails.

Other types of transactions also occur in a local disbursing system.[7] The bulk of these, however, relates to authorizations, changes, and other grant adjustments, which must continue regardless of disbursing procedure. A centralized system likewise does not eliminate all audit activities when documents substantiating the authorization remain in

---

[7] The additional transactions are generally those having to do with making claims for, and the payment of, state and federal grants-in-aid when the cost of assistance is shared by the locality. If no local funds are involved, requests for, and the payment of, advances from state and federal funds to the locality are a prerequisite to the issuance of assistance checks by the locality.

the local agency. The state must weigh the advantages of simplicity in central disbursing against a possible procedural rigidity necessitated by both volume and distant operations.

To compensate somewhat for remote operation and slowness in making changes in warrants, one state agency returns warrants to the local agencies for delivery. The local agencies may then make any necessary address changes or withhold payments of grants canceled for any reason during the preparation of warrants. Changes in amounts of grants and in grants authorized too late for inclusion in current payments cannot under this plan be adjusted by the local agency, but must await the succeeding period. Another state agency permits the locality to telephone or telegraph changes and new authorizations made during the warrant preparation period. This arrangement permits flexibility in a central disbursing system that equals the best local systems observed.

The relative desirability of central and local disbursement cannot be determined dogmatically. If grants are determined by the state agency, as in Iowa and Connecticut, centralization of disbursement is logical. If local agencies authorize assistance, only careful study of the total administrative system can furnish a basis for judgment. Centralizing disbursement for all units except those few local agencies with large case loads would be an interesting experiment.

SPECIAL PROBLEMS

To protect both recipient and agency, considerable emphasis is placed on the proper endorsement of assistance checks. One state agency made an examination of endorsements early in the program that revealed at least one wrong endorsement in each county. This much publicized report made clear that the authorities would countenance no loose practices. Some agencies send written instructions on proper endorsement along with checks. Others require recipients themselves to pick up the first check, or arrange for its personal delivery. Either system affords an opportunity to explain proper use of the checks. One state agency stamps a notice on the back of its checks to the effect that endorsements other than by signature must be witnessed, and provides spaces for the signatures of witnesses. Card files of recipients' endorsements are universally kept for comparison, although the actual value of thus guarding against improper check use is more theoretical than practical.

Some of the agencies examine check endorsements and bank cancellations from time to time to see whether recipients are using deposit accounts, and, if so, whether the agency has a record of them. One large city department regularly scans check cancellations and occasionally uncovers previously unrecorded assets, such as bank accounts and insurance policies. As a routine practice this is time consuming, although occasionally worth while. Some agencies investigate outstanding checks after a specified period, assuming that if the recipient needs the grant, the check will not long remain uncashed.

Despite requirements by law or regulation that assistance be paid directly to aged individuals, this procedure is not always expedient. Recipients may be incapable of handling funds or too infirm to cash checks conveniently. To meet these situations, guardianship may be established, its nature depending on state law. In some instances, the legal procedure for appointing a guardian is cumbersome. To avoid lengthy or expensive court procedures, some welfare laws provide that persons may be designated as "trustee" for relief recipients. Where this method is used, the check is frequently made payable to the recipient as well as to the trustee, who may cash the check. Such informal fiduciary relationships are seldom assured by bond or other evidence of trust. Although the amounts involved are individually small, they are nevertheless important to the beneficiary. His interests, as well as those of the public, should be protected in trusteeships.

The Social Security Act provides that payments must be made to recipients. This has been interpreted as limiting federal matching to assistance payments made directly to the recipient or a legally appointed guardian. Trusteeships or guardianships without formal legal status are not honored by the Social Security Board in determining grants eligible for federal matching in accordance with the Act. The Act is interpreted to prohibit acceptance of these informal relationships. If the recipient himself is unable to act, procedure for the appointment of legal guardians should be simplified. The volume of work handled by public assistance agencies and the rapid and frequent changes in the status of recipients make a simpler procedure desirable. Moreover, abuses can easily arise where informal procedures are used, which the appointment of legal guardians might prevent. So long, however, as federal matching is withheld on grants to responsible persons not legal guardians of recipients, the use of the trusteeship device is minimized.

CHAPTER 14

AUDITING AND SETTLEMENT OF CLAIMS

MANY STATE PROGRAMS for old age assistance provide for their administration by local agencies under the supervision of the state assistance agency, funds for this purpose being supplied either partly or wholly by the state. Under this arrangement the state agency's responsibility is to see that local agencies carry out the program within legal limitations and supplementary regulations. To accomplish this objective the state agency establishes supervisory controls, some of which are fiscal. While this chapter is limited mainly to auditing control, the discussion concerns primarily those jointly financed state-local systems of old age assistance administration in which disbursement of assistance payments occurs locally.

The exact nature of state supervision is difficult to determine, yet there are obviously differences in the techniques applied. The concept of supervision held by some state agencies is aptly described by the term "concurrent," or "dual," administration. In these plans control is focused on the end products of administrative operation. Hence the aim both of state supervisory efforts and of local administrative activities is leveled at similar objects. In the other concept of supervision state efforts are focused on the functioning of local administration: the state agency oversees the performance of the job rather than controlling the end product. The aim is not the approval or disapproval of each completed task but control of administrative processes and their improvement. The former is negative in approach, the latter, positive and constructive. The distinction made here is not sharply drawn in present methods of state supervision. Confusion of the two concepts often results; it seems to exist especially in state audit of local financial operations. Concepts of financial supervision and control, moreover, have been difficult to swing from detail control to positive supervision.

All state agencies observed disbursing funds on account of locally authorized grants build up records in the state office against which local claims are audited. The manner in which these records are established and the extent to which the state agency relies on the audit of claims from these records differentiate the two major plans of auditing. The relative merits of the audit controls in operation under these major plans and their actual net acomplishments will be examined.

In state supervisory agencies records are established for each recipient on which local claims for funds or credits against advances are audited. The records reflect the amount of grant authorized and date effective, identifying information about the recipient, and the effective date of subsequent grant changes. In addition, other information may be recorded, such as the amount of property, insurance, or other assets of the recipient. The data on grants must be kept up to date to serve the purpose of the state agency in examining the details of claims for correctness. For this purpose local agencies report currently all administrative actions affecting grants and recipients. The states may or may not accept this information without further examination as evidence that a grant has been made to a client in the amount reported; that the client is eligible according to all requirements of law and regulations; that all duly required procedures have been complied with; and that the amount of the grant as made is necessary. Of course, where assistance administration is delegated to local agencies, officials in charge presumably administer the activity in accordance with state laws and regulations, even though devices of state supervision and control are lacking.

In general, two types of auditing plans are observed in the states where assistance is administered locally but state supervised and supported. One plan correlates audit activities with state review of individual cases, utilizing the case-review operations as an integral part of audit control. The other type is not predicated on review of cases, but provides only for an audit of financial transactions.

AUDIT OF CLAIMS BY INDIVIDUAL CASE CONTROL

Some state plans for supervising local operations take as a point of departure questioning the capability of local administrators to grant assistance in accordance with law and regulations. This concept of state supervision probably intends not to reflect on the ability of local administrators and their staff but rather to recognize the difficulty of administering assistance in accordance with eligibility and need requirements subject to wide interpretation. To assure full compliance with grant requirements, these state agencies do not accept local authorizations as sufficient sanction for disbursing state funds. They feel that additional confirmation of the legality of local grants is required since theirs is the responsibility for allowing state aid on account of local expenditures. Consequently, these states, prior to allowing claims for state aid focus their supervisory efforts on reviewing all grants locally authorized.

This method of supervising is aptly termed "social audit," for it questions the local authorization of assistance and examines the data behind local actions for proof of compliance with state law and regulations.[1] Under this plan the state social service staff concentrates on continuous and current case review, frequently with the avowed object of improving local techniques of social investigation and administrative interpretation of social data, but actually to approve or disapprove the action in each case to allow claims for state aid. The findings of state case reviewers are reflected in case-audit records, which become a register of state grant authorizations for which aid may be allowed. The audit of local claims against records established in this manner gives the appearance of a thorough and intensive examination in which all items not allowable for state aid have been caught by the case review.

Audit of claims from individual case records has weaknesses that are often obscured by the superficial precision of state procedure. Predicated on a review of local records—often made from transcripts submitted to the state by local agencies—the audit is no more valid as a means of assuring the disbursement of state assistance funds to eligible cases in amounts actually needed than are the records on which social review and state authorization of aid are based. This fact is partially recognized in some instances in which the review of cases is carried to the local agencies, where social facts in addition to those recorded may be obtained by discussion with local workers. In one state the state case reviewers visit all clients at least once prior to the granting of state aid in order to verify the contents of local case records by consulting original data. The duplication by the state of activities for which local agencies are established is obvious. In all instances current state review of eligibility and of need substitutes state discretion for local discretion in the interpretation of data. Moreover, there is no guarantee that decisions of state case reviewers, based on recorded data alone, are more equitable than those of local administrators.[2]

[1] For further discussion of this technique of supervising the local service program and an appraisal of its effectiveness for this purpose see chap. 8.

[2] It should be noted that prior acceptance of individual cases for state aid gives the state agency some control over local commitments of state-aid funds since the state agency may reduce these potential claims by a stricter interpretation of eligibility requirements and need in the case-review process.

Control by detailed social and financial audit before granting state aid has many defects besides stimulating unwarranted confidence in its results. The process is costly, cumbersome, and destructive to local initiative. As analyzed in one state for a given period the cost of personnel to carry on the examination of claims was ten times as much as the total of disallowed claims. Furthermore, the time of the social service staff engaged in case review, the time of local staffs in duplicating local records for reporting to the state, and the time consumed in adjusting misunderstandings of the interpretation of local reports all add to the costs of advance review. The examination of claims is frequently delayed because full case data are not reported to state case reviewers by the local agencies; thus the financial data in the state office that result from action of the case reviewers may not agree with claims on all individual cases submitted by local agencies. The unfortunate effects on local administrative initiative and operations are the strongest arguments against financial control by case review.

In several states where aid depends upon the case reviewers' acceptance of local authorizations, some local agencies withhold payment of grants until state approval has been obtained.[3] State agencies are frequently unaware of this practice, but try to discourage it when brought to their attention. Local agencies, on the other hand, realize that detailed case audit by the state prior to approving claims for aid offers an opportunity to obtain a pre-audit of local expenditures. Since state case review is a continuous and current operation, the local agencies can often await state approval without too much delay in paying new or revised grants. This practice amounts to shifting determinative responsibilities from the local administrator to the state staff. In one state that reimbursed monthly, a large county did not make payments of grants until state aid was received for the assistance roll submitted, thus enabling it not only to obtain a pre-audit of all state relief expenditures but also to receive its reimbursement in advance of expenditure. This practice is equivalent to state administration under the guise of state supervision.

The audit records in several of these states include not only state approvals or disapprovals of cases but also ledger accounts of payments to individuals posted from audited monthly assistance reports. Attention to establishing its own detailed records often blinds the state agency

[3] Although observations of methods of pre-auditing claims based on intensive case review were limited to states granting state aid by the reimbursement method, there is no apparent reason to believe that granting state aid in advance of local expenditures will necessarily eliminate this particular practice.

to local record conditions. In one instance the state had much more detailed records of individual payments than one of its large counties. Apparently the state was either unaware or unconcerned that this anomalous situation existed.

Concentrating the state's supervisory efforts on case review is not a satisfactory means of improving local administrative methods and techniques. Some states attempt to combine positive assistance to, and supervision of, local agencies with individual case review. For example, several state agencies supervising by case control review the reasons for withdrawing and denying assistance, although such matters as guaranteeing proper use of state funds are beyond the scope of a financial audit. Advice on administrative matters and questions of local procedure is sometimes given local agencies. The extent of the case-review task, however, precludes placing much emphasis on positive supervision of local administrative methods. Combining administrative supervision with case review generally tends to lessen the intensity of the latter and hence to destroy much of its validity as a control device.

AUDIT OF CLAIMS WITHOUT CASE CONTROL

The other major plan of supervision places administrative responsibility upon local agencies, leaving the state accountable for advising local agencies on policies and procedures. With the emphasis of state supervision on broad administrative practices, it is impossible to audit local claims for state-aid funds by intensive case reviews without establishing a dual social service staff to perform this work. The aim of state supervision is sound administration by strengthening local investigative and administrative staffs. The audit process nevertheless utilizes much the same machinery as case-control.

Under this plan centrally maintained audit records are established from reports of locally authorized grants or changes of grants. Several state agencies receive copies of applications as well.[4] The reports on authorized grants are generally copies of individual authorizations. These data are posted on cards against which local claims are periodically audited. The content of this type of audit may be readily analyzed. Copies of the local grant lists are received and audited regularly against the state audit cards—a monthly procedure in the states observed. If grants listed do not conform to the record of authorized amounts exception is taken and the inconsistency reported to the local

[4] If copies of applications are received, they may be evidence that a person exists who has requested a grant. But there is no assurance that this evidence is more valid than a certification to the same-effect by a local administrator.

agency for adjustment. Claims are paid local agencies immediately when due, including any items excepted. If the exceptions cannot be subsequently adjusted, disallowed amounts are deducted from succeeding claims. Since the records against which the state agency checks local grant lists are established from documents upon which the local grant list is based, this state audit is for all practical purposes a verification of the accuracy of local computations but not a check on the validity of claims.

State agencies using this type of claims audit do not rely solely on a cursory examination. In several a field-audit staff works with the local agencies. The field audit in one state consists of examining local disbursement records to verify amounts reported to the state. In another a more comprehensive field examination embodies reconciling local assistance expenditures with amounts reported for state aid, an examination of canceled checks, including test checks of endorsements, names of payees, and an investigation of outstanding warrants to determine whether assistance is needed. Field auditors often give advice to local agencies on financial methods. Misunderstandings are set straight on the spot; consequently delays entailed in adjustment by mail are avoided.

The type of state financial control which accepts local administrative grant actions as sufficient basis for payment of state-aid claims releases the field staff from case-review activities and allows time to improve local operations by consultation with local agencies. It cannot be claimed that this plan is a less effective control of local expenditures of state funds than the plan previously described. The intensive office claims audit subsequent to approvals of individual cases is no more reliable than the local records from which state audit records are established. Furthermore, these intensive case-audit plans make no provision for verifying that expenditures have actually been made locally. The validity of audit plans that eliminate individual case approval prior to audit rests not on office examination of claims but on subsequent post-audits in the field or on the threat of a post-audit. The assurance of adequate financial control rests on verification of essential facts about expenditures by examining original records and documents. By each step that the audit is removed from local records, its value as a financial control is diminished. Nevertheless, much confidence is still placed in remote examination of record transcripts. The intricacies of the process seem to lend authority to its results and at the same time obscure its inherent weaknesses.

OFFICE-AUDIT VERSUS FIELD-AUDIT METHODS

An examination of centralized office auditing and of field auditing is necessary to determine which offers the more satisfactory solution to the problem of protecting public funds. The method of auditing must also be considered in its effects on local financial operations and the extent to which settlement of claims is delayed.

At first hearing, defenses of remote examination of state-aid claims by an office audit based on individual financial data cards often seem plausible, but the arguments do not stand up under analysis. A state official of an agency carrying on an office audit of old age assistance claims—for which purpose over 30,000 individual records were being maintained in addition to a field examination after payment—justified this claims audit by the following arguments:

First, if the detailed pre-audit were abandoned in favor of a thorough plan of post-auditing local expenditures, county auditors would demand a larger staff. The implication that state examination relieves local officials of maintaining an adequate organization does not merit consideration as an argument in favor of a claim-auditing system.

Second, by means of the office audit the state agency could check the legality of payments for proper authorization, since copies of such certificates and of the formal action of the local board were received by the state office. This argument may be accepted in favor of the plan, although a test check of authorizations is an essential part of a field examination and much more reliable when done in the field where it is coupled with a corresponding test check of applications, accounting entries, and cashed checks.

Third, the office audit might not control fraud in expenditures, but it would exert a psychological check upon county administrators. This argument also has a certain validity, but the anticipation of a field audit would have an even more salutary effect on local practice.

Fourth, claims examination in the state office would promote balanced operation of the several locally administered assistance programs, since it is readily apparent to the state office from the grant lists if one program is emphasized to the detriment of others. Such administrative data, however, may be obtained in greater detail and more readily from current statistical reports on local agency operations. The development of audit methods to supply data that are properly the responsibility of the statistical staff is either a duplication of effort or a grave reflection on the caliber and effectiveness of the statistical staff.

Fifth, an adequate staff to carry on the field audit would increase personnel costs not only for additional salaries and travel costs but for time consumed in travel. It is true that the cost of clerical work entailed in examining grant lists and claims for state aid against individual audit records in the state office and of establishing and maintaining these records as well as the expense of duplicating and transmitting required local records, authorizations, and grant lists would probably amount to a sum less than the cost of a field-audit staff. But a small field staff offers much more value for the amount expended even though audits may not be made so frequently as might be desired. A fairly detailed audit of financial records and documents in the counties is made by one state agency quarterly with a staff of three field auditors for a total case load of over 50,000 in three categories.

Finally, it was argued that a small clerical staff in the state office could perform the routine examination of local grant lists and claims more expediently; thus the field staff would have more freedom for consultation with the local agencies and for carrying on the discretionary part of the audit. In this instance the discretionary part of the audit apparently referred to verification of the entire local financial situation by test check. The time saved the field auditors by routine examination of monthly grants case by case in the state office is probably exaggerated. A complete test check of selected cases through all procedures and transactions would adequately review the local situation in contrast to the superficial examination of grant lists and authorizations in the state agency. As for guidance to the local agencies, the more complete the review of local procedures by field auditors, the better the basis for advice.

Centralization of audit control in the state agency, remote from original local records, obscures the effect of audit procedures on local financial operations. The development of the audit based on individual case review—in conjunction with reimbursing state aid—offers opportunity for a detailed examination of data supporting local claims prior to allowing state aid. A detailed pre-audit impedes local operations by holding up claims payment for periods of six months to a year or longer. The effect on local finances is obvious. To avoid these delays one state agency takes exception to claim items but allows payment for the net claim, with subsequent adjustment of irreconcilable differences. In effect, this method is a pre-audit of the regularity and correctness of the claim itself and a post-audit of the propriety of the claim by means of case review. This practice, however, resulted from circumstance rather than analysis of the problem. A change in the reimbursement period to monthly settlement forced the state agency to expedite its pre-audit, for the counties' financial condition did not permit a long lapse between expenditures and reimbursement.

State agencies not utilizing individual case-review audit methods have a clearer conception of what is administratively practicable in a pre-audit of state-aid claims and of what should be left for later examination. The routine examination of social data in individual cases is discarded, and the pre-audit of claims by the state agency amounts to an examination of computations and of the regularity of individual grant authorizations. Obvious disallowances for grants in excess of legal limitations can, of course, be made. Receipt and examination of individual applications in several states have no actual significance despite protestations to the contrary by officials in these state agencies. On the basis of this pre-audit, claims are paid. Verification, however, is made by field post-audit of local records of disbursements and balances. This method of auditing permits relatively speedy payment of claims and defers detailed verifications for post-auditing.

When state aid is advanced to local agencies, the procedure for settling claims does not distress current financial operations in the local agencies for lack of anticipated state aid. Several states that reimburse their share of assistance costs now advance the funds received in federal grants-in-aid. In one state, formerly an exponent of the detailed pre-audit of claims and individual case review, the pre-audit has been reduced to a brief examination of compliance with prescribed form, and verification of claims has been established through later field examinations. Several other states have shifted to an advance granting of state aid with subsequent reconciliation by audit.

Examination of state audit plans leads to the conclusion that greater responsibility is placed in office examinations than is warranted; that office examinations require excessive record-keeping and duplication of original records found in local agencies; that detailed audits before paying state aid strain local financial operations by delaying reimbursements; and, that if the state agencies have established a field post-audit the pre-audit in the state office offers no protection. Consequently, a logical development is the replacement of all office auditing by a field post-audit. Payment may be made on the receipt of local claims supported by schedules detailing individual grants. These schedules may then serve as the basis for verification of claims by the subsequent field audit. Experience with this type of audit control in emergency relief administration recommends it for categorical assistance programs.

SCOPE OF THE AUDIT

In general the question of what data are subject to audit has not been clarified by state agencies. Old age assistance laws prescribe eligibility qualifications.[5] Verifying an applicant's eligibility requires searching out and evaluating social data—processes of social case work. Moreover, authentication of many items may rest upon an evaluation of inferential data. The acceptance of what may constitute proof of certain items is frequently discretionary. The responsibility for this is placed on the local administrator—within the limits of state regulation—and often delegated by him to a trained staff. In addition to eligibility the law or regulations generally prescribe procedures to be followed by the local agency.[6] An investigation of the applicant's claims to eligibility must be made and recorded, and formal action taken on this information.

Which of the limitations on granting assistance are proper subjects of a fiscal audit is debatable.[7] To question a local administrator's discretion in determining all phases of need and eligibility after thorough investigation is not within the scope of the financial audit in verifying local claims to state aid. The distinction between auditing claims and inquiring into the propriety of local administrative decisions is clearly marked in states that review individual cases as part of state-aid control. For case-review purposes these states employ personnel specialized in social work techniques; for the remaining audit financial staffs are employed. States auditing claims against local grant-authorization reports perform a purely financial audit. If the audit goes behind the authorization to question the action of the local administrators, a staff trained in social work techniques is necessary.

In an audit for claim verification items that may properly be examined are those in which the discretion of the local authority is not replaced by that of the state auditing staff in matters of social work practice and administrative judgment. A distinction must be made between the area requiring professional supervision and that in which

---

[5] See chap. 6.

[6] See chap. 7.

[7] It must be kept in mind that the type of audit discussed here is designed to maintain state control of the amounts of state aid due localities and of its payment on account of assistance granted to recipients. It is conceivable that the audit might extend to every action in granting assistance. If this were done as a routine matter, it would be much more expedient for the state agency to assume all operating functions. The state agency, however, must delegate some of the operations—some responsibility must be imposed on subordinate units. Therefore, to question the propriety of all local decisions seems unnecessary and undesirable unless evidence of maladministration appears.

the audit staff may function without presuming on social work aspects of local operations. Since it is impractical for auditors to determine the existence of recipients by visit, in their current verification of the validity of claims for state aid, and since it is not their general responsibility to question administrative evaluation of social data and evidence, the results an audit can show conclusively are two: that the reported local assistance funds have actually been disbursed, and that expenditures have been within the legal maximum, if any. Beyond these, the certification of responsible local authorities must be accepted as evidence of legality unless a thorough investigation is made by a staff professionally competent to review local decisions. Certain matters of procedure, however, may be included in the scope of the audit. If formal applications are required, the audit may ascertain that one is on file for each case receiving a grant. If a record of investigation is required, the audit may determine that such a record exists, but to go further impinges on the area of professional supervision. A certification should be evidence that investigation as required by law has been made. Since such a statement in conjunction with a certification that the individual is eligible for assistance is generally a part of the grant authorization, examination of supplementary certifications by the audit staff seems unnecessary. The audit should verify grant authorizations, of course, as well as subsequent accounting entries, cashed checks or warrants, and balances, indicating that payments in the amounts authorized and to the extent reported have been made.

If a thorough examination of local expenditures is contemplated, the audit staff should be supplemented by professional staff familiar with problems and techniques of social case work. The financial staff may then examine local financial records and practices while the professional staff inquires into investigational records and procedures to evaluate the propriety of awards. If evidence is insufficient, the professional staff may visit clients to confirm or supplement the investigational record. This means of examining local operations is not practicable as a routine method of verifying claims, but it may be resorted to whenever the state agency has doubts about local efficiency.[8]

AUDIT OF SPECIAL TYPES OF CLAIMS

Of the twelve states observed[9] only New York and Colorado gave state aid toward local administrative expenses. Mississippi, Florida,

---

[8] Such a procedure should be considered an investigation rather than an audit.

[9] As of December, 1936.

Washington, and Iowa granted all financial support excepting limited local contributions for quarters and occasional supplies.

In New York and Colorado the localities were responsible for their own administrative costs, and state aid was granted only on a matching basis for specified expenditures. The problem of determining items eligible for state aid was partly resolved by law and regulation.

In Colorado the law limited aid to one-half local expenditures for personnel administering assistance, including both salary and traveling expenses. New York legally limited state aid to one-half the salary and traveling expenses of old age assistance staff and to one-half of other administrative costs approved by the state department of social welfare. Although items of administrative expense seem clear cut in contrast to assistance expenditures, it has been difficult to define proper expenses of administration for state-aid purposes. For example, anomalous situations have arisen in which equipment rentals were proper claims for state aid while capital expenditures for similar items were not, although the rentals might exceed purchase cost. Likewise, it has been difficult to determine definitely what personnel are engaged in the task of administering assistance. A broad construction of administrative costs would consider as proper objects of state aid the personal service items of many local authorities, such as the county treasurer, county clerk, etc., engaged in rendering service to the local assistance agency. But cost analyses have been largely limited to administrative expenses of the local assistance agency alone.

In New York the audit of local claims for administrative expenditures was performed in the state office in much the same manner as that of claims for assistance. Since this state applied case review or social audit to all items submitted, approval of local administrative expenditures by state administrative officials formed the basis for the audit of these claims. The same delays entailed by individualized state review in the audit of assistance claims were also encountered in the audit of administration claims. Since such items as personnel and equipment, which served several local programs, had to be allocated proportionately, the state agency utilizing the office audit had no means of verifying the correctness of allocations or of assuring that the amounts claimed had actually been spent.

Colorado depended on field audits to verify claims after payment. Aid for local administration was limited by law to one-half the expenditure for personnel and travel made in accordance with regulations of the state agency. Although no audit had been made at the time this plan was observed, field-audit schedules had been prepared. They provided for verifying actual expenditure transactions and checking such matters as the method of computing mileage and their correctness. The schedule, however, ignored the vastly more important questions whether personnel had been approved by the state agency and whether salary schedules followed the state-prescribed classification.

With the advent of federal aid for administration, many states allotted a portion of it to local agencies but made little attempt to control its use. Audits were, therefore, confined primarily to verifying the total expenditures reported without regard to object of expenditure.[10] The federal agency, of course, had not intimated that the states should use this money in any particular manner or to improve local administration. Without state definitions of use, audit control of objects of expenditure was ineffective.

The major emphasis of state audit plans was on the verification of local claims for state aid. The state agency, however, was at times in the position of holding claims against the localities for its share of recoveries from estates of deceased recipients, of refunds of aid granted, and of cancellations of checks or warrants issued for assistance for which state aid had been claimed. Several state agencies recorded on state audit cards at the time of local grants the amount of liens against holdings of assistance recipients. Upon notice of death or withdrawal of assistance these data afforded a clew to the state's share of potential recoveries.

The audit plans based on case reviews were additionally checked by the state supervisors' examination of the case record to ascertain potentially recoverable assets. Local actions subsequent to death were thus reviewed, and the case was held open by the state until its share was received or until a satisfactory explanation of the disposition of the claim was made by the local administrator. In this connection the social audit gives the state information about potential assets through which pressure may be brought on local agencies to collect all possible recoveries. But this advantage over audit controls not employing individual case review is outweighed by the fact that no field audits are provided whereby actual revenue items can be verified and proper accounting of the state's share of such recoveries can be assured.

State agencies not utilizing individual case control relied primarily upon field-audit verification of local reports of recoveries, cancellations, and refunds. If local agencies do not enforce recovery provisions, the

[10] Wisconsin required that this aid be applied against local personnel costs. Current reports were received on local administrative expenditures and verified by field audit.

state, of course, may have no knowledge of potential losses of revenue from this source. Nevertheless, examination of local revenues from recoveries and cancellations of warrants assures the state its due share if any income is received locally. In view of the relatively small amounts involved, this seems the soundest plan.

Payment of funeral expenses out of old age assistance funds is a local charge, reimbursable in some instances from state funds. The same audit procedure is applied to such claims as for other items. In states using social case-review control, detailed local reports on the deceased recipient's assets, ability of relatives to pay, etc., are received and examined by the case-review staff before the financial audit. The audit of claims for funeral and burial expenses in other states generally consists of a financial examination of the claim and its payment and a subsequent field audit. Yet in one state the state social work staff reviewed detailed reports on relatives' ability to pay and the value of the deceased recipient's estate before aid was allowed. The field audits, on the other hand, were not intensive in scope, and much reliance was placed on the state agency's audit cards. This situation shows a confusion of the concepts of control by supervision and control by dual administration.

In these miscellaneous claims it seems evident that the most effective plan of control is the payment of claims after examination, with subsequent post-audit at the place of expenditure for final verification.

RELATION OF AUDIT STAFF TO OTHER STATE SUPERVISORY PERSONNEL

The state financial staff audits claims to verify details of expenditures. State agencies have the problem of integrating this control with other administrative controls. Since the audit's direct effect may be an allowance or disallowance of state aid, local agencies often ask the audit staff for advance opinions to avoid potential disallowances.

To conduct general supervisory control of local administration, state agencies have a social service staff [11] operating in the agency or, more generally, in the field. As the main contact between state and local agencies, this staff is generally regarded by the localities as the personification of the state agency. The addition of staff to perform audit functions either in the office or in the field tends to confuse this relationship.

---

[11] As indicated in chap. 4, most state agencies cannot afford both a social service staff and an administrative staff; hence the social service staff is generally clothed with the responsibility for administrative relations with local units. In this section, this staff will usually be referred to as the social service field staff for purposes of emphasis.

The audit operation inevitably raises questions that can be settled only after consultation with the local agency. Frequently the reconciliation of differences involves establishing new policy or interpreting current policy, for the local agency tends to revise its practices to assure state aid.

Those state agencies subordinating the financial audit of claims to review of requests for state aid by a state case-review staff have generally maintained a single line of control between the state and local agencies through the state social service staff. Financial questions are taken up with localities through the case-review staff rather than by the audit staff directly. At times, this coordination of all negotiations with local agencies by one staff is circumvented. The development of administrative field staffs in states not utilizing case-review controls tends to separate the audit of claims and local financial transactions from such staffs. In these states the audit is exclusively fiscal and not concerned with local case-record content. Consequently, the separation of the state's financial staff from the technical and professional staff is distinct. The financial staff, however, may gain entirely different impressions of local operation and the acceptability of local administration for state aid than the professional field staff and as a result conflicting opinions may be given to local agencies. To avoid this, coordination of state supervisory activities is essential.

The professional state social service staff is generally recognized as the paramount representative of the state agency and is generally held responsible for supervising the promulgation of state policy. It is this staff with which local administrators regularly come in contact and to which they look for professional advice and leadership. As such, it should be the medium for all state agency transactions with localities. But to burden this staff with technical financial matters is impractical. The solution of the problem, therefore, seems to lie in working out a dual relationship in financial matters by which the financial staff handles technical fiscal problems with the full knowledge and approval of the state social service staff. Of course, the audit staff should be free to discuss doubtful matters with the local administrator and give whatever technical advice and assistance it can, informing the social service staff of any important matters. This type of relationship has recently been adopted by Wisconsin, where much of the state auditing work is carried on in the field. Seldom can the social service field staff be in the county during the audit process; but it is informed, nevertheless, of the agencies in which audits are to be made and of the findings. The social service field staff or the audit staff—with the full knowledge and approval of the social service staff—interprets these findings to the local administrator. Contradictory state opinions are thus forestalled, and the social service field staff maintains its function as the channel through which state supervision of local agency operations flows.

It is inadvisable for an audit staff to examine the discretionary basis of local assistance authorizations. When the financial audit or the social service field staff uncovers situations indicative of faulty administration, provision must be made for an intensive coordinate examination of local operations by a state staff composed of both types of personnel— the financial staff covering financial transactions and records, the social service staff examining social case-work techniques, records, and local administrative decisions. To perform this examination, coordination of the state social service and financial staffs is essential. Working concurrently in the local agency, this combined staff can produce more reliable facts on all phases of local-agency operations than any system of routine state case review or remote financial audit.

Thus a program of state supervision subordinating audit control to general supervisory control serves to protect the integrity of state policy and prevent the confusion that results from dealing with several state staffs. In addition, this coordination of audit control with social service supervision gives the state agency a means to investigate thoroughly all local operations whenever necessary.

STATE AUDIT CONTROL AND OTHER AUDITS

In analyzing the state audit of local-agency transactions as a means of assuring regularity and the verification of claims for state aid, one cannot ignore other audit controls that frequently apply to local assistance agencies. Except where funds are disbursed by the state agency on local authorizations—under centrally administered state programs— local agencies are generally subject to some local audit. Disbursement of assistance funds is generally by local fiscal officials upon the assistance agency's authorization. Often the local disbursing official is responsible for auditing the financial operations of local spending agencies. If not, other provision is made for audit either by the local governing body, such as the board of supervisors, by a local auditor, or by an independent agency on a contractual basis. The local audit is often unsatisfactory, but the duty to perform it remains. In most instances the responsible local official takes part in disbursing assistance. Although a complete and regular post-audit of local assistance transactions is the exception, an examination of grant authorizations prior to payment is often made.

It may be no more than a review of individual authorizations for form and a comparison of the current grant schedule with approved authorizations, but it is potentially as effective as the state comparison of grant lists against copies of local authorizations prior to payment of claims for state aid. One argument for this type of state examination—that otherwise local auditors would demand more staff—indicates that state audit methods tend either to reduce the responsibility of local audit authorities or to duplicate local work. Even if the local audit is only made occasionally, it may be a valuable safeguard against abuses and irregularities.

In addition to local audits, an audit of all local expenditures is sometimes made by a state agency, such as the Bureau of Municipal Accounts of the New York State Department of Audit and Control and the Indiana State Board of Accounts. Although these agencies may not perform this function regularly, nevertheless liability to such an examination may induce better local financial administration. Consequently, local spending agencies may often find themselves subject to general examinations of financial transactions by local and state authorities in addition to the specialized state and federal audits. Although each audit authority may have a different concept of purpose, complete duplication of activities does not of itself lead to economical operation and effective control. It is unnecessary for the state assistance agency or other audit authorities to give up the auditing function entirely; its importance as a device in a well-rounded supervisory and control pattern is too great. A state assistance agency should, however, be aware of the scope and purpose of other audit authorities, state and local, and should eliminate unnecessary duplication of operations.

An important phase of audit control needs mention here: the audit of state assistance activities by state audit authorities. The amount of funds now involved in state public assistance programs demands the safeguards that an audit can provide. It is not within the province of this brief discussion to consider the merits of such state auditing controls. Whatever audit safeguards are provided for other state spending agencies should obviously apply to the assistance agency. In those states with long-established programs this principle is apparently observed, but in others the recently established agencies seem to be divorced from general state financial controls. The constructive aid of such an audit depends largely on the administrator. If he recognizes that it is a protection to himself and to his administration, as well as to the state, the results may be more significant than if he merely considers it a necessary inquisition. A constructive and impartial audit may yield the state administrator side lights on his administration that he himself would be unable to obtain otherwise.

THE FEDERAL AUDIT

Purpose and Organization

Federal audit of state old age assistance expenditures is one of the Social Security Board's important controls designed to assure strict observance of the Social Security Act's provisions, as well as to maintain a check upon the accuracy of state accounts in the settlement of federal-aid claims. The audit is conducted by a field staff of the Bureau of Accounts and Audits and involves inspection of four classes of records: [12]

> (a) Fund accounts of the State, in which a summary review is made to determine the accountability for Federal funds as to receipt, expenditure, and balance on hand; (b) individual case files or history cards of beneficiaries, in which a verification is made of the eligibility of persons granted assistance; (c) disbursement accounts and supporting records in which a detailed audit is made of payments to beneficiaries in accordance with the requirements of the Social Security Act and the State Act and plan as approved by the Social Security Board; and (d) receipt accounts or related records in which an audit is made respecting any recoveries from estates of recipients of old age assistance. The books of accounts and records examined by the Federal auditors usually include: The general ledgers for appropriations, allotments, or funds, and related subsidiary records; case files of beneficiaries (application, investigators report and certificate of award); payrolls of beneficiaries; warrant or check registers; redeemed warrants or checks; and bank or other depository statements.

Schedules of federal auditors' exceptions are submitted to the state agency and to the regional representative of the Bureau of Public Assistance. After examining these exceptions, the state agency may present supplementary information to the auditors, who will, if satisfied, withdraw the exceptions. The revised report is then submitted to the Bureau of Public Assistance, and further adjustments may be made. The remaining exceptions considered fair and reasonable by the Bureau are submitted to the Board for its approval. It may accept the report, or, if the state appeals, may undertake further consideration of the evidence.

Relation of Federal and State Audits

When state old age assistance operations are decentralized, the federal audit often duplicates the state's. When as extensive and as thorough as

[12] From statement of instructions to federal auditors.

that of the state, the federal audit undermines the state audit and weakens state supervision. Local as well as state officials frequently attribute to the federal audit requirements for which they do not wish responsibility. State agencies may even use the federal audit as an excuse for forcing administrative practices or standards upon local agencies. Obviously, such a procedure vitiates initiative and responsibility in the state agency.

Overlapping of federal and state audits has been of concern to the Board, and steps have been taken to solve this problem by cooperative relations with state audit staffs.[13] No uniform method has been adopted, but if the state audit meets a satisfactory standard, an arrangement along one of the following lines may be made:

1. Mixed staff of federal and state auditors performing the audit under joint federal and state supervision.

2. Separate staffs of federal and state auditors performing different audit functions under divided supervision.

3. Separate staffs of federal and state auditors performing entire audits in specific local units, or for alternate periods in all local units.

4. Federal auditors using acceptable state reports and modifying their procedures accordingly.

Function of the Audit as a Control Device

The audit as a control device is especially important when grants of millions of dollars are involved. Federal administrative supervision is not, and can never be, a static and clearly defined control. A strong, well organized, and efficient state government may need only an occasional suggestion and routine checkup to see that satisfactory standards are maintained; the weaker states, however, with lower standards of administration, need a strong guiding hand and more intensive investigation. The audit may be a valuable source of information to both state and federal agencies when they are working in harmony, as well as a device for enforcing adherence to standards. It may reveal significant weaknesses in state administrative procedures.

[13] Although cooperative working relationships may eliminate some duplication of staff effort, there remains the question whether the federal audit by auditing in accordance with the state plan as well as the federal Act should thereby give force to matters purely in the province of state law and regulation. The nature of a state plan, whether a contract or a statement of objectives, has not been categorically determined by the Social Security Board. The informality by which many state actions are incorporated in plans and the frequency of revisions seem to mark the plan as an informational statement of practices, procedures, and objectives so far as the Bureau of Public Assistance is concerned; but the audit of state accounts, by the Bureau of Accounts and Audits, for conformity with plan material conceives the plan as a contract.

On the other hand, let us point out that the very simplicity and sanction of the audit may give it a predominance not entirely desirable. This tendency toward overemphasis is particularly strong because adjustment of federal grants results directly from the audit. Since individual assistance grants depend to a great extent upon administrative determinations of evidence of variable significance,[14] examination of single cases is apt to project the auditors into a review of administrative discretion and decisions beyond the scope of their function.

The extent of the audit will necessarily vary from state to state, depending on administrative standards. In a program's early years, when standards and precedents have not been fully developed, it is justifiable to conduct a more detailed audit than may be necessary or appropriate after the program is well established. The federal audit should be sufficiently intensive to provide a reasonable degree of protection against illegal or improper expenditures. If the quality of the state administration is in question, it may be advisable to extend the audit beyond ordinary fiscal investigation and inquire into the eligibility of assistance recipients. In this event, the status of recipients should be inspected by staff experienced in evaluating social evidence, with a concurrent examination of pertinent financial records by auditors.

The Federal Audit as a Supervisory Technique

It has already been pointed out that one of the fundamental problems of audit use in supervision is the difficulty of adapting it to a program in which many of the factors determining disbursement of funds are dependent upon evaluation of social evidence. While facts about purchase of equipment, for example, can be verified by relatively objective criteria, a subjective evaluation operating to qualify an individual for a specific assistance grant may be difficult to review by an objective standard. To a certain extent, the uniform application of objective criteria is incompatible with individual treatment of each applicant. The federal audit originally encompassed all factors of eligibility including need. For the most part, however, subsequent audits have presumed need and have not undertaken to review the case worker's findings in this respect. Examination of other eligibility items, however, continues to be a point of contention. In a program which is still experimental, policies and rules and regulations are broadly stated; until more specific interpretations are developed through experience, auditors, if they review in-

---

[14] The process of establishing eligibility for assistance and of determining grants is described in chap. 8.

dividual case records, must inevitably evaluate eligibility factors to some extent. When these interpretations are accepted by the supervisory agency and result in financial adjustment, they tend to become established as future operating policy. Interpretation of state and federal requirements is the function of state and federal service staffs, and the feeling that an auditor may make decisions independently tends toward confusion and antagonism.

The relation of the Social Security Board to state operating units in a public assistance program differs from that of the state to the local agency. The state generally exercises some current control through its review of methods and procedures and its examination of records by a field staff trained in such supervisory work. On the other hand, the field staff attached to the Bureau of Public Assistance does not function in a case-supervisory relationship but exercises supervision designed to establish satisfactory administrative standards. The representatives of the Bureau of Public Assistance are careful not to supersede state field supervisors, recognizing that sound administration requires the development of a strong state organization. The federal audit, however, to the extent that it inspects the method determining eligibility of individual cases tends to break down state audit and state administrative supervision. Federal auditors have insisted that such inspection is necessary to safeguard expenditures of federal funds and to enforce adherence to provisions of both the federal act and the federally approved state plan, although the state administrative officials have at times objected because decisions of federal auditors inevitably influence general administrative matters. As a step toward resolving problems arising from this situation, some states are adopting the device of having the local units file a certificate in the central state office vouching for all items of eligibility.

Integration of the federal audit with other supervisory and control techniques in the public assistance program is an important aspect of administration requiring continual and prompt attention. Precisely what relation the audit shall bear to other types of control, whether federal or state, can no more be stated with finality than what its scope shall be. The tendency to extend the use of certifications of eligibility in place of case-record data for audit purposes and to exclude from the audit consideration of such elements as amount of grant and the treatment of applicant resources are desirable modifications. In the long run strengthening of administrative supervision and development of better administrative standards and techniques will operate to reduce the necessity of utilizing the audit except as a purely fiscal check.

Regardless of the development in administrative techniques, the large amount of federal funds involved in matching state grants makes it imperative to establish a thorough audit, and if the state audit is inadequate, a detailed federal audit must be conducted. It should be varied to suit the situation in the individual state and should be recognized as a flexible control device rather than as a routine procedure. It is not the function of auditors to review administrative evaluations of social evidence, and yet their exceptions have at times been more influential upon local and state administration than the supervision of responsible administrative authorities. Even when auditors exercise care in adhering to administrative precedents, their exceptions, particularly upon points not definitely regulated, assume a directive character.

Integration of Auditing with Administrative Supervision

Because the federal audit is the controlling factor in settling state claims for federal aid, the Bureau of Accounts and Audits looms large in the federal-state relationship. While the Bureau of Public Assistance is charged with administering public assistance grants to the states, its authority and responsibility are threatened by the administrative significance of the audit conducted by the coordinate Bureau. This conflict is mitigated, but not removed, by the establishment of satisfactory working relations between audit field staff and representatives of the Bureau of Public Assistance; it will probably not be eliminated until responsibility for all administrative matters relating to the states is placed in one bureau.

An audit by a staff entirely independent of the bureau administering grants to the states tends to set up a double system of supervision. Differences between the two bureaus must be settled by negotiation, often by referral to the Board itself. This procedure is slow and cumbersome at best and increases difficulties with state agencies. An alternative would be to place the federal audit within a division of the Bureau of Public Assistance. This arrangement would maintain the advantages of an independent audit under an experienced accountant as the head of the division and at the same time avoid present conflicts. The auditing division would be subject to the general direction and supervision of the bureau chief. Thus would be provided closer integration of auditing with administrative supervision than is now possible, since coordination of the two separate bureaus is in the hands of the Board itself. As in other federal agencies administering grants-in-aid, one bureau would then be responsible for all public assistance relations with the states.

PART IV
Other Administrative Problems

CHAPTER 15

PERSONNEL CONTROL AND STAFF DEVELOPMENT

REGARDLESS OF the adequacy of financial support and of administrative arrangements, unless a public assistance program is conducted by competent personnel, effective performance is not apt to be attained. It would be assumed that any supervisory agency, either federal or state, which is to share in the administration of assistance should have some part in the selection and management of personnel. In no area, however, does a lower level of government so resent interference from a superior body as in personnel selection. The very tenacity with which communities endeavor to retain complete independence in the appointment of workers is of itself indicative of how vital the personnel factor is in public administration. The politician knows that if he can control personnel he can manipulate the operation of a program despite the stringency of the law and regulations. The excessive use of detailed and expensive methods of control observed in several states is usually accounted for by the fact that the state agency has little or nothing to say about the type of workers who are to administer the program. In the absence of a constructive personnel program the state supervisory agency has frequently increased its regulation of the mechanics of operation because it is aware that it has so little fundamental control. The methods used by federal and state bodies to insure the employment and development of qualified personnel in the agencies over which they have supervisory responsibility are, therefore, the phases of personnel management that require particular emphasis in a discussion of old age assistance administration.

PERSONNEL ACTIVITIES OF THE SOCIAL SECURITY BOARD

In his recent book on the administration of federal grants to the states, V. O. Key summarizes the limited power of the Social Security Board over personnel matters in the states:[1]

[1] Key, op. cit., pp. 273-74.

All but two of the eight types of grants to the states under the Social Security Act are made under statutory provisions which specifically prohibit the establishment of federal standards for state personnel. The phraseology in the section which authorizes grants for old age assistance requires that state plans shall "provide such methods of administration (other than those relating to selection, tenure of office, and compensation of personnel) as are found by the [Social Security] Board to be necessary for the efficient operation of the plan." Identical clauses appear in the sections relating to grants for unemployment compensation administration, aid to dependent children, and aid to the blind. Similar prohibitions are made in the sections of the act relating to grants for child- and maternal-health services and services for crippled children administered by the Children's Bureau. Only the grants for child welfare services and public-health services are made without such specific limitation on the federal administrative agency. These standing invitations to partisan and factional spoilsmen were written into the Act partly as the result of traditional congressional hostility towards the merit system, but more particularly as a reaction against the vigorous measures which had been taken by the F.E.R.A. and U.S.E.S. to control the personnel standards and procedures of the states.

The congressional prohibition refers only to formalized conditions governing the method of selection, tenure, and compensation of personnel. The statute cannot be interpreted to prohibit informal influence in support of the merit system or assistance to states in the installation of personnel procedures. Nevertheless, the definite character of the statutory clause tends to limit whatever persuasive effect recommendations of the representatives of the Board might have, and prevents the adoption of a clean-cut policy.

Despite the statutory limitation, the Board has made every effort to emphasize the importance of personnel. Its present position is clearly stated in its *Second Annual Report:*[2]

> The Federal Act . . . makes the Board responsible for seeing that State plans are efficiently administered. Since efficient administration depends largely upon the quality of personnel employed, the Board does not approve any State plan unless it contains provisions developed by the State which establish minimum objective standards for the selection of both State and Local staffs.

Although the Board may not say what the standards are, it has usually insisted that states must establish personnel requirements. The Board has also employed experts to advise the states on the operation of merit systems and on training programs. The Bureau of Public Assistance has issued two handbooks for the use of state welfare departments in

[2] 1937, p. 34. The discussion of state merit systems that follows shows that this has not uniformly been carried out.

establishing and operating merit systems.[3] Recently the Board has organized a "state technical advisory service," which is preparing an elaborate manual on the operation of merit systems for the benefit of state welfare departments and state unemployment compensation agencies.

In the states observed during federal participation in old age assistance, the representatives of the Social Security Board, through an active and cooperative interest in developing effective state administration, have been able to exert considerable influence to the end that the state employ qualified persons for key positions. The approach of the federal representatives has, of necessity, not been directly setting personnel standards or passing upon the appointment of specific individuals, but rather indirect—through an emphasis upon sound administration. For example, in some states representatives of the Board have found that the state agency had no staff member competent to direct the collection and compilation of social statistics. Consequently they have insisted that such a person be employed before the state plan be approved. To make such a suggestion concrete the Board representatives must indicate the content of the job that is to be done and the kind of person needed for it. Although the federal staff members have been scrupulous to refrain from volunteering the suggestion of particular persons, many states have felt free to call upon them for advice on the specific qualifications required for a particular position. Thus, despite its limited power, the Board's concern for adequate standards of administration has without doubt had a salutary effect upon the quality of personnel selected in many of the states.

MERIT APPOINTMENT OF STATE AND LOCAL EMPLOYEES

A wide variety of plans are now in effect by which state, local, or state and local employees in old age assistance are selected mainly on the basis of competence rather than personal or political preference. In some instances these state plans operate in connection with existing civil service systems; in others, the state personnel plan consists primarily of a system of merit selection operated by the state welfare de-

---

[3] See Social Security Board, "Suggestions relating to the requirements and selection of personnel for the use of State agencies administering or supervising assistance under the Social Security Act—with illustrative material for State agencies and departments handling similar work, August, 1936" and "The Personnel Unit; for use of State Agencies administering or supervising the administration of public assistance under the Social Security Act" (lithoprinted).

partment; in still others, both a general civil service agency and a system of departmental control of local appointment of personnel exist, with little or no relationship between the two. For purposes of clarification, the general civil service systems and the departmental merit plans will be discussed separately, and interaction between the two systems in certain states will be indicated.

Civil Service Systems

The Civil Service Assembly of the United States and Canada in its 1937 census of civil service agencies established the following qualifications to distinguish such an agency: It "must be established by formal legal provisions as the central personnel agency of a governmental jurisdiction," and "must, among its other functions, administer a merit system of appointments based upon open competitive examination."[4] Fourteen states, according to this census, now operate civil service systems. Seven of them were included in the scope of this study: New York, Massachusetts, Wisconsin, Colorado, New Jersey, California, and Connecticut.[5] With the occasional exception of a department head or bureau head, the professional and administrative employees of the state old age assistance agencies in these seven states are appointed in accordance with civil service rules.[6]

The crux of a merit system in a public assistance program is to be found in its application to employees on the operating level. To be sure, the state staff is important, but the local workers perform the basic activities in an assistance program; they carry on direct relations with the beneficiaries; and they outnumber the state staff frequently by a ratio as high as twenty to one. Furthermore, since the operating workers are usually appointees of local political subdivisions, unless some plan exists by which standards are established to insure local appointment of competent employees, no constructive state supervisory program can be said to exist. It is desirable, therefore, to see to what degree these state civil service systems are applicable to the operating agencies.

In Connecticut, the majority of the operating activities are carried on by state workers who are now selected from state civil service lists. The remaining operating activities in this state plan are handled by employees of towns and cities. The state agency has no power to determine

---

[4] Civil Service Assembly of the United States and Canada, *Civil Service Agencies in the United States: a 1937 Census.*

[5] The civil service law in Connecticut was passed in 1937, after the field visit in that state.

[6] In Colorado, members of the state field staff still have the status of provisional employees.

the quality of these local workers; state officials regard this as a serious limitation on their ability to maintain a satisfactory program.[7] In only two states—New Jersey and New York—have the state civil service facilities been used as the machinery through which the state's power to establish standards for certain local welfare positions has been carried out. The division of old age assistance in the New Jersey Department of Institutions and Agencies has the following authority over local employes: "Said division shall have the power to, and shall require adequate personnel standards for the county welfare boards, as county bureaus of old age assistance with respect to both the number of employees and their qualifications."[8] The standards established by the state division are put into effect through the examinations conducted by the State Civil Service Commission in the ten counties that have placed their personnel functions under the Commission. In the remaining eleven counties, the Commission conducts special examinations for the old age assistance positions at the request of the state old age assistance division.

The New York State Department of Social Welfare has the following authority over standards of local welfare personnel:[9]

> In consultation with the [state] civil service commission it [the State Department of Social Welfare] shall establish minimum qualifications for positions in the state and local welfare departments, having due regard for the requirements and varying types of communities within the state.
>
> No state reimbursement shall be made for the salary of any person who, in the opinion of the [state] department, at the time of appointment, lacks the qualifications necessary for the work for which employed or who, after a reasonable trial period, is considered by the department unable to do satisfactory work.

The standards worked out jointly by the State Department of Social Welfare and the State Department of Civil Service are put into effect directly by the latter agency in the seventeen counties where it operates the civil service system. In thirty-nine cities that operate their own personnel agency, the examinations for welfare positions are conducted under a joint arrangement between the state and city commissions; this

---

[7] See statement of Edward H. Reeves, head of the Connecticut Bureau of Old Age Assistance, quoted in chap. 2. The operating activities are carried on by state employees, appointed under state civil service regulations, in Michigan, Ohio, and Arkansas. These plans have not been examined, but serious charges have been leveled against the operation of the state civil service system in relation to old age assistance in Ohio.

[8] New Jersey, *Laws,* 1936, chap. 31, sec. 4.

[9] New York, *Laws,* 1936, chaps. 873 and 693.

The Administration of Old Age Assistance

insures uniform testing and grading of the candidates throughout the state.[10]

In most instances the state civil service system bears no relationship to whatever plan exists, if any, for establishment of qualifications by the state old age assistance agency for locally employed personnel. The Massachusetts State Department of Civil Service and Registration operates civil service arrangements for all or part of the employees of 121 of the 355 towns and cities in the state. Since the State Department of Public Welfare has no authority over local personnel standards, there in no interaction between the two bodies. Standards for local old age assistance employees are no better or worse for the fact that the state participates financially in the program. Local employees are selected on a merit basis only if the local municipality chooses to bring them under civil service.[11]

In California and Wisconsin, the state civil service agency has no authority over county personnel activities, nor does the state assistance agency establish standards for the county welfare units.[12] In the former state, four of the largest counties have civil service agencies of their own, and Milwaukee County, the largest county in Wisconsin, has its own civil service commission. For some positions in these counties, higher qualifications have been established than exist for equivalent jobs in the state agency, but participation by the state in state-wide assistance programs has had no effect whatsoever on these local standards. The Colorado Civil Service Commission has no authority over county personnel matters.[13]

[10] The qualifications of workers employed in local jurisdictions not included in either of these arrangements are verified directly by the Department of Social Welfare through the submission of qualifications of workers employed by the local welfare departments. According to the Department, 95 per cent of the local welfare employees whose qualifications are subject to the Department's approval are selected through civil service.

[11] An indirect relationship exists in Massachusetts resulting from the fact that the Department of Civil Service frequently uses a single examination to select candidates for both city and state positions. Thus the state welfare department by insisting upon high standards for its own workers might incidentally affect the standards in the towns and cities under civil service. No evidence could be found that the state welfare department had ever recognized the constructive possibilities of this arrangement.

[12] The California State Board of Social Welfare, in connection with a revision of plans for public assistance in 1937, agreed to establish minimum personnel standards and job specifications. In 1938 standards were established to be applied "at the earliest possible date," but the State Board further provided that "the procedure putting the standards into effect shall not affect those now employed or who continue in the employment of the social welfare agencies of the counties of California or the state of California." Furthermore, the standards thus established were too low to assure competency of personnel and were, therefore, not accepted as a part of the state plan by the Social Security Board.

[13] The Colorado State Welfare Department has statutory authority affecting the appointment of county welfare employees. See p. 281.

Some observers have assumed that because there was a state civil service agency, the state could be said to have a merit system in its public assistance program. The most important function of a merit system in a state-wide public assistance program is to provide a means by which the state welfare agency, either directly or indirectly, may insure that qualified workers are employed on the operating level. The above analysis of specific states shows that the mere coincidence of a state civil service agency does not necessarily meet this fundamental purpose. The type of merit system needed in a state-wide public assistance program is achieved in relationship to a state civil service system only when, as in Connecticut, the principal operating employees are state workers selected through the state personnel agency; or when, as in New Jersey and New York, the state commission has authority to conduct personnel activities in the localities and the state welfare agency in turn has power to establish local personnel standards that are enforced through the state personnel body.

Departmental Merit Systems

In the absence of civil service systems, many states have established plans for selection on a merit basis of personnel administering certain types of public assistance including aid to the aged. These plans may be called departmental merit systems since they are ordinarily operated by one department, and their jurisdiction is usually limited to one service of government. They show a wide variety of patterns, ranging from highly organized to very informal systems. For purposes of discussion, these plans may be divided into two groups: statutory and nonstatutory plans. The former are those provided for in the state welfare law; the latter are those that have been set up under the general rule-making authority of the state agency. Most departmental plans have been established to govern the appointment of both state and local employees, but some have been designed primarily to regulate the selection of workers in the operating units regardless of whether these units are branches of the state agency or instruments of local political subdivisions.[14]

[14] Although from the standpoint of public welfare administration these departmental plans represent an important development, no general study of their operation has been made. Neither a complete index of the number and coverage of these systems nor a standards classification of them is available. Some experts will quarrel with the classification of these systems used in this report. The Indiana plan, which is classed here as departmental, is regarded by some as a general civil service agency because it serves two state departments, but it is not so classified by the Civil Service Assembly. The authors are indebted to Mr. Jack Stipe, who, while a student at the New York School of Social Work, gathered material on merit systems in public welfare and made his findings available to supplement the observations of the survey staff.

The most highly organized of the statutory departmental merit systems in the states visited are those in Indiana and Washington. In Indiana, a personnel division is maintained under the joint control of the State Department of Public Welfare and the State Division of Unemployment Compensation. This personnel agency conducts examinations for the selection of state and certain county workers. The Washington State Department of Social Security is responsible for public welfare, employment services, and unemployment compensation activities; a division of personnel in this Department conducts examinations for both state and local workers in these programs. Unfortunately neither of these plans had been fully developed at the time of the staff visit so that a description of the methods of operation is lacking. In both instances, qualified personnel officers have been in charge of the classification, testing, and rating procedures.

The Iowa law provides for the selection of all employees of the State Board of Social Welfare through "an examination given by the state board or under its direction, covering character, general training, and experience."[15] Under a similar statutory provision, the Iowa Old Age Assistance Commission prior to 1937 administered a system for the selection of local workers, who, although appointed by the county boards, were paid by the state. The operation of this plan is described as follows in an official publication,[16] according to which the Commission

> . . . held a series of eleven examinations, at various and convenient points in the state, for those who desired to become eligible for employment as local investigators during the ensuing year. Those meeting the required standards in the written examination were submitted to a further test as to "character, training and experience" at which time inquiries of a confidential nature were made by the commission of persons given as references by the applicants and to others knowing said applicants. On the basis of written examination and the inquiries just outlined, certificates setting forth the eligibility of certain persons to conduct investigations of applicants for old age assistance have been issued. . . . From this list thus certified, the various county boards have selected their local investigators, the number of whom may be increased or decreased as necessity demands.

Examinations used in this system consisted largely of questions to determine the applicants' knowledge of the old age assistance law and of state administrative procedures. Although a few questions were aimed to test the judgment of the applicant, the examination was mainly

[15] Iowa, *Laws,* 1937, chap. 151, sec. 8.

[16] Iowa State Old Age Assistance Commission, *Handbook for Old Age Assistance,* 1934, pp. 16-17.

legalistic. Apparently no stated experience qualifications were required for certification, although it was understood that the following areas of experience were regarded as helpful: work in a bank, employment as an insurance agent, or relief work. It was customary to give a training course prior to the examination; candidates for it were suggested by the county boards. The course stressed legal, financial, and property problems rather than methods of administration.

Some of the statutory departmental merit plans are informal in their operation and are in reality certification plans.[17] For example, the Colorado State Department of Public Welfare has the following authority over appointments in the county welfare units:[18]

> The state board shall have the power and it shall be its duty to fix minimum standards of service and personnel, and to formulate salary schedules for the classified service based upon training, experience, and general ability for persons selected for positions in the State Department and in the County Departments of Public Welfare hereinafter created.

The law differentiates between the procedure of state control to be applied in the appointment of county directors as compared with the procedure in appointment of subordinate county employees. The county director must be appointed from a list of eligibles nominated by the county board and certified by the state department as meeting the qualifications that it has established. Appointees to staff positions in the counties must meet qualifications prescribed by the state, but such appointments need not be submitted to the state for approval.

In administering these provisions of the law, the state agency has set up a system of classification for all county positions; it includes a grouping of the counties into classes according to size of case load and total population, and the establishment within each class of a series of positions with qualifications and salary range indicated. The procedure followed in the approval of county directors is as follows:

[17] The term "certification plan" is used to apply to systems of limitation of selection of personnel in which a supervisory or standard-setting body either establishes qualifications to which the appointing authority must adhere in selecting employees or furnishes lists of persons meeting certain qualifications from which the appointing authority must select employees. One distinguishing feature of a certification plan is that the element of competition or competitive rating is usually absent. Confusion in nomenclature arises from the fact that in the civil service merit systems, "certification" is used to describe that part of the process by which the personnel agency furnishes lists of eligibles, after the examinations have been held and graded, to the appointing authority. Eligibles on a certification list in civil service are ranked in accordance with their achievement on the examination, and appointments must be made from the list in some specified order usually determined by the civil service law.

[18] Colorado, *Laws*, 2nd spec. sess., 1936, chap. 5, sec. 4.

The county submits to the state agency the name and qualifications of one or more candidates for the position of county director; the state department requires that the record of each be investigated by one of the state field supervisors; with a report of this investigation in its hands, the state department indicates its approval or disapproval of the nominees, and the county may appoint from the list of those approved.[19] State review of many of the appointments to staff positions occurs through the application of the state system of standards to these positions. The qualifications set for staff employees establish basic standards of training and experience for the various jobs, but "equivalent" experience may be substituted in most instances. The state department retains the right to interpret equivalent experience whenever it is offered in lieu of the basic requirements.

In the absence of statutory provision for a merit system some state welfare agencies, acting under their general rule-making or supervisory authority, have established plans to provide for personnel selection on the basis of competence. An example of a nonstatutory merit system is found in Florida: the State Board of Social Welfare conducts examinations through which all employees of the state agency and of the district boards must be selected. One state staff member, who is assisted by both state-wide and district advisory committees, is responsible for the operation of the program; one member of the state committee is a test expert. The examination consists of three parts: a rating of experience and training, a written examination, and a personal interview or oral examination. Experience and training qualifications are definitely specified; hence if a person does not measure up to them he is immediately disqualified. If he meets the minimum requirements and has additional experience and training, he receives a proportionately higher rating. The written tests used are partly of the true-false type and partly problems to test the judgment of the applicant. The written examinations are aimed to test the applicant's general intellectual background and understanding of social and economic problems. Since the personal interviews had not been held at the time of the staff visit, it is not known of what they consisted. Ratings under the first two parts of the examination had been established, however, and workers who had not qualified on these sections of the test were not allowed to continue in the employ of the districts. When the district staffs had to be reduced early in 1937, these ratings were used as an objective measure to determine which workers were to be retained.

[19] Actually, the county usually submits the name of only a single candidate.

The Florida plan as seen in operation at the time of the staff visit was superior to some of the statutory systems in that it was well-organized, recognized personnel techniques were used, and the competitive factor was maintained throughout. Most nonstatutory plans, however, are simply means of establishing qualifications for workers in operating units on a certification basis. The rigidity of the enforcement of the standards seems to depend entirely upon the zeal of the state agency. Under a plan of this type in operation in the state of Washington prior to 1937, the qualifications set for workers assigned to the local offices were being adhered to with considerable uniformity. In contrast, the personnel standards for county workers of Mississippi's old age assistance plan, which had been approved by the Social Security Board, were not being met uniformly. For example, the minimum requirements for the position of county director were either high-school graduation plus one year of experience in social work or public welfare, or college graduation with no previous experience. Nevertheless, in February, 1937, forty-three of the eighty-one county administrators had had no previous welfare experience, although only fifteen of the total group were college graduates.[20]

Any complete evaluation of departmental merit systems requires more intensive observation than was possible in this survey. Furthermore, their effectiveness needs to be judged after more experience with their operation than had been gained at the time of the staff visit. There is no question that more competent employees have been obtained under these plans than would have been selected had no restrictions been placed upon local and state appointing officers. A departmental system, to say the least, is a constructive force toward attaining good administration when no general personnel agency exists. The greatest weakness in both the statutory and nonstatutory plans is that none of them provides for tenure of office for those workers selected on a merit principle.[21] With this exception, the departmental plans of Indiana and Florida are potentially as effective devices for obtaining competent public welfare workers as the general state personnel system in Connecticut. Because the problem of measuring competence in social work has to date

---

[20] There is some question whether the standards in the Mississippi plan were intended to be mandatory. No record of formal approval of the state plan by the state welfare board was found in the minutes of that body. It is reported that there has been considerable improvement in the qualifications of local workers since the staff visit.

[21] There is not, however, an inherent limitation of a statutory merit plan. It is understood that the statutory merit plans for public assistance employees in Arizona, Idaho, Montana, and Texas contain provisions for tenure in office.

proved such a baffling problem to personnel agencies, the departmental system that can focus upon the needs of one particular service may be expected to develop better techniques and methods of selection than the general civil service agencies that can give less time to the specialized personnel problems of a single governmental activity.

Salary and Residence Limitation

State participation in establishing and enforcing qualifications for employees in the operating units may be limited in its effect unless some attention is given to salary scales and residence requirements. These factors frequently play an important part in determining the quality of workers who are employed in the local agencies.

In the public service there is usually a close correlation between salary scales and qualifications of workers. Some general issues enter into the determination of salaries: sectional living costs, current standards of remuneration in the governmental unit, public opinion, local tradition, and the degree of recognition achieved by a professional group. In the main, however, salary standards are determined by duties and responsibilities attached to positions plus the qualifications required to carry out these duties and responsibilities.

Most state agencies that have been active in establishing systems for the merit selection of operating personnel have also taken some part in setting salary scales for the operating units. In the most effective merit plans observed, a classification scheme, drawn up by the state agency in order to establish qualifications and salaries for the local staffs, was based upon objective statements of duties and responsibilities. Usually the local agency is given a range within which the salary for a given position must be fixed. States frequently establish different compensation schedules for groups of local units classed according to total population, case load, and other significant factors.

In general, the salaries paid to local workers in old age assistance were found to be low. Table 3 shows samples of salaries paid in different types of localities, taken from personnel schedules filled out during field visits.

The limitation of employment to local residents is a factor operating against obtaining the best personnel for an old age assistance program. The use of this type of restriction appears to be increasing, particularly in the field of public welfare, partly because of the general scarcity of jobs and partly—in some states at least—as a reaction against the importation of social workers for the unemployment relief programs. An

TABLE 3. SALARIES OF PROFESSIONAL WORKERS IN SELECTED LOCAL UNITS OF ELEVEN STATES *

Annual Salary	In 13 cities—150,000 or more population Professional Workers Receiving Specified Salary		In 139 counties and towns	
	Number	Per Cent	Number	Per Cent
TOTAL	340	100.0	274	100.0
Less than $750	1	0.3	25	9.1
$ 750-$ 999	—	—	42	15.3
1,000- 1,249	113	33.2	69	25.2
1,250- 1,499	44	12.9	50	18.3
1,500- 1,749	62	18.2	52	19.0
1,750- 1,999	78	23.0	21	7.7
2,000- 2,499	33	9.7	10	3.6
2,500- 2,999	7	2.1	2	0.7
3,000- 3,499	—	—	3	1.1
3,500- 3,999	1	0.3	—	—
4,000- 4,499	1	0.3	—	—

* Does not include Iowa.

extreme example of this restriction is a recent local ordinance in New York City prohibiting the employment in the city service of any person who has not been a resident of the city for three years immediately prior to appointment.

Of the states observed, the only ones not greatly affected by a local residence policy are those in which the state pays the salaries of the workers in the operating units. Employees of the Connecticut Bureau of Old Age Assistance who work out of district offices established by the state agency need only be residents of the state. Under the state-operated plan in effect until 1937, the Washington State Department gave preference to a county resident only if he possessed the training and experience required for a position. Much the same practice was followed in Florida. The Iowa State Commission officially informed the county boards that they need not employ county residents and added, "In fact, it may not always be desirable to do so." The original intent in Mississippi was not to assign workers to their own counties, but this policy had to be abandoned because the salaries were so low that the workers could not afford to accept positions away from home and had to work in the counties where they lived.[22]

In all the other states visited, the question of local residence was a matter left entirely to each county or city. So far as could be determined,

[22] One worker was compelled to resign a position in his own county because he lived so far from the county seat that he could not afford to pay out of his slender salary the cost of daily transportation from his home to the county seat.

most localities insisted upon local residents.[23] The fortuitous matter of domicile remains the preeminent qualification for rendering service to the aged in the local jurisdictions in these states despite the following facts: Two of the states, Colorado and New York, pay half the salaries of the local workers; all but one of the states pass on to the localities some share of the federal grants for administration; and one, New Jersey, distributes all this sum among the counties; from 75 to 100 per cent of assistance costs is paid from state and federal sources.

STAFF DEVELOPMENT

To assist the states in developing the employed personnel, the Bureau of Public Assistance of the Social Security Board has established a division of training. The Bureau has taken the position that to operate training programs for the states is not a federal responsibility, but that the Board's greatest contribution might be to aid states to undertake their own training programs. Thus the head of the division of training has served as a consultant to the states and in addition has worked with various national agencies that are concerned with the development of social work personnel, such as the American Public Welfare Association, the American Association of Schools of Social Work, and the American Association of Social Workers.

The emphasis on the development of state programs has undoubtedly been wise. During a period of emergency it is sometimes necessary in the interests of quick results to give the states, especially those inclined to lag, more direct help than should be provided in a long-time program which, for sound and enduring growth, needs a more indigenous effort. States vary in the extent to which they value trained service, but a sound state program must be rooted in understanding of the purposes of a training program and of the results to be expected from a well-organized and properly directed plan. The establishment of a training program involves stimulating interest, desire, and understanding of the value of trained service, as well as providing or suggesting suitable methods and procedures.

Staff Development Through Training

Basically the objective of a training program is improvement of the functioning of an agency by increasing the competence of the operating staff. The kinds of training provided for the social work staff are usually

[23] One county dismissed a well trained worker, a life-long resident of the state, who was doing a highly satisfactory job, merely because he did not have local residence.

three: professional, preprofessional, and nonprofessional—often called in-service training. Professional training is that given by a recognized school of social work through courses of the prescribed curriculum that are recognized as being on a professional level and, when completed successfully in the order and amount prescribed by the school and the American Association of Schools of Social Work, entitle the student to the degree or certificate conferred by the school upon its graduates. The purpose of such educational effort is to provide broad, fundamental professional training which will equip the worker not only for the work of the specific agency to which he is attached but will also qualify him for service in similar agencies. Professional training is sometimes undertaken by a student as a part-time activity while continuing to work, full or part time, on the agency staff; but it is most satisfactorily pursued as a full-time occupation during a period or periods of leave. In-service training, on the other hand, is undertaken while continuing regular work with the agency. It may include courses in a school of social work or other institution of higher learning in either the regular or the extension curriculum. Any training given to staff members on the job, whether by the agency itself or by outsiders, for the purpose of improving the immediate skill of the staff in their day-by-day activities may be classed as in-service training. Preprofessional training is that necessary for admission to a school of social work as a candidate for a professional degree (or certificate).

Obviously training is only one of the methods of improving staff competence. To be sound, the training program must be articulated into a larger program of staff development and improvement. It is also related to other general personnel activities. For example, personnel selection is one means of improving the quality of personnel. It is extremely wasteful for an agency to spend its money to provide professional training for untrained workers when without great difficulty it could recruit workers already well trained and competent, often within its state borders, or at least among its native sons.[24] Although there are not enough trained persons available the country over, this fact makes it all the more wasteful for a state interested in improving its work through staff development to ignore available trained personnel.

[24] In some instances state agencies have alleged that no trained workers were available; yet even a superficial canvass of the situation revealed workers, native to the state making such allegations, who were taking advantage of technical residence elsewhere to secure work in states with better appreciation of what they had to offer in training and skill. Many such workers would be glad to return to their native states if agencies in those states showed any disposition to recognize their competence.

The selection of trainable personnel, when the roster of trained and competent persons is exhausted, is also important in relation to professional training. It is unquestionably wasteful to attempt training of persons who cannot possibly become competent owing to lack of intellectual ability or defects in personality or character. This sort of waste is fairly obvious; less obvious, perhaps, is the fact that, if professional training is planned, it would be wise to select, so far as possible, persons who have the necessary preprofessional training.[25] Even when provision for professional training is not contemplated, a state agency should be able to see that its best chances for development of staff competence lie in recruitment and selection of the ablest, best-educated, and best-trained personnel it can find.

Although it is necessary to stimulate interest in training in connection with development of staff competence, administrators must also be aware of the limitations of training programs. Failure to exercise discretion in selection may grow out of an excessive faith in potential results of training. Sometimes this is found in relation to professional training, but more often regarding in-service training. Not infrequently the notion seems to have support that a staff of less-than-average competence can somehow be made over by a few lectures or special classes or some more elaborate but fairly painless training course that workers attend while also carrying on their regular duties. Unfortunately there is no magic in training courses whatever their content and method.

The content of a program of staff development includes, after proper selection of personnel, suitable induction into the duties of the positions involved. If new workers are not adequately instructed about their duties when they first join the staff, they inevitably waste time and may make serious and costly mistakes. At the beginning of the program, when large numbers of visitors were added to the local agency staffs, special classes were found to be very useful as a method of giving necessary instructions. In an agency large enough to justify a special training supervisor, orientation courses for beginners, combined with definite procedural instructions, may be valuable as a current activity. Usually after the initial period the volume of accessions to staff is

---

[25] Schools of social work are now on a graduate basis. A worker who has not completed his undergraduate work has therefore much farther to go in order to secure complete training than one who has already received his degree. It is not usual to provide preprofessional training for such persons at agency expense, but even if the worker finances himself, the agency waiting for him to complete his training has lacked trained service for a longer period than would have been necessary if a better prepared employee had been appointed in the first place.

too small to justify such classes.[26] Hence individual instruction must be given by the administrator, by a special training supervisor, or by the supervisor under whom the new staff member is to work.[27] A manual of procedures and special literature prepared for beginners can be very useful in starting a new visitor, local supervisor, or state field worker.

Furthermore, a well rounded program of staff development includes adequate supervision,[28] with administrative support, and as much opportunity for growth as can be provided through staff and other group conferences, and through opportunity to present the results of study and experience as a contribution toward shaping the total program of the agency.

Supervision and Staff Development

Although principles and general methods of supervision are similar for state and local agencies, the dispersion of the work of the state field staff over a wide area and other problems peculiar to state agencies suggest separate consideration of the special supervisory problems of state agencies. In relation to the state field staff, supervision must include instruction, direction, and support as needed, and the exercise of some control over the activities of the field staff. Field workers need to be fully informed on state policies, plans, and resources. They also must have the security of adequate backing in carrying out the policies of the state agency.[29] In addition they need to have an opportunity to report back to the state agency the reaction of local agencies to new policies and procedures established by the state, their own observations on the results of previously established policies, and problems discovered in the field for which no policies exist or for which existing policies or procedures are inadequate.

[26] The Social Security Board requires all administrative staff workers to attend a "basic training course" of two weeks, which is designed to give workers a comprehensive survey of the three diverse programs that the Board administers. Special groups of workers are required to attend classes of instruction in the basic procedures of the programs in which they are to work after the basic course is completed. Public assistance employees attend only the basic course.

[27] The instruction may be given jointly by two or more of the supervisory or administrative staff, but if accessions are infrequent, only one person will receive instruction at a time and so, in this sense, the instruction will be "individual" whether given by one person or by several.

[28] For a more detailed discussion of the value of supervision of the social service staff see chap. 8.

[29] Field workers cannot carry out a state policy effectively if a protest from the local unit to the state office immediately produces an exemption for that unit, or if a unit following a state policy under the direction of the field worker finds that clients obtain individual exemptions from the requirements by applying to the state office.

In order to function effectively in the development and execution of state policies, members of the state field staff must have suitable written instructions covering official policies and procedures, preferably in manual form, and sufficient oral interpretation of the written material to ensure clear understanding of any controversial points. As for support, field workers must have not only assurance of backing if policies and instructions are followed, but also practical demonstrations, when occasions arise, that this support will be forthcoming and will not disappear at the first breath of opposition. Many other faults in administration are forgiven if the field worker can count on real backing from his chief in carrying out policies.

Another need of the state field staff is periodical conferences. Opportunity should be given for individual consultation with the state case supervisor about troublesome points and for reporting back orally on various problems; thus the written reports submitted for supervision may be supplemented, elaborated, and interpreted. If special consultants are available, opportunity for individual conference with them must be planned. Group conferences with fellow workers, supervisors, and special consultants are also helpful and stimulating, as are general staff meetings attended by the director and other administrative officials. If the field staff has general responsibility for administrative supervision rather than for supervision solely over social service functions, it is particularly important for both field and office staff that there be ample opportunity for conferences of persons responsible for administrative activities. Staffs serving several programs, sometimes called integrated or generalized field staffs, have similarly a need for conference with directors of the various programs.

To attain the best results, group conferences should be planned and programmed carefully and scheduled well ahead of time; copies of the agenda should be circulated to those who are expected to attend, in order that each may have time to organize his material for presentation to the group.[30] In this way exchange of ideas can take place. The directors and other members of the state administrative staff have an opportunity for pooling their ideas and for checking them with the field workers who are in a position to present the results of thinking from the field or local point of view. This corrective of the inevitable "desk point of

[30] This does not mean that occasionally unplanned meetings will not be needed to consider problems growing out of emergent conditions, but staff meetings should not be entirely of this character as they too frequently are. Neither should they be devoted exclusively to procedural and technical matters better handled by individuals or by small committees.

view" of persons whose work flows, largely from others, over an office desk is always greatly needed in a state office if a program is to be kept realistic and practical. The field staff needs, on the other hand, to become aware of the state perspective of local problems and of the relation of seemingly isolated phenomena discovered in their districts to the total state trend.

A special consultant on training attached to the state staff might well undertake responsibility for assisting in the planning and programing of staff meetings. Such a consultant may also be useful in planning reading courses and special discussion groups and for advising state staff members about opportunities for advanced professional training or for special courses, acting as liaison between the state agency and schools of social work, as well as between agency and representatives of various organizations interested in professional standards. The chief duties of such a consultant will, however, be to assist in the development of suitable programs of staff development and training in the local units.[31]

Staff Development in Local Agencies

A program of staff development in local agencies may, in many respects, follow the pattern suggested for state agencies. Because a larger proportion of its staff usually lacks adequate training and experience at the time of recruitment, the local agency may need to place more emphasis on the training aspects of the task, but in general the problems of the two are much the same. Local as well as state workers must be carefully selected, properly inducted, well supervised and supported, sufficiently serviced, and given opportunity for growth.[32] In planning for staff development, local agencies, especially larger ones, will usually find value in planned staff meetings, in committee study of selected problems with results later reported to the larger staff groups, and in special courses related to the day-by-day activities of the staff. If the agency is large, a special training supervisor may be needed to plan programs of meetings to arrange for class and committee sessions, to teach or to arrange for the teaching of whatever classes are held, and to consult with workers on their individual developmental needs. If

---

[31] In no state was a well organized training program being operated by the state agency for the benefit of the localities at the time of the visit, although agencies previously responsible for unemployment relief had usually had some sort of training program, and one had had an effective director whose accomplishments were still noticeable in the quality of the local staff retained from the earlier program.

[32] For a discussion of supervision in local agencies see chap. 8.

workers are allowed time off to attend classes at a nearby school of social work while continuing to carry all or part of their usual duties, given "educational leave" in order to take full-time training, or are granted scholarships for this purpose, the training supervisor will have additional duties, such as aiding in the selection of workers likely to profit by training, acting as liaison with the schools offering courses available to staff members, and conferring with workers on their individual progress.[33]

Function of State Field Staff in Local Training Programs

Small agencies cannot usually employ a special training supervisor. The director or case-work supervisor upon whom these duties fall is sometimes poorly qualified to carry on such activities and often too busy to give sufficient time to them. The small agencies also frequently suffer from isolation, particularly the lack of opportunity for comparing results with others of like experience and for the stimulation of group thinking on agency problems. The state agency has an opportunity and a special responsibility for service to these small agencies. Regular visits and conferences between state worker and local staff are useful, especially if the time does not have to be given to procedural minutiae. If the state agency itself has a good program of staff development and a supervisor of training activities, consultative service can be given through the field staff. If training opportunities are available through educational leave or scholarships, some local workers may be able to take advantage of them. Special short courses, such as those given in connection with district and state conferences in several states, have been useful in offsetting the effects of isolation.[34] Attendance at conferences—district, state, regional, and even national—is particularly desirable for isolated workers. Visits to the state office and to other agencies may be valuable although such trips can easily degenerate into mere junkets. One state-operated agency has found publication of a "house organ" useful in its staff development program. Small agencies sometimes give workers a sense of participation in the program not attainable in very large ones through close association with the director and with other administrative

[33] One large local agency had a well trained supervisor who was giving practically full time to training problems. In most agencies the responsibilities for training and staff development are not centered in one person, and, partly for this reason, are frequently less effective than they should be.

[34] It is always necessary to avoid, so far as possible, overemphasis on the value of these and other courses which tend to be regarded as "professional training" instead of opportunities for "development."

officials. On the whole, the smaller agencies are in a less favorable situation regarding staff development than are larger ones; they are, therefore, in greater need of state service.

Staff Development and Agency Administration

A program of staff development must conform to established lines of administrative responsibility if it is to be constructive. Such a program should support and strengthen other supervisory and personnel activities. Since staff development is not a separate, specialized activity but an intimate and integral part of the administrative function, its general direction is largely the responsibility of the executive. The detailed activities usually should be delegated, but their coordination must remain chiefly the task of the agency director. If a special training consultant is employed by the state, he is usually immediately responsible to the head of the field staff, as are other technical consultants, since most of his activities will be carried on for the benefit of the social service staff. Thus consultants on a state staff are available for technical service to the central office staff, to the field workers, and through the latter to the local staffs.

It should be obvious that programs of training, staff development, or ordinary field supervision of the social service program should be channeled through director, case supervisor (and intermediate supervisory staff, if any), down to the visitor on the job. It was astonishing to find in practice how often this fundamental principle of sound administration was violated by state agencies.[35] The problem is not, however, so simple as it seems. State agencies are charged with re-

[35] In one state the field staff held training classes in the jurisdiction of the largest local agency. These classes were taught by state workers although the local agency had several workers as well qualified for this task as the state workers. The plan was later abandoned in favor of a plan of assisting the agency in developing a training program of its own. The latter program was showing indications of being more effective than the state program. Besides providing classes as well or better taught, it had the advantage of offering more continuity and better adaptation to the special needs of the agency. Its greatest advantage appeared to be that of maintaining the normal lines of administrative responsibility within the agency.

In this agency the supervisory staff was, with a few exceptions, very weak. Some of the staff workers and junior supervisors were, in fact, better trained than many of the senior supervisors. The state staff had proceeded on the theory that what was needed to improve staff competence was to work with the younger and more hopeful group and ignore the supervisors. The effect was, of course, to increase the cleavage between the two groups and further disrupt staff morale. The state therefore made two mistakes: first, it ignored administrative lines and began at the bottom instead of at the top, and second, it ignored the facilities which the agency possessed for assuming the training function. Both appeared inexcusable errors, but it must be said, in fairness to the state agency, that it promptly abandoned its plan when error became apparent.

sponsibility for proper administration of the funds appropriated for the old age assistance program, but in many cases are denied authority to set standards which will ensure "the efficient operation of the plan" required by the Social Security Act. The state is peculiarly helpless, if like the Social Security Board, it does not have authority to provide methods of administration "relating to selection, tenure of office, and compensation of personnel" of the local agencies. The case-by-case method of supervision made more necessary by a lack of constructive supervisory power brings to the attention of the state the inadequacies of individual local workers and increases the temptation to direct action to correct the individual lapses instead of the slower and sounder method of all-around agency development through normal administrative channels.

In large agencies with efficient supervision there should be little excuse for short-cutting the agency's supervisors to deal directly with the visiting staff, though such intervention was found to be all too frequent. Even if the supervisory staff of a large unit is below standard, little can be gained by weakening it still further—the inevitable result of the short-cut method. The problem in small units is somewhat different: if there is only one worker, the state field worker can give direct supervision with good results, provided he is skilful. If, however, there are two or more workers, the problem of staff relationships exists and must be taken into account in any plans for improving the competence of the workers. The wise field worker, whatever the size of the agency he is supervising, remembers that he must not let his enthusiasm for improvement in technical skill blind him to the dangers of compensating loss of staff morale and disorganization of agency administration which usually more than offset his efforts when he directs them counter to, instead of along, the lines of administrative responsibility. The extent to which state agencies recognize and act on this principle appears to measure the effectiveness of their functioning in relation to their operating units.

FISCAL PERSONNEL

Most of the personnel activities of the states have been concerned primarily with the social service and administrative employees, and little or no attention has been given to the local fiscal employees. When there is a civil service system in the locality or the state, these employees are usually selected through this medium, but no state agency observed has attempted to establish qualifications for the local fiscal employees or to develop training courses for them. One of the difficulties is that governmental finance officers have done less than other professional groups to establish professional standards. Hence any state welfare agency that might attempt to improve standards in this field would receive little support from the employees whose interests it was seeking to advance. In addition, there is a popular notion that anyone with private business experience can handle the business of government—that any accountant can do governmental accounting and any auditor can do governmental auditing. Experienced public administrators recognize that this popular generalization does not uniformly hold true.

The result of lack of objective standards for fiscal employees is shown in the experience of one of the state departments studied. In this state, with a change of governor came a complete turnover in the membership of the state board that administered the state welfare program. The state agency had established a merit system governing the appointment of its social service personnel, and the new board was quick to recognize that since these employees had been selected by this impartial rating device they should be retained and the merit system continued to insure that future appointments be made on an objective basis. The board was completely helpless, however, regarding financial employees. The state agency had at the head of its financial activities a competent business manager who was an expert in governmental accounting and auditing, and particularly in the administrative requirements of a public assistance program. He was immediately removed when a powerful politician sought a place for a henchman. No objective qualifications had been established for the position, and the board could not refute the argument that after all any person with business experience could make good in governmental fiscal affairs.

The point of view that state supervisory agencies might well assume toward the financial employees in subordinate agencies is that expressed by the State Department of Finance in California in its manual of accounting for state agencies:[36]

> *Responsibility of Accounting Personnel.* The system of accounting and budgetary control in the California state government places a heavy responsibility upon the departmental accounting personnel. The system is based on the theory that the operating management has the greatest need for prompt and detailed information and that the accounting personnel "on the job" is best situated to record

[36] State of California, *Manual for Uniform System of Accounting for State Department, Institutes, and other Agencies,* issued by the Division of Budget and Accounts of the California State Department of Finance (1934), p. 5. This manual also contains a clear statement of the features of governmental accounting which distinguish it from commercial accounting.

transactions accurately and promptly; that with an efficient accounting system in the departments and institutions there is not the necessity
for duplicating many of the detailed operations in the central office.
A completely centralized system with the proper operation of the type
of decentralized system now in use is very greatly dependent upon
reliable accounting personnel in the spending agencies. Reliance must
be placed upon them to properly maintain records, to correctly certify as
to budget allotment balances; in general to comply with regulations
and to guide and advise the executive officers in fiscal affairs. Without
competent and trustworthy accounting personnel in the departments,
institutions and other agencies, the decentralized "home-rule" system
cannot succeed.

Many state welfare agencies could dispense with much of their detailed
financial inspection and routine requirements if they were able to
have some assurance that qualified fiscal employees were doing the
primary work in the local welfare agencies.[37]

★   ★   ★

Many employees administering old age assistance in the localities
within the group of states visited are not equipped for the work. With
the exception of the states having effective merit systems and training
programs and a few local units of government which have themselves
established high standards of personnel administration, the employment
of qualified personnel for the complex tasks of old age assistance administration is left largely to chance. Some local employees in old age
assistance are no more enlightened than the old type of poor-law officials,
who made poor-relief administration in this country a national disgrace.
Today the local officials in the special programs of public assistance are
spending state and federal moneys in addition to local funds. It is no
longer, therefore, a personnel problem that can be left to the individual
initiative of thousands of local communities. Unless the states in cooperation with the Social Security Board can establish satisfactory
systems of personnel selection and training, the national program of
care for the dependent aged will become ineffective and corrupt.

[37] The state welfare agencies, of course, are powerless to affect local financial administration when this work is carried on by the fiscal officers of the city or county, rather
than by the welfare department.

CHAPTER 16

FAIR HEARING AND APPEAL

A FEW OF THE early old age assistance statutes provided that a dissatisfied applicant could have his case reviewed by the state administrative agency. Fair-hearing or appeal procedures are now universal in old age assistance programs owing to the fact that the federal Social Security Act requires that all state plans must provide for fair hearings to persons whose claims to assistance have been denied. Because an appeal provision gives the state agency the right to make a mandatory decision on individual cases brought to its attention, it has more far-reaching implications as a measure of control than almost any other power of the state agencies in those states where the program is locally administered. The widespread application of these procedures to public assistance is such a recent phenomenon, however, that it is one of the least standardized areas of administration in the field of old age assistance. Some states have developed elaborate appeal machinery; others are groping to find the best way to carry out this requirement; a few appear to be avoiding entirely its use.

Definitions

The common meaning of the term "fair hearing" is generally accepted and requires no elaboration. In contrast, "appeal" is frequently misused; therefore its meaning must be clarified. According to Webster's New International Dictionary,[1] an appeal is "a proceeding by which a cause is brought from an inferior to a superior court for re-examination or review and reversal, retrial, or modification." Implicit in this definition is the sense of action taken by a superior jurisdiction whereby the decision of a lower body is opened up for review; the term is so used in this report. In many instances, "fair hearing" and "appeal" have come to be used interchangeably in state old age assistance plans. Although this is loose usage, it is not incorrect if the procedures for giving an aggrieved person an opportunity formally to protest his treatment involve a state agency's review of an administrative decision previously

[1] Second Edition, Unabridged, 1937.

made by a local unit. In some state plans, however, no appeal in a strict sense of the term is possible since a single body, the state agency, makes all decisions on individual old age assistance grants; hence there is no superior administrative authority to review the action. Under these circumstances, a "fair hearing" may be granted by which the agency reviews its own action, but the term "appeal" cannot be applied to the proceeding.

The term "complaint" must carefully be distinguished from fair hearing and appeal. In most states a complaint is regarded as the first evidence of dissatisfaction of an applicant or recipient of old age assistance. In terms of procedure, a complaint is usually distinguished from an appeal in that it is disposed of by a written or oral response; moreover, if the response does not satisfy the complainant, he may protest again, and his grievance will subsequently be handled by a more formal review.

Three state laws—New Jersey, New York, and Washington—attach a special meaning to the term "complaint." For example, the New York State old age assistance statute provides that "Any person who has knowledge that old age relief is being improperly granted or administered under this article, may file a complaint in writing with the state department setting forth the particulars of such violation." In its administration of the law, the New York State Department has emphasized this distinction—as indicated in the following statement from an official in the Department:

> We have considered appeals to cover protests made by a recipient of old age relief, or his representative, or someone for him in which he asks for more favorable consideration than has been given, while complaints have been considered as covering only objections to what is considered unnecessary expenditure of public funds.

Complaints in this special use will not be discussed in this chapter.[2]

Purpose

The primary purpose of a fair hearing is to prevent discrimination against, or unjust treatment of, applicants or beneficiaries of old age assistance. An appeal procedure, which may be conducted by the method of fair hearing, may be established also for the purpose of giving the central or state agency an opportunity to review the action of local units. In this latter usage, it serves as a means of state control through

---

[2] Some states also use the term "inquiry" to include requests from applicants, recipients, or other citizens for information about individual grants or for interpretations of the law.

the adjustment of errors made by the local unit in individual cases. In addition, an appeal procedure may be used by a state agency to establish policy on a case-by-case basis. Although this is not one of the major purposes, it is a by-product of an appeal procedure that is of considerable importance in some states.

Scope

According to the federal Act, a state plan of old age assistance in order to be approved by the Social Security Board must "provide for granting to any individual whose claim for old age assistance is denied an opportunity for a fair hearing" before the state agency that administers or supervises the administration of the plan.[3] The scope of this requirement should be noted carefully. Literally, in order to comply with this provision the state need only provide a fair hearing for persons whose applications for old age assistance have been rejected; however, as pointed out below, many states have provided for a review of almost any type of grievance that may be brought to the state agency's attention by an applicant or recipient.[4] Moreover, since the provision of the federal law is applicable to both state-administered and state-supervised programs, an appeal is not required; only when a fair hearing is conducted by a state supervisory agency does it constitute an appeal. Since the Security Act specifies that the state agency which administers or supervises the old age assistance plan must be the body to provide the opportunity for a hearing, any plan that limits the avenue of appeal to the courts would not be approved.

The state provisions for fair hearing or appeal are found either in the state law, in the state rules, or in both. The old age assistance law in all but two of the states studied contains some requirement for a fair hearing or appeal. In the two states that do not have a statutory provision— Florida and Washington—the state agency under its rule-making power has authorized such action. In the majority of states, either regulations promulgated by the state agency or legal interpretations have extended the scope of the law.

Three of the state laws—California, Wisconsin, and Iowa—provide for an appeal only in case of denial of assistance. The California State Department has by regulation extended the area of appeals to those

---

[3] 49 *Stat. L.* 622, chap. 531, Tit. 1, sec. 2.

[4] It is understood that the Social Security Board has interpreted the language of the Act liberally, holding that any dissatisfaction of applicant respecting the amount of assistance granted is the equivalent of a "denial of an individual's claim." No formal interpretation to this effect, however, has been promulgated by the Board.

"whose aid has been decreased or discontinued by the [county] board of supervisors." The Wisconsin Attorney General has ruled in effect that if the applicant has not been granted the amount of assistance which he thinks he deserves, the grant decision should be considered a *partial denial* of his claim for assistance, and hence subject to appeal.[5]

The Iowa law provides that a person denied assistance by the state agency may appeal to the district court of the county in which he filed his application. According to the state plan furnished by Iowa to the Social Security Board, the state agency has by regulation provided that any individual whose claim has been denied may request a fair hearing before the state agency.[6]

The provisions found more commonly in the old age assistance laws studied grant the right of appeal or fair hearing to applicants whose claims to assistance have been denied or not acted upon within a reasonable time (defined in three state laws as thirty days), or whose grant of assistance has been modified or revoked. Two of the state laws— New Jersey and New York—go further and include instances when "the grant is deemed inadequate by the applicant." The Connecticut

[5] Opinion of J. E. Finnegan, Attorney General of Wisconsin, in letter of March 25, 1936, to Louis W. Cattau, District Attorney of Shawno County, Wisconsin:
"The word 'denial' as used in sec. 49.50 (4) is not confined to an absolute denial of assistance. Sec. 49.50 (4) Stats. provides in part:
" '(4) To enable this state to receive federal aid for old-age assistance, aid to dependent children, and blind pensions, any persons whose applications for any of these forms of assistance has been denied by the county officer charged with the administration of such form of assistance may apply to the state pension department for a review of such denials. . . .' Applicants for old age assistance are entitled to have their assistance 'fixed with due regard to the conditions in each case' Sec. 49.21. The discretion given to the administrative agency by the assistance statutes must be used in a reasonable manner so as to carry out the intent of the law. (See opinion of State Pension Department, dated March, 1936.) Although the administrative agency allows a person a certain amount of assistance, such allowance may, in fact, be a denial of the assistance to which the person is entitled under the law. Therefore, the word 'denial' as used in sec. 49.50 (4) Stats. is not confined to an absolute denial of assistance."
The Wisconsin law also stipulates that if an application has not been acted upon in ninety days, it shall be considered a denial.

[6] It was impossible for the survey staff to find any record of the promulgation of any such rule or regulation. Under the heading of "Investigation" in the Iowa law there is a provision for hearing the applicant before the county board if applicant "so requests" prior to the decision (recommendation) of the county board. The State Commission (which makes final decisions on cases) may make an investigation through the superintendent or through the Commission itself and "may direct a hearing before the board, of which the applicant shall have at least ten days' notice, and at which he may appear and offer evidence." This provision of hearings prior to decision is quite different from a requirement of a fair hearing after a decision has been reached. In several of the early plans of old age assistance which were administered locally by a judge, such as those in Colorado and Wisconsin, it was customary to have a hearing as a device for assembling evidence prior to the decision; this practice is still used in modified form in Milwaukee County, Wisconsin, and perhaps elsewhere.

statute is the simplest and most direct. It merely provides the right to a hearing for "any applicant or beneficiary aggrieved by the decision" of the state agency. The two states studied that have no statutory provision for appeals or fair hearings—Florida and Washington—both provide in rules and regulations for fair hearings for persons whose applications have been denied or whose grants have been modified or suspended.

Despite the fact that most state laws or regulations specify the circumstances under which persons may appeal, in actual practice, wherever a genuine fair-hearing or appeal procedure exists, no evidence has been found of a strict construction of the statute or rules. One of the most common types of protest received is that in which an individual complains about the size of his award; all state agencies that have an appeal or fair-hearing procedure seem to accept these cases even though there may be no provision for them in the law or regulations.[7]

Basic Methods

In some states no appeal within the administrative system is possible since the final decision on all grants of assistance is made by the state agency, and no higher administrative authority is empowered to act upon protests from applicant or beneficiary. Consequently, a fair hearing only is provided. The dissatisfied applicant or recipient in these states must present his case to the officials who bear the administrative responsibility for the decision against which he is protesting.[8] It is perhaps not accidental that the laws in Connecticut and Iowa—two states of this type—provide for an appeal to a court for persons aggrieved by the administrative decision. In Connecticut, a person who is dissatisfied with the result of the review of his case by the state agency may appeal to the superior court of the county in which he resides. In Iowa, a person whose application has been denied by the state commission may appeal to the district court of the county in which the application was filed.[9]

In those states in which the decision on individual grants is made

[7] Prior to the amendment of the old age assistance statutes in 1936, the Massachusetts State Department was limited in its appeal procedure to cases of applicants who had been denied assistance by the local agencies. This limitation was rigidly adhered to, and the department made no attempt to review formally any other appeal cases.

[8] Some measure of detachment was secured in the Washington plan at the time it operated on a centralized basis by the fact that decisions on individual cases were made in the first instance by the head of the division of old age assistance, whereas fair hearings were conducted by the head of the welfare department. Of course, the director of the department was in fact responsible for decisions made by his subordinate in the first instance; hence the levels of authority created by this arrangement were largely artificial.

[9] See discussion of appeals to the court, below, p. 314.

in the local unit and the state agency maintains a supervisory responsibility, the methods of conducting appeals differ chiefly in the degree of formality attached to the procedure, which in turn appears to depend upon the emphasis given to appeals in the total state supervisory program. In states with a weak or undeveloped supervisory program, great significance is attached to the appeal proceedings, and a highly formalized procedure has been worked out. In contrast, in states that have developed constructive supervisory programs, the appeal provisions are given less prominence, the range varying from states which have established some formal procedure to three states which for all practical purposes had no genuine appeal or fair-hearing procedure in operation at the time of the staff visit. Without longer and more intense observation than was possible in this study, it would be difficult to say whether the latter three states have developed no formal procedure designedly or because no protests have arisen that required formal review by the state agency.

ELEMENTS IN ADMINISTRATION OF FAIR HEARING OR APPEAL

If effective provision is to be made for dissatisfied persons to present their grievances, there must, of necessity, be some measure of formality attached to the arrangement. Primarily there must be an established procedure that is well understood by the state agency, by the local units, by applicants and recipients, and by the public. Many states describe their appeal procedure in a special bulletin to local agencies. The bulletin usually contains the rules and regulations of the state department regarding fair hearing, and enumerates the steps followed by the state agency in acting upon protests from applicants or beneficiaries. For example, the New Jersey bulletin first cites the applicable section of the law; this is followed by a statement of the policy of the department pursuant to the statutory provision. It then sets forth the role of the local agency in the proceedings, which includes the option of a local hearing prior to the matter's being handled by the state. The elements of the state hearing are outlined in detail and include a statement of the manner in which the final decision will be issued. Several states provide a special form on which a request for appeal may be submitted; nevertheless, in these instances, it is usually also provided that the applicant may make his request for a fair hearing in his own words in a direct communication.

In three of the states studied it was impossible to find any material that had been circulated to the staff of the state agency or to the local units indicating the procedure to be followed in appeal cases. Although in two of these states a method appeared to have been established, it apparently had deliberately been left vague in order to avoid its receiving undue attention. These two states were evidently working on the theory that to establish too definite a procedure would tend to make the fair-hearing device overly prominent in the eyes both of the administrative officers and of the public. An informal plan was being followed in one of these states, which consisted almost entirely of a special investigation by a state worker, who visited the complainant and endeavored to settle the matter with him. The state officials considered that this was technically within the federal requirement for a fair hearing, since the person with a grievance was given an opportunity to explain his difficulties directly to a state worker. Strictly speaking, this method might be considered within the letter of the law in the absence of more specific definition by the Social Security Board of the requirements for a satisfactory fair hearing.[10]

Limiting fair hearing to personal visitation by a state worker, genuine though its intent may be, appears to be unsatisfactory from several points of view. In the first place, the appellant does not necessarily recognize the state worker as a person who can satisfy him or as one of higher authority than a local worker, for the state worker may not appear any more important or impressive than the local worker. Furthermore, although undue formality in a hearing is to be avoided, it is desirable to have some semblance of an established procedure so that the appellant may realize that he is actually being given an opportunity to have his case reviewed by persons in authority. A home visit does not usually accomplish this since the appellant may be only too accustomed to home visits. The opportunity to be summoned to an office where he may speak before several persons may cloak the occasion with sufficient dignity to make it more impressive for the appellant.

A second objection is that the informal visit by a state worker leaves the local agency out entirely. On occasion the state worker may make promises, or at least give the complainant assurances, which, either through intent or neglect, are not reported to the local agency. The local agency, which must carry on day-by-day relations with the appellant

---

[10] The Social Security Board as yet has not officially defined its requirements for a fair-hearing procedure. The Bureau of Public Assistance has made available to its field staff and to the states a memorandum entitled "Some Factors to Be Considered in Developing Procedures for Fair Hearing," which is suggestive rather than mandatory. It is understood that rules are now in the process of formulation.

after the visit of the state worker, is left in the dark about what decision was reached and what was said to complainant. This makes for difficult relationships between the local agency and the local beneficiaries.[11]

Information Regarding Right to Appeal

In order that dissatisfied persons may have an opportunity to have their cases reviewed, they must be aware that a procedure has been established by which their protest will receive consideration. The question of how much emphasis to place upon the right to a fair hearing has proved one of the most perplexing problems in the administration of appeal procedures. The majority of the states visited have not established a system of formal *individual* notification that a plan is in effect for considering grievances, but several have made some arrangement of this sort. Two states, both of which make the final decision on eligibility in the state office, have included on the form used as a notice of rejection a printed statement of the rejected applicant's privilege to file a protest with the state office if he is not satisfied with the decision. One state supervisory agency requires the county units to notify all rejected applicants that they have been refused assistance and to include in the notification a statement of the right to appeal to the state department.[12] A fourth state has prepared a leaflet for prospective applicants containing information about provisions of the old age assistance law and including a statement of the right of the individual to appeal to the state department if he is dissatisfied with the decision of the local unit. It is impossible to know how widely such a booklet is circulated.[13] A fifth state includes in the prescribed form for the notification of rejected applicants a sentence requesting the individual concerned to file any additional information with the local unit which he feels would warrant a reconsideration of his case. The other states visited apparently considered it unwise to place too much stress on the opportunity to appeal. Some claim that prospective applicants are usually told orally by the local agency of their right to appeal and that information on the provisions of the law has received such wide circulation that most applicants and recipients are well aware of their rights.

[11] One state that uses state workers to conduct local hearings has avoided these difficulties by providing that the local worker is always to be brought in at the conclusion of the hearing so that there may be a clear understanding among the state worker, the local worker, and the appellant regarding the decision reached.

[12] This state agency does not prescribe a form for the counties to use for this purpose.

[13] A number of states have prepared similar pamphlets but have felt that it was unwise to suggest the possibility of unjust action in material sent to prospective applicants.

That the public may be informed about appeal procedures through other sources than the administrative agencies is shown by the fact that of the twelve visited the one that has had the most appeal cases does not require any formal notification to rejected applicants of their right to appeal. Apparently the information about appeal provisions was, in this instance, circulated by state political leaders.

If state officials are convinced that adequate investigations are made of applications and that decisions are reached only after careful consideration of all pertinent facts, they believe, quite naturally, that there is little that the rejected applicant can gain by an appeal procedure. Furthermore, many state officials think that a great disservice is done to individuals if false hopes are raised about what can be gained through a reconsideration by the state. The experience in one state that has placed great emphasis upon the appeal procedure as a means of state control with little attention proportionately to constructive supervision of local efforts illustrates the point. In this state many appeal cases have been instigated by politicians, not without the tacit approval of state officials, to whom rejected applicants have protested and to whom the existence of a state appeal procedure has presented a convenient "out" when they have been harassed by constituents objecting to decisions of local welfare officials. The state appeal authority ruled against the appellant in over two-thirds of the seven hundred cases on which hearings were conducted in a ten-month period. Were the time and emphasis given to the appeal procedure in this state directed to the improvement of local administration, applicants would be less likely to be led to believe that they were entitled to benefits that could not legally be granted.

Nevertheless it is obvious that an appeal or fair-hearing procedure is meaningless if there is no way that a person may know about it. Actually, however, the fact that a state receives a large number of appeal cases in which the appellant has little or no possibility to gain the end he desires does not appear to revolve primarily around the question of whether he is formally notified of his right to appeal. The most important contributing factor seems to be the manner in which he is informed of the decision regarding his application, particularly when his claim for assistance has to be denied. This point has been recognized by the Wisconsin Department:[14]

> Notification of denial should include a careful explanation of the reason therefor. The experience of the state pension department in hearing

[14] State Pension Department of Wisconsin, Bulletin No. WS.T.-A.D.11, April 3, 1936.

appeals warrants the view that many appeals can be avoided if the applicant is afforded a clear understanding of the reasons for denial. Other appeals can be avoided if care is taken to explain to the applicant the provisions of the statutes.

Care and patience in the explanation of the rejection or of any decision not granting the full request of the applicant are the most effective preventives of appeal action that may be disappointing to the appellant. The best local agencies attempt wherever possible to make the announcement of adverse decisions a matter of personal interview in which a careful explanation is made to the applicant of the reasons for not granting his request. Some agencies endeavor to bring in his friends and relatives for the final interview in which the decision on his application is announced. Upon this occasion the applicant is given every opportunity to inquire into the reasons for the decision, and the provisions of the law are explained to him in detail. If he thoroughly understands the reasons he is not likely to seek recourse to a higher authority.[15]

Opportunity for Local Agency to Review Its Action

The authority of the state agency to conduct fair hearings is not weakened if the state, before it holds its own hearing, submits appeal cases for reconsideration to the local unit that made the original decision. This is the procedure followed in the majority of the states visited in which the decision on eligibility and size of grant is made in the local units. Compelling reasons are offered for this practice. If some mistake appears to have been made in arriving at the original decision, if the appellant has new information pertaining to his claim to present, or if he feels that his circumstances have not been clearly understood, the agency that made the initial decision should have the opportunity to review the facts and to reconsider its previous decision before a superior body takes action. Some critics have interpreted the plan of referring appeal cases back to the local agency as an attempt by the state agency either to avoid responsibility or to make it more difficult for the appellant to present his case to the state. Actually, from the standpoint of the appellant's convenience, it is usually much simpler for him to present his case locally—backed by a request from the state agency—than to have to participate in the more involved and slower moving state

[15] Ideally the personal interview should be used in informing applicant or beneficiary of all administrative decisions affecting his circumstances, but it is particularly desirable when the decision is a denial or partial denial of his claim for assistance. For further discussion see chap. 9.

procedures. Furthermore, to preserve the administrative authority of the local unit, the local officials should have an opportunity to reconsider their action. When this practice is not followed, it is found that many cases are acted upon by the state agency which could have been cleared up without a state hearing had the local agency had the additional facts or the opportunity to explain its decisions more fully to the appellant or his friends.[16]

When the local agency is given an opportunity to review its action prior to a state hearing, the state may easily determine whether the local agencies are making a genuine review of the case by requesting appellants to inform the state agency if they are not satisfied with the results of the local review and by requiring prompt reporting from the localities on the disposition of these cases. If cases from a particular jurisdiction on return to the state agency show both that the appellant is frequently in the right and that the local agency is failing to give a fair review of cases, it is conclusive evidence of the need to reorganize the local work. In short, if the local agency is given an opportunity to reconsider its action prior to formal review by the state agency, the local prerogatives are properly respected, the interests of the appellants are safeguarded, the state agency is relieved of much useless activity, and the state-control aspects of the appeal procedure are made much more effective.

Timeliness of Action

Whether the state agency itself conducts the fair hearings in the first instance or whether requests for a hearing are first referred to the local units, it is important that the appellant's protest be given prompt attention. The Wisconsin law provides that the hearing must be held within thirty days from the time when the complaint has been filed. Although the state agency has looked upon this provision as directing rather than mandatory, nevertheless it has carried out the requirements in spirit, and the hearings are scheduled systematically and promptly. In other states it has been observed that the appellant is frequently required to wait for months before his case is given consideration. This aggravates the appellant's dissatisfaction and, if an injustice has been done, it postpones too long the correction of the mistake. The speed with which action is taken on requests for a state review depends in some

---

[16] To be effective, this initial local referral of appeal cases implies that the local agency must make a genuine reinvestigation of the appellant's circumstances. This does not always happen.

states upon the staff organization for handling appeals—a point which will be discussed subsequently. In other states requests for hearings are not acted upon promptly because the state agency is swamped with appeals. This congestion could have been relieved in some instances by insistence upon improvements in administration in local jurisdictions, and in others, by having many of the cases reviewed in the localities prior to formal state consideration.

Authority of a State Ruling

In most of the states in which the state agency is a supervisory rather than an administrative body, the law provides that the ruling of the state agency in appeal cases is binding upon the locality. In the states visited, no local jurisdiction had formally raised a question about the state's power to make mandatory its decision in appeal cases, although several state officials expressed concern whether the courts, if appealed to by a local agency, would uphold the state decision in all instances. In a locally administered plan, the issue would be sharpest in an appeal case in which the locality had rejected an applicant's claim to assistance. If the state upholds the claim of the applicant, the locality is compelled to grant assistance to a person it considers ineligible. Thus the state is forcing the expenditure of local funds contrary to the judgment of local officials. This seems clearly to be the power of the state agency under the old age assistance statutes, but if state action is inhibited in any state through fear of the actual power of the state agency, it would be wholesome to encourage a locality to carry a case to court in order to secure a directive ruling.

Conduct of the State Hearing

A memorandum regarding fair hearings, prepared by the Bureau of Public Assistance of the Social Security Board, lists the following "essential elements of fair hearing which should be observed with respect to the right of the appellant." These are given in full as representing the best experience of the states to date in the conduct of hearings on appeals.

a. The individual whose claim is denied and who requests a hearing must be given due notice of the time and place of hearing with a reasonable time in which to prepare his case.

b. The hearing must be held within a reasonable time after application for it has been made.

c. The individual must be given an opportunity to present his claim in oral or written form, to produce witnesses, and to review the basis of denial of his claim.

1. Presentation of a claim to the reviewing body by a representative of the state or local agency is not an acceptable substitute for direct presentation by the individual.

2. One of the primary purposes of fair hearing is to give the applicant assurance that his claim, whether accepted or denied, has received intelligent and sympathetic consideration. If he wishes to have his claim presented by an attorney he should be permitted to do so. Such service, however, should not be necessary and specific instructions with regard to this possibility may give the appellant the impression that it is expected, and create a feeling of dissatisfaction on the part of the individual who is unable to engage an attorney. The State Plan should provide that the use of lawyers is permissible but not necessary and not recommended for the purpose of furthering a claim. The problem in individual cases can be better handled by administrative practice than by specific instruction or formal procedure.

This is also true of admission of witnesses. An appellant should be permitted to produce witnesses who can support his claim. These witnesses may include members of pressure groups who in some instances can give important information with respect to the claim. The routine admission of group testimony may tend to create the impression that pressure and special influence are necessary to leadership; group pressure may tend to obscure the facts on the basis of which decision should be made, prejudice the reviewing body and weaken rather than support the claim of the appellant. Witnesses can be most effective if their testimony is heard individually.

d. Fair hearing shall be privately conducted and shall be open only to the claimant, designated representatives of the state agency, and individuals who have evidence bearing directly on the claim.

e. The decision of the state agency must be based solely upon the evidence introduced at the hearing and such other documents as are referred to at the hearing and which the claimant has had an opportunity to inspect.

f. The individual must be fully informed of the basis of denial of his claim. It is not necessary that confidential case records be produced at the hearing. If they are produced the claimant would be entitled to examine them. For this reason, it may be desirable that documents from the record rather than the entire record be produced.

The choice of the members of the state agency staff to conduct fair hearings is determined largely by the purpose of the hearings. If the main objective is justice for individual applicants, with little or no concern for correcting the conditions out of which the injustice has arisen, appeals can most conveniently be handled by persons selected specifically for this purpose and who are required to perform this duty and no other. If the hearings are intended to be an integral part of the total supervisory effort of the state, the staff arrangements for hearings must include participation by workers responsible for relations with the localities involved. Only a minimum of value is derived from the appeal procedure if the state supervisory staff is limited to the records of the hearings to learn of the results and of the conditions disclosed by the testimony, but a dual advantage is gained by having the representative of the state agency responsible for the supervision of a particular locality present when an appeal case is considered that affects the administration in that jurisdiction. On the one hand, the state supervisor may be able to contribute illuminating information on the factors leading to the claim of abuse. It may frequently happen that the very circumstances which developed this particular appeal case are those which the state worker has been trying to correct. Or, the hearing may reveal local conditions which have not otherwise come to the attention of the state supervisor, and only by being present at the hearing and learning both the case of the appellant and the defense of the locality can he get an accurate picture of these circumstances.

There is an additional weakness in an appeal procedure conducted by officials other than those assigned to supervise the locality involved. The local agencies and the beneficiaries of the program may come to look upon the appeal authorities as the most influential arm of the state agency. Even though the contact of officials conducting appeals is only with individual cases and individual abuses, the fact that they seem to have final authority in these instances may give undue emphasis to their importance in the state agency. In the long run this would tend to lessen the supervisors' influence with the localities, especially if they have been attempting to improve local administration through an educational rather than an authoritarian approach.

When many requests for review are being presented to the state agency, it may be impossible for the state supervisors to give the time necessary to the conduct of the hearings. Under these circumstances, the state office should at least require that the supervisor be notified of hearings to be held involving his jurisdiction so that he may attend if possible. This practice is followed in Wisconsin.

Even though hearings may be conducted by minor officials, most states place the final responsibility for the settlement of appeal cases in the administrative head of the state agency or of the old age assistance division—a single executive or a board, as the case may be. One board assumed this responsibility in the early days of the program in order to establish a set of case rulings as precedent to be followed by the state staff. In another state the law specifies an appeal board of which the head of the state welfare department and the chief of the old age assistance division are members. Other executives or boards have assumed the responsibility for final adjudication of appeal cases in order to keep in direct touch with some of the problems arising in the administration of the law and to have some check on the effectiveness of the state staff itself. Only a few agencies, however, appear to have decided upon this assignment of responsibility because they have recognized the relationship of appeal decisions to their rule-making authority.

Appeal cases frequently involve a challenge to a state regulation. Often the local unit must reject an application, even though it may think that the applicant should be awarded a grant, because acceptance would mean a technical violation of a state rule. In such instances the local agency is as anxious as the appellant to have the case adjudicated by the state agency. In other cases the local agencies face problems of eligibility on which there is no clear ruling by the state, and they may encourage applicants to appeal to the state in order to obtain a ruling. Although in a well operated state program it should not be necessary to go through an appeal procedure in order to obtain policy rulings, such tactics are likely to be necessary in many states at the present time, particularly in the formative stages of the program. When an appeal case is carried to the state for purposes of policy determination, it is well to have the decision made or reviewed by the highest administrative authority in the department.[17]

One difficulty involved in having the head of the state agency (whether this be a single executive or a board) act on appeal cases is the time-consuming nature of a fair hearing. Ordinarily, if the head of the agency or the board is to function in these cases, provision must be made for genuine hearings with due regard for the convenience of the appellant and local officials. Most busy executives and boards, particularly in the larger states, do not have the time required by these

[17] State agencies frequently fail to realize that their action on appeal cases establishes precedent for the local units; were they to look upon their action in this light they might make more judicious and thoughtful decisions. Some state officials appear to be naive about the effect of appeal decisions. In one state where the head of the state agency insisted that the state had no real power to supervise or control the activities of the local agencies, two units were found to be keeping track of all rulings on appeal cases which they could obtain. These rulings were used as a body of precedent by which subsequent action of the local agency was determined.

proceedings.[18] The procedure followed in Wisconsin is the only plan observed by which the head of the agency (in this instance a board) can make rulings fairly without also being compelled to take up the time required by the conduct of hearings. Under this plan, two state staff members who have no other responsibilities conduct the hearings in various parts of the state. These officials submit a summary report of each hearing documented by a statement of the legal aspects of the case and by a complete stenographic record of the proceedings. Thus the state board is furnished with all the facts and opinions presented at the hearing in a form that can readily be reviewed.

The conduct of appeal hearings by the lay board of a state department presents some disadvantages. One argument frequently made for having this type of board conduct appeal hearings is that it will make a more impartial review than a paid official. But in no instance observed have board members appeared to be more judicious than trained public officials in handling appeal cases. Moreover, paid officials have seemed more alert than board members to the significance of appeal cases for the total administrative and supervisory responsibility of the state agency. Citizen board members, who meet once a month to consider appeal cases along with other business of the department, do not always appreciate that their decision on an individual case may have widespread policy implications. Since they are not actively engaged in the work, they are likely to look only upon the particular needs or circumstances in an individual case without regard to questions of policy. One instance reported to the staff, while undoubtedly exceptional, illustrates the problem of lay authority in appeal cases. A state board was called upon to consider a case in which the appellant was seeking a larger grant of assistance to care for his medical needs. In the course of the hearing it was disclosed that his poor physical condition was the result of an early luetic infection. When this fact was discovered, some of the board members took the position that the appellant should be given no grant at all because they believed that no person who had had syphilis should be granted old age assistance, although there was no legal sanction for such a moralistic ruling.[19]

[18] One state board which was attempting to pass on appeals was constantly falling behind in this task as the following record of appeal cases pending at the end of four successive months in 1937 shows:

April 30	36 cases pending
May 31	65 cases pending
June 30	83 cases pending
July 31	89 cases pending

[19] For further discussion of the participation of boards in case decisions see chap. 17.

Records

In view of the importance of fair-hearing procedure to the state agency, it was astonishing to find how few state agencies had made an attempt to keep track of the work being done in this field. At the time of the staff visit only four states were able to furnish simple current figures showing the number of fair hearings requested, the number of hearings conducted, the disposition of the cases that had been considered, and the number still pending. The importance of such records appears obvious but apparently needs to be emphasized. Figures of this sort furnish a record of the amount of appeal activity and the speed with which cases are being disposed of. Statistics on the reasons for appeal and on disposition give some indication of the factors causing discontent to applicants and beneficiaries. Additional statistics showing the localities from which appeals have come would give the state agency clues to whether dissatisfaction was greater in some localities than in others.

At least seven of the states, at the time of the staff visit, kept some record of the individual hearings. Two states kept stenographic reports of each hearing as a matter of protection to the appellant, the local agency, and the state agency; others maintained less complete reports. Two state agencies were unable to tell how many cases had been handled through the fair-hearing procedure because once the case had been dismissed the papers were filed in the state case record on the individual, and no index list was maintained for reference. As a consequence, officials in these two states could discuss specific appeal cases only if they happened to remember the names of the individuals who had been granted fair hearings. In one of these states the claim that a fair-hearing procedure was in operation could not be substantiated to the satisfaction of the survey staff because the state officials were unable to recall the names of persons who had been granted hearings and hence they could not produce any records.

The question of how complete a record should be kept cannot be answered dogmatically. The filing of a complete report on each case, including all papers and a stenographic record of the proceedings, is the ideal, but many states cannot afford to prepare so complete a record.[20] Certainly the report of an individual hearing should contain

[20] It is interesting to note that the hearings on workmen's compensation cases in one state labor department are recorded by a stenographer, but the notes are never written up unless some question is raised about the content of the hearing. A municipal personnel agency has recently recorded oral examinations for an important position by a mechanical recording device.

all available data including the original complaint, the state investigation of the claim of the applicant, the report of the local agency on its decision, and the material presented by the appellant and his associates at the hearing. This latter, if presented orally, need not be preserved verbatim but at least a summary should be kept. The decision reached and the reasons for the decision should complete the record. If the state office keeps individual case records for the state as a whole, this appeal record may be filed in the individual's folder, providing that a separate index of appeal cases is maintained. Otherwise, the records of the appeal hearings should be maintained in a separate folder file and copies furnished to the local agencies involved.

No state agency can claim to be giving serious consideration to the legal or regulatory provisions requiring fair hearings for aggrieved applicants or beneficiaries if they do not keep track of the work done under this heading. Furthermore, since the local agencies are very alert to the decisions of state agencies in fair hearings and use them as precedent for subsequent action, it is wise for the state agency to protect itself by keeping its own record of the individual cases. Finally, since the appeal procedure is potentially an important factor in state supervision, the experience under fair hearings should be subject to careful, current analysis.

Appeals to the Courts

The old age assistance laws of Iowa and Connecticut, where both eligibility and the size of the grant are decided in the state office, provide for an appeal to the court under special circumstances. In Iowa this recourse is limited to persons whose applications have been denied;[21] in Connecticut an appeal may be made only after the state has granted a fair hearing.[22] In Iowa, according to state officials, there had been at the

[21] *Code of Iowa,* 1935, chap. 266-F1, sec. 5296: "The commission shall decide upon the application and fix the amount of the assistance, if any. Any applicant whose application for assistance has been rejected may within thirty days appeal from the decision of the commission to the district court of the county in which the application was filed by serving a ten days' notice of such appeal upon the superintendent or upon any member of the commission, in the manner required for service of an original notice. Upon service of such notice, the commission shall furnish the applicant a copy of the application, a copy of all supporting papers, a transcript of the testimony and a copy of its decision. The court shall hear and determine said application on its merits."

[22] Connecticut, *Public Acts,* 1935, chap. 110: "Any applicant or beneficiary aggrieved by a decision of the bureau made without a hearing may make application in writing to the bureau for a hearing and shall state, in such application, in simple language, the reasons why he claims to be aggrieved. Such application for a hearing shall be mailed to the bureau within ten days after the rendition of such decision. The bureau, upon receipt of such application, shall hold a hearing, and shall, at least ten days prior to the date

time of the staff visit only seven persons in the course of about two years who had attempted to appeal to the court. Although no records of these cases were available, it was reported that six of them withdrew their appeals and the seventh was thrown out on a review of the brief by a judge because the protest was entirely on the grounds of the size of the award, over which the court claimed it had no jurisdiction. In Connecticut no cases have been carried to court to date.

Apparently no state law would prevent an individual who is aggrieved by the decision of an administrative agency from resorting to court action, particularly if he thinks that the law has been interpreted incorrectly and to his detriment by an administrative officer. Aside from the Iowa experience, record of court action was encountered in only one state. In Massachusetts, two cases involving an interpretation of the law have been carried to the state supreme court. In one, the court was called upon to interpret the meaning of the word "deserving" —then in the law; it held that such interpretation was a matter of administrative discretion. In the other, the court decided that under the then existing residence requirements a person must have resided in the state for the twenty years immediately preceding his reaching the age of seventy rather than prior to the filing of his application; this ruling was a reversal of the decision of the administrative officer. This latter case was carried to the supreme court with the encouragement of the state agency, which was anxious to have a court ruling on the point involved.

The use of appeal to courts has been so slight to date that no final judgment can be reached of its value to applicants and beneficiaries of old age assistance. There is no reason to believe, however, that citizens should need to go to the expense and trouble of appealing cases to courts, if the states establish adequate facilities for fair hearings.

THE APPEAL AND ADMINISTRATION

The appeal procedure has come to stay in old age assistance administration, but it is a delicate matter that must be handled intelligently

---

set for such hearing, mail a notice, giving the time and place thereof, to the applicant or beneficiary and to the chief executive authority, or his appointee, of the town in which such applicant resides. After such hearing, the bureau shall render a final decision, which shall supersede the decision made without a hearing, and of which final decision notice shall be given the applicant for hearing as hereinbefore provided. Such decision after hearing shall be final except that the applicant for such hearing, if aggrieved, may appeal therefrom, within thirty days from the date of its rendition, to the superior court for the county wherein he resides, in accordance with the provisions of section 5465 of the general statutes. No appeal may be taken from a decision made without a hearing."

and judiciously as well as sympathetically. Ideally it is a means of insuring justice for aged citizens of the state; practically it may easily be the means of superseding established executive authority. The British system of noncontributory pensions furnishes the executive officer with rigid rules of eligibility. Some flexibility in the scheme occurs through the power of the local committee which hears appeals to be liberal in the determination of fact, although the committee is not empowered to permit express variations from the prescribed limitations. In the matter of verification of age, for example, the administrative officer must refuse a grant if documentary proof of age is lacking, but the committee may "determine" an applicant's age by fiat. In contrast, most of the state laws in the United States allow the administrator flexibility in the determination both of the amount of the grant and, within certain general rules, of eligibility.

The decisions reached by local units, and by the state administrations in review of local action, are judgments largely based upon an investigation of social and economic facts, tempered always by state policy and by the total amount of money made available by the appropriating bodies. The quality of these judgments varies with the officer making them, and it is only fair that the state administration be empowered to provide a special review of the local judgment when a person presents a grievance.

The establishment of extra-administrative appeal boards is frequently urged. For example, a special commission in Massachusetts recommended the establishment of an appeal board with mandatory powers in disputes "in the matter of eligibility of those seeking old age assistance" and with the additional duty of acquainting "applicants with their rights under the laws." One member of this board was to be the superintendent of the bureau of old age assistance, but the other two— that is, the majority—were to be citizens appointed for four years by the governor at annual salaries of $1,000 plus expenses.[23] Advocates of such detached judicial bodies apparently fail to distinguish between the decisions of administrators that are judgments based upon facts and those based upon an interpretation of the law. An independent body with power to review the former type of administrative action would inevitably assume the role of making all important executive decisions, and in effect, of determining all significant policies, although it would bear no responsibility for their execution. A remedy for unsympathetic

[23] Commonwealth of Massachusetts, *Report of the Special Commission Established to Study and Revise the Laws Relating to Public Welfare.* House Doc., No. 1551, 1936.

or inept administration of a law is not to set up more machinery to review the actions and correct the mistakes of reactionary or stupid public officials but rather to replace them with intelligent public servants. The same administrative difficulty is not inherent in an appeal board used solely for the purpose of passing on cases involving interpretation of the law, but undoubtedly the strongest advocates of the independent appeal board would be the first to protest that this would be usurping the function of the courts.[24]

★　★　★

Conclusions drawn from the experience with fair hearings in the states to date are:

1. A definite procedure should be established for the filing and hearing of appeals.

2. Fair hearings should be permitted for reconsideration of the size of the grant as well as of the rejection of applicants.

3. The state administration should be the final authority in appeals, but where local units of government participate in the administration of old age assistance they should be given an opportunity to modify decisions previously made before the state takes mandatory action.

4. The state should keep a record of the individual proceedings, an index to these records, and statistics showing the number, source, and disposition of cases.

5. Hearings resulting in mandatory action should be conducted by persons having administrative responsibility.

[24] The British system, where separation of powers is not so strictly adhered to, permits no court appeal but instead grants final appeal from the local committee to the National Ministry of Health, whose decision is final. No attorney may be retained at any point in the proceedings.

CHAPTER 17

THE PLACE OF BOARDS IN THE MANAGEMENT OF STATE AND LOCAL AGENCIES

ADMINISTRATIVE CONTROL of state and local welfare agencies is assigned by many state welfare laws to uncompensated or compensated boards, which usually select an executive to perform the tasks of management under their direction. The use of boards is so prevalent in the field of public welfare that a discussion of the administration of aid to the aged must give consideration to the types of these boards, the nature of their authority, and the methods of board operation.

In terms of the legal powers under which they operate, and the degree of authority retained or delegated, public welfare boards may be classified under three groups. *Executive boards* are those which by law are given the administrative responsibility for the operation of a public agency and in which the members themselves perform many major duties involved in the direct operation of the agency. An example of an executive board is found in a small political subdivision where the board, designated as responsible for a particular activity, does not hire staff but performs the activity itself. The principle is the same, however, when in a much larger agency, board members perform major direct activities themselves and delegate to the staff only secondary responsibilities. In larger agencies members of such a board are usually compensated for their services.[1]

Administrative boards are those which have the final responsibility for the operation of a public agency but delegate the executive duties to an employed staff. Members of a board of this type ordinarily are not compensated for their services over and above necessary expenses. The uncompensated administrative board is the most common type of

[1] The usual classification of public welfare boards includes a type known as the "board of control," a small paid board with executive responsibilities. In the classifications employed here, the board of control is included under "executive boards," the latter term covering all boards, compensated or uncompensated, which perform direct executive functions.

board found in public welfare. A wide variety of practice, however, is found among administrative boards, marked chiefly by the degree of responsibility delegated to the executive. *Advisory boards,* the third type, have little or no administrative responsibility; their chief duty is to advise on administrative policies and other matters.

BOARDS OF STATE AGENCIES: TYPES AND COMPOSITION

Of the eleven state boards observed, seven are clearly administrative boards.[2] They are in California, Colorado, Florida, Indiana, Mississippi, New Jersey, and New York. The board of the State Pension Department in Wisconsin is difficult to classify. Legally, it has the administrative responsibility for the execution of the program, but of its three members, two are state officials serving ex officio and the third is the director of the Department.[3] It is difficult, therefore, to distinguish between the activities of the director as a member of the board and as director of the Department. Since the other two board members do not perform executive duties in the Department, the board is classed as administrative.

The Iowa Old Age Assistance Commission, which was abolished in 1937, was clearly an executive board since it met three or four times a week and performed detailed executive functions including the final review and approval of all assistance grants. Apparently the intent of the law was to provide an administrative board of citizens, but in actual performance the board became a compensated, executive board. The law provided a per diem of ten dollars in addition to expenses for each meeting attended, but the Commission met so frequently that each member received a considerable sum for his services during a year.[4]

The state board in Massachusetts is by definition in the law an advisory

[2] Washington is the only state studied which does not provide for some kind of state welfare board.

[3] "There is created within the industrial commission a state pension department consisting of a member of the industrial commission, selected by such commission, the director of the budget and the administrative head of said department who shall be known as the supervisor of pensions." Wisconsin, *Stat.,* 1935, sec. 49.50.

[4] For the fiscal year ending June 30, 1936, the members of this Commission received for per diem and expenses the following amounts: $2,511.53; $3,606.65; and $2,126.65. Most state laws provide a per diem and expenses for citizen boards so that no person may be precluded from serving because of his economic circumstances. Usually, however, a sum from $500 to $1,000 is fixed as the maximum payment which may be made to any individual board member during a calendar year. The Iowa Commission was abolished in 1937 when the administration of old age assistance became by law a function of a newly established state welfare agency.

board. It is called into play chiefly upon the initiative of the state commissioner. In recent years it has functioned little, although at one time it was a vital force. At the present time, its chief function is to consider policies of the department, and it is required to review all rules and regulations issued by the department which presumably include those formulated by the bureau of old age assistance. Until 1937, one member served on the appeal board for old age assistance.[5]

The Public Welfare Council in Connecticut may be classed as an advisory board although its power is more extensive than that of most advisory groups. In one sense it is a state agency separate from the office of the Commissioner of Welfare, since it has its own budget and staff; but it is not clear in the law whether the two are to be regarded as parts of a single agency or separate agencies. A recent official state report speaks of them as parts of a whole: "The department of public welfare consists of the public welfare council and the commissioner of welfare."[6] The Public Welfare Council may also be regarded as a supervisory body since it has the authority to report on the administration and operation of any state welfare laws and because the Commissioner of Welfare (although otherwise he has full executive authority) must secure the approval of the Council for the appointment of all personnel.[7]

The members of the boards in all these states except Wisconsin are selected by the governor, usually for overlapping terms. The number of board members is indicated in the following table:

State	Number of Members	Type of Board
California	7a	administrative
Colorado	7a	administrative
Connecticut	5	advisory
Florida	7	administrative
Indiana	5	administrative
Iowa	3	executive
Massachusetts	7a	advisory
Mississippi	3	administrative
New Jersey	9b	administrative
New York	15	administrative
Wisconsin	3a	administrative

a Includes the executive officer of the department.
b Includes the governor, ex officio.

[5] An amendment to the old age statute enacted in May, 1937, limited the membership in the appeal board to three executive staff members.

[6] *Report of the Connecticut Commission Concerning the Reorganization of the State Departments* (1937), p. 473.

[7] This arrangement resulted from a compromise between advocates of an administrative board and their opponents when the welfare laws were amended in 1935.

Some legal restrictions are placed on the governor in the appointment of the state welfare board. In Florida three members of the board must be women and only one member may be appointed from any one of the twelve welfare districts. In Indiana no more than three members of the board of five may be from a single political party; in Iowa no more than two of the three members of the state commission may have the same party affiliation. In Mississippi one of the three members of the board must reside in each of the three judicial districts of the state. Three members of the Public Welfare Council in Connecticut must be men, and two, women. In New York State a board member must be appointed from each of the nine judicial districts of the state. One member of the New Jersey Board must be a woman.

BOARDS OF LOCAL AGENCIES: TYPES AND COMPOSITION

The predominating type of board in local agencies is the uncompensated, administrative board, that is, a board which appoints an executive to perform the detailed duties of the department, but which retains the final authority. The local boards in Florida, Indiana, Iowa, Mississippi, Colorado, and New Jersey are uniformly of this type, which is also found in some localities in California, New York, and Wisconsin. In a few instances the county board in Wisconsin includes one paid member who performs the detailed duties of the board.

Executive boards are found in some Massachusetts towns, the members of which are frequently elected. In most of the larger towns and cities an agent is employed; hence the boards are administrative.

Advisory committees were organized in connection with most of the county branches in Washington, though there was no statutory sanction for them.[8] Advisory committees have been appointed locally in certain instances in Wisconsin counties though they are usually subcommittees of the county boards of supervisors.

Florida is the only state observed in which the state agency participates in the selection of the members of the local board: the district board members are appointed by the governor upon recommendation of the state welfare department. County welfare boards in Mississippi, Iowa, New Jersey, and Wisconsin are selected by the governing board of the county, but in Indiana the county welfare board is appointed by the circuit court judge of the county. Where boards appear in New York

---

[8] The 1937 welfare law in Washington provides for an advisory committee in each county welfare department.

State, they are usually of city agencies, with members selected by the chief executive of the municipality—namely, the mayor or city manager.[9]

An, example of an ex officio local board is found in Colorado, where the state law provides that the county board of commissioners shall constitute the county board of public welfare. This means that the board of county commissioners at stated times sits officially as the county welfare board. As a matter of fact, it is difficult to distinguish this plan from that which prevails in California. There the board of supervisors of the county serves, in a sense, as the county welfare board since it appoints the welfare executive and authorizes grants of assistance.[10] Actually, however, the boards of supervisors in California are really performing the duties of governing officials of the county when they act on welfare matters. The only advantage of the Colorado scheme is that it definitely focuses the attention of the county board of commissioners upon the welfare problem. If the purpose of a system of local boards is to secure citizen participation and nonpartisan control, this ex officio arrangement does not gain that end. One observer has pointed out, however, that in many Colorado counties it would be difficult to find citizens qualified to serve on county welfare boards.[11]

> . . . it is regrettable that the administration of these [welfare] services should remain wholly under the control of officials who can only be retained in office by popular vote. This may make it easy for them to allow political considerations, rather than good standards of welfare administration, to dictate their policies. On the other hand, it is questionable whether it would be possible to secure, in many of the counties of the state, a sufficient number of interested, competent, and informed lay people to serve on non-political boards if such had been established.

Most state laws prescribe the number of members which may be appointed to the local board and also place certain limitations on the selection. The district board in Florida must consist of one representative from each county included in the district, and for counties with a population of 25,000 or more, one member must be appointed for each population unit of 25,000. In Indiana, the sole requirement is that the membership of the county board must consist of five members. The county board in Iowa is made up of three persons, one of whom must

[9] In New York State, aid to dependent children is usually administered by a county board of child welfare appointed by the county children's court judge. These boards have not been studied in this project.

[10] Some California counties have established uncompensated citizen welfare boards, but they are advisory rather than administrative.

[11] D. S. Howard, "The 1936 Public Welfare Legislation of Colorado" (mimeographed).

be a woman, and one, the overseer of the poor of the county ex officio. (If the overseer of the poor is a woman, this meets both requirements of the law.) In Mississippi, the law provides that the board must be composed of from three to five members representing the various supervisory districts of the county; practically every board has the full quota of five members. The county welfare board in New Jersey must have at least two women members and must include two members of the county board of freeholders. In addition, the county adjuster is an ex officio member of the board unless he is serving as director. There are no general legislative provisions governing the appointment of whatever citizen boards are used locally in the administration of old age assistance in New York and Wisconsin.

POWERS AND DUTIES OF BOARDS OF STATE AGENCIES

State laws indicate in some detail the powers of the state boards and of the local boards wherever the latter are provided for. Some statutes distinguish between the specific powers of the board and those duties that are intended for delegation to the staff, but this formal differentiation has not been particularly successful. Actually, most of the powers of the boards enumerated in the statutes are intended to be the broad legal responsibilities of those bodies; the law does not attempt to specify whether the board itself is to perform the duties or delegate them to an executive or his subordinates. From observation of the operation of the boards, certain significant areas in which the boards participate directly stand out as important to the administration of old age assistance.

In seven of the states studied the state boards select the chief executive officer of the department, although in some of these there are statutory limitations on their authority to appoint or to remove this official.[12]

[12] In Iowa, New Jersey, and New York, the state board selects the executive without any qualifications prescribed in the act, and he serves at the pleasure of the board. In four states—Florida, Colorado, Indiana, and Mississippi—the selection of the executive is made by administrative boards, but with some limitations on their authority to hire or fire. The Florida law sets forth certain qualifications which the commissioner must meet. In Colorado the commissioner must be chosen from among the members of the state board, and, since all members of the board serve at the "pleasure of the governor," the latter official would seem to have power to remove the commissioner if he so desired. In Indiana the law requires that the selection be made "with the advice and approval of the governor"—language which might be interpreted to give the governor actual control over the appointment rather than the board. In Mississippi the law requires that the director be appointed by the board for a four-year term, although the official minutes of the board in this state record that the present director was originally appointed for a one-year term. The Wisconsin statute prescribes that the official who had been handling old age assistance under the previous state law, a civil service employee, should be director

The state boards in these states, and in Iowa and Wisconsin, have the final responsibility for all staff appointments, but most of them have delegated this task to the chief executive even though they may formally ratify his selections. Several state boards select heads of the principal subdivisions in the agencies, with the result that the executive is occasionally forced to accept as a major assistant a person who is not his own choice. One state board insists that it must review and ratify all appointments to the department regardless of their importance; consequently when a vacancy occurs in a minor but essential position a person must be appointed provisionally, subject to later ratification by the board. Although the board has usually accepted the director's recommendations, employment is precarious until the formality of board approval has taken place. In the best managed state agencies observed, the chief executive is given the responsibility for the appointment of all staff members; as a matter of wisdom, he usually seeks the board's advice on major appointments but does not bother it with the selections for lesser posts.

Most of the state boards observed take some part in the formulation of policy for the administration of the old age assistance program, generally to the extent of approving the rules and regulations. The usual procedure is that the rules and regulations are prepared in advance by the staff and are approved by the board after detailed consideration. Although it is advisable that the board participate in this activity, the staff, which is daily faced with the problems of administration, must take the leadership in the formulation of rules. In one state the board set forth on its own to revise the rules and regulations, but few members were in close touch with the administrative problems involved, and their attempt to reshape the rules and regulations was abortive. The staff and the board should also distinguish between procedural and policy regulations. Board members can contribute little to the content of regulations on the mechanical operation of the program. Furthermore, if the board devotes its efforts to the consideration of large numbers of procedural regulations, it cannot give proper time to weighing important questions of policy.

The old age assistance laws in Iowa, Indiana, and Wisconsin make the board of the state agency responsible for the conduct of appeals,

of the State Pension Department, but that any subsequent vacancy should be filled by the State Industrial Commission from a civil service list. This is the only state observed in which the state director is selected in accordance with civil service requirements, although the Colorado director acquired civil service status after his appointment.

but the board in Indiana has by formal action delegated this responsibility to the staff. In two other states, California and Colorado, the state board has on its own motion assumed the responsibility for handling appeals. This activity is a staff responsibility by board action in Florida, Mississippi, New Jersey, and New York, and by law in Massachusetts.[13]

In Wisconsin the board of the State Pension Department has been spending a good deal of time on appeal cases for the purpose of developing a case policy, but with the intention of later delegating this activity entirely to the staff. The detailed hearings are conducted by two staff members and the board considers summaries, which these officials prepare.

The consideration of appeal cases has been a time-consuming task for the state boards in California and Colorado. There is no evidence that this activity is regarded by either board as a temporary function, but both seem to have assumed that it is a duty to be performed by the board itself. Both boards meet monthly and have fairly heavy agenda, and the consideration of individual appeal cases has taken a disproportionate amount of time. As indicated previously in the discussion of appeals,[14] there is no evidence that these boards make any special contribution to the appeal procedure or that their hearing of appeals is any more impartial than that of staff workers in other states.

Although many state administrative boards concern themselves with some details of operation, it is surprising to find that several of them pay little attention to the budget of the agency. For example, one state board which passes on many appointments of the staff and which considers many other matters of detail gives no time to the state budget. Another state board which concerns itself with personnel selection and administrative details leaves the consideration of the budget to an informal committee without board ratification. The lack of attention given to the department's budget in these states may be attributable partly to the state's having an elaborate budgetary procedure that requires constant executive attention. One reason, however, for having citizen participation in the management of a welfare agency is to secure support for the agency itself. It would appear, therefore, that members of the board should be familiar with the financial requirements of the

---

[13] The appeal board in Massachusetts formerly was composed of three executive staff members and one member of the advisory board, but by an amendment enacted in May, 1937, it was limited to the three staff members.

[14] See chap. 16.

agency and should help defend the department's estimates before the appropriating bodies.

The conduct of relations with the local units in old age and other assistance programs is the principal function of, and one of the most complex supervisory problems faced by, most state departments. The state boards observed have shown varying degrees of concern with this problem. The newer state programs show more active participation of the state boards in developing the policy of the department's relations with the operating units. The boards of some of the older agencies, in contrast, appear to be much less interested in local relations. Most of the older state departments have a varied program, and the board appears to be more concerned with the inspectional or institutional activities of the department than with the newer public assistance programs. Many board members were, in fact, originally appointed because of their interest in private social work or institutional affairs. The conclusion is inescapable that some of them have not come to appreciate the significance of the problem of state-local relationships. Although it is assumed that the day-by-day state-local relationships should be conducted by the staff, the board, nevertheless, so long as it retains administrative authority, should concern itself with the policies involved in state supervision of local administration.[15]

Individual board members have been active in interpreting the state program throughout the state, though in the state agencies it appears that a successful interpretative program must be carried on as a professional staff function since the area to which educational efforts must be extended is so large. Individual board members can only have a limited influence because of the proportionately small sphere that can be reached by personal efforts. Members of the board can serve as effective media for the release of material prepared by the staff.[16]

As one glances from state to state the choice of the particular duties which state boards have reserved to themselves appears to have been made haphazardly. Under similar statutes one state board concerns

[15] It should not be assumed that the authors believe that citizen board members are more impartial and more judicious in handling state-local relationships. Where they are appointed on a sectional basis board members are sometimes inclined to favor the interests of the localities which they represent rather than to defend the position of the state.

[16] One state department has had a, long controversy over basic legislation with a new governor who was not in sympathy with the plans of the agency. The leadership in the department's campaign was taken by the board, and public statements always appeared in the chairman's name; thus the staff was protected from the appearance of openly opposing the chief executive of the state. The material used by the board, however, was usually prepared within the department by staff members acquainted with the facts.

itself with considerable administrative detail, while another delegates all executive duties to the director. For most state departments the control of the administration of public assistance is a new and baffling problem requiring a careful reconsideration of the board's function. That the final solution has not been found is clear to any impartial student of state welfare administration.

POWERS AND DUTIES OF BOARDS OF LOCAL AGENCIES

The selection of the chief executive is a common responsibility of the local board of the administrative type. Prior to state participation in administration of old age assistance, most local boards had complete freedom from any state authority in appointing the chief executive officer, although a few of them were subject to the limitations prescribed by a local civil service commission. With the establishment of state plans of administration in which the state shares with the local subdivisions the responsibility for the program, some state agencies have been given a measure of control over the selection of personnel in the operating units.[17]

Having appointed a chief executive, some local boards are content to leave with him the responsibility for appointment of his subordinates. Other boards, however, participate directly in the appointment of staff members. Strict interpretation of some state statutes leads to the conclusion that the local board is expected to approve all appointments of subordinates. Even under these statutes the practice ranges from mere ratification of appointments by the board to actual selection without reference to the wishes of the executive. When the latter practice prevails, the director is deprived of real staff control.

The principal operating function of the local agency in old age assistance is the authorization and payment of grants to eligible applicants for aid. The degree to which the board participates in the final decision on individual cases varies greatly among the local agencies. The board ordinarily possesses the power to pass on every case, but the difference arises from the board's idea of how literally this responsibility is to be taken.

In one state the old age assistance statute requires the county board to approve all old age assistance cases, but the attorney general, in an unofficial opinion, stated that the board could delegate this responsibility under the following provision of the welfare act:[18]

[17] See chap. 15.
[18] Indiana, *Acts,* spec. sess., 1936, chap. 3, sec. 27.

Whenever, by any of the provisions of this act, or of any other act, any right, power or duty is imposed or conferred on the state department of public welfare or the county department of public welfare, the right, power or duty so imposed or conferred shall be possessed and exercised by the state board of public welfare, or the county board of public welfare, as the case may be, unless otherwise provided in this act, or unless any such right, power or duty is delegated to the duly appointed agents or employees of such department, or any of them, by an appropriate rule, regulation or order of the state board or the county board.

The approval of individual cases by a local board involves a long, tedious process. The executive of the agency or one of his staff must present the cases, the board members must bring out any points which they feel they need for clarification, and then a decision must be reached. In smaller communities, board members occasionally contribute from personal knowledge new information about an applicant, though if an adequate investigation is made by the staff this knowledge should be elicited earlier and should be included in the facts leading to the staff recommendation. In larger units the board members pass upon the circumstances of persons whom they do not know at all and whose records must of necessity be presented to them in summary form. If the board of the local agency includes members from the governing body of the county, these officials are apt to be concerned particularly about applicants who come from their districts. This concern may arise from genuine motives, for these officials are often well acquainted with the circumstances of their constituents and they wish to be sure that their needs have been considered fairly. At the same time, this participation in case review may be used to secure preferential treatment for the constituents of the elected official, and the possibilities of political trading in the system are obvious.

The participation of the board in the detailed approval of individual cases consumes so much time that the board may have little time left for its other responsibilities. One local board in its first year of operation was interested in a wide variety of policy and administrative matters. It had developed an active program of interpretation and had concerned itself about matters of relationships with other agencies and other broad questions. Once it became responsible for passing upon individual cases, however, it had time for little else; the broader activities of the board were neglected.

In some of the largest units the board perfunctorily fulfils the legal requirement to approve cases. At official board meetings long lists of cases are presented which are approved *in toto* without individual consideration. Some agencies have arrived at a compromise between consideration of each case and a mere formal approval of schedules of cases. The Essex County (New Jersey) Welfare Board has instructed the executive (and these instructions have officially been incorporated in the minutes) to submit in a group at each monthly meeting for formal approval all cases presenting no particular problem. The board reserves for individual consideration those cases that puzzle the staff or that involve some policy on which the staff desires an expression of opinion by board members. At the meetings of this board four or five problem cases are usually discussed, each of which may lead to a policy decision by the board to guide subsequent actions of the staff. This practice gives the board an opportunity to appreciate the major problem that the agency is confronting, and affords the staff an opportunity to discuss policies with the board in concrete terms.

Since the administrative or executive board is the head of the local agency, one of its responsibilities is to see that the agency has sufficient money with which to do business. Within the observation of this study local welfare boards have, on the whole, been more active on the problem of finance than have state boards. This situation has several possible explanations. In the first place, the financial administration of smaller political subdivisions is less subject to complicated budgetary procedures that require constant staff attention. Secondly, the whole matter of raising and appropriating funds in local units of government is a more intimate concern of the citizens, and the board members, as local taxpayers, are in direct touch both with the financial procedures and with the officials responsible. Finally, in counties particularly, the appropriating body is usually also the executive body to which the executive is directly or indirectly responsible; hence he is inhibited from any aggressive measures to obtain support, whereas members of a citizen board can put up an independent fight for the agency's needs.

The device of having the county board made up in whole or in part of members of the county governing body may greatly ease the problem of financial support. When the members of the board are themselves the county governing body, they are familiar with the problems and needs of the county welfare agency. Undoubtedly this has been one factor leading to this method of board composition. In New Jersey the county welfare board includes both citizen members and representatives of the governing board of the county. This arrangement provides the welfare agency with informed representatives on the appropriating body and at the same time with citizen members who from an independent position can exert their influence in favor of adequate funds.

One value of having citizen board members in charge of local agencies is that they may interpret the program to the community. Community education is needed not alone to secure support for an adequate appropriation: public understanding of the aims of the agency simplifies the day-by-day administration of the program. A few of the local boards have undertaken an active educational program, but this activity has not been developed extensively in the communities visited.

One observes that the local agencies which have been established longest seem to pay the least attention to public relations. This result may be attributable to the fact that new agencies have a hard struggle to gain community recognition. In addition, the board members of the established agencies sometimes become so firmly entrenched that they regard the agency as their own property, and they see no reason why they should explain to the public what they are doing. Actually, some of these older agencies are more in need of community understanding than are some of the newer organizations which have been established after a state-wide program of interpretation.

The cultivation of effective public relations is not something that takes place automatically. Local agencies that have gained community acceptance have done so through a program of interpretation that has been carefully planned and executed. The board of a small county department in Indiana, for example, has on its own initiative made public relations its primary task. Each board member assumes responsibility for definite assignments, such as speaking engagements, preparation of reports for the local paper, etc., and the county is thus made aware of its welfare needs and the steps being taken to meet them. Some state agencies have recognized the importance of local interpretation, and the state staffs assist the local units in developing an educational program.

BOARD OPERATION

The experience with administrative boards on both state and local levels has led to the gradual development of accepted practices of board operation. It is impossible in this type of report to discuss the question of board management exhaustively, but since successful board operation has a direct effect upon the quality of administrative performance in public assistance agencies, it is desirable to indicate briefly some of the best practices. The differences between the board-management problem of an operating unit and of a state supervisory agency are so slight that the problem of the two levels may be discussed simultaneously.

Relationship of Board to the Executive

Under a well thought out plan the board should be regarded as the policy-making body, which employs a director to perform the executive tasks. Basic to a satisfactory relationship between the board and the executive is a clear-cut understanding of the fields of activity of each arrived at by mutual agreement. In the development of a public agency, boards ordinarily come first, and the members become accustomed to performing some executive duties prior to the organization of the staff. As soon as an executive officer is appointed, however, the board must look to him for leadership in the program; its members should thereafter perform direct activities only with the knowledge and approval of the executive.

Board interference with executive responsibility occurs more often in the smaller agencies, whose executive officer may not be so experienced and whose board members feel more of a personal trusteeship over the program. Although it is frequently necessary for the board members of small agencies to assist the executive, no excuse exists for their performing administrative tasks on their own initiative and without previous consultation with the director.

The best board-executive relationships have been noted in three state departments in which the boards have delegated the major executive responsibility to the commissioner and therefore are able to devote themselves to broad policy questions. These boards are careful, however, to be clear and precise about what delegation is made. The channel of the board's relationship to the staff in these agencies is entirely through the chief executive.

The determination of staff participation in board meetings should be primarily in the hands of the director; other staff should appear only at his suggestion or upon a request which comes directly from the board to him and not to the subordinate. In several state agencies a large number of the staff attends the board meetings. This has become a routine procedure, and no one seems to question it. From the standpoint of economy of staff effort alone, one can certainly challenge the wisdom of having twelve staff members present at a meeting at which five board members are in attendance—a common occurrence in one state.[19]

The provision in the law that the director is a member of the state board results in a lack of clear distinction between the function of the board and that of the executive. In two of the states where this obtains, the board acts upon a large number of detailed administrative matters rather than confining itself to policy matters. In one state the executive seldom takes a decisive stand on day-to-day matters that should be settled immediately, and usually puts off these questions for consideration at the monthly board meeting.

Frequency of Meetings

Most state boards have found it possible to meet regularly only once a month. A monthly meeting is usually sufficient for the conduct of the major business of a state welfare department when the work is well organized and the board meeting is well planned. In some state agencies the monthly meeting lasts two days; in others, only one day; the difference depends largely on the amount of detail considered and the organization of the meeting. In two boards that hold a two-day meeting, much of the time is given over to routine reports of seven or eight division heads of the department. One state which expedites its monthly meetings handles such reports in a more satisfactory manner. The director sends monthly reports of division directors to the board in advance of the meeting, and during the board session the members are given an opportunity to raise questions on the aspects of the reports which interest them. Thus the time devoted to individual staff reports is focused on the material which seems of importance to board members or to which the executive wishes to direct their attention; the group as a whole is relieved of listening to a long recitation of statistics and routine activities.

One new state board had had only three meetings in the course of ten months, ostensibly because the state agency was so short of funds that it could not afford traveling expenses for frequent meetings. Some communications on important matters passed between the executive and the board members in the interim between the meetings, but this infrequency of meeting has meant that the board has served its purpose inadequately.

[19] Apparently in one state in which a group of staff members attends board meetings, these occasions are used as a substitute for staff meetings. Such substitution is a clear indication of a confusion between the policy-making functions of the board and the executive nature of staff duties.

The state boards which meet monthly need to provide for interim authority to be vested either in the chairman of the board or in a small executive committee. In some state agencies this arrangement is routine, but no official delegation of authority is made by the board. In others, however, there is a clear-cut arrangement for an executive committee to function in interim periods. Usually members who live near the state capital or who are otherwise more readily available to the commissioner serve on such a committee.

The question of frequency of meetings is not a matter of so great concern in local agencies, for, with few exceptions, the problem of travel time of members is not a factor. The local boards usually meet at stated monthly periods and in emergencies may meet more frequently. In several states in which recently established local boards have taken considerable responsibility for the review of individual cases, the boards have met as frequently as two or three times a week over a period of several months. Obviously, this requires more time than citizen members should be expected to devote to the work and, if continued, it would deprive the local agency of the best people who should be recruited for board service. In some of the large counties and in districts such as those in Florida, the geographical factor affects the frequency of meetings. In one Florida district, board members have to travel as much as 100 to 150 miles by automobile to attend meetings. This board attempted to have only quarterly meetings to conserve the time of the members and to save transportation costs. This arrangement, however, did not prove satisfactory, since too many questions of policy requiring board action arose in the interim; the board reverted to the earlier practice of monthly meetings.

Agenda of Meetings

All well organized boards observed conduct their meetings in accordance with an agenda, which is usually drawn up by the director of the department, in consultation with the chairman of the board, and sent to the members in advance. To conserve time at the meeting, some executives send reports or summaries, which will be useful background, along with the agenda, but many agencies have not recognized the advantage of this procedure. The reading of material in advance requires a little more effort of the board members than listening to reports at a meeting, but it makes possible a more economical use of the meeting time. When a detailed statement of policy is to be considered, members should be given a draft of the proposal prior to the meeting.

Recording of Meetings

The action of boards is of considerable significance both to the immediate and to the future operation of the public agency. Consequently, great care must be given to the accurate recording of the decisions made at board meetings. It is almost impossible for any member of the board or for the executive to keep an accurate record of official motions or of significant points of discussion and at the same time participate in the proceedings; hence most large agencies have found it desirable to have a stenographer present. This employee may be designated as secretary to the board, or if the executive of the agency is the official board secretary, he assigns an office assistant to take the minutes. A detailed stenographic record of meetings is not necessary, but a record that is limited to the motions formally adopted frequently excludes from the minutes important matters brought up in the discussion. The best practice calls for the inclusion of significant points of discussion and summaries of oral reports along with formal action in the record of the meeting.

It is desirable to file with the board minutes copies of official rules and regulations which have been promulgated by the board and of other official communications resulting from board actions. One of the best plans for preserving the records of a board's activity in a large agency is to maintain two separate records: a formal report of all meetings, including attendance, major points of discussion, and all formal action taken; and a concurrent journal, in which to file a transcript of the discussions of each meeting, copies of important communications, and copies of all official bulletins and reports. Although all boards cannot keep a detailed running account of deliberations, a journal is certainly a convenient device for the preservation of many essential documents which, if filed with the formal minutes, would produce a record too bulky for ready reference, but which should be kept intact as an administrative record.[20]

Adjudication Activities

When state boards give considerable time to formal appeal hearings, formal adjudication of state-local or intercounty disputes, and other quasi-judicial activities, the problem of management of the board sessions is much more difficult. As compared with the executive business of a board, these deliberative activities consume considerable time. If

[20] As a part of the state supervisory program, several state agencies give detailed attention to the form and content of the records of the board meetings of local agencies. ·

a fair hearing is to be given to an individual or to the representatives of a community, ample time must be allowed for the presentation of the case and for discussion. When proceedings of this sort are combined on the agenda with the transaction of other business, the pressure of time is likely to compel too hasty action in performing the adjudicating functions. Operating boards that pass on a great many cases have usually found it desirable to hold special sessions for case review. Likewise, state agencies handling appeals of various sorts may find it wise to put aside a specified period of the monthly meeting for business of this nature.

INDEX

INDEX